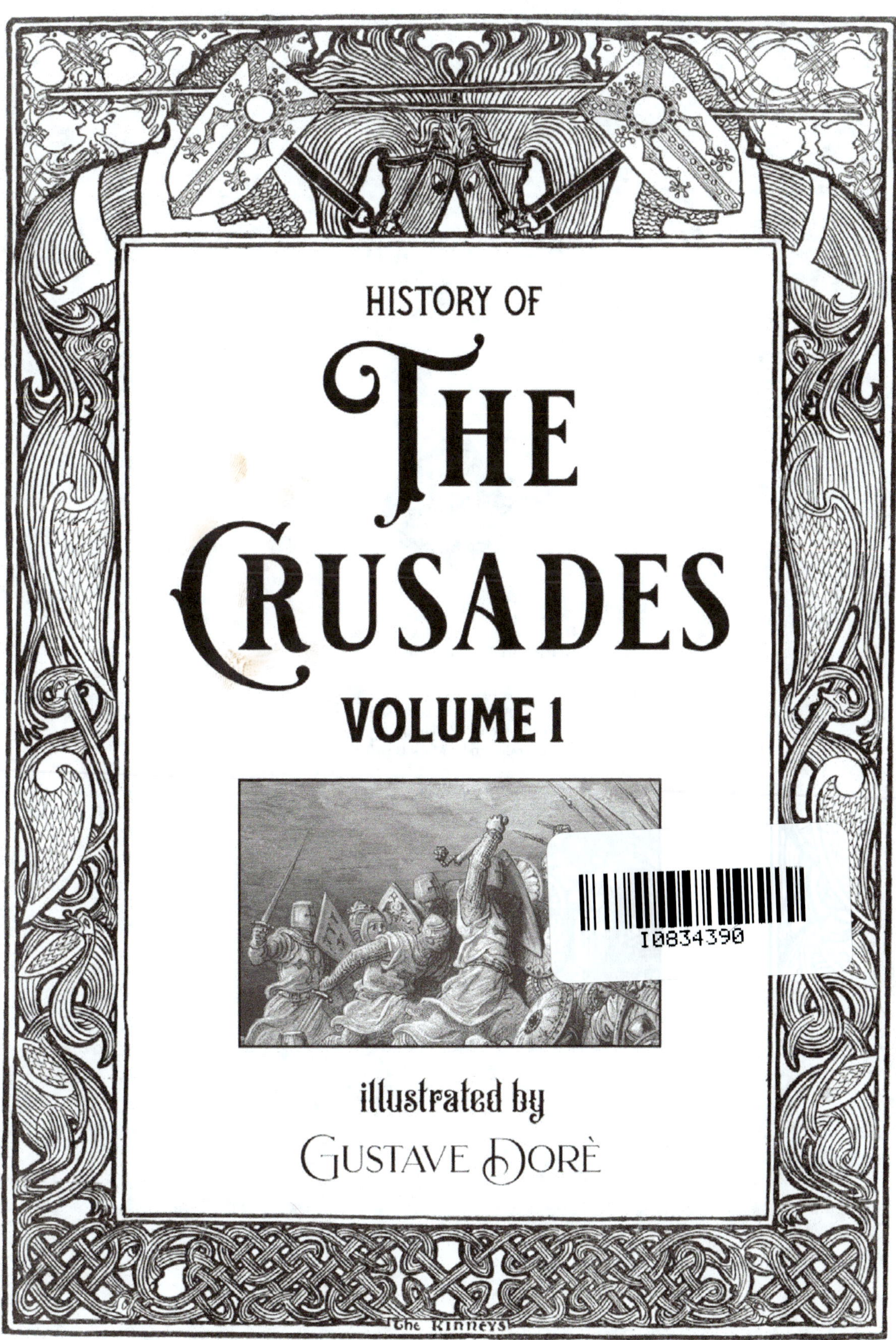

HISTORY OF

THE CRUSADES

VOLUME 1

illustrated by

GUSTAVE DORÈ

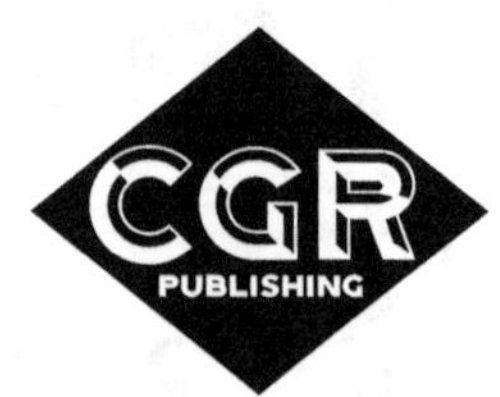

History of the Crusades Volume 1:
Gustave Doré Restored Special Edition

By Michaud
Illustrations by Gustave Doré
Translated by William Robson
Cover design by Mark Bussler

www.CGRpublishing.com

HISTORY

OF THE

CRUSADES

BY MICHAUD

Member of the Academy of France

ILLUSTRATED WITH ONE HUNDRED GRAND COMPOSITIONS

BY

GUSTAVE DORÉ

ENGRAVED BY

BELLENGER, DOMS, GUSMAN, JONNARD, PANNEMAKER, PISAN, QUESNEL

VOLUME I

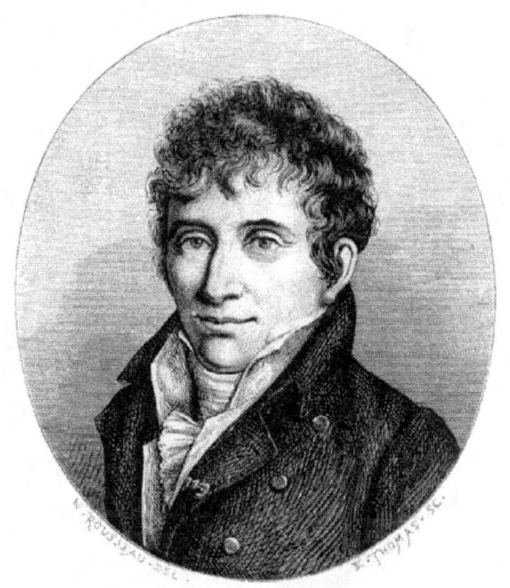

PHILADELPHIA

GEORGE BARRIE PUBLISHER

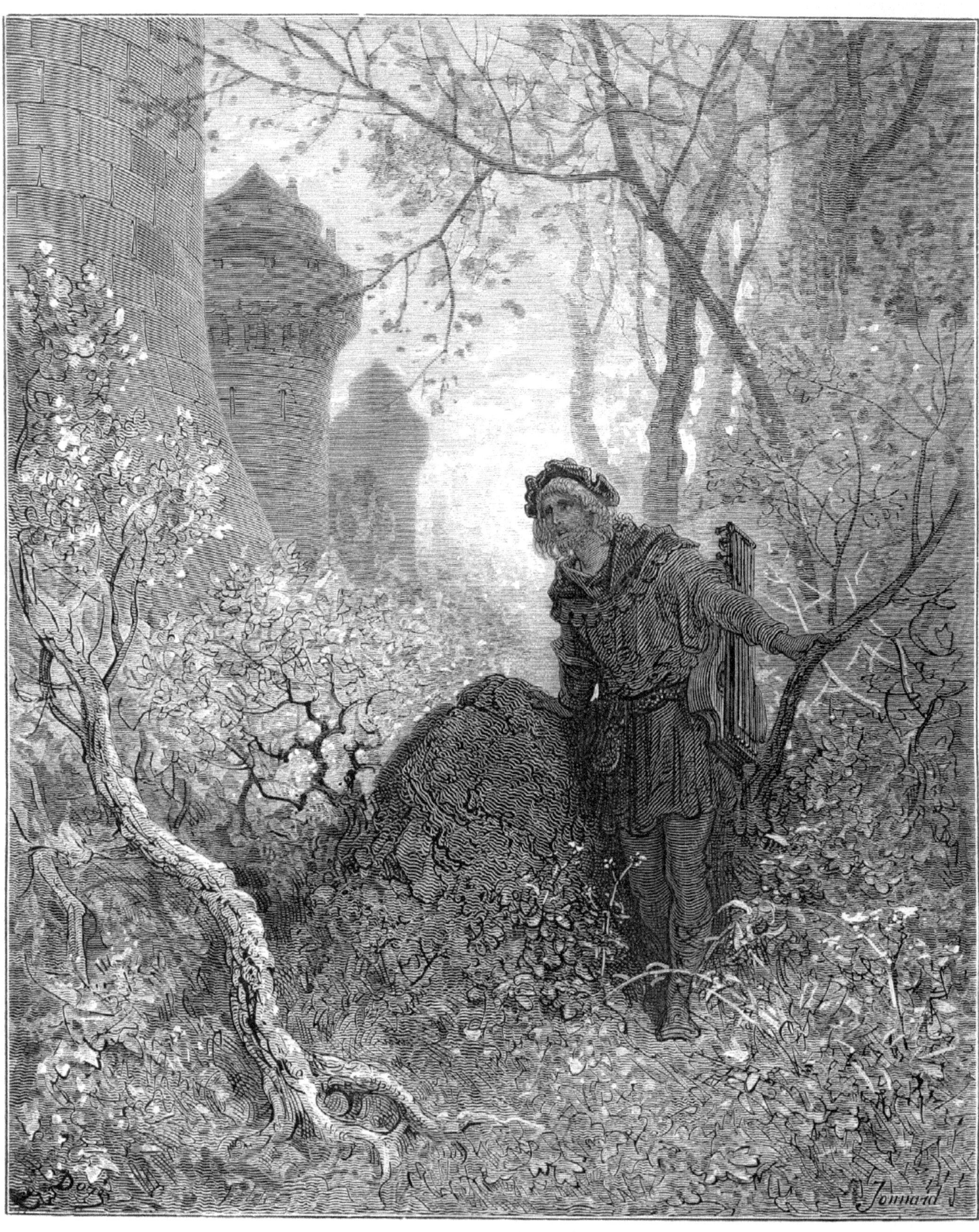

BLONDEL HEARS THE VOICE OF RICHARD.

A long captivity awaited Richard on his return to Europe. The vessel in which he embarked was shipwrecked on the coast of Italy, and fearing to pass through France, he took the route of Germany, concealed under the habit of a simple pilgrim. His liberality betrayed the monarch, and as he had enemies everywhere, he was seized by the soldiers of the duke of Austria. It was not known in Europe what had become of King Richard, when a gentleman of Arras, named Blondel, set out in search of his master, and traversed Germany in the dress and with the lyre of a minstrel. On his arrival before a castle, in which, it was said, languished an illustrious captive, Blondel began to sing the first couplet of a song which he had composed in conjunction with Richard. From the top of a high tower a voice answered him, and sang the second couplet. Then the faithful troubadour returned into England to announce that he had discovered the prison of the king.—Book VIII.

INTRODUCTION

THE history of the middle ages presents no spectacle more imposing than the Crusades, in which are to be seen the nations of Asia and of Europe armed against each other, two religions contending for superiority, and disputing the empire of the world. After having been several times threatened by the Mussulmans, and a long time exposed to their invasions, all at once the West arouses itself, and appears, according to the expression of a Greek historian—Anna Comnena—to tear itself from its foundation, in order to precipitate itself upon Asia. All nations abandon their interests and their rivalries, and see upon the face of the earth but one single country worthy of the ambition of conquerors. One would believe that there no longer exists in the universe any other city but Jerusalem, or any other habitable spot of earth but that which contains the tomb of Jesus Christ. All the roads which lead to the holy city are deluged with blood, and present nothing but the scattered spoils and wrecks of empires.

In this general confusion we may contemplate the sublimest virtues mixed with all the disorders of the wildest passions. The Christian soldiers have at the same time to contend against famine, the influence of climate, and enemies the most formidable; in the greatest dangers, in the midst of their successes and their constant discords, nothing can exhaust either their perseverance or their resignation. After four years of fatigue, of miseries, and of victories, Jerusalem is taken by the Crusaders; but as their conquests are not the work of wisdom and prudence, but the fruit of blind enthusiasm and ill-directed heroism, they create nothing but a transient power.

The banner of the cross soon passes from the hands of Godfrey de Bouillon into those of his weak and imbecile successors. Jerusalem, now a Christian city, is obliged again to apply for succour to the West. At the voice of St. Bernard, the Christians take arms. Conducted by an emperor of Germany and a king of France, they fly to the defence of the Holy Land; but they have no longer great captains among them; they have none of the magnanimity or heroic resignation of their fathers. Asia, which beholds their coming without terror, already presents a new spectacle. The disciples of Mahomet awaken from their apathy; they are at once seized with a frenzy equal to that which had armed their enemies; they oppose enthusiasm to enthusiasm, fanaticism to fanaticism, and in their turn burn with a desire to shed their blood in a religious war.

The spirit of discord which had destroyed their power is no longer felt but among the Christians. Luxury and the manners of the East weaken the courage of the defenders of the cross, and make them forget the object even of the holy war. Jerusalem, which had cost the Crusaders so much blood, falls again into the power of the infidels, and becomes the conquest of a wise and warlike prince, who had united under his banner the forces of Syria and Egypt.

The genius and fortune of Saladin inflict a mortal blow upon the ill-assured power of the Christians in the East. In vain an emperor of the West, and two kings celebrated for their bravery, place themselves at the head of the whole powers of their states to deliver Palestine; these new armies of Crusaders meet everywhere with brave enemies and invincible barriers, and all their united efforts produce nothing but illustrious disasters. The kingdom of Jerusalem, for whose ruins they contend, is no longer anything but a vain name; soon even the captivity and the miseries of the holy city cease to inspire the sentiments of piety and enthusiasm that they had given birth to among the Christians. The Crusaders, who had taken up arms for its deliverance, suffer themselves to be seduced by the wealth of Greece, and stop short to undertake the conquest of Constantinople.

From that time the spirit of the Crusaders begins to change; whilst a small number of Christians still shed their blood for the deliverance of the tomb of Jesus Christ, the princes and the knights are deaf to everything but the voice of ambition. The popes complete the corruption of the true spirit of the Crusaders, by urging them on, by their preaching, against other Christian people, and against their own personal enemies. The holy wars then degenerate into civil wars, in which both religion and humanity are outraged.

These abuses of the crusades, and the dire passions which had mixed themselves with them, plunge Europe in disorder and anarchy; when a pious king undertakes once more to arm the powers of the West against the infidels, and to revive among the Crusaders the spirit which had animated the companions of Godfrey. The two wars directed by this pious chief, are more unfortunate than all the others. In the first, the world is presented with the spectacle of a captive army and a king in fetters; in the second, that of a powerful monarch dying in its ashes. Then it is that the illusion disappears, and Jerusalem ceases to attract all the attention of the West.

Soon after, the face of Europe is changed; intelligence dissipates barbarism; the crusades no longer excite the same degree of enthusiasm, and the first effect of the civilization it begins to spread is to weaken the spirit of the fanaticism which had given them birth. Some few useless efforts are at times made to rekindle the fire which had burnt so furiously in Europe and Asia. The nations are so completely recovered from the pious delirium of the Crusades, that when Germany finds itself menaced by the Mussulmans, who are masters of Constantinople, the banner of the cross can with difficulty gather an army around it; and Europe, which had risen in a mass to attack the infidels in Asia, opposes but a feeble resistance to them on its own territories.

Such is, in a few words, the picture of the events and revolutions which the historian of the crusades has to describe. A writer who has preceded us by two centuries, and who calls the history of the Crusades *a right royal history*, is surprised at the silence preserved to his time. "I esteem it," says he, "a deplorable thing that such persons, inferior in no way to those who have been so much celebrated by the Greeks and the Romans, should have fallen into such obscurity, that we search in vain to discover who they were and what they did; and they appear to me highly culpable, who, possessing learning and the skill to write, have left these histories neglected." Everybody ought now to be of this opinion, and regret that our great writers have not entertained the noble subject of the Crusades. When I undertake to supply the want created by their silence, I am duly impressed with the difficulty of the task.

They who, among us, have written ancient history, had for guides the historians of Rome and Athens. The brilliant colours of Livy, of Tacitus, of Thucydides presented themselves naturally to their pencils; but I have no models to follow, and am compelled to make those historians of the middle ages speak whom our times despise. They have rarely sustained me in my labour by the charm of their style, or the elegance of their narrations; but if they have afforded me no lessons in the art of writing, they transmit to me at least events whose interest will make up for the deficiency of their talent or mine. Perhaps it will be found, in the perusal of this history, that a period in which everything is astonishing, loses nothing by being presented in a simple and faithful picture. The unaffected style of our old historians, in my view, appears to reanimate the persons and the characters they describe; and if I have profited by that which they have taught me, the age in which they lived will not be ill represented in my pages. It would have been easy for me to have censured with severity, as has usually been done, their ignorance and their credulity, but I respect in them the frankness and the candour of the periods of which they are the interpreters. Without yielding faith to all they say, I have not disdained the fables they relate to us, and which were believed by their contemporaries ; for that which was thought worthy of credit then serves to picture to us the manners of our ancestors, and forms an essential part of the history of past ages.

We do not now require much sagacity to discover in our ancient chronicles what is fabulous and what is not. A far more difficult thing is to reconcile, upon some points, the frequent contradictory assertions of the Latins, the Greeks and the Saracens, and to separate, in the history of the crusades, that which belongs to religious fanaticism, to policy, or to human passions. I do not pretend to resolve more skilfully than others these difficult problems, or to elevate myself above my subject, by offering positive judgments upon the nations and ages which will present themselves before me. Without giving myself up to digressions in which it is always easy to make a display of learning, after having scrupulously examined the historical monuments which remain to us, I will tell honestly what I believe to be the truth, and will leave dissertations to the erudite, and conjectures to philosophers.

In an age in which some value is set upon an opinion of the crusades, it will be first asked, if the wars of the Crusades were just. Upon this head we have but little to answer : whilst the Crusaders believed that they were obeying God himself, by attacking the Saracens in the East, the latter, who had invaded a part of Asia possessed by Christian people, who had got possession of Spain, who threatened Constantinople, the coasts of Italy, and several countries of the West, did not reproach their enemies with making an unjust war, and left to fortune and victory the care of deciding a question almost always useless.

We shall think it of more importance in this history to examine what was the cause and the nature of these remote wars, and what has proved to be their influence on civilization. The crusades were produced by the religious and military spirit which prevailed in Europe during the middle ages. The love of arms and religious fervour were two dominant passions, which, mingled in some way, lent each other a mutual energy. These two great principles, united and acting together, gave birth to the holy war ; and carried, among the Crusaders, valour, resignation and heroism of character to the highest degree of eminence.

The part which the union of these two principles necessarily had in the undertaking of the holy wars will be plainly perceived in our narration. It will be much less easy for us to make all the results of the crusades appreciated. Some writers have seen nothing in these great expeditions but the most deplorable excesses, without any advantage to the ages that succeeded them ; others, on the contrary, maintain that we owe to them all the benefits of civilization. It is not, at present, my business to examine these two conflicting opinions. Without believing that the holy wars have done either all the good or all the harm that is attributed to them, it must be admitted that they were a source of bitter sorrow to the generations that saw them or took part in them ; but like the ills and tempests of human life, which render man better, and often assist the progress of his reason, they have forwarded the experiences of nations ; and it may be said, that after having for a time seriously agitated and shaken society, they have, in the end, much strengthened the foundations of it. This opinion, when stripped of all spirit of exaggeration or system, will, perhaps, appear the most reasonable ; I, besides, experience some pleasure in adopting it, from its being consolatory to the age in which we live. The present generation, which has witnessed the outbreak of so many passions on the political scene, which has passed through so many calamities, will not see without interest that Providence sometimes employs great revolutions to enlighten mankind, and to ensure the future prosperity of empires.

BIOGRAPHICAL NOTICE.

WE are not of those who think that readers are without curiosity as to the position in life, actions, and fortunes of the authors who afford them instruction or pleasure; the eagerness with which the birthplaces of men of genius are sought for and commemorated; the fondness with which their most trifling actions are dwelt upon; and the endless collections that are made of their conversations and sayings, prove that this cannot be the case.

In a prefatory memoir, we can scarcely go into so many details of the life of Michaud, as, perhaps, the subject deserves. Michaud was not a mere author, whose history may be read in his works. He lived at a momentous period, and was no idle spectator of passing events. A complete life of Michaud would, indeed, swell to a history of France from 1790 to 1839.

Joseph François Michaud, born at Albens, in Savoy, on the 19th of June, in the year 1767, was descended from a family that traced its nobility beyond the tenth century. One of his ancestors, Hugh Michaud de Corcelles, was deservedly distinguished by the Emperor Charles V. The father of Joseph was obliged to leave his country in consequence of what is termed by his biographer a piece of boyish rashness, but which we prefer relating to any of the warlike deeds of the above-named Hugh. Whilst on a shooting party, he sought refreshment in a cottage, and found the mistress of it in the greatest distress; for, at the moment of his entrance, officers were bearing away her humble furniture for the paltry sum of sixty francs. He offered to pay the amount if they would come with him to his home, but they refused, and continued their operations in his presence. This irritated him to such a degree that he threatened to make use of his gun, and at length struck one of them so severe a blow with the stock of it, that the fellow died immediately. He retired to a place near Bourg, in Bresse, where he married; and he afterwards established himself as a notary and commissary at Terrier, in that province. An early death left his widow burdened with a numerous family, of which Joseph was the oldest. Notwithstanding this calamity, he received an excellent education at the college of Bourg, and acquired great credit as a rhetorician and a composer of French verses. His studies and some juvenile travels completed, it became necessary for him to fix upon a mode of getting a living; and the narrowness of his mother's resources confining his efforts to trade, he went into the house of a bookseller at Lyon, attracted, no doubt, by the affinity between the bookseller and the man of letters. He remained here till 1790, when the passage of the rich, influential and intellectual Countess Fanny de Beauharnais through that city aroused all the provincial muses to make their offerings to the great lady. Among the poets, Michaud was so successful, that he thought himself warranted in following her to Paris, with the view of pursuing a literary career under her auspices. Immediately on his arrival he laid the contents of his poetical portfolio before the public, and soon became the associate of Cerisier, in the *Gazette Universelle*, and with Esménard, in the *Postillon de la Guerre*. His opinions and early associations led him towards the Royalist party, to which the accession of his talents was very acceptable. He may be said to have been faithful to his colors through all the disasters of the unhappy cause he had embraced, for, in spite of imprisonment, banishment and repeated concealments, we find him, in 1799, publishing two satirical pamphlets against Buonaparte, by the orders of Louis XVIII. One of his escapes was so well managed, and so opportunely effected, that we will offer an account of it to our readers. He had been sent prisoner to Paris, walking between two mounted gendarmes, who were directed not to spare him, and if fatigue relaxed his speed, they were to refresh him with the flat sides of their sabres. As he entered Paris in this forlorn condition, he was met by his zealous friend Giguet, whose sorrow only set his fertile brain to work to devise means for his escape. As Michaud was, during many days, conducted from his prison to the Tuileries, to undergo examination, Giguet at first thought that the best way would be to blow out the brains of the two gendarmes that escorted him, but this he rejected as unworthy of a man of genius. Choosing a point in Michaud's passage that would answer his purpose, he stopped the party, and affecting to know nothing of the matter, and not to have seen his friend since his arrival in Paris, was eager in his inquiries as to how his health was, what he was doing, where he was going, and insisted upon his breakfasting with him. "No, no," answered Michaud ; "I have a little affair yonder at the Tuileries, just a few words of explanation to give, only the business of a minute or two. Begin breakfast without me ; I shall be back presently." "That won't do, that won't do ; they do not despatch people so quickly as all that. Perhaps they won't begin with you ; let us have our breakfast first. I dare say these gentlemen (pointing to the gendarmes) have not breakfasted, and will have no objection to a cutlet and a glass of Bordeaux wine, and here's the best house in Paris close at hand." The gendarmes, after a little faint hesitation, suffered themselves to be seduced, and prisoner, guards and friend were soon comfortably seated at table. They eat, they drink, they pass bumper toasts, and talk a little about everything, but most particularly about Bresse and the good cheer that was there always to be met with—but the pullets of Bresse ! never was such eating as the pullets of Bresse ! The mouths of the gendarmes watered at the bare description of them. "Parbleu, gentlemen," cried Giguet, "since you have never partaken of our country pullets, I will undertake to convince you that there are none such in the eighty-three departments. We have plenty of time ; you can eat a little bit more, and appetite comes with—drinking (and he filled the glasses). Waiter, here ! a Bresse pullet ! no tricks, mind; it must be from Bresse, not from Mans. But stop. Michaud, you understand these things better than anybody ; have an eye to these fellows ; go down into the kitchen, and see that they don't cheat us. Good health to you, gentlemen." Whilst they are drinking, Michaud rises, and is soon out of the house. Giguet had the art to keep the guards another half hour at table, by saying his friend was only watching the cooking, for a Bresse pullet was worth nothing if not roasted *à la* Bresse ; and when they discovered Michaud was not in the kitchen, he asserted it must either be a joke, or else he was ill and gone home, and contrived to lead them a long, useless search in a way directly opposite to that which he knew the late prisoner had taken. Michaud's escape was a happy one, for that very day the council had condemned him to death. Poor Giguet's friendly zeal cost him nearly a month's imprisonment, and placed his life even in jeopardy.

The career of Buonaparte was so successful that, at length, further resistance seemed useless, and Michaud even wrote complimentary verses on the marriage of Napoleon with Maria Louisa, and upon the birth of the young King of Rome. But this submission to circumstances was no voluntary homage ; he was still at heart faithfully attached to the Bourbons. For a length of time he resisted the tempting offers of the emperor, and one of his refusals, for its wit, if not for its patriotism, almost deserves to be placed by the side of Andrew Marvel's. Fontaines, Buonaparte's emissary, said to him : "There must be an end to all resistance ; it is diminishing every day. Come, do as other men do. Look at Delille, for instance ; he has just accepted a pension of six thousand francs." "Oh ! as to that," replied Michaud, "he is so frightened that he would accept a pension of a hundred thousand francs if you were to offer it to him." Posterity, perhaps, may be thankful that he was driven from politics to literature. During one of his necessary exiles he had written his beautiful poem of "Le Printemps d'un Proscrit." He afterwards became associated with his brother as a bookseller, and planned and executed the works of which we will furnish a list. Whatever opinion might be entertained of his talents, it is more than probable that, without his implied submission to Buonaparte, he never would have obtained that object of the hopes of all French authors, the immortal *fauteuil* in the Academy. This honor he attained in 1813, and upon the publication of his fourth volume of the "History of the Crusades," had the gratification of signing himself "Knight of the Order of St. John of Jerusalem" and "Knight of the Holy Sepulchre"—titles bestowed upon him, unasked, by the commanders representing the Order of St. John of Jerusalem in France.

He watched with intense anxiety the madly ambitious career of Buonaparte, and hailed with unfeigned delight the return of his patrons, the Bourbons. He had no cause to complain of their ingratitude, and occupied as good a position as a literary man could expect, when the escape from Elba, during a hundred days, disturbed his occupations, and placed him in considerable danger. He left Paris ; returned again, and put himself forward for a struggle ; but finding resistance dangerous and useless, he retired to the department of the Ain, where he concealed himself till the tempest had blown over ; his celebrated journal, the *Quotidien*, in the mean time, degenerating into the *Feuille du Jour*, or rather, as a wit said, "la Feuille de la veille (last night's journal) ; for it was only edited by scissors, and contained nothing but scraps from the *Moniteur* and other inoffensive journals." The *Nain Jaune* (yellow dwarf) took unfair advantage of an enemy who, he knew, could not answer him, and bestowed upon Michaud the sobriquet of "Grand Master of the Order of the Extinguishers," which stuck to him, with the bur-like pertinacity of sobriquets, for many years after the second restoration of the Bourbons. He welcomed this last event by the publication of a pamphlet entitled "The History of the Fifteen Weeks, or the Last Reign of Buonaparte," which had a great sale, twenty-seven editions of it appearing in a very short period. Having, since his success as an author, separated from his brother as a bookseller, and sold his share in the printing office, he, after 1815, gave himself up to the prosecution of his great work on the Crusades, and even parted with his portion of "La Biographie Universelle." His love of politics led him, at this time, to get returned as deputy for the department of the Ain ; but alas ! he found it a very different thing for a man with a weak voice, and totally "unaccustomed to public speaking," to sit and write uncontrolled and unobserved in his closet, and to be subject to the "retort courteous" of an enemy who watches for your mistakes, corrects your errors, and mercilessly refutes all your favourite arguments. After the trial of one sessions, he retired from his deputyship, and gave up all hopes of fame as an orator.

During the celebrity of his journal, the *Quotidien*, he was made reader to the king, with a salary of 3,000 francs ; to which appointment was attached the somewhat strange stipulation that he should never be called upon to perform its duties. After 1819, when a plan was devised of buying up the influential journals, Michaud and his fellow-proprietors were offered 500,000 francs for theirs, which our author declined. "Monseigneur," said he to the excellency who solicited him, "there is but one thing for which I could be tempted to sell the *Quotidien*, and that would be a little health. If you could give me that, I might allow myself to be corrupted." The minister, Villèle, returned repeatedly to the charge, but when, in consequence of the increasing weakness of his health, the sexagenarian Michaud parted with the greater part of his shares of the journal, it was only to pass them over to another self, his friend Laurentie.

Whilst carrying on his great work, he had been surprised to meet with a vast quantity of matter which he had not dreamt of when he began it ; and he conceived the idea of not only reconstructing his history, but of going to the Holy Land in search of more information. Although it was too late for such an attempt, his fame procured him encouragement ; and the king, Charles X., so far favoured it as to give him 25,000 francs to defray his expenses. He set out at the beginning of 1830. Whatever gratification he derived from his voyage, it must have been sadly damped by the news he received from France during that eventful year. To complete his griefs, he likewise at this period lost 200,000 francs, the greater part of his fortune, which he had imprudently placed in unsafe hands. He still, however, had a moderate competence, and might have passed the remainder of his days in ease, but for that mismanagement to which the families of literary men are so frequently subject. On his return from the Holy Land he sojourned for a time in Italy, where he was kindly welcomed by his natural sovereign, Charles Albert. In 1837 he was named member of the Académie des Inscriptions ; but honours from monarchs and academies could not put off the fatal hour, and he died at the elegant village of Passy on the 30th of September, 1839. On this occasion was exhibited an instance of what our poet calls "the ruling passion strong in death."

Few authors had received more adulation, and no one could be more covetous of it. Extraordinary instances are told of the copious draughts of this intoxicating beverage that were offered to him, and of the greediness with which he swallowed them. "Never," says his biographer, "although he loved to be called the *La Fontaine of journalism*, did he think of the second fable of the good man—*The Crow and the Fox*." One of the most extravagant of his flatterers said to a friend, admitted for a last interview : "With all his weakness, not the least trace of decline of intellect ; still the same facility of expression, still the same lucidity." This aroused Michaud, upon whom the affectionate words of a sincere friend had just before produced no effect. He started, and sitting upright in his bed, exclaimed, in a tremulous voice : "Yes ! yes ! *still* the same ! still ——" and he sunk exhausted and dying on his pillow. These were his last words !

To criticise the works of Michaud properly would require a volume ; we can, therefore, only lay before our readers a list of such as from their merit and celebrity are ever likely to fall under the eye of English readers. His greatest claim to the attention of posterity is doubtless the one before us, "The History of the Crusades," of which his biographer, who is certainly less of an eulogist than any one we ever saw assume a similar task, very justly says : "It may be said, without exaggeration, that it is one of the most valuable historical works that our age has produced. To its completion he sacrificed almost every moment of twenty of the best years of his life." No reader requires to be told that it was a labour of love. He was the founder of, and a considerable contributor to, "La Biographie Universelle;" and if to these we add his beautiful poem of "Le Printemps d'un Proscrit," we think we name all that he wrote that would be interesting at the present day. As a journalist he is supposed to have excelled. Mixed up from an early age with politics and journalism ; possessed of a lively imagination and great facility of expression ; constantly in the world, and deeply interested in its movements—we can fancy his *vers de société*, of which so much is said to have been piquant and sparkling. We subjoin a specimen, written upon Buonaparte's expedition to Egypt :

Que de lauriers tombés dans l'eau,
Et que de fortunes perdues !
Que d'hommes courent au tombeau,
Pour porter Bonaparte aux nues !
Ce héros vaut son pesant d'or ;
En France, personne n'en doute ;
Mais il vaudrait bien plus encore,
S'il valoit tout ce qu'il nous coute.

What laurels in the waters fall,
What fortunes sink no more to rise !
What men lie shrouded in death's pall,
That Bonaparte may gain the skies !
This hero's worth his weight in gold ;
In France of that there's no one doubts ;
But greater far his worth, if sold
At what he costs—or thereabouts !

As a conversationalist his reputation stands even higher than that of Coleridge ; for the stream was quite as constant and abundant, and at the same time much more pellucid. An English biographical dictionary says he was censor of the press under Louis XVIII., but this, we believe, is not correct ; indeed, it was an office scarcely suitable for the editor and proprietor of such a journal as the *Quotidien*. He was a member of the Academy and of the Institute ; a Knight of St. John of Jerusalem and of the Holy Sepulchre, and for a short time representative of the department of the Ain. These were his temporary honours. Much more durable and brilliant ones belong to him as the author of the work before us.

W. R.

HISTORY

OF THE

CRUSADES

HOSPITALITY OF BARBARIANS TO PILGRIMS.

When the world was ravaged by the Goths, the Huns and the Vandals, the pilgrimages to the Holy Land were not at all interrupted. Pious travellers were protected by the hospitable virtues of the barbarians, who began to respect the cross of Christ, and sometimes even followed the pilgrims to Jerusalem. In these times of trouble and desolation a poor pilgrim, who bore his scrip and staff, often passed through fields of carnage, and travelled without fear amidst armies which threatened the empires of the East and West.—Book I.

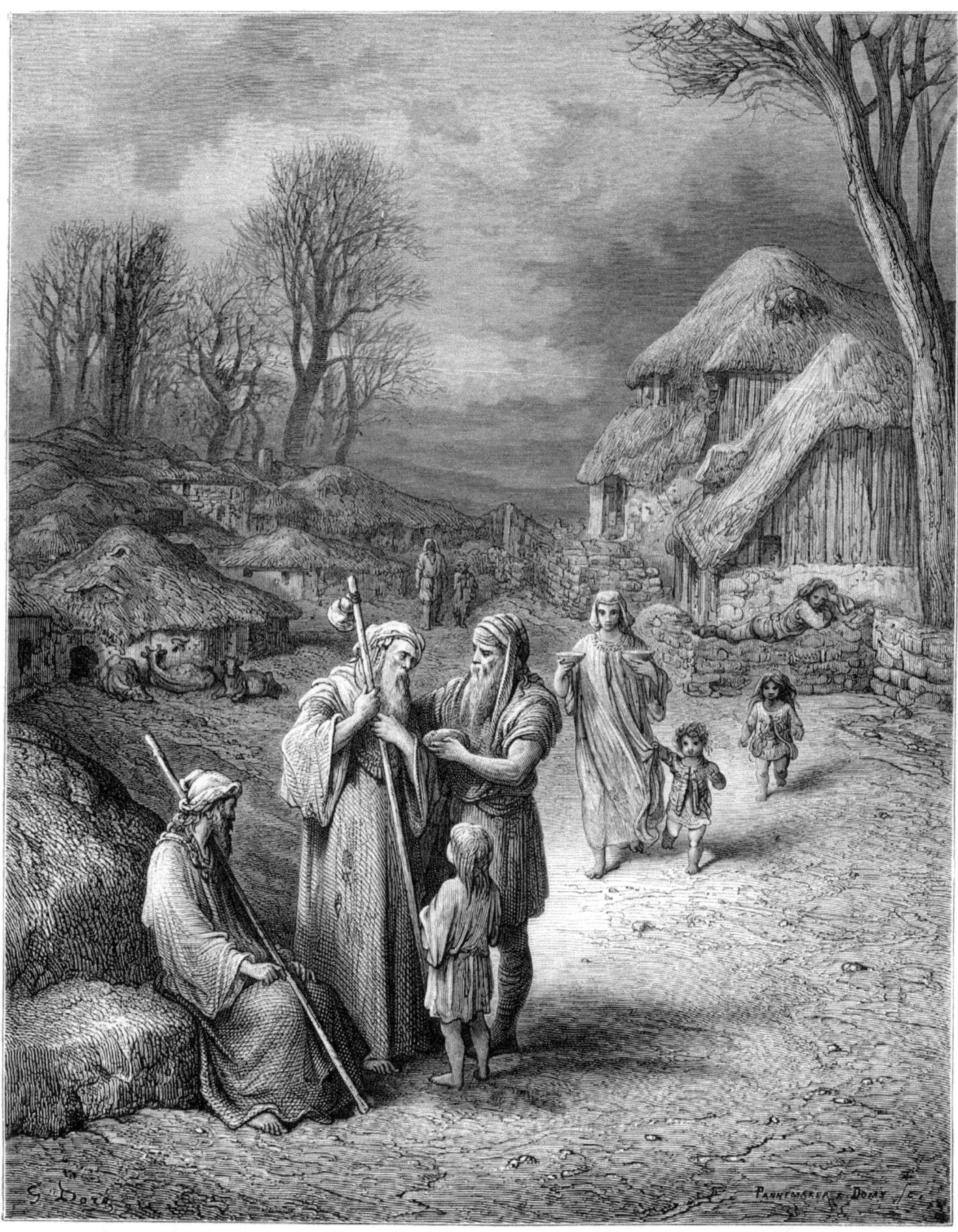

BOOK I

The Birth of the Crusades

300 to 1095

HISTORY OF THE CRUSADES.

BOOK I.

BIRTH OF THE CRUSADES.

A. D. 300–1095.

Early pilgrimages to the Holy Land—Veneration for the Holy Sepulchre—Palestine visited by the early Christians—Profaned by Fire Worshippers—Worship of the Magi annihilated by Mohammedanism—Fanaticism and bravery of the Saracens—Their conquests—Paganism annihilated by Mohammedanism—Christians persecuted by the Mussulmans—Pilgrimages of Peter the Hermit, &c.—Siege of Constantinople—Caliphs of Bagdad—The Fatimites—Fatimite Caliphs capture Jerusalem—William of Tyre—Persecutions of the Jews—Pilgrims welcomed everywhere—Monasteries for the pilgrims—Pilgrimages of distinguished persons the forerunner of the Crusades—Victorious career of the Turks—Jerusalem captured—Eleven emperors of Constantinople put to death—Pope Gregory VII.—Power of the popes—Pope Hildebrand—Pope Victor III. incites the Christians to take arms against the infidels—Conquests of the Genoese and Pisans—Peter the Hermit—His interviews with the patriarch of Jerusalem and Pope Urban II.—The crusades instigated by Peter—First determined on at the council of Clermont, convoked by Urban II.—Enthusiasm in their favour.

FROM the earliest ages of the Church, a custom had been practised of making pilgrimages to the Holy Land. Judea, full of religious remembrances, was still the promised land of the faithful; the blessings of heaven appeared to be in store for those who visited Calvary, the tomb of Jesus Christ, and renewed their baptism in the waters of the Jordan. Under the reign of Constantine, the ardour for pilgrimages increased among the faithful; they flocked from all the provinces of the empire to worship Jesus Christ upon his own tomb, and to trace the steps of their God in that city which had but just resumed its name, and which the piety of an emperor had caused to issue from its ruins. The Holy Sepulchre presented itself to the eyes of the pilgrims surrounded by a magnificence which redoubled their veneration. An obscure cavern had become a marble temple, paved with precious stones and decorated with splendid colonnades. To the east of the Holy Sepulchre appeared the church of the Resurrection, in which they could admire the riches of Asia, mingled with the arts of Greece and Rome. Constantine celebrated the thirty-first year of his reign by the inauguration of this church, and thousands of Christians came, on occasion of this solemnity, to listen to the panegyric of Christ from the lips of the learned and holy bishop Eusebius.

St. Helena, the mother of the emperor, repaired to Jerusalem, at a very advanced age, and caused churches and chapels to be built upon Mount Tabor, in the city of Nazareth, and in the greater part of the places which Christ had sanctified by his presence and his miracles. From this period pilgrimages to the Holy Land became much more frequent. The pilgrims, no longer in dread of the persecutions of the Pagans, could now give themselves up, without fear, to the fervour of their devotion; the Roman eagles, ornamented with the cross of Jesus Christ, protected them on their march; they everywhere trampled under-foot the fragments of idols, and they travelled amidst the abodes of their fellow-Christians.

When the emperor Julian, in order to weaken the authority of the prophecies, undertook to rebuild the temple of the Jews, numerous were the prodigies related by which God confounded his designs, and Jerusalem, for that attempt even, became more dear to the disciples of Jesus Christ. The Christians did not cease to visit Palestine. St. Jerome, who, towards the end of the fourth century, had retired to Bethlehem, informs us in one of his letters that pilgrims arrived in crowds in Judea, and that around the holy tomb the praises of the Son of God were to be heard, uttered in many languages. From this period, pilgrimages to the Holy Land were so numerous, that several doctors and fathers of the Church thought it their duty to point out the abuses and danger of the practice. They told Christians that long voyages might turn them aside from the path of salvation; that their God was not confined to one city; that Jesus Christ was everywhere where faith and good works were to be found; but such was the blind zeal which then drew the Christians towards Jerusalem, that the voice of the holy doctors was scarcely heard. The counsels of enlightened piety were not able to abate the ardour of the pilgrims, who believed they should be wanting in faith and zeal, if they did not adore Jesus Christ in the very places where, according to the expression of St. Jerome, the light of the gospel first shone from the top of the holy cross.

As soon as the people of the West became converted to Christianity, they turned their eyes to the East. From the depths of Gaul, from the forests of Germany, from all the countries of Europe, new Christians were to be seen hastening to visit the cradle of the faith they had embraced. An itinerary for the use of pilgrims served them as a guide from the banks of the Rhone and the Dordogne to the shores of the Jordan, and conducted them, on their return, from Jerusalem to the principal cities of Italy.

When the world was ravaged by the Goths, the Huns, and the Vandals, the pilgrimages to the Holy Land were not at all interrupted. Pious travellers were protected by the hospitable virtues of the barbarians, who began to respect the cross of Christ, and sometimes even followed the pilgrims to Jerusalem. In these times of trouble and desolation, a poor pilgrim, who bore his scrip and staff, often passed through fields of carnage, and travelled without fear amidst armies which threatened the empires of the East and the West.

Illustrious families of Rome came to seek an asylum at Jerusalem, and upon the tomb of Jesus Christ. Christians then found, on the banks of the Jordan, that peace which seemed to be banished from the rest of the world. This peace, which lasted several centuries, was not troubled before the reign of Heraclius. Under this reign, the armies of Cosroës, king of Persia, invaded Syria, Palestine, and Egypt; the holy city fell into the hands of the worshippers of fire; the conquerors bore away into captivity vast numbers of Christians, and profaned the churches of Jesus Christ. All the faithful deplored the misfortunes of Jerusalem, and shed tears when they learned that the king of Persia had carried off, among the spoils of the vanquished, the cross of the Saviour, which had been preserved in the church of the Resurrection.

Heaven, at length, touched by the prayers and affliction of the Christians, blessed the arms of Heraclius, who, after ten years of reverses, triumphed over the enemies of Christianity and the empire, and brought back to Jerusalem the Christians whose chains he had broken. Then was to be seen an emperor of the East, walking barefooted in the streets of the holy city, carrying on his shoulders to the summit of Calvary, the wood of the true cross, which he considered the most glorious trophy of his victories. This imposing ceremony was a festival for the people of Jerusalem and the Christian church, which, latter still, every year celebrates the memory of it. When Heraclius re-entered Constantinople, he was received as the liberator of the Christians, and the kings of the West sent ambassadors to congratulate him.

But the joy of the faithful was not of long duration. Towards the beginning of the seventh century there had arisen, in an obscure corner of Asia, a new religion, opposed to all others, which preached dominion and war. Mahomet had promised the conquest of the world to his disciples, who had issued almost naked from the deserts of Arabia. By his passionate doctrine he was able to inflame the imagination of the Arabs, and on the field of battle knew how to inspire them with his own impetuous courage. His first successes, which must have greatly exceeded his hopes, were like so many miracles, increasing the confidence of his partisans, and carrying conviction to the minds of the weak and wavering. The political state of the East seemed to offer no obstacle to the progress of a sect, which, from its birth, showed itself everywhere with fire and sword. The worship of the Magi was sinking into contempt; the Jews scattered throughout Asia were opposed to the Sabeans, and divided amongst themselves; and the Christians, under the names of Eutychians, Nestorians, Maronites, and Jacobites, were engaged in heaping, reciprocally, anathemas upon one another. The empire of Persia, torn by intestine wars, and attacked by the barbarous races of Tartary, had lost both its power and splendour; that of the Greeks, weakened both within and without, was hastening to its fall; "everything was perishing in the East," says Bossuet. A new religion, a new empire, sprang up easily in the midst of ruins. The armed doctrine of Mahomet invaded, within a very short period, the three Arabias, a part of Syria, and a large division of Persia.

After the death of the Prophet of Mecca, his lieutenants and the companions of his first exploits carried on his great work. The sight of conquered provinces only increased the fanaticism and the bravery of the Saracens. They had no fear of death in the field of battle, for, according to the words of their prophet, paradise, with all its voluptuous pleasures, awaited those who precipitated themselves upon the enemy, and behind them hell opened its abysses. Their conquests were so much the more rapid, from their uniting, in their military and religious government, the prompt decision of despotism with all the passions that are met with in a republic. Masters of Persia and Syria, they soon took possession of Egypt; their victorious battalions flowed on into Africa, planted the standard of the Prophet upon the ruins of Carthage, and carried the terror of their arms to the shores of the Atlantic. From India to the Straits of Cadiz, and from the Caspian Sea to the ocean, language, manners, religion, everything was changed; what had remained of Paganism was annihilated, together with the worship of the Magi; Christianity scarcely subsisted, and Europe itself was threatened with a similar destruction. Constantinople, which was the bulwark of the West, saw before its walls innumerable hordes of Saracens: several times besieged both by sea and land, the city of Constantine only owed its safety to the Greek fire, to the assistance of the Bulgarians, and to the inexperience of the Arabs in the art of navigation.

During the first age of the Hegira, the conquests of the Mussulmans were only bounded by the sea which separated them from Europe; but when they had constructed vessels, no nation was safe from their invasion; they ravaged the isles of the Mediterranean, the coasts of Italy and Greece; fortune or treason made them masters of Spain, where they overturned the monarchy of the Goths; they took advantage of the weakness of the children of Clovis to penetrate into the southern provinces of Gaul, and were only stopped in their invasions by the victories of Charles Martel.

Amidst the first conquests of the Saracens, they had turned their eyes towards Jerusalem.

According to the faith of the Mussulmans, Mahomet had been in the city of David and Solomon; it was from Jerusalem that he set out to ascend into heaven in his nocturnal voyage. The Saracens considered Jerusalem as the house of God, as the city of saints and miracles. A short time after the death of the Prophet, the soldiers of Omar besieged it. The Christians, animated by despair, swore to defend the city. The siege lasted four months, each day being marked by sorties or attacks; the Saracens approaching the walls repeating the words of the Koran—"Let us enter into the holy land which God has promised us." After enduring all the miseries of a long siege, the inhabitants of Jerusalem at length surrendered to the caliph Omar, who himself came into Palestine to receive the keys and the submission of the conquered city.

The Christians had the grief of seeing the church of the Holy Sepulchre profaned by the presence of the chief of the Infidels. The patriarch Sophronius, who accompanied the caliph, could not refrain from repeating these words of Daniel,—"The abomination of desolation is in the holy place." Jerusalem was filled with mourning, a gloomy silence reigned in the churches, and in all the places in which the hymns of the Christians had so long resounded. Although Omar had left them the exercise of their worship, they were obliged to conceal their crosses and their sacred books. The bell no longer summoned the faithful to prayer; the pomp of ceremonies was interdicted, and religion appeared but as a desolate widow. The caliph ordered a mosque to be erected on the spot whereon the temple of Solomon had been built. The aspect of this edifice, consecrated to the worship of the infidels, still further increased the affliction of the Christians. History relates that the patriarch Sophronius was unable to support the sight of so many profanations, and died in despair, deploring the misfortunes and captivity of the holy city.

In the mean time, the presence of Omar, of whose moderation the East boasts, restrained the jealous fanaticism of the Mussulmans. After his death the faithful had much more to suffer; they were driven from their houses, insulted in their churches; the tribute which they had to pay to the new masters of Palestine was increased, and they were forbidden to carry arms or to mount on horseback. A leathern girdle, which they were never allowed to be without, was the badge of their servitude; the conquerors would not permit the Christians to speak the Arab tongue, sacred to the disciples of the Koran; and the people who remained faithful to Jesus Christ had not liberty even to pronounce the name of the patriarch of Jerusalem without the permission of the Saracens.

All these persecutions could not stop the crowd of Christians who repaired to Jerusalem; the sight of the holy city sustaining their courage as it heightened their devotion. There were no evils, no outrages, that they could not support with resignation, when they remembered that Christ had been loaded with chains, and had died upon the cross in the places they were about to visit. Among the faithful of the West who arrived in Asia in the midst of the early conquests of the Mussulmans, history has preserved the names of St. Arculphus and St. Antoninus of Plaisance. The latter had borne arms with distinction, when he determined to follow the pilgrims who were setting out for Jerusalem. He traversed Syria, Palestine, and Egypt. On his arrival on the banks of the Jordan, Judea had not yet fallen into the hands of the infidels; but the fame of their victories already filled the East, and their armies were threatening the holy city. Several years after the pilgrimage of St. Antoninus, Arculphus, accompanied by Peter, a French hermit, set out from the coast of England in a vessel bound for Syria. He remained nine months at Jerusalem, then under the dominion of the enemies of Christ. On his return to Europe, he related what he had seen in Palestine, and in all the sacred spots visited by the pilgrims of the West. The account of his pilgrimage was drawn up by a holy monk of the Hebrides, for the information and edification of the faithful.

The Christians of Palestine, however, enjoyed some short intervals of security during the civil wars of the Mussulmans. If they were not freed from their bondage, they could at least weep in peace upon the tomb of Christ. The dynasty of the Ommiades, which had established the seat of the Mussulman empire at Damascus, was always odious to the ever-formidable party of the Alides, and employed itself less in persecuting the Christians than in preserving its own precarious power. Merwan II., the last caliph of this house, was the most cruel towards the disciples of Christ; and when he, with all his family, sunk under the power of his enemies, the Christians and the infidels united in thanks to heaven for having delivered the East from his tyranny.

The Abassides, established in the city of Bagdad, which they had founded, persecuted and tolerated the Christians by turns. The Christians, always living between the fear of persecution and the hope of a transient security, saw at last the prospect of happier days dawn upon them with the reign of Haroun al Raschid, the greatest caliph of the race of Abbas. Under this reign the glory of Charlemagne, which had reached Asia, protected the churches of the East. His pious liberality relieved the indigence of the Christians of Alexandria, of Carthage, and Jerusalem. The two greatest princes of their age testified their mutual esteem by frequent embassies: they sent each other magnificent presents; and, in the friendly intercourse of two powerful monarchs, the East and the West exchanged the richest productions of their soil and their industry. The presents of Haroun created a lively surprise in the Court of Charlemagne, and gave a high idea of the arts and riches of Asia. The monarch of the Franks took pleasure in showing to the envoys of the caliph the magnificence of the religious ceremonies of the Christians. Witnesses, at Aix-la-Chapelle, of several processions, in which the clergy had exhibited all their most precious ornaments, the ambassadors, on their return to Bagdad, reported that they had seen *men of gold.*

There was no doubt policy in the marks of esteem which Haroun lavished upon the most powerful of the princes of the West. He was making war against the emperors of Constantinople, and might justly fear that they would interest the bravest among Christian people in their cause. The popular traditions of Byzantium foretold that the Latins would some day be the liberators of Greece; and in one of the first sieges of Constantinople by the Saracens, the report only of the arrival of the Franks had re-animated the courage of the besieged, and carried terror into the ranks of the Mussulmans. In the time of Haroun, the name of Jerusalem already exercised so powerful an influence over the Christians of the West, that it was sufficient to rouse their warlike enthusiasm, and raise armies to serve against the infidels. To take from the Franks every pretext for a religious war, which might make them embrace the cause of the Greeks, and draw them into Asia, the caliph neglected no opportunity of obtaining the friendship of Charlemagne; and caused the keys of the holy city and of the holy sepulchre to be presented to him. This homage, rendered to the greatest of the Christian monarchs, was celebrated with enthusiasm in contemporary legends, which afterwards caused it to be believed that this prince had made the voyage and completed the conquest of Jerusalem.

Haroun treated the Christians of the Latin Church as his own subjects; and the children of the caliph imitated his moderation. Under their sway, Bagdad was the abode of the sciences and the arts. The caliph Almamon, says an Arabian historian, was not ignorant that they who labour in the advancement of reason are the elect of God. Intelligence polished the manners of the chiefs of Islamism, and inspired them with a toleration till that time unknown to Mussulmans. Whilst the Arabians of Africa were pursuing their conquests towards the West, whilst they took possession of Sicily, and Rome itself saw its suburbs and its churches of St. Peter and St. Paul invaded and pillaged by infidels, the servants of Jesus Christ prayed in peace within the walls of Jerusalem. The pilgrims of the West, who arrived there without danger, were received in an hospital, the foundation of which was attributed to Charlemagne. According to the report of the monk Bernard, who himself performed the pilgrimage to the Holy Land, about the middle of the ninth century, the hospital for the pilgrims of the Latin Church was composed of twelve houses or hostelries. To this pious establishment were attached fields, vineyards, and a garden, situated in the Valley of Jehoshaphat. This hospital, like those which the emperor of the West founded in the north of Europe, had a library always open to Christians and travellers. From the tenth century there existed in the neighbourhood of the Fountain of Siloë, a cemetery, in which were interred the pilgrims who died at Jerusalem. Among the tombs of the faithful dwelt the servants of God. This place, says the relation of St. Antoninus, covered with fruit-trees, dotted with sepulchres and humble cells, brings together the dead and the living, and presents at once a cheerful and a melancholy picture.

To the desire of visiting the tomb of Jerusalem was joined the earnest wish to procure relics, which were then sought for with eagerness by the devotion of the faithful. All who returned from the East made it their glory to bring back to their country some precious remains of Christian antiquity, and above all the bones of holy martyrs, which constituted the ornament and the riches of their churches, and upon which princes and kings swore to respect truth and justice. The productions of Asia likewise attracted the attention of the people of Europe. We read in Gregory of Tours, that the wine of Gaza was celebrated in France in the reign of Gontran; that the silk and precious stones of the East added to the splendour of the dresses of the great and the noble; and that St. Eloi, at the court of Dagobert, did not disdain to clothe himself in the rich stuffs of Asia. Commerce attracted a great number of Europeans to Egypt, Syria, and Palestine. The Venetians, the Genoese, the Pisans, —the merchants of Amalfi and Marseilles,—had all stores at Alexandria, in the maritime cities of Phenicia, and in the city of Jerusalem. Before the church of St. Marie-la-Latine, says the monk Bernard, already quoted, extended a large place or square, which was called the Market of the Franks. Every year, on the 15th of September, a fair was opened on Mount Calvary, in which were exchanged the productions of Europe for those of the East.

Greek and Syrian Christians were established even in the city of Bagdad, where they devoted themselves to trade, exercised the art of medicine, and cultivated the sciences. They attained by their learning the most considerable employments, and sometimes even obtained the command of cities and the government of provinces. One of the caliphs of the race of Abbas [Mohamed] declared that the disciples of Christ were the most worthy to be trusted with the administration of Persia. In short, the Christians of Palestine and the Mussulman provinces, the pilgrims and travellers who returned from the East, seemed no longer to have any persecutions to dread, when all at once new storms broke out in the East. The children of Haroun soon shared the fate of the posterity of Charlemagne, and Asia, like the West, was plunged into the horrors of anarchy and civil war.

As the empire founded by Mahomet had for its principle the spirit of conquest; as the state was not defended by any provident institution; and as all depended upon the personal character of the prince, it might easily be perceived that symptoms of decay began to appear as soon as there remained nothing else to conquer, and the chiefs ceased either to make themselves feared or to inspire respect. The caliphs of Bagdad, rendered effeminate by luxury, and corrupted by long prosperity, abandoned the cares of empire, buried themselves in their seraglios, and appeared to reserve to themselves no other right than that of being named in the public prayers. The Arabians were no longer governed by that blind zeal, and that ardent fanaticism which they had brought from the desert. Degenerated, like their chiefs, they no longer resembled their warlike ancestors, who would weep at not having been present at a battle. The authority of the caliphs had lost its true defenders; and when despotism surrounded itself with slaves purchased on the banks of the Oxus, this foreign militia, called in to defend the throne, only precipitated its fall. New sectaries, seduced by the example of Mahomet, and persuaded that the world would obey those who should change its manners or opinions, added the danger of religious dissensions to that of political troubles. In the midst of the general confusion, the emirs or lieutenants, of whom several governed vast kingdoms, no longer offered anything beyond a vain homage to the successor of the Prophet, and refused to send him either money or troops. The gigantic empire of the Abassides crumbled away on all sides, and the world, according to the expression of an Arabian writer, was within the reach of him who would take possession of it. The spiritual power was itself divided; Islamism beheld at one time five caliphs, each of whom assumed the title of commander of the faithful, and vicar of Mahomet.

The numerous dynasties which sprung up amidst the troubles of Asia, shared amongst them the spoils of the sovereigns of Bagdad; those which ruled over Persia and upon the banks of the Tigris, under the pretence of defending the Mussulman religion, subjected their spiritual chiefs to the most humiliating subserviency. At the same time the Fatimites, who pretended to be descended from Aly, and who had usurped the title of caliph, raised armies, and launched anathemas against the Abassides; they had taken possession of Egypt, and they threatened to invade Syria, and to march to Bagdad, and dethrone the vicars of the Prophet.

The Greeks then appeared to rouse themselves from their long supineness, and sought to take advantage of the divisions and the humiliation of the Saracens. Nicephorus Phocas took the field at the head of a powerful army, and recaptured Antioch from the Mussulmans. Already the people of Constantinople celebrated his triumphs, and styled him "*the star of the East, the death and the scourge of the infidels.*" He might, perhaps, have merited these titles, if the Greek clergy had seconded his efforts. Nicephorus was desirous of giving to this war* a religious character, and to place in the rank of martyrs all who should fall in prosecuting it. The prelates of his empire condemned his design as sacrilegious, and opposed to him a canon of St. Basil, the text of which recommended to him who had killed an enemy to abstain during three years from a participation in the holy mysteries. Deprived of the powerful stimulus of fanaticism, Nicephorus found among the Greeks more panegyrists than soldiers, and could not pursue his advantages against the Saracens, to whom, even in their decline, religion prescribed resistance and promised victory. His triumphs, which were celebrated at Constantinople with enthusiasm, were confined to the taking of Antioch, and only served to create a persecution against the Christians of Palestine. The patriarch of Jerusalem, accused of keeping up an understanding with the Greeks, expired at the stake, and several churches of the holy city were consigned to the flames.

A Greek army, under the command of Temelicus, had advanced to the gates of Amida, a city situated on the banks of the Tigris. This army was attacked, in the midst of a hurricane, by the Saracens, who routed it, and made a great number of prisoners. The Christian soldiers who fell into the hands of the infidels, heard, in the prisons of Bagdad, of the death of Nicephorus; and as Zimisces, his successor, gave no attention to their deliverance, their chief wrote to him in these terms:—"You who leave us to perish in an accursed land, and who do not deem us worthy to be buried, according to Christian usages, in the tombs of our fathers, we cannot recognize you as the legitimate chief of the holy Greek empire. If you do not avenge those who fell before Amida, and those who now sigh in foreign lands, God will demand a strict account of them of you, at the terrible day of judgment."

---

* Lebeau, in his "History of the Lower Empire," relates, after contemporary historians, an incident which plainly shows what was the spirit of the Greeks at that time. "A small town of Silicia being invaded by the Saracens, the curé of the place, named Themal, was saying mass at the time. At the noise which he hears he descends briskly from the altar, without taking off his pontificals, arms himself with a hammer which served for a bell in many eastern churches, goes straight to meet the enemy, wounds, knocks down, crushes all that he meets, and puts the rest to flight. Although he had delivered his town from an invasion of the Saracens, the curé Themal was censured and suspended by his bishop. He was so ill treated that he sought refuge with the Saracens, and embraced the religion of Mahomet."

When Zimisces received this letter at Constantinople, says an Armenian historian, he was penetrated with grief, and resolved to avenge the outrage inflicted upon religion and the empire. On all sides preparations were set on foot for a fresh war against the Saracens. The nations of the West were no strangers to this enterprize, which preceded, by more than a year, the first of the Crusades. Venice, which then enjoyed the commerce of the East, forbade her people, under pain of death, to convey to the Mussulmans of Africa and Asia, either iron, wood, or any species of arms. The Christians of Syria and several Armenian princes repaired to the standard of Zimisces, who took the field, and carried war into the territories of the Saracens. So great was the confusion which then prevailed among the Mussulman powers, and with such rapidity did one dynasty succeed to another, that history can scarcely distinguish what prince, or what people ruled over Palestine and Jerusalem. After having defeated the Mussulmans on the banks of the Tigris, and forced the caliph of Bagdad to pay a tribute to the successors of Constantine, Zimisces penetrated, almost without resistance, into Judea, took possession of Cesarea, of Ptolemaïs, of Tiberias, Nazareth, and several other cities of the Holy Land. He was encamped upon Tabor when he received a deputation of the inhabitants of Ramala and Jerusalem, who promised him obedience, and required of him troops to defend their cities. Zimisces received their submission and their request favourably,* and pursued the wreck of the Saracen army, which had sought refuge in some cities of Phenicia and in the mountains of Libanus.

After this first campaign, the Holy Land appeared to be on the eve of being delivered entirely from the yoke of the infidels, when the emperor died poisoned. His death at once put a stop to the execution of an enterprize of which he was the soul and the leader. The Christian nations had scarcely time to rejoice at the delivery of Jerusalem, when they learnt that the holy city had again fallen into the hands of the Fatimite caliphs, who, after the death of Zimisces, had invaded Syria and Palestine.

The caliphs of Cairo, who had taken advantage of the transient conquests of the Greeks to extend their empire, at first treated the Christians as allies and auxiliaries. In the hope of enriching their new dominions and repairing the evils of war, they favoured the commerce of the Europeans, and tolerated the devotion of pilgrimages to the Holy Land. The markets of the Franks were re-established in the city of Jerusalem; the Christians re-built the hospitals of the pilgrims, and the churches which were falling to decay. They began to forget the peaceful domination of the Abassides, and felicitated themselves upon living under the laws of the sovereigns of Cairo; and still greater right had they to hope that all their troubles were about to be at an end, when they saw the caliph Hakim, whose mother was a Christian, ascend the throne. But God, who, according to the expression of contemporary authors, wished to try the virtues of the faithful, did not long delay to confound their hopes and raise new persecutions against them.

Hakim, the third of the Fatimite caliphs, signalized his reign by all the excesses of fanaticism and outrage. Unfixed in his own projects, and wavering between two religions, he by turns protected and persecuted Christianity. He respected neither the policy of his predecessors nor the laws which he himself had established. He changed, on the morrow, that which he had ordained the preceding day, and spread disorder and confusion throughout his dominions. In the extravagance of his mind and the intoxication of power, he carried his madness so far as to believe himself a god. The terror which he inspired procured him worshippers, and altars were raised to him in the neighbourhood of Fostat, which he had given up to the flames. Sixteen thousand of his subjects prostrated themselves before him, and adored him as sovereign of the living and the dead.

* Whilst reading the letter of Zimisces, which gives an account of these events, we feel astonished that he does not show more eagerness to see Jerusalem; but such was the character of the Greeks, that they set more value on the acquisition of relics, which were borne in triumph to Constantinople, than in delivering the holy city and the tomb of Christ. It is thence apparent that this expedition was not at all directed by the same spirit as the crusades.

Hakim despised Mahomet, but the Mussulmans were too numerous in his states to allow him to think of persecuting them. The god trembled for the authority of the prince, and allowed all his anger to fall upon the Christians, whom he gave up to the fury of their enemies. The places which the Christians held in the administration, and the abuses introduced into the mode of levying the imposts, with which duty they were charged, had drawn upon them the hatred of all the Mussulmans. When the caliph Hakim had once given the signal for persecution, he found himself at no loss for executioners. At first, they who had abused their power were the objects of pursuit; the Christian religion became the next crime, and the most pious among the faithful were deemed the most guilty. The blood of the Christians flowed in all the cities of Egypt and Syria, their courage in the midst of torments only adding to the hatred of their persecutors. The complaints which escaped them in their sufferings, the prayers, even, which they addressed to Jesus Christ to put an end to their evils, were considered as a revolt, and punished as the most guilty treasons.

It is probable that motives of policy joined with those of fanaticism in the persecution of the Christians. Gerbert, archbishop of Ravenna, who had become pope, under the name of Sylvester II., had witnessed the ills to which the faithful were subjected in their pilgrimages to Jerusalem. On his return he excited the nations of the West to take up arms against the Saracens. In his exhortations, he made Jerusalem herself speak, made her deplore her misfortunes, and conjure her Christian children to hasten and break her chains. The people were deeply moved with the complaints and groans of Sion. The Pisans, the Genoese, with Boson, king of Arles, undertook a maritime expedition against the Saracens, and made an incursion upon the coasts of Syria. These hostilities, and the number of the pilgrims, which increased every day, might well create distrust in the masters of the East. The Saracens, alarmed by sinister predictions, and by the imprudent menaces of the Christians, saw nothing but enemies in the disciples of Christ; from that time terror and death guarded the gates of Jerusalem.

It is impossible, says William of Tyre, to describe all the species of persecutions to which the Christians were then exposed. Among the instances of barbarity cited by the historians, there is one which gave to Tasso the idea of his affecting episode of Olindus and Sophronia. One of the bitterest enemies of the Christians, in order to increase the hatred of their persecutors, threw, in the night, a dead dog into one of the principal mosques of the city. The first who repaired thither to morning prayer were seized with horror at the sight of this profanation, and proclaimed their anger aloud. Threatening clamours soon resounded in every part of the city; the crowd assembled in a state of tumultuous excitement around the mosque; the Christians were at once accused of this act of sacrilege, and all swore to wash out the outrage to their prophet in the blood of the perpetrators. All Christians were about to be immolated to the revenge of the Mussulmans, and already were they prepared for death, when a young man, whose name history has not preserved, presented himself in the midst of them. ‘The greatest misfortune that could happen," said he, "would be that the church of Jerusalem should perish. When a people is threatened with destruction, it is just that a single man should sacrifice himself for the salvation of all; I here and now offer myself as a victim to die for you; to you I leave the charge of doing justice to my memory, and I recommend myself to your prayers." After pronouncing these words, which dissolved the assembly in tears, he quitted them, and repaired to the chiefs of the Mussulmans; he declared himself alone to be the author of the crime imputed to the Christians, and invoked upon himself the death with which his brethren were menaced. The Mussulmans, without being in the least touched by his generous devotion, were satisfied with the victim who offered himself to their vengeance: the sword was no longer suspended over the heads of the Christians, and he who had immolated himself for their safety, went, according

FOULQUE-NERRA ASSAILED BY THE PHANTOMS OF HIS VICTIMS.

Foulque-Nerra, Count of Anjou, charged with crimes, and stained with blood, thought to efface all his cruelties by a voyage to Jerusalem. His brother, whom he had caused to perish in a dungeon, presented himself, wherever he went, before his eyes; it appeared to him that the numerous victims sacrificed to his ambition in unjust war issued from their tombs to disturb his sleep, and reproach him for his barbarity.—Book I.

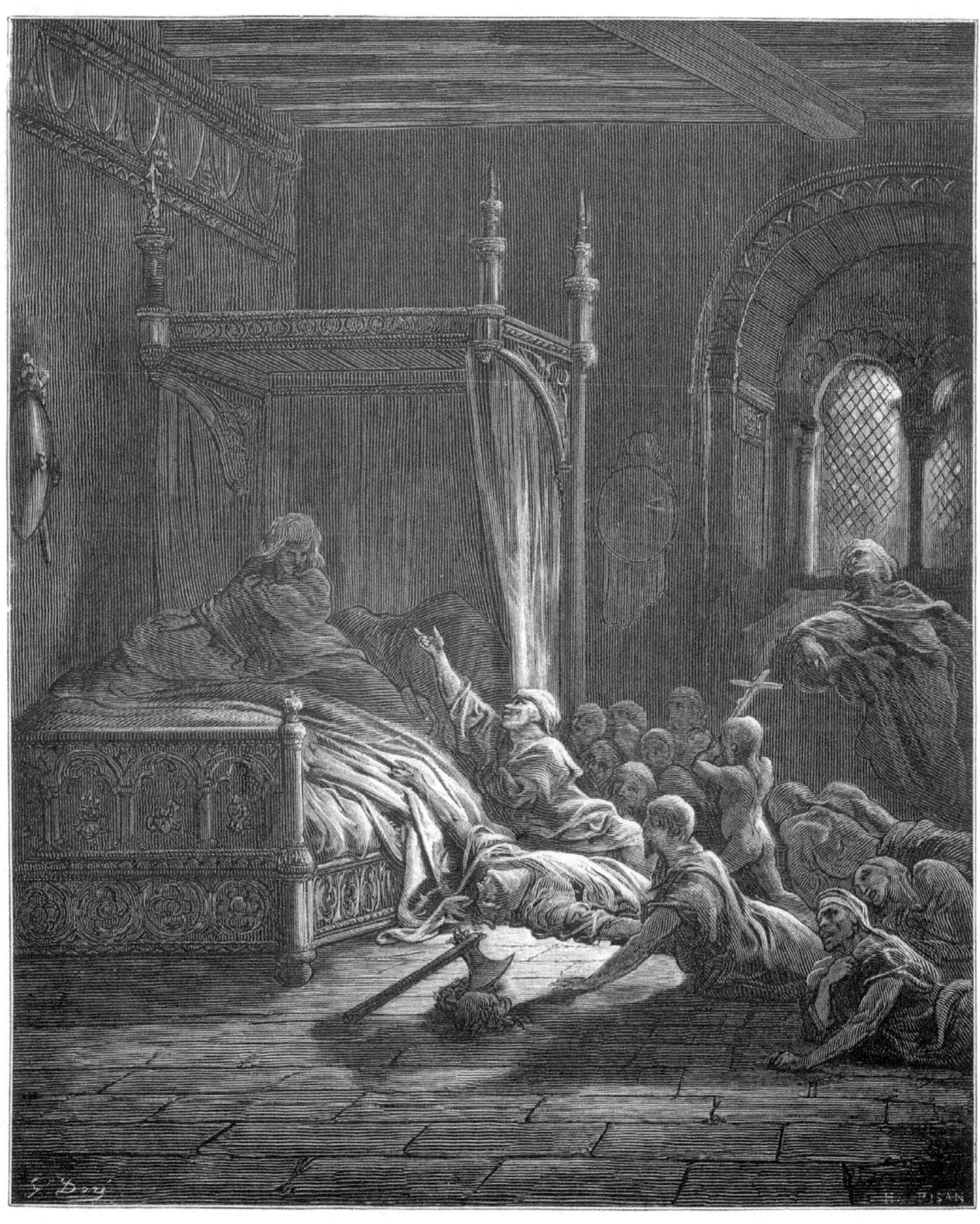

to the expression of William of Tyre, to receive in heaven the reward reserved for those whose minds burn with a love of perfect charity.

Nevertheless, other misfortunes awaited the Christians of Palestine; all religious ceremonies were interdicted; the greater part of the churches were converted into stables; that of the Holy Sepulchre was completely destroyed. The Christians, driven from Jerusalem, were scattered throughout the countries of the East. Old historians relate, that the world took part in the mourning of the holy city, and was seized with trouble and consternation. Winter, with its frosts and storms, showed itself in regions where, till that time, it had been unknown. The Bosphorus and the Nile bore sheets of ice upon their bosoms. Earthquakes were felt in Syria and Asia Minor; and their shocks, which were repeated during two months, destroyed several large cities. When the account of the destruction of the holy places arrived in the West, it drew tears from all true Christians. We read in the chronicle of the monk Glaber, that Europe had likewise been presented with signs which foreboded great calamities: a shower of stones had fallen in Burgundy, and a comet and threatening meteors had appeared in the heavens. The agitation was extreme among all Christian nations; nevertheless, they did not take up arms against the Mussulmans, but the whole of their vengeance fell upon the Jews, whom all Europe accused of having provoked the fury of the infidels.

The calamities of the holy city rendered it still more venerable in the eyes of the faithful; persecution redoubled the pious delirium of those who went into Asia to contemplate a city covered with ruins, and to behold an empty sepulchre. It was in Jerusalem, filled with mourning, that God most manifestly distributed his blessings and delighted to point out his will. Impostors constantly took advantage of this opinion of the Christian people, to mislead the credulity of the multitude. To gain credit for their words, it was quite sufficient to exhibit letters which, they said, had fallen from heaven into Jerusalem. At this period, a prediction, which announced* the end of the world and the approaching coming of Jesus Christ into Palestine, very much increased the veneration of the people for the holy places. The Christians of the West arrived in crowds at Jerusalem, with the design of dying there, or there awaiting the coming of the sovereign judge. The monk Glaber informs us, that the affluence of pilgrims surpassed all that could be expected from the devotion of these remote times. First were seen on the holy march the poor and the lower classes, then counts, barons, and princes, all reckoning as nothing the grandeurs of the earth.

The inconstancy of Hakim had, in a degree, mitigated the misfortunes of Jerusalem, and he had just granted liberty to the Christians to rebuild their churches, when he died by the hand of the assassin. His successor, guided by a wiser policy, tolerated both pilgrimages and the exercise of the Christian religion. The church of the Holy Sepulchre was not entirely rebuilt till thirty years after its destruction; but the spectacle of its ruins still inflamed the zeal and the devotion of the Christians.

In the eleventh century the Latin Church allowed pilgrimages to suffice instead of canonical penitences; sinners were condemned to quit their country for a time, and to lead a wandering life, after the example of Cain. This mode of performing penance agreed better with the active and restless character of the people of the West. It ought to be added, that the devotion of pilgrimages, whatever may be the opinion of an enlightened philosophy, has been received, and even encouraged, in all religions. It belongs, too, to a sentiment natural to man. If the sight of a land once inhabited by heroes and sages awakens in us touching and noble remembrances; if the soul of the philosopher finds itself agitated at the sight of the ruins of Palmyra, Babylon, or Athens; what lively emotions must

* It was pretended that the thousand years of which the Scripture speaks, were about to be accomplished, and that the end of the world was approaching. In an act of donation made by St. Géraud, Baron d'Aurillac, are these words, "*Appropinquante mundi termino.*"

not the Christians have felt on beholding places which God had sanctified by his presence and his blessings?

The Christians of the West, almost all unhappy in their own countries, and who often lost the sense of their evils in long voyages, appeared to be only employed in seeking upon earth the traces of a consoling and helpful divinity, or of some holy personage. There existed no province without its martyr or its apostle, whose support they went to implore; there was no city or secluded spot which did not preserve the tradition of a miracle, or had not a chapel open to pilgrims. The most guilty of sinners, or the most fervent of the faithful, exposed themselves to the greatest perils, and repaired to the most distant places. Sometimes they directed their steps to Apulia and Calabria, they visited Mount Gargan, celebrated by the apparition of St. Michael, or Mount Cassin, rendered famous by the miracles of St. Benedict; sometimes they traversed the Pyrenees, and, in a country given up to the Saracens, esteemed themselves happy in praying before the relics of St. Jago, the patron saint of Galicia. Some, like King Robert, went to Rome, and prostrated themselves on the tombs of the apostles St. Peter and St. Paul; others travelled as far as Egypt, where Christ had passed his infancy, and penetrated to the solitudes of Scete and Memphis, inhabited by the disciples of Anthony and Paul.

A great number of pilgrims undertook the voyage to Palestine; they entered Jerusalem by the gate of Ephraim, where they paid a tribute to the Saracens. After having prepared themselves by fasting and prayer, they presented themselves in the church of the Holy Sepulchre, covered with a funeral cloth or robe, which they preserved with care during the remainder of their lives, and in which they were buried after their death. They viewed with holy respect Mount Sion, the Mount of Olives, and the Valley of Jehoshaphat; they quitted Jerusalem to visit Bethlehem, where the Saviour of the world was born; Mount Tabor, rendered sacred by the transfiguration; and all the places memorable for his miracles. The pilgrims next bathed in the waters of the Jordan, and gathered in the territory of Jericho palms which they bore back as evidences and relics to the West.

Such were the devotion and spirit of the tenth and eleventh centuries, that the greater part of the Christians would have thought themselves wanting in the duties of religion if they had not performed some pilgrimage. He who had escaped from a danger, or triumphed over his enemies, assumed the pilgrim's staff, and took the road to the holy places; he who had obtained by his prayers the preservation of a father or of a son, went to return his thanks to heaven far from his domestic hearth, in places rendered holy by religious traditions. A father often devoted his child in the cradle to a pilgrimage, and the first duty of an affectionate and obedient son, when past the age of childhood, was to accomplish the vow of his parents. More than once a dream, a vision in the midst of sleep, imposed upon a Christian the obligation of performing a pilgrimage. Thus, the idea of these pious journeys mixed itself up with all the affections of the heart, and with all the prejudices of the human mind.

Pilgrims were welcomed everywhere, and in return for the hospitality they received, they were only asked for their prayers; often, indeed, the only treasure they carried with them. One of them, desirous to embark at Alexandria for Palestine, presented himself with his scrip and staff on board a ship, and offered a book of the holy Evangelists in payment for his passage. Pilgrims, on their route, had no other defence against the attacks of the wicked but the cross of Christ, and no other guides but those angels whom God has told "*to watch over his children, and to direct them in all their ways.*"

The greatest merit in the eyes of the faithful, next to that of pilgrimage, was to devote themselves to the service of the pilgrims. Hospitals were built upon the banks of rivers, upon the heights of mountains, in the midst of cities and in desert places, for the reception of these travellers. In the ninth century, the pilgrims who left Burgundy to repair to Italy, were received in a monastery built upon Mount Cenis. In the following century, two monasteries, in which were received travellers who had strayed from their way, occupied the places of the temples of idolatry on Montes Jovis,* and thence lost the name they had received from Paganism, and took that of their pious founder, St. Bernard de Menton. Christians who travelled to Judea, found on the frontiers of Hungary, and in the provinces of Asia Minor, a great number of asylums raised by charity.

Christians established at Jerusalem went to meet the pilgrims, and often exposed themselves to a thousand dangers whilst conducting them on their route. The holy city contained hospitals for the reception of all travellers. In one of these hospitals the women who performed the pilgrimage to Palestine, were received by religious females devoted to the offices of charity. The merchants of Amalfi, Venice, and Genoa, the richest among the pilgrims, and several princes of the West, furnished, by their benevolence, the means of keeping these houses open for all poor travellers. Every year monks from the East came into Europe to collect the self-imposed tribute of the piety of the Christians. A pilgrim was a privileged being among the faithful. When he had completed his journey, he acquired the reputation of particular sanctity, and his departure and his return were celebrated by religious ceremonies. When about to set out, a priest presented to him his scrip and staff, together with a gown marked with a cross; he sprinkled holy water over his vestments, and accompanied him, at the head of a procession, as far as the boundaries of the next parish. On his return to his country, the pilgrim gave thanks to God, and presented to the priest a palm-branch, to be deposited on the altar of the church, as an evidence of his undertaking being happily terminated.

The poor, in their pilgrimages, found certain resources against misery; when coming back to their country, they received abundant alms. Vanity sometimes induced the rich to undertake these long voyages, which made the monk Glaber say, that many Christians went to Jerusalem to make themselves admired, and to be enabled, on their return, to relate the wonders they had seen. Many were influenced by the love of idleness and change, others by curiosity and an inclination to see various countries. It was by no means rare to meet with Christians who had spent their lives in holy pilgrimages, and had visited Jerusalem several times.

Every pilgrim was obliged to carry with him a letter from his prince or his bishop, a precaution which must have prevented many disorders. History does not record a single act of violence committed by one of the travellers who absolutely covered the route to the East. A Mussulman governor, who had seen a vast number of them pass to Emessa, said: "They have not left their homes with any bad design; they only seek to fulfil their law."

Every year, at the period of the festivals of Easter, numberless troops of pilgrims arrived in Judea to celebrate the mystery of the Redemption, and to behold the miracle of the sacred fire, which a superstitious multitude believed they saw descend from heaven upon the lamps of the holy sepulchre. There existed no crime that might not be expiated by the pilgrimage to Jerusalem, and acts of devotion at the tomb of Christ. We find in the "Acts of the Saints," that, in the time of Lothaire, this opinion was established among the Franks. An old relation, preserved by a monk of Redon, informs us that a powerful lord of the duchy of Brittany, named Frotmonde, the murderer of his uncle and his brother, presented himself in the habit of a penitent before the king of France and an assembly of bishops. The monarch and the prelates, as an expiation for the blood he had shed, caused him to be tightly bound with chains of iron, and ordered him to visit the holy places, his brow marked with

* These mountains, called Monts de Joux (Montes Jovis), now bear the names of the Great and Little St. Bernard. When St. Bernard founded these two hospitals, the inhabitants of the Alps were still idolaters, and the Saracens had penetrated into Le Valais, where they constantly annoyed the march of the pilgrims.

ashes, and his body clothed in a winding-sheet. Frotmonde, accompanied by his servants and the accomplices of his crime, set out for Palestine; after having for some time sojourned at Jerusalem, he crossed the desert, went to the banks of the Nile, traversed a part of Africa, proceeded as far as Carthage, and came back to Rome, where Pope Benedict III. advised him to commence a new pilgrimage, to complete his penance and obtain an entire remission of his sins. Frotmonde saw Palestine a second time, penetrated as far as the shores of the Red Sea, remained three years on Mount Sinai, and went into Armenia, to visit the mountain on which the ark of Noah had rested after the deluge. On his return to his country he was received as a saint; he shut himself up in the monastery of Redon, and died regretted by the cenobites whom he had edified by the relation of his pilgrimages.

Many years after the death of Frotmonde, Centius, prefect of Rome, who had used violence to the Pope in the church of St. Mary the Great, who had dragged him from the altar, and placed him in a dungeon, needed nothing more to expiate this sacrilege than to perform the pilgrimage to the Holy Land. Foulque-Nerra, count of Anjou, charged with crimes, and stained with blood, thought to efface all his cruelties by a voyage to Jerusalem. His brother, whom he had caused to perish in a dungeon, presented himself wherever he went, before his eyes; it appeared to him that the numerous victims sacrificed to his ambition in unjust wars issued from their tombs to disturb his sleep, and reproach him for his barbarity. Pursued everywhere by these frightful images, Foulque left his states, and repaired to Palestine, in the garb of a pilgrim. When he arrived at Jerusalem, he passed through the streets of the holy city with a cord about his neck, beaten with rods by his domestics, repeating in a loud voice these words: "Lord, have pity on a perjured and fugitive Christian." During his abode in Palestine he bestowed numerous benefactions, comforted the miseries of the pilgrims, and left everywhere testimonials of his devotion and charity. He returned to his duchy, bringing with him a portion of the true cross, and the stone upon which he had knelt when he prayed before the tomb of Christ.

Foulque, on returning to his dominions, was desirous of having always under his eyes an image of the places he had visited, and caused to be built, near the castle of Loches, a monastery and a church, which bore the name of the Holy Sepulchre. In the midst of the remembrances of his pilgrimage, he still heard the voice of remorse, and set off a second time for Jerusalem. He once more edified the Christians of the holy city by the expressions of his repentance and the austerities of his penance. As he was returning to his duchy, in passing through Italy, he delivered the Roman state from a brigand who plundered the towns and villages, and made war upon all merchants and pilgrims. The pope praised his zeal and his bravery, gave him absolution for his sins, and permitted him to bear about with him the relics of two holy martyrs. When he left Rome, he was conducted in triumph by the people and the clergy, who proclaimed him their liberator. On his arrival in Anjou, he re-established peace in his dominions, which had been in great confusion during his absence. Restored to his country, his family, and his subjects, who had forgotten his cruelties; reconciled with the Church, which declared him its benefactor, he appeared to have no more crimes to expiate, or wishes to form for his old age; but neither the absolution of the pope, nor the peace of his states, nor the blessings of the people—nothing could calm his soul, for ever torn with remorse. He could not escape from the image of his brother, which pursued him still, and recalled to his mind the crimes with which he had stained himself. Without cessation he was before him, pale, disfigured, dragging his chains, and invoking heaven to take vengeance on the fratricide. Foulque resolved to make a third pilgrimage to Jerusalem; he returned into Palestine, watered anew the tomb of Christ with his tears, and made the holy places resound with his groans. After having visited the Holy Land, and recommended his soul to the prayers of the anchorites charged to receive and console pilgrims, he quitted Jerusalem to return to his country, which he was doomed never to see again. He fell sick, and died at Metz. His body was transported to Loches, and buried in the monastery of the Holy Sepulchre, which he had caused to be built. His heart was deposited in a church at Metz, where was shown, for many ages after his death, a mausoleum, which was called the tomb of Foulque, count of Anjou.

At the same period, towards the middle of the eleventh century, Robert-le-Frison, count of Flanders, and Berenger II., count of Barcelona, resolved likewise to expiate their sins by the voyage to the Holy Land. The latter died in Asia, not being able to support the rigorous penances he had imposed upon himself. Robert came back to his dominions, where his pilgrimage caused him to find grace in the eyes of the clergy, whom he had wished to plunder. These two princes had been preceded in their pilgrimage by Frederick, count of Verdun. Frederick was of the illustrious family which was one day to reckon among its heroes Godfrey de Bouillon. On setting out for Asia, he renounced earthly grandeur, and gave up his county to the bishop of Verdun. Returned into Europe, he resolved to terminate his days in a monastery, and died prior of the abbey of St. Wast, near Arras.

The weak and timid sex was not deterred by the difficulties and the perils of a long voyage. Helena, born of a noble family of Sweden, quitted her country, which was buried in idolatry, and travelled on foot into the East. When, after having visited the holy places, she returned to her country, she was sacrificed to the resentment of her relations and her compatriots, and gathered, says an old legend, the palm of martyrdom. A few of the faithful, touched with her piety, raised a chapel to her memory in the isle of Zealand, near a fountain, which is still called the Fountain of St. Helena. The Christians of the North for a long time went in pilgrimage to this island, where they contemplated a grotto which Helena had inhabited before her departure for Jerusalem.

Among the celebrated pilgrims of this age we observe the name of Robert II., duke of Normandy, father of William the Conqueror. History accuses him of having caused his brother Richard to be poisoned. Remorse urged him to make the pilgrimage to Palestine; and he set out accompanied by a great number of knights and barons, bearing the scrip and staff, walking barefoot, and clothed in the sack of penitence. He attached, he said, more value to the pains he suffered for Christ's sake than to the richest city of his dukedom. On his arrival at Constantinople, he despised the luxury and the presents of the emperor, and appeared at court in the guise of the humblest of the pilgrims. Having fallen sick in Asia Minor, he refused the services of the Christians of his suite, and caused himself to be carried in a litter by Saracens. Meeting a pilgrim from Normandy, the latter asked him if he had any message that he could deliver for him to his country. "Go and tell my people," said the duke, "that you have seen a Christian prince being carried to Paradise by devils." When he arrived at Jerusalem, he found a crowd of pilgrims, who, not having the means of paying the tribute to the infidels, awaited the arrival of some rich lord who might deign, by his charity, to open for them the gates of the holy city. Robert paid a piece of gold for each of them, and followed them into Jerusalem amidst the acclamations of the Christians. During his sojourn here he caused himself to be remarked for his devotion, and still more for his charity, which he extended even to the infidels. As he was returning into Europe, he died at Nicea, in Bithynia, regarding only the relics he had brought with him from Palestine, and regretting that he had not finished his days in the holy city.

The greatest blessing for the pilgrims, and that which they demanded of Heaven as a reward for their labours and fatigues, was to die, like Jesus Christ, in the holy city. When they presented themselves before the holy sepulchre, they were accustomed to offer up this prayer:—"Thou who died for us, and wast buried in this holy spot, take pity of our misery, and withdraw us at once from this valley of tears." History tells of a Christian, born in the territory of Autun, who, on his arrival at Jerusalem, sought death in the excess of his fastings and mortifications. One day he remained a long time in prayer on the Mount of Olives, with his eyes and his hands raised towards heaven, whither God seemed to call him. On his return to the hospital of the pilgrims, he cried three times, "*Glory to thee, oh God!*" and died suddenly in the sight of his companions, who envied him his fate, and believed themselves witnesses of a miracle.

The inclination to acquire holiness by the journey to Jerusalem became at length so general, that the troops of pilgrims alarmed by their numbers the countries through which they passed, and although they came not as soldiers, they were designated "*the armies of the Lord.*" In the year 1054, Litbert, bishop of Cambrai, set out for the Holy Land, followed by more than three thousand pilgrims from the provinces of Picardy and Flanders. When he began his march, the people and the clergy accompanied him three leagues from the city, and with eyes bathed in tears, implored of God the happy return of their bishop and their brethren. The pilgrims traversed Germany without encountering any enemies, but on reaching Bulgaria, they found none but men who inhabited the forests and subsisted upon plunder. Many were massacred by these barbarous people, and some perished with hunger in the midst of the deserts. Litbert arrived with much difficulty at Laodicea, embarked with those who followed him, and was cast upon the coast of Cyprus by a tempest. He had seen the greater part of his companions perish, and the remainder were nearly sinking under their various miseries. Returned to Laodicea, they learnt that still greater dangers awaited them on the route to Jerusalem. The bishop of Cambrai felt his courage abandon him, and believed that God himself was opposed to his pilgrimage. He returned through a thousand dangers to his diocese, where he built a church in honour of the holy sepulchre, which he had never seen.

Ten years after the voyage of Litbert, seven thousand Christians, among whom were the archbishop of Mayence and the bishops of Spires, Cologne, Bamberg, and Utrecht, set out together from the banks of the Rhine, to repair to Palestine. This numerous caravan, which was the forerunner of the Crusades, crossed Germany, Hungary, Bulgaria, and Thrace, and was welcomed at Constantinople by the emperor Constantine Ducas. After having visited the churches of Byzantium, and the numerous relics which were the objects of the veneration of the Greeks, the pilgrims of the West traversed Asia Minor and Syria without danger; but when they approached Jerusalem, the sight of their riches aroused the cupidity of the Bedouin Arabs, undisciplined hordes, who had neither country nor settled abode, and who had rendered themselves formidable in the civil wars of the East. The Arabs attacked the pilgrims of the West, and compelled them to sustain a siege in an abandoned village; and this was on a Good Friday. On such a sacred day, the pilgrims even who had arms employed them with much hesitation and scruple. Enclosed within the ruins of an old castle, they resisted for a time, but on the third day famine compelled them to capitulate. When they came to the arrangement of the conditions of the peace, there arose a violent quarrel, which was near leading to the massacre of all the Christians by the Arabs. The emir of Ramala, informed by some fugitives, came happily to their rescue, delivered them from the death with which they were threatened, and permitted them to continue their journey. As the report of their combats and their perils had preceded them, their arrival created a great sensation in Jerusalem. They were received in triumph by the patriarch, and conducted, to the sound of timbrels and by the light of torches, to the church of the Holy Sepulchre. During their abode at Jerusalem, the misery into which they were fallen excited the pity of the Christians. They could not visit the banks of the Jordan, or the places most renowned in Judea, as these were all now infested by the Arabs and exposed to their incursions. After having lost more than three thousand of their companions, they returned to Europe, to relate their tragical adventures, and the dangers of a pilgrimage to the Holy Land.

New perils and the most violent persecutions at this period threatened both the pilgrims of the West and the Christians of Palestine. Asia was about once again to change masters, and tremble beneath a fresh tyranny. During several centuries, the rich countries of the East had been subject to continual invasions from the wild hordes of Tartary. As fast as the victorious tribes became effeminated by luxury and prosperity, they were replaced by others retaining all the barbarism of the deserts. The Turks, issuing from countries situated beyond the Oxus, had rendered themselves masters of Persia, where the uncalculating policy of Mamouh had received and encouraged their wandering tribes. The son of Mamouh fought a battle with them, in which he performed prodigies of valour; "but fortune," says Feristha, "had declared herself unpropitious to his arms; he looked around, during the fight, and except the body which he immediately commanded, his whole army had *devoured the paths of flight.*" Upon the very theatre of their victory the Turks proceeded to the election of a king. A large number of arrows were collected into a bundle. Upon each of these arrows was inscribed the name of a tribe, of a family, and of a warrior. A child drew three of the arrows in the presence of the whole army, and chance assigned the throne to Togrul-Beg, grandson of Seldjouc. Togrul-Beg, whose ambition equalled his courage, embraced, together with his soldiers, the faith of Mahomet, and soon joined to the title of conqueror that of protector of the Mussulman religion.

The banks of the Tigris and the Euphrates were then troubled by the revolt of the emirs, who shared the spoils of the caliphs of Bagdad: the caliph Cayem implored the assistance of Togrul, and promised the conquest of Asia to the new master of Persia. Togrul, whom he had named his temporal vicar, marched at the head of an army, dispersed the factious and the rebellious, ravaged the provinces, and entered Bagdad, to prostrate himself at the feet of the caliph, who proclaimed the triumph of his liberators and their sacred claims to the empire. In the midst of an imposing ceremony, Togrul was successively clothed with seven robes of honour; and seven slaves born in the seven climates of Arabia were presented to him. Two crowns were placed upon his head, and, as an emblem of his dominion over the East and the West, they girded him with two scimitars. This ceremony rendered the usurpation of the Turks legitimate in the eyes of the Mussulmans. The empire which the vicar of Mahomet pointed out to their ambition was speedily conquered by their arms. Under the reign of Alp-Arsland, and that of Malek-Scha, the successors of Togrul, the seven branches of the dynasty of Seldjouc shared amongst them the largest kingdoms of Asia. Thirty years had scarcely passed away since the Tartars conquered Persia, and already their military and pastoral colonies extended from the Oxus to the Euphrates, and from the Indus to the Hellespont.

One of the lieutenants of Malek-Scha carried the terror of his arms to the banks of the Nile, and wrested Syria from the hands of the Fatimite caliphs. Palestine yielded to the power of the Turks, and the black flag of the Abassides floated triumphantly over the walls of Jerusalem. The conquerors spared neither the Christians nor the children of Aly, whom the caliph of Bagdad represented to be the enemies of God. The Egyptian garrison was massacred, and the mosques and the churches were delivered up to pillage. The holy city was flooded with the blood of Christians and Mussulmans.

The possession of Jerusalem in no degree arrested the barbarous fury of the Turks. As their empire was recent and ill-established, as they were threatened with the armies of Cairo, and even with those of the West, their tyranny became restless, jealous, and violent. The Christians trembled under the hardest and most humiliating subjugation; they were despoiled of their property, and reduced to the most frightful degree of misery. They underwent much greater evils than they had suffered during the reign of Hakim.

A great number of those who had quitted their families and their country to visit the tomb of Christ, lost their lives before they were able to enjoy the felicity of saluting the holy city; and they who arrived at Jerusalem after having escaped a thousand dangers, found themselves exposed to the insults and cruelties of the new masters of Judea. The pilgrims of the Latin Church who returned into Europe, related all that they had suffered in their voyage, and told, with groans, of the outrages committed upon the religion of Christ. They had seen the holy sepulchre profaned, and the ceremonies of the Christians become the sport of the infidels; they had seen the patriarchs of Jerusalem and the venerable guardians of the holy places dragged from their sanctuary and cast ignominiously into dungeons. These recitals, exaggerated by repetition, flew from mouth to mouth, and drew tears from the eyes of the faithful.

Whilst the Turks, under the command of Toutousch and Ortock, were desolating Syria and Palestine, other tribes of that nation, led by Soliman, nephew of Malek-Scha, had penetrated into Asia Minor. They took possession of all the provinces through which pilgrims were accustomed to pass on their way to Jerusalem. These countries, in which the Christian religion had first shone forth, and the greater part of the Greek cities whose names were conspicuous in the annals of the primitive church, sunk under the yoke of the infidels. The standard of the prophet floated over the walls of Edessa, Iconium, Tarsus, and Antioch. Nicea had become the seat of a Mussulman empire, and the divinity of Christ was insulted in that city wherein the first œcumenic council had declared it to be an article of faith. The modesty of the virgins had been sacrificed to the brutal lust of the conquerors. Thousands of children had been circumcised.* Everywhere the laws of the Koran took place of those of the Evangelists and of Greece. The black or white tents of the Turks covered the plains and the mountains of Bithynia and Cappadocia, and their flocks pastured among the ruins of the monasteries and churches.

The Greeks had never had to contend against more cruel and terrible enemies than the Turks. Whilst the court of Alp-Arslan and Malek-Scha blazed with magnificence and cultivated the knowledge and intelligence of the ancient Persians, the rest of the people remained in a state of barbarism, and preserved, amidst the conquered nations, all the ferocious and savage manners of Tartary. The children of Seldjouc loved better to abide under their tents than in the walls of cities; they lived upon the milk of their flocks, disdaining both agriculture and commerce, in the conviction that war would supply all their wants. For themselves, their home was every region in which their arms could prevail and their flocks find rich pastures. When they passed from one country into another, all the members of the same family marched together; they took with them all that they loved, and all that they possessed. A constantly wandering life, and frequent quarrels among themselves and with their neighbours, kept up their military spirit. Every warrior carried his name inscribed upon his javelin, and swore to make it respected by his enemies. So eager were the Turks for battle, that it was quite sufficient if a chief sent his bow or his arrows among his tribe, to make them all instantly fly to arms.

The patience with which they supported hunger, thirst, and fatigue, rendered them invincible. No nation of the East surpassed them in horsemanship, or in skill with the bow; nothing could exceed the impetuosity of their attack, and they were at the same time redoubtable in flight, and implacable in victory. They were not guided in their expeditions by a desire for glory or a sense of honour, but simply by a love of destruction and pillage.

The report of their invasions had spread among the nations of Caucasus and the Caspian Sea,

* A picture of the excesses and shameless debaucheries committed by the Turks after the conquest of Asia Minor, may be found in a letter of Alexis, quoted by the Abbé Guibert, lib. i., cap. 4:—"Dicit eos quemdam abusione sodomiticâ intervenisse episcopum, matres correptæ in conspectu filiarum multipliciter repetitis diversorum coitibus vexabantur. Filiæ existentiæ terminum præcinere saltando cogebantur,—mox eadem passio ad filias," &c.

and new migrations appeared to arrive every day to strengthen their armies. As they were docile in war, and turbulent and rebellious in peace, it was the policy of their chiefs to lead them constantly on to new conquests. Malek-Scha, with a view to get rid of his lieutenants rather than to reward them, had given them permission to attempt the conquest of the lands of the Greeks and Egyptians. It was an easy matter to raise armies, to which were promised the spoils of the enemies of the prophet and his legitimate vicar. All who had not shared in the booty of preceding wars flocked to the standards, and the wealth of Greece soon became the prey of turkish horsemen, who had but recently issued from their deserts with woollen caps and stirrups of wood. Of all the hordes subject to the dynasty of Seldjouc, the troops that invaded Syria and Asia Minor were the poorest, the most wild, and the most intrepid.

In the depth of their misery, the Greeks of the conquered provinces scarcely dared to lift their eyes to the sovereigns of Byzantium, who had not had the courage to defend them, and therefore left them no hope that they would assist them in their troubles. In the midst of revolutions and civil wars, the Greek empire was hastening to its fall. Since the reign of Heraclius, Constantinople had seen eleven of its emperors put to death in their own palace. Six of these masters of the world had terminated their days in the obscurity of cloisters; several had been mutilated, deprived of sight, and sent into exile; the purple, stained and degraded by so many revolutions, decorated only wicked and contemptible princes, or men without character or virtue. Their whole employment was their own personal safety; and they were compelled to share their power with the accomplices of their crimes, of whom they lived in a constant state of dread. They frequently sacrificed cities and provinces, to purchase from their enemies a few moments of security, and appeared to have nothing to ask of fortune beyond the existence of the empire during their own worthless lives.

The Greeks still cherished great names and great remembrances, of which they were proud, but which only served to show their present weakness and degradation. In the midst of the luxury of Asia and the monuments of Greece and Rome, they were scarcely less barbarous than other nations. In their theological disputes they had lost the true spirit of the Evangelists; among them everything was corrupted, even religion. A universal bigotry, says Montesquieu, depressed their courage and paralyzed the whole empire. They neglected the dangers of their country, and became zealous for a relic or for a sect. In war, superstition pointed out to the Greeks lucky and unlucky days, in which a general ought or ought not to give battle; and as religion inspired in them nothing beyond an apathetic resignation in reverses, they consoled themselves for the loss of provinces by accusing their inhabitants of heresy.

Among the Greeks, stratagem and perfidy were decorated with the name of policy, and received the same encomiums as valour; they esteemed it as glorious to deceive their enemies as to conquer them. Their soldiers were followed to the seat of war by light chariots, which carried their arms; and they had perfected every machine which could supply the place of courage in either sieges or battles. Their armies displayed great military pomp, but were deficient in soldiers. The only thing they inherited from their ancestors was a turbulent and seditious spirit, which mixed itself with their effeminated manners, and was sure to break out when their country was threatened with danger. Discord unceasingly reigned among both the army and the people; and they continued madly to dispute the right to an empire whose very existence was menaced, and blindly gave up its defence to barbarians and strangers. In short, the corruption of the Greeks was so great, that they could neither have endured a good prince nor good laws. Nicephorus Phocas, who had formed the project of re-establishing discipline, died assassinated. Zimisces had also paid with his life for his efforts to rouse the Greeks from their pusillanimous degradation. When the emperor Romanus-Diogenes was made prisoner by the Turks, his misfortunes were the signal for a fresh revolt against his person. Sent back with honours by the sultan of Persia, he met with nothing but executioners in an empire he had endeavoured to defend, and died with misery and despair in a desert island of the Propontis.

Whilst the empire of the East approached near to its fall, and appeared sapped by time and corruption, the institutions of the West were in their infancy. The empire and the laws of Charlemagne no longer existed. Nations had no relations with each other, and mistaking their political interests, made wars without considering their consequences or their dangers, and concluded peace, without being at all aware whether it was advantageous or not. Royal authority was nowhere sufficiently strong to arrest the progress of anarchy and the abuses of feudalism. At the same time that Europe was full of soldiers, and covered with strong castles, the states themselves were without support against their enemies, and had not an army to defend them. In the midst of general confusion, there was no security but in camps and fortresses, by turns the safeguards and the terror of the towns and the country. The largest cities held out no asylum to liberty, and the life of man was reckoned so trifling an object, that impunity for murder could be purchased with a few pieces of money. Frequently, to detect crime, the judges had recourse to water, fire, and iron; upon the blind and dumb evidence of the elements, victims were condemned to death; it was sword in hand that justice was invoked; it was by the sword that the reparation of wrongs and injuries was to be obtained. No one would then have been understood who would have spoken of the rights of nature, or the rights of man; the language of the barons and the lords comprised only such words as treated of *war;* war was the only science, the only policy of either princes or states.

Nevertheless, this barbarism of the nations of the West did not at all resemble that of the Turks, whose religion and manners repelled every species of civilization or cultivation, nor that of the Greeks, who were nothing but a corrupted and degenerated people. Whilst the one exhibited all the vices of a state almost savage, and the other all the corruption of decay; something heroical and generous was mingled with the barbarous manners of the Franks, which resembled the passions of youth, and gave promise of a better future. The Turks were governed by a gross barbarism, which made them despise all that was noble or great; the Greeks were possessed by a learned and polished barbarism, which filled them with disdain for heroism or the military virtues. The Franks were as brave as the Turks, and set a higher value on glory than any other people. The principle of *honour*, which gave birth to chivalry in Europe, directed their bravery, and sometimes assumed the guise of justice and virtue.

The Christian religion, which the Greeks had reduced to little formulæ and the vain practices of superstition, was, with them, incapable of inspiring either great designs or noble thoughts. Among the nations of the West, as they were yet unacquainted with the disputed dogmas of Christianity, it had more empire over their minds, it disposed their hearts more to enthusiasm, and formed amongst them, at once, both saints and heroes.

Although religion might not always preach its doctrines with success, and its influence was subject to abuse, it had a tendency to soften the manners of the barbarous people that had invaded Europe; it afforded a holy authority to the weak; it inspired a salutary fear in the strong, and frequently corrected the injustice of human laws.

In the midst of the darkness which covered Europe, the Christian religion alone preserved the memory of times past, and kept up some degree of emulation among men. It preserved, also, for happier days, the language of the royal people, the only one capable of expressing the grand and noble ideas of moral virtue, in which the genius of legislation had elevated its most splendid monuments. Whilst despotism and anarchy pervaded the cities and the kingdoms of the West, the people invoked religion against tyranny, and the princes called in its aid against license and revolt. Often, mid the troubles of states, the title of Christian inspired more respect, and awakened more enthusiasm than did the name of citizen in ancient Rome. As the Christian religion had preceded all the then existing institutions, it naturally remained for a long time surrounded by the veneration and love of the people. Under more than one relation the nations appeared to recognise no other legislators than the fathers of the councils, no other code than that of the gospel and the holy Scriptures. Europe might be considered as a religious society, wherein the preservation of the faith was the principal interest, and in which men belonged more to the church than to the country. In such a state of things it was easy to inflame the minds of the people, by showing them that the cause of religion and of Christians stood in need of defence.

Ten years before the invasion of Asia Minor by the Turks, Michael Ducas, the successor of Romanus-Diogenes, had implored the assistance of the pope and the princes of the West. He had promised to remove all the barriers which separated the Greek from the Roman Church, if the Latins would take up arms against the infidels. Gregory VII. then filled the chair of St. Peter, and his talents, his knowledge, his activity, his boldness, together with the inflexibility of his character, rendered him capable of the greatest undertakings. The hope of extending the religion and the empire of the Holy See into the East, made him receive kindly the humble supplications of Michael Ducas. He exhorted the faithful to take up arms against the Mussulmans, and engaged to lead them himself into Asia. The misfortunes of the Christians of the East, said he, in his letters, had moved him even to feel a contempt for death; he would rather expose his life to deliver the holy places, than live to command the entire universe. Excited by his discourses, fifty thousand pilgrims agreed to follow Gregory to Constantinople, and thence to Syria; but he kept not the promise he had made, and the affairs of Europe, in which the ambition of the pontiff was more interested than in those of Asia, suspended the execution of his projects.

Every day the power of the popes was augmented by the progress of Christianity, and by the ever-increasing influence of the Latin clergy. Rome was become a second time the capital of the world, and appeared to have resumed, under the monk Hildebrand, the empire it had enjoyed under the Cæsars. Armed with the two-edged sword of Peter, Gregory loudly proclaimed that all the kingdoms of the earth were under the dominion of the Holy See, and that his authority ought to be as universal as the church of which he was the head. These dangerous pretensions, fostered by the opinions of his age, engaged him immediately in violent disputes with the emperor of Germany. He desired also to dictate laws to France, Spain, Sweden, Poland, and England; and thinking of nothing but making himself acknowledged as the great arbiter of states, he launched his anathemas even against the throne of Constantinople, which he had undertaken to defend, and gave no more attention to the deliverance of Jerusalem.

After the death of Gregory, Victor III., although he pursued the policy of his predecessor, and had at the same time to contend against the emperor of Germany and the party of the anti-pope Guibert, did not neglect the opportunity of making war against the Mussulmans. The Saracens, inhabiting Africa, disturbed the navigation of the Mediterranean, and threatened the coast of Italy. Victor invited the Christians to take arms, and promised them the remission of all their sins if they went to fight against the infidels. The inhabitants of Pisa, Genoa, and several other cities, urged by their zeal for religion, and their desire to defend their commerce, equipped fleets, levied troops, and made a descent upon the coasts of Africa, where, if we are to believe the chronicles of the time, they cut in pieces an army of one hundred thousand Saracens. That we may not doubt, says Baronius, that God interested himself in the cause of the Christians, on the very day on which the Italians triumphed over the enemies of Christ, the news of the victory was carried miraculously beyond the seas. After having given up to the flames two cities, Al-Mahadia and Sibila, built within the territories of ancient Carthage, and forced a king of Mauritania to pay a tribute to the Holy See, the Genoese and the Pisans returned to Italy, where the spoils of the conquered were employed in ornamenting the churches.

The pope Victor, however, died without realizing his promise of attacking the infidels in Asia. The glory of delivering Jerusalem belonged to a simple pilgrim, possessed of no other power than the influence of his character and his genius. Some assign an obscure origin to Peter the Hermit; others say he was descended from a noble family of Picardy; but all agree that he had an ignoble and vulgar exterior. Born with a restless, active spirit, he sought, in all conditions of life, for an object which he could meet with in none. The study of letters, bearing arms, celibacy, marriage, the ecclesiastical state, offered nothing to him that could fill his heart or satisfy his ardent mind. Disgusted with the world and mankind, he retired amongst the most austere cenobites. Fasting, prayer, meditation, the silence of solitude, exalted his imagination. In his visions he kept up an habitual commerce with heaven, and believed himself the instrument of its designs, and the depositary of its will. He possessed the fervour of an apostle, with the courage of a martyr. His zeal gave way to no obstacle, and all that he desired seemed easy of attainment. When he spoke, the passions with which he was agitated animated his gestures and his words, and communicated themselves to his auditors.* Such was the extraordinary man who gave the signal to the Crusaders, and who, without fortune and without name, by the ascendancy of his tears and prayers alone, succeeded in moving the West to precipitate itself in a mass upon Asia.

The fame of the pilgrimages to the East drew Peter from his retreat, and he followed into Palestine the crowd of Christians who went to visit the holy places. The sight of Jerusalem excited him much more than any of the other pilgrims, for it created in his ardent mind a thousand conflicting sentiments. In the city, which exhibited everywhere marks of the mercy and the anger of God, all objects inflamed his piety, irritated his devotion and his zeal, and filled him by turns with respect, terror, and indignation. After having followed his brethren to Calvary, and the tomb of Christ, he repaired to the patriarch of Jerusalem. The white hairs of Simeon, his venerable figure, and, above all, the persecution which he had undergone, bespoke the full confidence of Peter, and they wept together over the ills of the Christians. The hermit, his heart torn, his face bathed in tears, asked if there was no termination to be looked for, no remedy to be devised, for so many calamities? "Oh, most faithful of Christians!" replied the patriarch, "is it not plain that our iniquities have shut us out from all access to the mercy of the Lord? All Asia is in the power of the Mussulmans, all the East is sunk into a state of slavery; no power on earth can assist us." At these words Peter interrupted Simeon, and pointed out to him the hope that the warriors of the West might one day be the liberators of Jerusalem. "Yes, without doubt," replied the patriarch, "when the measure of our afflictions shall be full, when God will be moved by our miseries, he will soften the hearts of the princes of the West, and will send them to the succour of the holy city." At these words Peter and Simeon felt their hearts expand with hope, and embraced each other, shedding tears of joy. The patriarch resolved to implore, by his letters, the help of the pope and the princes of Europe, and the hermit swore to be the interpreter of the Christians of the East, and to rouse the West to take arms for their deliverance.

---

* Anna Comnena calls Peter the Hermit *Cucupièttore*, which appears to be taken from the Picard word *kiokio*, little, and from the word Petrus, Peter, little Peter. If we are to believe Oderic-Vital, the hermit had still another name, and was called Peter of Achiris. He is styled in this manner in the chronicle of the counts of Anjou: "Heremita quidam *Petrus Achiriensis*." William of Tyre informs us that he was a hermit in name and in fact: "*Heremita nomine et effectu*."

PETER THE HERMIT PREACHING THE CRUSADE.

The singularity of his appearance was a spectacle for the people, whilst the austerity[1] *of his manner, his charity, and the moral doctrines that he preached, caused him to be revered as a saint. . . . They who touched his vestments esteemed themselves happy, and a portion of hair pulled from the mule he rode was preserved as a holy relic. At the sound of his voice differences in families were reconciled, the poor were comforted, the debauched blushed at their errors.*—BOOK I.

[1] *When the Crusaders were besieging Antioch and dying from starvation, Peter ran away, but was caught and brought back in disgrace to camp. Vide* BOOK III. *See also his disastrous leadership of the First Crusade,* BOOK II.

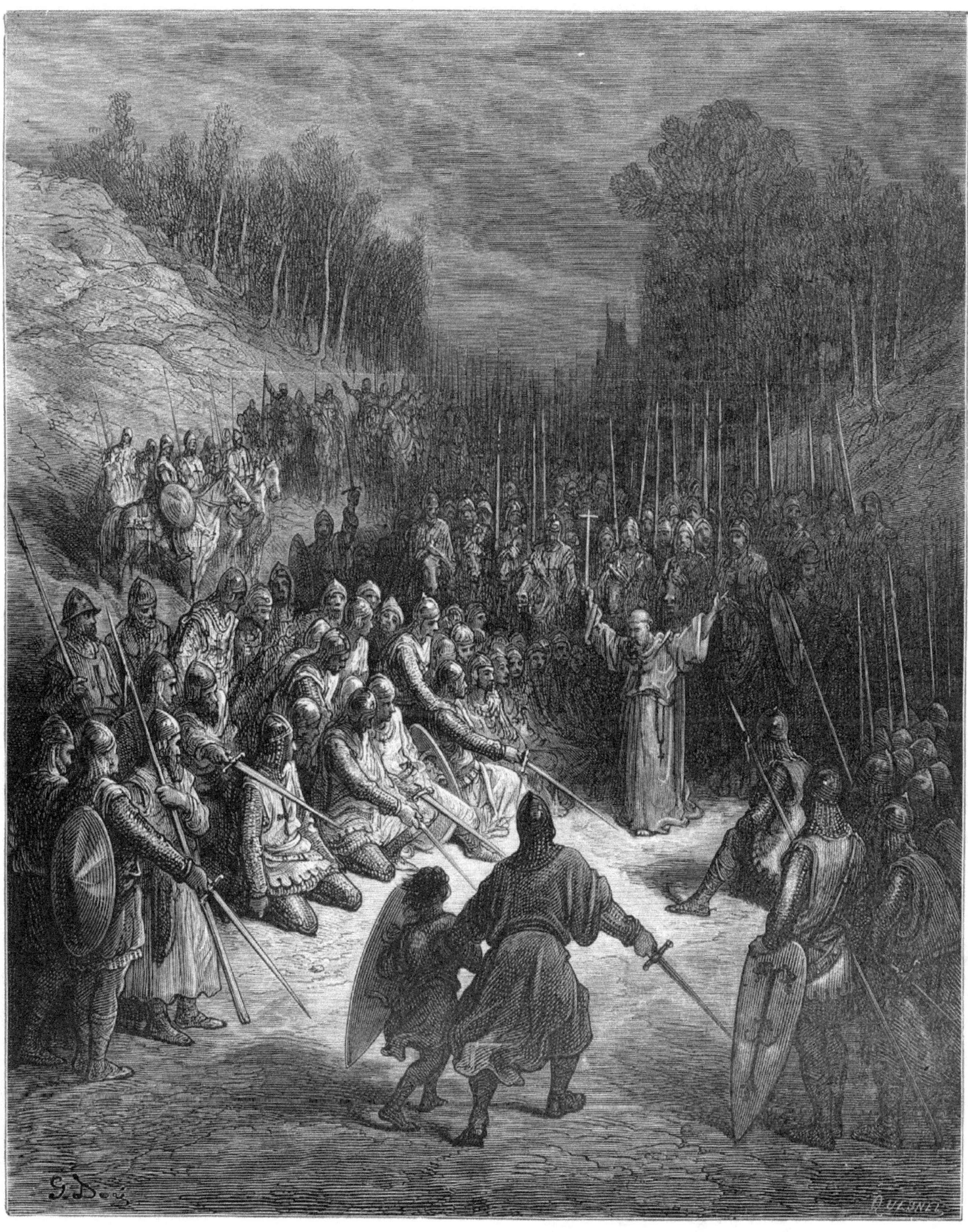

After this interview, the enthusiasm of Peter knew no bounds; he was persuaded that Heaven itself called upon him to avenge its cause. One day, whilst prostrated before the holy sepulchre, he believed that he heard the voice of Christ, which said to him, —"Peter, arise! hasten to proclaim the tribulations of my people; it is time that my servants should receive help, and that the holy places should be delivered." Full of the spirit of these words, which sounded unceasingly in his ears, and charged with letters from the patriarch, he quitted Palestine, crossed the seas, landed on the coast of Italy, and hastened to cast himself at the feet of the pope. The chair of St. Peter was then occupied by Urban II., who had been the disciple and confidant of both Gregory and Victor. Urban embraced with ardour a project which had been entertained by his predecessors; he received Peter as a prophet, applauded his design, and bade him go forth and announce the approaching deliverance of Jerusalem.

Peter the Hermit traversed Italy, crossed the Alps, visited all parts of France, and the greatest portion of Europe, inflaming all hearts with the same zeal that consumed his own. He travelled mounted on a mule, with a crucifix in his hand, his feet bare, his head uncovered, his body girded with a thick cord, covered with a long frock, and a hermit's hood of the coarsest stuff. The singularity of his appearance was a spectacle for the people, whilst the austerity of his manners, his charity, and the moral doctrines that he preached, caused him to be revered as a saint wherever he came.

He went from city to city, from province to province, working upon the courage of some, and upon the piety of others; sometimes haranguing from the pulpits of the churches, sometimes preaching in the high roads or public places. His eloquence was animated and impressive, and filled with those vehement apostrophes which produce such effects upon an uncultivated multitude. He described the profanation of the holy places, and the blood of the Christians shed in torrents in the streets of Jerusalem. He invoked, by turns, Heaven, the saints, the angels, whom he called upon to bear witness to the truth of what he told them. He apostrophized Mount Sion, the rock of Calvary, and the Mount of Olives, which he made to resound with sobs and groans. When he had exhausted speech in painting the miseries of the faithful, he showed the spectators the crucifix which he carried with him; sometimes striking his breast and wounding his flesh, sometimes shedding torrents of tears.

The people followed the steps of Peter in crowds. The preacher of the holy war was received everywhere as a messenger from God. They who could touch his vestments esteemed themselves happy, and a portion of hair pulled from the mule he rode was preserved as a holy relic. At the sound of his voice, differences in families were reconciled, the poor were comforted, the debauched blushed at their errors; nothing was talked of but the virtues of the eloquent cenobite; his austerities and his miracles were described, and his discourses were repeated to those who had not heard him, and been edified by his presence.

He often met, in his journeys, with Christians from the East, who had been banished from their country, and wandered over Europe, subsisting on charity. Peter the Hermit presented them to the people, as living evidences of the barbarity of the infidels; and pointing to the rags with which they were clothed, he burst into torrents of invectives against their oppressors and persecutors. At the sight of these miserable wretches, the faithful felt, by turns, the most lively emotions of pity, and the fury of vengeance; all deploring in their hearts the miseries and the disgrace of Jerusalem. The people raised their voices towards heaven, to entreat God to deign to cast a look of pity upon his beloved city; some offering their riches, others their prayers, but all promising to lay down their lives for the deliverance of the holy places.

In the midst of this general excitement, Alexius Comnena, who was threatened by the Turks, sent ambassadors to the pope, to solicit the assistance of the Latins. Some time before this embassy he had addressed letters to the princes of the West, in which he had described to them, in a most lamentable manner, the conquests of the Turks in Asia Minor. These savage hordes, in their debauches and in the intoxication of victory, had outraged both nature and humanity.* They were now at the gates of Byzantium, and without the prompt assistance of all the Christian states, Constantinople must fall under the most frightful domination of the Turks. Alexius reminded the princes of Christianity of the holy relics preserved in Constantinople, and conjured them to save so sacred an assemblage of venerated objects from the profanation of the infidels. After having set forth the splendour and the riches of his capital, he exhorted the knights and barons to come and defend them; he offered them his treasures as the reward of their valour, and painted in glowing colours the beauty of the Greek women, whose love would repay the exploits of his liberators. Thus, nothing was spared that could flatter the passions, or arouse the enthusiasm of the warriors of the West. The invasion of the Turks was, in the eyes of Alexius, the greatest misfortune that the chief of a Christian kingdom had to dread; and to avert such a danger, everything appeared to him just and allowable. He could support the idea of losing his crown, but not the shame of seeing his states subjected to the laws of Mahomet; if he was doomed one day to lose his empire, he could console himself for that loss, provided Greece escaped the Mussulman yoke, and became the prize of the Latins.

In compliance with the prayers of Alexius and the wishes of the faithful, the sovereign pontiff convoked a council at Plaisance, in order there to expose the dangers of the Greek and Latin Churches in the East. The preachings of Peter had so prepared the minds and animated the zeal of the faithful, that more than two hundred bishops and archbishops, four thousand ecclesiastics, and thirty thousand of the laity obeyed the invitation of the Holy See. The council was so numerous that it was obliged to be held in a plain in the neighbourhood of the city.

At this assembly all eyes were turned upon the ambassadors of Alexius; their presence in the midst of a Latin council, announced sufficiently plainly the disastrous condition of the East. When they had exhorted the princes and the warriors to save Constantinople and Jerusalem, Urban supported their discourse and their prayers with all the reasons which the interests of Christianity and the cause of religion could furnish. The council of Plaisance, however, came to no determination upon the war against the infidels. The deliverance of the Holy Land was far from being the only object of this council: the declarations of the empress Adelaide, who came to reveal her own shame, and that of her husband, anathemas against the emperor of Germany and the anti-pope, Guibert, occupied, during several days, the attention of Urban and the assembled fathers.

It must be added, too, that among the states of Italy, in which country this council was held, the spirit of commerce and liberty began to weaken the enthusiasm of religion. The greater part of the cities only thought of the advantages that might accrue to them from the troubles; some entertaining hopes they would increase their wealth, others looking to them as a means of securing their independence, and none yielding so freely as other nations to the influence of the popes. Whilst the Christian world revered in Urban the formidable successor of Gregory, the Italians, whose charity he had frequently implored, were best acquainted with his disgraces and misfortunes: his presence did not in any degree warm their zeal, and his decrees were not always laws for them, who had seen him, from the depths of misery and in exile, launch his thunders against the thrones of the West.

* This letter of Alexius, quoted in extract by the Abbé Guibert, and the whole of it by Robert the Monk. M. Heeren, in his learned Latin commentary on the Greek historians, doubts its authenticity. The principal reason he gives for his opinion is, that this letter differs too strongly from the known character of the Greek emperors. This reason does not appear to me sufficient; we know very well that the Greek emperors affected great haughtiness in their correspondence, but we know also that they spared no prayers when they were in any danger, or wanted assistance: nothing suits better with vanity than servility. Some critics cannot believe that Alexius should have spoken in his letters of the beautiful women of Greece; the thing may, however, well be believed, when we recollect that the Turks, who were invading the empire of Byzantium, sought with great eagerness to obtain Greek women. Montesquieu remarks it, when speaking of the decline of the empire. It seems then very natural that Alexius should speak of the beautiful women of Byzantium, when addressing the Franks, whom the Greeks considered barbarians, and governed by the same tastes as the Turks.

The prudent Urban avoided trying to arouse the ardour of the Italians; he did not think their example at all likely to lead on other nations. In order to take a decided part in the civil war, and to interest all Europe in its success, he resolved to assemble a second synod, in the bosom of a warlike nation, which, from the most distant times, had been accustomed to give impulsion to Europe. The new council assembled at Clermont, in Auvergne, was neither less numerous nor respectable than that of Plaisance; the most renowned holy men and learned doctors came to honour it with their presence, and enlighten it with their counsels. The city of Clermont was scarcely able to contain within its walls all the princes, ambassadors, and prelates who had repaired to the council; "so that," says an ancient chronicle, "towards the middle of the month of November, the cities and villages of the neighbourhood were so filled with people, that they were compelled to erect tents and pavilions in the fields and meadows, although the season and the country were extremely cold."

Before it gave up its attention to the holy war, the council at first considered the reform of the clergy and ecclesiastical discipline; and it then occupied itself in placing a restraint upon the license of wars among individuals. In these barbarous times even simple knights never thought of redressing their injuries by any other means than arms. It was not an uncommon thing to see families, for the slightest causes, commence a war against each other that would last during several generations; Europe was distracted with troubles occasioned by these hostilities. In the impotence of the laws and the governments, the Church often exerted its salutary influence to restore tranquillity: several councils had placed their interdict upon private wars during four days of the week, and their decrees had invoked the vengeance of Heaven against disturbers of the public peace. The council of Clermont renewed the truce of God, and threatened all who refused "*to accept peace and justice*" with the thunders of the Church. One of its decrees placed widows, orphans, merchants, and labourers under the safeguard of religion. They declared, as they had already done in other councils, that the churches should be so many inviolable sanctuaries, and that crosses, even, placed upon the high roads should become points of refuge against violence.

Humanity and reason must applaud such salutary decrees; but the sovereign pontiff, although he presented himself as the defender of the sanctity of marriage, did not merit the same praises when he pronounced in this council an anathema against Philip I.: but such was then the general infatuation, that no one was astonished that a king of France should be excommunicated in the very bosom of his own kingdom. The sentence of Urban could not divert attention from an object that seemed much more imposing, and the excommunication of Philip scarcely holds a place in the history of the council of Clermont. The faithful, gathered from all the provinces, had but one single thought; they spoke of nothing but the evils the Christians endured in Palestine, and saw nothing but the war which was about to be declared against the infidels. Enthusiasm and fanaticism, which always increase in large assemblies, were carried to their full height. Urban at length satisfied the impatience of the faithful, impatience which he, perhaps, had adroitly excited, and which was the surest guarantee of success.

The council held its tenth sitting in the great square or place of Clermont, which was soon filled by an immense crowd. Followed by his cardinals, the pope ascended a species of throne which had been prepared for him; at his side was Peter the Hermit, clad in that whimsical and uncouth garb which had everywhere drawn upon him the attention and the respect of the multitude. The apostle of the holy war spoke first of the outrages committed against the religion of Christ; he reverted to the profanations and the sacrileges of which he had been a witness; he pictured the torments and persecutions which a people, enemies to God and man, had caused those to suffer who had been led by religion to visit the holy places. He had seen, he said, Christians loaded with irons, dragged into slavery, or harnessed to the yoke, like the vilest animals; he had seen the oppressors of Jerusalem sell to the children of Christ permission to salute the temple of their God, tear from them even the bread of their misery, and torment their poverty itself to obtain their tribute; he had seen the ministers of God dragged from their sanctuaries, beaten with rods, and condemned to an ignominious death. Whilst describing the misfortunes and degradation of the Christians, the countenance of Peter was cast down, and exhibited feelings of consternation and horror; his voice was choked with sobs; his lively emotion penetrated every heart.

Urban, who spoke after Peter, represented, as he had done, the holy places as profaned by the domination of the infidels. That land, consecrated by the presence of the Saviour, that mountain whereon he expiated our sins by his sufferings,—that tomb in which he deigned to be enclosed as a victim to death, had all become the heritage of the impious. The altars of false prophets were raised within those walls which had contained the august assembly of the apostles. God had no longer a sanctuary in his own city; the East, the cradle of the Christian religion, now witnessed nothing but sacrilegious pomps; impiety had spread its darkness over all the richest countries of Asia. Antioch, Ephesus, Nicea, had become Mussulman cities; the Turks had carried their ravages and their odious dominion even to the Straits of the Hellespont, to the very gates of Constantinople, and from thence they threatened the West.

The sovereign pontiff addressed himself to all the nations that were represented at the council, and particularly to the French, who formed the majority:—"Nation beloved by God," said he, "it is in your courage that the Christian church has placed its hope; it is because I am well acquainted with your piety and your bravery, that I have crossed the Alps, and am come to preach the word of God in these countries. You have not forgotten that the land you inhabit has been invaded by the Saracens, and that but for the exploits of Charles Martel and Charlemagne, France would have received the laws of Mahomet. Recall, without ceasing, to your minds the danger and the glory of your fathers; led by heroes whose names should never die, they delivered your country, they saved the West from shameful slavery. More noble triumphs await you, under the guidance of the God of armies; you will deliver Europe and Asia; you will save the city of Jesus Christ,—that Jerusalem which was chosen by the Lord, and from whence the law is come to us."

As Urban proceeded, the sentiments by which he was animated penetrated to the very souls of his auditors. When he spoke of the captivity and the misfortunes of Jerusalem, the whole assembly was dissolved in tears; when he described the tyranny and the perfidy of the infidels, the warriors who listened to him clutched their swords, and swore in their hearts to avenge the cause of the Christians. Urban redoubled their enthusiasm by announcing that God had chosen them to accomplish his designs, and exhorted them to turn those arms against the Mussulmans which they now bore in conflict against their brothers. They were not now called upon to revenge the injuries of men, but injuries offered to divinity; it was now not the conquest of a town or a castle that was offered to them as the reward of their valour, but the riches of Asia, the possession of a land in which, according to the promises of the Scriptures, flowed streams of milk and honey.

The pontiff sought to awaken in their minds, by turns, ambition, the love of glory, religious enthusiasm, and pity for their Christian brethren. "There scarcely exists," said he, "a Christian family into which the Mussulmans have not brought mourning and despair. How many Christians every year leave the West, to find in Asia nothing but slavery or death! Bishops have been delivered over to the executioner; the virgins of the Lord have been outraged; holy places have been despoiled of their ornaments; the offerings of piety have become the booty of the enemies of God; the children of the faithful have forgotten in bondage the faith of their fathers, and bear upon their bodies the impression of their opprobrium. Witnesses of so many calamities, the Christians of Jerusalem would long since have left the holy city, if they had not imposed upon themselves the obligation of succouring and consoling pilgrims, if they had not feared to leave without priests, without altars, without worshippers, a land where still smokes the blood of Jesus Christ.

"I will not seek to dry the tears which images so painful for a Christian, for a minister of religion, for the common father of the faithful, must draw from you. Let us weep, my brethren, let us weep over the errors which have armed the anger of God against us; let us weep over the captivity of the holy city! But evil be to us, if, in our sterile pity, we longer leave the heritage of the Lord in the hands of the impious! Why should we taste here a moment's repose whilst the children of Jesus Christ live in the midst of torments, and the queen of cities groans in chains?

"Christian warriors, who seek without end for vain pretexts for war, rejoice, for you have to-day found true ones. You, who have been so often the terror of your fellow-citizens, go and fight against the barbarians, go and fight for the deliverance of the holy places; you who sell for vile pay the strength of your arms to the fury of others, armed with the sword of the Machabees, go and merit an eternal reward. If you triumph over your enemies, the kingdoms of the East will be your heritage; if you are conquered, you will have the glory of dying in the very same place as Jesus Christ, and God will not forget that he shall have found you in his holy ranks. This is the moment to prove that you are animated by a true courage; this is the moment in which you may expiate so many violences committed in the bosom of peace, so many victories purchased at the expense of justice and humanity. If you must have blood, bathe your hands in the blood of the infidels. I speak to you with harshness, because my ministry obliges me to do so: SOLDIERS OF HELL, BECOME SOLDIERS OF THE LIVING GOD! When Jesus Christ summons you to his defence, let no base affections detain you in your homes; see nothing but the shame and the evils of the Christians; listen to nothing but the groans of Jerusalem, and remember well what the Lord has said to you: '*He who loves his father and his mother more than me, is not worthy of me; whoever will abandon his house, or his father, or his mother, or his wife, or his children, or his inheritance, for the sake of my name, shall be recompensed a hundred-fold, and possess life eternal.*'"

At these words the auditors of Urban displayed an enthusiasm that human eloquence had never before inspired. The assembly arose in one mass as one man, and answered him with a unanimous cry,—"*It is the will of God! It is the will of God!*" "Yes, without doubt, it is the will of God," continued the eloquent Urban; you to-day see the accomplishment of the word of our Saviour, who promised to be in the midst of the faithful, when assembled in his name; it is He who has dictated to you the words that I have heard. Let them be your war-cry, and let them announce everywhere the presence of the God of armies." On finishing these words, the pontiff exhibited to the assembled Christians, the sign of their redemption. "It is Christ himself," said he to them, "who issues from his tomb, and presents to you his cross; it will be the sign raised among the nations, which is to gather together again the dispersed children of Israel. Wear it upon your shoulders and upon your breasts; let it shine upon your arms and upon your standards; it will be to you the surety of victory or the palm of martyrdom; it will unceasingly remind you that Christ died for you, and that it is your duty to die for him."

When Urban had ceased to speak, loud acclamations burst from the multitude. Pity, indignation, despair, at the same time agitated the tumultuous assembly of the faithful: some shed tears over Jerusalem and the fate of the Christians; others swore to exterminate the race of the Mussulmans; but, all at once, at a signal from the sovereign pontiff, the most profound silence prevailed. Cardinal Gregory, who afterwards occupied the chair of St. Peter under the name of Innocent II., pronounced, in a loud voice, a form of general confession, the assembly all fell upon their knees, beat their breasts, and received absolution for their sins.

Adhémar de Monteil, bishop of Puy, demanded to be first allowed to enter into the *way of God,* and took the cross from the hands of the pope; several other bishops following his example. Raymond, count of Thoulouse, excused himself by his ambassadors for not being able to be present at the council of Clermont; he had already, he said, fought against the Saracens in Spain, and he promised to go and fight against them in Asia, followed by the bravest and most faithful of his warriors. The barons and knights who had heard the exhortations of Urban, all took a solemn oath to revenge the cause of Jesus Christ; they forgot their private quarrels, and even they who were at actual war had no longer any enemies than the Mussulmans. All the faithful promised to respect the decrees of the council, and decorated their garments with a red cross. From that time, all who engaged to combat the infidels were termed "*Bearers of the Cross,*"* and the holy war took the name of *Crusade.* The faithful solicited Urban to place himself at their head; but the pontiff, who had not yet triumphed over the anti-pope Guibert, who was dealing out at the same time his anathemas against the king of France and the emperor of Germany, could not quit Europe without compromising the power and the policy of the Holy See. He refused to be chief of the crusade, and named the bishop of Puy apostolic legate with the army of the Christians.

He promised to all who assumed the cross, the entire remission of their sins. Their persons, their families, their property, were all placed under the protection of the Church, and of the apostles St. Peter and St. Paul. The council declared that every violence exercised upon the soldiers of Christ should be punished by anathema, and recommended its decrees in favour of the bearers of the cross to the watchful care of all bishops and priests. It regulated the discipline and the departure of those who had enrolled themselves in the holy ranks, and for fear reflection might deter any from leaving their homes, it threatened with excommunication all those who did not fulfil their vows.

Fame soon spread everywhere the war that had just been declared against the infidels. When the bishops returned to their dioceses, they still continued to bestow their blessings upon the crosses of the crowds of Christians that required to be led to the conquest of the Holy Land. Urban went through several provinces of France, to finish the work he had so happily begun. In the cities of Rouen, Tours, and Nîmes he held councils, in which he deplored the fate of the Christians of the East: everywhere the people and the great, the nobles and the clergy, obeyed the pressing exhortations of the pontiff, and promised to take arms against the Mussulmans.

It might be said that the French had no longer any other country than the Holy Land, and that to it they were bound to sacrifice their ease, their property, and their lives. This enthusiasm, which had no bounds, was not long in extending itself to the other Christian nations; the flame which consumed France was communicated to England, still disturbed by the recent conquest of the Normans; to Germany, troubled by the anathemas of Gregory and Urban; to Italy, agitated by its factions; to Spain even, although it had to combat the Saracens on its own territory. Such was the ascendancy of the religion outraged by the infidels, such was the influence of the example given by the French, that all Christian nations seemed to forget, at once, the objects of their ambition or their fears, and furnished, for the crusade, soldiers that they absolutely required to defend themselves. The entire West resounded with these words: "*He who will not take up his cross and come with me, is not worthy of me.*"

* The cross which the faithful wore in this crusade was of cloth, and sometimes even of red-coloured silk. Afterwards they wore crosses of different colours. The cross, a little in relief, was sewed upon the right shoulder of the coat or mantle, or else fastened on the front of the helmet, after having been blessed by the pope or some bishop. On returning from the Holy Land, they removed this mark from the shoulder and placed it on the back, or else wore it at the neck.

The devotion for pilgrimages, which had been increasing during several centuries, became a passion and an imperative want for most Christians; every one was eager to march to Jerusalem, and to take part in the crusade, which was, in all respects, an armed pilgrimage. The situation in which Europe was then placed, no doubt contributed to increase the number of pilgrims: "all things were in such disorder," says William of Tyre, "that the world appeared to be approaching to its end, and was ready to fall again into the confusion of chaos." Everywhere the people, as I have already said, groaned under a horrible servitude; a frightful scarcity of provisions, which had, during several years, desolated France and the greater part of the kingdoms of the West, had given birth to all sorts of brigandage and violence; and these proving the destruction of agriculture and commerce, increased still further the horrors of the famine. Villages, towns even, became void of inhabitants, and sank into ruins. The people abandoned a land which no longer nourished them, or could offer them either repose or security: the standard of the cross appeared to them a certain asylum against misery and oppression. According to the decrees of the council of Clermont, the Crusaders were freed from all imposts, and could not be pursued for debts during their voyage. At the name of the cross, the very laws suspended their menaces, tyranny could not seek its victims, nor justice even the guilty, amidst those whom the Church adopted for its defenders. The assurance of impunity, the hope of a better fate, the love of license, and a desire to shake off the most sacred ties, actuated a vast proportion of the multitude which flocked to the banners of the crusade.

Many nobles who had not at first taken the cross, and who saw their vassals set out, without having the power to prevent them, determined to follow them as military chiefs, in order to preserve some portion of their authority. The greater part of the counts and barons had no hesitation in quitting Europe, which the council had declared to be in a state of peace, as it no longer afforded them an opportunity of distinguishing themselves by their valour; they had all many crimes to expiate; "they were promised," says Montesquieu, "expiation in the indulgence of their dominant passion,—they took up, therefore, the cross and arms."

The clergy themselves set the example. Many of the bishops, who bore the titles of counts and barons, and who were accustomed to make war in defence of the rights of their bishoprics, thought it their duty to arm for the cause of Jesus Christ. The priests, to give greater weight to their exhortations, themselves assumed the cross; a great number of pastors resolved to follow their flocks to Jerusalem; not a few of them, as we shall see hereafter, having in their minds the rich bishoprics of Asia, and allowing themselves to be led by the hope of some day occupying the most celebrated sees of the Eastern church.

In the midst of the anarchy and troubles which had desolated Europe since the reign of Charlemagne, there had arisen an association of noble knights, who wandered over the world in search of adventures; they had taken an oath to protect innocence, to fight against infidels, and, by a singular contrast, called themselves *the Champions of God and of Beauty*. The religion which had consecrated their institution and blessed their sword, called them to its defence, and the order of chivalry, which owes a great part of its splendour and progress to the holy wars, saw its warriors hasten to range themselves under the banners of the cross.

Ambition was, perhaps, not foreign to the devotion for the cause of Christ. If religion promised its rewards to those who were going to fight for it, fortune promised them, likewise, riches and the thrones of the earth. All who returned from the East, spoke with enthusiasm of the wonders they had seen, and of the rich provinces they had traversed. It was known that two or three hundred Norman pilgrims had conquered Apulia and Sicily from the Saracens. The lands occupied by the infidels appeared to be heritages promised to knights whose whole wealth consisted in their birth, their valour, and their sword.*

We should nevertheless deceive ourselves if we did not believe that religion was the principle which acted most powerfully upon the greater number of the Crusaders. In ordinary times men follow their natural inclinations, and only obey the voice of their own interest; but in the times of the Crusades, religious fever was a blind passion, which spoke louder than all others. Religion permitted not any other glory, any other felicity to be seen by its ardent defenders, but those which she presented to their heated imagination. Love of country, family ties, the most tender affections of the heart, were all sacrificed to the ideas and the opinions which then possessed the whole of Europe. Moderation was cowardice, indifference treason, opposition a sacrilegious interference. The power of the laws was reckoned as nothing amongst men who believed they were fighting in the cause of God. Subjects scarcely acknowledged the authority of princes or lords in anything which concerned the holy war; the master and the slave had no other title than that of Christian, no other duty to perform than that of defending his religion, sword in hand.

They whom age or condition appeared to detain in Europe, and whom the council had exempted from the labours and perils of the crusade, caused the heaven which called them to the holy war to speak aloud. Women and children imprinted crosses upon their delicate and weak limbs, to show the will of God.† Monks deserted the cloisters in which they had sworn to die, believing themselves led by a divine inspiration; hermits and anchorites issued from forests and deserts, and mingled with the crowd of Crusaders. What is still more difficult to believe, thieves and robbers, quitting their secret retreats, came to confess their crimes, and promised, whilst receiving the cross, to go and expiate them in Palestine.

Europe appeared to be a land of exile, which every one was eager to quit. Artisans, traders, labourers, abandoned the occupations by which they subsisted; barons and lords even renounced the domains of their fathers. The lands, the cities, the castles for which they had but of late been at war, all at once lost their value in the eyes of their possessors, and were given up, for small sums, to those whom the grace of God had not touched, and who were not called to the happiness of visiting the holy places and conquering the East.

Contemporary authors relate several miracles which assisted in heating the minds of the multitude. Stars fell from the firmament; traces of blood were seen in the heavens; cities, armies, and knights decorated with the cross, were pictured in the clouds. The monk Robert asserts that on the very day on which the council of Clermont determined on the holy war, that decision was proclaimed beyond the seas. "This news," adds he, "raised the courage of the Christians in the East, and caused despair among the nations of Arabia." As the most effective of prodigies, saints and kings of preceding ages were said to have issued from their tombs, and many Frenchmen declared they had seen the shade of Charlemagne exhorting the Christians to fight against the Mussulmans.

We will not relate all the other miracles reported by historians, which were believed in an age in which nothing was more common than prodigies, in which, according to the remark of Fleury, the taste for the wonderful prevailed greatly over that for the true. The readers of this history will find quite enough of extraordinary things in the description of so many great events, for which the moral

* Robert le Frisin, second son of the count of Flanders, not being allowed a share of the wealth of his house, said to his father, "Give me men and vessels, and I will go and conquer a state among the Saracens of Spain."

† The Abbé Guibert quotes the example of a monk who made a large incision on his forehead in the form of a cross, and preserved it with prepared juices. He took care to report that an angel had made this incision, which procured for him, during both the voyage and the war, all the help he could desire. He became archbishop of Cæsarea. Foulque, of Chartres, relates that a vessel laden with Crusaders having been wrecked on the coast of Brundusium, all the shipwrecked bodies appeared with a kind of cross imprinted on their flesh, and on the very part on which it had been worn on their clothes when they were alive.

THE WAR CRY OF THE CRUSADERS.

As soon as the spring appeared nothing could restrain the impatience of the Crusaders, and they set forward. . . . The crowd presented a whimsical and confused mixture of all ranks and all conditions; women appeared in arms in the midst of warriors, prostitution not being forgotten in the austerities of penitence; old age was to be seen with infancy, opulence next to misery; the helmet was confounded with the frock, the mitre with the sword. . . . On all parts resounded the war cry of the Crusaders—"IT IS THE WILL OF GOD! IT IS THE WILL OF GOD!"—BOOK I.

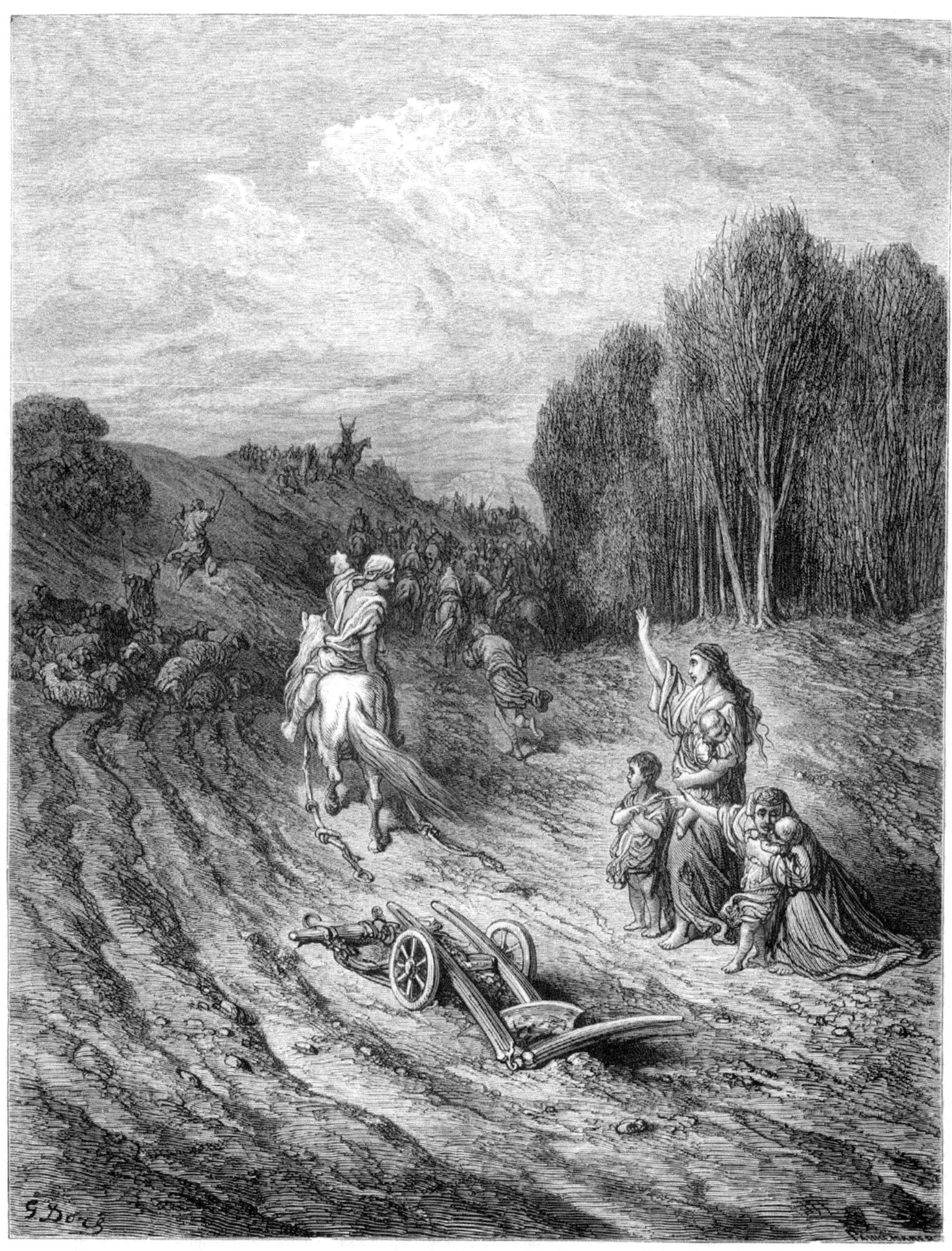

world, and even nature herself seemed to have interrupted their laws. What prodigy, in fact, can more astonish the philosopher, than to see Europe, which may be said to have been agitated to its very foundations, move all at once, and like a single man, march in arms towards the East?

The council of Clermont, which was held in the month of November, 1095, had fixed the departure of the Crusaders for the festival of the Assumption of the following year. During the winter nothing was thought of but preparations for the voyage to the Holy Land; every other care, every other labour was suspended in the cities and the plains. In the midst of the general excitement, the religion, which animated all hearts, watched over public order. All at once there was no more robbery or brigandage heard of. The West was silent, to employ an expression from the Scripture, and Europe enjoyed during several months a peace that it had never before known.

They who had taken the cross encouraged each other, and addressed letters and sent ambassadors to hasten their departure. The benedictions of the heavens appeared to be promised to those who should be first ready to march to Jerusalem. Men even, who at the first had found fault with the delirium of the crusade, accused themselves of indifference for the cause of religion, and showed no less fervour than those who had given the example. All were eager to sell their possessions, but could find no purchasers. The Crusaders despised everything they could not carry with them; the productions of the earth were sold at a low price, which all at once brought back abundance even in the midst of scarcity.

As soon as the spring appeared, nothing could restrain the impatience of the Crusaders, and they set forward on their march to the places at which they were to assemble. The greater number went on foot; some horsemen appeared amongst the multitude; a great many travelled in cars; they were clothed in a variety of manners, and armed, in the same way, with lances, swords, javelins, iron clubs, etc., etc. The crowd of Crusaders presented a whimsical and confused mixture of all ranks and all conditions; women appeared in arms in the midst of warriors, prostitution not being forgotten among the austerities of penitence. Old age was to be seen with infancy, opulence next to misery; the helmet was confounded with the frock, the mitre with the sword. Around cities, around fortresses, in the plains, upon the mountains, were raised tents and pavilions; everywhere was displayed a preparation for war and festivity. Here was heard the sound of arms or the braying of trumpets; whilst at a short distance the air was filled with psalms and spiritual songs. From the Tiber to the ocean, and from the Rhine to the other side of the Pyrenees, nothing was to be seen but troops of men marked with the cross, who swore to exterminate the Saracens, and were chanting their songs of conquest beforehand. On all parts resounded the war-cry of the Crusaders—"*It is the will of God! It is the will of God!*"

Fathers themselves conducted their children, and made them swear to conquer or die for Jesus Christ. Warriors tore themselves from the arms of their wives and from their families, promising to return victorious. Women or old men, whose weakness was left without support, accompanied their sons or their husbands to the nearest city, and there, not being able to separate themselves from the objects of their affections, determined to follow them to Jerusalem. They who remained in Europe envied the fate of the Crusaders, and could not restrain their tears; they who went to seek death in Asia were full of hope and joy. Families, whole villages set out for Palestine, and drew into their ranks all they met with on their passage. They marched on without forethought, and would not believe that he who nourishes the sparrow would leave pilgrims clothed with the holy cross to perish with want. Their ignorance added to their illusion, and lent an air of enchantment to everything they saw; they believed at every moment they were approaching the end of their pilgrimage. The children of the villagers, when they saw a city or a castle, asked *if that was Jerusalem?* Many of the great lords, who had passed their lives in their rustic donjons, knew very little more on this head than their vassals; they took with them their hunting and fishing appointments, and marched with their falcons on their wrists, preceded by their hounds. They expected to reach Jerusalem, enjoying themselves on the road, and to exhibit to Asia the rude luxury of their castles.

In the midst of the general delirium, no sage caused the voice of reason to be heard; nobody was then astonished at that which now creates so much surprise. These scenes, so strange, in which every one was an actor, could only be a spectacle for posterity.

BOOK II.

DEPARTURE AND MARCH OF THE CRUSADERS.

A. D. 1096–1097.

Immense armies collected in various parts of Europe—Peter the Hermit chosen general of the crusade—Opposed by the Hungarians and Bulgarians—Semlin—Nissa—The Crusaders reach Constantinople—Alexius Comnenus—Rapacity and cruelties of the Crusaders—Their defeat and slaughter—Fresh armies sent from Europe—Their distinguished leaders—They wage war against the Greeks—Alliance of Godfrey de Bouillon with Alexius of Constantinople—Wretched situation of the remains of Peter's army in Bithynia—The Turkish power—Kingdom of Ezeroum—Siege of Nice—Battle of Gorgoni—The Turks defeated by the Crusaders—Sultan of Nice desolates the country—Antiochetta—Iconium—Tarsus captured by Baldwin—His conflicts with Tancred—Capture of Alexandretta and Edessa by the Crusaders—They arrive in Mesopotamia.

THE number of Christians who had taken the cross in the greater part of the countries of Europe were quite sufficient to form many large armies. As these armies might exhaust the countries through which they had to pass, the princes and captains who were to conduct them agreed among themselves that they should not all set out at one time, but should pursue different routes, and meet again at Constantinople.

Whilst they were engaged in preparations for departure, the multitude who followed Peter the Hermit in his preachings, became impatient to advance before the other Crusaders; and being without a chief, they cast their eyes upon him whom they considered as an envoy from heaven. They chose Peter for their general; the cenobite, deceived by the excess of his zeal, believed that enthusiasm could alone answer for all the successes of war, and that it would be easy to conduct an undisciplined troop which had taken up arms at the sound of his voice. He yielded to the prayers of the multitude, and, clothed in his woollen mantle, a hood over his head, sandals on his feet, and only mounted on the mule upon which he had traversed Europe, he took upon himself the command. His troop, which set out from the banks of the Meuse and Moselle, proceeded towards Germany, and was increased upon the road by a vast number of pilgrims hastening from Champagne, Burgundy, and other parts of France. Peter soon saw from eighty to a hundred thousand men under his standard. These first Crusaders, dragging in their train women, children, old men, and numerous sick, began their march upon the faith of the miraculous promises made them by their general; in the persuasion they were filled with, that God himself called upon them to defend his cause, they hoped that rivers would open before their battalions, and that manna would fall from heaven to feed them. The army of Peter the Hermit was divided into two bodies; the vanguard marched under the orders of Walter the Penniless, whose surname, preserved by history, proves that the chiefs were as miserable as the soldiers. This vanguard only reckoned eight horsemen; all the rest went to the conquest of the East asking charity by the way. As long as the Crusaders were upon the French Territory, the charity of the faithful who were on their route provided for their wants. They warmed the zeal of the Germans, amongst whom the crusade had not been preached. Their troop, which was considered everywhere as the people of God, met with no enemies on the banks of the Rhine; but new Amalekites, the Hungarians and the Bulgarians, awaited them on the shores of the Morava and the Danube.

The Hungarians, who had issued from Tartary, had a common origin with the Turks, and, like them, had rendered themselves formidable to the Christians. In the tenth century they had invaded Pannonia, and carried the ravages of war into the richest countries of Europe. Nations terrified at the progress of their arms, considered them as a scourge which was sent as a forerunner of the end of the world. Towards the middle of the eleventh century they embraced the Christianity they had persecuted. Once obedient to the faith of the Gospel, they began to build cities and cultivate their land; they felt what it was to have a country, and ceased to be the terror of their neighbours. At the period of the first crusade, the Hungarians boasted of having a saint among their kings, but, still separated from the Christian republic by their position, they did not at all partake of the fervour of the Crusaders, and looked on with indifference at the preparations of Europe for the conquest of Asia.

The Bulgarians, who were descended from the ancient people of the Sclaves, had by turns protected and ravaged the empire of Constantinople. Their warriors had killed Nicephorus in battle, and the skull of an emperor, enchased in gold, served for a long time as a cup for their chiefs in the orgies of victory. They were afterwards conquered by Basil, who put out the eyes of fifteen thousand of his prisoners, and by this act of barbarity roused the whole nation against Greece. At the time of the crusade, Bulgaria was under the power of the Greek empire, but it despised the laws and the power of its masters. The Bulgarian people spread along the southern banks of the Danube, in the midst of inaccessible forests, preserved their savage independence, and only recognized the emperors of the East when they saw their armies. Although they had embraced Christianity, the Bulgarians did not consider the Christians as their brothers; they neither respected the laws of nations nor the rights of hospitality, and during the eleventh century they were the terror of the pilgrims of the West who journeyed to Jerusalem.

Such were the people whose territories the Crusaders were about to cross, and among whom want of discipline must necessarily expose them to the most direful reverses. When the vanguard entered Hungary, they were only disturbed in their march but by a few insults, which Walter had the prudence not to avenge; but the resignation of the pilgrims could not hold out long against the misery which every day increased. Want and its attendant evils soon dispersed all the sentiments of moderation to which religion had for a moment given birth in the hearts of its defenders. The governor of Bulgaria not having been able to furnish provisions, they spread themselves about over the country, carried off the flocks, burnt the houses, and massacred several of the inhabitants who opposed their violences. The irritated Bulgarians ran to arms, and fell upon the soldiers of Walter loaded with their booty. A hundred and forty Crusaders perished in the midst of flames, in a church in which they had taken refuge; the rest sought safety in flight. After this defeat, which he did not endeavour to repair, Walter continued his march through the forests of Bulgaria, pursued by famine, and dragging along the wreck of his army. He presented himself as a supplicant before the governor of Nissa, who was touched with the misery of the Crusaders, and gave them provisions, arms, and clothing.

The soldiers of Walter, tried by merited reverses, conducted by a chief who was wanting in neither skill nor courage, became again attentive to the voice of religion, and passed through Thrace without committing any disorders. After two months of fatigue and misery, they arrived under the walls of Constantinople, where the Emperor Alexis permitted them to wait for the army of Peter the Hermit.

WALTER THE PENNILESS IN HUNGARY.

When the vanguard entered Hungary, they were only disturbed in their march but by a few insults, which Walter had the prudence not to avenge; but the resignation of the pilgrims could not hold out long against the misery which every day increased. Want and its attendant evils soon dispersed all the sentiments of moderation to which religion had for a moment given birth in the hearts of its defenders. The governor of Bulgaria not having been able to furnish provisions, they spread themselves about over the country, carried off the flocks, burnt the houses, and massacred several of the inhabitants who opposed their violence. The irritated Bulgarians ran to arms, and fell upon the soldiers of Walter, loaded with their booty.—Book II.

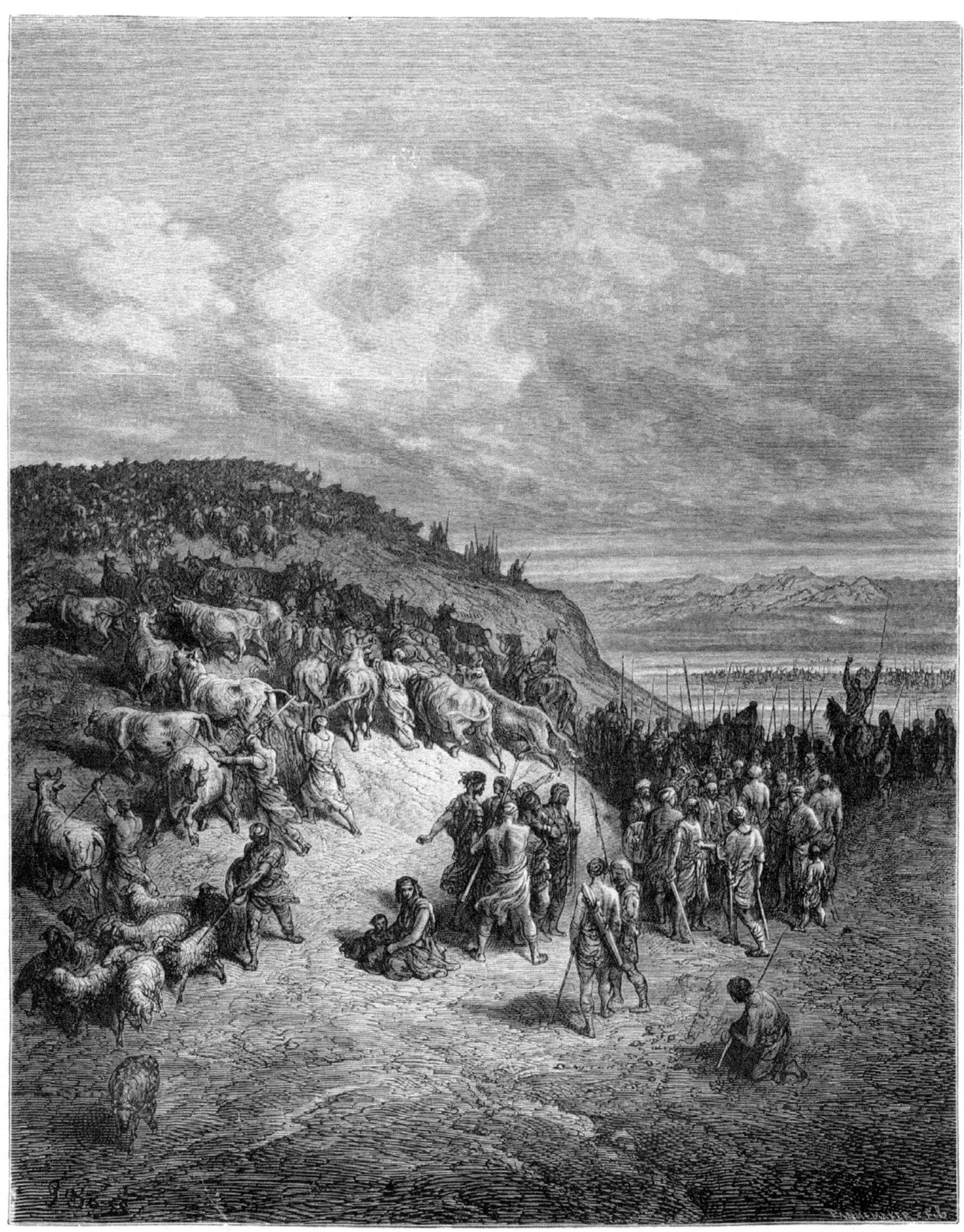

This army, which was then passing through Germany, was about to be treated worse than its vanguard had been. The cenobite, Peter, more enthusiastic than his soldiers, was more skilful in exciting their zeal than in directing it. He showed neither the moderation nor the prudence of his lieutenant, and had no idea how to avoid the dangers which awaited him on his route. On arriving on the frontiers of Hungary, he learnt the ill-fortune that his companions had met with, and the projects of hostilities formed, as he was told, against the army of the pilgrims. The bodies of several of the Crusaders hung at the gates of Semlin, which the historians of the crusades call *Malleville*, attracted his regard and drew forth his indignation. At this sight, he gave the signal for vengeance and war. The trumpets sounded, the soldiers seized their arms, and hastened to the carnage. Terror preceded them into the city. On their first attack the people took to flight, and sought refuge upon a hill, one side of which was defended by woods and rocks, and the other by the Danube. They were pursued and forced into this last asylum by the furious multitude of the Crusaders. More than four thousand of the inhabitants of Semlin fell under the swords of the conquerors. The bodies carried down by the river bore the tidings of this horrible victory as far as Belgrade.

At this intelligence the Bulgarians and Hungarians were seized with grief and indignation, and in all parts flew to arms. The Crusaders still remained in Semlin, and were glorifying themselves upon their triumph, when all at once an army, assembled in haste by Coloman, king of Hungary, presented itself to their view. Peter had nothing to oppose to his enemies but the soldiers whose blind fury he had himself excited, and with whom it was impossible to make any military disposition. He did not dare to wait for the army of Coloman, and hastened to cross the Morava.

On gaining the territories of the Bulgarians, the Crusaders found the villages and cities abandoned; even Belgrade, the capital, was without inhabitants; they had fled into the forests and mountains. Peter's soldiers, after a painful march, in want of provisions, and with difficulty finding guides to conduct them, arrived at last at the gates of Nissa, a place sufficiently well fortified to be secure from a first attack. The Bulgarians showing themselves upon their ramparts, and the Crusaders leaning on their arms, inspired each other with a mutual fear. This fear at first prevented hostilities; but harmony could not last long between an army without discipline and a people that had been irritated by violence.

The pilgrims, after having obtained provisions, had just set forward on their march, when a quarrel between the inhabitants and some of the soldiers caused war to break forth with inveteracy. A hundred German Crusaders, whom William of Tyre styles *children of Belial*, and who fancied they had cause of complaint against some merchants, wishing to avenge themselves, set fire to seven mills placed upon the Nissava. At the sight of this fire, the inhabitants of Nissa rushed from their ramparts, and falling upon Peter's rear-guard, massacred all who fell in their way, bore off two thousand carriages, and made a great number of prisoners. Peter, who had already quitted the territory of Nissa, warned of the disaster of his companions, returned immediately with the bulk of his army. The eyes of the Crusaders, on approaching the city, were shocked everywhere by beholding the most sorrowful spectacle. They recognized among the dead friends and brothers, and burned to revenge them.

The cenobite, however, who feared fresh reverses, had recourse to negotiations and prayers. Deputies were sent into Nissa, to demand the prisoners and the baggage of his army, which had been taken by the Bulgarians. These deputies reminded the governor that they had taken up the cross, and that they were going to fight in the East for the cause of Jesus Christ. They appealed to the religion and humanity of the inhabitants of Nissa, whom they called their brethren.

The governor, who saw nothing in these peaceful words but the language of fear, showed himself inflexible to their prayers. He sternly sent them back to their general, telling them that the Crusaders had themselves given the signal for the war, and that he could see in them nothing but enemies. When this answer was reported to the army of Peter, every soldier was fired with indignation. In vain the cenobite endeavoured to calm their spirits and attempt fresh negotiations; they accused his fidelity, they suspected his courage. The most ardent flew to arms; nothing was heard but complaints and menaces; and no Crusader would submit to any directions but those of his own angry will. Whilst Peter was conferring with the governor of Nissa, two thousand soldiers approached the ramparts, and endeavoured to scale them. They were repulsed by the Bulgarians, and supported by a great number of their companions. The fight became general, and the fire of carnage blazed on all parts around the chiefs, who were still speaking of conditions of peace. In vain the hermit had recourse to supplications, to stop the mad progress of his soldiers, in vain he placed himself between the combatants; his voice, so well known to the Crusaders, was lost in the din of arms. They braved his authority; they despised his prayers. His army, which fought without order and without leaders, was routed and cut to pieces. The women, the children, who followed the Crusaders, their horses, their camp equipages, the chest of the army, which contained the numerous offerings of the faithful, all became the prey of an enemy whose fury and vengeance nothing could stop.

The hermit Peter, with the wreck of his troop, took refuge on a hill in the neighbourhood of the city. He passed the night in alarms, deploring his defeat, and the sad effects of the violences of which he had himself given the signal and the example among the Hungarians. He had around him no more than five hundred men. The trumpets and the clarions were sounded without ceasing, to recall those who had escaped the carnage, and had lost themselves in their flight.

Whether it was that the Crusaders could find no safety but under their own standards, or whether they were still mindful of their oath, none turned back from the crusade. On the day following their defeat, seven thousand fugitives came to rejoin their general. A few days after, Peter mustered beneath his command thirty thousand combatants. All the rest had perished in the battle fought under the walls of Nissa. The army of the Crusaders, reduced to a deplorable condition, sought no opportunity of avenging their defeat, but marched with melancholy steps towards the frontiers of Thrace. They were without the means either of subsisting or fighting. They had to fear a fresh defeat if they encountered the Bulgarians, and all the horrors of famine if they came to a desert country. Misfortune rendered them more docile, and inspired them with sentiments of moderation. The pity which their misery excited was more serviceable to them than the terror which they had wished to create. When they ceased to be an object of dread, assistance was afforded them. When they entered the territories of Thrace, the Greek emperor sent deputies to complain of their disorders, but at the same time to announce his clemency. Peter, who dreaded new disasters, wept with joy when he learnt that he had found favour with Alexis. Full of confidence and hope, he pursued his march, and the Crusaders, carrying palms in their hands, arrived without further obstacles under the walls of Constantinople.

The Greeks, who entertained no love for the Latins, were more prodigal and kind in the assistance they afforded them from finding them less formidable. They secretly applauded the courage of the Bulgarians, and contemplated with complacency the warriors of the West covered with the rags of indigence. The emperor was desirous of seeing the extraordinary man who had roused the western world by his eloquence, and Peter was admitted to an audience of Alexis. In the presence of all his court, the emperor extolled the zeal of the preacher of the crusade; and as he had nothing to fear from the ambition of a hermit, he loaded him with presents, caused arms, money, and provisions to be distributed among his army, and advised him to defer the commencement of the war to the arrival of the princes and illustrious captains who had assumed the cross.

This advice was salutary, but the most renowned heroes of the crusade were not yet ready to leave Europe; they were to be preceded by fresh troops of Crusaders, who, marching without forethought and without discipline in the steps of the army of Peter, should commit the same excesses, and be exposed to the same reverses. A priest of the Palatinate had preached the crusade in several provinces of Germany. At his voice fifteen or twenty thousand men had taken the oath to fight the infidels, and had assembled in an armed body. As the preachers of the holy war passed for men inspired by God, the people believed they were obeying the will of heaven in taking them for chiefs of the crusade. Gotschalk obtained the same honour that had been conferred on Peter the Hermit, and was elected general by the men he had prevailed upon to take arms. This army arrived in Hungary towards the end of summer. The harvest, which was abundant, furnished the Germans with a ready opportunity of giving themselves up to intemperance. In the enjoyment of tumultuous scenes of debauchery, they forgot Constantinople, Jerusalem, and Christ himself, whose worship and laws they were marching to defend. Pillage, violation and murder were everywhere left as the traces of their passage. Coloman assembled troops to chastise their license, and to recall them to a sense of the maxims of justice and the laws of hospitality. The soldiers of Gotschalk were full of courage, and, at first, defended themselves with advantage. Their resistance even inspired serious alarm among the Hungarians, who resolved to employ stratagem to reduce them. The general of Coloman feigned to be desirous of peace. The chiefs of the Hungarians presented themselves in the camp of the Crusaders, no longer as enemies, but as brothers. By dint of protestations and caresses, they persuaded them to allow themselves to be disarmed. The Germans, slaves of the most brutal passions, but simple and credulous, yielded to the promises of a Christian people, and abandoned themselves to a blind confidence, of which they very shortly became the victims. Scarcely had they laid down their arms when the chief of the Hungarians gave the signal for the carnage. The prayers, the tears of the Crusaders, the sacred sign which they bore upon their breasts, could not divert the blows of a perfidious and barbarous enemy. Their fate was worthy of pity, and history might have shed tears over it if they had themselves respected the laws of humanity.

We are doubtless the less astonished at the excesses of the first Crusaders, when we reflect that they belonged to the lowest class of the people, always blind, and always ready to abuse names and things the most holy, when not restrained by laws or leaders. The civil wars, which had so long disturbed Europe, had greatly increased the number of vagabonds and adventurers. Germany, more troubled than the other countries of the West, was filled with men trained in brigandage, and became the scourge of society. They almost all enrolled themselves under the banners of the cross, and carried with them into a new expedition the spirit of license and revolt with which they were animated.

There assembled on the banks of the Rhine and the Moselle a new troop of Crusaders, more seditious, more undisciplined, even, than those of Peter and Gotschalk. They had been told that the crusade procured the forgiveness of all sins; and in this persuasion they committed the greatest crimes with security. Animated by a fanatical pride, they believed themselves entitled to despise and ill-treat all who did not join in the holy expedition. The war they were about to wage appeared to them so agreeable to God, and they thought by it to render such a signal service to the Church, that all the wealth of the earth would be scarcely sufficient to pay them for their devotion. Everything which fell into their hands appeared a conquest over the infidels, and became the just reward of their labours.

No captain durst place himself at the head of this ferocious troop; they wandered on in disorder, and obeyed none but those who partook their wild delirium. A priest named Volkmar, and a Count Emicio, who thought to expiate the wildness of his youth by the excess of his fanaticism, attracted, by their declamations, the attention and confidence of the new Crusaders. These two chiefs were astonished that people should go so far to make war upon the Mussulmans, who kept up under their own law the tomb of Jesus Christ, whilst they left in peace a nation which had crucified its God. To inflame men's passions still more, they took care to make heaven speak, and to support their opinions by miraculous visions. The people, for whom the Jews were everywhere an object of hatred and horror, had already shown themselves but too ready to persecute them. Commerce, which they almost alone carried on, had placed in their hands a great part of the gold then circulating in Europe. The sight of their wealth necessarily irritated the Crusaders, who were, for the most part, reduced to implore charity of the faithful to procure the means for undertaking their voyage. It is probable, likewise, that the Jews, by their railleries, insulted the enthusiasm of the Christians for the crusade.

All these motives, joined to the thirst for pillage, lit up the fires of persecution. Emicio and Volkmar gave both the signal and the example. At their voice a furious multitude spread themselves through the cities of the Rhine and the Moselle, massacring pitilessly all the Jews that they met with in their passage. In their despair, a great number of these victims preferred being their own destroyers, to awaiting certain death at the hands of their enemies. Several shut themselves up in their houses, and perished amidst flames which they themselves had kindled; some fastened large stones to their garments, and precipitated themselves and their treasures into the Rhine or the Moselle. Mothers stifled their children at the breast, saying that they preferred sending them thus to the bosom of Abraham, to seeing them given up to the fury of the Christians. Women and old men implored pity to assist them to die; all these wretched creatures calling upon death as earnestly as other men ask for life. In the midst of these scenes of desolation, history takes pleasure in doing justice to the enlightened zeal of the bishops of Worms, Trèves, Mayence, and Spiers, who raised the voice of religion and humanity, and opened their palaces as so many asylums for the Jews against the pursuit of murderers and villains.

The soldiers of Emicio prided themselves upon their exploits, and scenes of carnage filled them with exultation. As proud as if they had conquered the Saracens, they set out on their march, loaded with booty, invoking the heaven they had so cruelly outraged. They were slaves to the most brutal superstition, and caused themselves to be preceded by a goat and a goose, to which they attributed something divine. These mean animals at the head of the battalions were as their chiefs, and shared the respect and confidence of the multitude, with all those who furnished examples of the most horrible excesses. All people fled at the approach of these dreaded champions of the cross. Christians who met them on their route were forced to applaud their zeal, whilst trembling for fear of becoming victims to it. This unrestrained multitude, without being acquainted with the people or the countries through which they had to pass, ignorant even of the disasters of those who had preceded them in this perilous career, advanced like a hurricane towards the plains of Hungary. Mersbourg shut its gates upon them, and refused them provisions. They were indignant that so little respect should be shown to the soldiers of Christ, and deemed it their duty to treat the Hungarians as they had treated the Jews. Mersbourg, situated on the Leytha, a river which flows into the Danube, was defended by marshes. The Crusaders crossed the river, cut down a forest, and formed a causeway, which conducted them close under the walls of the place. After some preparation the signal was given, the ladders were raised against the ramparts, and the general assault was begun. The besieged opposed a spirited resistance, and showered upon their enemies a tempest of darts and arrows, with torrents of boiling oil. The besiegers, encouraging each other, redoubled their efforts. Victory appeared to be about to declare for them, when suddenly several ladders yielded to the weight of the assailants, and dragged down with them in their fall the parapets and the fragments of the towers that the rams had shaken. The cries of the wounded, and the rattling of the falling ruins, spread a panic among the

THE ARMY OF PRIEST VOLKMAR AND COUNT EMICIO ATTACK MERSBOURG.[1]

Mersbourg shut its gates upon them, and refused them provisions. They were indignant that so little respect should be shown to the soldiers of Christ, and deemed it their duty to treat the Hungarians as they had treated the Jews. Mersbourg, situated on the Leytha, a river which flows into the Danube, was defended by marshes. The Crusaders crossed the river, cut down a forest, and formed a causeway, which conducted them close under the walls of the place. After some preparation the signal was given, the ladders were raised against the ramparts, and the general assault was begun. The besieged opposed a spirited resistance, and showered upon their enemies a tempest of darts and arrows, with torrents of boiling oil. The besiegers, encouraging each other, redoubled their efforts. Victory appeared to be about to declare for them, when suddenly several ladders yielded to the weight of the assailants, and dragged down with them in their fall the parapets and the fragments of the towers that the ram had shaken. The cries of the wounded and the rattling of the falling ruin spread a panic among the Crusaders.—Book II.

[1] *Now called Altenburgh.*

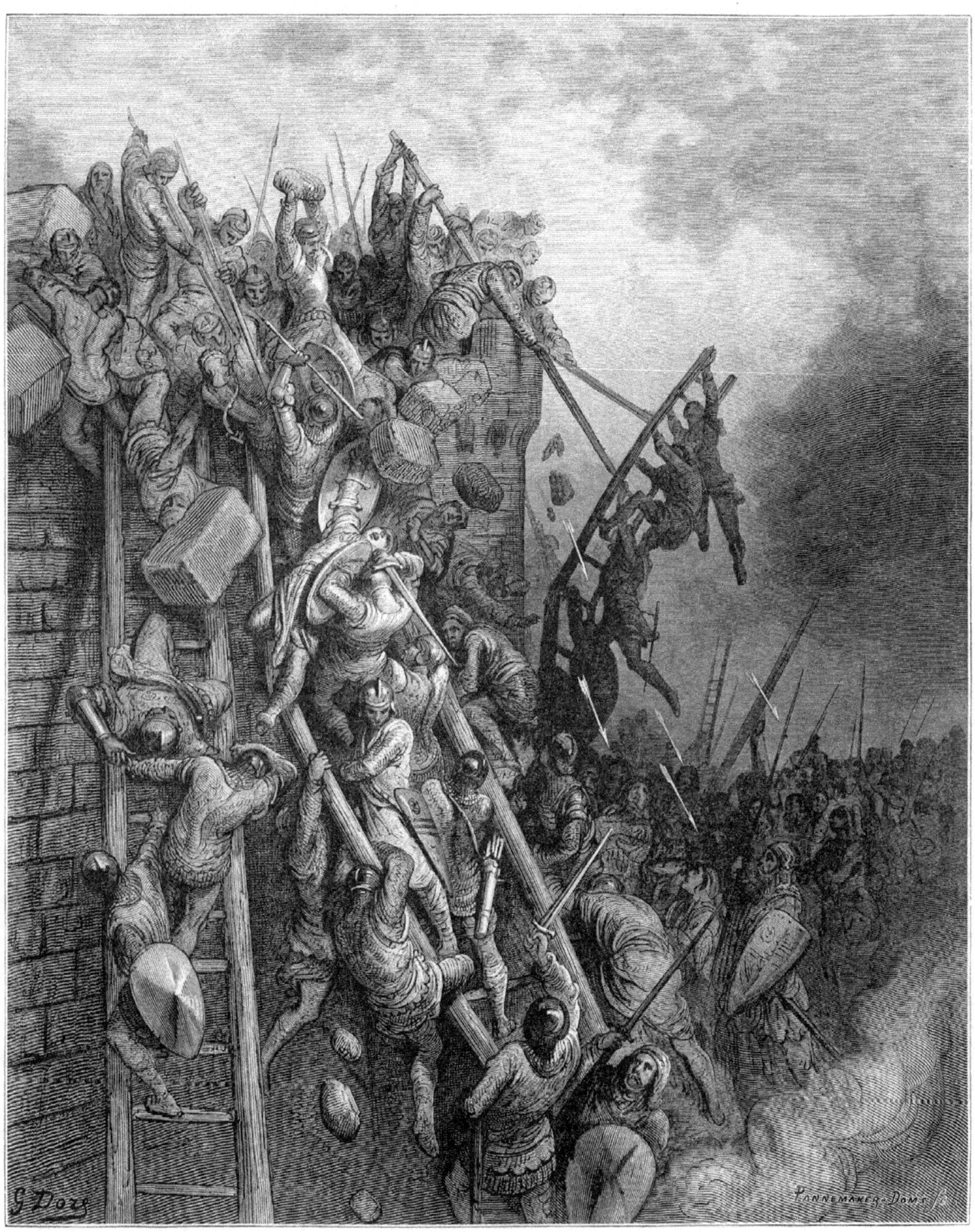
G. Doré
PANNEMAKER-DOMS

Crusaders. They abandoned the half-destroyed ramparts, behind which their enemies trembled, and retired in the greatest disorder.

"God himself," says William of Tyre, "spread terror through their ranks, to punish their crimes, and to accomplish that word of the wise man: 'The impious man flies without being pursued.'" The inhabitants of Mersbourg, astonished at their victory, at length quitted the shelter of their ramparts, and found the plain covered with the fliers, who had cast away their arms. A vast number of these furious beings, whom, recently, nothing could resist, allowed themselves to be slaughtered without resistance. Many perished, swallowed up in the marshes. The waters of the Danube and the Leytha were reddened with their blood, and covered with their bodies.

The vanguard of this army met with the same fate among the Bulgarians, whose territories they had gained. In the cities and the plains, these unworthy Crusaders found everywhere men as ferocious and implacable as themselves, who appeared—to employ the words of the historians of the times—to have been placed upon the passage of the pilgrims as instruments of divine wrath. A very small number escaped the carnage. Among the few who found safety in flight, some returned into their own country, where they were welcomed by the scorn and jeers of their compatriots; the rest arrived at Constantinople, where the Greeks learnt the new disasters of the Latins, with so much the more joy, from having suffered greatly from the excesses committed by the army of Peter the Hermit.

This army, united to that of Walter, had received under its standard an accession of Pisans, Venetians, and Genoese, and might amount to about a hundred thousand combatants. The remembrance of their misery caused them for a time to respect the commands of the emperor and the laws of hospitality; but abundance, idleness, and the sight of the riches of Constantinople, brought back to their camp, license, insubordination, and a thirst for plunder. Impatient to receive the signal for war, they pillaged the houses, the palaces, and even the churches, of the suburbs of Byzantium. To deliver his capital from these destructive guests, Alexis furnished them with vessels, and transported them to the other side of the Bosphorus.

Nothing could be expected from a band composed of a confused mixture of all nations, and the wrecks of several undisciplined armies. A great number of the Crusaders, on quitting their country, had thought of nothing but accomplishing their vow, and only sighed for the happiness of beholding Jerusalem; but these pious dispositions had all vanished on their route. Whatever may be the motive that brings them together, when men are not confined by any restraint, the most corrupted gain the ascendancy, and bad examples constitute the law. As soon as the soldiers of Peter had passed the straits, they considered all they met their enemies, and the subjects of the Greek emperor suffered much more than the Turks from their first exploits. In their blindness, they allied superstition with license, and under the banners of the cross, committed crimes which make nature shudder. But discord soon broke out amongst them, and retaliated upon them all the evils they had inflicted upon Christians.

They had established their camp in the fertile plains which border the Gulf of Nicomedia. Every day parties strayed into the neighbourhood, and returned loaded with booty. The partition of the spoil excited frequent quarrels among them. The French, of an assuming and bantering character, attributed to themselves all the success of this commencement of the war, and treated the Italians and Germans with contempt. The latter separated themselves from the army, and under the conduct of a chief named Rinaldo,* advanced towards the mountains which border upon Nicea. There they

* This Rinaldo, of whom nothing else is known, except that he was an Italian, is the only personage so called who has any event of importance in the first crusade attached to his name. Tasso, who has taken most of his characters from history, has borrowed the person and character of Rinaldo, in the "Jerusalem Delivered," entirely from his imagination.

rendered themselves masters of a fort, whose garrison they massacred, and although their troop was not numerous, and stood in great want of provisions, they were bold enough to await the army which was approaching to besiege them. They were not able to resist even the first attacks of the Turks, and were almost all put to the sword ; their general, and some few of his soldiers, only saved their lives by embracing the faith of Mahomet, and by taking a disgraceful oath to fight against the Christians.

When the news of this disaster reached the camp of the Crusaders, it brought with it agitation and trouble. The French, who, a few days before, could not endure the Germans and the Italians, wept over their tragical fate, and were eager to march to avenge them. In vain Walter, who commanded them, represented to them that the Crusaders whose loss they deplored had fallen victims to their own imprudence, and that their principal duty was to avoid their example ; nothing could restrain the impatience and the blind ardour of his soldiers. The latter believed that they already saw the Turks flying before them, and feared they should not be able to overtake them. Murmurs arose in the Christian army against a general whom they accused of want of courage, because he foresaw reverses. From murmurs they passed to revolt, and the order for departure and attack was forced from him by violence. Walter, groaning, followed a headstrong multitude, who marched in disorder towards Nicea, and whom the Turks would soon punish for the contempt with which they had treated the advice of their leaders.

The sultan of Nicea, foreseeing their imprudence, had concealed a part of his army in a forest, and waited for them with the rest of his troops in a plain at the foot of the mountain. After a march of some hours, in a country which was unknown to them, the Christians were unexpectedly attacked by the Turks, whom they believed to be in flight. They formed in haste, and at first defended themselves valiantly. But the enemy had the advantages of position and numbers, and they were soon surrounded on all sides, and completely routed. The carnage was horrible ; Walter, who was worthy of commanding better soldiers, fell pierced by seven arrows. With the exception of three thousand men, who took refuge in a castle close to the sea, the whole army perished in a single battle, and there soon remained no more of them than a confused heap of bones, piled up in the plains of Nicea, as a deplorable monument to point out to other Crusaders the road to the Holy Land.

Such was the fate of that multitude of pilgrims who threatened Asia, and yet never beheld the places they went to conquer. By their excesses they had prejudiced the whole of Greece against the enterprize of the crusades, and by their manner of fighting had taught the Turks to despise the arms of the Christians of the West.

Peter, who had returned to Constantinople before the battle, and who had long lost all authority among the Crusaders, declaimed against their indocility and their pride, and beheld in them nothing but brigands, whom God had deemed unworthy to contemplate or adore the tomb of his Son. From that time it was quite evident that the apostle of the holy war possessed no quality to enable him to act as its chief. Coolness, prudence, inflexible firmness, alone could conduct a multitude whom so many passions impelled, and who listened to nothing but enthusiasm. The cenobite Peter, after having prepared the great events of the crusade by his eloquence, lost in the crowd of pilgrims, played nothing but an ordinary part, and was in the end scarcely to be perceived in a war that was his work.

Europe, without doubt, learnt with terror and astonishment the unhappy end of three hundred thousand Crusaders, whom she had seen depart ; but they who were to follow were not at all discouraged, and resolved to profit by the lessons which the disasters of their companions had given them. The West soon saw on foot armies more regular and more formidable than those which had been destroyed on the banks of the Danube, and in the plains of Bithynia.

When describing their march and their exploits, we are about to trace much nobler pictures. Here the heroic spirit of chivalry will display itself in all its splendour, and the brilliant period of the holy war will commence.

The leaders of the Christian armies which now quitted the West were already celebrated by their valour and their deeds. At the head of the great captains who commanded in this crusade, history, as well as poetry, must place Godfrey de Bouillon,* duke of the Lower Lorraine. He was of the illustrious race of the counts of Boulogne, and descended on the female side from Charlemagne. From his earliest youth he had distinguished himself in the open war carried on between the Holy See and the emperor of Germany. On the field of battle he had killed Rodolphe de Rhenfield, duke of Suabia, to whom Gregory had sent the imperial crown. When the war broke out in Italy for the cause of the anti-pope Anaclet, Godfrey was the first to enter the city of Rome, besieged and taken by the troops of Henry. He afterwards repented of having embraced a party which victory itself could not make triumphant, and which the greater part of Christendom considered sacrilegious. To expiate exploits condemned as useless by the spirit of the age, he made a vow to go to Jerusalem, not as a simple pilgrim, but as a liberator.

Contemporary history, which has transmitted his portrait to us, informs us that he joined the bravery and virtues of a hero to the simplicity of a cenobite. His prowess in fight and his extraordinary strength of body made him the pride of camps. Prudence and moderation tempered his valour; his devotion was sincere and disinterested; and in no instance during the holy war did he employ his courage or inflict his vengeance but upon the enemies of Christ. Faithful to his word, liberal, affable, full of humanity, the princes and knights looked upon him as their model, the soldiers as their father—all were eager to fight under his standard. If he was not the leader of the crusade, as some writers pretend, he at least obtained that empire which virtue bestows. Amidst their quarrels and divisions, the princes and barons constantly appealed to the wisdom of Godfrey, and in the dangers of war his counsels became absolute orders.

At the signal of the duke of Lorraine, the nobility of France and the borders of the Rhine were prodigal of their treasures in preparing for the crusades. All things serviceable in war mounted to so exorbitant a price, that the produce of an estate was scarcely sufficient to defray the equipment of a single knight. The women despoiled themselves of their most precious ornaments to furnish forth their sons and their husbands for the expedition. Men even, say the historians, who in other times would have suffered a thousand deaths rather than give up their hereditary domains, either sold them for a low price or exchanged them for arms. Gold and steel appeared to be the only desirable objects in existence.

Now appeared the stores of riches which had been concealed by fear or avarice. Ingots of gold, coined pieces, says the Abbé Guibert, were to be seen in heaps in the tents of the principal Crusaders, like the most common fruits in the cottages of villagers.

Many barons, having neither lands nor castles to sell, implored the charity of the faithful who did not take up the cross, and might hope to participate in the merits of the holy war by assisting in the equipment of the Crusaders. Some ruined their vassals; others, like William, viscount de Melun, pillaged the burghs and villages to place themselves in a condition to combat the infidels. Godfrey de Bouillon, guided by a more enlightened piety, was content with alienating his domains. We read in Robert Gaguin that he permitted the inhabitants of Metz to redeem their city, of which he was suzer-

* Godfrey of Bouillon was born at Baysy, a village of Wallon Brabant, now in the department of La Dyle, two leagues south-east of Nevilles, and not far from Fleurus. Aubert le Mire, and the Baron Leroy, in the geography of Brabant, report that in their time the remains of the castle in which Godfrey was brought up were to be seen.

ain. He sold the principality of Stenai to the Bishop of Verdun, and ceded his rights over the duchy of Bouillon to the bishop of Liège for the small sum of four thousand silver marks and a pound of gold, which makes an historian of the Crusaders say that the secular princes ruined themselves for the cause of Jesus Christ, whilst the princes of the Church took advantage of the fervour of the Christians to enrich themselves.

The duke de Bouillon had gathered under his standard eighty thousand foot-soldiers and ten thousand horsemen. He began his march eight months after the council of Clermont, accompanied by a great number of German and French nobles. He took with him his brother Eustace de Boulogne, his other brother Baldwin, and his cousin Baldwin de Bourg. These two last, who were destined one day, like Godfrey de Bouillon, to become kings of Jerusalem, held then the rank of simple knights in the Christian army. They were all less animated by sincere piety than by the hope of achieving a great fortune in Asia, and quitted without regret the mean possessions that they held in Europe. Still further were to be remarked in the train of the duke de Lorraine, Baldwin, count de Hainaut; Garnier, count de Grai; Conon de Montaigu, Dudon de Contz, so celebrated in the "Jerusalem Delivered;" the two brothers Henri and Godfrey de Hache, Gérard de Cherisi, Rinaldo and Peter de Toul, Hugh de St. Paul, and his son Engelran. These chiefs brought with them a crowd of other knights, less known, but not less formidable by their valour.

The army commanded by the duke of Lorraine, composed of soldiers formed by discipline and tried in battle, offered to the Germans a very different spectacle from the troop of Peter the Hermit, and re-established the honour of the Crusaders in all the countries they passed through. They met with assistance and allies where the first champions of the cross had found nothing but obstacles and enemies. Godfrey deplored the fate of those who had preceded him, without seeking to avenge their cause. The Hungarians and the Bulgarians, on their part, forgot the violences committed by the soldiers of Peter, Gotschalk, and Emicio; they admired the moderation of Godfrey, and offered up vows for the success of his arms.

Whilst the duke de Lorraine was advancing towards Constantinople, France was raising other armies for the holy war. A few months after the council of Clermont, the nobles of the kingdom assembled to deliberate upon the affairs of the crusade. In this assembly, held in the presence of Philip I., who had just been excommunicated, no one was opposed to the war preached under the auspices of the Holy See; no one even thought of invoking policy either to moderate or direct the passions which agitated Europe. The cabinets of princes were as much infatuated as the multitude, and it may be said that the fortune of France took charge alone of these great events, which, though unfortunate at first, afterwards concurred to raise the monarchy which had fallen into ruins under the feeble successors of Charlemagne.

Towards the middle of the tenth century, the chief of the third dynasty had consecrated the usurpation of the nobles, and to obtain the title of king, had almost abandoned the little that remained of the rights of the crown. Philip I., grandson of Hugh Capet, found that his dominions extended but little beyond Paris and Orleans; the rest of France was governed by the great vassals, of whom several surpassed the monarch in power. Royalty, the only hope of the people against the oppressions of the nobles and the clergy, was so feeble, that we are at the present time astonished that it did not fall, so numerous were the difficulties and the enemies that surrounded it on all sides. As the monarch was exposed to the censures of the Church, it was an easy matter to lead his subjects to disobedience, and to legitimatize any sort of revolt, by giving it the colour of a sacred pretext.

The crusade removed far from Europe all who could have taken advantage of the unhappy situation in which the kingdom was placed; it saved the country from a civil war, and prevented such san-

THE SECOND CRUSADERS ENCOUNTER THE REMAINS OF THE FIRST CRUSADERS.

Peter the Hermit and Walter the Penniless crossed the Bosphorus with an army which might amount to about a hundred thousand combatants. . . . After a march of some hours, in a country which was unknown to them, the Christians were unexpectedly attacked by the Turks, whom they believed to be in flight. They formed in haste, and at first defended themselves valiantly. But the enemy had the advantage of position and numbers, and they were soon surrounded on all sides and completely routed. The carnage was horrible; Walter, who was worthy of commanding better soldiers, fell pierced by seven arrows. With the exception of three thousand men, who took refuge in a castle close to the sea, the whole army perished in a single battle, and there soon remained no more of them than a confused heap of bones, piled up in the plains of Nicea, as a deplorable monument to point out to other Crusaders the road to the Holy Land.—Book II.

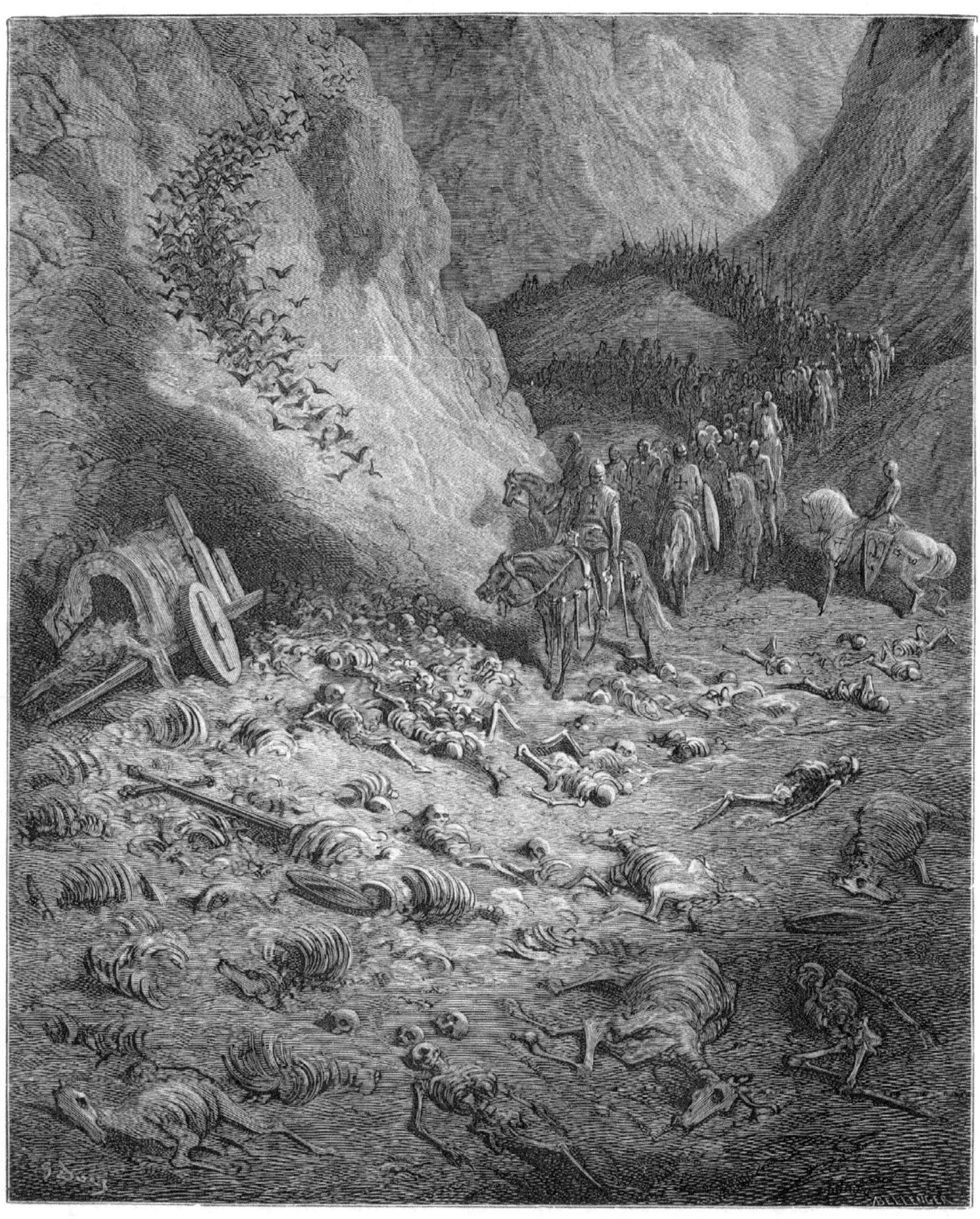

guinary discords as had broken out in Germany under the reign of Henry and the pontificate of Gregory.

Such were the considerations which might present themselves to the most enlightened men, and which must strike us more strongly than they would the contemporaries of Philip. It would be difficult to believe that any one of the counsellors of the king of France perceived, in all their extent, these salutary results of the crusade, which were recognized long after, and which have only been properly appreciated in the age in which we live. On the other hand, they had no conception that a war in which all the most dangerous passions should be brought into action would be accompanied by great misfortunes and calamitous disorders. Ambition, license, the spirit of enthusiasm, all so much to be dreaded by the country, might also bring about the ruin of armies. Not one of the enemies of Philip, not one of those who remained at home, made this reflection. Everybody, as we have already said, they who were of the party of the Holy See and they who adhered to royalty, allowed themselves to be carried along by the current of events, without either perceiving the causes of them or foreseeing their consequences. The most wise blindly followed that invisible destiny which orders the world as it pleases, and makes use of the passions of men as of an instrument to accomplish its designs.

In a superstitious age the sight of a prodigy or of an extraordinary phenomenon had more influence over the minds of men than the oracles of wisdom or reason. Historians inform us, that whilst the barons were assembled, the moon, which was in eclipse, appeared of the colour of blood. When the eclipse was over, its disc was surrounded by an unprecedented splendour. Some weeks after, says the Abbé Guibert, the northern horizon was seen to be all on fire, and the terrified people rushed from the houses and cities, believing that the enemy was advancing, fire and sword in hand. At another time the stars assembled in the form of a cross and a wreath of thorns, and appeared to rise into the sky in conjunction with the moon. These phenomena, with several others, were regarded as signs of the will of God, and presages of the terrible war about to be made in his name. They everywhere redoubled the enthusiasm for the crusade. Men who had hitherto remained indifferent now partook of the general delirium. All Frenchmen called to the profession of arms, and who had not yet taken the oath to fight against the infidels, hastened now to take the cross.

The men of the Vermandois marched with the subjects of Philip under the colours of their count Hugh, a young prince whose brilliant qualities had been much admired by the court. Proud of being a brother of the king of France and the first of the French knights, he distinguished himself by his bravery and the ostentation of his manners. He displayed invincible courage in the field of battle, but allowed himself to be too easily overcome by flattery, and was wanting in perseverance in reverses. Although fortune was not too kind to him, not one of the heroes of the crusade exhibited more honourable and disinterested intentions. If he had not merited by his exploits the surname of *Great*, which history has given him, he would have obtained it for having only listened to his zeal, and for having sought nothing but glory in a war which offered kingdoms to the ambition of princes and simple knights.

Robert, surnamed *Courte-heuse*, duke of Normandy, who led his vassals to the holy war, was the eldest son of William the Conqueror. He joined to noble qualities some of the faults the most reprehensible in a prince. He could not, even in his early youth, endure paternal authority; but, drawn away more by a desire for independence than by a real ambition, after having made war against his father for the sake of reigning in Normandy, he neglected the opportunity of ascending the throne of England on the death of William. His levity, his inconstancy, and his weakness, caused him to be despised both by his subjects and his enemies. His profusion ruined his people, and reduced him, if we may credit the monk Oderic Vital, to a condition bordering upon absolute poverty. The historian

I have just quoted relates a trait, which, although difficult to be believed, at the same time describes both Robert and the age he lived in. "He was often compelled to remain in bed for want of clothes, and frequently was absent from mass because his nudity prevented him from assisting at it." It was not an ambition for conquering kingdoms in Asia, but his inconstant, chivalric disposition, that made him assume the cross, and take up arms. The Normans, a wandering and warlike people, who had made themselves remarkable among all the nations of Europe for their devotion to pilgrimages, hastened in crowds to his banner. As Duke Robert had not the means of providing for the expenses of an army, he pledged Normandy with his brother William Rufus. William, whom his age accused of impiety, and who laughed at the knight errantry of the Crusaders, seized with joy the opportunity of governing a province which he hoped one day to unite to his kingdom. He levied taxes upon the clergy, whom he did not like, and caused the silver plate of the churches to be melted to pay the sum of ten thousand silver marks to Robert, who set out for the Holy Land, followed by almost all the nobility of his duchy.

Another Robert, count of Flanders, placed himself at the head of the Frisons and the Flemings. He was son of Robert, surnamed *the Frison*, who had usurped the principality of Flanders from his own nephews, and who, to expiate his victories, had performed, some time before the crusade, the pilgrimage to Jerusalem. The young Robert easily found soldiers for his enterprize in a country where everybody had borne arms during the civil wars, and where the people were animated by the tales of a great number of pilgrims returned from the Holy Land. He exhausted the treasures of his father, to embark in an expedition which procured him the reputation of a bold knight, together with the surname of "*The Lance and Sword" of the Christians.* Five hundred horsemen sent by Robert the Frison to the emperor Alexis had already preceded him to Constantinople.

Stephen, count of Blois and Chartres, had also taken up the cross. He passed for the richest noble of his times. The number of his castles was said to be equal to that of the days of the year. What might be really considered a phenomenon in the eleventh century, this prince loved and cultivated letters. He proved to be the soul of the councils by his eloquence and his intelligence; but he could not long together support the fatigues of war, and he sometimes was but timid in the field of battle.

These four chiefs were accompanied by a crowd of knights and nobles, among whom history names Robert of Paris, Evrard of Prusaiè, Achard de Montmerle, Isouard de Muson, Stephen, count d'Albermarle, Walter de St. Valery, Roger de Barneville, Fergant and Conan, two illustrious Bretons, Guis de Trusselle, Miles de Braiës, Raoul de Baugency, Rotrou, son of the count de Perche; Odo, bishop of Bayeux, uncle of the duke of Normandy; Raoul de Gader, Yve and Albéric, sons of Hugh de Grandménil. The greater part of the counts and barons took with them their wives and children, and all their war equipages. They crossed the Alps, and directed their march towards the cities of Italy, with the intention of embarking for Greece. They found in the neighbourhood of Lucca Pope Urban, who gave them his benediction, praised their zeal, and offered up prayers for the success of their enterprize. The count de Vermandois, after having received the standard of the Church from the hands of the sovereign pontiff, repaired to Rome, with the other princes, to visit the tombs of St. Peter and St. Paul. The capital of the Christian world was then the theatre of a civil war. The soldiers of Urban and those of the anti-pope Guibert, disputed, arms in hand, for the church of St. Peter, and by turns carried off the offerings of the faithful. Whatever some modern historians may say, the Crusaders took no part in the troubles which divided the city of Rome; and what is still more astonishing, Urban did not call to the defence of his own cause one of the warriors whom his appeal had induced to take up arms. For the rest, the spectacle which presented itself in the city of St. Peter must have been a subject of scandal to the greater part of the French knights. Some, satisfied with having saluted the tomb of the apostles, and perhaps cured of their holy enthusiasm by the sight of the violences which profaned the sanctuary, abandoned the standard of the cross, and returned into their own country. Others pursued their march towards Apulia; but when they arrived at Bari, the winter beginning to render the navigation dangerous, they were forced to wait during several months for a favourable moment to embark.

The passage of the French Crusaders, however, had awakened the zeal of the Italians. Bohémond, prince of Tarentum, was the first who resolved to associate himself with their fortunes, and to partake of the glory of the holy expedition. He was of the family of those knights who had founded the kingdom of Naples and Sicily. Fifty years before the crusade, his father, Robert Guiscard (the subtle) had quitted the castle of Hauteville, in Normandy, with thirty foot-soldiers and five horsemen. Seconded by some of his relations and compatriots, who had preceded him into Italy, he fought with advantage against the Greeks, the Lombards, and the Saracens, who disputed Apulia and Calabria with him. He soon became sufficiently powerful to be by turns the enemy and the protector of the popes. He beat the armies of the emperors of the East and the West, and when he died he was engaged in the conquest of Greece.

Bohémond had neither less cunning nor less talents than his father, Robert Guiscard. Contemporary authors, who never fail to describe the physical qualities of their heroes, inform us that his height was so great that it exceeded by a cubit that of the tallest man in his army; his eyes were blue, and appeared full of passion and haughty pride. His presence, says Anna Comnena, was as astonishing to the eyes as his reputation was to the mind. When he spoke, his hearers believed that eloquence had been his only study; when he appeared under arms, he might be supposed to have done nothing but wield the lance and the sword. Brought up in the school of the Norman heroes, he concealed the combinations of policy beneath an exterior of violence; and although of a proud and haughty character, he could put up with an injury when vengeance would not have been profitable to him. Everything that could contribute to the success of his designs appeared to him to be just. He had learnt from his father to consider every man whose wealth or states he coveted as his enemy; he was neither restrained by the fear of God, the opinion of men, nor his own oaths. He had followed Robert in the war against the emperor Alexis, and had distinguished himself in the battles of Durazzo and Larissa; but, disinherited by a will, he had nothing at his father's death but the memory of his exploits, and the example of his family. He had declared war against his brother Roger, and had recently compelled him to cede to him the principality of Tarentum, when the expedition to the East began to be talked of in Europe. The deliverance of the tomb of Christ was not the object that kindled his zeal, or induced him to assume the cross. As he had sworn an eternal hatred to the Greek emperors, he smiled at the idea of traversing their empire at the head of an army; and, full of confidence in his own fortunes, he hoped to win a kingdom before he should arrive at Jerusalem.

The little principality of Tarentum could not supply him with an army; but in the name of religion, a leader had then the power of raising troops in all the states. Enthusiasm for the crusade soon seconded his projects, and brought a great number of warriors to his standard.

He had accompanied his brother and his uncle Roger to the siege of Amalfi, a flourishing city which refused with contempt the protection of the new masters of Apulia and Sicily. Bohémond, who knew well how to speak in proper season the language of enthusiasm, and to conceal his ambition beneath the colours of religious fanaticism, preached himself the crusade in the army of the besiegers. He went among the soldiers, talking of the princes and the great captains who had taken the cross. He spoke to the most pious warriors of the religion which was to be defended, and exalted before others the glory and fortunes which would crown their exploits. The army was won over by his discourses, and the camp soon resounded with the cry of *"It is the will of God! It is the will of God!"* Bohémond congratulated himself in secret on the success of his eloquence, and tore his coat of arms into strips, of which he made crosses, and ordered his officers to distribute them among the soldiers. There now only wanted a chief to command the holy expedition, and the new Crusaders came to solicit the prince of Tarentum to place himself at their head. Bohémond appeared at first to hesitate; he refused that which he ardently desired; and the soldiers assembled around him redoubled their solicitations. At length he seemed to yield to their importunities, and obey their will. Instantly the eagerness and enthusiasm became more animated and more general. In an incredibly short space of time the whole army swore to follow him into Palestine. Roger was obliged to raise the siege of Amalfi, and the happy Bohémond gave himself up entirely to the preparations for his voyage.

A short time after he embarked for the coasts of Greece with ten thousand horsemen and twenty thousand foot. Every illustrious knight of Apulia and Sicily followed the prince of Tarentum. With him marched Richard, prince of Salerno, and Randulf, his brother; Herman de Cani, Robert de Hanse, Robert de Sourdeval, Robert the son of Tristan, Boile de Chartres, and Humphrey de Montaigu. All these warriors were celebrated for their exploits, but no one amongst them was more worthy to attract the attention of posterity than the brave Tancred. Although he belonged to a family in which ambition was hereditary, he was fired by no other passion than a desire to fight against the infidels. Piety, glory, and perhaps his friendship for Bohémond alone, led him into Asia. His contemporaries admired his romantic pride and his haughty austerity. He yielded to no superiority but that of virtue, with the exception of occasional submission to the power of beauty. A stranger to all the motives and interests of policy, he acknowledged no other law but religion and honour, and was always ready to die in their cause. The annals of chivalry present no model more accomplished; poetry and history have united to celebrate him, and both have heaped upon him the same praises.

The Crusaders from the southern provinces of France had marched under the command of Adhémar de Monteil and Raymond, count de St. Gilles and Thoulouse. Bishop Adhémar acted as the spiritual chief of the crusade; his title of apostolic legate, and his personal qualities, earned for him in the holy war the confidence and respect of the pilgrims. His exhortations and his counsels contributed greatly to the maintaining of order and discipline. He consoled the Crusaders in their reverses, he animated them amidst dangers; clothed at the same time with the insignia of a pontiff and the armour of a knight, he exhibited in the tent a model of the Christian virtues, and in the field often gave proofs of undaunted valour.

Raymond, who marched with Adhémar, had had the glory of fighting in Spain by the side of the Cid; and of conquering several times the Moors under Alphonso the Great, who had bestowed his daughter Elvira upon him in marriage. His vast possessions on the banks of the Rhone and the Dordogne, and still more his exploits against the Saracens, rendered him one of the most remarkable among the great leaders of the crusade. Age had not extinguished in the count of Thoulouse either the ardour or the passions of youth. Hasty and impetuous, of a character haughty and inflexible, he had less ambition to conquer kingdoms than to make every will bend beneath his own. Both Greeks and Saracens have acknowledged his bravery. His subjects and his companions in arms hated him for his obstinacy and violence. Unhappy prince, he bade eternal farewell to his country, which was one day to be the theatre of a terrible crusade preached against his own family!

All the nobility of Gascony, Languedoc, Provence, the Limousin, and Auvergne, accompanied Raymond and Adhémar. Contemporary historians name among the knights and lords who had taken the cross, Héracle, count de Polignac, Pons de Balazan, Guillaume de Sabran, Eléazar de Castrie,

CELESTIAL PHENOMENA.

In a superstitious age the sight of a prodigy or of an extraordinary phenomenon had more influence over the minds of men than the oracles of wisdom or reason. Historians inform us that whilst the barons were assembled, the moon, which was in eclipse, appeared of the color of blood. When the eclipse was over, its disc was surrounded by an unprecedented splendor. Some weeks after, says the Abbé Guibert, the northern horizon was seen to be all on fire, and the terrified people rushed from the houses and cities, believing that the enemy was advancing, fire and sword in hand. At another time the stars assembled in the form of a cross and a wreath of thorns, and appeared to rise in the sky in conjunction with the moon. These phenomena, with several others, were regarded as signs of the will of God, and the presages of the terrible war about to be made in his name. They everywhere redoubled the enthusiasm of the Crusade. Men who had hitherto remained indifferent now partook of the general delirium. All Frenchmen called to the profession of arms, and who had not yet taken the oath to fight against the infidels, hastened now to take the cross.—BOOK II.

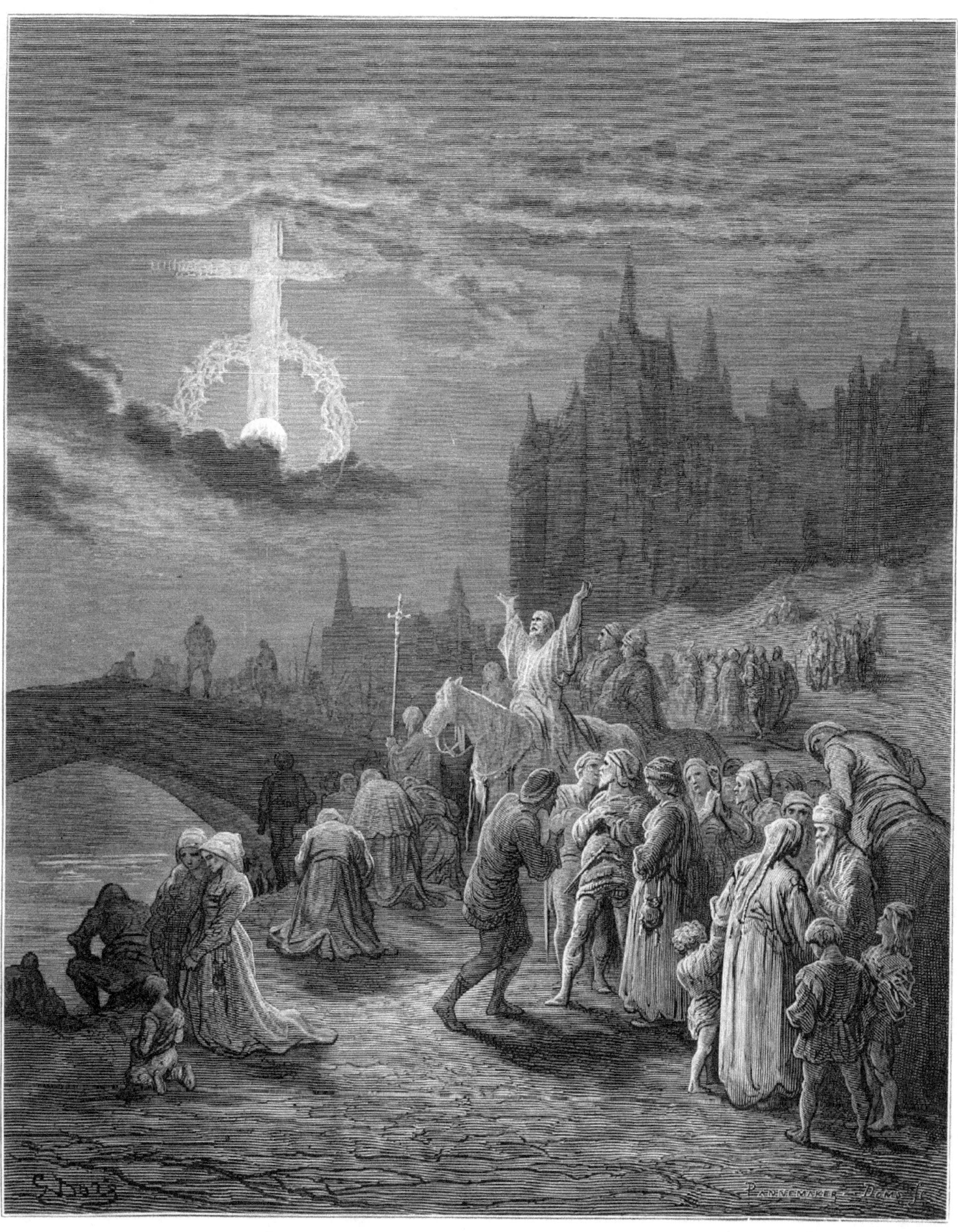

Eléazar de Montrédon, Pierre Bernard de Montagnac, Raymond de Lille, Pierre Raymond de Hautpool, Gouffier de Lastours, Guillaume V., lord of Montpellier, Roger, count de Foix, Raymond Pelet, Seigneur d'Alais, Isard, count de Diè, Raimbaud, count d'Orange, Guillaume, count de Ferez, Guillaume, count de Clermont, Gerard, son of Guillabert, count de Roussillon, Gaston, viscount de Béarn, Guillaume Amanjeu d'Albret, Raymond, viscount de Turenne, Raymond, viscount de Castillon, Guillaume d'Urgal, and the count de Fortcalquier. After the example of Adhémar, the bishops of Apt, Lodève, and Orange, and the archbishop of Toledo, had taken up the cross, and led a part of their vassals to the holy war.

Raymond, count of Thoulouse, followed by his wife Elvira and his sons, placed himself at the head of a hundred thousand Crusaders, advanced to Lyons, where he crossed the Rhone, traversed the Alps, Lombardy, and Frioul, and directed his march towards the territory of the Greek empire, over the savage mountains and through the equally savage nations of Dalmatia.

Alexis, who had implored the assistance of the Latins, was terrified when he learnt the numbers of his liberators. The leaders of the crusade were only princes of the second order, but they drew with them all the forces of the West. Anna Comnena compares the multitude of the Crusaders to the sands of the sea or the stars of the heavens, and their innumerable bands to torrents which unite to form a great river.* Alexis had learned to dread Bohémond on the plains of Durazzo and Larissa. Although he was less acquainted with the courage and ability of the other Latin princes, he repented of having imparted to them the secret of his weakness by asking their aid. His alarms, which were increased by the predictions of astrologers and the opinions spread among his people, became more serious as the Crusaders advanced towards his capital.

Seated on a throne from which he had hurled his master and benefactor, he could have no faith in virtue, and was better aware than another what ambition might dictate. He had displayed some courage in gaining the purple, but only governed by dissimulation,—the ordinary policy of the Greeks and all weak states. If Anna Comnena has made an accomplished prince of him, the Latins have represented him as a perfidious and cruel monarch. Impartial history, which alike rejects the exaggerations of eulogy or satire, can see nothing in Alexis but a weak ruler, of a superstitious character, led away much more by a love of vain splendour and display than by any passion for glory. He had it in his power to put himself at the head of the Crusaders, and reconquer Asia Minor, by marching with the Latins to Jerusalem. This great enterprize alarmed his weakness. His timid prudence made him believe that it would be sufficient to deceive the Crusaders to have nothing to fear from them, and to receive a vain homage from them in order to profit by their victories. Everything appeared good and just to him which would assist in extricating him from a position of which his policy increased the dangers, and which the unsteadiness of his projects made every day more embarrassing. The more earnestly he endeavoured to inspire confidence, the more suspicious he rendered his good faith. By seeking to inspire fear, he discovered all the alarms which he himself experienced. As soon as he had notice of the march of the princes of the crusade, he sent them ambassadors to compliment them, and to penetrate their intentions. In the meanwhile, he placed troops everywhere to harass them on their passage.

The count de Vermandois, cast by a tempest on the shores of Epirus, received the greatest honours from the governor of Durazzo, and was led a prisoner to Constantinople by the orders of Alexis. The Greek emperor hoped that the brother of the king of France would become, in his hands, a hostage that might protect him from the enterprizes of the Latins; but he only awakened suspicion, and

* An Armenian historian says of the preparations for this crusade, "The gates of the Latins were opened, and the inhabitants of the West saw issuing from their countries armies and soldiers numerous as locusts or the sands of the sea."

provoked the hatred of the leaders of the crusade. Godfrey de Bouillon had arrived at Philippopoli, when he heard of the captivity of the count de Vermandois. He sent to the emperor to demand instant reparation for this outrage; and as the deputies reported but an unfavourable answer, he restrained neither his own indignation nor the fury of his army. The lands through which they passed were treated as an enemy's country, and during eight days the fertile plains of Thrace became the theatre of war. The crowd of Greeks who fled towards the capital soon informed the emperor of the terrible vengeance of the Latins. Alexis, terrified at the fruits of his own policy, implored the pardon of his prisoner, and promised to restore him his liberty when the French should have arrived at the gates of Constantinople. This promise appeased Godfrey, who caused the war to cease, and resumed his march, treating the Greeks everywhere as friends and allies.

In the meanwhile, Alexis employed every effort to obtain from the count de Vermandois the oath of obedience and fidelity, hoping that his submission would lead to that of the other princes of the crusade, and that he should have less to fear from their ambition if he could reckon them in the number of his vassals. The brother of the king of France, who, on arriving in the territories of the empire, had written letters filled with pride and ostentation, could not resist the caresses and presents of the emperor, and took all the oaths that were required of him. On the arrival of Godfrey, he appeared in the camp of the Crusaders, who rejoiced at his deliverance, but could not pardon him for having yielded submission to a foreign monarch. Cries of indignation arose around him when he endeavoured to persuade Godfrey to follow his example. The more gentle and submissive he had shown himself in his captivity, the more strong became the opposition and resistance to the will of the emperor of his companions, who had drawn their swords to avenge the insult offered to him.

Alexis refused them provisions, and thought to reduce them by famine; but the Latins were accustomed to obtain all they wanted by violence and victory. At the signal of their leader, they dispersed themselves over the surrounding country, pillaged the villages and the palaces near the capital, and, by force, brought abundance to their camp. This disorder lasted several days; but the festival of Christmas was approaching, and the epoch of the birth of Christ revived generous sentiments in the breasts of the Christian soldiers and the pious Godfrey. Advantage was taken of these feelings to bring about peace. The emperor granted provisions, and the Crusaders sheathed their swords.

But it was impossible for harmony to subsist long between the Greeks and the Latins. The Latins haughtily boasted of having come to the rescue of the empire. On all occasions they spoke and acted as masters. The Greeks despised the barbarous courage of the Latins, and placing all their glory in the refinement of their manners, believed that they disgraced the language of Greece when pronouncing the names of the warriors of the West. The rupture which had for a long time subsisted between the churches of Rome and Constantinople, increased the antipathy which the difference of manners and customs had given birth to. On both sides anathemas were launched, and the theologians of Greece and Italy detested each other more than they detested the Saracens. The Greeks, who employed themselves in nothing but vain subtleties, had never been willing to place in the list of martyrs those who had died fighting against the infidels. They abhorred the martial character of the Latin clergy, boasted that they possessed in their capital all the relics of the East, and could not understand what they could be going to seek at Jerusalem. On their side, the Franks could not pardon the subjects of Alexis for not partaking in their enthusiasm for the crusade, and reproached them with a culpable indifference for the cause of God. All these motives of discord and hatred provoked frequent scenes of violence, in which the Greeks displayed more perfidy than courage, and the Latins more valour than moderation.

Throughout all these divisions Alexis constantly sought to obtain from Godfrey the oath of obedience and fidelity; sometimes he employed protestations of friendship, sometimes he threatened to exercise powers that he did not possess. Godfrey braved his menaces, and placed no faith in his promises. The imperial and the Latin troops were twice called to arms, and Constantinople, badly defended by its soldiers, had cause to fear beholding the standard of the Crusaders floating over its walls.

The report of these serious quarrels conveyed joy to the heart of Bohémond, who had just landed at Durazzo. He believed the time was come to attack the Greek empire, and to divide the spoils. He sent envoys to Godfrey, to invite him to take possession of Byzantium, promising to join him with all his forces, for the prosecution of this great enterprize. But Godfrey did not forget that he had taken up arms for the defence of the holy sepulchre, and rejected the proposal of Bohémond, reminding him of the oath he had taken to fight against the infidels.

This embassy to Bohémond, the object of which could not be concealed, redoubled the alarm of Alexis, and made him employ every means to subdue the firmness of Godfrey de Bouillon. He sent his own son as a hostage to the army of the Crusaders. From that time all mistrust was dissipated. The princes of the West swore to respect the laws of hospitality, and repaired to the palace of Alexis. They found the emperor surrounded by a splendid court, and entirely occupied in endeavouring to conceal his weakness under an exterior of vain magnificence. The chief of the Crusaders, and the princes and knights who accompanied him, in an apparel on which shone the martial luxury of the West, bowed before the throne of the emperor, and bent the knee to a mute and motionless majesty. After this ceremony, during which the Greeks and the Latins must have afforded each other a strange spectacle, Alexis adopted Godfrey for his son, and placed the empire under the protection of his arms. The Crusaders engaged to replace the cities they had taken belonging to the empire in the hands of the emperor, and to pay him homage for the other conquests they might make. Alexis, on his part, promised to aid them by land and by sea, to furnish them with provisions, and to share the perils and the glory of their expedition.

Alexis considered this homage of the Latin princes as a victory. The leaders of the Crusaders returned beneath their tents, where his gratitude loaded them with presents. Whilst Godfrey caused it to be proclaimed in his army by sound of trumpet, that the most profound respect for the emperor and the laws of Constantinople should be preserved, Alexis ordered all his subjects to carry provisions to the Franks, and to observe the laws of hospitality. The alliance they had just made appeared to have been sworn to in good faith on both sides; but Alexis could not destroy the prejudices the Greeks entertained against the Latins, nor could Godfrey restrain the turbulent multitude of his soldiers. Besides, the emperor of Byzantium, although he might feel reassured as to the intentions of the duke of Lorraine, still dreaded the arrival of Bohémond, and the union of several large armies in the neighbourhood of his capital. He engaged Godfrey to pass with his troops over to the Asiatic shore of the Bosphorus, and turned his attention to whatever means his policy could suggest to abate the pride, and even to diminish the powers of the other Latin princes who were marching towards Constantinople.

The prince of Tarentum was advancing through Macedonia, now listening to the harangues of the deputies from Alexis, and now contending with the troops which opposed his passage. Several provinces and several cities had been ravaged by the Italian and Norman Crusaders, when their chief received an invitation from the emperor to precede his army, and come to Constantinople. Alexis made Bohémond protestations of friendship, in which the latter placed no faith, but from which he hoped to reap some advantage. He, on his part, declared his good feeling, and went to meet Alexis. The emperor received him with a magnificence proportionate to the fear he entertained of his arrival.

These two princes were equally skilled in the arts of seducing and deceiving. The greater cause they had to complain of each other, the warmer were their protestations of friendship. They complimented each other publicly on their victories, and concealed their suspicions, and perhaps their contempt, under an exterior of reciprocal admiration. Both unscrupulous on the subject of oaths, Alexis promised vast domains to Bohémond, and the Norman hero swore without hesitation to be the most faithful of the vassals of the emperor.

Robert, count of Flanders, the duke of Normandy, and Stephen, count of Chartres and Blois, as they arrived at Constantinople, rendered their homage, in their turn, to the Greek emperor, and received, as others had done, the reward of their submission. The count of Thoulouse, who arrived the last, at first answered the messengers of Alexis, that he was not come into the East to seek a master. The emperor, to bend the pride of Raymond and his Provençals, was obliged to stoop to them. He flattered by turns their avarice and their vanity, and took more pains to show them his treasures than his armies. In states in their decay it is not uncommon for wealth to be mistaken for power, and the prince believes he reigns over all hearts as long as he possesses the means of corrupting them. Ceremonial was, besides, at the court of Constantinople, the most serious and the most important of all things; but whatever value may be attached to vain formulæ, we cannot but be astonished to see warriors so haughty, who went to conquer empires, on their knees before a prince who trembled with the fear of losing his own. They made him pay dearly for an uncertain and transient submission, and not unfrequently contempt was apparent through their outward marks of respect.

During a ceremony in which Alexis received the homage of several French princes, Count Robert of Paris advanced to seat himself by the side of the emperor. Baldwin of Hainaut pulled him by the arm, and said, "You should remember, when you are in a foreign country, you ought to respect its customs." "Truly!" replied Robert, "this is a pleasant clown who is seated, whilst so many illustrious captains are standing!" Alexis was desirous of having his words explained to him, and when the counts were gone, he retained Robert, and asked him what were his birth and country. "I am a Frenchman," replied Robert, "and of the most illustrious rank of nobles. I only know one thing, and that is, that in my country there is a place near a church to which all repair who burn with a desire to signalize their valour. I have often been there without anybody yet having dared to present himself before me." The emperor took care not to accept this kind of challenge, and endeavoured to conceal his surprise and vexation by giving some useful advice to the daring warrior. "If you waited then," said he, "without meeting enemies, you are now going where you will find enough to satisfy you. But do not put yourself either at the head or the tail of the army; remain in the centre. I have learnt how to fight with the Turks; and that is the best place you can choose."

The policy of the emperor, however, was not without effect. The pride of a great number of the counts and barons was not proof against his caresses and his presents. There still exists a letter which Stephen of Blois addressed to Adela his wife, in which he felicitates himself on the welcome he had received at the court of Byzantium. After having described all the honours with which he had been received, he exclaims, whilst speaking of Alexis, "Truly there is not at this time such a man beneath the heavens!" Bohémond could not have been less struck with the liberality of the emperor. At the sight of an apartment filled with riches, "There is here," said he, "enough to conquer kingdoms with." Alexis immediately ordered these treasures to be conveyed to the tent of the ambitious Bohémond, who at first refused them with a kind of modesty, and finished by accepting them with joy. He went so far as to demand the title of grand domestic or of general of the empire of the East. Alexis, who had himself held that dignity, and who knew that it was the road to the throne, had the courage to refuse him, and contented himself with promising the office to the future services of the prince of Tarentum.

ASTONISHMENT OF THE CRUSADERS AT THE WEALTH OF THE EAST.

At the sight of an apartment filled with riches, Bohemond, prince of Tarentum, said: "There is here enough to conquer kingdoms with." The Emperor Alexis, who wished to bribe him, immediately ordered them to be conveyed to the tent of the ambitious Bohemond, who at first refused them with a kind of modesty, and finished by accepting them with joy. . . . An abode at Byzantium might become otherwise dangerous for the Crusaders; the spectacle of the luxury of the East, which they beheld for the first time, was calculated to corrupt them. The Christian knights were never weary of admiring the palaces, the splendid edifices, the riches, and perhaps the beautiful women of whom Alexis had spoken in his letters addressed to the princes of the West.—Book II.

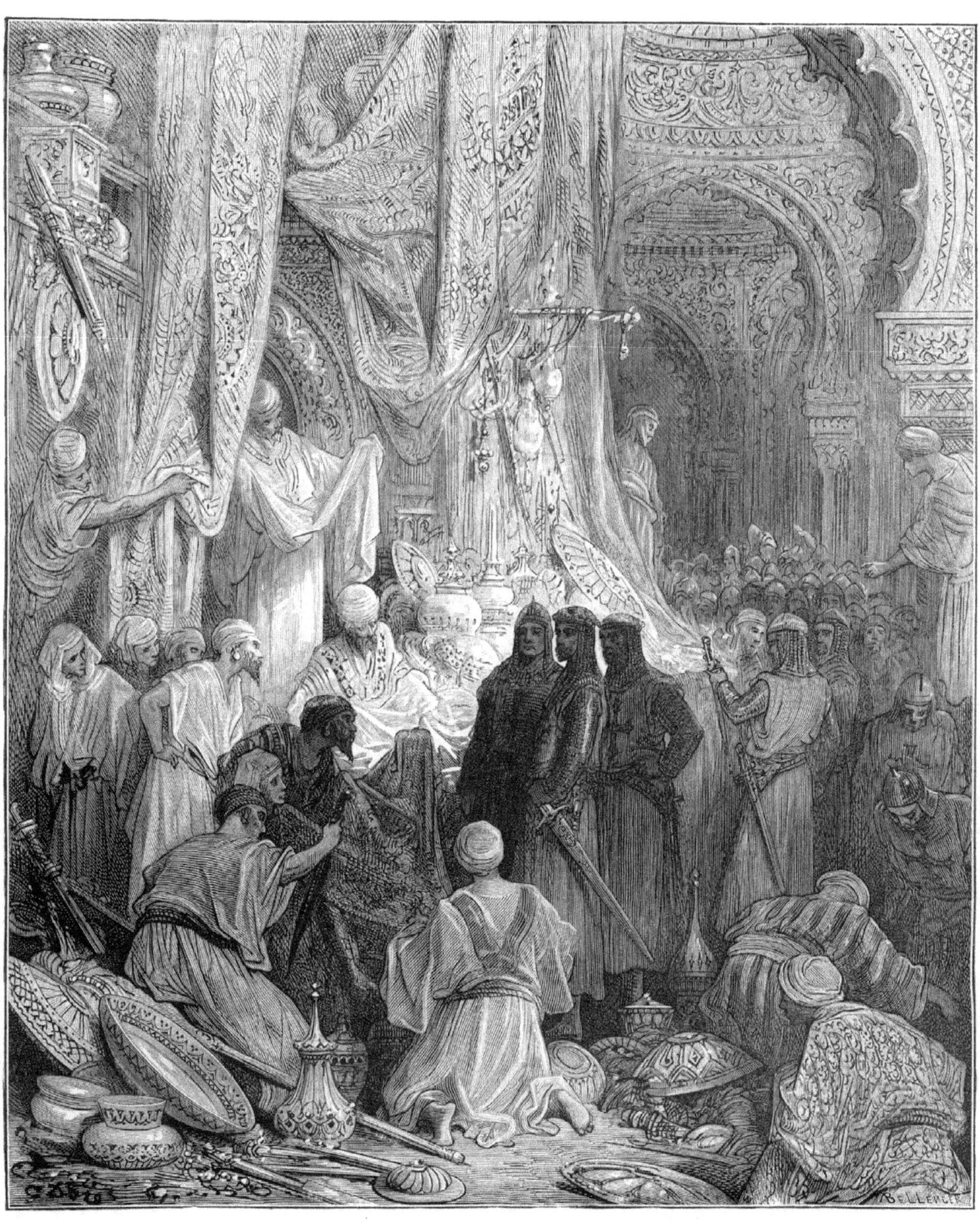

Thus the promises of the emperor retained for a short period the Latin princes under his laws. By his skilfully-distributed favours and flatteries he created a spirit of jealousy among the leaders of the crusade. Raymond de St. Gilles declared himself against Bohémond, whose projects he revealed to Alexis; and whilst this prince debased himself thus before a foreign monarch, the courtiers of Byzantium repeated with warmth, that he excelled all the other chiefs of the crusade, as the sun excels the stars.

The Franks, so dreaded in the field of battle, were powerless against the skill and address of Alexis, and could not sustain their advantage amidst the intrigues of a dissolute court. An abode at Byzantium might become otherwise dangerous for the Crusaders; the spectacle of the luxury of the East, which they beheld for the first time, was calculated to corrupt them. The Christian knights, according to the report of the historians of the times, were never weary of admiring the palaces, the splendid edifices, the riches, and perhaps the beautiful Greek women, of whom Alexis had spoken in his letters addressed to the princes of the West. Tancred alone, inflexible to all solicitations, would not expose his virtue to the seductions of Byzantium. He deplored the weakness of his companions, and, followed by a small number of knights, hastened to quit Constantinople, without having taken the oath of fidelity to the emperor.

The departure and resistance of Tancred disturbed the joy which the success of his policy had given Alexis. He applauded himself for having softened, by his presents, the principal leaders of the crusade; but he did not so entirely depend upon his means of corruption as to be perfectly free from apprehension. Every day brought new Crusaders, whom he must seduce and load with presents; the very riches he displayed to them might, in the end, awaken their ambition, and inspire them with most fatal designs. He felt by no means secure against their enterprizes until all the armies of the West were on the other side of the Bosphorus. There, without the power of insulting the capital of the empire, they turned all their attention to their preparations for the war against the Saracens.

As the Crusaders advanced across the plains of Bithynia, they saw, seeking refuge in their tents, several soldiers of Peter's army, who having escaped from the sword of the Saracens, had lived concealed in the mountains and forests. They were clothed in the rags of misery, and with lamentations and tears related the disasters of the first army of the Christians. On the east they pointed to the fortress in which the companions of Rinaldo, pressed by hunger and thirst, had surrendered to the Turks, who had massacred them all. Near to that they showed them the mountains, at the foot of which had perished Walter and his whole army. Everywhere the Crusaders encountered the remains of their brethren; everywhere they found reason to deplore the imprudence and disasters of the first soldiers of the cross; but nothing affected them so deeply as the sight of the camp in which Walter had left the women and the sick, when he was forced by his soldiers to advance to the city of Nicea. There the Christians had been surprised by the Mussulmans, at the moment their priests were celebrating the sacrifice of the mass. Women, children, old men, all whom weakness or sickness detained in the camp, pursued to the foot of their altars, had been either borne away into slavery, or slaughtered by a pitiless enemy. The remembrance of so great a calamity stifled discord, silenced ambition, and rekindled zeal for the deliverance of the holy places. The leaders profited by this terrible lesson, and laid down useful regulations for the maintenance of discipline. The formidable army of the Crusaders advanced in the best order through the country of the infidels, and commenced the war with the first days of the spring.

Although the empire of the Seljoucide Turks, at the period of the arrival of the Crusaders in Asia, already inclined towards its fall, it nevertheless presented a formidable barrier to the warriors of the West. The kingdom of Ezeroum, or Roum, extended from the Orontes and the Euphrates to the neighbourhood of the Bosphorus, and comprised the richest provinces of Asia Minor. The Turks were animated by the double enthusiasm of religion and victory. Abandoning the cares of agriculture and commerce to the Greeks, their slaves, they knew no profession but that of arms, or desired other wealth but the booty obtained from their enemies. Their present chief was the son of Soliman, whose victories over the Christians had procured him the name of *the Sacred Champion.* David, surnamed Kilidge-Arslan, or *the Sword of the Lion*, brought up amidst the troubles of civil war, and for a long time detained a prisoner in the fortress of Koraçan by the orders of Malek-Scha, had ascended the throne of his father, and maintained his position by his valour. He possessed a genius rich in resources, and a character not to be subdued by reverses. On the approach of the Crusaders, he summoned his subjects and his allies to his defence. From all the provinces of Asia Minor, and even from Persia, the bravest defenders of Islamism hastened to range themselves beneath his banner.

Not content with assembling an army, he at first gave all his attention to the fortifying of the city of Nice, to which the earliest attempts of the Christians would be directed. This city, the capital of Bithynia, and celebrated by the holding of two councils, was the seat of the empire of Roum; and it was there that the Turks, as in an advanced post, awaited an opportunity to attack Constantinople, and precipitate themselves upon Europe. High mountains defended the approach to it. Towards the west and the south the Lake of Ascanius bathed its ramparts, and preserved to the inhabitants an easy communication with the sea. Large ditches, filled with water, surrounded the place. Three hundred and seventy towers of brick or stone protected the double enclosure of its walls, which were wide enough for the passage of a chariot. The chosen of the Turkish warriors composed its garrison, and the sultan of Roum, ready to defend it, was encamped upon the neighbouring mountains, at the head of an army of a hundred thousand men.

Full of just confidence in their own strength, and ignorant of that which could be opposed to them, the Crusaders advanced towards Nice. Never had the plains of Bithynia presented a more magnificent or a more terrible spectacle. The numbers of the Crusaders exceeded the population of many great cities of the West, and were sufficient to cover the largest plains. The Turks, from their encampments on the summits of the mountains, must have beheld, with terror, an army composed of more than a hundred thousand horse and five hundred thousand foot, the picked men of the warlike nations of Europe, who were come to dispute with them the possession of Asia.*

When it had been determined to besiege Nice, the posts were distributed to the various bodies of the Christian army. The camp of the Crusaders extended over a vast plain, intersected by rivulets which fell from the mountains. Fleets from Greece and Italy transported provisions, and kept the besiegers in a state of abundance. Foulcher de Chartres reckons in the camp of the Christians nineteen nations, differing in manners and language. Each nation had its quarters, which they surrounded with walls and palisades, and as they were without wood or stone for the divisions, they employed the bones of the Crusaders lying unburied in the country round Nice; "by which," Anna Comnena says, "they at once constructed a tomb for the dead and an abode for the living." In each quarter they quickly raised magnificent tents, which served as churches, in which the chiefs and the soldiers assembled to perform the ceremonies of religion. Different war-cries, drums, the use of which had been introduced into Europe by the Saracens, and sonorous horns, pierced with several holes, summoned the Crusaders to their military exercises.

The barons and knights wore a hauberk, or coat of mail, a sort of tunic, composed of small rings of iron or steel. Over the coat of arms of every squire floated a blue, red, green, or white scarf. Every warrior wore a casque, covered with silver for the princes, of steel for the knights and nobles,

* Such might be the character of the hundred thousand horse; but the five hundred thousand foot by no means merited such a description.—Trans.

and of iron for the common men. The knights bore round or square bucklers, and long shields covered the foot-soldiers. The arms employed in fight by the Crusaders were the lance, the sword, a species of knife, a poniard, called *miséricorde*, the club, the *masse d'armes*, with which a warrior could, at a single blow, strike an enemy to the earth; the sling, from which were thrown stones and balls of lead; the bow, and the cross-bow, a murderous weapon, till that time unknown to the Orientals. The warriors of the West did not then cover themselves with that heavy iron armour described by the historians of the middle ages, which they afterwards borrowed from the Saracens.

The princes and knights bore upon their shields figures or signs of different colours, which served as rallying-points for their soldiers. Here might be seen, painted on the bucklers and standards, leopards and lions; there, stars, towers, crosses, Asiatic trees, and European trees. Several caused to be represented on their shields the birds of passage which they had met with on their route, which birds, by changing their climate annually, presented to the Crusaders a symbol of their own pilgrimage. These distinctive marks at the time served to animate their valour in the field of battle, and were destined, at a future day, to be one of the attributes of rank among the nations of the West.

In the immense crowd of Crusaders, no count, no prince, deigned to receive orders from any one. The Christians presented the image of a republic under arms. This republic, in which everything appeared to be in common, recognized no other law but that of honour, no other tie but that of religion. So great was their zeal, that chiefs performed the duties of common men, and the latter required no signal to rush to victory or encounter death. The priests passed continually amongst the ranks, to recall to the Crusaders the maxims of scriptural morality. Their discourses were not thrown away; for, if we may credit contemporary authors, who seldom spare the champions of the cross, the conduct of the Christians during the siege of Nice offered nothing but examples of warlike virtue and subjects of edification.

In the first days of the siege the Christians made several assaults, in which they uselessly displayed prodigies of valour. Kilidge-Arslan, who had placed both his family and his treasures in Nice, animated the garrison by his letters, and resolved to spare no efforts to succour the besieged. He called together the chiefs of his army; he reminded them of the advantages they had gained over the Christians, and predicted still more brilliant trophies to their valour. "The greatest disorder," he told them, "reigned in the Christian army, and the numbers of their enemies assured them the victory. They were going to fight for their wives, their children, and the country which they owed to the conquests of their fathers; the religion of the prophet implored their help, and the richest booty would be the reward of their exploits." The Mussulmans, animated by the speeches and the example of their chief, prepared for battle, and descended the mountains. Their army, divided into two bodies, attacked with impetuosity the quarter of Godfrey de Bouillon and that of Raymond de Thoulouse, who had just arrived before Nice. The Provençals were not able to resist the first shock, but they rallied soon at the voices of Raymond and Adhémar. "Then the two armies," says Matthew of Edessa, who speaks of this battle, "joined, mingled, and attacked each other with equal fury. Everywhere glittered casques and shields; lances rung against cuirasses; the air resounded with piercing cries; the terrified horses recoiled at the din of arms and the hissing of arrows; the earth trembled beneath the tread of the combatants, and the plain was for a vast space bristling with javelins." Godfrey, Tancred, and the two Roberts, appeared to be everywhere at once, and carried death and terror into the ranks of the infidels. The Turks could not long withstand the impetuous valour of the Crusaders; they were put to the rout, and pursued by the conquerors even to the mountains which served them as a place of refuge.

The sultan, instead of deploring his defeat, only thought of avenging the disgrace of his arms, and on the very morrow, at break of day, led back his troops to the combat. The Turks attacked the Christians, uttering loud cries. Sometimes they rushed with fury into the ranks of the Crusaders, sometimes they fought at a distance, pouring in showers of arrows. Then they feigned to fly, only to return to the charge with greater fury. This second battle, in which the Turks showed the courage of despair seconded by all the stratagems of war, lasted from morning till night. The victory, which was for a long time doubtful, cost the Christians two thousand lives. The Crusaders made a great many prisoners; four thousand Mussulmans fell on the field of battle; the heads of a thousand were sent to Alexius; and the rest, by the aid of machines, were cast into the city, to inform the garrison of this fresh defeat of the Turks.

Kilidge-Arslan, despairing to save Nice, retired with the wreck of his army, and hastened to gather together in the provinces new forces, with which to oppose the Christians. The Crusaders, having no longer to dread the neighbourhood of an enemy's army, pushed on the siege with vigour. Sometimes they made approaches by galleries covered by a double roof of boards and hurdles; sometimes they dragged towards the walls towers mounted on a number of wheels, constructed with several stages, and loaded with arms and soldiers. Here the rams beat against the walls with redoubled shocks; at a short distance balistas vomited, without ceasing, beams of wood and showers of arrows; and catapultas cast into the air combustible matters and enormous stones, which fell with a crash into the city.

The Christians employed in this siege all the machines* known to the Romans. The Greeks were better acquainted with the construction of them than the Latins, and directed their operations. It is likewise probable that the Greeks who were in Nice, and subject to the power of the Mussulmans, instructed the latter in the means of defending the place.

The Christians allowed the besieged no respite, and they defended themselves with obstinate fury. All the inhabitants of Nice had taken arms. Their ramparts were covered with formidable machines, which hurled destruction among the assailants. Fiery darts, beams, enormous pieces of stone, launched from the height of the walls, destroyed, day after day, the labours of the Crusaders. When the Christians had made a breach in the ramparts, another wall arose from the bosom of the ruins, and presented a new barrier to the besiegers.

As the Crusaders attacked without order or precaution, their imprudence and their rashness were often very fatal to them. Some were crushed beneath the fragments of their own machines; others fell pierced with poisoned darts; sometimes, even, says an historian, the besieged sported with their efforts, catching them with *iron hands*,† or hooks, which, falling upon them, seized them, and lifted them alive into the city. After having stripped them, the Turks hung them upon their ramparts, and then launched them, by means of their machines, stark naked into the camp of the Christians.

A Saracen, whom history describes to us as a giant, performed during this siege exploits which surpass those related of fabulous antiquity. He was not less remarkable for his skill than for the strength of his arm; he never cast a javelin in vain, and all whom he hit were sure to sink beneath the blow. When he had exhausted his arrows, and could make no more use of his bow, he seized masses of rock, and rolled them down upon the assailants. One day, when he was standing on the platform of a tower attacked by Raymond, he alone defied the efforts of the enemies. At one time he hurled a shower of stones upon the besiegers; then, raising his voice, he defied the bravest of the Christians to the combat, loading them with the most violent abuse. All eyes were turned towards him, and a

* The Pisans, the Genoese, and the greater part of the nations of Italy, after the Greeks, showed themselves most skilful in the construction of machines for war.

† These *iron hands* were nothing more than the machine called the *raven* by the Romans, which they employed in grappling vessels: they likewise made use of it in sieges.

GODFREY MEETS THE REMAINS OF THE ARMY OF PETER THE HERMIT.

As the Crusaders advanced across the plains of Bithynia, they saw, seeking refuge in their tents, several soldiers of Peter's army, who, having escaped the swords of the Saracens, had lived concealed in the mountains and forests. They were clothed in the rags of misery, and with lamentations and tears related the disasters of the first army of the Christians. On the east they pointed to the fortress in which the companions of Rinaldo, pressed by hunger and thirst, had surrendered to the Turks, who had massacred them all. Near to that they showed them the mountains, at the foot of which had perished Walter and his army. There the Christians had been surprised by the Mussulmans at the moment their priests were celebrating the sacrifice of the mass.—Book II.

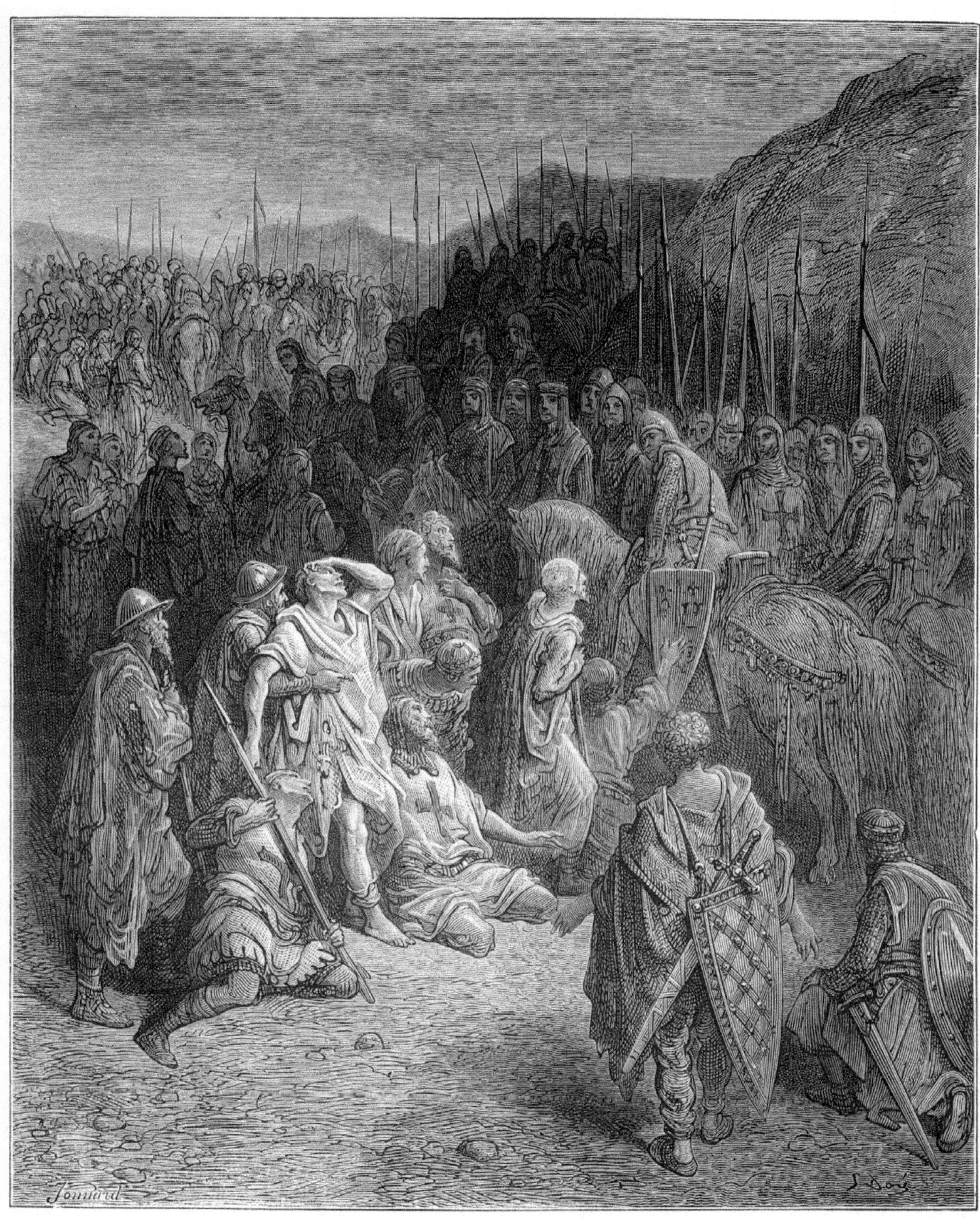

thousand arrows flew at once from the Christian army to punish his audacity. For a moment all the efforts of the besiegers were directed against a single man. His body was covered with wounds and bristling with arrows; but he defended himself skilfully, and was still braving the crowd of his enemies, when Godfrey, attracted by the noise of this general attack, seized a cross-bow, and taking aim at the redoubtable Saracen, shot him through the heart, and his immense body rolled from the platform into the ditch.

This victory, which appears rather to belong to the heroes of the epopea than to those of history, was celebrated by the acclamations of the Christian army. The Crusaders, who gained several other advantages, redoubled their zeal and their valorous efforts, and the besieged began to offer a less animated resistance. As the Saracens received provisions and reinforcements by the Lake Ascanius, it was resolved to cut off this last resource. A large number of boats, furnished by the Greeks, were transported by land, and launched into the water in the night-time. When day appeared, the lake was covered with barks, each bearing fifty combatants; the flags were displayed, and floated over the waters, and the lake and its shores resounded with the various war-cries and the noise of the trumpets and drums. At this sight the besieged were struck with surprise and terror; and the Christians renewed their attacks with greater success. The soldiers of Raymond had undermined the foundations of one of the principal towers of Nice. This tower sank down in the middle of the night, and its fall was accompanied by so frightful a noise, that both the Christians and the Mussulmans were aroused from their sleep, and believed that an earthquake had taken place. On the following day the wife of the sultan, with two infant children, endeavoured to escape by the lake, and fell into the hands of the Christians. When the news of this reached the city, it greatly increased the general consternation. After a siege of seven weeks, the Mussulmans had lost all hopes of defending Nice, and the Christians were expecting every day to be able to take it by assault, when the policy of Alexius intervened to deprive their arms of the honour of a complete conquest.

This prince, who has been compared to the bird who seeks his food in the tracks of the lion, had advanced as far as Pelecania. He had sent to the army of the Crusaders a weak detachment of Greek troops, and two generals intrusted with his confidence, less for the purpose of fighting than to negotiate, and seize an opportunity to get possession of Nice by stratagem. One of these officers, named Butumitus, having got into the city, created in the inhabitants a dread of the inexorable vengeance of the Latins, and advised them to surrender to the emperor of Constantinople. His propositions were listened to, and when the Crusaders were preparing to begin a last assault, the standards of Alexius all at once appeared upon the ramparts and towers of Nice.

This sight created the most lively surprise in the Christian army. The greater part of the leaders could not restrain their indignation, and the soldiers who were preparing for the assault returned to their tents trembling with rage. Their fury was increased when they found they were prohibited from entering more than ten at a time into a city which they had conquered at the price of their blood, and which contained riches which had been promised to them. In vain the Greeks alleged the treaties made with Alexius, and the services they had rendered the Latins during the siege; the murmurs were never silenced for a moment, except by the largesses of the emperor.

This prince received the greater part of the chiefs at Pelecania, where he duly praised their bravery and loaded them with presents. After having taken possession of Nice, he gained a new victory, perhaps not less flattering to his vanity; he at length triumphed over the pride of Tancred, who took the oath of fidelity and obedience to him. Nevertheless, he did not stifle the suspicions they had conceived of his perfidy. The liberty to which he restored the wife and children of the sultan, and the kind manner in which he treated the Turkish prisoners, gave the Latins good reason to believe that he sought to conciliate the enemies of the Christians. Nothing more was necessary to renew former hatreds, and from this period war was almost declared between the Greeks and the Crusaders.

A year had passed away since the Crusaders had quitted the West. After having reposed some time in the neighbourhood of Nice, they prepared to set forward on their march towards Syria and Palestine. The provinces of Asia Minor which they were about to cross were still occupied by the Turks, who were animated by fanaticism and despair, and who formed less a nation than an army, always ready to fight and to pass from one place to another. In a country so long ravaged by war, the roads were scarcely to be seen, and all communication between cities was stopped. In the mountains, defiles, torrents, precipices, must constantly create impediments to the march of a numerous army; in the plains, mostly uncultivated and barren, famine, the want of water, the burning heat of the climate, were inevitable evils. The Crusaders fancied they had conquered all their enemies at Nice, and without taking any precaution, without any other guides than the Greeks, of whom they had so much reason to complain, they advanced into a country with which they were totally unacquainted. They had no idea of the obstacles they should encounter in their march, and their ignorance created their security.

They had divided their army into two bodies, which marched at some distance the one from the other, across the mountains of Lesser Phrygia. By marching thus separately they could more easily procure provisions; but they ran the risk of being surprised by an active and vigilant enemy. Kilidge-Arslan, twice conquered by the Christians, had gathered together new forces. At the head of an army, which the Latin historians say amounted to two hundred thousand men, he followed the Crusaders, watching for an opportunity to surprise them, and to make them pay dearly for the conquest of Nice.

Whilst the main army, commanded by Godfrey, Raymond, Adhémar, Hugh the Great, and the count of Flanders, was crossing the plain of Dorylæum, the other body, which was commanded by Bohémond, Tancred, and the duke of Normandy, directed its march to the left. It was following the banks of a little river, and was advancing into a valley to which the Latin historians have given the name of Gorgoni or Ozellis. Some intimations had been given by the Greeks that the enemy was nigh, but the Crusaders believed they had nothing to fear. After a day's march, on the evening of the 30th of June, they arrived at a place which offered them abundant pasturage, and they resolved to encamp. The Christian army passed the night in the most profound security; but on the morrow, at daybreak, the scouts and clouds of dust on the heights announced to them the presence of the enemy. Immediately the camp was roused, and all flew to arms. Bohémond, thus become the leader of the army in the midst of peril, hastened to make the necessary dispositions for receiving the Turks. The camp of the Christians was defended on one side by the river, and on the other by a marsh covered with reeds. The prince of Tarentum caused it to be surrounded with chariots, and with palisades made of the stakes employed in erecting the tents. He next assigned the posts to the infantry, and placed the women, the children, and the sick in the centre of them. The cavalry, divided into three bodies, advanced to the head of the camp, and prepared to dispute the passage of the river. One of these bodies was commanded by Tancred, and William his brother, and another by the duke of Normandy and the count de Chartres. Bohémond, who commanded the centre, placed himself with his horsemen upon a height, whence he might observe everything, and follow the order of the battle.

Scarcely had the prince of Tarentum finished his preparations, when the Saracens, uttering loud cries, descended from the mountains, and, when within bow-shot, discharged a shower of arrows upon the Christians. This did very little harm to the horsemen, who were defended by their shields and their armour, but it wounded a great many of the horses, which threw the ranks into disorder. The

PRIESTS EXHORTING THE CRUSADERS.

In the immense crowd of Crusaders, no count, no prince, deigned to receive orders from any one. The Christians presented the image of a republic under arms. This republic, in which everything appeared to be in common, recognized no other law but that of honor, no other tie but that of religion. So great was their zeal that chiefs performed the duties of common men, and the latter required no signal to rush to victory or encounter death. The priests passed continually amongst the ranks, to recall to the Crusaders the maxims of Scriptural morality. Their discourses were not thrown away; for, if we may credit contemporary authors, who seldom spare the champions of the cross, the conduct of the Christians during the siege of Nice offered nothing but examples of warlike virtue and subjects of edification.—BOOK II.

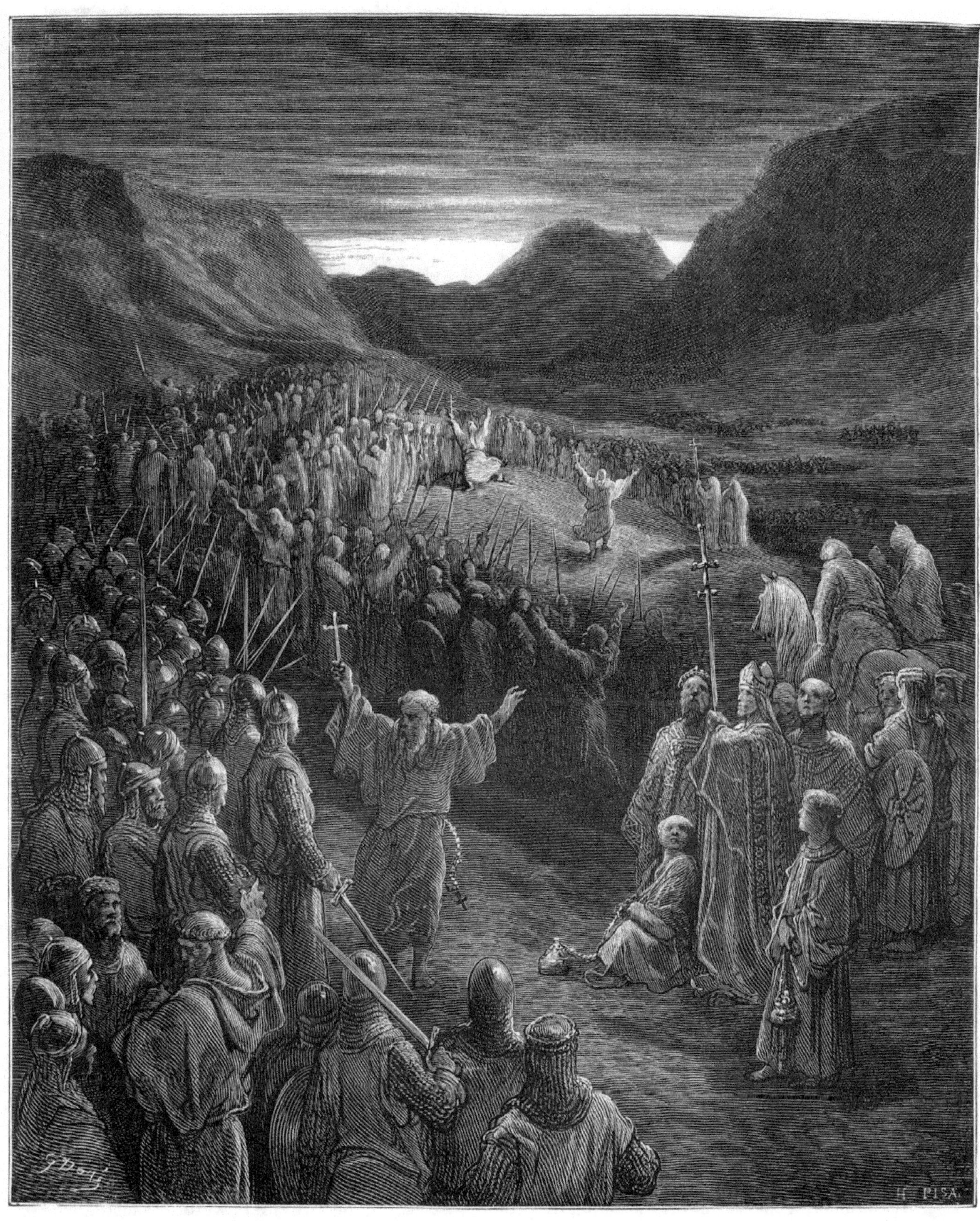

archers, the slingers, the crossbow-men, scattered here and there upon the flanks of the Christian army, were not able to return to the Turks all the arrows that were launched at them. The horsemen becoming impatient to make use of the lance and the sword, the most eager of them imprudently crossed the river and fell upon the Saracens. But the latter avoided the *mêlée;* as fast as the Crusaders presented themselves before them, they opened their ranks, dispersed, rallied at some distance, and darkened the air with a fresh cloud of arrows. The speed of their horses seconded them in these evolutions, and secured them from the pursuit of the Crusaders, whom they fought whilst appearing to fly.

This manner of fighting was quite in favour of the Turks, and rendered the disposition the Christian army made before the battle, entirely useless. Every leader, every horseman, took counsel only of his own courage, and abandoned himself to its dictates. The Christians fought in disorder upon ground with which they were quite unacquainted, and the bravest ran the greatest risks. Robert of Paris, the same who had seated himself on the imperial throne by the side of Alexius, was mortally wounded, after having seen forty of his companions fall around him. William, the brother of Tancred, fell pierced with arrows. Tancred himself, whose lance was broken, and who had no weapon left but his sword, only owed his safety to Bohémond, who came to his succour, and extricated him from the hands of the infidels. Whilst the victory between strength and agility remained uncertain, new troops of Saracens descended from the mountains and joined the fight. The sultan of Nice took advantage of the moment at which the cavalry of the Crusaders could scarcely resist the shock of the Turkish army, to attack their camp. He ordered a body of his choicest soldiers to draw their swords and follow him. He crossed the river, and overcame every obstacle that was placed in his way. In an instant the camp of the Christians was invaded and filled by the Turks. The Saracens massacred all who came within reach of their swords; sparing none but young and beautiful women, whom they destined for their seraglios. If we are to believe Albert of Aix, the daughters and the wives of the barons and knights preferred on this occasion slavery to death; for they were seen, in the midst of the tumult, decking themselves in their most beautiful vestments, and presenting themselves thus before the Saracens, seeking by the display of their charms to soften the hearts of a pitiless enemy. In the meanwhile Bohémond, rendered aware of the attack upon the camp, came promptly to its succour, and forced the sultan to rejoin the body of his army. Then the conflict recommenced on the banks of the river with increased fury. The duke of Normandy, who had remained alone with some of his knights on the field of battle, snatched his white pennon embroidered with gold from the hand of him who bore it, and rushed into the thickest of the fight, crying aloud, "*It is the will of God! It is the will of God!*" He cut down with his sword all who were in his path; among the victims to his valour being one of the principal Turkish emirs. Tancred, Richard prince of Salerno, Stephen count of Blois, and other chiefs, followed Robert's example and seconded his valour. Bohémond, who was pursuing the sultan of Nice, met a troop of soldiers who were flying, and stopped them, saying, "Whither are you flying, Christian soldiers? Do you not see that their horses have more speed than ours? Follow me, I will show you a safer road than flight!" Scarcely had he spoken these words, than he rushed with them into the midst of the Saracens, and renewed the fight. In the disorder of the *mêlée,* the women, who had been liberated from the hands of the Saracens, and who were eager to revenge their outraged modesty, went through the ranks bearing refreshment to the soldiers, and exhorting them to redouble their courage to save them from slavery.

But so many generous efforts were nearly proving useless. The Crusaders were exhausted with fatigue, and could not long resist an enemy whose force was being constantly renewed, and who overwhelmed them with numbers. The Christian army, surrounded on all sides, was compelled to retreat fighting and to retire to the camp, into which the Turks were upon the point of entering with them. It is impossible to paint the confusion and the despair which reigned at that moment among the Crusaders. Priests were seen imploring, by their groans and their prayers, the assistance of the God ot armies; women filled the air with lamentations for the dead and the wounded; whilst soldiers fell on their knees to the priests to obtain absolution for their sins. Amid this frightful tumult the voices of the leaders were but little attended to; the most intrepid were covered with wounds, burning with thirst and heat, and could fight no longer. They despaired of seeing Jerusalem, and were in momentary expectation of death, when all at once a thousand voices proclaimed the approach of Raymond and Godfrey, who were advancing with the other division of the Christian army.

Before the commencement of the battle, Bohémond had sent messengers to inform them of the attack of the Turks. On learning this, the duke of Lorraine, the count de Vermandois, and the count of Flanders, at the head of the main body of their army, had directed their march towards the valley of Gorgoni, followed by Raymond and Adhémar, who brought up the baggage, at the head of the rear-guard. When they appeared upon the ridge of the mountains on the eastern side, the sun was in the midst of his course, and his light shone full upon their shields, their helmets, and their naked swords; the ensigns were displayed; the noise of their drums and clarions resounded afar; and fifty thousand horsemen, fully armed and eager for the fight, advanced in good order. This splendid sight revived the hopes of the Crusaders, and cast fear and dread among the infidel ranks.

Scarcely had Godfrey, who, followed by fifty knights, had preceded his army, mixed with the combatants, when the sultan sounded a retreat and retired to the heights, where he hoped the Crusaders would not dare to follow him. The second body of the Christian army soon arrived on the plain smoking with the blood of the Christians. The Crusaders, recognising their brothers and companions stretched in the dust, became impatient to revenge their death, and with loud cries demanded to be led to the fight. Even the combatants who had been fighting from morning, now would not hear of repose. The Christian army immediately formed in order of battle. Bohémond, Tancred, and Robert of Normandy, placed themselves on the left; Godfrey, the count of Flanders, and the count of Blois led on the right wing. Raymond commanded the centre, and the rear-guard, or body of reserve, was placed under the orders of Adhémar. Before the leaders gave the word, the priests passed among the ranks, exhorting the Crusaders to fight manfully, and giving them their benedictions. The soldiers and the leaders, drawing their swords, and threatening the enemy, cried with one voice, "*It is the will of God! It is the will of God!*" and this animating war-cry was repeated by the echoes of the mountains and the valleys. At length the Christian army advanced, marching full of confidence against the Turks, for whom the rocks and the hills appeared to be a sure place of refuge.

The Saracens remained motionless on the mountains, and had apparently exhausted their arrows. The nature of the ground did not allow them to perform their rapid evolutions or pursue their usual tactics. Neither were they animated by the hopes of victory; but, in an attitude which expressed fear, they awaited their enemies in silence. The count of Thoulouse, who attacked them in front, broke through their ranks at the first charge. Tancred, Godfrey, Hugh, and the two Roberts, attacked them on their flanks with the same advantage. Adhémar, who had gone round the mountains, directed his attack upon the rear of the enemies, and completed the disorder. The Saracens found themselves surrounded by a forest of lances, and became only solicitous to secure safety by escaping over the rocks and through the woods. A great number of emirs, three thousand officers, and more than twenty thousand soldiers, lost their lives in the battle and the flight.

The camp of the enemy, which was at two leagues' distance, fell into the hands of the Crusaders. The conquerors there found abundance of provisions, magnificently ornamented tents, immense trea-

CRUSADERS THROWING HEADS INTO NICE.

This second battle, in which the Turks showed the courage of despair, seconded by all the stratagems of war, lasted from morning till night. The victory . . . cost the Christians two thousand lives. The Crusaders made a great many prisoners; four thousand Mussulmans fell on the field of battle; the heads of a thousand were sent to Alexius, and the rest, by the aid of machines, were cast into the city, to inform the garrison of this fresh defeat of the Turks.—Book II.

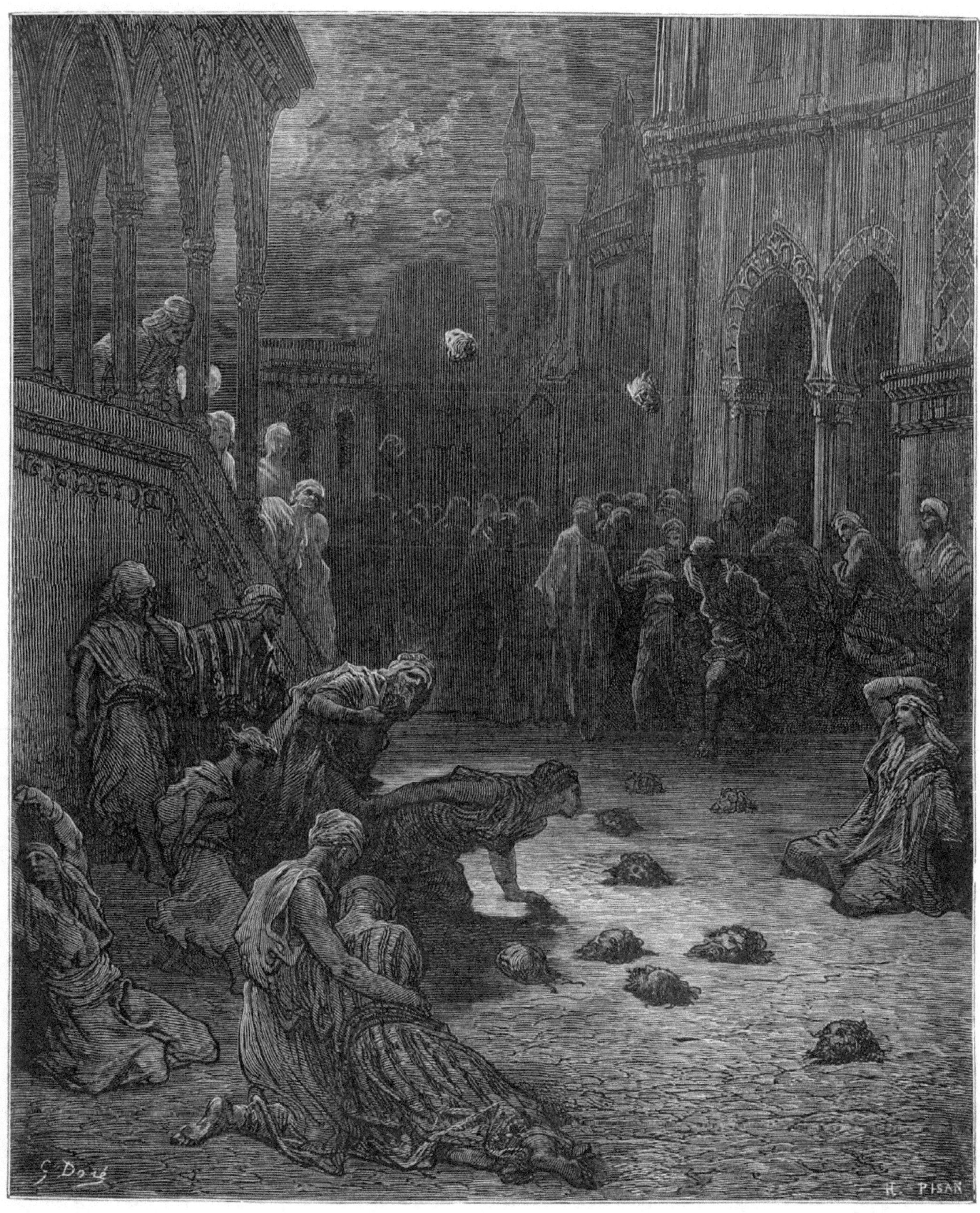
G. Doré
H. PISAN

sures, all sorts of beasts of burthen, and above all, a great number of camels. The sight of these animals, which were then unknown in the West, caused them as much surprise as joy. They mounted the horses of the Saracens, to pursue the remains of the conquered army. Towards nightfall they returned to their camp loaded with booty, preceded by their priests, singing hymns and canticles of thanksgiving. Both leaders and soldiers had covered themselves with glory in this great conflict. We have named the principal leaders of the army; historians point out many more, such as Baldwin of Beauvais, Galon de Calmon, Gaston de Béarn, Gerard de Chérisi, all of whom signalized themselves by exploits, says William of Tyre, the remembrance of which will never perish.

The day after the victory the Crusaders repaired to the field of battle for the purpose of burying the dead. They had lost four thousand of their companions, and they paid them the last duties in tears; the clergy offered up their prayers for them, and the army honoured them as martyrs. They soon, however, passed from funeral ceremonies to transports of the wildest joy. On stripping the Saracens, they quarrelled for their blood-stained habits. In the excess of their delight, some of the soldiers would put on the armour of their enemies, and clothing themselves in the flowing robes of the Mussulmans, would seat themselves in the tents of the conquered, and, with imitative gestures, ridicule the luxury and customs of Asia. Such as were without arms took possession of the swords and crooked sabres of the Saracens, and the archers filled their quivers with the arrows which had been shot at them during the fight.

The intoxication of victory, however, did not prevent their doing justice to the bravery of the Turks, who, from that time, boasted of having a common origin with the Franks. Contemporary historians, who praise the valour of the Turks, add, that they only wanted to be Christians to make them quite comparable to the Crusaders. That which, otherwise, proves the high idea the Crusaders entertained of their enemies, is, that they attributed their victory to a miracle. Two days after the battle, says Albert of Aix, although no one was pursuing them, the infidels continued flying, exclaiming as they went, "*It is the will of God! It is the will of God!*" After the victory, the Christian army invoked the names of St. George and St. Demetrius, who had been seen, as they said, fighting in the ranks of the Christians. This pious fable was accredited among both the Latins and Greeks. A long time subsequent to the victory, the Armenians erected a church in the neighbourhood of Dorylæum, where the people were accustomed to assemble on the first Friday of March, and believed that they saw St. George appear on horseback, lance in hand.

Whilst the Crusaders were felicitating themselves on their victory, the sultan of Nice, who did not dare again to encounter the Christians in the field, undertook to desolate the country which he could not defend. At the head of the wreck of his army, and ten thousand Arabs who had joined him, he preceded the march of the Christians, and laid waste his own provinces. The Turks burnt the harvests, pillaged the cities, the bourgs, and the houses of the Christians, and carried away in their train the wives and children of the Greeks, whom they detained as hostages. The banks of the Meander and the Caïster, Cappadocia, Pisidia, Isauria, and all the country as far as Mount Taurus, were given up to pillage, and entirely laid waste.

When the Crusaders resumed their march, they determ.ned not to separate again, as they had done on entering Phrygia. This resolution certainly rendered them safe from surprise or hostile attack, but it exposed so numerous an army to the risk of perishing by famine and misery in a country devastated by the Turks.* The Christians, who marched without forethought, and were never provisioned for more than a few days, were not long before they felt the want of food. They found

* I have made earnest researches to discover by what means the Christian army was provisioned, and I can learn nothing beyond the fact that the Crusaders carried hand-mills with them.

nothing on their route but deserted fields, and soon had no other subsistence but the roots of wild plants and the ears of corn which had escaped the ravages of the Saracens. By far the greater number of the horses of the army perished for want of water and forage.

Most of the knights, who were accustomed to look with contempt on foot-soldiers, were obliged, like them, to march on foot, and carry their arms, the weight of which was enough to exhaust them. The Christian army presented a strange spectacle—knights were seen mounted on asses and oxen, advancing at the head of their companies; rams, goats, pigs, dogs, every animal they could meet with, was loaded with baggage, which, for the most part, was left abandoned on the roads.

The Crusaders then traversed that part of Phrygia which the ancients called "burning Phrygia." When their army arrived in the country of Sauria, they endured all the horrors of thirst, of which the most robust soldiers could not resist the terrible power. We read in William of Tyre, that five hundred perished in one day. Historians say that women were seen giving premature birth to their offspring in the midst of burning and open fields; whilst others, in despair, with children they could no longer nourish, implored death with loud cries, and, in the excess of their agony, rolled naked on the earth in the sight of the whole army. The authors of the time do not forget to mention the falcons and birds of prey which the knights had brought with them into Asia, and which almost all perished under the burning sun. In vain the Crusaders called for a repetition of the miracles which God had formerly wrought for his chosen people in the desert. The sterile valleys of Pisidia resounded during several days with their prayers, with their complaints, and perhaps, likewise, with their blasphemies.

In the midst of these burning countries they at length made a discovery which saved the army, but which was very near becoming as fatal to them as the horrors of thirst.

The dogs which had followed the Crusaders had abandoned their masters, and wandered over the plains and into the mountains in search of a spring. One day several of them were seen returning to the camp with their paws and their hides covered with moist sand, and it was judged that they had found water. Several soldiers observed their track, and discovered a river. The whole army rushed towards it in a mass. The Crusaders, famishing with heat and thirst, cast themselves headlong into the water, and quenched the inward heat without moderation or precaution. More than three hundred of them died almost immediately, and many fell seriously ill, and could not continue their march.

At length the Christian army arrived before Antiochetta, which opened its gates to them. This city, the capital of Pisidia, was situated in the midst of a territory interspersed with fields, rivers, and forests. The sight of a smiling and fertile country invited the Christians to repose for a few days, and made them soon forget all the evils they had undergone.

As the fame of their victories and their march had spread throughout the neighbouring countries, the greater part of the cities of Asia Minor, some from fear, and others from affection to the Christians, sent deputies to offer them supplies and to swear obedience to them. Thus they found themselves masters of several countries of whose names or geographical position they were perfectly ignorant. Most of the Crusaders were far from being aware that the provinces they had just subdued had seen the phalanx of Alexander and the armies of Rome, or that the Greeks, the inhabitants of these countries, were descended from the Gauls, who, in the time of the second Brennus, had left Illyria and the shores of the Danube, had crossed the Bosphorus, pillaged the city of Heraclea, and founded a colony on the banks of the Halys. Without troubling themselves with traces of antiquity, the new conquerors ordered the Christian churches to be rebuilt, and scoured the country to collect provisions.

During their abode at Antiochetta, the joy of their conquests was, for a moment, disturbed by the

THE BATTLE OF NICEA.

"Then the two armies," says Matthew of Edessa, who speaks of this battle, "joined, mingled, and attacked each other with equal fury. Everywhere glittered casques and shields; lances rung against cuirasses; the air resounded with piercing cries; the terrified horses recoiled at the din of arms and the hissing of arrows; the earth trembled beneath the tread of the combatants, and the plain was for a vast space bristling with javelins." Godfrey, Tancred, and the two Roberts appeared to be everywhere at once, and carried death and terror into the ranks of the infidels. The Turks could not long withstand the impetuous valor of the Crusaders; they were put to the rout and pursued by the conquerors even to the mountains, which served them as a place of refuge.—BOOK II.

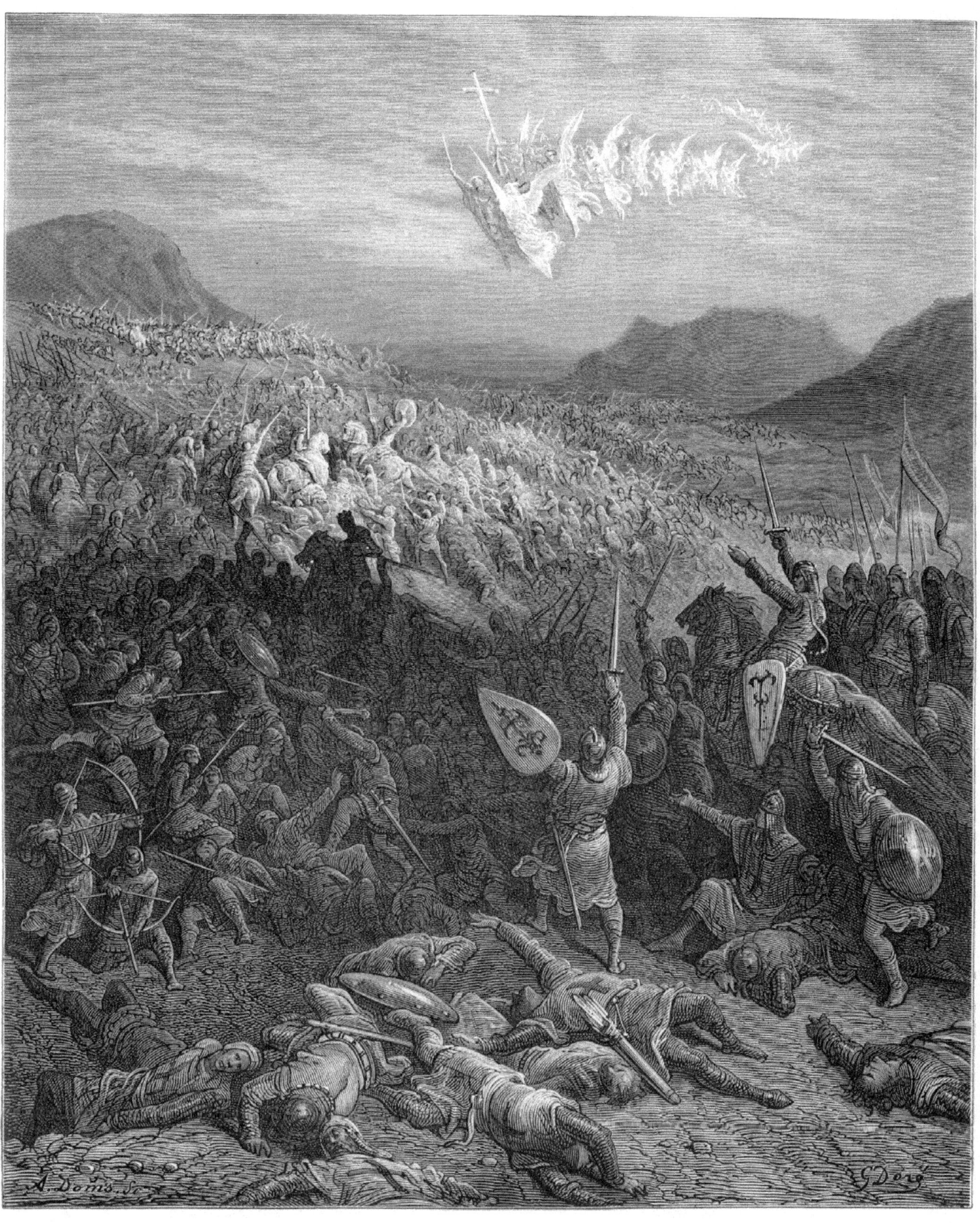
A. Doms Sc
G. Doré

fear of losing two of their most renowned chiefs. Raymond, count of Thoulouse, fell dangerously ill. As his life was despaired of, they had already laid him upon ashes, and the bishop of Orange was repeating the litanies of the dead, when a Saxon count came to announce that Raymond would not die of this disease, and that the prayers of St. Gilles had obtained for him *a truce with death.* These words, says William of Tyre, restored hope to all the bystanders, and soon Raymond showed himself to the whole army, which celebrated his cure as a miracle.

About the same time, Godfrey, who had one day wandered into a forest, was in great danger from defending a soldier who was attacked by a bear. He conquered the bear, but being wounded in the thigh, and the blood flowing copiously, he was carried in an apparently dying state into the camp of the Crusaders. The loss of a battle would have spread less consternation than the sad spectacle which now presented itself to the eyes of the Christians. All the Crusaders shed tears, and put up prayers for the life of Godfrey. The wound did not prove dangerous, but weakened by the loss of blood, the duke de Bouillon was a length of time before he regained his strength. The count de Thoulouse had likewise a long convalescence, and both were obliged during several weeks to be borne in a litter in the rear of the army.

Greater evils threatened the Crusaders. Hitherto peace had reigned amongst them, and their union constituted their strength. All at once, discord broke out amongst some of the leaders, and was on the point of extending to the whole army. Tancred and Baldwin, the brother of Godfrey, were sent out on a scouring party, either to disperse the scattered bands of Turks, or to protect the Christians, and obtain from them assistance and provisions. They advanced at first into Lycaonia as far as the city of Iconium; but having met with no enemy, and finding the country abandoned, they directed their march towards the sea-coast, through the mountains of Cilicia. Tancred, who marched first, arrived without obstacle under the walls of Tarsus, a celebrated city of antiquity, which takes great pride from having been the birthplace of St. Paul. The Turks who defended the place consented to display the flag of the Christians on their walls, and promised to surrender if they were not speedily relieved. Tancred, whom the inhabitants, for the most part Christians, already considered as their deliverer, was encamping without the walls, when he saw the detachment commanded by Baldwin approach. The leaders and the soldiers congratulated each other on their reunion, and expressed the greater joy from having, reciprocally, taken each other for enemies.

But this harmony was soon troubled by the pretensions of Baldwin. The brother of Godfrey was indignant at seeing the colours of Tancred and Bohémond flying on the walls of Tarsus. He declared that as his troop was the more numerous, the city ought to belong to him. He demanded, at least, that the two parties should enter together into the place, and should share the spoils of the garrison and the inhabitants. Tancred rejected this proposition with scorn, and said that he had not taken arms for the purpose of pillaging Christian cities. At these words Baldwin broke into a rage, and bestowed the grossest abuse upon Tancred, Bohémond, and the whole race of Norman adventurers. After long debates, it was agreed on both sides, that the affair should be decided by the inhabitants, and that the city should belong to whichever they should choose for master The assembled people at first appeared inclined towards Tancred, to whom they thought they owed their deliverance; but Baldwin made the Turks and the inhabitants sensible of the superiority of his numbers, and threatened them with his anger and his vengeance. The fear which he inspired decided the suffrages in his favour; and the flag of Tancred was cast into the ditches of the town, and replaced by that of Baldwin.

Blood was about to flow to avenge this outrage, but the Italians and Normans, appeased by their chief, listened to the voice of moderation, and quitted the disputed city to seek other conquests elsewhere. Baldwin entered in triumph into the place, of which the fortress and several towers were still in possession of the Turks. He so much feared that his new conquest would be disputed, that he refused to open the gates to three hundred Crusaders whom Bohémond had sent to the assistance of Tancred, and who demanded an asylum for the night. These latter, being obliged to pass the nigh in the open field, were surprised and massacred by the Turks. The following morning, at the sight of their brethren stretched lifeless, and stripped of their arms and vestments, the Christians could not restrain their indignation. The city of Tarsus resounded with their groans and complaints. The soldiers of Baldwin flew to arms, they threatened the Turks who still remained in the place, and vowed vengeance upon their own leader, whom they accused of the death of their companions. At the first outbreak of this danger Baldwin was obliged to fly, and take refuge in one of the towers. A short time after he appeared surrounded by his own people, mourning with them the death of the Crusaders, and excused himself by saying, that he had bound himself by an oath that none but his own soldiers should enter the town. Thus speaking, he pointed to several towers which were still occupied by the Turks. In the midst of the tumult, some Christian women, whose noses and ears the Turks had cut off, by their presence added to the fury of the soldiers of Baldwin, and they immediately fell upon the Turks who remained in the city, and massacred them all without pity.

In the midst of these scenes of violence, Baldwin received an unexpected reinforcement. A fleet was seen approaching the coast full sail. The soldiers of Baldwin, who expected to have to deal with more infidels, hastened fully armed to the shore. As the fleet drew near, they interrogated the crew of the first ship. The crew replied in the Frank language. Soon they learnt that these, whom they had taken to be Mussulmans, were pirates from the ports of Flanders and Holland. These corsairs had for ten years cruised in the Mediterranean, where they had made themselves remarkable by their exploits, and still more frequently by their piracies. Upon hearing of the expedition of the Christians of the West, they had made sail for Syria and Palestine. On the invitation of the Crusaders, they joyfully entered the port of Tarsus. Their chief, Guymer, who was a Boulonnais, recognised Baldwin, the son of his ancient master, and promised with his companions to serve under him. They all took the cross, and with it the oath to share the glory and the labours of the holy war.

Aided by this new reinforcement, and leaving a strong garrison in the city of Tarsus, Baldwin resumed his march, following the route of Tancred, and soon came in sight of Malmistra, of which the Italians had just taken possession. The latter, on seeing Baldwin, were persuaded that he was come to dispute their new conquest, and prepared to repulse force by force. When Tancred endeavoured to appease his irritated soldiers, murmurs arose against him. They accused him of having forgotten the honour of chivalry, his moderation being in their eyes nothing but a shameful weakness. The effect that such reproaches must have had upon a spirit like that of Tancred, may be easily imagined. The moment they suspected his courage, he no longer made an effort to restrain his anger, and swore to avenge his wrongs in the blood of his rival. He himself led the soldiers, and rushed out of the town at their head to encounter the troops of Baldwin. They at once came to blows. On both sides courage was equal; but the fury of revenge doubled the efforts of the Italians. The soldiers of Baldwin had the advantage in numbers. They fought with the animosity peculiar to civil wars; but at length the troops of Tancred were forced to give way; they left many of their companions in the hands of their adversaries and upon the field of battle, and re-entered the town deploring their defeat in silence.

Night restored calm to their excited spirits. The soldiers of Tancred had acknowledged the superiority of the Flemings, and believed, as blood had flowed, they had no longer any outrage to avenge, whilst the followers of Baldwin remembered that the men whom they had conquered were

THE BATTLE OF DORYLÆUM.

Bohémond ordered a body of his choicest soldiers to draw their swords and follow him. He crossed the river, and overcame every obstacle that was placed in his way. In an instant the camp of the Christians was invaded and filled by the Turks. The Saracens massacred all who came within reach of their swords; sparing none but young and beautiful women, whom they destined for their seraglios. If we are to believe Albert of Aix, the daughters and the wives of the barons and knights preferred on this occasion slavery to death; for they were seen, in the midst of the tumult, decking themselves in their most beautiful vestments, and presenting themselves thus before the Saracens, seeking by the display of their charms to soften the hearts of a pitiless enemy. In the mean while Bohémond, rendered aware of the attack upon the camp, came promptly to its succour, and forced the sultan to rejoin the body of his army. Then the conflict recommenced on the banks of the river with increased fury. The duke of Normandy, who had remained alone with some of his knights on the field of battle, snatched his white pennon embroidered with gold from the hand of him who bore it, and rushed into the thickest of the fight, crying aloud, "IT IS THE WILL OF GOD! IT IS THE WILL OF GOD!" *He cut down with his sword all who were in his path; among the victims to his valour being one of the principal Turkish emirs.*

BOOK II.

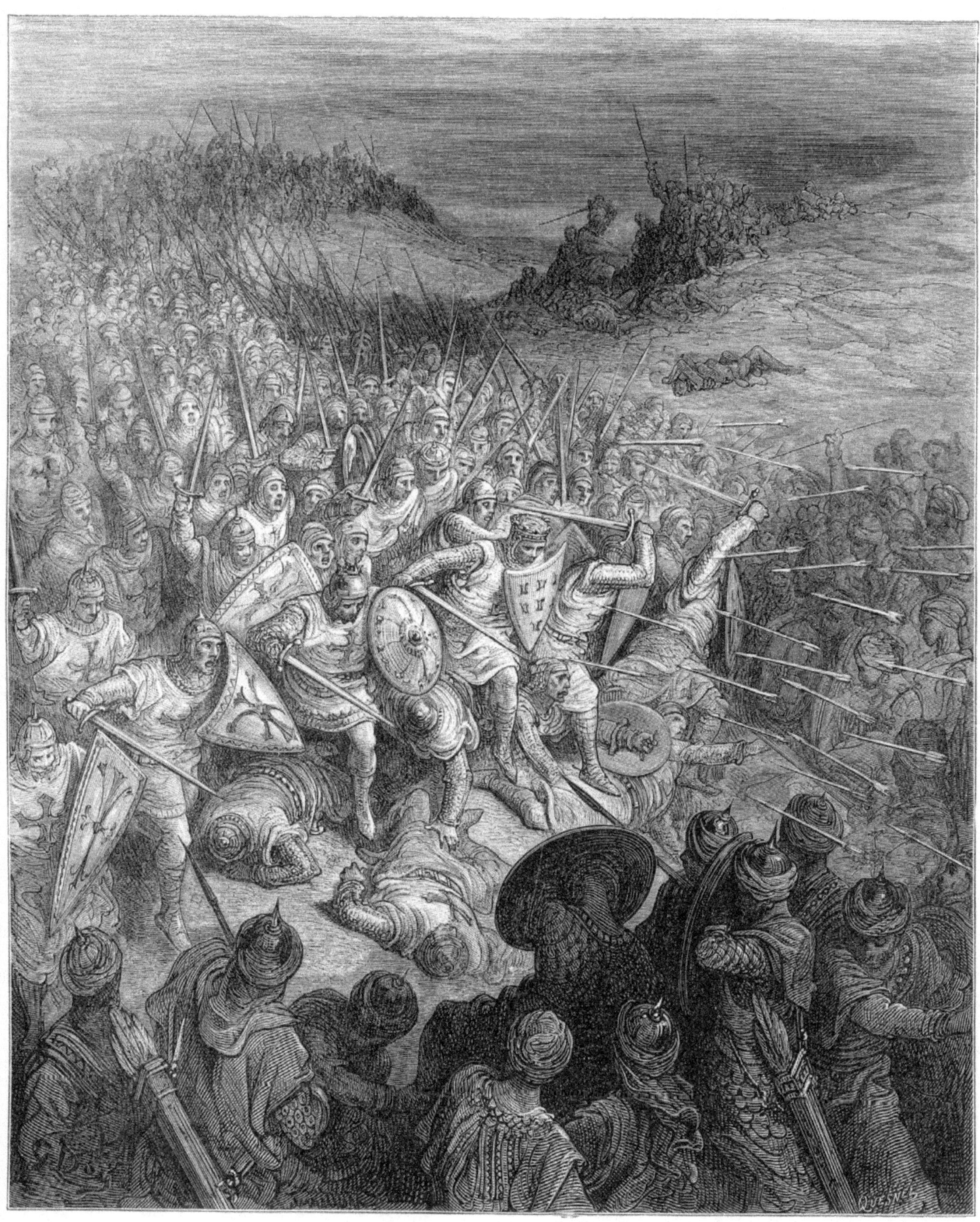

Christians. On the morrow nothing was heard on either side but the voice of humanity and religion. The two chiefs at the same time sent deputies, and in order to avoid an appearance of asking for peace, both attributed their overtures to the inspiration of Heaven. They swore to forget their quarrels, and embraced in sight of the soldiers, who reproached themselves with the sad effects of their animosity, and longed to expiate the blood of their brothers by new exploits against the Turks.

Tancred with his troop departing from Malmistra, passed in triumph along the coasts of Cilicia, and penetrated as far as Alexandretta, of which he easily took possession. In proportion as he made himself dreaded by his enemies, he made himself the more beloved by his companions. When he rejoined the Christian army covered with glory and loaded with booty, he heard all around him nothing but praises of his moderation and valour. The presence of Baldwin, who had preceded him, on the contrary, only excited murmurs, as they attributed to him the death of so many Christian soldiers. Godfrey loudly blamed the ambition and avarice of his brother. But caring little for these reproaches, Baldwin yielded to his rival, without pain, the suffrages of the army, and preferred a principality to the love and esteem of the Crusaders; and fortune soon offered him an opportunity of realizing his ambitious projects.

During the siege of Nice, an Armenian prince named Pancratius had come to join the Christian army. In his youth he had been king of northern Iberia. Driven from his kingdom by his own subjects, and for a length of time a prisoner at Constantinople, he had followed the Crusaders in the hope of re-conquering his states. He had particularly attached himself to the fortunes of Baldwin, whose aspiring character he understood, and whom he hoped to associate in his designs. He spoke to him continually of the rich provinces which extended along the two shores of the Euphrates. These provinces, he said, were inhabited by a great number of Christians, and the Crusaders had but to present themselves there to make themselves masters of them. These discourses inflamed the ambition of Baldwin, who resolved a second time to quit the main army of the Christians, and to go to the banks of the Euphrates, to conquer a country of such boasted wealth.

He had just lost his wife Gundechilde, who had accompanied him to the crusade, and who was buried with great pomp by the Christians. This loss did not stop him in the execution of his projects. As he was not beloved in the Christian army, when he was ready to set out no leader was willing to join him, and several even of his own soldiers refused to accompany him. He could only take with him from a thousand to fifteen hundred foot-soldiers, a troop despised in the army, and two hundred horsemen, seduced by the hopes of pillage. But nothing could abate his ardour, and as the chiefs of the crusade had decided in a council that nobody should be allowed to withdraw from the standard of the army, he set out the day before this decision was published in the camp of the Christians. At the head of his little army he advanced into Armenia, finding no enemy able to impede his march. Consternation reigned among the Turks, and the Christians, everywhere eager to throw off the yoke of the Mussulmans, became powerful auxiliaries to the Crusaders.

Turbessel and Ravendel were the first cities that opened their gates to the fortunate conqueror. This conquest soon produced a separation between Baldwin and Pancratius, who both entertained the same projects of ambition; but this difference did not at all delay the march of the brother of Godfrey. The Crusader prince opposed violence to cunning; he threatened to treat his rival as an enemy, and thus drove him away from the theatre of his victories. Baldwin wanted neither guide nor assistance in a country of which the inhabitants all flocked out to meet him. As he pursued his march, fame carried his exploits into the most distant places; the intelligence of his conquests preceded him beyond the Euphrates, and reached even the city of Edessa.

This city, so celebrated in the times of the primitive church, was the metropolis of Mesopotamia.

As it had escaped the invasion of the Turks, all the Christians of that neighbourhood had, with their riches, taken refuge within its walls. A Greek prince, named Theodore,* deputed by the emperor of Constantinople, was the governor of it, and maintained his power by paying tribute to the Saracens. The approach and the victories of the Crusaders produced the most lively sensations in the city of Edessa. The people and the governor joined in soliciting the aid of Baldwin. The bishop and twelve of the principal inhabitants were deputed to meet the Crusader prince. They described to him the wealth of Mesopotamia, the devotion of their fellow-citizens to the cause of Jesus Christ, and conjured him to rescue a Christian city from the domination of the infidels. Baldwin readily yielded to their prayers, and immediately prepared to cross the Euphrates.

He had the good fortune to escape the Turks, who were waiting for him on his passage, and without drawing a sword he arrived in the territories of Edessa. As he had placed garrisons in the cities which had fallen into his power, he had no greater force with him than one hundred horsemen. As soon as he drew near to the city, the whole population came out to meet him, bearing branches of olive and singing hymns. It must have been a curious spectacle to behold so small a number of warriors, surrounded by an immense multitude, who implored their support and proclaimed them their liberators. They were welcomed with so much enthusiasm, that the prince or governor of Edessa, who was not beloved by the people, took umbrage, and began to see in them enemies more to be dreaded by him than the Saracens. In order to attach their chief to himself, and engage him to support his authority, he offered him great riches. But the ambitious Baldwin, whether because he expected to obtain more from the affections of the people and the fortune of his arms, or that he considered it disgraceful to place himself in the pay of a foreign prince, refused with contempt the offers of the governor of Edessa, and even threatened to retire and abandon the city. The inhabitants, who dreaded his departure, assembled in a tumultuous manner, and implored him with loud cries to remain among them; the governor himself made new efforts to detain the Crusaders, and to interest them in his cause. As Baldwin had made it pretty clearly understood that he would never defend states that were not his own, the prince of Edessa, who was old and childless, determined to adopt him for his son and nominate him his successor. The ceremony of the adoption was performed in the presence of the Crusaders and the inhabitants. According to the custom of the Orientals, the Greek prince made Baldwin pass between his shirt and his naked skin, and kissed him as a sign of alliance and paternity. The aged wife of the governor repeated the same ceremony, and from that time Baldwin, considered as their son and heir, neglected nothing for the defence of a city which was to belong to him.

An Armenian prince, named Constantine, who governed a province in the neighbourhood of Mount Taurus, had also come to the assistance of Edessa. Baldwin, seconded by this useful auxiliary, and followed by his own horsemen and the troops of Theodore, took the field, in order to attack the nearest Turkish cities. He defeated the troops of the emir Baldoukh in several encounters, and forced them to retire into the city of Samosata. The Christians approached the place, pillaged the suburbs, and the houses of the neighbourhood, without meeting with the least resistance; but as they were engaged in dividing their booty, they were attacked unexpectedly by the infidels and routed. After having lost two thousand fighting men, they returned to Edessa, where the news of their defeat spread the greatest consternation.

Misunderstandings soon broke out between Theodore and Baldwin, who mutually reproached each other with their reverses. The Edessenians, who had declared for the Crusader prince, would not hear of any other master, and were not long in satisfying his impatience to reign. They forgot

* None of the Latin historians have given us the name of the governor of Edessa. The name of Theodore is found in the History of Matthew of Edessa, from which we have taken, according to the translation of M. Corbied, several curious details, which would be sought for in vain elsewhere.

BURYING THE DEAD AFTER THE BATTLE OF DORYLÆUM.

The day after the victory the Crusaders repaired to the field of battle for the purpose of burying the dead. They had lost four thousand of their companions, and they paid them their duties in tears; the clergy offered up their prayers for them, and the army honoured them as martyrs. They soon, however, passed from funeral ceremonies to transports of the wildest joy. On stripping the Saracens, they quarrelled for their blood-stained habits. In the excess of their delight, some of the soldiers would put on the armour of their enemies, and clothing themselves in the flowing robes of the Mussulmans, would seat themselves in the tents of the conquered, and, with imitative gestures, ridicule the luxury and customs of Asia. Such as were without arms took possession of the swords and crooked sabres of the Saracens, and the archers filled their quivers with the arrows which had been shot at them during the fight.—Book II.

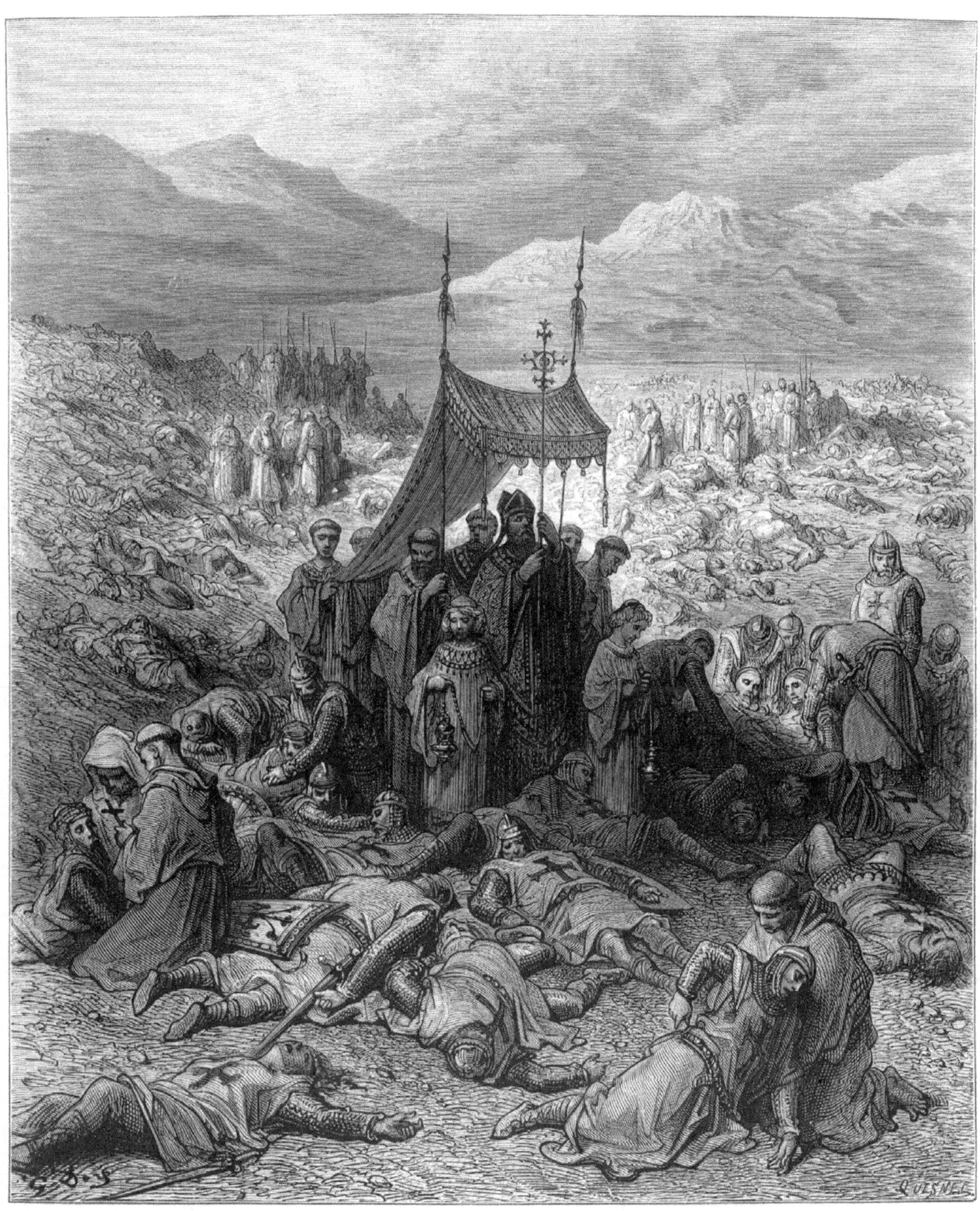

that Theodore, by his courage and skill, had maintained their independence in the centre of a country constantly exposed to the invasions of the Mussulmans. They accused him of having burdened his subjects with imposts, to satisfy the avidity of the Turks, and with having employed the power of infidels to oppress a Christian people. They formed, says Matthew of Edessa, a plot against his life, of which Baldwin was not ignorant. Warned of the danger which threatened him, Theodore retired into the citadel, which commanded the city, and placed no reliance on anything but force to defend himself against the seditious.

Upon this a most furious tumult was created among the people. The enraged multitude flew to arms, and pillaged the houses of the inhabitants who were suspected of being the partisans of Theodore. They swore to treat him as a declared enemy. They attacked the citadel, some beating in the gates, and others scaling the walls. Theodore seeing that his enemies were masters of one part of the ramparts, no longer endeavoured to defend himself, but proposed to capitulate. He agreed to abandon the place, and to renounce the government of Edessa, requesting permission to retire, with his family, to the city of Melitene. This proposition was accepted with joy; the peace was signed, and the inhabitants of Edessa swore upon the cross and the Evangelists to respect the conditions of it.

On the following day, whilst the governor was preparing for his departure, a fresh sedition broke out in the city. The factious repented of having allowed a prince whom they had so cruelly outraged, to live. New accusations were brought against him. It was said that he had only signed the peace with perfidious intentions. The fury of the people soon rose above all bounds, and a thousand voices demanded the death of Theodore. They penetrated, tumultuously, into the citadel, seized the aged governor in the midst of his family, and precipitated him from the heights of the ramparts. His bleeding body was dragged through the streets by the multitude, who prided themselves upon having murdered an old man as much as if they had gained a victory over the infidels.

Baldwin, who may, at least, be accused of not having defended his adoptive father, was soon surrounded by all the people of Edessa, who offered him the government of the city. He refused it at first, "but in the end," says an old historian, "they combated his objections with so many reasons, that they forced him to consent, and established him instead of the other." Baldwin was proclaimed liberator and master of Edessa. Seated on a blood-stained throne, and in constant dread of the fickle nature of the people, he soon inspired his subjects with as much fear as his enemies. Whilst the seditious trembled before him, he extended the limits of his territories. He purchased the city of Samosata with the treasures of his predecessor, and obtained possession of several other cities by force of arms. As fortune favoured him in everything, the loss even, which he had lately experienced, of his wife, Gundechilde, promoted his projects of aggrandizement. He espoused the niece of an Armenian prince, and by that new alliance he extended his possessions as far as Mount Taurus. All Mesopotamia, with both shores of the Euphrates, acknowledged his authority, and Asia then beheld a French knight reigning without dispute over the richest provinces of the ancient kingdom of Assyria.

Baldwin thought no more of the deliverance of Jerusalem, but gave all his attention to the defence and aggrandizement of his states.* Many knights, dazzled by such a rapid fortune, hastened to Edessa, to increase the army and the court of the new monarch. The advantages which resulted to the Crusaders from the foundation of this new state, have made their historians forget that they were the fruit of injustice and violence. The principality of Edessa served as a check upon the Turks and the Saracens, and was, to the period of the second crusade, the principal bulwark of the power of the Christians in the East.

* In the first book of the *Jerusalem Delivered*, when the Eternal turns his eyes on the Crusaders, he sees in Edessa the ambitious Baldwin, who only aspires to human grandeurs, with which he is solely occupied.

BOOK III

The March to, and Siege of Antioch

1097 to 1099

BOOK III.

THE MARCH TO, AND SIEGE OF ANTIOCH.

A. D. 1097–1099.

The Crusaders everywhere triumphant—Their sufferings in passing Mount Taurus—Enter Syria—Damascus—Aleppo—Capture of Chalcis and Artesia—Siege of Antioch—Sweno, king of Denmark—Barbarous treatment of the Turks—Ambassadors from Egypt—City of Harem—The Crusaders relieved by the Pisans and Genoese—Baldwin, prince of Edessa—Antioch captured—Quarrel of Godfrey de Bouillon and Bohémond—Kerbogha, sultan of Mossoul—Sultan of Persia sends an immense army against the Crusaders—Contests before Antioch—Sufferings of the Crusaders—Subtle policy of Alexius—Kerbogha besieges Antioch—Pretended miracles—The sacred lance—Speech of Peter the Hermit to the Saracen leaders, and Kerbogha's haughty reply—Saracens defeated by the Crusaders—Instances of heroic bravery—Magnificent encampment of Kerbogha—The miraculous influence of the holy lance doubted—Death of Baldwin count of Hainault—Fatal epidemic at Antioch—Death of Bishop Puy—Docility of a lion—Geoffrey de la Tour—Foulque and his widow—Hezas, the emir, allies himself with the Crusaders, and defeats the sultan of Aleppo—Letters conveyed by pigeons—Miraculous prodigies—Capture of Maarah—Conquests in Syria by the Crusaders.

THE great army of the Crusaders had traversed the states of the sultan of Nice and Iconium; throughout its passage the mosques were given up to the flames or converted into churches; but the Christians had neglected to fortify the cities of which they had rendered themselves masters, or to found a military colony in a country wherein the Turks were always able to rally and re-establish their formidable power. This fault, which must be attributed to a too great confidence in victory, became fatal to the Crusaders, who, in the midst of their triumphs, lost the means of communication with Europe, and thus deprived themselves of the assistance they might have received from Greece and the West.

Terror opened to the pilgrims all the passages of Mount Taurus. Throughout their triumphant march the Christians had nothing to dread but famine, the heat of the climate, and the badness of the roads. They had, particularly, much to suffer in crossing a mountain situated between Coxon and Marash, which their historians denominate "*The Mountain of the Devil.*" This mountain was very steep, and offered only one narrow path, in which the foot-soldiers marched with difficulty; the horses, which could not keep their footing, dragged each other down the abysses; and the army lost a great part of its baggage. In the course of this disastrous march, says an historian who was an eye-witness, the soldiers gave themselves up to despair, and refused to proceed. Being encumbered with their arms, they either sold them at a low price or cast them down the precipices. On all sides were to be seen warriors wounded by their frequent falls, and pilgrims exhausted with fatigue, who could not continue their route, and filled the air and mountains with their cries and groans. The passage of the Christian army across this mountain occupied several days; but when they had at length passed the chains of Mount Taurus and Mount Amanus, the sight of Syria revived their courage, and made them quickly forget all their fatigues. That country into which they were about to enter embraced within its territories PAL-

ESTINE, the object of all their wishes, prayers, and labours. In all ages Syria has attracted conquerors, by the fertility of its soil and its wealth. In the time of David and Solomon, it already boasted several flourishing cities. At the period of the crusades it had undergone a great many revolutions, but its fields, though covered with celebrated ruins, still preserved some portion of their fecundity.

The first of the Syrian provinces that presented itself to the eyes of the Christians was the territory of Antioch. Towards the east extended the states of the sultans of Aleppo and Mousoul. Further, at the foot of Mount Libanus, was seen the principality of Damascus; on the coast stood Laodicea, Tripoli, and the cities of Sidon and Tyre, so celebrated in both sacred and profane antiquity. All these cities, which scarcely maintained a shadow of their former splendour, were governed by emirs who had shaken off the yoke of the sultans of Persia, and reigned as sovereign princes over the ruins of the empire of Malek-Scha.

The Crusaders advanced as far as the ancient Chalcis, then called Artesia, of which they made themselves masters. To arrive before Antioch they had to pass over a bridge built over the Orontes, and defended by two towers masked with iron. Nothing could resist the van, commanded by the duke of Normandy. The Normans soon got possession of the bridge, and passed the river. Terror seized upon the Mussulman ranks, and they sought shelter, with the greatest haste, within the walls of the city. The whole Christian army, drawn up in battle array, with trumpets sounding and flags flying, marched towards Antioch and encamped within a mile of its walls.

The sight of this city, so celebrated in the annals of Christianity, revived the enthusiasm of the Crusaders. It was within the walls of Antioch that the disciples of Jesus Christ first assumed the title of Christians, and the apostle Peter was named the first pastor of the young church. No city had contained within its bosom a greater number of martyrs, saints, and doctors; no city had beheld more miracles worked for the faith. During many centuries, the faithful had been accustomed to come into one of its suburbs to pray at the tomb of St. Babylas, who, during the reign of Julian, had silenced the oracles of Apollo. For a long time Antioch was considered in Christendom as the eldest daughter of Sion; it bore the name of Theopolis (the city of God), and pilgrims visited it with no less respect than Jerusalem.

Antioch was as much celebrated in the annals of Rome as in those of the Church. The magnificence of its edifices and the residence of several emperors had obtained it the name of the Queen of the East. Its situation, amidst a smiling and fertile country, attracted strangers to it at all times. At two leagues eastward was a lake abounding in fish, which communicated with the Orontes; whilst on the south were the suburbs and the fountain of Daphne, so renowned in paganism. Not far from this arose the mountain of Orontes, covered with gardens and country houses; on the north was another mountain, sometimes called the Black Mountain, on account of its forests, and sometimes the Water Mountain, on account of its numerous springs. The river Orontes,* flowed at the foot of the ramparts of Antioch towards the west, and fell into the sea at a distance of three or four leagues from the city.

Within the walls were four hills separated by a torrent, which cast itself into the river. Upon the western hill was built a very strong citadel, which dominated over the city. The ramparts of Antioch, whose solidity equalled that of a rock, were three leagues in extent. "This place," says an old author, "was an object of terror to those who looked upon it, for the number of its strong and vast towers, which amounted to three hundred and sixty." Wide ditches, the river Orontes and marshes, still further protected the inhabitants of Antioch, and cut off an approach to the city.

* At the present day named *Aassy* (the Rebel), or *el Macloub*, the Reversed, because it flows from south to north, an opposite direction to that of the other rivers of the same country.

In spite of all these fortifications of nature and art, Antioch had been several times taken. It fell at once into the power of the Saracens, in the first age of the Hegira; it was afterwards retaken by the Greeks, under Nicephorus Phocas; and, fourteen years before, the Turks had rendered themselves masters of it. At the approach of the Christians, the greater part of the Saracens of the neighbouring cities and provinces had sought security in Antioch for themselves, their wives, and treasures. Baghisian, or Accien, grandson of Malek-Scha, who had obtained the sovereignty of the city, had shut himself up in it, with seven thousand horse and twenty thousand foot-soldiers.

The siege of Antioch presented many difficulties and dangers. The chiefs of the Crusaders deliberated upon the propriety of undertaking it; and the first who spoke in the council thought that it would be imprudent to commence a siege at the beginning of winter. They did not dread the arms of the Saracens, but the rains, the tempests, and the horrors of famine. They advised the Crusaders to await in the provinces and neighbouring cities the arrival of the aid promised by Alexius, and the return of spring, by which time the army would have repaired its losses, and received beneath its standards fresh reinforcements from the West. This counsel was listened to with much impatience by the greater part of the leaders, among whom were conspicuous the legate Adhémar and the duke of Lorraine. "Ought we not, at once," said they, "to take advantage of the terror spread among the enemy? Is it right to leave them time to rally and recover from their alarm? Is it not well known that they have implored the succour of the caliph of Bagdad and the sultan of Persia? Every moment of delay may strengthen the armies of the Mussulmans, and rob the Christians of the fruits of their victories. You talk of the arrival of the Greeks; but do we stand in need of the Greeks to attack enemies already many times conquered? Was it necessary to await for new Crusaders from the West, who would come to share the glories and the conquests of the Christian army, without having shared its dangers and its labours? As to the rigours of winter, which they appeared so much to dread, it was an insult to the soldiers of Jesus Christ to think them incapable of enduring cold and rain. It was, in some sort, to compare them to those birds of passage which fly away and hide themselves in secret places, when they see the bad season approach. It was, besides, impossible to think that a siege could be protracted to any length with an army full of ardour and courage. The Crusaders had only to remember the siege of Nice, the battle of Dorylæum, and a thousand other exploits. Why should they be restrained by the fear of want and famine? Had they not hitherto found in war all the resources of war? They must know that victory had always supplied the wants of the Crusaders, and that abundance awaited them in that city of Antioch, which would not be long in opening its gates to them."

This discourse won over the most ardent and the most brave. Such as entertained a contrary opinion dreaded to be accused of timidity, and remained silent. The council decided that the siege of Antioch should at once be commenced; and on that very day the whole Christian army advanced under the walls of the city. Bohémond and Tancred took their posts on the east, opposite the gate of St. Paul; to the right of the Italians were the Normans, the Bretons, the Flemings, and the French, commanded by the two Roberts; the count de Vermandois and the count de Chartres encamped towards the north, opposite the gate of the Dog; the count of Thoulouse, the bishop of Puy, and the duke of Lorraine, with the troops they commanded, occupied the space which extended from the gate of the Dog to the spot where the Orontes turning towards the west approaches the walls of Antioch. The Crusaders left open the southern part, defended by the mountain of Orontes, and likewise neglected to invest the western side of the city, which the river protected, and thus gave the besieged liberty to make sorties or receive succours.

The Turks had shut themselves up within their walls; not a soul appeared upon the ramparts, and not the least noise was heard in the city. The Crusaders fancied that they saw in this appearance of inaction and this profound silence the discouragement and terror which had taken possession of their enemies. Blinded by the hope of an easy conquest, they took no precautions, and spread themselves about over the neighbouring country. The abundance of provisions, the beautiful sky of Syria, the fountain and the shades of Daphne, and the banks of the Orontes, famous in Pagan antiquity for the worship of Venus and Adonis, made them lose sight of the holy war, and spread license and corruption among the soldiers of Christ.

Whilst they thus neglected, amongst scenes of intemperance and debauchery, the laws of discipline and the precepts of the Scriptures, they were attacked by the garrison of Antioch, which surprised them, some scarcely guarding the camp, and the rest scattered about in the neighbouring country. All whom the hopes of pillage or the attractions of pleasure had drawn into the villages and orchards bordering upon the Orontes, met with either slavery or death. Young Albéron, archdeacon of Metz, and son of Conrad, count of Lunebourg, paid with his life for the enjoyment of amusements which accorded but very little with the austerity of his profession. He was surprised by the Turks at the moment when, stretched upon the grass, he was playing at dice with a Syrian courtezan. His head was struck off with one blow of a sabre. The courtezan was not killed till she had satisfied the brutal passion of their conqueror. Their heads, with those of a great number of Christians, were cast into the camp of the Crusaders, who now deplored their disorders, and swore to take revenge for their defeat.

The desire to repair one fault made them commit another. They resolved upon scaling the walls of Antioch, without having either ladders or machines of war. The signal was given for a general assault. Vengeance and fanaticism animated both soldiers and leaders ; but their efforts could neither shake the walls of the city, nor disturb the security of the besieged. Their attacks, though renewed several times and at several points, were always unsuccessful. Experience, for whose lessons they always paid so dearly, at length taught them, that if they wished to make themselves masters of the place, no other means were left them but to invest it completely, and prevent the arrival of any succour from without.

They established a bridge of boats upon the Orontes, and passed some troops over towards the western side of the city. All the means in their power were employed to stop the sorties of the enemy —sometimes they erected wooden fortresses near the ramparts, whilst at others they prepared balistas, which launched large stones upon the besieged. The Crusaders, in order to close the gate of the Dog upon the Turks, were obliged to heap up against it enormous beams and fragments of rock. At the same time they intrenched their camp, and redoubled their efforts to secure themselves against surprise on the part of the Saracens.

The Christian army was now solely occupied with the blockade of the city. Although this determination was dictated by imperious necessity, the slowness of a siege did not at all agree with the impatience of the warriors of the West. On their arrival before Antioch, the Christian soldiers had dissipated in a few days the provisions of several months ; they had only thought of fighting the enemy in the field of battle, and, ever full of confidence in victory, they had neither sought to protect themselves against the rigours of winter, nor to prevent the approaches of the famine with which they were threatened.

The want of provisions was not long before it was felt. As soon as winter had set in, they found themselves a prey to every species of calamity. Torrents of rain fell daily, and the plains, an abode upon which had rendered the soldiers of Christ effeminate, were almost all buried beneath the waters. The Christian camp, particularly in the valley, was submerged several times ; tempests and inundations carried away the pavilions and tents; moisture relaxed the bows; and rust gnawed into both lances and swords. The greater part of the soldiers were without clothes; and contagious diseases carried off both men and animals. Rains, cold, famine, epidemic diseases made such ravages, that, according to the report of William of Tyre, the Crusaders had not either time or space to bury thei: dead.

In the midst of the general distress, Bohémond and the duke of Normandy were commissioned to go and scour the country in search of provisions. In the course of their incursion they defeated several detachments of Saracens, and returned to the camp with a considerable booty. But the provisions they brought could not be sufficient to support a large army for any length of time; every day they made fresh incursions, and every day were less successful. All the country of Upper Syria had been ravaged by the Turks and Christians. The Crusaders who were sent on these foraging parties often put the infidels to flight; but victory, which was almost always their only resource in moments of want, could not bring back abundance to their camp.

To fill up the measure of their miseries, all communication was stopped with Constantinople; the fleets of the Pisans and Genoese no longer coasted the countries occupied by the Crusaders. The port of St. Simeon, situated at three leagues from Antioch, saw no vessel now arrive from either Greece or the West. The Flemish pirates, who had taken up the cross at Tarsus, after possessing themselves of Laodicea, had been surprised by the Greeks, and were detained prisoners during several weeks. The darkest future lay before the Christians; they no longer talked of anything but of the losses they had sustained, and of the evils with which they were threatened; each day the most afflicting intelligence was spread through the army.

It was said that the son of Sweno, king of Denmark, who had assumed the cross, and was leading fifteen hundred horsemen to the holy war, had been surprised by the Turks whilst advancing rapidly across the defiles of Cappadocia. Attacked by an enemy superior in numbers, he had defended himself during a whole day, without being able to repulse the infidels, with all the efforts of his courage or the battle-axes of his warriors. Florine, daughter of Eudes I., duke of Burgundy, who accompanied the Danish hero, and to whom he was to be married after the taking of Jerusalem, had valiantly fought by his side. Pierced by seven arrows, but still fighting, she sought with Sweno to open a passage towards the mountains, when they were overwhelmed by their enemies. They fell together on the field of battle, after having seen all their knights and their most faithful servants perish around them. "Such were the news that came to the camp of the Christians," says William of Tyre, "and so full were they of sadness and grief, that more than ever were their hearts depressed with the increase of their calamities."

Each succeeding day famine and disease made greater ravages. The provisions* brought to the camp by a few Syrians were at so high a price that the soldiers could not obtain any; the multitude filled the camp with lamentations, and there was not a Crusader who had not to weep for the death of several of his companions. Desertion was soon added to the other scourges. The greater part of the Crusaders had lost all hope of taking Antioch, or of ever reaching the Holy Land. Some sought refuge from misery in Mesopotamia, now governed by Baldwin; whilst others repaired to the cities of Cilicia which had fallen into the hands of the Christians.

The duke of Normandy withdrew to Laodicea, and did not return until he had received three summonses from the army in the name of religion and of Jesus Christ. Tatius, the general of Alex-

---

* According to William of Tyre, the bread which sufficed for the daily food of one man cost two sous instead of a denier; an ox two marks of silver, instead of five sous; a kid or a lamb five or six sous, instead of three or four deniers; the expense of a horse for a single night arose as high as eight sous, whilst it had only been two or three deniers at the commencement of the siege.

THE BATTLE OF ANTIOCH.

The sight of this city, so celebrated in the annals of Christianity, revived the enthusiasm of the Crusaders. It was within the walls of Antioch that the disciples of Jesus Christ first assumed the title of Christians, and the apostle Peter was named the first pastor of the young church. For a long time Antioch was considered in Christendom as the eldest daughter of Sion; it bore the name of Theopolis (the city of God), and the pilgrims visited it with no less respect than Jerusalem. The ramparts of Antioch, whose solidity equaled that of a rock, were three leagues in extent. "This place," says an old author, "was an object of terror to those who looked upon it, for the number of its strong and vasty towers, which amounted to three hundred and sixty." Wide ditches, the river Orontes, and marshes still further protected the inhabitants of Antioch, and cut off an approach to the city.—Book III.

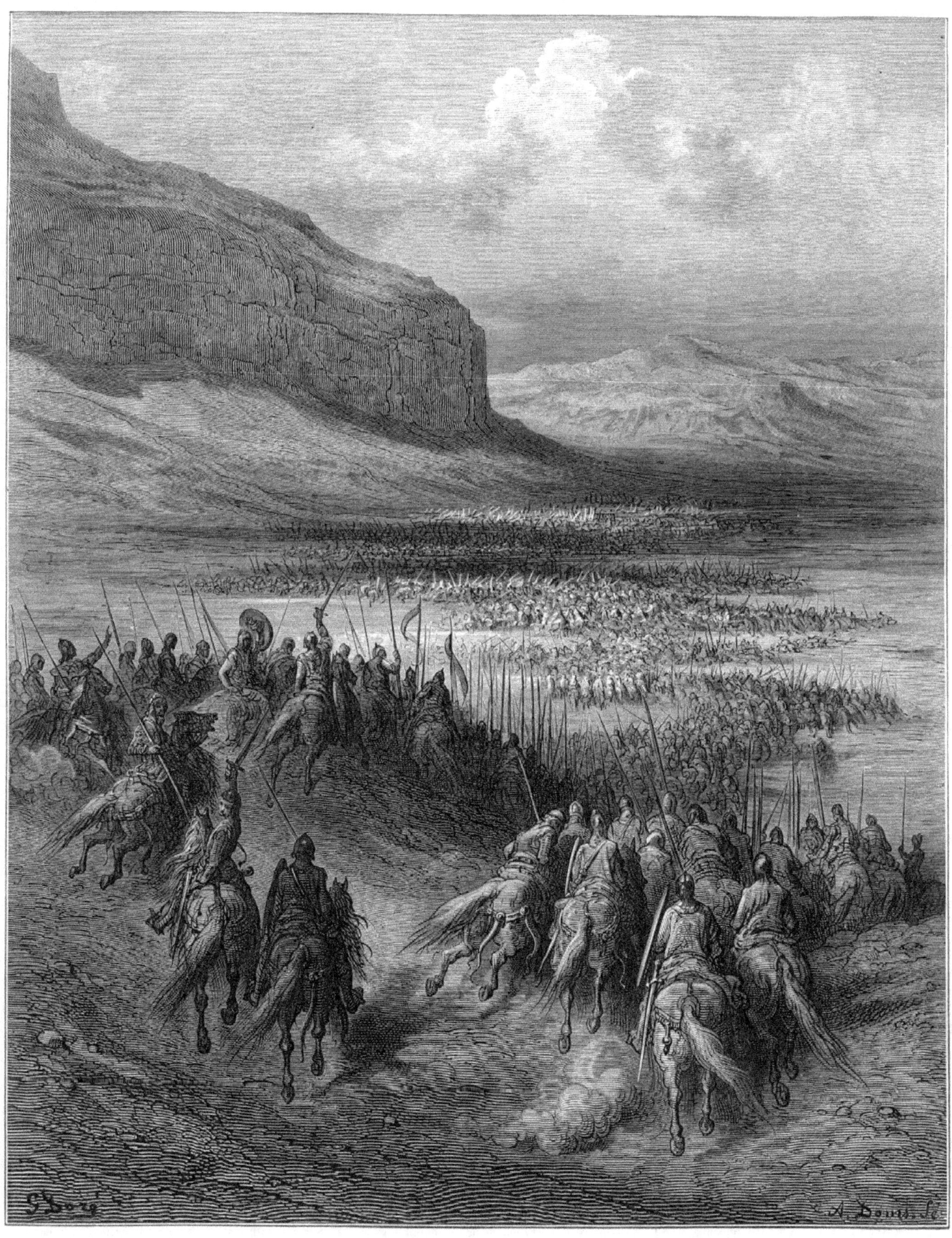

iux, quitted the camp of the Crusaders with the troops he commanded, promising to return with reinforcements and provisions. His departure caused little regret, and his promises, in which they had no confidence, did not at all alleviate the despair of the sufferers. This despair was carried to its height among the defenders of the cross when they saw those who ought to have set them an example of patience and courage desert them. William, viscount de Melun, whose extraordinary exploits with the battle-axe had procured him the name of *the Carpenter*, could not support the miseries of the siege, and deserted the standard of Christ. The preacher of the crusade, Peter the Hermit, whom the Christians, doubtless, blamed for all the miseries of the siege, was unable to bear their complaints or share their misfortunes; and despairing of the success of the expedition, he fled secretly from the camp.* His desertion caused a great scandal among the pilgrims, "and did not astonish them less," says Abbot Guibert, "than if the stars had fallen from the heavens." Pursued and overtaken by Tancred, he and William the Carpenter were brought back disgraced to the camp. The army reproached Peter with his base desertion, and made him swear upon the Scriptures that he would never again abandon a cause which he had preached. They threatened with the punishment usually inflicted upon homicides all who should follow the example he had given to his companions and brothers.

But in the midst of the corruption which reigned in the Christian army, virtue itself might have thought of flight, and have excused desertion. If contemporary accounts are to be credited, all the vices of the infamous Babylon prevailed among the liberators of Sion. Strange and unheard-of spectacle! Beneath the tents of the Crusaders famine and voluptuousness formed a hideous union; impure love, an unbounded passion for play, with all the excesses of debauch, were mingled with images of death. In their misfortunes, the greater part of the pilgrims seemed to disdain the consolations that might have been derived from piety and virtue.

And yet the bishop of Puy, and the more virtuous portion of the clergy, used every effort to reform the manners of the Crusaders. They caused the voice of religion to hurl its thunders against the excesses of libertinism and licentiousness. They recalled to their minds all the evils that the Christian army had suffered, and attributed them entirely to the vices and debaucheries of the defenders of the cross. An earthquake which was felt at this time, an aurora borealis, which was a new phenomenon to great part of the pilgrims, were pointed out to them as an announcement of the anger of Heaven. Fasts and prayers were ordered, to avert the celestial indignation. The Crusaders made processions round the camp, and hymns of penitence resounded from all parts. The priests invoked the wrath of the Church against all who should betray the cause of Christ by their sins. To add to the terrors which the threats of religion inspired, a tribunal, composed of the principal leaders of the army and the clergy, was charged with the pursuit and punishment of the guilty. Men surprised in a state of intoxication had their hair cut off; whilst blasphemers, or such as gave themselves up to a passion for play, were branded with a hot iron. A monk accused of adultery, and convicted by the ordeal of fire, was beaten with rods, and led naked through the camp. As the judges became aware of the guilty, they must have been terrified at their numbers. The severest punishments could not entirely stop the prostitution which had become almost general. They determined upon shutting up all the women in a separate camp—an extreme and imprudent measure, which confounded vice and virtue, and produced crimes more disgraceful than those they desired to prevent.

Among all these calamities, the camp of the Crusaders was filled with Syrian spies, who daily bore into the city accounts of the plans, the distress, and the despair of the besiegers. Bohémond, in order

* This great faster, says Maimbourg, who by a voluntary austerity which had acquired him such a great reputation of sanctity, made profession to eat neither bread nor meat, could not endure a necessary fast.

to deliver the army, employed a means of a nature to disgust even barbarians. My pen refuses to trace such pictures, and I leave William of Tyre, or rather his old translator, to speak. "Bohémond," says he, "commanded that several Turks, whom he held in close confinement, should be brought before him. These he caused instantly to be executed by the hands of the officers of justice, and then ordering a great fire to be lighted, he had them spitted and roasted, as flesh prepared for the supper of himself and his troops; at the same time commanding, that if any one made inquiries about what was going on, that they should be answered in this fashion: '*The princes and rulers of the camp have this day decreed in council, that all Turks or spies that shall henceforward be found in their camp, shall be, in this manner, forced to make meat with their own bodies, as well for the princes as the whole army.*'"

The servants of Bohémond executed exactly the orders and instructions which he had given them. The strangers who were in the camp soon flocked to the quarters of the prince of Tarentum, and when they saw what was going on, adds our ancient author, *were marvellously terrified,* fearing to share the fate of the victims. They made haste to quit the camp of the Christians, and everywhere on their road spread an account of that which they had seen. Their story flew from mouth to mouth, even to the most distant countries: the inhabitants of Antioch, and all the Mussulmans of the Syrian cities, were seized with terror, and no more ventured to approach the camp of the Crusaders. "By these means," says the historian we have above quoted, "it ensued from the cunning and conduct of the seigneur Bohémond, that the pest of spies was banished from the camp, and the enterprises of the Christians were not divulged to the enemy."

The bishop of Puy, at the same time, employed a stratagem much more innocent and conformable with the spirit of his ministry and his profession. He caused the lands in the neighbourhood of Antioch to be ploughed and sowed, in order to protect the Christian army from the attacks of famine, and, at the same time, to lead the Saracens to believe that nothing could exhaust the perseverance of the besiegers.

In the meanwhile the winter was stealing away; the contagious diseases committed fewer ravages; and the princes and the monasteries of Armenia sent provisions to the Christians.* The famine began to be less felt. The amelioration in the condition of the pilgrims was attributed to their penitence and their conversion; and they returned thanks to Heaven for having made them better and more worthy of its protection and mercy.

It was at this period that ambassadors from the caliph of Egypt arrived in the camp of the Crusaders. In the presence of the infidels the Christian soldiers endeavoured to conceal the traces and remembrances of the lengthened miseries they had undergone. They clothed themselves in their most precious vestments, and displayed their most brilliant arms. Knights and barons contended for the glory of strength and skill in tournaments. Nothing was seen but dancing and festivity, amidst which abundance and joy appeared to reign. The Egyptian ambassadors were received in a magnificent tent, in which were assembled all the principal leaders of the army. They did not disguise, in their address, the extreme aversion that their master had always entertained for an alliance with the Christians; but the victories which the Crusaders had gained over the Turks, those eternal enemies of the race of Ali, had led him to believe that God himself had sent them into Asia, as the instruments of his vengeance and justice. The Egyptian caliph was disposed to ally himself with the victorious Christians, and was preparing to enter Palestine and Syria. As he had learnt that the wishes of the Crusaders were confined to an ardent desire to behold Jerusalem, he promised to restore the Christian churches, to protect their worship, and open the gates of the Holy City to all the pilgrims, upon con-

* This circumstance is taken from an Armenian manuscript of Matthew of Edessa. It is surprising that the Latin historians have made no mention of it; but they never speak of any means of providing provisions employed by the Crusaders.

dition that they would repair thither without arms, and would remain there no longer than one month. If the Crusaders submitted to these conditions, the caliph promised to become their most generous supporter; if they declined the blessing of his friendship, the nations of Egypt and Ethiopia, with all those that inhabit Asia and Africa, from the Straits of Gades to the gates of Bagdad, would arise at the voice of the legitimate vicar of the prophet, and would show the warriors of the West the power of their arms.

This discourse excited violent murmurs in the assembly of the Christians; one of the chiefs arose to answer it, and addressing himself to the deputies of the caliph: "The religion that we follow," said he to them, "has inspired us with the design of re-establishing its empire in the places in which it was born; and we stand in no need of the concurrence of the powers of the earth to accomplish our vows. We do not come into Asia to receive laws or benefits from Mussulmans, nor have we forgotten, besides, the outrages committed by Egyptians upon the pilgrims of the West; we still remember that Christians, under the reign of the caliph Hakem, were delivered over to executioners, and that their churches, particularly that of the Holy Sepulchre, were razed to the ground. Yes, without doubt, we have the intention of visiting Jerusalem, but we have also taken an oath to deliver it from the yoke of the infidels. God, who has honoured it by his sufferings, wills that he shall be there served by his people. The Christians resolve to be both its guardians and its masters. Go and tell him who sent you to make choice of peace or war; tell him that the Christians encamped before Antioch fear neither the nations of Egypt, nor those of Asia, nor those of Bagdad, and that they only ally themselves with powers which respect the laws of justice and the standards of Jesus Christ."

The orator who spoke thus expressed the opinion and sentiments of the assembly; nevertheless, they did not entirely reject the alliance with the Egyptians. Deputies were chosen from the Christian army to accompany the ambassadors of Cairo on their return, and to bear to the caliph the definitive propositions of peace of the Crusaders.

Scarcely had the deputies left the camp of the Christians, when the latter obtained a fresh victory over the Turks. The sultans of Aleppo and Damascus, with the emirs of Cæsarea, Emessa, and Hieropolis, had raised an army of twenty thousand horse to succour Antioch; and this army was already on its march towards the city, when it was surprised and cut to pieces by the prince of Tarentum and the count de St. Gilles, who had gone out to meet it. The Turks lost in this battle two thousand men and one thousand horses; and the city of Harem, in which they in vain sought an asylum after their defeat, fell into the hands of the Christians. At the moment the ambassadors from Egypt were about to embark at the port of St. Simeon, the heads and spoils of two hundred Mussulmans were brought to them upon four camels. The conquerors cast two hundred other heads into the city of Antioch, whose garrison was still in expectation of succour; and they stuck a great number upon pikes round the walls. They exhibited thus these horrible trophies, to avenge themselves of the insults the Saracens had, on their ramparts, heaped upon an image of the Virgin which had fallen into their hands.

But the Crusaders were soon to signalize tnemselves in a much more perilous and murderous battle. A fleet of Genoese and Pisans had entered the port of St. Simeon, and the news of their arrival causing the greatest joy in the army, a great number of soldiers left the camp and hastened towards the port, some to learn news from Europe, and others to buy the provisions of which they stood so much in need. As they were returning loaded with provisions, and for the greater part unarmed, they were unexpectedly attacked and dispersed by a body of four thousand Turks, who laid wait for them on their passage. In vain the prince of Tarentum, the count de St. Gilles, and Bishop Adhémar flew to their aid with their troops; the Christians could not resist the shock of the infidels, and retreated in disorder.

The account of this defeat soon spread alarm among the Crusaders who had remained before the city. Immediately Godfrey, to whom danger gave supreme authority, ordered the leaders and soldiers to fly to arms.* Accompanied by his brother Eustace, the two Roberts, and the count de Vermandois, he crossed the Orontes, and hastened to seek the enemy, still engaged in following up their first advantage. As soon as he came in presence of the Saracens, he commanded the other chiefs to follow his example, and rushed, sword in hand, into the thickest of the enemy's ranks. The latter, accustomed to fight at a distance, and principally to employ the bow and arrow, could not resist the sword and lance of the Crusaders. They took to flight, some towards the mountains, and others towards the city. Accien, who, from the towers of his palace, had witnessed the victorious attack of the Crusaders, immediately sent a numerous detachment to renew the fight. He accompanied his soldiers as far as the gate of the Bridge, which he caused to be shut after them, telling them it should only be opened to them when they returned victorious.

This new body of Saracens were soon beaten and dispersed; and there remained no hope to them but to endeavour to regain the city. But Godfrey, who had foreseen everything, had posted himself upon an eminence between the fugitives and the gates of Antioch. It was there that the carnage was renewed; the Christians were animated by their victory, and the Saracens by their despair and the cries of the inhabitants of the city, who were assembled on the ramparts. Nothing can paint the frightful tumult of this fresh conflict. The clashing of arms and the cries of the combatants would not permit the soldiers to hear the orders of their leaders. They fought man to man, and without order, whilst clouds of dust covered the field of battle. Chance directed the blows of both the conquerors and the conquered, and the Saracens, heaped as it were together by their terror, impeded their own flight. The confusion was so great that several of the Crusaders were killed by their companions and brothers in arms. A great number of Saracens fell almost without resistance under the swords of the Christians, and more than two thousand, who sought safety in flight, were drowned in the Orontes. "The old men of Antioch," says William of Tyre, "whilst contemplating this bloody catastrophe from the height of their walls, grieved that they had lived so long, whilst the women who witnessed the death of their children, lamented their own fecundity." The carnage continued during the whole day; and it was not till night-fall that Accien allowed the gates to be opened for the reception of the miserable remains of his troops, still hotly pursued by the Crusaders.

The leaders and soldiers of the army had performed prodigies of valour. Bohémond, Tancred, Adhémar, Baldwin du Bourg, and Eustace had appeared everywhere, leading their warriors in the paths of danger. The whole army spoke of the lance-thrusts and marvellous feats of arms of the count de Vermandois and the two Roberts. The duke of Normandy sustained a single combat with a leader of the infidels, who advanced towards him surrounded by his troop. With one blow of his sword he split his head to the shoulder, and, as the Saracen fell dead at his feet, exclaimed, "*I devote thy impure soul to the powers of hell.*" Tancred, says Raoul de Caen, distinguished himself amongst the most intrepid of the knights. In the heat of the *mêlée*, the Christian hero, as modest as he was brave, made his squire swear to preserve silence upon the exploits of which he was a witness. "Godfrey, who, in this memorable day, had displayed the skill of a great captain, signalized his bravery and vast strength by actions which both history and poetry have celebrated. No armour seemed proof against his trenchant blade; lances, helmets, and cuirasses flew in shivers beneath its strokes. A Sar-

* A chronicle printed at Paris in 1517, which bears for title, "Grand Voyage d'Outre-Mer," places the following speech in the mouth of Godfrey:—"Brave seigneurs, my brothers and companions in Jesus Christ; if the news we hear be true, that for our sins these cruel dogs have thus killed these valiant men, and of great consideration, I only perceive two things, that we shall die with them as good and loyal Christians, assured of receiving our guerdon from our Lord and Saviour Jesus Christ, for whose service we came here and have quitted our native lands and our kindred; or if it should please him, that he allow us to take vengeance and obtain victory over these vile dogs who have thus degraded and weakened Christianity in its valiant men."

FLORINE OF BURGUNDY.

It was said that the son of Sweno, king of Denmark, who had assumed the cross, and was leading fifteen hundred horsemen to the holy war, had been surprised by the Turks whilst advancing rapidly across the plains of Cappadocia. Attacked by an enemy superior in numbers, he had defended himself during a whole day, without being able to repulse the infidels, with all the efforts of his courage or the battle-axes of his warriors. Florine, daughter of Eudes I., duke of Burgundy, who accompanied the Danish hero, and to whom he was to be married after the taking of Jerusalem, had valiantly fought by his side. Pierced by seven arrows, but still fighting, she sought with Sweno to open a passage towards the mountains, when they were overwhelmed by their enemies. They fell together on the field of battle, after having seen all their knights and most faithful servants perish around them.—Book III.

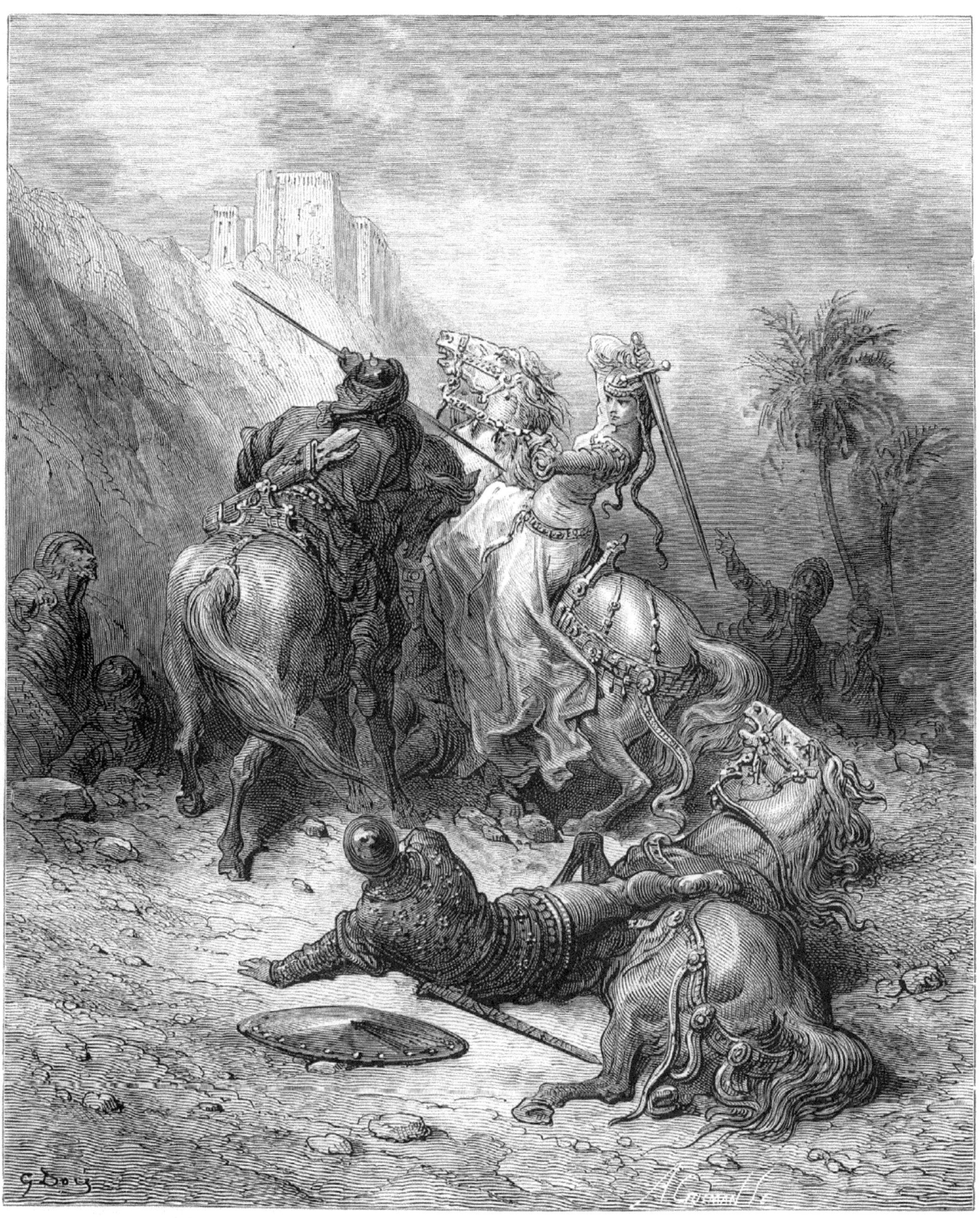

acen of surpassing strength and stature offered him single combat in the midst of the *mêlée*, and with his first blow dashed the shield of Godfrey in pieces. Indignant at such audacity, the Christian hero raised himself in his stirrups, and rushing on his antagonist, dealt him so terrible a blow on the shoulder, that he divided his body into two parts. One part, say the historians, fell to the ground, whilst the other remained on the horse, which returned to the city, where this spectacle redoubled the consternation of the besieged. In spite of these astonishing exploits, the Christians sustained a considerable loss. Whilst celebrating the heroic valour of the Crusaders, contemporary history is astonished at the multitude of martyrs which the Saracens sent to heaven, and who, on arriving in the abodes of the elect, with crowns upon their heads, and palm branches in their hands, addressed God in these words: "Why have you not spared our blood which has flowed for you this day?"

The infidels passed the night in burying such as had been killed under the walls of the city. They interred them near a mosque built on the outer side of the bridge of the Orontes. After the funeral ceremonies, they returned into Antioch. As, according to the custom of the Mussulmans, these bodies had been buried with their arms, their ornaments, and their vestments, this plunder held out too strong a temptation for the gross multitude that followed the army of the Crusaders. They crossed the Orontes, precipitated themselves in a crowd upon the graves of the Saracens, exhumed the dead bodies, and tore off the arms and habiliments with which they were covered. They quickly returned to exhibit in the camp the silk stuffs, bucklers, lances, javelins, and rich swords found in the coffins; nor did this spectacle at all disgust the knights and barons. On the day following the battle, among the spoils of the vanquished, they contemplated with joy fifteen hundred heads separated from their trunks, which were paraded in triumph through the army, recalling to them their own victory, and the loss they had inflicted on the infidels. All these heads were cast into the Orontes, and, together with the bodies of the Mussulmans drowned in the conflict of the preceding day, carried the news of the victory to the Genoese and Pisans disembarked at the port of St. Simeon. The Crusaders, who, at the commencement of the battle, had fled towards the sea or the mountains, and who had been lamented as dead, returned to the camp, and joined their brethren in the thanks offered to heaven for the triumphs of the Christian army. From this time the chiefs thought of nothing but taking advantage of the terror with which they had inspired the Saracens. Masters of the cemetery of the Mussulmans, the Crusaders destroyed the mosque which had been built outside the walls of the city, and employed the stones of the tombs even in erecting a fortress before the gate of the bridge, by which the besieged made their sorties. Raymond, who had been accused of want of zeal for the holy war, caused the fort to be constructed, and charged himself with the defence of this dangerous post. It was proposed to raise another fortress near the first, and as no other of the leaders presented himself to forward the construction of it, Tancred offered his services to the Crusaders. But, generous and loyal knight as he was, he possessed nothing but his sword and his renown. He asked the necessary money of his companions, and himself undertook the dangers of the enterprise. All were eager to second his courageous devotedness; the labours which he directed were soon finished, and from that period the besieged found themselves completely enclosed within the circle of their walls.

The Crusaders, after having thus finished the blockade of the place, surprised the Syrians who had been accustomed to bring provisions into Antioch, and only gave them liberty and life upon their swearing to supply the Christian army. Having learnt that Accien had sent a great part of the horses of his garrison into a valley at a few leagues from the city, they repaired thither by circuitous routes, and got possession of this rich booty. Two thousand horses, and as many mules, were led in triumph into the camp of the Christians.

As the fleet of the Pisans and Genoese had brought with them a great number of labourers and engineers, they were employed in directing and carrying on the works of the siege. Machines of war were constructed, and the city of Antioch was pressed more vigourously, and threatened on all sides. Whilst despair supplied the place of courage among the Saracens, the zeal and emulation of the Crusaders were redoubled. Many whom misery or fear had driven from the Christian army rejoined their standards, and sought by their exertions to obliterate the remembrance of their desertion. The besiegers allowed themselves no repose, and only seemed to live to fight. The women seconded the valour of the warriors. Some mingled with them in the ranks, whilst others bore them food and ammunition to the battle-field. Children even formed themselves into troops, exercised themselves in military evolutions, and took up arms against the Saracens. The inhabitants of Antioch opposed their children to those of the Christians, and several times these young combatants came to blows in the presence of the besiegers and the besieged, who animated them with voice and gesture, and joined the combat even to support such of their party as seemed to yield.

There was formed at the same time another military force still more formidable to the Saracens. The mendicants and vagabonds who followed the Christian army were employed in the labours of the siege, and worked under the orders of a captain, who took the title of "*Roi truant*," or king of the beggars. They received pay from the general treasury of the Crusaders, and as soon as they were in a condition to purchase arms and clothes, the king renounced them as his subjects, and forced them to enter into one of the troops of the army. This measure, whilst forcing the vagabonds to abandon a life of dangerous idleness, changed them into useful auxiliaries. As they were accused of violating tombs and feeding on human flesh, they inspired great terror among the infidels, and the sight of them alone put to flight the defenders of Antioch, who trembled at the thoughts of falling into their hands.

Antioch was so closely pressed, and the garrison had so little means of defence left, that the Crusaders expected every day to become masters of it. Accien demanded a truce of them, and promised to surrender if he were not soon relieved. The Crusaders, ever full of blind confidence, had the imprudence to accept the proposals of the governor. As soon as they had concluded a truce with the Saracens, the leaders of the army, who scarcely ever agreed, except upon the field of battle, and whom the presence of danger did not always unite, were upon the point of declaring war against one another.

Baldwin, prince of Edessa, had sent magnificent presents to Godfrey, the two Roberts, the count de Vermandois, and the counts of Blois and Chartres, but in the distribution of his favours had, designedly, omitted Bohémond and his soldiers. Nothing more was necessary to create division. Whilst the rest of the army were celebrating the liberality of Baldwin, the prince of Tarentum and his warriors breathed nothing but complaints and murmurs.

At this time a richly-ornamented tent, which an Armenian prince destined for Godfrey, and which, falling into the hands of Pancracius, was sent to Bohémond, became a fresh subject of trouble and discord. Godfrey haughtily claimed the present which had been intended for him, and Bohémond refused to give it up. On each side they proceeded to injurious terms and threats; they were even ready to have recourse to arms, and the blood of the Christians was about to flow for a miserable quarrel; but at length the prince of Tarentum, abandoned by the greater part of the army, and overcome by the prayers of his friends, gave up the tent to his rival, consoling himself in his vexation, with the hope that war would soon put him in possession of a richer booty.

William of Tyre, who has transmitted to us this account, is astonished to see the wise Godfrey claim such a frivolous object with so much heat; and in his surprise he compares the weakness of the hero to the slumbers of the good Homer. His thought would have been more just if he had compared the discords and quarrels of the leaders of the crusade to those which troubled the camp of the Greeks, and so long retarded the taking of Troy. Whilst these quarrels engaged the attention of the whole Christian army, the inhabitants of Antioch were introducing reinforcements into the city, and preparing for a fresh resistance. When they had received the succours and provisions necessary to defend themselves and prolong the siege, they broke the truce, and again began the war, with all the advantages that a peace too easily granted them had procured.

Antioch, after a siege of seven months, would have escaped from the hands of the Christians, if stratagem, policy, and ambition had not effected for them that which patience and bravery had been unable to achieve. Bohémond, whose sole motive for undertaking the crusade had been a desire to improve his fortunes, was constantly on the watch for an opportunity of realizing his projects. Baldwin's great success had awakened his jealousy, and haunted him even in his sleep. He dared to direct his views to the possession of Antioch, and was so far favoured by circumstances, as to meet with a man who might be able to place this city in his power. This man, whose name was Phirous, was, whatever some historians who give him a noble origin may say, the son of an Armenian, who was by trade a maker of cuirasses. Of a restless and busy character, he was constantly anxious to change and improve his condition. He had abjured the Christian religion from a spirit of inconstancy, and in the hope of advancing his fortune; he was endowed with admirable self-possession, and with audacity proof against any accident; and was at all times ready to perform that for money which could only have been expected from the most ardent fanaticism. Nothing appeared unjust or impossible to him that promised to gratify his ambition or his avarice. Being active, adroit, and insinuating, he had wormed himself into the confidence of Accien, and was admitted into his council. The prince of Antioch had intrusted him with the command of three of the principal towers of the place. He defended them at first with zeal, but without any advantage to his fortune, and he grew weary of a barren fidelity the moment his busy brain suggested that treason might be more profitable. In the intervals of the various conflicts he had had many opportunities of seeing the prince of Tarentum. These two men divined each other's character at the first glance, and it was not long before this sympathy produced mutual confidence. In their first meetings Phirous complained of the outrages he had experienced from the Mussulmans; he deeply regretted having abandoned the religion of Christ, and wept over the persecutions the Christians had suffered in Antioch. No more than this was required to place the prince of Tarentum in possession of the secret thoughts of Phirous. He commended both his remorse and his good feeling, and made him the most magnificent promises. Then the renegado opened his heart to him. They swore an inviolable friendship to each other, and planned an active correspondence. They met several times afterwards, but always with the greatest secrecy. At every interview Bohémond told Phirous that the fate of the Christians was in his hands, and that it only rested with himself to merit their gratitude, and receive from them vast recompenses. On his side, Phirous protested that he was anxious to serve the Christians, whom he considered as his brothers, and, in order to assure the prince of Tarentum of his fidelity, or else to excuse his treason, he said that Jesus Christ had appeared to him, and had advised him to give up Antioch to the Christians. Bohémond required no such protestation. He had no difficulty in believing what he so ardently desired, and as soon as he had agreed with Phirous upon the means of executing the projects they had so long meditated, he called an assembly of the principal leaders of the Christian army. He began by laying before them with much earnestness both the evils with which the Crusaders had hitherto been afflicted, and the still greater evils with which they were threatened. He added, that a powerful army was advancing to the assistance of Antioch; that a retreat could not be effected without disgrace and danger; and that there remained no safety for the Christians but in the capture of the city.

It was true, the place was defended by impregnable ramparts; but they should recollect that all victories were not obtained by force of arms or in the field of battle; and that such as were won by address were neither the least important nor the least glorious. They, then, who could not be conquered must be deceived, and the enemy must be overcome by a great but skilful enterprise. Among the inhabitants of Antioch, so diverse in their manners and religions, so opposed in their interests, there must be some to be found who would be accessible to the bait of gold, or the allurements of brilliant promises. The question of a service so important to the Christian army, was of such magnitude that it was right to promote every kind of undertaking. The possession of Antioch itself did not appear to him to be too high a reward for the zeal of him who should be sufficiently adroit, or sufficiently fortunate, as to throw open the gates of the city to the Crusaders.

Bohémond was careful not to explain himself more clearly, but his purpose was easily divined by the jealous ambition of some of the leaders, who perhaps entertained the same views as himself. Raymond, particularly, warmly refuted the artful insinuations of the prince of Tarentum. "We are all," said he, "brothers and companions, and it would be unjust, after all have run the same risks, that one alone should gather the fruits of our joint labours. For myself," added he, casting a look of anger and contempt upon Bohémond, "I have not traversed so many countries, braved so many perils, lavished so much blood and treasure, or sacrificed so many of my soldiers, to repay with the price of our conquests some gross artifice or shameful stratagem worthy only of women." These vehement words had all the success to be expected among warriors accustomed to prevail by force of arms, and who esteemed no conquest that was not the reward of valour. The greater number of the leaders rejected the proposition of the prince of Tarentum, and added their railleries to those of Raymond. Bohémond, whom history has surnamed the Ulysses of the Latins, did all in his power to restrain himself and conceal his vexation. He went out from the council smiling, persuaded that necessity would soon bring the Crusaders to his opinion.

As soon as he had regained his tent, he sent emissaries through all the quarters of the camp to spread secretly the most alarming intelligence. As he foresaw, consternation seized the Christians. Some of the leaders were sent to ascertain the truth of the reports prevalent in the camp; and soon returned with an account that Kerboghâ, sultan of Mossoul, was advancing towards Antioch with an army of two hundred thousand men, collected on the banks of the Euphrates and the Tigris. This army, which had threatened the city of Edessa and ravaged Mesopotamia, was at a distance of only seven days' march. At this recital the fears of the Crusaders were redoubled. Bohémond passed through the ranks, exaggerating the danger, and affecting to show more depression and terror than all the rest; but in his heart he was delighted, and smiled at the idea of soon seeing all his hopes accomplished. The leaders again assembled to deliberate upon the means necessary to be taken in such perilous circumstances. Two opinions divided the council. Some wished that the siege should be raised, and that they should march to meet the Saracens; whilst others were of opinion that the army should be formed into two bodies, one of which should act against Kerboghâ, whilst the other should remain to guard the camp. This last opinion appeared likely to prevail, when Bohémond demanded permission to speak. He had not much difficulty in making them sensible of the impracticability of both the plans proposed. If they raised the siege, they would be placed between the garrison of Antioch and a formidable army. If they continued the blockade of the city, and half of the army only went to meet Kerboghâ, they were almost certain of a defeat. "The greatest perils," added the prince of Tarentum, "surround us. Time presses; to-morrow, perhaps, it will be too late to act; by to-morrow we may have lost the fruits of all our labours and all our victories; but no, I cannot think so; God, who has led us hitherto by the hand, will not allow that we shall have fought for his cause in vain. He *will* save the Christian army, he *will* conduct us to the tomb of his Son. If you will accept the proposal I have made to you, to-morrow the standard of the cross shall float over the walls of Antioch, and we will march in triumph to Jerusalem."

When he had finished these words, Bohémond showed the letters of Phirous, who promised to give up the three towers which he commanded. Phirous said that he was ready to perform this promise, but he declared he would have nothing to do with any one but the prince of Tarentum. He required, as the price of his services, that Bohémond should remain master of Antioch. The Italian prince added that he had already given considerable sums to Phirous; that he alone had obtained his confidence, and that a reciprocal confidence was the surest guarantee of the success of so difficult an enterprise. "As for the rest," continued he, "if a better means of saving the army can be found, I am ready to approve of it, and willingly renounce my share in a conquest upon which the safety of all the Crusaders depends."

The danger became every day more pressing; it was shameful to fly, imprudent to fight, and dangerous to temporize. Fear silenced all interests and all rivalry. The more opposition the leaders had shown at first to the project of Bohémond, the more eagerly did they now produce cogent reasons for adopting it. A divided conquest became no longer a conquest. To divide or share Antioch might give birth to a crowd of divisions in the army, and lead to its ruin. They only gave that which was really not yet their own; and they gave it to secure the lives of the Christians. It were better that one man should profit by the labours of all, than that all should perish for opposing the good fortunes of that one. Moreover, the taking of Antioch was not the object of the crusade—they had taken up arms to deliver Jerusalem. Every delay was opposed to that which religion looked for from its soldiers, to that which the West expected from its bravest knights. All the leaders, with the exception of the inflexible Raymond, united in according the principality of Antioch to Bohémond, and conjured him to hasten the execution of his project.

Upon leaving the council, the prince of Tarentum sent information of the resolution of the leaders to Phirous, who placed his own son in the prince's hands as a hostage. The execution of the plan was fixed for the next day. To lull the garrison of Antioch in the greatest security, it was agreed that the Christian army should quit the camp, and direct its march at first towards the route by which the prince of Mossoul was expected to arrive, and that at nightfall it should meet under the walls of Ascalon. On the following day, early in the morning, the troops received orders to prepare for their departure. At some hours before night the Crusaders issued from their camp, and marched away, trumpets sounding and standards flying. After a march of a short distance, they retraced their steps, and returned in silence under the walls of Antioch. At a signal given by the prince of Tarentum, they halted in a valley on the west, and near to the tower of the Three Sisters, in which Phirous commanded. It was there that the leaders revealed to the army the secret of the great expedition which was to open to them the gates of the city.

The projects of Phirous and Bohémond, however, were very near failing. At the moment that the Christian army quitted their camp, and all was prepared for carrying out the plot, a report of treason all at once was spread throughout Antioch. The Christians and newly-converted Mussulmans were suspected; the name of Phirous even was whispered, and he was accused of keeping up an intelligence with the Crusaders. He was obliged to appear before Accien, who interrogated him closely, and fixed his eyes intently upon him in order to penetrate his thoughts; but Phirous dispersed all his suspicions by his firm countenance. He himself proposed the proper measures to be taken against the traitors, and advised his master to change the commanders of the principal towers. This advice was approved of, and Accien determined to follow it on the morrow. In the mean time orders were given to load with chains and put to death, during the darkness of the night, all the Christians that should be found in the city. The renegade was then sent back to his post, loaded with praises for his carefulness and fidelity. At the approach of night everything appeared tranquil in Antioch, and Phirous, escaped from such threatening danger, awaited the Crusaders in the tower which he had agreed to surrender to them.

As his brother commanded a tower near his own, Phirous went to find him, and sought to engage him in the plot. "Brother," said he to him, "you know that the Crusaders have quitted their camp, and that they are gone to meet the army of Kerboghâ. When I think of the miseries they have endured, and on the death which threatens them, I cannot help feeling a sort of pity for them. You are not ignorant, likewise, that this night all the Christian inhabitants of Antioch, after having undergone so many outrages, are going to be massacred by the orders of Accien. I cannot help pitying them; I cannot forget that we were born in the same religion, and that we were formerly brothers." These words did not produce the effect he expected. "I am surprised," replied his brother, "that you should pity men who ought to be objects of horror to us. Before the Christians appeared under the walls of Antioch, we were loaded with benefits. Since they have besieged the city, we have passed our lives in dangers and alarms. May all the evils they have brought upon us recoil upon them! As to the Christians who live amongst us, do you not know that the greater part of them are traitors, and that they think of nothing but delivering us up to the sword of our enemies?" On finishing these words, he cast a threatening look upon Phirous. The renegade saw that he was suspected. He could not acknowledge a brother in the man who refused to be his accomplice, and as his only answer, plunged his dagger into his heart.

At length the decisive moment arrived. The night was dark, and a rising storm increased the depth of the obscurity. The wind, which rattled among the roofs of the buildings, and the peals of thunder, prevented the sentinels from hearing any noise around the ramparts. The heavens seemed inflamed towards the west, and the sight of a comet which then appeared in the horizon, seemed to announce to the superstitious minds of the Crusaders the destined moment for the ruin and destruction of the infidels.*

They awaited the signal with impatience. The garrison of Antioch was plunged in sleep; Phirous alone watched, and meditated his conspiracy. A Lombard named *Payen,* sent by Bohémond, mounted the tower by a ladder of leather. Phirous received him, telling him all was ready; and as an evidence of his fidelity, pointed to the dead body of his brother, whom he had just slain. Whilst they were conversing, an officer of the garrison came to visit the posts. He presented himself, with a lantern in his hand, before the tower Phirous commanded. The latter, without appearing the least disturbed, made the emissary of Bohémond conceal himself, and went forward to meet the officer. After receiving praise for his vigilance, he hastened to send Payen back with instructions for the prince of Tarentum. The Lombard, on his return to the army, related what he had seen, and, on the part of Phirous, conjured Bohémond not to lose another moment.

But all at once fear took possession of the soldiers; at the moment of execution all saw the whole extent of the danger, and not one of them put himself forward to mount the rampart. In vain Godfrey and the prince of Tarentum employed by turns promises and threats; both leaders and soldiers remained motionless. Bohémond himself ascended by a ladder of ropes, in the hope that he should be seconded by the most brave; but nobody felt it his duty to follow in his footsteps. He reached the tower alone, where Phirous reproached him warmly for his delay. Bohémond hastily descended to his soldiers, and repeated to them that all was ready to receive them. His discourse, and still more,

* A comet appeared on the very night of the taking of Antioch, June 3, 1098.

his example, at length reanimated their courage, and sixty of them commenced the escalade. They ascended by the ladder of leather, led on by one Foulcher de Chartres, whom the historian of Tancred compares to an eagle conducting her young ones, and flying at their head. Among these sixty brave men was the count of Flanders, together with several of the principal chiefs. Very soon sixty more Crusaders quickly pressed upon the heels of the first,* and these again were followed by such numbers and with such precipitation, that the parapet to which the ladder was fixed tottered, and at length fell with a loud crash into the ditch. Such as were nearly attaining the summit of the tower fell upon the lances and swords of their companions who were following them. Disorder and confusion prevailed among the assailants, nevertheless the leaders of the plot viewed everything with a tranquil eye. Phirous embraced his new companions over the bloody corpse of his brother; he even yielded to their swords another brother who happened to be with him, and then surrendered to the Crusaders the three towers intrusted to his command. Seven other towers soon fell into their hands, and Phirous loudly summoned the whole Christian army to his aid. He fixed a new ladder to the rampart, by which the most impatient ascended, and he pointed out to others a gate which they might easily burst open, and by it crowds rushed into the city.

Godfrey, Raymond, and the duke of Normandy were soon in the streets of Antioch at the head of their battalions. All the trumpets were sounded, and from the four hills the city resounded with the terrible cry of "*It is the will of God! It is the will of God!*" At the first report of the tumult, the Christians dwelling in Antioch all believed that their last hour was come, and that the Mussulmans were about to sacrifice them. The latter, half asleep, poured out of their houses to ascertain the cause of the noise they heard, and died without knowing who were the traitors, or by whose hands they were slain. Some, when aware of the danger, fled towards the mountain upon which the citadel was built, whilst others rushed out at the gates of the city. All who could not fly fell beneath the swords of the conquerors.

In the midst of this bloody victory, Bohémond did not neglect taking formal possession of Antioch, and at dawn his red standard was seen floating over one of the highest towers of the city. At the sight of this the Crusaders who were left in charge of the camp broke into loud acclamations of joy, and hastened to take a part in this fresh conquest of the Christians. The slaughter of the Mussulmans was continued with unabated fury. The greater part of the Christians of Antioch, who, during the siege, had suffered much from the tyranny of the infidels, joined their liberators, several exhibiting the fetters by which they had been loaded by the Turks, and thus further provoking the vindictive spirit of the victorious army. The public places were covered with dead bodies, and blood flowed in torrents in the streets. The soldiers penetrated into the houses; religious emblems pointed out such as were Christians, sacred hymns indicated their brethren; but everything that was not marked with a cross became the object of vengeance, and all who pronounced not the name of Christ were massacred without mercy.

In a single night more than six thousand of the inhabitants of Antioch perished. Many of those who had fled into the neighbouring fields were pursued and brought back into the city, where they found either slavery or death. In the first moments of the confusion, Accien, seeing that he was betrayed, and no longer daring to trust any of his officers, resolved to fly towards Mesopotamia, and go to meet the army of Kerboghâ. Escaping through one of the gates, he proceeded without an escort over mountains and through forests, till he fell in with some Armenian wood-cutters. These

* All these details of the siege and the taking of Antioch, which appear to belong to the epopea, are taken literally from the ancient historians of the crusades. See *Albert d'Aix*, lib. iii. and iv.; *William of Tyre*, lib. v.; *Robert the Monk*, lib. v. and vi.; and the authors of the *Collection of Bongars*. All these historians agree in the principal circumstances.

men at once recognised the prince of Antioch, and as he bore upon his countenance marks of depression and grief, they judged that the city must be taken. One of them, drawing near to him, snatched his sword from him, and plunged it into his body. His head was carried to the new masters of Antioch, and Phirous had an opportunity of contemplating without fear the features of him who, the day before, might have sentenced him to death. After having received great riches as the reward of his treachery, this renegade embraced the Christianity he had abandoned, and followed the Crusaders to Jerusalem. Two years afterwards, his ambition not being satisfied, he returned to the religion of Mahomet, and died abhorred by both Mussulmans and Christians, whose cause he had by turns embraced and betrayed.

When the Christians were tired of slaughter, they prepared to attack the citadel; but as it was built upon a mountain, inaccessible on most sides, all their efforts were useless. They contented themselves with surrounding it with soldiers and machines of war, in order to confine the garrison, and then spread themselves throughout the city, giving way to all the intoxication which their victory inspired. The pillage of Antioch had yielded them immense riches; and although they had found but a small stock of provisions, they abandoned themselves to the most extravagant excesses of intemperance and debauchery.

These events passed in the early days of June, 1098; the siege of Antioch had been begun in the month of October of the preceding year. After this victory, three days passed quickly away in the midst of rejoicings, but the fourth was a day of fear and mourning.

A formidable army of Saracens was drawing near to Antioch. From the earliest period of the siege, Accien, and the sultan of Nice, whom the Christians had despoiled of his dominions, had applied to all the Mussulman powers to procure assistance against the warriors of the West. The supreme head of the Seljoucides, the sultan of Persia, had promised to aid them; and at his voice all Corassan, says Matthew of Edessa, Media, Babylon, a part of Asia Minor, and all the East, from Damascus and the sea-coast to Jerusalem and Arabia, had arisen at once to attack the Christians.* Kerboghâ, sultan of Mossoul, commanded this army of the Mussulmans. This warrior had fought for a length of time, at one period for the sultan of Persia (Barkiarok), at others for the various princes of the family of Malek-Scha, who contended for the empire. Often defeated, and twice a prisoner, he had grown old amidst the tumults of civil war. As full of contempt for the Christians as of confidence in himself, a true model of the fierce Circassian celebrated by Tasso, he considered himself the liberator of Asia, and traversed Mesopotamia with all the pomp and splendour of a conqueror. The sultans of Nice, Aleppo, and Damascus, with the governor of Jerusalem and twenty-eight emirs from Persia, Palestine, and Syria, marched under his command. The Mussulman soldiers were animated by a thirst for vengeance, and swore by their prophet to exterminate all the Christians. On the third day after the taking of Antioch, the army of Kerboghâ pitched its tents on the banks of the Orontes.

The Christians were made aware of its arrival by a detachment of three hundred horsemen, who came to reconnoitre the place, and advanced even under the walls. Inquietude and alarm succeeded immediately to festivity and rejoicing. They found that they had not stores to sustain a siege; and several of their leaders were sent with their troops towards the port of St. Simeon, and into the neighbouring country, to collect all the provisions they could find; but the territory of Antioch had been so completely ravaged during many months, that they could not procure anything like enough for the maintenance of a numerous army. The return of all who had been sent in quest of provisions completed the terror of the Christians. At the very moment of their arrival the infidels attacked the

* Matthew of Edessa estimates this army at a hundred thousand horse and three hundred thousand foot. Abulfaradge speaks of "*mille mille*" horse. The Latin historians do not exaggerate so much, but do not at all agree in their accounts.

BOHÉMOND ALONE MOUNTS THE RAMPART OF ANTIOCH

The night was dark, and a rising storm increased the depth of the obscurity. The wind, which rattled among the roofs of the buildings, and the peals of thunder, prevented the sentinels from hearing any noise around the ramparts. The heavens seemed inflamed towards the west, and the sight of a comet, which then appeared in the horizon, seemed to announce to the superstitious minds of the Crusaders the destined moment for the ruin and destruction of the infidels.

But all at once fear took possession of the soldiers; at the moment of execution all saw the whole extent of the danger, and not one of them put himself forward to mount the rampart. In vain Godfrey and the prince of Tarentum employed by turns promises and threats; both leaders and soldiers remained motionless. Bohémond himself ascended by a ladder of ropes, in the hope that he should be seconded by the most brave; but nobody felt it his duty to follow in his footsteps.—Book III.

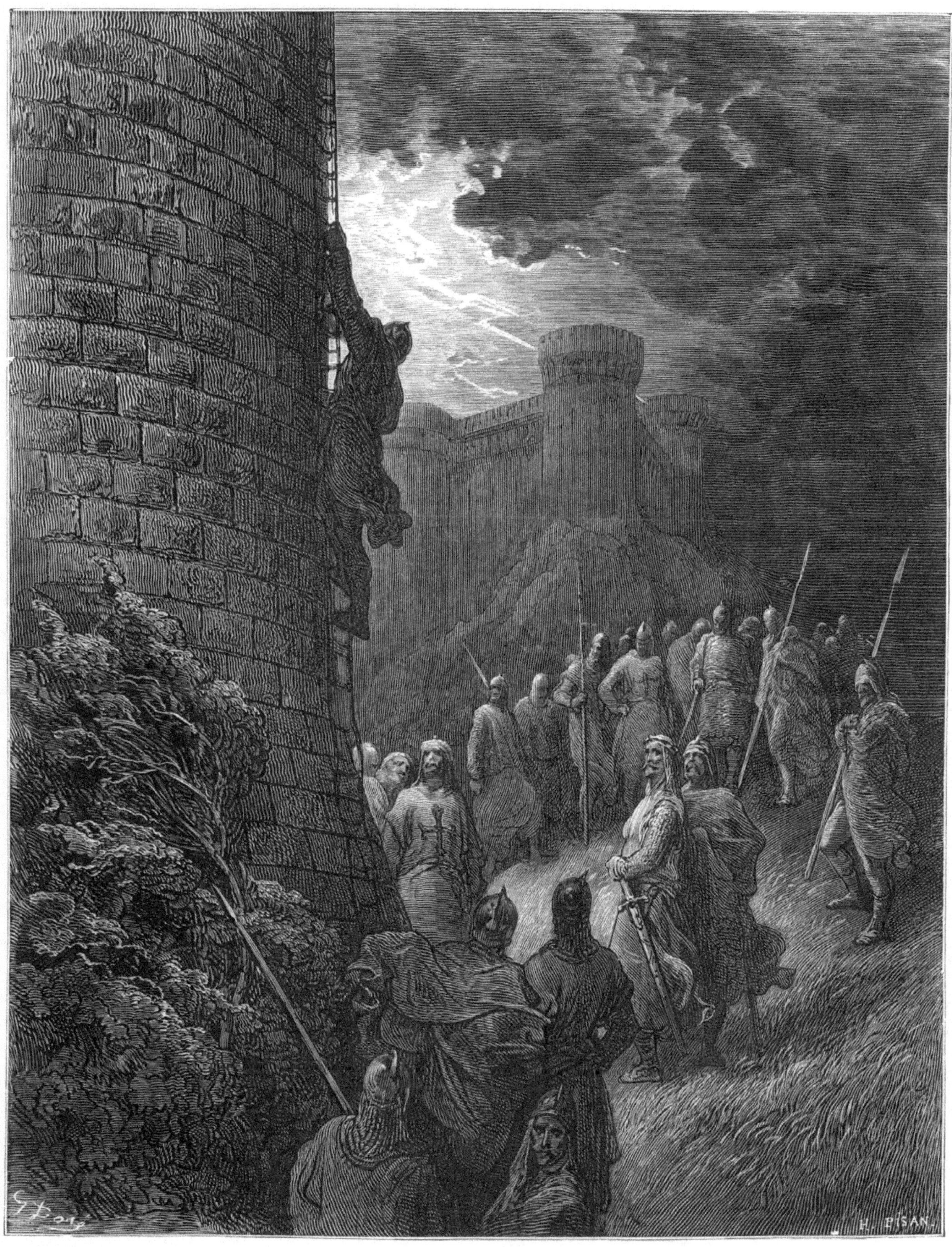
H. PISAN

advanced posts of the Crusaders; and, even in these early contests, the Christian army had to lament the loss of several of its bravest warriors. Bohémond was wounded in a sortie; in vain Tancred and Godfrey performed prodigies of valour; the Mussulmans forced the Christians to shut themselves up in a place of which the latter had but just made themselves masters, and in which they were soon closely besieged in their turn.

Placed between the garrison of the citadel and a besieging army, the Crusaders found themselves in a most critical position. To prevent their being relieved by any supplies by sea, two thousand Mussulmans were sent by Kerboghâ to take possession of the port of St. Simeon, and of all vessels which brought provisions to the Christian army. Famine was not long in making its appearance, and soon exercised cruel ravages among the besieged.

From the earliest period of the siege the Crusaders could scarcely procure the common necessaries of life at their weight in gold. A loaf of moderate size sold at a bezant, an egg was worth six Lucquese deniers, whilst a pound of silver was given for the head of an ox, a horse, or an ass. Godfrey bought for fifteen silver marks a half-starved camel, and gave three marks for a goat, which at other times would have been rejected by the poorest soldiers of his army. Surrounded by the vast riches conquered from the Saracens, the Crusaders were thus condemned to all the horrors and miseries of famine. After having killed most of their horses, they were compelled to make war upon unclean animals. The soldiers and the poor who followed the army supported themselves on roots and leaves; some went so far as to devour the leather of their bucklers and shoes, whilst the most wretched exhumed the bodies of the Saracens, and, to support their miserable existence, disputed with death for his prey. In this frightful distress, disconsolate mothers could no longer nourish their babes, and died with famine and despair. Princes and knights, whose pride and haughtiness had been the most conspicuous, were brought to the necessity of asking alms. The count of Flanders went begging to the houses and in the streets of Antioch for the commonest and coarsest orts, and often obtained none. More than one leader sold his arms and all his appointments for food to support him a single day. As long as the duke of Lorraine had any provisions he shared them with his companions; but at length he made the sacrifice of his last war-horse, and found himself, as were all the other Crusaders, reduced to the most cruel necessities.

Many of the Crusaders endeavoured to fly from a city which presented to them nothing but the image and the prospect of death; some fled by sea, through a thousand dangers, whilst others cast themselves amongst the Mussulmans, where they purchased a little bread by the abandonment of Christ and his religion. The soldiers necessarily lost courage when they saw that count de Melun, who so often defied death in the field, a second time fly from famine and misery. His desertion was preceded by that of the count de Blois, who bore the standard of the Crusaders, and presided at their councils. He had quitted the army two days before the taking of Antioch, and when he learned the arrival of Kerboghâ, he, with his troops, immediately marched towards Constantinople.

Deserters made their escape during the darkness of night. Sometimes they precipitated themselves into the ditches of the city, at the risk of their lives; sometimes they descended from the ramparts by means of a cord. Every day the Christians found themselves abandoned by an increasing number of their companions; and these desertions added to their despair. Heaven was invoked against the dastards; God was implored that they might, in another life, share the fate of the traitor Judas. The ignominious epithet of *rope-dancers* (sauteurs de corde) was attached to their names, and devoted them to the contempt of their companions. William of Tyre refuses to name the crowd of knights who then deserted the cause of Jesus Christ, because he considers them as blotted out from the book of life for ever. The wishes of the Christians against those who fled were but too completely fulfilled; the greater part perished from want, and others were killed by the Saracens. Stephen, count of Chartres, more fortunate than his companions, succeeded in reaching the camp of Alexius, who was advancing with an army towards Antioch. To excuse his desertion, he did not fail to paint, in the darkest colours, all the misfortunes and dangers of the Christians, and to make it appear by his accounts that God had abandoned the cause of the Crusaders. The despair of several Latin pilgrims who followed the army of the Greeks was so violent, that it urged them to horrible blasphemies. They, groaning, asked why the true God had permitted the destruction of his people? why he had allowed them, who were going to deliver the tomb of his Son, to fall into the hands of his enemies? Nothing was heard among the Latin Crusaders but such strange speeches, and Guy, the brother of Bohémond, exceeded all the rest in his despair. In the excess of his grief, he blasphemed more than any, and could not understand the mysteries of Providence, which betrayed the cause of the Christians. "O God," cried he, "what is become of thy power? If thou art still an all-powerful God, what is become of thy justice? Are we not thy children, are we not thy soldiers? Who is the father of a family, who is the king who thus suffers his own to perish when he has the power to save them? If you abandon those who fight for you, who will dare, henceforward, to range themselves under your sacred banner?" In their blind grief, all the Crusaders repeated these impious words. Such was the frenzy of despair in which sorrow had plunged them, that, according to the report of contemporary historians, all ceremonies of religion were suspended, and no priest or layman during many days pronounced the name of Jesus Christ.

The emperor Alexius, who had advanced as far as Philomelium, was so terrified by all he heard, that he did not dare to continue his march towards Antioch. He thought, says Anna Comnena, it was rash to attempt to succour a city whose fortifications had been ruined by a long siege, and whose only defenders were soldiers reduced to the lowest state of misery. Alexius further reflected, says the same historian, upon the indiscretion and the inconstancy of the Franks, upon their manner of making war without art or rules, and upon the imprudence with which, after having conquered their enemies, they allowed themselves to be surprised by the very same people whom they had conquered. He likewise thought of the difficulty he should have in making his arrival known to the Crusaders, and of the still greater difficulty of making their leaders agree with him upon the best means to save them. All these motives appeared reasonable; but it is easy to believe that Alexius was not sorry to see a war going on which destroyed at the same time both Turks and Latins. However it may be, the resolution which he took of returning to Constantinople threw all the Christians of Phrygia and Bithynia into the greatest alarm. The report then current was (and if we may believe Anna Comnena, it was from the insinuations of Alexius) that the Mussulmans were approaching with numerous armies. They were constantly believed to be coming, and the soldiers of the emperor themselves laid waste all the country round Philomelium, which, they said, the Saracens were about to invade. Women, children, all the Christian families followed the army of Alexius, as it returned to Constantinople. They bade an eternal adieu to their native country, and deplored the loss of their property of all kinds. Nothing was heard in the army but lamentations and groans; but they who evinced the greatest grief were the Latins, whose wishes were all centred in Syria, and who lost all hope of assisting their brethren besieged in the city of Antioch.

When the news of this retreat reached Antioch, it greatly augmented the depression of the Crusaders. Not a hope remained to them; famine carried off every day a great number of soldiers; their weakened arms could scarcely lift the lance or the sword; they had neither strength to defend their own lives nor to bury their dead. In the midst of such frightful misery, not a tear was seen, not a sob was heard; the silence was as complete in Antioch as if the city had been buried in the most profound night, as if not one living person was left in it. The Crusaders had not even the courage of despair left. The last feeling of nature, the love of life, was becoming daily extinct in their hearts; they feared to meet each other in the public places, and concealed themselves in the interior of the houses, which they looked upon as their tombs.

The towers and the ramparts remained almost without defence. Bohémond, who had taken the command of the place, sought in vain by his speeches to raise the courage of the Crusaders; in vain the trumpets and the serjeants-at-arms called them to the combat. Whilst the Mussulmans shut up in the citadel, and those who besieged the city, every day renewed their attacks, the Christian warriors remained immovable in their dwellings. In order to drive them from their retreats, Bohémond was obliged to give several quarters of the city up to the flames. Raoul de Caen deplores, in pompous verses, the conflagration and the ruin of churches and palaces, *built with the cedars of Mount Lebanon,* and in which shone *the marble of Mount Atlas, the crystal of Tyre, the brass of Cyprus, the lead of Amanthontis, and the iron of England.* The barons who could no longer enforce the obedience of their soldiers, had not strength to offer them an example. Then they bitterly remembered their families, their castles, their wealth, all which they had quitted for this unfortunate war; they could not comprehend the reverses of the Christian army, and little was wanting, says William of Tyre, to make them accuse God of ingratitude, for having refused so many sacrifices made to the glory of his name.

Matthew of Edessa relates that the Christian leaders offered to give up the city to Kerboghâ, upon the single condition that he would allow them and their soldiers to return to their own countries, taking with them their baggage. As the Saracen general rejected their proposal, several of them, actuated by despair, formed the project of abandoning the army, and flying by night towards the coast, but were prevented by the exhortations of Godfrey and Bishop Adhémar, who pointed out to them the disgrace which such a step would bring upon them in the eyes of both Europe and Asia.

The famine had continued its ravages for more than two weeks, and the Mussulmans pressed on the siege with the greater ardour, from the conviction that they should soon be masters of the city. Fanaticism and superstition, which had precipitated the Crusaders into the abyss in which they were now plunged, alone had the power to re-animate their courage, and extricate them from such fearful perils. Prophecies, revelations, and miracles became every day the more frequent subjects of report in the Christian army. St. Ambrose had appeared to a venerable priest, and had told him that the Christians, after overcoming all their enemies, would enter Jerusalem as conquerors, and that God would there reward their exploits and their labours. A Lombard ecclesiastic had passed the night in one of the churches of Antioch, and had there seen Jesus Christ, accompanied by the Virgin and the prince of the apostles. The Son of God, irritated by the conduct of the Crusaders, rejected their prayers, and abandoned them to the fate they had too richly merited; but the Virgin fell at the knees of her son, and by her tears and lamentations appeased the anger of the Saviour. "Arise," then said the Son of God to the priest, "go and inform my people of the return of my commiseration; hasten and announce to the Christians, that if they come back to me, the hour of their deliverance is at hand."

They whom God had thus made the depositaries of his secrets and his will, offered, in attestation of the truth of their visions, to precipitate themselves from a lofty tower, to pass through flames, or to submit their heads to the executioner; but these proofs were not necessary to persuade the Crusaders, always ready to believe in prodigies, and who had become more credulous than ever in the moment of danger and in the excess of their misfortunes. The imagination of both leaders and soldiers was easily led away by the promises which were made to them in the name of Heaven. The hopes of a more prosperous future began to re-animate their courage. Tancred, as a good and loyal knight, swore, that as long as he had sixty companions left, he would never abandon the project of delivering Jerusalem. Godfrey, Hugh, Raymond, and the two Roberts took the same oath. The whole army, after the example of their leaders, promised to fight and to suffer until the day appointed for the deliverance of the holy places.

In the midst of this reviving enthusiasm, two deserters came before the Christian army, and related that, when endeavouring to escape from Antioch, they had been stopped, the one by his brother, who had been killed in fight, the other by Jesus Christ himself. The Saviour of mankind had promised to deliver Antioch. The warrior who had fallen under the sword of the Saracens had sworn to issue from the grave with all his companions, equally dead as himself, to fight with the Christians. In order to crown all these heavenly promises, a priest of the diocese of Marseilles, named Peter Barthélemi, came before the council of the leaders, to reveal an apparition of St. Andrew, which had been repeated three times during his sleep. The holy apostle had said to him: "Go to the church of my brother Peter at Antioch. Near the principal altar you will find, by digging up the earth, the iron head of the lance which pierced the side of our Redeemer. Within three days this instrument of eternal salvation shall be manifested to his disciples. This mystical iron, borne at the head of the army, shall effect the deliverance of the Christians, and shall pierce the hearts of the infidels."* Adhémar, Raymond, and the other leaders believed, or feigned to believe, in this apparition, an account of which soon spread throughout the army. The soldiers said among themselves that nothing was impossible to the God of the Christians; they further believed that Jesus Christ was interested in their welfare, and that God ought to perform miracles to save his disciples and defenders. During three days the Christian army prepared itself by fasting and prayer for the discovery of the holy lance.

On the morning of the third day, twelve Crusaders, chosen from amongst the most respected of the clergy and the knights, repaired to the church of Antioch with a great number of workmen provided with the necessary instruments. They began by digging up the earth under the principal altar. The greatest silence prevailed in the church; the spectators expecting every instant to see the glitter of the miraculous lance. The whole army, assembled round the doors, which they had had the precaution to shut, awaited with impatience the results of the search. The diggers worked during several hours, and had gone to the depth of twelve feet without any appearance of the lance. They continued their operations till evening without discovering anything. The impatience of the Christians still increased. In the middle of the night another attempt was made. Whilst the twelve witnesses were at prayers around the sides of the hole, Barthélemi precipitated himself into it, and in a short time re-appeared, holding the sacred iron in his hands. A cry of joy arose among the spectators, which was repeated by the soldiers who waited at the doors, and which soon resounded through all quarters of the city. The iron on which all the hopes of the Christians were centred, was exhibited in triumph to the Crusaders, to whom it appeared a celestial weapon with which God himself would disperse his enemies. Every mind became excited, and doubts were no longer entertained of the protection of Heaven. Enthusiasm gave new life to the army, and restored strength and vigour to the Crusaders. All the horrors of famine, and even the numbers of their enemies were forgotten. The most pusillanimous thirsted for the blood of the Saracens, and all demanded with loud cries to be led forth to battle.

The leaders of the Christian army who had prepared the enthusiasm of the soldiers, now

* The discovery of this lance and the prodigies that it operated are related by all the historians of the Crusades. The Arabian historian Aboul-Mahaçen agrees, in the principal circumstances, with the Latin historians. The most credulous of the latter, and he who gives the greatest number of details, is Raymond d'Agiles. Albert d'Aix, William of Tyre, Guibert, and Robert, raise not the least doubt about the authenticity of the lance. Anna Comnena says nothing about the lance, but speaks of the *nails* which had been used to nail Christ to the cross. Albu-faradge commits the same error. In general the accounts of both the Greeks and the Arabians of this war must be read with much precaution; they furnish us with very few positive ideas.

employed themselves in taking advantage of it. They sent deputies to the general of the Saracens, to offer him either a single combat or a general battle. Peter the Hermit, who had evinced more exaltation than any other person, was chosen for this embassy. Although received with contempt in the camp of the infidels, he delivered himself no less haughtily or boldly. "The princes assembled in Antioch," said Peter, addressing the Saracen leaders, "have sent me to demand justice of you. These provinces, stained with the blood of martyrs, have belonged to Christian nations, and as all Christian people are brothers, we are come into Asia to avenge the injuries of those who have been persecuted, and to defend the heritage of Christ and his disciples. Heaven has allowed the cities of Syria to fall for a time into the power of infidels, in order to chastise the offences of his people; but learn that the vengeance of the Most High is appeased; learn that the tears and penitence of the Christians have turned aside the sword of divine justice, and that the God of armies has arisen to fight on our side. Nevertheless we still consent to speak of peace. I conjure you, in the name of the all-powerful God, to abandon the territory of Antioch and return to your own country. The Christians promise you, by my voice, not to molest you in your retreat. We will even put up prayers for you that the true God may touch your hearts, and permit you to see the truth of our faith. If Heaven deigns to listen to us, how delightful it will be to us to give you the name of brethren, and to conclude with you a lasting peace! But if you are not willing to accept either the blessings of peace or the benefits of the Christian religion, let the fate of battle at length decide the justice of our cause. As the Christians will not be taken by surprise, and as they are not accustomed to steal victories, they offer you the choice of combat."* When finishing his discourse, Peter fixed his eyes upon the leader of the Saracens, and said, "Choose from amongst the bravest of thy army, and let them do battle with an equal number of the Crusaders; fight thyself with one of our Christian princes; or give the signal for a general battle. Whatever may be thy choice, thou shalt soon learn what thy enemies are, and thou shalt know what the great God is whom we serve!"

Kerboghâ, who knew the situation of the Christians, and who was not aware of the kind of succour they had received in their distress, was much surprised at such language. He remained for some time mute with astonishment and rage, but at length said, "Return to them who sent you, and tell them it is the part of the conquered to receive conditions, and not to dictate them. Miserable vagabonds, extenuated men, phantoms may terrify women; but the warriors of Asia are not intimidated by vain words. The Christians shall soon learn that the land we tread upon belongs to us. Nevertheless I am willing to entertain some pity for them, and if they will acknowledge Mahomet, I may forget that this city, a prey to famine, is already in my power; I may leave it in their hands, and give them arms, clothes, bread, women, in short, all that they have not; for the Koran bids us pardon all who submit to its laws. Bid thy companions hasten, and on this very day take advantage of my clemency; to-morrow they shall only leave Antioch by the sword. They will then see if their crucified God, who could not save himself from the cross, can save them from the fate which is prepared for them."

This speech was loudly applauded by the Saracens, whose fanaticism it rekindled. Peter wished to reply, but the sultan of Mossoul, placing his hand upon his sword, commanded that these miserable mendicants, who united blindness with insolence, should be driven away. The Christian deputies retired in haste, and were in danger of losing their lives several times whilst passing through the army of the infidels. Peter rendered an account of his mission to the assembled princes and barons; and all immediately prepared for battle. The heralds-at-arms proceeded through the different quarters of the city, and battle was promised for the next day to the impatient valour of the Crusaders.

* This speech is reported by most of the Latin historians of the crusades. We have preserved the spirit of it, with the most scrupulous exactness.

The priests and bishops exhorted the Christians to render themselves worthy of fighting for the cause of Jesus Christ; and the whole army passed the night in prayer and acts of devotion. Injuries were forgiven, alms were bestowed, and all the churches were filled with warriors, who humbled themselves before God, and implored a remission of their sins. The preceding evening some provisions had been found, and this unexpected abundance was considered as a species of miracle. The Crusaders repaired their strength by a frugal meal; and towards the end of the night, that which remained of bread and meal in Antioch served for the sacrifice of the mass. A hundred thousand warriors approached the tribunal of penitence, and received, with all the evidences of piety, the God for whom they had taken up arms.

At length day appeared; it was the festival of St. Peter and St. Paul. The gates of Antioch were thrown open, and the whole Christian army marched out in twelve divisions, symbolical of the twelve apostles. Hugh the Great, though weakened by a long illness, appeared in the foremost ranks, and bore the standard of the Church. All the princes, knights, and barons were at the head of their men-at-arms. The only one of all the leaders that did not appear in the ranks was the count de Thoulouse; detained in Antioch by the consequences of a wound, he was charged with the duty of watching the garrison of the citadel, whilst his companions went to give battle to the army of the Saracens.

Raymond d'Agiles, one of the historians of the crusade, bore the holy lance, and directed the attention of the soldiers to it. Adhémar marched by the side of Raymond, announcing to the Crusaders the help of the celestial legions which God had promised them. A part of the clergy advanced in procession at the head of the army, singing the martial psalm, "*Let the Lord arise, and let his enemies be dispersed.*" The bishops and priests who had remained in Antioch, surrounded by the women and children, from the top of the ramparts blessed the arms of the Crusaders, praying the Lord to preserve his people and confound the pride of his enemies. The banks of the Orontes and the neighbouring mountains appeared to answer to these invocations, and resounded with the war-cry of the Crusaders, "*It is the will of God! It is the will of God!*"

Amidst this concert of acclamations and prayers, the Christian army advanced into the plain. To judge only by the state of misery to which they had been reduced, they had rather the appearance of a conquered army than of an army of men marching to victory. A great number of the Crusaders were without clothes. The greater part of the knights and barons marched on foot. Some were mounted on asses and camels, and, what is not an indifferent circumstance on this day, Godfrey de Bouillon had been obliged to borrow a horse of the count de Thoulouse. In the ranks were sick and attenuated soldiers, weakened by famine, and marching with difficulty, who were only supported by the hope of conquering or of dying for the cause of Jesus Christ.

The whole country round Antioch was covered with the Mussulman battalions. The Saracens had divided their army into fifteen bodies arranged in *échelons*. In the midst of all these, the division of Kerboghâ, says the Armenian historian, appeared like *an inaccessible mountain*. The Saracen general, who had no expectation of a battle, at first believed that the Christians were come to implore his clemency. A black flag flying over the citadel of Antioch, which was the signal agreed upon to announce the resolution of the Crusaders, soon informed him that he had not to deal with supplicants. Two thousand men of his army, who guarded the passage of the bridge of Antioch, were cut in pieces by the count de Vermandois. The fugitives carried terror to the tent of their general, who was playing at chess. Aroused from his false security, the sultan of Mossoul ordered the head of a deserter to be cut off who had announced to him the speedy surrender of the Christians, and then set himself seriously to the task of fighting an enemy whose auxiliaries were fanaticism and despair.

On marching out of Antioch the Christians advanced westwards towards the spot where the mountains draw near to the Orontes. Ranged in order of battle, in a vast space where the mountains formed a semicircle around them and secured them from surprise, they extended across the plain a league from the city. Hugh, the two Roberts, the count de Belesme, and the count of Hainaut placed themselves at the head of the left wing; Godfrey was on the right, supported by Eustace, Baldwin du Bourg, Tancred, Rinaldo de Toul, and Erard de Puyset. Adhémar was in the centre, with Gaston de Béarn, the count de Die, Raimbaut of Orange, William of Montpellier, and Amanjeu d'Albret. Bohémond commanded a body of reserve, ready to act upon all points where the Christians might require assistance. Kerboghâ, who saw the disposition of the Crusaders, ordered the sultans of Nice, Damascus, and Aleppo, to make the tour of the mountain and then reascend the Orontes, so as to place themselves between the Christian army and the city. He at the same time drew his army up in line of battle to receive the Christians and repulse their attack. He placed his troops partly on the heights and partly on the plain. His right wing was commanded by the emir of Jerusalem, and his left wing by one of the sons of Accien. For himself he remained upon a high hill, to give his orders and watch the movements of the two armies.

At the moment of the commencement of the battle, Kerboghâ was seized with fear, and sent to propose to the Christian princes, that in order to spare the effusion of blood, they should select some of their knights to fight against an equal number of Saracens. This proposal, which had been rejected the day before, could not be adopted by the leaders of an army full of ardour and confident of victory. The Christians entertained no doubt that Heaven had declared itself in their favour, and this persuasion must render them invincible. In their enthusiasm, they looked upon the most natural events as prodigies announcing to them the triumph of their arms. A globe of fire, which on the preceding evening had passed across the horizon and burst over the camp of the Saracens, appeared to them a sign foretelling their victory. As they left Antioch a light rain refreshed the burning air of the climate and the season, and was in their eyes a fresh proof of the favour of Heaven. A strong wind, which assisted the flight of their javelins and impeded that of the arrows of the Turks, was for them as the wind of heavenly anger raised to disperse the infidels. Animated by this persuasion, the Christian army showed the greatest impatience to begin the fight. They marched towards the enemy in perfect order. A profound silence reigned over the plain, on all parts of which shone the arms of the Christians. No sound was heard in their ranks but the voices of the leaders, the hymns of the priests, and the exhortations of Adhémar.

All at once the Saracens commenced the attack by discharging a cloud of arrows and then rushing on the Crusaders, uttering barbarous cries. In spite of their impetuous shock, their right wing was soon repulsed and penetrated by the Christians. Godfrey met with greater resistance in their left wing; he succeeded, however, in breaking it and carrying disorder among their ranks. At the moment that the troops of Kerboghâ began to give way, the sultan of Nice, who had made the tour of the mountain and returned along the banks of the Orontes, fell with impetuosity upon the rear of the Christian army, and threatened destruction to the body of reserve commanded by Bohémond. The Crusaders, who fought on foot, could not resist the first charge of the Saracen cavalry. Hugh the Great, warned of the danger of Bohémond, abandoned the pursuit of the fugitives, and hastened to the succour of the body of reserve. Then the battle was renewed with redoubled fury. Kilidj Arslan, who had to avenge the shame of several defeats as well as the loss of his states, fought like a lion at the head of his troops. A squadron of three thousand Saracen horse, clothed in steel and armed with clubs, carried disorder and terror through the ranks of the Christians. The standard of the count de Vermandois was carried away, and retaken, covered with the blood of Crusaders and infidels. Godfrey and Tancred, who flew to the assistance of Hugh and Bohémond, signalized their strength and valour by the death of a great many Mussulmans. The sultan of Nice, whom no reverse could overcome, firmly withstood the shock of the Christians. In the heat of the combat he ordered lighted flax to be thrown amongst the low bushes and dried grass which covered the plain. Immediately a blaze arose which enveloped the Christians in masses of flame and smoke. Their ranks were for a moment broken; they could no longer either see or hear their leaders. The sultan of Nice was about to gather the fruits of his stratagem, and victory was on the point of escaping from the hands of the Crusaders.

At this moment, say the historians, a squadron was seen to descend from the summit of the mountains, preceded by three horsemen clothed in white and covered with shining armour. "Behold!" cried Bishop Adhémar, "the heavenly succour which was promised to you. Heaven declares for the Christians; the holy martyrs George, Demetrius, and Theodore come to fight for you." Immediately all eyes were turned towards the celestial legion. A new ardour inspired the Christians, who were persuaded that God himself was coming to their aid, and the war-cry "*It is the will of God!*" was heard as at the beginning of the battle. The women and children who had remained in Antioch, and were collected on the walls, animated the courage of the Crusaders by their cries and acclamations, whilst the priests continued to raise their hands towards heaven, and returned thanks to God by songs of praise and thanksgiving for the succour he had sent to the Christians. Of the Crusaders themselves each man became a hero, and nothing could stand before their impetuous charge. In a moment the ranks of the Saracens were everywhere broken, and they only fought in confusion and disorder. They endeavoured to rally on the other side of a torrent and upon an elevated point whence their trumpets and clarions resounded; but the count de Vermandois attacked them in this last post and completely routed them. They had now no safety but in flight, and the banks of the Orontes, the woods, the plains, the mountains were covered with the fugitives, who abandoned both their arms and their baggage.

Kerboghâ, who had been so certain of victory as to have announced the defeat of the Christians to the caliph of Bagdad and the sultan of Persia, fled towards the Euphrates, escorted by a small body of his most faithful soldiers. Several of the emirs had taken to flight before the end of the battle. Tancred and some others, mounted on the horses of the conquered enemy, pursued till night-fall the sultans of Aleppo and Damascus, the emir of Jerusalem, and the scattered wreck of the Saracen army. The conquerors set fire to the intrenchments behind which the enemy's infantry had sought refuge, and a vast number of Mussulmans perished in the flames.

According to the account of several contemporary historians, the infidels left a hundred thousand dead on the field of battle. Four thousand Crusaders lost their lives on this glorious day, and were placed among the ranks of the martyrs.

The Christians found abundance beneath the tents of their enemies; fifteen thousand camels and a great number of horses fell into their hands. As they passed the night in the camp of the Saracens, they had leisure to admire the luxury of the Orientals, and they examined with the greatest surprise the tent of the king of Mossoul,* resplendent with gold and precious stones, which, divided into long streets flanked by high towers, resembled a fortified city. They employed several days in carrying the spoils into Antioch. The booty was immense, and every Crusader, according to the remark of Albert d'Aix, found himself much richer than he was when he quitted Europe.

The sight of the Saracen camp after the battle proved plainly that they had displayed much more splendour and magnificence than true courage. The veteran warriors, the companions of Malek-Scha, had almost all perished in the civil wars which had for so many years desolated the empire of the Seljoucides. The army that came to the succour of Antioch was composed of raw troops, levied in haste,

* This tent was able to contain more than two thousand persons. Bohémond sent it into Italy, where it was preserved for a length of time.

THE MASSACRE OF ANTIOCH.

The Crusaders had obtained possession of the city by treachery. The soldiers penetrated into the houses. . . . Everything that was not marked with a cross became the object of vengeance, and all who pronounced not the name of Christ were massacred without mercy. In a single night more than six thousand of the inhabitants of Antioch perished. . . . Phirous, the betrayer, received from the Christians great riches as the reward of his treachery; this renegade now embraced the Christianity he had abandoned; two years afterwards, his ambition not being satisfied, he returned to the religion of Mahomet, and died abhorred by Christians and Mussulmans, whose cause he had by turns embraced and betrayed.—Book III.

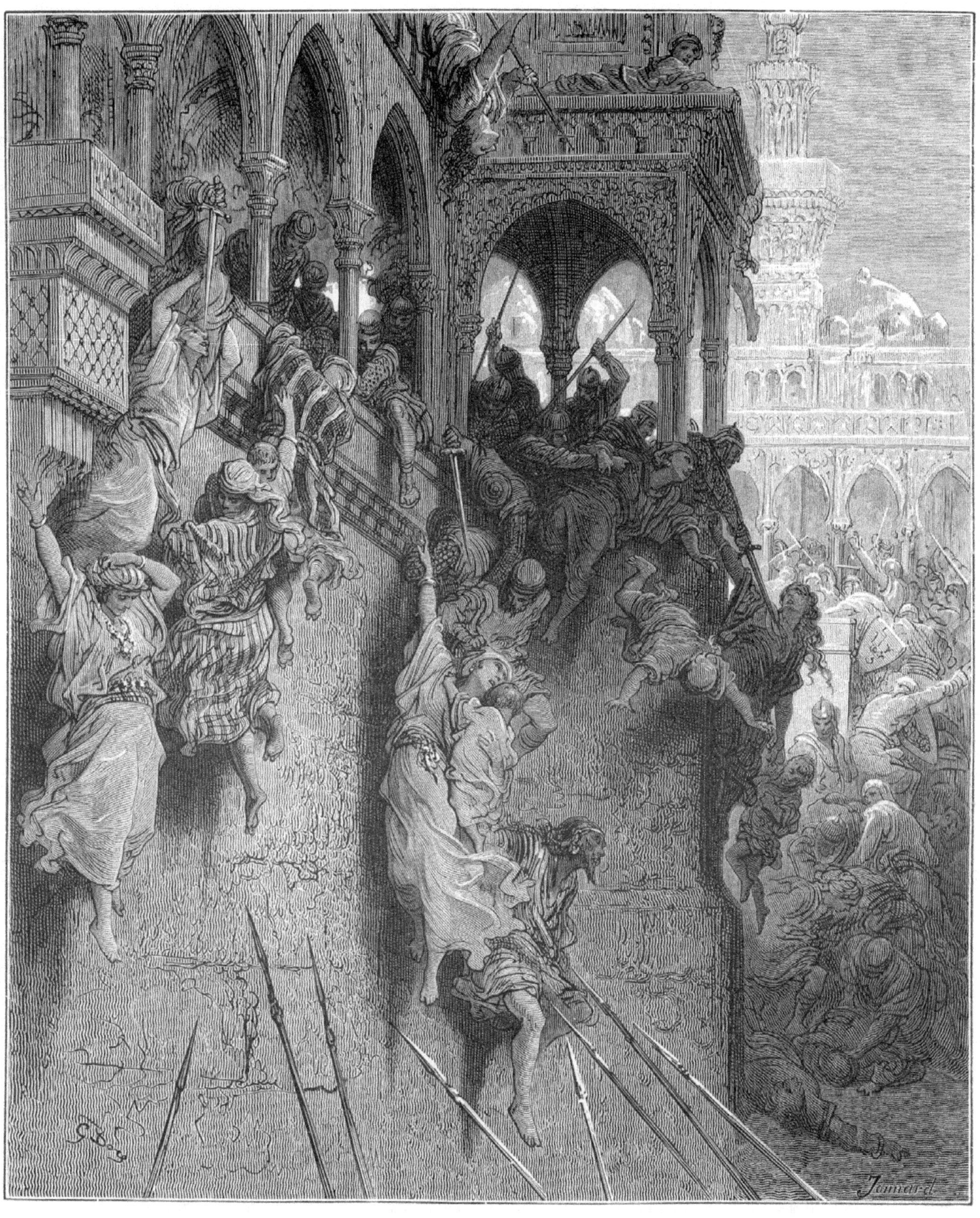

and reckoned under its standards several rival nations, always ready to take up arms against each other.* It is the duty of the historian to admit that the twenty-eight emirs who accompanied Kerboghâ were almost all at variance with one another, and scarcely acknowledged the authority of a chief. On the contrary, the greatest union prevailed on this day among the Christians. The different bodies of their army fought upon one single point, and afforded each other mutual support, whereas Kerboghâ had divided his forces. In this battle, but more particularly in the circumstances which preceded it, the sultan of Mossoul showed more presumption than skill; by the slowness of his march he lost the opportunity of assisting Accien or of surprising the Crusaders. Afterwards, too certain of victory, he never dreamt of what despair and fanaticism are able to effect. These two powerful principles greatly increased the natural bravery of the Franks. The horrible distress to which they had been reduced only tended to make them invincible, and in that we shall find the miracle of the day.

When the danger was past, the holy lance which had given so much confidence to the Crusaders during the battle, no longer excited their veneration, and lost all its marvellous influence. As it remained in the hands of the count of Thoulouse and his Provençals, to whom it brought a great number of offerings, the other nations were not willing to leave them the sole advantage of a miracle which augmented their consideration and their wealth; and, as we shall soon see, it was not long before doubts were raised upon the authenticity of the lance which had effected such wonders, and the spirit of rivalry did that which reason might have done in a more enlightened age.

The victory of Antioch appeared to the Saracens to be so extraordinary an event that many of them abandoned the religion of their prophet. Those who defended the citadel were so struck with terror and surprise, that they surrendered to Raymond the very day of the battle. Three hundred of them embraced the faith of the holy Gospel, and many went among the cities of Syria declaring that the God of the Christians must be the true God.

After this memorable day the Turks made scarcely any effort to impede the march of the Christians. This last triumph of the Franks appeared to them like a decision of heaven that men ought not to contend against. Most of the emirs of Syria who had shared the spoils of the sultan of Persia, considered the invasion of the Christians as a passing calamity, without thinking of the consequences it might leave behind, and only sought to take advantage of it to assure their own domination and independence. The dynasty of the Seljoucides was every day losing its strength and its splendour. The vast empire of Togrul, Alp-Arslan, and Malek-Scha was crumbling away on all sides amidst civil and foreign wars. This empire, created towards the middle of the eleventh century, whose sudden increase had alarmed Constantinople and carried terror even among the nations of the West, was soon doomed to see other states elevate themselves upon its ruins; for, according to the remark of an historian, it might be said that God was pleased to show how insignificant the earth is in his eyes, by thus causing to pass from hand to hand, like a child's toy, a power so monstrous as to threaten the universe.

The first care of the Crusaders after their victory was to put, if we may say so, Jesus Christ in possession of the countries they had just conquered, by re-establishing his worship in Antioch. The capital of Syria had all at once a new religion, and was inhabited by a new people. A considerable part of the spoils of the Saracens was employed in repairing and ornamenting the churches which had been converted into mosques. The Greeks and the Latins mingled their vows and their hymns, and

* Gemaleddin, who of all the Oriental historians gives the greatest number of details upon the taking and the battle of Antioch, reports that a violent quarrel had broken out between the Turks and the Arabs; he even adds that the Arabs had retired before the battle, and that in the course of it the Turks turned their arms against their allies.

prayed together to the God of the Christians to conduct them to Jerusalem. The leaders of the army then joined in addressing a letter to the princes and nations of the West, in which they made a relation of their labours and their exploits. That they might not trouble the joy that the news of their victories must create, they took care to conceal the losses they had sustained;* but they must have made them apparent by calling new warriors to their aid. They solicited by prayers, and even by threats, the immediate departure of all who had assumed the cross, and yet still remained in the West.

The Crusaders sent at the same time an embassy to Constantinople, composed of Hugh, count of Vermandois, and Baldwin, count of Hainault. The object of this embassy was to remind the emperor Alexius of the promise he had made to accompany the Christians with an army to Jerusalem. The count of Hainault perished, with all his train, in Asia Minor. The count of Vermandois, who took a different route, arrived safely at Constantinople; but could obtain nothing from Alexius. Hereupon, whether he was ashamed of having failed in his mission, or whether he feared to rejoin an army in which he could not maintain the splendour of his rank, he determined to return to Europe, where his desertion caused him to be compared to the raven of the ark.

Some days after the battle of Antioch, the greater part of the pilgrims entreated the leaders to conduct them towards the Holy City, the principal object of their expedition. The council of the princes and barons being assembled, the opinions were at first divided. Some of the leaders thought that they ought to take advantage of the terror which the victory of Antioch had created in the Saracens. "Both the East and the West," said they, "have their eyes upon us; Christ calls us to the deliverance of his tomb; the Christians who still groan in the chains of the infidels implore the assistance of our arms; we have seen the emir of Jerusalem, and the soldiers who ought to defend the approach to the Holy Sepulchre, fly before us; all the routes are open to us; let us hasten then to comply with the impatience of the Crusaders, an impatience which was always so fatal to our enemies; let us depart from an abode whose pleasures have several times corrupted the soldiers of Christ; let us not wait till discord shall disturb our peace and rob us of the fruits of our labours."

This advice seemed to be dictated by wisdom and prudence, but the majority of the leaders were full of blind security; they could not resolve still to dread enemies they had so often conquered, and the hopes of extending their conquests in Syria made them forget Jerusalem. Specious reasons were not wanting wherewith to combat the opinions they had heard. The Christian army was deficient in horses; it was exhausted by fatigue, by long miseries, and even by its own victories. As it was now the height of summer, though the Crusaders might have no enemies, they had to dread during a long march the want of water, and the heat of both the season and the climate. It was well known that new warriors from the West were expected in Asia, and prudence commanded them to wait for them. By the beginning of winter everything would be prepared for the conquest of Jerusalem, and the united Crusaders would then march without obstacles or dangers towards Palestine. This opinion obtained a majority of the suffrages.

The Crusaders had soon cause to repent of their determination. An epidemic disease made fearful ravages in their army. Nothing was to be seen in Antioch, says an ancient chronicle, but buryings and funerals, and death there reigned, neither more nor less, than in some great battle or defeat. Most of the women and the poor who followed the army were the first victims to this calamity. A great number of Crusaders who came from Germany and other parts of Europe met with death immediately on their arrival at Antioch. Within one month, more than fifty thousand pilgrims perished by this epidemic. The Christians had to regret among their leaders Henry d'Asques, Renaud d'Amerbach, and several other knights renowned for their exploits. In the midst of the general mourning,

* The leaders of the Crusades declared that the siege and the battle of Antioch had scarcely cost them ten thousand men.

the bishop of Puy, who comforted the Crusaders in their misery, himself gave way under his fatigue and died,* like the leader of the Hebrews, without having seen the promised land. His remains were buried in the church of St. Peter of Antioch, in the very spot where the miraculous lance had been discovered. All the pilgrims, whose spiritual father he had been, honoured his funeral with their presence and their tears. The leaders, who sincerely regretted him, wrote to the pope to inform him of the death of his apostolic legate. They at the same time solicited Urban to come and place himself at their head, to sanctify the standards of the crusade, and to promote union and peace in the army of Jesus Christ.

But neither the respect they entertained for the memory of Adhémar, nor the spectacle of the scourge which was devouring the Christian army, could close their hearts against ambition and discord. The count of Thoulouse, who still maintained his claims to the possession of Antioch, refused to deliver up to Bohémond the citadel of which he had become master on the day the Christians had defeated the army of Kerboghâ. These two haughty rivals were several times on the point of coming to blows, Raymond accusing the new prince of Antioch of having usurped that which belonged to his companions, whilst Bohémond threatened to bathe his sword, red with the blood of infidels, in blood which he said he had too long spared. One day that the princes and leaders were assembled in the basilica of the church of St. Peter, engaged in regulating the affairs of the crusade, their deliberations were disturbed by the most violent quarrels. Notwithstanding the sanctity of the place, Raymond, in the midst of the council, gave way to his passion and resentment. Even at the foot of the altar of Christ, Bohémond hesitated not to make false promises in order to draw the other chiefs to his party, and repeated several times an oath which he never meant to keep, that of following them to Jerusalem.

Every day trouble and disorder increased in the Christian army, some only thinking of aggrandising the states which victory had given them, whilst others wandered about Syria in search of cities over which they might unfurl their standards. Bands were seen dispersed in all parts where there was a chance of a rich booty, fighting among themselves for their conquests when they were victorious, and a prey to all sorts of horrors and miseries when they met with unforeseen resistance. The jealousy which prevailed among the chiefs extended to the soldiers; the latter quarrelling for the booty gained from the enemy, in the same manner that the princes and barons contended for the possession of cities and provinces. Those whom fortune had not favoured complained of their companions, until some lucky chance allowed them in their turn to take advantage of all the rights of victory. On all sides the Crusaders accused each other reciprocally of having enriched themselves by injustice and violence, although everybody envied the most guilty.

And yet, amidst their conflicts or their misfortunes, the Christians continued to show the most heroic bravery and resignation; they endured hunger, thirst, and fatigue without a complaint, and neither deserts, rivers, precipices, the heat of the climate, nor any other obstacle, could stop them in their incursions. In every kind of peril they sought all opportunities of proving their strength and skill, or of signalizing their valour. Sometimes in the forests or mountains they encountered savage animals. A French knight, named Guicher, rendered himself celebrated in the army by overcoming a lion. Another knight, Geoffrey de la Tour, gained great renown by an action which doubtless will appear incredible. He one day saw in a forest a lion which a serpent held within its monstrous folds, and which made the air resound with his roaring. Geoffrey flew to the assistance of the animal, which appeared to implore his pity, and with one blow of his sword killed the serpent, which was intent upon his prey. If we may believe an old chronicle, the lion thus delivered attached himself to

* Tasso makes Adhémar die at the siege of Jerusalem, and makes him die by the hands of a woman.

his liberator as to a master; he accompanied him during the war, and when, after the taking of Jerusalem, the Crusaders embarked to return into Europe, he was drowned in the sea whilst following the vessel in which Geoffrey was.*

Several Crusaders, whilst waiting for the signal of departure for Jerusalem, went to visit their brethren who had established themselves in the conquered cities. Many of them repaired to Baldwin, and joined with him in contending against the Saracens of Mesopotamia. A knight, named Foulque, who went with several of his companions to seek adventures on the banks of the Euphrates, was surprised and massacred by the Turks. His wife, whom he had taken with him, was brought before the emir of Hazart or Hezas. Being of rare beauty, one of the principal officers of the emir fell in love with her, and asked her of his master in marriage, who yielded her to him, and permitted him to espouse her. This officer, deeply in love with a Christian woman, avoided all occasions of fighting against the Crusaders, and yet, zealous in the service of his master the emir, made incursions into the territories of the sultan of Aleppo. Redowan, wishing to avenge himself, marched with an army of forty thousand men to attack the city of Hezas. Then the officer who had married the widow of Foulque advised the emir to implore the assistance of the Christians.

The emir proposed an alliance to Godfrey de Bouillon. Godfrey at first hesitated, but the Mussulman returned to the charge, and to disperse all the suspicions of the Christian princes, sent them his son Mahomet as an hostage. The treaty was then signed, and two pigeons, says a Latin historian, charged with a letter, brought the news to the emir, at the same time announcing to him the early arrival of the Christians.† The army of the sultan of Aleppo was beaten in several encounters by Godfrey, and forced to abandon the territory of Hezas, that it had begun to pillage. A short time after this expedition the son of the emir died at Antioch of the epidemic so fatal to the pilgrims of the West. Godfrey, according to the custom of the Mussulmans, had the body of the young prince enveloped in rich purple stuff, and sent it to his father. The deputies who accompanied this funeral convoy were ordered to express to the emir the regrets of Godfrey, and to tell him that their leader had been as much afflicted by the death of the young prince Mahomet, as he could have been by that of his brother Baldwin. The emir of Hezas wept for the death of his son, and never ceased to be the faithful ally of the Christians.

The leaders of the crusades still thought no more about setting forward on their march to Jerusalem, and the autumn advanced without their being engaged in any expedition of importance. In the midst of the idleness of the camps, a celestial phenomenon offered itself to the eyes of the Crusaders, and made a lively impression upon the minds of the multitude. The soldiers who guarded the ramparts of Antioch saw during the night a luminous mass, which appeared to be fixed in an elevated point of the heavens. It seemed as if all the stars, according to the expression of Albert d'Aix, were united in a space scarcely more extensive than a garden of three acres. "These stars," says the same historian, "shed the most brilliant light,‡ and *shone like coals in a furnace.*" They appeared for a long time as if suspended over the city of Antioch; but the circle which seemed to contain them being broken, they dispersed in the air. At the sight of this prodigy, the guards and sentinels uttered loud cries, and ran to awaken the citizens of Antioch. All the pilgrims issued from their houses, and found in this phenomenon a manifest sign of the will of Heaven. Some believed they saw in the

* This anecdote, which is here quoted without giving it any more importance than it merits, is related in the *Magnum Chronicon Belgicum*, which is found in the collection of the historians of Germany of Pistorius. The author says the lion followed Geoffrey *like a hare*.

† Some learned writers cannot trace messages by pigeons further back than the reign of Saladin. It is true that it was in the reigns of Nouradin and Saladin that regular posts, served by pigeons, were organized in Egypt; but this means of communication was very ancient in the East. The recital of Albert d'Aix cannot be doubted. The historian speaks of the surprise that this sort of messengers produced among the Crusaders; and as the fact appeared remarkable to him, he has not neglected the smallest details of it.

‡ Globes of fire, or ignited globes, as naturalists call them, might have produced this appearance.

united stars an image of the Saracens, who were assembled at Jerusalem, and who would be dispersed at the approach of the Christians; others, equally full of hope, saw in them the Christian warriors uniting their victorious forces, and then spreading themselves over the earth to conquer the cities ravished from the empire of Christ; but many of the pilgrims did not abandon themselves to these consolatory illusions. In a city where the people had much to suffer, and had dwelt during many months amidst death and its funeral rites, the future naturally presented itself under the most sad and disheartening colours. All who suffered, and had lost the hope of ever seeing Jerusalem, saw nothing in the phenomenon presented to their eyes but an alarming symbol of the multitude of pilgrims, which was every day diminishing, and which promised soon to be entirely dispersed, like the luminous clouds which they had seen in the heavens. "Things, however," says Albert d'Aix, "turned out much better than was expected; for, a short time afterwards, the princes, on their return to Antioch, took the field, and brought under their dominion several cities of Upper Syria."

The most important of their expeditions was the siege and capture of Maarah, situated between Hamath and Aleppo. Raymond was the first to sit himself down before this city, where he was soon joined by the duke of Normandy and the count of Flanders and their troops. The Christians met with the most obstinate resistance from the besieged during several days. The infidels poured arrows and stones upon them in clouds, together with floods of an inflammable matter, which several historians pretend to have been the Greek fire. William of Tyre says that they hurled from the summits of the towers upon the assailants quick lime and hives filled with bees. Want of provisions soon began to be felt, and the Crusaders at length experienced such distress, that many among them subsisted upon the dead bodies of their enemies. History ought, however, to relate with hesitation the extremes to which famine is said to have carried them, and to throw great doubt upon the account of the public sale of human flesh in the camp of the Christians. This circumstance is related by Mailly, but he does not say upon what authority.

The Crusaders endured all their misfortunes with patience, but they could not support the outrages committed by the inhabitants of Maarah upon the religion of Jesus Christ. The infidels raised crosses upon the ramparts, covered them with ordure, and heaped all sorts of insults upon them. This sight so irritated the Christians, that they resolved to redouble their efforts to get possession of the city. They constructed machines which shook the walls, whilst the soldiers mounted to the assault; and they succeeded, after a lengthened resistance, in making themselves masters of the towers and the ramparts. As they were overtaken by night in the midst of their victory, they did not venture to penetrate into the place; and when, with the break of day, they spread themselves through the streets, not a sound was to be heard,—every part of the city was deserted. The army pillaged the uninhabited houses, but soon discovered, to their great surprise, that the whole population of Maarah had taken refuge in subterranean places. A large quantity of straw, set on fire at the mouths of the caverns in which the infidels were concealed, soon forced them to issue from their retreats, and such was the animosity of the conquerors, that the bewildered and trembling multitude implored their pity in vain. All the inhabitants of Maarah were either put to the sword or led into slavery; the city was completely razed to the ground, "which so terrified the neighbouring cities," says an historian, "that of their own free will, and without force, they surrendered to the Crusaders."

This conquest became the subject of fresh discord. Bohémond, who had come to the siege, was desirous of keeping a portion of the city, whilst Raymond pretended to reign over Maarah as its sovereign. The debate grew warm; the camp of the Christians was filled with confusion and factions, and the Crusaders were very near shedding their own blood to ascertain who should be master of a city which they had just entirely deprived of inhabitants, and given up to pillage. "But God, who was the leader of this great enterprise," says le Père Maimbourg, "repaired by the zeal of the weak and the lowly that which the passions of the great and the wise of this world had destroyed." The soldiers at length became indignant at the thoughts of shedding, for miserable quarrels, the blood which they had sworn to dedicate to a sacred cause. Whilst they were most loud in their complaints and murmurs, the report reached them that Jerusalem had fallen into the hands of the Egyptians; they had taken advantage of the defeat of the Turks, and of the unfortunate delay of the Christian army in their invasion of Palestine. This news redoubled the discontent of the Crusaders, and they loudly accused Raymond and their other leaders of having betrayed the cause of God. They announced their intention of choosing fresh leaders, who should have no other ambition but that of accomplishing their vows, and would conduct the Christian army to the Holy Land.

The count of St. Gilles and the prince of Antioch, the latter of whom was, perhaps, no stranger to the general movement, went through the ranks, and addressed the soldiers, the one upon the necessity of obedience, the other upon the glory which awaited them at Jerusalem. The tumult soon became more violent. The clergy menaced Raymond with the anger of Heaven, whilst his soldiers threatened to abandon his standard. The Provençals themselves at length refused to obey the inflexible count of Thoulouse, and the army set seriously to work to demolish the ramparts of Maarah, the possession of which was the object of contention.

Whilst this was going on, Tancred had, by either force or address, got possession of the citadel of Antioch, and planted the standard of Bohémond in place of that of the count of St. Gilles. Raymond, thus left alone, and without any hopes of realizing his pretensions, was obliged to yield to the wishes of the army, and appeared to listen to the voice of God. After having set fire to the city of Maarah, he marched out of it by the light of the flames, barefooted, and shedding tears of repentance. Followed by the clergy, who sang the psalms of penitence, he abjured his ambition, and renewed the oath he had so often made, and so often forgotten, of delivering the tomb of Jesus Christ.

BOOK IV.

THE SIEGE OF JERUSALEM.

A. D. 1099–1103.

The Crusaders take their departure from Antioch, and march for Palestine—Siege of Archas—Pons de Balasu—Arnold de Rohés, and his disbelief in prodigies—Fanaticism of Barthélemi—The holy lance—Ordeal by fire—Hatred of the Latins towards the Greeks—Caliph of Cairo—Emir of Tripoli defeated—Palestine—Phœnicia—Plain of Berytus—Serpents—Ptolemaïs—Emmaus and Bethlehem—Alarm from an eclipse—The city of Jerusalem—Enthusiasm of the Crusaders on first beholding it—Siege of Jerusalem—Indignities heaped upon the Christians—Fountain of Siloë—The Genoese fleet enter the port of Jaffa—Gaston de Béarn—Mount of Olives—Address of Arnold de Rohés—Speech of Peter the Hermit to the Crusaders—Tower of Tancred—Machines used at the siege of Jerusalem—The Saracen magicians—Miraculous appearance of St. George—The Crusaders enter Jerusalem by storm—Creton Rheimhault—Everard de Puysaie—Mosque of Omar—Slaughter of the Mussulmans, and pious fervour of the Christians—Destruction of the Jews—Wealth found in Jerusalem—Discovery of the "true cross"—Speech of the count of Flanders—Prophetic visions—Godfrey elected king of Jerusalem—Rejoicings among the Christians, and despair of the Mussulmans—Elegy of Modhaffer Abyverdy—Afdhal, the Mussulman commander—Signal defeat of the Saracens at Ascalon—Tasso—Godfrey's quarrel with Raymond—Siege of Ascalon—Riou de Loheac—Stephen de Salviac—Peter de Salviac—Death of Gaston de Béarn—Peter the Hermit and many of the Christian leaders return to Europe—William IX., count of Flanders, sets out for the East—William, count de Nevers, defeated by the Turks—Eude, duke of Burgundy, slain—Conrad, Marshal of Henry I. of Germany—Wolf IX., duke of Bavaria—Humbert II., count of Savoy, departs for the Holy Land—Alexius, emperor of Constantinople, opposes the Crusaders—City of Ancyra captured—The Crusaders defeated by the Turks—Capture of Tortosa—Invasions of the Tartars—Tasso's "Jerusalem Delivered"—Ordinances of Gaston de Béarn.

MORE than six months had passed away since the taking of Antioch, and several of the leaders of the crusade still thought nothing of commencing their march to Jerusalem. As soon as Raymond gave the signal for departure, his soldiers, and the knights who accompanied him, broke into loud demonstrations of joy and a revived enthusiasm. The count of Thoulouse was followed by Tancred and the duke of Normandy, who were both impatient to accomplish their vow and conquer Palestine. Conducted by these three leaders, a great part of the Christian army traversed the territories of Cæsarea in Syria, Hamath, and Edessa. From all parts both Christians and Mussulmans came eagerly to meet them, the former to beg their assistance, the latter to implore their clemency. Many emirs came to conjure Raymond to plant his standard on their cities' walls, to protect them from pillage, and render them safe from the enterprises of the other Crusaders. The pilgrims everywhere on their passage received provisions and rich tributes without the trouble and risk of fighting for them. In the course of their triumphant march, the sweetest fruit of their labours and the terror that their arms inspired was the return of a vast number of Christian prisoners, whose death they had mourned, who were sent to them from the neighbouring cities by the Mussulman chiefs.

They drew near to the sea-coast, and advanced, almost without obstacle, as far as the vicinity of Archas. This city was situated at the foot of Libanus, two leagues from the sea, in a territory covered with olive-trees, and rich with corn. The count of Thoulouse, either from a desire to conquer so rich a country, or from being provoked by the insults and threats of the infidels, resolved to besiege

Archas. In order to inflame the courage of his soldiers, and associate them with him in his project, he promised them as a reward for their labours, the pillage of the city and the deliverance of two hundred Christian prisoners confined in the citadel.

In the mean time Godfrey, Eustace, and Robert, count of Flanders, had not yet set out from Antioch. They did not begin their march before the early days of spring. Bohémond accompanied them as far as Laodicea, and then returned to his capital, after having promised his companions to rejoin them before Jerusalem. At Laodicea the Crusaders liberated the Flemish pirates who had taken the cross at Tarsus, and who, for more than a year, had been detained prisoners by the Greeks, the masters of that city. At the same place the Christian army received a reinforcement of new Crusaders from the ports of Holland and Flanders, and the British isles. Among these new defenders of the cross was Edgar Atheling, who, after the death of Harold, had disputed the crown of England with William the Conqueror. He came to endeavour to forget the misfortunes of his country under the banners of the holy war, and at the same time to seek a refuge from the tyranny of the conqueror. The English and the new Crusaders from other countries were received with great joy into the ranks of the Christian army, which, however, pursued its march towards Palestine very slowly.

It grieved the greater part of the leaders to be obliged to traverse such rich provinces without establishing their domination in them. There was not a city in their route upon the walls of which one of them had not a strong secret inclination to plant his standard. These pretensions gave birth to rivalries which weakened the army, and prevented it from making useful conquests. Raymond still obstinately prosecuted the siege of Archas, which opposed to him the firmest resistance. Godfrey went to lay siege to Gibel or Gibelet, a maritime city situated some leagues from Laodicea. The leaders of the army never consented to unite their efforts against the Saracens, but sold to the emirs, by turns, their inaction and their neutrality.

The only expedition in which success crowned their bravery was the attack of Tortosa. Raymond, viscount de Turenne, the viscount de Castellane, the seigneur d'Albret, and some others of the principal leaders of the Gascons and Provençals, with a hundred horse and two hundred foot, presented themselves before this city. The inhabitants closed their gates, manned their ramparts, and forced the Christians to retreat. The leader of this expedition, Raymond de Turenne, who had not a sufficient number of troops to undertake a siege or force a city to surrender, had recourse to a stratagem which succeeded. At night he caused to be lighted in a neighbouring wood such a number of fires, that the inhabitants of Tortosa were persuaded that the whole Christian army was come to attack them, and before the break of day they all fled to the mountains, taking with them their most valuable effects. On the morrow the Christians approached the city, the ramparts of which they found deserted, and entered it without resistance. After having pillaged the houses, and given up to the flames a city they could not keep, they returned to the camp loaded with booty.

The Mussulmans shut up in Archas still held out against the Christians. Although the army was encamped in a fertile country, they soon began to experience the want of provisions. The poorest of the pilgrims were reduced, as at Antioch, to feed upon roots, and dispute with animals the leaves of the trees and the grass of the fields. The numerous clergy which followed the army sunk into the deepest distress. Such as could fight went to ravage the surrounding country, and lived on pillage ; but those whom age, sex, or infirmities would not permit to carry arms, had no hope but in the charity of the Christian soldiers. The army freely assisted them, and gave up to them the tenth part of the booty obtained from the infidels.

A great number of the Crusaders yielded to the fatigues of the siege, and perished with misery and disease, whilst many fell by the hands of the enemy, who defended themselves with obstinate val-

BARTHELEMI UNDERGOING THE ORDEAL OF FIRE.

The flames had already mounted to a height of twenty cubits, when Barthélemi was seen advancing, accompanied by the priests, who walked in silence, barefooted, and clothed in their sacerdotal habits. Covered by a simple tunic, the priest of Marseilles bore the holy lance, surrounded with floating streamers. When he arrived within a few paces of the pile, one of the principal of the clergy pronounced in a loud voice the following words: "If this man has seen Jesus Christ face to face, and if the apostle Andrew did reveal the divine lance to him, may he pass safe and sound through the flames; but if on the contrary, he is guilty of falsehood, may he be burnt, together with the lance which he bears in his hands." At these words all the spectators bowed, and answered as with one voice, "Be the will of God accomplished." Barthélemi threw himself on his knees, took Heaven to witness the truth of all that he had said, and, after recommending himself to the prayers of the bishops and priests, rushed through the funeral pile at a part where an opening of two feet wide had been made for his passage.

He was carried in a dying state to the tent of the count of Thoulouse, where he expired in a few days after, still protesting his innocence and veracity.—Book IV.

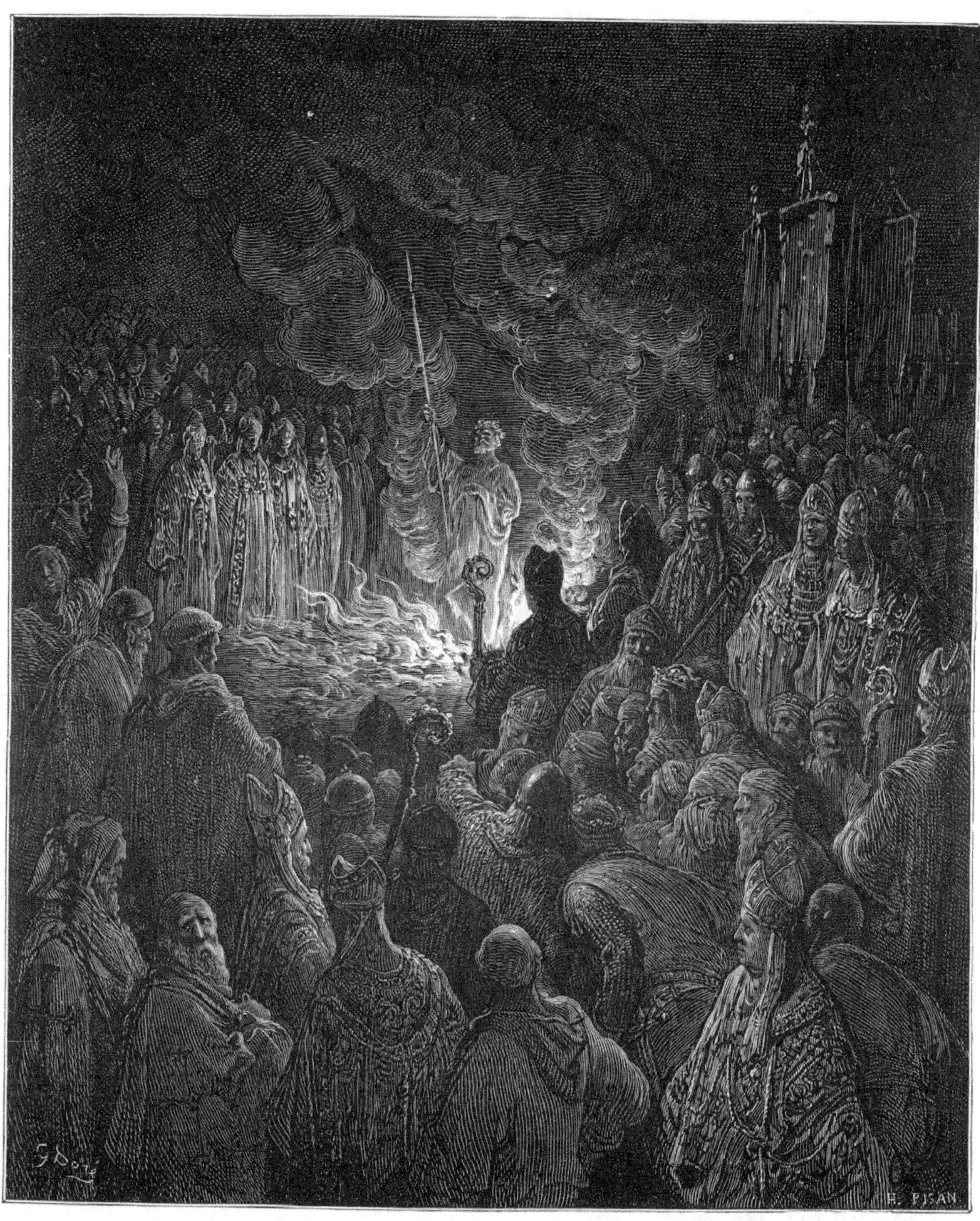
G Doré
H. PISAN

our. Among those whose loss was most regretted, history has preserved the name of Pons de Balasu; he was highly esteemed in the army for his intelligence, and up to his death had written the history of the crusade, in conjunction with Raymond d'Agiles. The Crusaders also gave their tears to the memory of Anselm de Ribemont, count de Bouchain, whose piety and courage are much praised in the chronicles of the times. Contemporary authors relate his death as attended with such wonderful circumstances as deserve to be preserved, because they afford a strong idea of the spirit which animated the Crusaders.

One day (we follow the relation of Raymond d'Agiles) Anselm saw enter into his tent young Angelram, son of the count de St. Paul, who had been killed at the siege of Maarah. "How is it," said he, "that I see you still living whom I saw dead on the field of battle?" "Know," replied Angelram, "that they who fight for Jesus Christ do not die." "But whence comes that strange splendour with which I see you surrounded?" Then Angelram pointed out to him in the heavens a palace of crystal and diamonds. "It is thence," he added, "that I derive the beauty which surprises you; that is my abode, and there is a much more beautiful one being prepared for you, which you will soon inhabit. Farewell; we shall meet again to-morrow." At these words, adds the historian, Angelram returned to heaven. Anselm, struck with this apparition, the next morning sent for several ecclesiastics, and received the sacraments; and, although in full health, took leave of his friends, telling them he was about to quit the world in which they had known him. A few hours afterwards, the enemy having made a sortie, Anselm flew, sword in hand, to meet them, and was struck on the forehead by a stone, which, say the historians, sent him to the beautiful palace in heaven that was prepared for him. This marvellous recital, which was credited by the Crusaders, is not the only one of the kind that history has collected. It is useless to remind our readers that extreme misery always rendered the Crusaders more superstitious and credulous. Although the siege of Archas had no religious aim, and even turned the pilgrims aside from the principal object of the holy war, it was not thence less abundant, according to Raymond d'Agiles, in miracles and prodigies of all sorts. The belief of the people was frequently supported by the most enlightened of the leaders, who found it necessary to warm the imaginations of the soldiers to preserve their authority. Every day fresh parties were formed in the Christian army, and the most powerful were always those who circulated a belief in the greatest number of miracles. It was during the siege of Archas that doubts arose among the pilgrims about the discovery of the lance which had had such an effect upon the courage of the Crusaders at the battle of Antioch, and the camp of the besiegers became all at once divided into two great factions, strongly opposed to each other. Arnold de Rohés, according to William of Tyre, a man of dissolute manners, but well versed in history and letters, was the first who dared openly to deny the truth of the prodigy. This ecclesiastic, who was chaplain to the duke of Normandy, drew into his party all the Normans and the Crusaders from the north of France; whilst those of the south ranged themselves on the side of Barthélemi, who was attached to the count de St. Gilles. The priest of Marseilles, a simple man, who himself believed that which he wished others to believe, had a new revelation, and related in the camp that he had seen Jesus Christ attached to the cross, cursing the incredulous, and devoting to the death and punishment of Judas the impious sceptics who dared to search into the mysterious ways of God. This apparition, and the menaces of Christ, highly excited the imaginations of the Provençals, who had no less faith, according to Raymond d'Agiles, in the tales of Barthélemi, than in the evidence of the saints and apostles. But Arnold was astonished that God should only reveal himself to a simple priest, whilst so many virtuous prelates were in the army; and, without denying the intervention of the divine power, he was not willing to admit any other prodigies than those performed by the valour and heroism of the Christian soldiers.

As the produce of the offerings made to the depositaries of the holy lance were distributed to the poor, the latter, who were in vast numbers in the army, were not sparing in murmurs against the chaplain of the duke of Normandy, and they attributed to his incredulity, and that of his partisans, all the evils that the Crusaders had suffered during the siege of Archas. Arnold and his party, which increased every day, on the contrary attributed the misfortunes of the Christians to their divisions, and to the turbulent spirit of a set of visionaries. Amongst these debates the Crusaders of the northern provinces reproached those of the south with want of bravery in fight, with being less anxious for glory than pillage, *and with passing their time in ornamenting their horses and mules.* The latter, on their side, did not cease to reproach the partisans of Arnold with their want of faith, and their sacrilegious railleries, and, without ceasing, opposed new visions to the reasonings of the incredulous. One had seen St. Mark the evangelist, another the holy Virgin, and both had attested the veracity of the priest of Marseilles. Bishop Adhémar had appeared to a third, informing him that he had been kept several days in hell for having entertained some doubts of the truth of the holy lance.

These recitals only served still more to inflame the minds of the army, and violence often came to the support of trickery and credulity. At length Barthélemi, seduced by the importance of the part he was made to play, and perhaps, also, by the miraculous tales of his partisans, which might strengthen his own illusions, resolved to terminate all debates by submitting to the ordeal by fire. This resolution restored calm to the Christian army, and all the pilgrims were convoked to be witnesses of the judgment of God. On the day fixed (it was Good Friday), a funeral pile, made of branches of olive, was erected in the middle of a vast plain. Most of the Crusaders were assembled, and everything was prepared for the terrible ordeal. The flames had already mounted to a height of twenty cubits, when Barthélemi was seen advancing, accompanied by the priests, who walked in silence, barefooted, and clothed in their sacerdotal habits. Covered by a simple tunic, the priest of Marseilles bore the holy lance, surrounded with floating streamers. When he arrived within a few paces of the pile, one of the principal of the clergy pronounced in a loud voice the following words:— "If this man has seen Jesus Christ face to face, and if the apostle Andrew did reveal the divine lance to him, may he pass safe and sound through the flames; but if, on the contrary, he is guilty of falsehood, may he be burnt, together with the lance which he bears in his hands." At these words all the spectators bowed, and answered as with one voice, "Be the will of God accomplished." Barthélemi threw himself on his knees, took Heaven to witness the truth of all that he had said, and, after recommending himself to the prayers of the bishops and priests, rushed through the funeral pile at a part where an opening of two feet wide had been made for his passage.

The numerous spectators lost sight of him for a moment, and many pilgrims, says Raymond d'Agiles, were beginning to lament him, when they saw him appear on the side opposite to that by which he had entered. He was immediately surrounded and pressed upon by an innumerable crowd, who cried out "miracle," and were eager to touch his vestments. But Barthélemi was covered with mortal wounds. He was carried in a dying state to the tent of the count of Thoulouse, where he expired a few days after, still protesting his innocence and veracity. He was buried beneath the spot where the funeral pile had been erected. Raymond of St. Gilles and the Provençals persisted in regarding him as an apostle and a martyr. The greater number of the pilgrims allowed themselves to be satisfied with *the judgment of God,* and the miraculous lance from that time ceased to work miracles.* In vain the Crusaders from the southern provinces endeavoured to substitute for it the ring and cross of Adhémar; they attracted neither the devotion nor the offerings of the pilgrims.

Whilst the Crusaders were detained before the fortress of Archas, they received an embassy from

* Accounts of this event may be read in William of Tyre, Robert d'Aix, and above all in Raymond d'Agiles, who does not omit the least circumstance.

Alexius. The Greek emperor wished to impose upon the Latins, by promising to follow them into Palestine with an army, if they would allow him time to make the necessary preparations. Alexius in his letters complained of the non-performance of the treaties by which he was to be made master of the cities of Syria and Asia Minor that had fallen into the hands of the Christians ; but he complained without bitterness, and showed so much circumspection in his reproaches as proved that he likewise had some wrongs to repair. This embassy was but ill received in the Christian army. The leaders accused the Greeks of the death of the count of Hainault, and reproached the emperor with his shameful flight during the siege of Antioch. They despised his complaints, and gave no faith to his so often broken promises.

The Latins hated Alexius ever since the siege of Nice. Hatred guided them on this occasion better than the most clear-sighted policy could have done ; for in the end, if we are to believe their historians, they learned that the emperor of Constantinople maintained a secret understanding with the caliph of Egypt, and that his design was to retard the march and the progress of the Christian army.

The caliph of Cairo, who was governed by the same policy as Alexius, kept up relations with the Crusaders which circumstances rendered more or less sincere, and which were subordinate to the fear which their arms inspired. Although he negotiated at the same time with the Christians and the Turks, he hated the former because they were the enemies of the prophet, and the latter because they had deprived him of Syria. His object was but to profit by the war, so as to regain his possessions and extend the limits of his empire. For several months he had been master of Jerusalem, and as he trembled for his new conquest, he sent ambassadors to the Christian army. This embassy arrived in the camp a short time after the departure of the deputies of Alexius.

It was accompanied by the deputies whom the Christians had sent into Egypt during the siege of Antioch. On their arrival at Cairo they had at first been well received by the caliph ; but as soon as he learned that the Christian army was in a desperate situation, they were thrown into dungeons, and only owed their liberation to the triumphant march of the Christian army, which filled the East with the fame of its victories. Their unexpected return gave the greatest delight to their brothers and companions. They listened with emotion to the account of their captivity, and loud cries of indignation arose throughout the army against the caliph of Cairo.

The Egyptian ambassadors did all in their power to justify their master and appease the anger of the Christians. They had brought with them magnificent presents, destined by the caliph for the principal leaders of the army. They were to present to Godfrey of Bouillon forty thousand pieces of gold, thirty mantles, and several vases of gold and silver ; to Bohémond they were to offer sixty thousand pieces of gold, fifty purple mantles, several precious vases, rich carpets, and an Arabian horse whose harness was covered with plates of gold. Each leader was to receive a present proportioned to his military reputation, and to the idea that was entertained of his importance in the Christian army. When the ambassadors had distributed the presents of the caliph according to his instructions, they demanded permission to speak in the council of the leaders. They announced that their master had delivered Jerusalem from the domination of the Turks, and that he anxiously desired to maintain peace with the Christians. After having declared the benevolent and friendly dispositions of the caliph, and after having repeated that it was his intention to protect pilgrimages and the exercise of the Christian religion, they finished by declaring that the gates of Jerusalem should only be opened to *unarmed Christians.* Upon hearing this proposition, which they had already rejected amidst the miseries of the siege of Antioch, the leaders of the Christian army could not restrain their indignation. As their only answer, they came to the resolution to hasten their march towards the Holy Land, and threatened the ambassadors of Egypt to carry their arms even to the banks of the Nile.

The Crusaders were drawing together their troops, which had so long been dispersed, to march together towards Jerusalem, when they were attacked by the emir of Tripoli. A prompt and bloody defeat was the reward of the temerity of the Mussulman prince. After having lost a great number of his soldiers, he was obliged to purchase peace and the safety of his capital by the payment of a considerable tribute to the Crusaders. He furnished them with provisions in abundance, sent back three hundred Christian prisoners to the camp, and, to leave no pretext for future hostilities, he engaged to surrender the places he possessed when their standards should float over the walls of Jerusalem.

The Crusaders, satisfied with this promise extracted from fear, had no more enemies to combat, and now only thought of that one conquest which was to assure them all others. Raymond alone did not partake of the new ardour of the Christian army; he was fixed in his determination to remain before Archas, and only gave up the siege when his soldiers had a second time threatened to abandon his colours.

The Crusaders commenced their march towards Palestine at the end of the month of May.* The inhabitants of Phœnicia had finished their harvest. The Christians found provisions everywhere, and admired on their passage the rich productions of Asia, which they already looked upon as the reward of their labours. On their left rose the mountains of Libanus, so often celebrated by the prophets; between the mountains and the sea, the fields they traversed were covered with olive-trees, which grew to the height of elms and oaks; in the plains and on the hills were oranges, pomegranates, and many other sorts of trees unknown in the West. Among these new productions one plant, the juice of which was sweeter than honey, above all attracted the attention of the pilgrims: this plant was the sugar-cane. It was cultivated in several of the provinces of Syria, and particularly in the territory of Tripoli, where they had found means of extracting from it the substance which the inhabitants called *zucra*. According to Albert d'Aix, this plant had afforded great assistance to the Christians when assailed by famine at the sieges of Maarah and Archas. This plant, now become of such importance in commerce, had been till this time unknown in the West. The pilgrims made it known in Europe, and towards the end of the crusades it was transported into Italy and Sicily, whilst the Saracens introduced it into the kingdom of Grenada, whence the Spaniards afterwards conveyed it to Madeira and the American colonies.†

When the pilgrims were all united to continue their march to Palestine, they must doubtless have been struck with terror as they contemplated the losses they had experienced. More than two hundred thousand Crusaders had been cut off by battles, famine, misery, and disease. A great number of them, unable to support the fatigues of the holy pilgrimage, and losing all hope of seeing Palestine, had returned to the West. Many had taken up their abode in Antioch, Edessa, and other cities from which they had driven the inhabitants, and which they were obliged to defend against the infidels. With all these deductions, the army which was to achieve the conquest of the Holy Land scarcely numbered fifty thousand fighting men under its banners.

The leaders, however, did not hesitate to pursue their enterprise. They who did remain in the ranks had borne every trial; they did not drag in their train a useless, embarrassing multitude; and it was much more easy to supply them with provisions and establish order and discipline amongst them. Strengthened in some sort by their losses, they were perhaps more formidable than they were at the siege of Nice. The remembrance of their exploits increased their confidence and courage, and

* The picture of the march and the impatience of the Christians is to be found in Tasso, in the same colours and almost the same circumstances as in the historians.

† Sanuti proposed to plant the sugar-cane in Sicily and Apulia. This idea was not carried into execution before the end of the fourteenth century. The sugar-cane did not pass, as has been said, from Sicily to America; it was transported to Madeira from the coast of Spain, whither it had been brought by the Saracens. The sugar-cane is still found in some parts of Grenada.

THE ROAD TO JERUSALEM.

Most of the princes whom the war had ruined were in the pay of the count of Thoulouse. This species of degradation was doubtless painful to their pride; but as they approached the holy city it might be said that they lost some of their indomitable arrogance, and that they forgot both their pretensions and their quarrels. The most perfect union now prevailed among the Crusaders. In their impatience to see Jerusalem, neither mountains, defiles, rivers, nor any other impediments at all damped their ardour; the soldiers would not even consent to take repose, and often, contrary to the wishes of their leaders, marched during the night, when they were directed by a luminous angel.—Book IV.

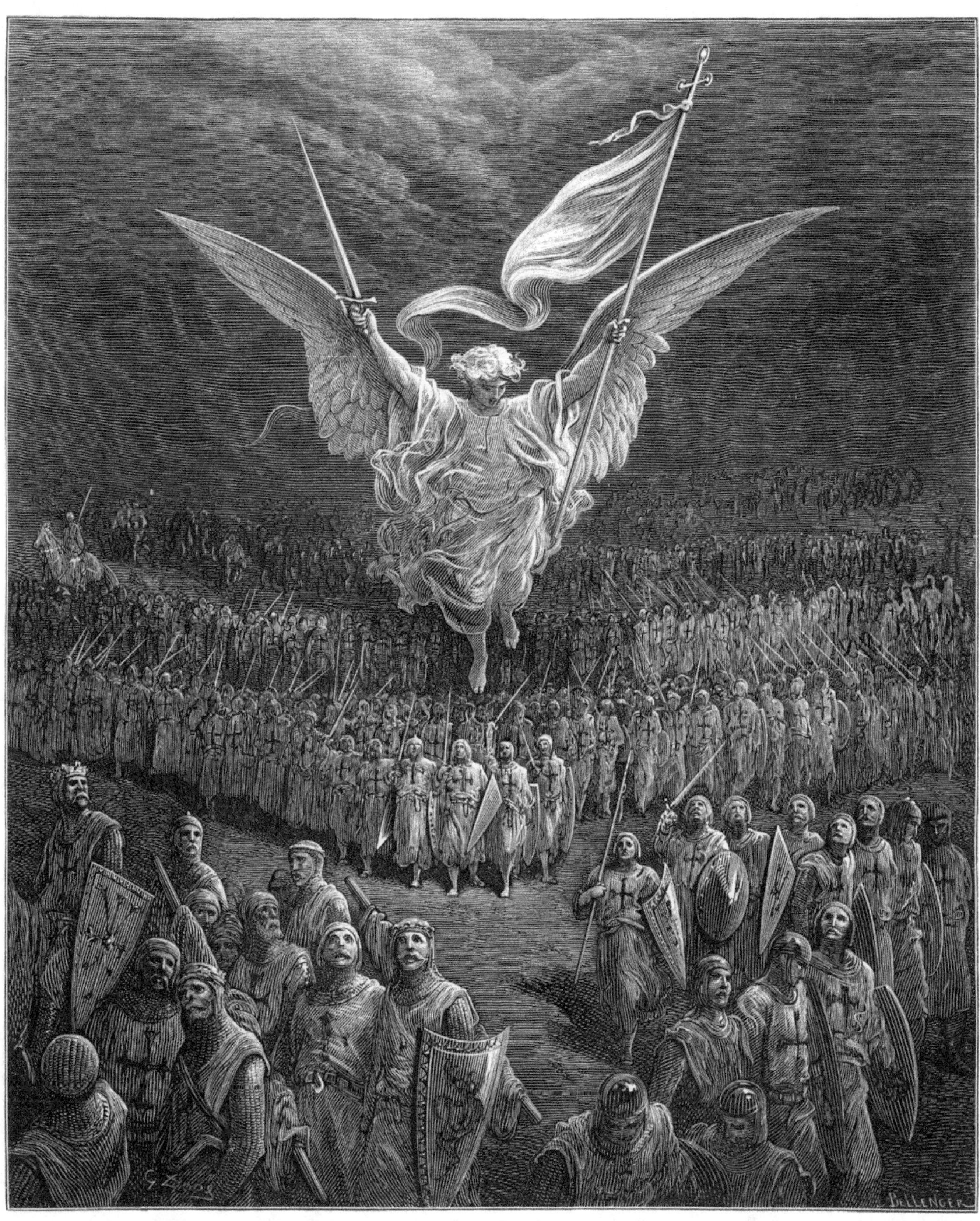

the terror which their arms inspired might well make the Saracens believe that their army was still innumerable.

Most of the princes whom the war had ruined were in the pay of the count of Thoulouse. This species of degradation was doubtless painful to their pride; but as they approached the holy city it might be said that they lost some of their indomitable arrogance, and that they forgot both their pretensions and their quarrels. The most perfect union now prevailed among the Crusaders. In their impatience to see Jerusalem, neither mountains, defiles, rivers, nor any other impediments at all damped their ardour; the soldiers would not even consent to take repose, and often, contrary to the wishes of their leaders, marched during the night, when they were directed by a luminous angel.

The Christian army followed the coasts of the sea, where they might be provisioned by the Pisan, Genoese, and Flemish fleets. A crowd of Christians and pious solitaries who inhabited the neighbouring mountains, hastened to meet their brethren of the West, brought them fresh provisions, and guided them on their way. After a painful march over rocks and along the declivities of precipices, they descended into the plain of Berytus, and traversed the territory of Sidon and Tyre.

Whilst they remained three days on the banks of the river Eleuctera, they were assailed by serpents called *tarenta*, whose bite produced death, attended by violent pain and unquenchable thirst. The sight of these reptiles, which they attempted to frighten away by striking stones one against another, or by the clashing of their bucklers, filled the pilgrims with fear and surprise; but that which must have more astonished them was the strange remedy for their bite which the inhabitants pointed out to them, and which without doubt must have seemed to them far more a subject of scandal than a means of cure.*

The Christians, having still continued to march along the coast, arrived before the walls of Accon, the ancient Ptolemaïs, at the present day St. Jean d'Acre. The emir who commanded in this city for the caliph of Egypt, sent them provisions, and promised to surrender as soon as they should become masters of Jerusalem. The Crusaders, who had no idea of attacking Ptolemaïs, received with joy the submission and promises of the Egyptian emir; but chance soon made them aware that he had no other intention but that of getting them out of his territories, and raising up enemies against them in the countries they were about to pass through. The Christian army, after having quitted the country of Ptolemaïs, had advanced between the sea and Mount Carmel, and were encamped near the port of Cæsarea, when a dove, which had escaped from the talons of a bird of prey, fell lifeless among the soldiers. The bishop of Apt, who chanced to pick up this bird, found under its wing a letter written by the emir of Ptolemaïs to the emir of Cæsarea. "The cursed race of the Christians," wrote the emir, "have just passed through my territories, and will soon cross yours; let the chiefs of all the Mussulman cities be warned of their march, and let them take measures to crush our enemies." This letter was read in the council of the princes, and before all the army. The Crusaders, according to the account of Raymond d'Agiles, an eye-witness, broke out into loud expressions of surprise and joy, no longer doubting that God protected their enterprise, since he sent the birds of heaven to reveal to them the secrets of the infidels. Filled with new enthusiasm, they continued their route, drawing away from the sea, and leaving Antipatride and Jaffa on their right. They saluted in the east the heights of Ephraim, and took possession of Lydda (the ancient Diospolis), celebrated by the martyrdom of St. George, and of Ramla, famous for the birth and tomb of Samuel.

---

* We may venture to quote the passage of Albert d'Aix in Latin, which speaks of the remedy advised by the inhabitants of the country against the bite of the *tarenta*:—Similiter et aliam edocti sunt medicinam, ut vir percussus sine morâ coiret cum muliere, cum viro mulier, et sic ab omni tumore veneni liberaretur uterque.—*Alb. Aq.* lib. iv. cap. 40. The same historian speaks of another remedy, which consisted in pressing strongly the place of the bite, to prevent the communication of the venom with the other parts of the system.

When arrived at this last-named city, the Christians had only a march of sixteen miles to be before Jerusalem. The leaders held a council, in which some of them proposed to go and attack the infidels in Egypt, instead of undertaking the siege of the holy city. "When," said they, "we shall have conquered the sultan of Egypt, the cities of Alexandria and Cairo, with Palestine and most of the kingdoms of the East, will fall under our power. If we go straight to Jerusalem, we shall want both water and provisions, and we shall be obliged to raise the siege, without having the power to undertake anything else." Such of the leaders as did not agree with this opinion, answered, "That the Christian army amounted to no more than fifty thousand combatants, and that it would be madness to begin a march to distant, and, to them, unknown regions, and where they could look for no assistance. On all sides they must expect dangers and obstacles; nowhere should they be free from the dread of want of provisions; but the route to Jerusalem was much more easy than that to Alexandria or Cairo. The Crusaders could pursue no wiser plan than to continue their march, and prosecute the enterprise they had begun, leaving it to Providence to provide for their wants, and protect them from thirst and famine."

This latter opinion was adopted, and the army received the signal for departure. In going from Lydda the Crusaders approached the mountains of Judea. These mountains, on which Jerusalem is situated, do not resemble those of Taurus or Lybia; the bluish summits of the Judean range have neither verdure nor shade, and its solitudes have no other inhabitant than the boar and the gazelle, the eagle and the vulture. Their physiognomy has something of the sadness of Israel, and recalls the austere and melancholy poetry of the prophets. The Christian army advanced through a narrow valley, between two mountains burning with the rays of the sun. The route which it followed had been cut into gullies by torrents of rain, which had also loosened large masses of rock, and these, descending into the valley, choked the narrow passages. In such difficult situations a few Mussulmans would attack and kill many of the Crusaders.

The cities which lay in the route of the Crusaders were all abandoned by the infidels. The greater part of the pilgrims endeavoured to get in advance of each other, that they might be the first to obtain possession of the places and castles that were thus left without inhabitants. The Crusaders, says Raymond d'Agiles, had agreed among themselves, that when one of the leaders had planted his standard upon a city, or had placed any mark whatever on the door of a house, he should become the legitimate possessor of it. This imprudent agreement had given birth to ambition and covetousness in the soldiers as well as the barons. Many, in the hope of obtaining rich possessions, abandoned their colours, wandered about the country, and spread themselves even as far as the banks of the Jordan. In the mean time, those to whom, according to the expression of the historians, *nothing was more dear than the commandments of God*, advanced, barefooted, under the standard of the cross, lamenting the error of their brethren. When they arrived at Emmaus, a considerable city in the times of the Maccabees, and which was then no more than a large village, known under the name of Nicopolis, some Christians of Bethlehem came to implore their assistance. Touched with their prayers, Tancred set out in the middle of the night with a detachment of three hundred men, and planted the flag of the Crusaders upon the walls of the city, at the same hour in which Christ was born and was announced to the shepherds of Judea.

During this same night a phenomenon appeared in the heaven, which powerfully affected the imagination of the pilgrims. An eclipse of the moon produced all at once the most profound darkness, and when she at length re-appeared she was covered with a blood-red veil. Many of the Crusaders were seized with terror at this spectacle; but those who were acquainted with the march and movements of the stars, says Albert d'Aix, reassured their companions by telling them that the sight of such a phenomenon announced the triumph of the Christians and the destruction of the infidels.

By the break of day, on the 10th of June, 1099, the Crusaders ascended the heights of Emmaus. All at once the holy city presented itself to their eyes.* The first who perceived it exclaimed together, "*Jerusalem! Jerusalem!*" The rear ranks rushed forward to behold the city that was the object of all their wishes, and the words, "*It is the will of God! It is the will of God!*" were shouted by the whole army, and resounded over Mount Sion and the Mount of Olives, which offered themselves to the eager gaze of the Crusaders. The horsemen dismounted from their horses, and marched barefooted. Some cast themselves upon their knees at beholding the holy places, whilst others kissed with respect the earth honoured by the presence of the Saviour. In their transports they passed by turns from joy to sadness, and from sadness to joy. At one moment they felicitated themselves with touching the last term of their labours; and then wept over their sins, over the death of Christ, and over his profaned tomb; but all renewed the oath they had so often made to deliver the holy city from the sacrilegious yoke of the Mussulmans.

History furnishes very few positive notions of the foundation and origin of Jerusalem. The common opinion is, that Melchisedec, who is called king of Salem in Scripture, made his residence there. It was afterwards the capital of the Jebusees, which procured it the name of the city of Jebus. It is probable that from the name of Jebus and that of Salem, which signifies *vision*, or *abode of peace*, was formed the name of Jerusalem, which it bore under the kings of Judah.

From the highest antiquity Jerusalem yielded in magnificence to none of the cities of Asia. Jeremiah names it *admirable city*, on account of its beauty; and David calls it *the most glorious and most illustrious city of the East.* From the nature of its entirely religious legislation, it always showed an invincible attachment for its laws; but it was often a prey to the fanaticism of its enemies as well as that of its own citizens. Its founders, says Tacitus, having foreseen that the opposition of their manners to those of other nations would be a source of war, had given their attention to its fortifications, and in the early times of the Roman empire it was one of the strongest places in Asia. After having undergone a great many revolutions, it was at length completely destroyed by Titus, and in accordance with the denunciations of the prophets, presented no more than a horrible confusion of stones. The emperor Adrian afterwards destroyed even its ruins, and caused another city to be built, giving it the name of Aëlia, so that there should remain nothing of the ancient Jerusalem. The Christians, but more particularly the Jews, were banished from it. Paganism there exalted its idols, and Jupiter and Venus had altars upon the tomb of Jesus Christ. In the midst of so many profanations and vicissitudes, the people of the East and the West scarcely preserved the memory of the city of David, when Constantine restored it its name, recalled the faithful, and made it a Christian city. Conquered afterwards by the Persians, and retaken by the Greeks, it had fallen a bloody prey into the hands of the Mussulmans, who disputed the possession of it, and subjected it by turns to the double scourge of persecution and war.

At the time of the crusades, Jerusalem formed, as it does at present, a square, rather longer than wide, of about a league in circumference. It extends over four hills; on the east the *Moriah*, upon which the mosque of Omar was built in the place of the temple of Solomon; on the south and west the *Acra*, which occupied the whole width of the city; on the north the *Bezetha*, or the new city; and on the north-west the *Golgotha*, or *Calvary*, which the Greeks considered to be the centre of the world, and upon which was built the church of the Resurrection. In the state in which Jerusalem then was it had lost much of its strength and extent. Mount Sion no longer arose within its enclosure and

* Tasso has spoken of the enthusiasm of the Crusaders at the sight of Jerusalem.

dominated over its walls between the south and west. The three valleys which surrounded the ramparts had been in many places filled up by Adrian, and the access to the place was much less difficult, particularly on the northern side. Nevertheless, as Jerusalem under the Saracens had had to sustain several sieges, and as it was at all times exposed to fresh attacks, its fortifications had not been neglected. The Egyptians, who had had possession of it for several months, took advantage of the tardiness of the Christian army to put it in a state of defence.

Whilst the Crusaders were advancing slowly towards the city, the lieutenant of the caliph, Iftikhar-Eddaulah, ravaged the neighbouring plains, burnt the villages, filled up or poisoned the cisterns, and surrounded himself with a desert in which the Christians must find themselves a prey to all kinds of misery. He caused provisions for a long siege to be transported into the place ; he called upon all Mussulmans to come to the defence of Jerusalem, and employed a great number of workmen, day and night, to construct machines of war, to raise the walls, and repair the towers. The garrison of the city amounted to forty thousand men, and twenty thousand of the inhabitants took up arms.

At the approach of the Christians, some detachments of infidels had come out from Jerusalem to observe the march and proceedings of the enemy, but were repulsed by Baldwin du Bourg and Tancred. The latter had hastened from Bethlehem, of which he had taken possession. After having pursued the fugitives up to the gates of the holy city, he left his companions and repaired alone to the Mount of Olives, from whence he contemplated at leisure the city promised to the arms and devotion of the pilgrims.* He was disturbed in his pious contemplations by five Mussulmans who came from the city, and finding him alone attacked him. Tancred made no effort to avoid the combat; three of the Saracens fell beneath his arm, whilst the other two took to flight. Without either hastening or retarding his speed, Tancred rejoined the army, which, in its enthusiasm, was advancing without order, and descended the heights of Emmaus, singing these words from Isaiah, "*Jerusalem, lift up thine eyes, and behold the liberator who comes to break thy chains.*"

On the day after their arrival the Crusaders employed themselves in regularly laying siege to the place. The duke of Normandy, the count of Flanders, and Tancred encamped towards the north, from the gate of Herod to the gate of Cedar or of St. Stephen. Near to the Flemings, the Normans, and the Italians, were placed the English, commanded by Edgar Atheling, and the Bretons, conducted by their duke, Alain Fergent, the sire de Chateau-Giron, and the viscount de Dinan. Godfrey, Eustace, and Baldwin du Bourg established their quarters between the west and the north, around the enclosure of Calvary, from the gate of Damascus to the gate of Jaffa. The count of Thoulouse placed his camp to the right of Godfrey between the south and the west; he had near to him Raimbaud of Orange, William of Montpellier, and Gaston of Béarn. His troops at first extended to the declivity of Sion, and a few days afterwards he pitched his tents upon the very summit of the mountain, at the place where Christ celebrated Easter. By these dispositions the Crusaders left free the sides of the city which were defended on the south by the valley of Gihon or Siloë, and towards the east by the valley of Jehoshaphat.†

Every step that the pilgrims took around Jerusalem brought to their minds some remembrance dear to their religion. In this territory, so revered by the Christians, there was not a valley, not a rock which had not a name in sacred history. All that they saw awakened or warmed their enthusiasm. They could not withdraw their eyes from the holy city, or cease to lament over the state of debasement into which it had fallen. This city, once so superb, looked as if buried in its own ruins,

* Tasso here makes Tancred contend with Clorinda. The personages of Clorinda and Herminia are the invention of the poet.

† In comparing the description of the siege of Jerusalem by the Crusaders with that of the siege which the Romans carried on under Vespasian, we find that the quarters of Godfrey were in the same place as those of Titus, when he directed his first attacks against the city. See the *History* of Josephus.

and they then might, to employ the expression of Josephus, have asked in Jerusalem itself where was Jerusalem? With its square houses without windows, surmounted by flat terraces, it appeared to the Crusaders like an enormous mass of stones heaped up between rocks. They could only perceive here and there in its bosom a few cypresses and some clumps of aloes and terebinthi, among which arose steeples in the quarter of the Christians, and mosques in that of the infidels. In the valleys and the fields adjacent to the city, which ancient traditions describe as covered with gardens and groves, there struggled into growth a few scattered olives and thorny shrubs. The sight of these sterile plains, and of the mountains burnt up by an ardent sun, offered to the pilgrims nothing but images of mourning, and mingled a melancholy sadness with their religious sentiments. They seemed to hear the voices of the prophets which had announced the servitude and the misfortunes of the city of God, and, in the excess of their devotion, they thought themselves called upon to restore it to its ancient greatness and splendour.

That which still further inflamed the zeal of the Crusaders for the deliverance of the holy city, was the arrival amongst them of a great number of Christians who had come out of Jerusalem, and being deprived of their property and driven from their homes, had sought assistance and an asylum among their brethren from the West. These Christians described the miseries which the Mussulmans had inflicted upon all the worshippers of Christ. The women, children, and old men were detained as hostages, whilst such as were of an age to bear arms were condemned to labours which surpassed their strength. The head of the principal hospital for pilgrims had, with a great many other Christians, been cast into prison, and the churches had been pillaged to furnish support for the Mussulman soldiers. The patriarch Simeon was gone to the isle of Cyprus to implore the charity of the faithful, and save his flock, which was menaced with destruction if he did not pay the enormous tribute imposed by the oppressors of the holy city. Every day new outrages were heaped upon the Christians of Jerusalem, and several times the infidels had formed the project of giving up to the flames and utterly destroying both the Holy Sepulchre and the church of the Resurrection.

The Christian fugitives, whilst making these melancholy recitals to the pilgrims, exhorted them to hasten their attack upon Jerusalem. In the very first days of the siege, a solitary, who had fixed his retreat on the Mount of Olives, came to join his prayers with those of the Christians driven from Jerusalem, and conjured the Crusaders, in the name of Christ, whose interpreter he declared himself, at once to proceed to a general assault. Although destitute of either ladders or machines of war, the Crusaders yielded to the counsels of the pious hermit, believing that their courage and their swords were sufficient to destroy the ramparts of the Saracens. The leaders, who had seen so many prodigies performed by the valour and enthusiasm of the Christian soldiers, and who had not forgotten the lengthened miseries of the siege of Antioch, yielded without difficulty to the impatience of the army; besides, the sight of Jerusalem had exalted the minds of the Crusaders, and disposed even the least credulous to hope that God himself would second their bravery by miracles.

At the first signal, the Christian army advanced in good order towards the ramparts. Never, say the historians, did the soldiers of the cross evince so much ardour; some, joined in close battalions, covered themselves with their bucklers, which formed an impenetrable vault over their heads, and endeavoured with pikes and hammers to destroy the wall; whilst others, ranged in long files, remained at some distance, and plied their slings and cross-bows in driving the enemy from the ramparts. Oil, boiling pitch, large stones, and enormous beams were cast upon the front ranks of the Christians without putting the least stop to their labours. The outer wall began to fall beneath their strokes, but the inner wall presented an insuperable obstacle, and nothing was left to them but escalade. This bold method was attempted, although only one ladder long enough to reach the top of the walls could be found. The bravest mounted, and fought hand to hand with the Saracens, who were confounded with such rash courage. It is probable that the Crusaders would have entered Jerusalem that very day if they had had the necessary instruments and machines; but so small a number of them could gain the top of the walls, that they could not maintain themselves there. Bravery was useless; Heaven did not perform the miracles which the solitary had promised, and the Saracens at length forced the assailants to retreat.

The Christians returned to their camp deploring their imprudence and credulity. This first reverse taught them that they must not always expect prodigies, and that before they proceeded further they must construct machines of war. But it was very difficult to procure the necessary wood in a country of barren sands and arid rocks. Several detachments were sent to search for materials; and chance discovered to one of them some large beams, which Tancred caused to be transported to the camp. They demolished the houses, and even the churches in the vicinity of the city which had not been given up to the flames, and every available bit of wood that had escaped the ravages of the Saracens was employed in the construction of machines.

In spite of their discoveries and exertions, the progress of the siege did not answer to the impatience of the Crusaders, nor did they appear likely to be able to avert the evils that threatened them. The most intense heats of the summer set in at the very time the pilgrims arrived before Jerusalem. A scorching sun and southern winds, loaded with the sands of the desert, inflamed the horizon. Plants and animals perished; the torrent of Kedron was dry, and all the cisterns had been filled up or poisoned.* Under a sun of fire, and amidst burning and arid plains, the Christian army soon became a prey to all the horrors of thirst.

The fountain of Siloë, which only flowed at intervals, could not suffice for such a multitude. A skinful of fetid water, brought from a distance of three leagues, cost as much as three silver deniers. Overcome by thirst and heat, the soldiers turned up the soil with their swords, and burying themselves in the freshly-moved earth, eagerly carried to their lips every moist clod that presented itself. During the day they looked anxiously for the night. and at night longed for the break of day, in the constantly disappointed hope that the return of either the one or the other would bring some little freshness, or a few drops of rain. Every morning they were seen to glue their parched lips to the marbles covered with dew. During the heat of the day the most robust languished beneath their tents, seeming not to have even strength left to implore the assistance of Heaven.

The knights and barons were not at all exempt from the scourge which devoured the army, and many of them exchanged for the water of which they stood in daily need, the treasures they had won from the infidels. "Pity, on account of this extreme thirst," says the old translator of William of Tyre, "was not so much due to the foot-soldiers as the horsemen; the foot-soldiers could be contented with a little, but the horsemen could only supply their horses with drink at great expense. As to the beasts of burthen," adds the same historian, "there was no more account taken of them than of things already dead; they were allowed to stray away in the fields, where they died for want of water."

In this general misery the women and children dragged their exhausted bodies across fields and plains, seeking sometimes a spring and sometimes shade, neither of which existed. Many who strayed from the army fell into the ambushes of the Saracens, and lost either their lives or their liberty. When some fortunate pilgrims discovered a spring or a cistern in a remote or obscure place, they concealed it from their companions, and prevented their approach to it. Quarrels of a violent nature broke out on this account daily; and not unfrequently the Crusaders drew their swords for the sake of a little

* An admirable picture is to be found in Tasso of this drought, which is also described by Robert the Monk, Baldric, Raymond d'Agiles, Albert d'Aix, William of Tyre, and by Gilles or Gilou, in his Latin poem upon the first crusade.

muddy water; in short, the want of water was so insupportable an evil, that they hardly noticed the scarcity of food. The intensity of thirst and the heat of the climate made them forget the horrors of the famine which seemed to pursue the Christians everywhere.

If the besieged had at this period made a *sortie*, they would have easily triumphed over the Crusaders, but the latter were defended by the remembrance of their exploits; and in the distress to which they were now reduced, their name alone still inspired the Saracens with dread. The Mussulmans likewise might entertain the belief that their enemies could not long resist the joint calamities of famine and thirst. The old historians here employ the most pathetic expressions to paint the frightful misery of the pilgrims. Abbot Guibert even goes so far as to say that men never suffered so many evils to obtain benefits which were not of this earth. Amidst such calamities, says Raymond d'Agiles, who was himself at the siege of Jerusalem, many forgot their God, and thought no longer of either gaining the city, or obtaining the divine mercy. The remembrance of their own country increased their sufferings; and so great was their discouragement, that some deserted the standards of the crusade entirely, and fled to the ports of Palestine and Syria to wait for an opportunity of returning to Europe.

The leaders clearly saw that there was no other remedy for the evils the army endured but the taking of Jerusalem; and yet the labours of the siege went on very slowly, for they had neither wood enough for the construction of machines, nor workmen with necessary implements. In addition, a report was current that a formidable army had left Egypt for the purpose of relieving the city. The wisest and the bravest were beginning, in such a critical situation, to despair of the success of the enterprise, when assistance was afforded them of an unexpected kind.

They learned that a Genoese fleet had entered the port of Jaffa, laden with provisions and ammunition of all sorts. This news spread the greatest joy through the Christian army, and a body of three hundred men, commanded by Raymond Pelet, set out from the camp to meet the convoy, which Heaven appeared to have sent the Crusaders in their misery. This detachment, after having beaten and dispersed the Saracens they met on their passage, entered the city of Jaffa, which, being abandoned by its inhabitants, was occupied by the Genoese. On their arrival, the Crusaders learnt that the Christian fleet had been surprised and burnt by that of the infidels, but they had had time to get out the provisions and a great quantity of instruments for the construction of machines of war. All they had been able to save was transported to the camp of the Christians. This convoy arrived under the walls of Jerusalem, followed by a great number of Genoese engineers and carpenters, whose presence greatly revived the emulation and courage of the army.

As they still had not sufficient wood for the construction of the machines, a Syrian conducted the duke of Normandy and the count of Flanders to a mountain situated at a distance of thirty miles from Jerusalem, between the Valley of Samaria and the Valley of Sechem. There the Christians found the forest of which Tasso speaks in the "Jerusalem Delivered." The trees of this forest were neither protected from the axe of the Crusaders by the enchantments of Ismen nor the arms of the Saracens. Oxen shod with iron transported them in triumph before Jerusalem.

None of the leaders, except Raymond of Thoulouse, had sufficient money to pay for the labours they had commanded, but the zeal and charity of the pilgrims came to their assistance. Many offered the remains of the spoil taken from the enemy; the knights and barons themselves became laborious workmen; and every arm was employed, and everything in motion throughout the army. The women, the children, even the sick, shared the toils of the soldiers. Whilst the more robust were engaged in the construction of rams, catapultas, and covered galleries, others fetched water in skins from the fountain of Elpira, on the road to Damascus, or from a rivulet which flowed beyond Bethlehem, towards the desert of St. John. Some prepared the skins that were to be stretched over the machines to render them fire-proof, whilst others traversed the plains and neighbouring mountains to collect branches of the olive, the fig, and some other trees of the country, to make hurdles and faggots.

Although the Christians had still much to suffer from thirst and the heat of the climate, the hope of soon seeing the end of their troubles gave them strength to support them. The preparations for the attack were pressed on with incredible activity; every day formidable machines appeared, threatening the ramparts of the Saracens. The construction of them was directed by Gaston of Béarn, of whose skill and bravery historians make great boast. Among these machines were three enormous towers of a new structure, each of which had three stages, the first for the workmen who directed the movements of it, and the second and third for the warriors who were to make the assault. These three rolling fortresses were higher than the walls of the besieged city. At the top was fixed a kind of drawbridge, which could be let down on the ramparts, and present a road by which to penetrate into the place.

But these powerful means of attack were not the only ones which were to second the efforts of the Crusaders. The religious enthusiasm which had already performed so many prodigies was again to augment their ardour and confidence in victory. The clergy spread themselves through all the quarters of the army, exhorting the pilgrims to penitence and concord. Misery, which almost always engenders complaints and murmurs, had soured their hearts, and produced division among the leaders and the soldiers, who at other times had disputed for cities and treasures, but for whom then the most common things had become objects of jealousy and quarrels. The solitary from the Mount of Olives added his exhortations to those of the clergy, and addressing himself to the princes and people: "You who are come," said he, "from the regions of the West to worship the God of armies, love one another as brothers, and sanctify yourselves by repentance and good works. If you obey the laws of God, he will render you masters of the holy city; if you resist him, all his anger will fall upon you." The solitary advised the Crusaders to march round Jerusalem, invoking the mercy and protection of Heaven.

The pilgrims, persuaded that the gates of the city were not less likely to be opened by devotion than bravery, listened with docility to the exhortations of the solitary, and were all eager to follow his counsel, which they regarded as the language of God himself. After a rigorous fast of three days, they issued from their quarters armed, and marched barefooted and bareheaded around the walls of the holy city. They were preceded by their priests clothed in white, carrying images of the saints, and singing psalms and holy songs. The ensigns were displayed, and the cymbals and trumpets sounded afar. It was thus that the Hebrews had formerly marched round Jericho, whose walls had crumbled away at the sound of their instruments.

The Crusaders set out from the Valley of Rephraim, which faces Calvary; they advanced towards the north, and saluted, on entering into the Valley of Jehoshaphat, the tombs of Mary, St. Stephen, *and the first elect of God.* On continuing their march towards the Mount of Olives, they contemplated with much respect the grotto in which Christ sweated blood, and the spot where the Saviour wept over Jerusalem. When they arrived at the summit of the mountain, the most imposing spectacle presented itself to their eyes. Towards the east were the plains of Jericho, the shores of the Dead Sea and the Jordan; and to the west they saw at their feet the holy city and its territory, covered with sacred ruins. Assembled on the very spot whence Christ ascended into heaven, and where they still sought for the vestiges of his steps, they listened to the exhortations of the priests and bishops.

Arnold de Rohés, chaplain to the duke of Normandy, addressed them in a pathetic discourse, conjuring them to redouble their zeal and perseverance. When terminating his discourse, he turned towards Jerusalem: "You see," said he to them, "the heritage of Christ trampled under foot by the

ENTHUSIASM OF CRUSADERS AT THE FIRST VIEW OF JERUSALEM.

By the break of day, on the 10th of June, 1099, the Crusaders ascended the heights of Emmaus. All at once the holy city presented itself to their eyes. The first who perceived exclaimed together, "JERUSALEM! JERUSALEM!" *The rear ranks rushed forward to behold the city that was the object of all their wishes, and the words,* "IT IS THE WILL OF GOD! IT IS THE WILL OF GOD!" *were shouted by the whole army, and resounded over Mount Sion and the Mount of Olives, which offered themselves to the eager gaze of the Crusaders. At one moment they felicitated themselves with touching the last term of their labors; and then wept over their sins, over the death of Christ, and over his profaned tomb; but all renewed the oath they had so often made to deliver the holy city from the sacrilegious yoke of the Mussulmans.*—BOOK IV.

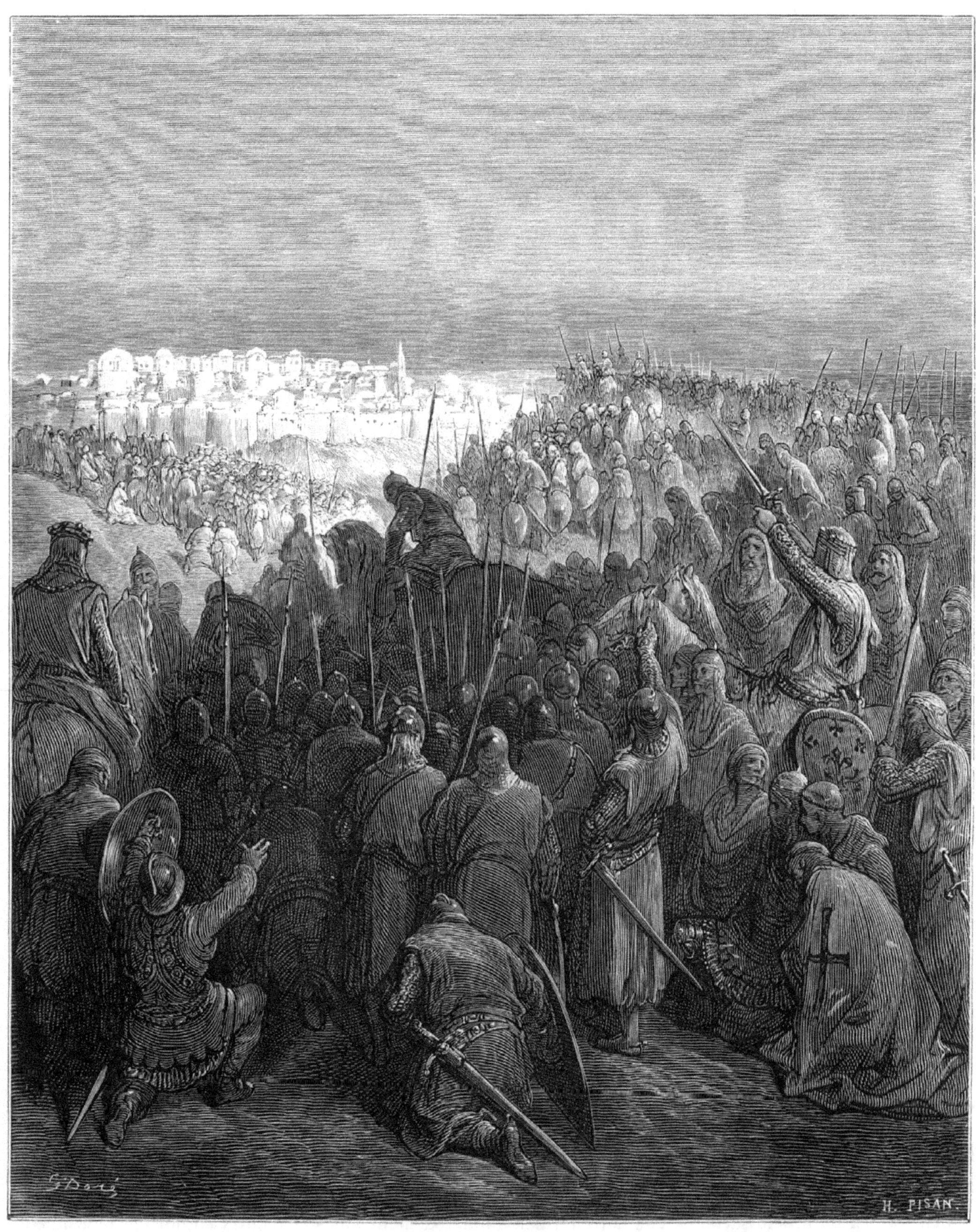

impious; here is, at last, the worthy reward of all your labours; here are the places in which God will pardon all your sins, and will bless all your victories." At the voice of the orator, who pointed out to them the church of the Resurrection and the rocks of Calvary, ready to receive them, the defenders of the cross humbled themselves before God, and kept their eyes fixed upon Jerusalem.

As Arnold exhorted them, in the name of Christ, to forget all injuries, and to love one another, Tancred and Raymond, who had had long and serious disputes, embraced each other in the presence of the whole Christian army. The soldiers and leaders followed their example. The most rich promised to comfort the poor by their alms, and to support the orphans of the bearers of the cross. All forgot their fatal discords, and swore to remain faithful to the precepts of evangelical charity.

Whilst the Crusaders were thus giving themselves up to transports of devotion and piety, the Saracens assembled on the ramparts of Jerusalem, raised crosses high in the air, and treated them with all kinds of outrages, at the same time insulting the ceremonies of the Christians by their gestures and their clamours. "You hear them," said Peter the Hermit; "you hear the menaces and the blasphemies against the true God; swear to defend Jesus Christ, a prisoner, and crucified a second time by the infidels. You see him who expires afresh upon Calvary for the redemption of your sins." At these words the cenobite was interrupted by the groans and cries of indignation which arose on all parts against the infidels. "Yes, I swear by your piety," continued the orator, "I swear by your arms, that the reign of the impious is near its end. The army of the Lord has only to appear, and all that vain mass of Mussulmans will disperse like a shadow. To-day they are full of pride and insolence, to-morrow they shall be frozen with fear, and shall fall motionless before you, like the guardians of the sepulchre, who felt their arms escape from their hands, and fell dead with fright, when an earthquake announced the presence of a God on that Calvary on which you are going to mount the breach. Still a few moments, and these towers, the last bulwark of the infidels, shall be the asylum of the Christians; these mosques, which stand upon Christian ruins, shall serve as temples for the true God, and Jerusalem shall only henceforward hear the praises of the Lord."

At these last words of Peter the most lively transports broke forth among the Christians; they embraced, shedding tears, and exhorting each other to support the evils and the fatigues of which they should so soon receive the glorious reward. The Christians at length descended the Mount of Olives to return to their camp, and, taking their route southward, they saluted on their right the tomb of David, and passed close to the pool of Siloë, where Christ restored sight to the man born blind. They perceived, further on, the ruins of the palaces of Judah, and marched along the declivity of Mount Sion, where other remembrances arose before them to add to their enthusiasm. Towards evening the Christian army returned to their quarters, repeating these words of the prophet: *The nations of the West shall fear the Lord; and the nations of the East shall see his glory.* When they had regained their camp, the greater part of the pilgrims passed the night in prayer; the leaders and the soldiers confessed their sins at the feet of their priests, and received their God, whose promises filled them with confidence and hope.

Whilst these things were passing in the Christian camp, the most profound silence reigned over the walls of Jerusalem; nothing was heard but the voices of the men who, from hour to hour, from the tops of the mosques of the city, called the Mussulmans to prayer. The infidels came in crowds to their temples to implore the protection of their prophet, and swore by the mysterious stone of Jacob to defend a city which they called the *House of God.* The besieged and the besiegers were stimulated by an equal ardour to fight and to shed their blood, the former to preserve, and the latter to conquer a city which both held sacred. The hatred which animated them was so violent, that during the whole siege no Mussulman deputy came into the Christian camp, nor did the Christians deign to summon the garrison to surrender. Between such enemies the shock must necessarily be terrible, and the victory implacable.

The leaders of the Christian army being assembled to decide upon the day for attacking the city, it was resolved to take advantage of the enthusiasm of the pilgrims, which was at its height, and to press forward the assault, the preparations for which were rapidly going on. As the Saracens had raised a great number of machines on the sides of the city most threatened by the Christians, it was agreed that they should change the dispositions of the siege, and that the principal attack should be directed towards the points where the enemy had made the least preparations for defence.

During the night Godfrey removed his quarters eastward, near to the gate of Cedar, and not far from the valley in which Titus was encamped when his soldiers penetrated into the galleries of the temple. The rolling tower, and the other machines of war which the duke of Lorraine had caused to be constructed, were transported with incredible difficulty in face of the walls he intended to attack. Tancred and the two Roberts got ready their machines, between the gate of Damascus and the angular tower, which was afterwards called the *tower of Tancred.**

When the Saracens, at daybreak, saw these new dispositions, they were seized with astonishment and affright. The Crusaders might have taken profitable advantage of the alarm which this change created in the enemy, but upon steep ground it was difficult to bring the towers up close to the walls. Raymond in particular, who was charged with the attack on the south, found himself separated from the rampart by a ravine, which it was necessary to have filled up. He immediately made it known, by a herald-at-arms, that he would pay a denier to every person who should cast three stones into it. A crowd of people instantly flew to second the efforts of his soldiers; nor could the darts and arrows, which were hurled like hail from the ramparts, at all relax the ardour and zeal of the assailants. At length, at the end of the third day, all was finished, and the leaders gave the signal for a general attack.

On Thursday, the 14th of July, 1099, as soon as day appeared, the clarions sounded in the camp of the Christians; all the Crusaders flew to arms; all the machines were in motion at once; the stone-machines and mangonels vomited showers of flints, whilst under the cover of tortoises and galleries, the rams were brought close to the walls. The archers and cross-bowmen kept up a continual discharge against the rampart; whilst the most brave planted their ladders in places where the wall seemed to offer least resistance. On the north, east, and south of the city, the three towers advanced towards the ramparts, amidst the tumult and shouts of the soldiers and the workmen. Godfrey appeared on the highest platform of his wooden fortress, accompanied by his brother Eustace and Baldwin du Bourg. He animated his people by his example; and every javelin that he cast, say the historians of the times, carried death among the Saracen host. Raymond, Tancred, the duke of Normandy, and the count of Flanders fought amidst their soldiers; whilst the knights and men-at-arms, animated by the same zeal as their principal chiefs, flew from place to place where danger called them.

Nothing could equal the impetuosity of the first shock of the Christians; but they were everywhere met by an obstinate resistance. Arrows, javelins, boiling oil, Greek fire, fourteen machines which the besieged had now time to oppose to those of their enemies, repulsed on all sides the attacks and the efforts of the assailants. The infidels issuing through a breach made in their rampart, attempted to burn the machines of the besiegers, and carried disorder among the Christian ranks. Towards the end of the day, the towers of Godfrey and Tancred could no longer be moved, whilst

* Raymond d'Agiles says that Godfrey's tower was transplanted by night a mile from the spot where it had been constructed; which leads us to believe that the principal attack was directed near the gate of Cedar, towards the entrance of the Valley of Jehoshaphat.

that of Raymond fell to pieces. The combat had lasted twelve hours, without victory having inclined to the side of the Crusaders, when night came to put a temporary end to the efforts of both parties. The Christians returned to their camp trembling with rage and grief; the leaders, but particularly the two Roberts, lamenting *that God had not yet thought them worthy of entering into his holy city, and adoring the tomb of his Son.*

The night was spent anxiously on both sides, each deploring their losses, and trembling at the idea of others they were likely to sustain. The Saracens dreaded a surprise; the Christians were afraid that the Saracens would burn the machines they had left under the walls. The besieged were employed without intermission in repairing the breaches made in the walls; whilst the besiegers were equally active in putting their machines in a state of service against a fresh attack. The following day brought a renewal of the same dangers and the same combats that the preceding one had witnessed. The chiefs endeavoured by their speeches to raise the courage of the Crusaders; whilst the priests and bishops indefatigably visited the tents of the soldiers, promising them the assistance of Heaven. The Christian army, filled with renewed confidence in victory, appeared under arms, and marched in profound silence towards the points of attack, whilst the clergy walked in procession round the city.

The first shock was impetuous and terrible. The Christians were indignant at the resistance they had met with the day before, and fought with fury. The besieged, who had learnt the approach of an Egyptian army, were animated by the hope of victory, and their ramparts were protected by machines of a formidable description. The mutually discharged javelins hissed on all sides; whilst stones and beams launched by both Christians and infidels were dashed against each other in the air with a frightful noise, and fell upon the assailants. From the height of the towers, the Mussulmans unceasingly hurled lighted torches and fire-pots. The wooden fortresses of the Christians approached the walls amidst a conflagration which was increasing on all parts around them. The infidels directed their attacks particularly against the tower of Godfrey, upon the summit of which shone a cross of gold, the sight of which provoked their utmost fury. The duke of Lorraine saw one of his esquires and many of his soldiers fall by his side; but although himself a mark for all the arrows of the enemy, he fought on amidst the dead and the wounded, and never ceased to exhort his companions to redouble their courage and ardour. The count of Thoulouse, who attacked the city on the south side, brought up all his machines to bear against those of the Mussulmans: he had to contend against the emir of Jerusalem, who animated his people by his words, and appeared upon the walls surrounded by the *élite* of the Egyptian soldiery. Towards the north, Tancred and the two Roberts stood motionless at the head of their battalions, on their rolling fortress, impatient to employ the lance and sword. Already their rams had, upon several points, shaken the walls, behind which the Saracens in close ranks presented themselves as a last rampart against the attacks of the Christians.

In the midst of the conflict two female magicians appeared upon the ramparts of the city, calling, as the historians say, upon the elements and the infernal powers. They could not, however, themselves avoid the death which they invoked upon the Christians, and fell dead beneath a shower of arrows and stones.* Two Egyptian emissaries, sent from Ascalon to exhort the besieged to persist in their defence, were surprised by the Crusaders as they were endeavouring to enter the city. One of them fell covered with wounds, and the other, having revealed the secret of his mission, was, by means of a machine, hurled upon the ramparts where the Saracens were fighting. But the combat had now lasted

* As Tasso often employs magic, we have sought with care for all that relates to this species of the marvellous in the contemporary historians. That which we have just quoted from William of Tyre, is the only instance we have been able to find. Some historians likewise have said that the mother of Kerboghâ was a sorceress, and that she had foretold to her son the defeat of Antioch. It is in vain to seek for similar incidents in the history of the first crusade. We ought to add that magic was much less in vogue in the twelfth century than in that in which Tasso lived.

half the day, without affording the Crusaders any hope of carrying the place. All their machines were on fire, and they wanted water, but more particularly vinegar,* which alone will extinguish the species of fire employed by the besieged. In vain the bravest exposed themselves to the greatest dangers to prevent the destruction of the wooden towers and the rams; they fell, buried under the ruins, and the flames consumed even their bucklers and vestments. Many of the most intrepid warriors had met with death at the foot of the ramparts; a great number of those who were upon the towers had been disabled; whilst the rest, covered with sweat and dust, fatigued by the weight of their arms and the heat, began to lose courage. The Saracens, who perceived this, uttered loud cries of joy. Among their blasphemies they reproached the Christians with worshipping a God who was not able to defend them. The assailants deplored their fate, and, believing themselves abandoned by Jesus Christ, remained motionless on the field of battle.

But the combat was destined soon to change its appearance. All at once the Crusaders saw a knight appear upon the Mount of Olives, waving his buckler, and giving the Christian army the signal for entering the city. Godfrey and Raymond, who perceived him first and at the same time, cried out aloud that St. George was come to the help of the Christians! The tumult of the fight allowed neither reflection nor examination, the sight of the celestial horseman fired the besiegers with new ardour; and they returned to the charge. Women, even children and the sick, mingled in the *mêlée*, bringing water, food, and arms, and joined their efforts to those of the soldiers to move the rolling towers, the terror of the enemy, nearer the ramparts. That of Godfrey, in spite of a terrible discharge of stones, arrows, and Greek fire, advanced near enough to have its drawbridge lowered upon the walls. Flaming darts flew, at the same time, in showers against the machines of the besieged, and against the sacks of straw and hay, and bags of wool which protected the last walls of the city. The wind assisted the fire, and drove the flames upon the Saracens, who, enveloped in masses of flame and smoke, retreated before the lances and swords of the Crusaders. Godfrey, preceded by the two brothers Lethalde and Engelbert of Tournai, and followed by Baldwin du Bourg, Eustace, Reimbault Creton,† Gunher, Bernard de St. Vallier, and Amenjou d'Albret, rushes upon the enemy, pursues them, and upon the track of their footsteps enters Jerusalem. All the brave men who fought with him on the platform of the tower, followed their intrepid chief, penetrated with him into the streets, and massacred all they met in their passage. At the same time a report was spread in the Christian army that the holy pontiff Adhémar, and several Crusaders who had fallen during the siege, had appeared at the head of the assailants, and had unfurled the standard of the cross upon the towers of Jerusalem. Tancred and the two Roberts, animated by this account, made fresh efforts, and at last threw themselves into the place, accompanied by Hugh de St. Paul, Gerard de Roussillon, Louis de Mouson, Conon and Lambert de Montaigu, and Gaston de Béarn. A crowd of heroes followed them closely; some entering by a half-opened breach; others scaling the walls with ladders; and many leaping from the tops of the wooden towers. The Mussulmans fled on all sides, and Jerusalem resounded with the cry of victory of the Crusaders,—"*It is the will of God! It is the will of God!*"

The companions of Godfrey and Tancred beat the gate of St. Stephen to pieces with axes, and the city was at once thrown open to the crowd of Crusaders, who pressed forward and contended for the honour of dealing the last blow to the conquered infidels.

Raymond alone still experienced some resistance. Warned of the success of the Christians, by

* We report this circumstance here, in order to give an idea of the fire which was launched against the Christians. Albert d'Aix expresses himself thus:—Qualiter ignis, aquâ inextinguibilis solo aceti liquore restingui valeat.—*Alb. Aq.* lib. vi. cap. 18.

† Oderic Vital attributes to Reimbault Creton of Cambresis the glory of having first entered Jerusalem. Other historians only name him among those who followed most closely the steps of the brothers Lethalde and Engelbert of Tournai.

the clashing of arms, and the tumult he heard in the city, he endeavoured still further to animate his soldiers. The latter, impatient to join their companions, abandoned their tower and machines, which they could no longer move. They planted ladders and swords, by the means of which they mounted the rampart, whither they were preceded by the count of Thoulouse, Raymond Pelet, the bishop of Bira, the count de Die, and William de Sabran. Nothing now could stop their progress; they dispersed the Saracens, who with their emir had taken refuge in the fortress of David, and soon all the Crusaders united in Jerusalem embraced, wept for joy, and gave all their attention to the completion of their victory.

Despair, however, for a moment forced the bravest of the Saracens to rally, and they charged with impetuosity the Christians, who, in the security of victory, were proceeding to the pillage. The latter were even beginning to give way before the enemy they had so recently conquered, when Everard de Puysaie, of whom Raoul de Caen has celebrated the bravery, revived the courage of his companions, placed himself at their head, and once more spread terror among the infidels. From that moment the Crusaders had no more enemies to contend with. History has remarked that the Christians entered Jerusalem on a Friday, at the hour of three in the afternoon; exactly the same day and hour at which Christ expired for the salvation of the human race. It might have been expected that this memorable epoch would have awakened sentiments of mercy in their hearts; but, irritated by the threats and protracted insults of the Saracens, incensed by the sufferings they had undergone during the siege, and by the resistance they had met with even in the city, they filled with blood and mourning that Jerusalem which they came to deliver, and which they considered as their own future country. The carnage soon became general, for all who escaped from the swords of Godfrey and Tancred, fell into the hands of the Provençals, equally thirsting for blood. The Saracens were massacred in the streets and in the houses; Jerusalem contained no place of refuge for the vanquished. Some sought to escape death by throwing themselves from the ramparts; others flocked in crowds to the palaces, the towers, but particularly to the mosques,—but nowhere could they escape the pursuit of the Christians.

When the Crusaders made themselves masters of the mosque of Omar, in which the Saracens defended themselves for some time, a frightful repetition ensued of the scenes of carnage which attended the conquest of Titus. Horse and foot entered the mosque *pêle-mêle* with the vanquished. In the midst of the most horrible tumult nothing was heard but groans, screams, and cries of death; the conquerors trampling over heaps of bodies in pursuit of all who endeavoured to escape. Raymond d'Agiles, an ocular witness, says that under the portico, and in the porch of the mosque, the blood rose up to the knees and the bridles of the horses. To paint the terrible spectacle which was presented at two periods in the same place, it will suffice to say, borrowing the words of the historian Josephus, that the number of the slain by far surpassed that of the soldiers who immolated them to their vengeance, and that the mountains near the Jordan in moans reëchoed the frightful sounds that issued from the temple.

The imagination turns with disgust from these horrible pictures, and can scarcely, amidst the carnage, contemplate the touching image of the Christians of Jerusalem, whose chains the Crusaders had broken. They flocked from all parts to meet the conquerors; they shared with them all the provisions they had been able to steal from the Saracens; and with them offered up thanks to God for having granted such a triumph to the arms of the Christians. Peter the Hermit, who, five years before, had promised to arm the West for the deliverance of the Christians of Jerusalem, must have profoundly enjoyed the spectacle of their gratitude and exultation. Amidst all the Crusaders, they appeared only to see him; they recalled his words and his promises; it was to him they addressed their songs of praise; it was him they proclaimed their liberator. They related to him the evils they had suffered during his absence; they could scarcely believe what was passing before them; and, in their enthusiasm, they expressed astonishment that God should thus have employed only a single man to stir up so many nations, and to effect such prodigies.

The sight of the brethren they had delivered, no doubt recalled to the minds of the pilgrims that they were come for the purpose of adoring the tomb of Christ; and the pious Godfrey, who had abstained from carnage after the victory, quitted his companions, and, followed by three attendants, repaired without arms and barefooted to the church of the Holy Sepulchre. The news of this act of devotion was soon spread through the Christian army, and immediately all vengeance and all fury were at an end; the Crusaders, casting away their bloody vestments, made the city resound with their groans and their sobs, and, conducted by the clergy, marched together, with their feet bare and their heads uncovered, towards the church of the Resurrection.

When the Christian army was thus assembled on Calvary, night began to fall; silence reigned over the public places and around the ramparts; nothing was heard in the holy city but hymns of penitence and these words of Isaiah, "*You who love Jerusalem, rejoice with her.*" The Crusaders exhibited a devotion so animated and so tender, that it might have been said, according to the remark of a modern historian, that these men who had just taken a city by assault, and had committed a horrible carnage, had come come forth from a long retirement, and a profound meditation upon our mysteries. These inexplicable contrasts are often to be observed in the history of the crusades. Some writers have believed that they found in them a pretext to accuse the Christian religion itself, whilst others, not less blind or passionate, have endeavoured to palliate the deplorable excesses of fanaticism; the impartial historian contents himself with relating them, and mourns in silence over the weaknesses of human nature.

The pious fervour of the Christians only suspended the scenes of carnage. The policy of some of the leaders might make them believe that it was necessary to inspire the Saracens with as much dread as possible; they thought, perhaps also, that if they released the men who had defended Jerusalem, they should have to fight them over again, and that it was not prudent for them, in a distant country and surrounded by enemies, to undertake the charge of prisoners whose number by far surpassed that of their own soldiers. The approach of the Egyptian army likewise was announced, and the dread of a new danger closed their hearts against pity. In their council, a sentence of death was decreed against all the Mussulmans that remained in the city.*

Fanaticism but too well seconded this barbarous policy. All the enemies whom humanity or the fatigue of carnage had at first spared, and even such as had been saved in hopes of a rich ransom, were slaughtered. They compelled the Saracens to cast themselves from the tops of the towers and the houses; they made them perish in the midst of flames; they dragged them from their subterranean concealments to the public places, and there immolated them upon heaps of dead. Neither the tears of women nor the cries of infants, not even the sight of the very place where Christ had pardoned his executioners, could soften the hearts of the angry conquerors. The carnage was so great that, according to the report of Albert d'Aix, bodies were seen heaped up, not only in the palaces, the temples, and the streets, but even in the most retired and solitary places. Such was the delirium of vengeance and fanaticism, that these scenes appear not to have been revolting to the eyes of those who beheld them. The contemporary historians describe them without thinking of excusing them, and amidst recitals of the most disgusting details, never allow a single expression of horror or pity to escape them.

* Albert d'Aix gives the sentence which emanated from the council of the leaders. This sentence is supported by the motives we have pointed out.

The few Crusaders who had preserved any feelings of humanity had not the power to check the fury of an army who thought they were avenging outraged religion. Three hundred Saracens, who had taken refuge on the platform of the mosque of Omar, were immolated on the day after the conquest, in spite of the prayers of Tancred, who had sent them his standard as a safeguard, and was indignant to find that so little respect was paid to the laws of honour and chivalry. The Saracens who had retreated to the fortress of David were almost the only persons that escaped death. Raymond accepted their capitulation, and had the good fortune and the glory to have it executed; but this act of humanity appeared so strange to the greater part of the Crusaders, that they expressed less admiration for the generosity of the count de St. Gilles than contempt for his avarice.

The carnage did not cease until the end of a week. Such of the Saracens as had been able to elude pursuit during this period were reserved for the service of the army. The Oriental and Latin historians agree in stating the number of the Mussulmans slain in Jerusalem to have been more than seventy thousand. The Jews met with no more mercy than the Saracens. The soldiers set fire to the synagogue in which they had taken refuge, and all perished in the flames.

But it began to be feared that the bodies heaped up in the public places, and the blood which had flooded the mosques and the streets might give rise to pestilential diseases, and the leaders gave orders that the streets should be cleansed, and that a spectacle which, now fury and fanaticism were satisfied, must have been odious to them, should be removed from before their eyes. Some Mussulman prisoners, who had only escaped the sword of the conquerors to fall into a horrible state of slavery, were ordered to bury the disfigured bodies of their friends and brothers. "They wept," says Robert the Monk, "and transported the carcases out of Jerusalem." They were assisted in this melancholy duty by the soldiers of Raymond, who, having entered last into the city, had not had a large share of the plunder, and sought to increase it by a close search of the bodies of the Saracens.

The city of Jerusalem soon presented a new spectacle. In the course of a few days only it had changed its inhabitants, laws, and religion. Before the last assault it had been agreed, according to the custom of the Crusaders in their conquests, that every warrior should remain master and possessor of the house or edifice in which he should present himself first. A cross, a buckler, or any other mark placed upon a door, was, for every one of the conquerors, a good title of possession. This right of property was respected by every soldier, however greedy of plunder, and the greatest order soon reigned in a city but recently given up to all the horrors of war. The victory enriched the greater part of the Crusaders. The conquerors shared the provisions and the riches they had found, and such as had not been fortunate in the pillage had no cause to complain of their companions. A part of the treasures was employed in assisting the poor, in supporting orphans, and in decorating the altars they had freed from the Mussulmans.

Tancred had as his share all the wealth found in the mosque of Omar. Among these riches were twenty candelabra of gold, a hundred and twenty of silver, a large lamp, and many other ornaments of the same metals. This booty was so considerable, that it would have been enough, say the historians, to load six chariots, and employed Tancred two days in removing it from the mosque. The Italian hero gave up a portion of this to his soldiers and another to Godfrey, to whose service he had attached himself. He distributed abundance of alms, and placed fifty gold marks in the hands of the Latin clergy for the reëstablishment and the decoration of the churches.

But the Crusaders soon turned their eyes from the treasures which victory had bestowed upon them to admire a conquest much more precious in their estimation; this was the true cross, which had been borne away from Jerusalem by Cosroës and brought back again by Heraclius. The Christians shut up in the city had concealed it from the Saracens during the siege. The sight of it excited the most lively emotions in the pilgrims. "*Of this thing*," says an old chronicle, "*the Christians were as much delighted as if they had seen the body of Christ hung thereupon.*" It was borne in triumph through the streets of Jerusalem, and then replaced in the church of the Resurrection.

Ten days after their victory the Crusaders employed themselves in restoring the throne of David and Solomon, and in placing upon it a leader who might preserve and maintain a conquest that the Christians had made at the expense of so much blood. The council of the princes being assembled, one of the leaders (history names the count of Flanders) arose in the midst of them, and spoke in these terms: "Brothers and companions; we are met to treat of an affair of the greatest importance; never did we stand in greater need of the counsels of wisdom and the inspirations of heaven. In ordinary times it is desirable that authority should be in the hands of the most able; with how much greater reason then ought we to seek for the man most worthy to govern this kingdom, still in a great measure in the power of the barbarians. Already we are told that the Egyptians threaten this city, for which we are about to choose a master. The greater part of the Christian warriors are impatient to return to their country, and to abandon to others the care of defending their conquests. The new people then who are going to inhabit this land will have in their neighbourhood no other Christian nations to assist them in their need or console them in their disgraces. Their enemies are near them, their allies are beyond the seas. The king we shall give them will be their only support amidst the perils which will surround them. He then who is called upon to govern this country must have all the qualities necessary to maintain his position with glory; he must unite with the bravery natural to the Franks, temperance, good faith, and humanity; for you know by such virtues great principalities are acquired and kept as well as by arms. Let us not forget, brothers and companions, that our object to-day is not so much to elect a king for Jerusalem, as to bestow upon it a faithful guardian. He whom we shall choose as leader must be as a father to all those who have quitted their country and their families for the service of Jesus Christ and the defence of the holy places. He must make virtue flourish in this land where God himself has given the model of it; he must win the infidels to the Christian religion, accustom them to our manners, and teach them to bless our laws. If you elect one who is not worthy, you will destroy your own work, and will bring ruin on the Christian name in this country. I have no need to recall to your minds the exploits or the labours which have placed us in possession of this territory; I will not remind you of the dearest wishes of our brothers who have remained in the West. What would be their sorrow, what would be ours, if, on our return to Europe, we should hear that the public good had been neglected and betrayed, or religion abolished in these places where we have restored its altars? Many would then not fail to attribute to fortune, and not to virtue, the great things we have done, whilst the evils which this kingdom would undergo would pass in the eyes of men as the fruit of our imprudence.

"Do not believe, however, brothers and companions, that I speak thus because I am ambitious of royalty, and that I am seeking your favour or suffrages. No; I have not sufficient presumption to aspire to such an honour; I take Heaven and men to witness, that even if you should offer me the crown, I would not accept it, being resolved to return to my own country. That which I have said to you is but for the good and glory of all. For the rest, I supplicate you to receive this advice as I give it to you, with affection, frankness, and loyalty, and to elect for king him who by his virtue shall be most capable of preserving and extending this kingdom, to which are attached both the honour of your arms and the cause of Jesus Christ."

Scarcely had the count of Flanders ceased speaking, than all the other leaders gave him the warmest praise for his prudence and good feelings. Most of them even thought of offering him the honour he had declined, for he who in such circumstances refuses a crown, always appears to be the most

SECOND ASSAULT OF JERUSALEM: THE CRUSADERS REPULSED.

Nothing could equal the impetuosity of the first shock of the Christians; but they were everywhere met by an obstinate resistance. Arrows, javelins, boiling oil, Greek fire, fourteen machines, which the besieged had now time to oppose to those of their enemies, repulsed on all sides the attacks and the efforts of the assailants. Toward the end of the day the towers of Godfrey and Tancred could no longer be moved, whilst that of Raymond fell to pieces. The combat had lasted twelve hours, without victory having inclined to the side of the Crusaders, when night came to put a temporary end to the efforts of both parties. The Christians returned to their camp trembling with rage and grief; the leaders, but particularly the two Roberts, lamenting THAT GOD HAD NOT YET THOUGHT THEM WORTHY OF ENTERING INTO HIS HOLY CITY, AND ADORING THE TOMB OF HIS SON.—BOOK IV.

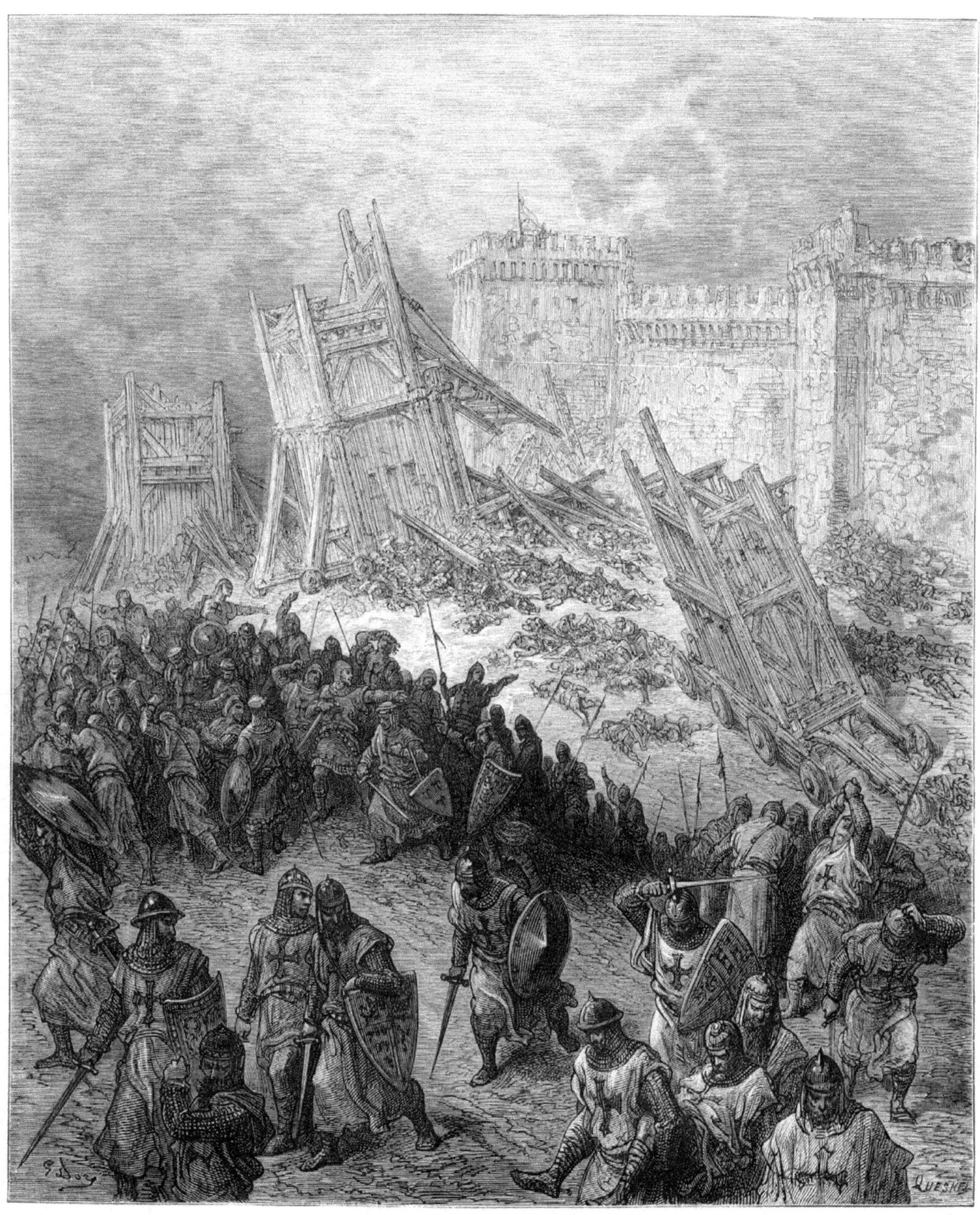
QUESNEL

worthy of it; but Robert had expressed himself with frankness and good faith; he longed to return to Europe, and was satisfied with the honour of bearing the title of "the Son of St. George," which his exploits in the holy war had obtained for him.

Among the leaders who could be called upon to reign over Jerusalem, we must place in the first rank Godfrey, Raymond, the duke of Normandy, and Tancred. The only object of Tancred was glory in arms, and he placed the title of knight far above that of king. The duke of Normandy, likewise, had evinced more bravery than ambition; after having disdained the kingdom of England, he was not likely to be anxious to gain that of Jerusalem. If we may believe an English historian, he might have obtained the suffrages of his companions; but he refused the throne of David from indolence, which so irritated God against him, says the same author, that nothing afterwards prospered with him during the remainder of his life. The count of Thoulouse had taken an oath never to return to Europe, but his companions dreaded his obstinate and ambitious character; and although several authors have said that he refused to ascend the throne on account of his great age, everything leads us to believe that the Christians feared to have him for king.

The opinions of the leaders and the army were various and uncertain. The clergy insisted that a patriarch should be named before they elected a king; the princes were not at all agreed among themselves, and of the body of the Crusaders, some would have wished to choose him whom they had followed through the holy war, whilst others, like the Provençals, who had no attachment for the count of St. Gilles, and were not desirous of remaining in Asia, gave all their efforts to keep the crown of Jerusalem from the prince under whose colours they served.

To terminate the debate, it was decided that the choice should be made by a special council of ten of the most highly respected men of the army. Prayers, fasts, and alms were commanded, in order to propitiate Heaven to guide them in the nomination they were about to make. They who were called upon to choose the king swore, in the presence of the whole Christian army, not to listen to any interest or any private affection, but to decree the crown to wisdom and virtue. These electors, whose names history has not preserved, gave the utmost attention to ascertain the opinion of the army upon the merits of each of the leaders. William of Tyre relates that they went so far as even to interrogate the familiar associates and servants of all who had any pretensions to the crown, and that they made them take an oath to reveal all they knew of the manners, characters, and secret propensities of their masters. The servants of Godfrey of Bouillon gave the most striking evidence of his mildness and humanity, but above all of his exemplary devotion.

To add to this honourable testimony, the exploits of the duke of Lorraine during the holy war were dwelt upon. They remembered that at the siege of Nice he had killed the most redoubtable of the Saracens; that he had split from shoulder to haunch a giant on the bridge of Antioch, and that in Asia Minor he had exposed his life to save that of a soldier who was overpowered by a bear. Many other feats of bravery were related of him, which in the minds of the Crusaders placed him above all the other competitors.

Godfrey was the leader decidedly in possession of the suffrages of the majority of the army and the people; and that he might not want anything in the expression of their wishes for his success, revelations were announced that God himself declared in his favour. "Many years before the crusade," says Albert d'Aix, "a soldier named Hezelon de Kintzveiler had fallen asleep in a forest, and, being conveyed in a dream to the summit of Sinai, he had seen Godfrey, covered with glory, and accompanied by two celestial messengers, who announced to him that God had chosen him, as he had done Moses, to be the conductor and chief of his people." A clerk, Giselbert (a canon of St. Mary, of Aix la Chapelle), related a vision not less miraculous. The duke of Lorraine had appeared to him seated upon the throne even of the sun. The birds of heaven from all climates and all points of the horizon, flew around him in numberless troops. The recital of this apparition was accompanied by many other circumstances which we have not space to repeat; but the Crusaders, who were much struck with them, did not fail to see in the throne of the sun a faithful image of that of Jerusalem, and in the birds of heaven the multitude of pilgrims who would come from all countries to do honour to the glorious reign of Godfrey.

These visions, which are despised in an enlightened age, had great power over the Christian army, and did not contribute less than the personal merit of the prince of Bouillon to draw upon him the attention of all. In this disposition of the general mind, the Crusaders looked with impatience for the decision of the council which was to give a king to Jerusalem.

At length the electors, after mature deliberations, and an anxious inquiry for all necessary information, proclaimed the name of Godfrey. This nomination caused the most lively joy throughout the Christian army, and was considered as an inspiration of heaven. By the authority given to him, Godfrey became the depositary of the dearest interests of the Crusaders. Every one among them had in some sort confided his own glory to him, by leaving him the care of watching over and guiding their conquests. They conducted him in triumph to the church of the Holy Sepulchre, where he took the oath to respect the laws of honour and justice. He refused the diadem and the insignia of royalty, saying that he would never accept a crown of gold in a city in which the Saviour of the world had been crowned with thorns. He contented himself with the modest title of defender and baron of the Holy Sepulchre. It has been pretended that in this he only acted in obedience to the insinuations of the clergy, who were afraid of seeing pride seated upon a throne over which the spirit of Christ ought to reign. However this may be, Godfrey richly merited by his virtues the title of king which history has given him, and which was far more due to him than the name of kingdom was to the feeble states he had to govern.

As the war had the triumph of religion for its object, the clergy employed themselves in naming bishops, consecrating churches, and sending pastors to all the cities that had submitted to the power of the Christians. Piety and disinterestedness ought to have presided in the choice of the ministers of Christ; but since the death of the virtuous Adhémar, the greater part of the Latin ecclesiastics, no longer restrained by his example, had forgotten the humility and simplicity of their profession. If William of Tyre may be believed, address and intrigue openly obtained the suffrages, and the spirit of the religion which had just given Jerusalem a good king, could not succeed in bestowing upon it prelates respectable either for their wisdom or their virtues. The clergy, who had ventured to disturb the election of the king by their intrigues, carried their pretensions as high as the sovereignty of the city, and claimed with arrogance the greatest part in the division of the booty won from the infidels.* The Greek priests, in spite of their rights, were sacrificed to the ambition of the Roman clergy, as they had been in the city of Antioch. The chaplain of the duke of Normandy caused himself to be proposed as patriarch of Jerusalem, in the place of Simeon, who had summoned the warriors from the West. Simeon was still in the isle of Cyprus, from whence he had continually sent provisions to the Crusaders during the siege. He died at the moment in which the Latin ecclesiastics were quarrelling for his spoils, and his death came very opportunely to excuse their injustice and ingratitude. Arnold, whose morals were more than suspected, and whose conduct has merited the censure of the gravest historians, was nominated pastor of the church of Jerusalem.

In the meanwhile fame had proclaimed the conquest of the holy city throughout all the neigh-

* We may see in Raoul de Caen the debates which arose on this subject, and particularly the accusation directed against Tancred by Arnold de Rohés, in the name of the Latin clergy.

bouring countries. In all the churches founded by the Crusaders in their passage, thanks were offered up to God for a victory which must necessarily cause the triumph of the worship and the laws of Christ in the East. The Christians of Antioch, Edessa, and Tarsus, with those who inhabited Cilicia, Cappadocia, Syria, and Mesopotamia, came in crowds to Jerusalem, some for the purpose of fixing their abode there, others to visit the holy places.

Whilst the faithful were rejoicing over their conquest, the Mussulmans gave themselves up to despair. The few who had escaped from the swords of the Crusaders spread consternation wherever they went. The historians Abul-Mahacam, Elmacin, and Aboul-Feda have described the desolation which reigned at Bagdad. Zeimeddin, cadhi of Damascus, tore out his own beard in the presence of the Caliph. The whole divan shed tears whilst listening to the recital of the misfortunes of Jerusalem. Fasts and prayers were ordered to mitigate the anger of heaven. The Imans and poets deplored in pathetic verses and discourses the fate of the Mussulmans who had become slaves of the Christians. "What blood," said they, "has not flowed? What disasters* have not befallen the true believers? Women have been obliged to fly, concealing their faces; children have fallen under the swords of the conquerors; and there remains no other asylum for our brothers, so lately masters of Syria, but the backs of their camels, or the entrails of the vultures."

The caliph of Bagdad, deprived of his authority, had nothing to offer but his prayers and tears, for the cause of the Mussulmans. The victories of the Christians had inflicted a mortal blow upon the dynasty of the Seldjoucides. The sultan of Persia, retired to the extremity of Coraçan, was occupied in appeasing civil wars, and scarcely gave a thought to the emirs of Syria, who had shaken off his authority, and shared his spoils amongst them. The greater part of the emirs were quarrelling among themselves for the cities and provinces threatened by the warriors of the West. The discords which accompany the fall of empires had everywhere sown trouble and division among the infidels; but such was their grief when they learnt the conquest of Jerusalem by the Christians, that they united in weeping together over the outrages committed upon the religion of Mahomet. The Turks of Syria, and the inhabitants of Damascus and Bagdad placed their last hope in the caliph of Cairo, whom they had so long considered an enemy to the prophet, and came in crowds to join the Egyptian army which was advancing towards Ascalon.

At Jerusalem they soon learnt that this army had reached Gaza, in the ancient country of the Philistines. Godfrey immediately caused his brother Eustace and Tancred, who had quitted the city to go and take possession of Naplouse, to be informed of this. He pressed the other leaders of the crusade to unite with him and march to meet the Saracens. The duke of Normandy at first refused to follow him, alleging that his vow was accomplished; and the count of Thoulouse, who had been forced to give up to the king the fortress of David, which he pretended belonged to him by right of conquest, rejected with haughtiness the prayers of Godfrey, and treated the news of the approach of the Saracens as a fable.

The refusal of the duke of Normandy and Raymond did not prevent Godfrey from commencing his march, followed by Tancred, the count of Flanders, and several other leaders. They learnt on their route that the emir Afdhal, the same that had taken Jerusalem from the Turks, commanded the

* We here give the translation of some passages of an elegy of the poet Modhaffer Abyverdy upon the taking of Jerusalem by the Crusaders, inserted by Aboul-Feda in his *Annales*, tom. iii. p. 319. This translation is by M. Jourdain.

"Our blood is mingled with our tears, and no part of our being remains to us that can be the object of the blows of our enemies.

"O misfortune! if tears take the place of true arms, when the fires of war break forth!

"How can the eye close its lids, when catastrophes such as ours would awaken even those who slept in the most profound repose!

"Your brethren have no other resting-places in Syria but the backs of their camels and the entrails of vultures!

"The Franks treat them like vile slaves, whilst you allow yourselves to be drawn carelessly along by the skirt of the robe of effeminacy, as people would do in perfect security!

"What blood has not flowed! how many women have been forced by modesty to conceal their beauty with their bracelets!"

army of the infidels. This general had under his standard an almost countless multitude of Mussulmans, from the banks of the Tigris and the Nile, the shores of the Red Sea, and the extremities of Ethiopia. A fleet had sailed from the ports of Alexandria and Damietta, laden with all sorts of provisions, and the machines necessary for the siege of Jerusalem.

Afdhal had taken a solemn oath before the caliph to annihilate for ever the power of the Crusaders in Asia, and to entirely destroy Calvary, the tomb of Christ, and all the monuments revered by the Christians.

The march and the intentions of Afdhal soon conveyed terror to Jerusalem. Raymond and the duke of Normandy were again pressed to join the Christian army. Women, old men, and priests with tears conjured the two princes to have pity on the holy city they had delivered. They represented to them the fatal consequences of their inaction, which rendered all the labours of the Crusaders useless, and closed for ever the doors of the East against pilgrims. The voices of all the nations of the West, they told them, would be raised against them, and the blood of the Christians would be on their heads. At last Robert and Raymond allowed themselves to be prevailed upon, and marched with their troops to join Godfrey. The new patriarch desired to follow them, bearing with him the wood of the true cross, the sight of which, like that of the holy lance, would redouble the enthusiasm and the bravery of the Crusaders.

All the Christians in a condition to bear arms quitted Jerusalem to go and fight the Mussulmans. There only remained in the holy city the women, the sick, and a part of the clergy, who, having Peter the Hermit at their head, addressed night and day prayers to Heaven to obtain the triumph of the defenders of the holy places, and the last defeat of the enemies of Christ.

The Christian army, which had at first assembled at Ramla, advanced across a sandy country, and encamped on the banks of the torrent of Sorex, in the plain of Saphœa, or Serfend, situated between Jaffa and Ascalon. The day after the Christians arrived on this plain, they perceived at a distance, towards seven o'clock in the evening, a vast multitude, which they took for the army of the enemy. Two hundred horsemen, who were sent out to reconnoitre, soon returned, however, with the agreeable intelligence that the multitude they had taken for the Egyptian army was nothing but a drove of oxen and camels. So rich a booty at first awakened the avidity of the soldiers, but the prudent Godfrey, who saw nothing in this circumstance but a stratagem of the enemy to throw the Christian army in disorder, forbade his soldiers to leave their ranks. The other leaders, after his example, endeavoured to restrain the men under their command, and all remained firm beneath their standards.

The Crusaders learned from some prisoners they had made, that the enemy were encamped at three leagues from them, and that they were preparing to come and attack the Christian army. Upon receiving this advice, the leaders made their dispositions to receive the infidels. The army was drawn up in nine divisions, and formed a sort of square battalion, so as to be able at need, to face the enemy at all points. The Crusaders passed the night under arms. On the following morning (it was the eve of the Assumption) the heralds announced by sound of trumpet that they were about to give battle to the infidels. At break of day the Crusaders received the benediction of the patriarch of Jerusalem. The wood of the true cross was carried through the ranks, and shown to the soldiers as a certain pledge of victory. The leaders then gave the signal, all the ensigns were unfurled, and the army marched to meet the Saracens.

The nearer the Christians approached the army of Egypt, the more were they filled with confidence and hope. Their drums, cymbals, hymns, and war-songs animated them to the fight. They marched towards the enemy, says Albert d'Aix, as to a joyous feast. An emir of Palestine, who followed the army as an auxiliary, could not sufficiently admire, if we may believe historians, this joy of

APPARITION OF ST. GEORGE ON THE MOUNT OF OLIVES.

Many of the most intrepid warriors had met with death at the foot of the ramparts; a great number of those who were upon the towers had been disabled; whilst the rest, covered with sweat and dust, fatigued by the weight of their arms and the heat, began to lose courage. The Saracens, who perceived this, uttered loud cries of joy. Among their blasphemies they reproached the Christians with worshipping a God who was not able to defend them. All at once the Crusaders saw a knight appear upon the Mount of Olives, waving his buckler, and giving the Christian army the signal for entering the city. Godfrey and Raymond, who perceived him first and at the same time, cried aloud that St. George was come to the help of the Christians! The tumult of the fight allowed neither reflection nor examination; the sight of the celestial horseman fired the besiegers with new ardour, and they returned to the charge. Women, even children and the sick, mingled in the mêlée, bringing water, food, and arms, and joining their efforts to those of the soldiers to move the rolling towers, the terror of the enemy, nearer the ramparts.—BOOK IV.

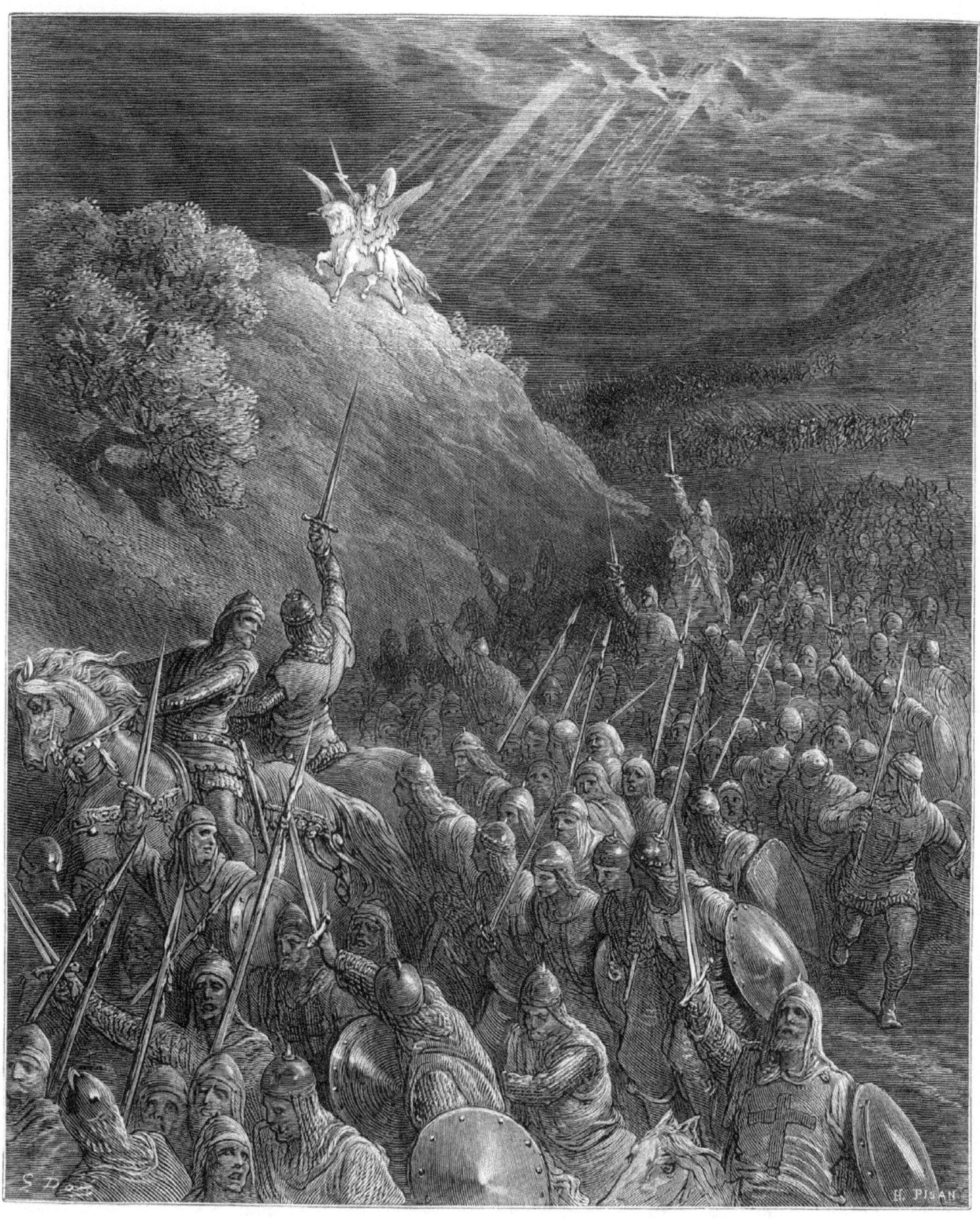
H. PISAN

the soldiers of the cross at the approach of danger. He came to express his surprise to the king of Jerusalem, and swore before him to embrace a religion which could give so much strength and bravery to its defenders.

The Christians soon arrived in the plain of Ascalon. This immense plain is bounded on the east and south by mountains, and extends on the west to the sea. On the coast was situated the city of Ascalon, over which the Mussulman standards floated. At the extremity of the plain the army of Egypt was drawn up, with the sea and the mountains behind it. The Crusaders advanced in two lines; the count of Thoulouse commanded the right wing, the two Roberts and Tancred were placed at the left. Godfrey commanded a body of reserve, which was at the same time to keep the garrison of Ascalon in check and fight with the army of Egypt.

Whilst the Christian army was thus marching in battle array, the drove of oxen and camels that they had met on their route came to their rear, and followed all their movements. The confused noise of these animals, mingled with the sound of the drums and trumpets, and the clouds of dust which arose under their steps, caused them to be taken for squadrons of horse, and the Mussulmans were persuaded that the Christian army was more numerous than their own. They were drawn up in two lines, as the Crusaders were. The Turks from Syria and Bagdad were on the right; the Moors and Egyptians on the left; the emir Afdhal occupied the centre with the main body of the Egyptian forces. This army covered an immense space, and, says Foulcher de Chartres, like a stag who projects his branching horns, it extended its wings to envelop the Christians; but a sudden terror rendered it motionless.

In vain the emir endeavoured to rouse the courage of his soldiers. They fancied that millions of Crusaders had arrived from the West; they forgot both their oaths and their threats, and only remembered the fate of the Mussulmans immolated after the conquest of Jerusalem.

Before engaging, all the Crusaders, fully armed, fell on their knees to implore the protection of Heaven; and rising full of ardour and hope, marched against the Saracens. If the most truthful historians are to be believed, they had not more than fifteen thousand foot and five thousand horse. When they had arrived within bow-shot, the foot-soldiers made several discharges of javelins, at the same time the cavalry, increasing their speed, precipitated themselves upon the enemy's ranks. At this first charge the duke of Normandy, the count of Flanders, and Tancred broke through the centre of the Egyptians. Duke Robert, followed by his bravest knights, penetrated to the place where Afdhal fought, and got possession of the great standard of the infidels. The foot-soldiers followed the horse into the *mêlée*, and cast away their bows and javelins to make use of sword and lance, arms much more terrible to the Mussulmans.

On all sides the Saracens were thrown into disorder. Towards the end of the battle Godfrey had had to contend with a troop of Ethiopians, who bent one knee to the ground to launch their javelins, and then, springing up, rushed upon the Crusaders with long flails armed with balls of iron. This redoubtable battalion could not alone resist the lances of the Christians, and were soon dispersed. An invincible terror seemed to paralyze the arms of the Mussulmans. Whilst the king of Jerusalem was pursuing the Ethiopians and Moors who fled towards the mountains in the vicinity of the field of battle, the Syrians and the Arabs, who fought in the left wing, were broken by the count of Thoulouse. Hotly pressed by the conquerors, a great number of them precipitated themselves into the sea, and perished in the waves; others sought an asylum in the city of Ascalon, and such was their eagerness, and so numerous were they, that two thousand were crushed to death upon the drawbridge. Amidst the general rout, Afdhal was on the point of falling into the hands of the conquerors; and, leaving his sword upon the field of battle, had great difficulty in gaining Ascalon. Historians add, that when, from the walls of that city, he contemplated the destruction of his army, he shed a torrent of tears. In his despair, he cursed Jerusalem, the cause of all his evils, and blasphemed Mahomet, whom he accused of having abandoned his servants and disciples.

This was a day of terror and death for the Mussulmans. From the beginning of the battle, the infidels, who had previously burned with a thirst of vengeance, appeared to have no purpose but to escape by flight from an enemy who granted no mercy to the conquered. In their mortal fear, they let fall their arms, and suffered themselves to be slaughtered without offering the least resistance. Their terrified crowd stood motionless on the field of battle, and the sword, to employ the expression of a contemporary, mowed them down like the grass of the field. Some cast themselves on the ground, and concealed themselves among heaps of slain; whilst others plunged into caverns, or scrambled up rocks or trees, where they were shot down with arrows, like birds. Afdhal, who did not believe himself to be in safety in Ascalon, embarked on board a fleet which had arrived from Egypt. Towards the middle of the contest, all the Egyptian vessels which were near the shore spread their sails, and gained the open sea. From that moment no hope of safety remained for the scattered army of these infidels, who were, as they had said, to deliver the East, and whose multitude was so great, that, according to the expression of old historians, God alone knew the number of them.

Such was this battle, whose prodigies poetry has taken delight in celebrating, but which was, in reality, nothing but an easy victory for the Christians, in which fanaticism even had not the least share. On this day the presence of celestial legions did not animate the battalions of the Crusaders, and the martyrs St. George and St. Demetrius, whom they always believed they saw in great perils, had no occasion to be present in this fight. The Christians must have learnt from this *rencontre* that their new adversaries were much less to be dreaded than the Turks. The Egyptian army was composed of many different nations, which were divided among themselves; the greater part of the Mussulman troops had been levied in haste, and fought for the first time. The army of the Crusaders, on the contrary, had been proved by many victories, and their leaders were as skilful as they were brave. The bold resolution that Godfrey had taken of going to meet the enemy, raised the confidence of the soldiers, and assisted in creating fear and disorder among the Egyptians.*

If William of Tyre and Robert the Monk may be believed, the Christians did not lose a single horseman. They might have made themselves masters of Ascalon, but want of union among the leaders prevented their taking due advantage of their victory.

After the defeat of the enemy, Raymond had sent a messenger into the place to summon the garrison to surrender. He wished to plant his standard on the walls of the city, and retain the conquest for himself. On the other hand, Godfrey claimed the possession of it and maintained that Ascalon ought to form part of the kingdom of Jerusalem. The debates became very warm. The count of Thoulouse, who found all the leaders of the Christian army against him, listened to nothing but the dictates of his blind anger; he recommended the garrison to defend themselves, and set forward with his troops to return to Jerusalem. Godfrey, after the desertion of Raymond, in vain attempted to besiege the city. The greater part of the Crusaders, impatient to return to their own country, abandoned his colours; and, after making the inhabitants and garrison of Antioch pay him a considerable sum, he was obliged to follow them to Jerusalem.

The quarrel which was begun between Raymond and Godfrey before Ascalon was renewed a few days after before the city of Arsouf, situated near the sea, twelve miles to the north of Ramla. The count of St. Gilles, who marched first with his troops, undertook to besiege this place, but as he met

* It is commonly believed that this battle of Ascalon served Tasso as a model for the great battle which terminates the *Jerusalem Delivered*. It is easy to see that the poet had also in view the battle of Antioch, which was fought at the gates of the city, of which the Christians were the masters.

with an obstinate resistance, he abandoned the siege, and continued his march, after having warned the garrison that they had nothing to fear from the king of Jerusalem. A short time after, Godfrey having besieged the city, found the Saracens determined to defend themselves, and as he learnt that their resistance was the fruit of the counsels of Raymond, he could not restrain his anger, but resolved to avenge this affront in the blood of his rival. He marched with his ensigns displayed, against the count de St. Gilles, who, on his part, was willing to meet him, and prepared for the conflict. The Christians were on the point of proceeding to extremities, when the two Roberts and Tancred threw themselves between Raymond and Godfrey, and used their utmost exertions to appease them. After a long altercation, the two rivals, overcome by the prayers of the other chiefs, embraced in the presence of their soldiers, who had taken part in their animosity.

The reconciliation was sincere on both sides. The pious Godfrey, says Albert d'Aix, conjured his companions to forget the dissension that had broken out among the Christian warriors, and implored them, with tears in his eyes, to remember that they had together delivered the holy tomb, that they were all brothers in Christ, and that concord was still necessary to defend Jerusalem. When the inhabitants of Arsouf learnt that the leaders of the Christian army were reconciled, they repented of their resistance, and engaged to pay a tribute to Godfrey.

After having received and given hostages as a guarantee of the treaty, Godfrey, followed by all the other chiefs, quitted the territory of Arsouf, to return to Jerusalem. The Christian army was loaded with an immense booty. It marched, followed by the droves of cattle it had met on the banks of the Sorec, and brought back all the riches found in the camp of the infidels. As they approached Jerusalem, all the trumpets were sounded, and their victorious flags were unfurled. A crowd of pilgrims, who came out to meet them, filled the air with their songs of gladness; these lively expressions of joy mingled with the hymns of the priests; the echoes, says Robert the Monk, repeated the sounds of the warlike instruments and the acclamations of the Christians, and appeared to offer an application of these words of Isaiah: "*The mountains and the hills shall sing before you the praises of the Lord.*" The Crusaders entered the holy city in triumph. The great standard and the sword of the sultan were suspended on the columns of the church of the Holy Sepulchre. All the pilgrims, assembled in the very places which the emir Afdhal had sworn utterly to destroy, returned thanks to Heaven for a victory which crowned all their labours.

The victory of Ascalon was the last of this crusade. At length, liberated from their vows, after four years of toils and dangers, the princes of the crusade quitted Jerusalem, whose sole means of defence now were three hundred knights, the wisdom of Godfrey, and the sword of Tancred, who had resolved to end his days in Asia. Some embarked on the Mediterranean, whilst others marched across Syria and Asia Minor. They arrived in the West bearing palm branches in their hands, and singing hymns of triumph on their way. Their return was considered as a miracle, a sort of resurrection, and their presence was everywhere looked upon as a subject of edification and enthusiasm. Most of them had been ruined by the holy war; but they brought back from the East precious relics, which were in the eyes of the faithful a veritable treasure. Their hearers were never tired of listening to the recital of their labours and exploits. Tears, doubtless, mingled with the transports of admiration and joy when they spoke of their numerous companions whom death had swept away in Asia. There was not a family that had not to weep a defender of the cross, or did not glorify itself with having a martyr in heaven. Ancient chronicles have celebrated the heroic devotion of Ida, countess of Hainault, who made the voyage to the East, and braved all dangers in search of her husband. Sent by the Crusaders to Alexius, the count of Hainault, with all the persons of his suite, had disappeared, without any one being able to say what had been their fate. Some said they were still prisoners among the Turks, others that they were killed. Ida sought through many countries of Asia, but returned to France without having obtained any tidings of her husband.

The count of Thoulouse, who had sworn never to return to the West, went to Constantinople, where the emperor received him with distinction, and gave him the city of Laodicea. Raymond of Orange determined to share the destiny of the count of Thoulouse, and finish his days in the East. Among the knights, companions of Raymond de St. Gilles, who returned to their own country, we must not forget Stephen and Peter de Salviac de Viel Castel, whom their age holds up as models of brotherly love. Stephen and Peter de Salviac were twins, and the tenderest affection united them from their infancy. Peter assumed the cross at the council of Clermont, and Stephen, although married, and the father of several children, determined to follow his brother into Asia, and share with him the perils of so long a voyage. In all battles they were seen fighting side by side, and they together were present at the sieges of Nice, Antioch, and Jerusalem. A short time after their return to Le Quercy, they both died in the same week, and were buried in the same tomb. On their tomb may still be read an epitaph which has transmitted to us the remembrance of their exploits and of their touching affection. Gaston de Béarn returned with them into Europe; but some years after, having re-entered upon his estates, he again took up arms against the infidels, and died in Spain, fighting against the Moors.

Peter the Hermit, on his return to his country, concealed himself from the eager curiosity of the faithful, and shut himself up in a monastery he had founded at Huy. He lived there in humility and penitence, and was buried among the cenobites he had edified by his virtues. Eustace, the brother of Godfrey and Baldwin, returned to take possession of the moderate inheritance of the family, and gave no further trouble to fame by his exploits. Alain Fergent, duke of Brittany, and Robert, count of Flanders, returned to their states, repaired the evils caused by their absence, and died regretted by their subjects.

The duke of Normandy was less fortunate than his companions. The sight of the holy places, or the long series of labours and evils he had endured in the cause of religion, had had no effect upon his indolent, undecided character. On his return from the Holy Land, he passed through Italy, where he fell in love with Sibylla, the daughter of the count of Conversana, and allowed his passion to detain him from his duchy more than a year. By this delay he lost the opportunity of ascending the throne of England, to which, after the death of his brother William Rufus, his birth, and the great renown he had acquired in the crusade, gave him undoubted right. When at length he returned to Normandy, he was received with transports of admiration and joy; but upon resuming the reins of government, he showed nothing but weakness; he gave himself up entirely to debauchery, and surrounded himself by none but dissipated, greedy courtiers, who drew upon him the hatred of his subjects. His brother, Henry I., who had succeeded William Rufus, took advantage of the degraded condition of Robert, and the contempt into which he was fallen, to take possession of Normandy. At the end of a battle this unfortunate prince was made prisoner by his brother, who led him in triumph to England, and caused him to be confined in the castle of Cardiff, in the province of Glamorgan. The remembrance of his exploits in the Holy Land had no effect in mitigating his misfortunes. After twenty-eight years of captivity, he died forgotten by his subjects, his allies, and the ancient companions of his glory.

The return of the Crusaders, and the account of their conquests, excited great enthusiasm, and renewed the eagerness for crusades and pilgrimages among the nations of the West. They were not now affected by the passion for delivering the holy places, but by that of visiting and defending them. Europe exhibited a second time the scenes which had followed the council of Clermont; new discourses were heard, and fresh miracles related. Cities, lands, and castles were again offered for sale.

GODFREY ENTERS JERUSALEM.

The rolling tower of Godfrey, in spite of a terrible discharge of stones, arrows, and Greek fire, advanced near enough to have its drawbridge lowered upon the walls. Flaming darts flew, at the same time, in showers against the machines of the besieged, and against the stacks of straw and hay, and bags of wool which protected the last walls of the city. The wind assisted the fire and drove the flames upon the Saracens, who, enveloped in masses of flame and smoke, retreated before the lances and swords of the Crusaders. Godfrey, preceded by the two brothers Lethalde and Engelbert of Tournai, and followed by Baldwin du Bourg, Eustace, Reimbault Creton, Gunher, Bernard de St. Vallier, and Amenjou d'Albret, rushes upon the enemy, pursues them, and upon the track of their footsteps enters Jerusalem: All the brave men who fought with them upon the platform of the tower, followed their intrepid chief, penetrated with him into the streets, and massacred all they met in their passage.—Book IV.

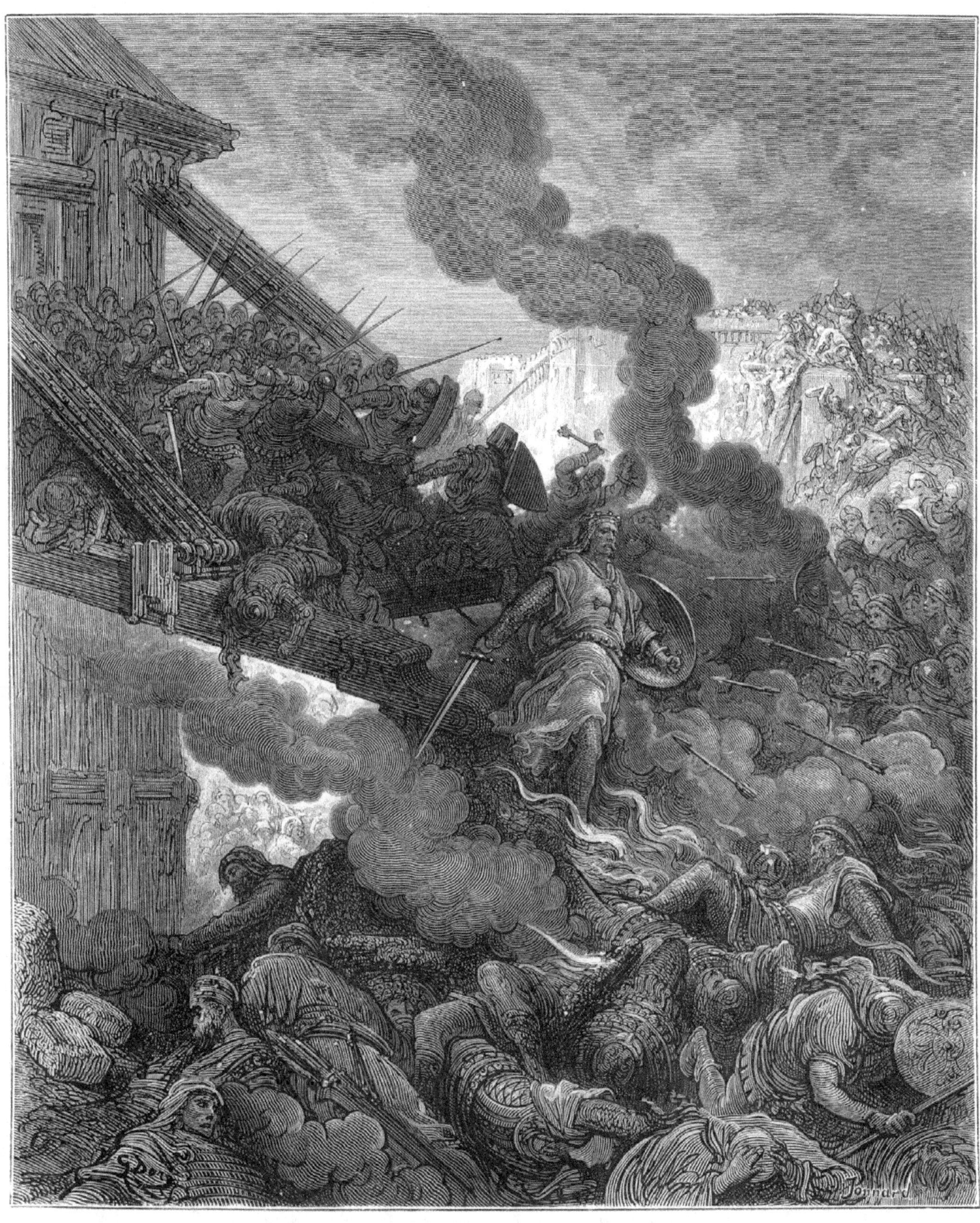

He who preferred repose and his country to the glory of the holy pilgrimage passed for a very lukewarm Christian; whilst all who had quitted the standard of the crusade were objects of contempt in the eyes of the faithful, and were threatened with the thunders of the Church.

A general cry was raised against the brother of the king of France, who could not be pardoned for having abandoned the Christian army in a cowardly manner, and returned to Europe without seeing Jerusalem. Stephen, count of Chartres and Blois, was not allowed to remain in peace in his states and family; his people were astonished at his shameful desertion, and his wife Adela reproached him with having shrunk from the duties of religion and chivalry. These unfortunate princes, and all who had deserted the standards of the holy war, were obliged to quit France, and again take the route for Asia.

Many of the princes and barons who had not partaken of the enthusiasm of the first Crusaders, accused themselves of culpable indifference, and were drawn into the general movement. Among these latter was William IX., count of Poictiers, a relation of the emperor of Germany, and the most powerful vassal of the king of France. An amiable and intelligent prince, of not at all a warlike character, he left, to take up the pilgrim's staff, a voluptuous and gallant court, which he had often delighted with his songs. He took upon him the cross at Limoges, and set out for the East, accompanied by a great number of his vassals, among whom were a vast many women and young girls.* His example was followed by William, count of Nevers, Orpin, count of Bourges, and Eude, duke of Burgundy. This last prince, perhaps, was influenced less by a desire of visiting Jerusalem than by his anxiety to recover the remains of his daughter Florine, who had been killed with Sweno in Asia Minor.

In Italy, Albert, count of Blandras, and Anselm, archbishop of Milan, placed themselves at the head of a countless multitude of pilgrims. Germany witnessed the departure of Conrad, marshal of the emperor Henry, Wolf IX., duke of Bavaria, the princess Ida, margravine of Austria, and a great number of lords and knights.

In this new expedition, as in the first, many of the Crusaders were led away by a desire for seeking adventures and visiting foreign countries. The brilliant success of Baldwin, Bohémond, and Godfrey aroused the ambition of the barons who had remained in Europe. Humbert II., count of Savoy, who set out for the Holy Land with Hugh the Great, made a donation to the monks of the Bourget, in order to obtain by their prayers, a fortunate establishment (*consulat*) in his foreign voyage. Many lords and knights made similar donations, whilst others founded monasteries and churches, setting out with the hope that God would bless their arms, and enable them to acquire rich principalities in the East.

The Crusaders assembled in several troops, and crossing the territories of the Hungarians and Bulgarians, united under the walls of Constantinople to the amount of two hundred thousand. These new pilgrims repeated the scenes of violence which had so seriously alarmed Alexius in the first expedition. The Greek emperor, faithful to his policy, opposed force by cunning; he flattered the vanity or the avarice of men he could not subdue, and paid very dearly for the insincere homage of the leaders of the crusade. He called Raymond to his assistance, who was then in his government of Laodicea. The presence and the persuasive discourses of the count of Thoulouse calmed the perturbed spirits of the Crusaders for a few days; and when they set forward on their march to Palestine, he was charged with conducting them across Asia Minor.

Among this confused mass of pilgrims was a crowd of monks, old men, women, and young girls.

* William IX. is the first troubadour known. He was a valorous and courteous knight, but *a great deceiver of ladies*. He bade adieu in a song to the Limousin, to Poitou, to chivalry, which he had loved so much, and to mundane vanities, which he describes as coloured habits and beautiful hose. On his return he sang the fatigues, the dangers, and the misfortunes of this expedition, in a poem which is lost. His usual gaiety pervaded it, according to Oderic Vital, in spite of the sadness of the subject.

They were without discipline, and marched without either precaution or order; but they had such perfect confidence in their arms, that they boasted, on leaving Constantinople, that they would go to Bagdad, and wrest Asia from the hands of the infidels. Their troop was divided into three bodies. At the head of the first were the duke of Burgundy, the count of Chartres, the archbishop of Milan, the count de Blandras, and Raymond de St. Gilles. "The archbishop of Milan," says Albert d'Aix, "had brought into Asia an arm of St. Ambrose, with which he gave his benediction to the Crusaders. Raymond carried with him the lance that had been found at Antioch, to which he looked for new miracles."

This first body, advancing towards Paphlagonia, took the city of Ancyra by assault, and laid siege to the fortress of Gangras. The garrison made a strong resistance, and forced the Christians to retire. They were in want of provisions, and entertained but little hopes of obtaining any in an enemy's country; and whilst sinking into despondency they quite unexpectedly found themselves confronted by a Turkish army.

Kilidge Arslan, who had retired to Iconium, which became the capital of his states, after the taking of Nice, had got together the remains of his army, and recruited his strength. The sultan of Mossoul, that same Kerboghâ who, three years before, had lost the battle of Antioch, had joined the son of Soliman, and burned to meet the Christians again.

Although they both had a considerable number of troops, they contented themselves, at first, with harassing the Crusaders in their march. Sometimes the infidels got before the Christians, and ravaged the country and filled up the wells and the cisterns; whilst at others, they laid ambushes for them, and massacred all who strayed away from the main body. The Christian army had suffered much in crossing the defiles of Paphlagonia; and fatigue, hunger, and thirst had greatly weakened the strength of the pilgrims, when the sultans of Mossoul and Iconium determined upon giving them battle on the banks of the Halys.

Raymond, before the engagement, caused the miraculous lance to be carried through the Christian ranks; whilst the archbishop of Milan, followed by his clergy, exhibited the arm of St. Ambrose, and offered up prayers for victory; but neither the prayers of the clergy, nor the sight of the holy lance, nor even the prodigies of valour displayed by the Crusaders, could secure them a triumph. After a sanguinary conflict, they retired to their camp in great disorder. The Turks, who had met with a determined resistance, did not at first dare to follow up their victory, and satisfied themselves with remaining masters of the field of battle, and plundering the dead. During the night the Crusaders became aware of the extent of their loss. Raymond and the other terrified leaders sought safety in flight. As soon as their absence was discovered, terror and despair pervaded the camp of the Christians; every one attempted to fly, abandoning the baggage, the sick and the wounded. The roads were soon covered with soldiers, women, and children, who embarrassed each other in their confusion, and were ignorant where they might meet with the enemy, or where they should look for the Christian army. The Turks, rendered aware of their victory by the cries and groans which resounded from the neighbouring mountains, hastened to the camp of the Crusaders, massacring or making prisoners all they met. They then hotly pursued the fugitives, slaughtering them without mercy. The darkness of the night added to the horrors of this scene of carnage. The pilgrims lost themselves in their confusion, and seemed to seek the swords they wished to avoid; others stopped exhausted by fatigue, and awaited death as an end of their calamities.

When day appeared, the country was covered with the bloody, plundered bodies of the Christians. Raymond de St. Gilles, the duke of Burgundy, the count of Chartres, the count of Blandras, and some other leaders who had fled by different routes, met at Sinope, where they could scarcely gather around them a few thousand men, the remains of an army which had counted under its standards more than a hundred thousand pilgrims.

A second army of Crusaders, led by the count de Nevers and the count de Bourges, advanced as far as Ancyra, and directed its course towards Heraclea. This army looked for traces of that which had preceded it; but instead of finding the Christians, they soon met with the victorious army of the Turks, which came to meet them, attacked them, and routed them. The count de Nevers with great difficulty found refuge in Germanicopolis. Taking for guides some Greek soldiers, he was pillaged and abandoned by them in a desert. He went through the greatest dangers for several days; and, exhausted with fatigue and covered with rags, he at length arrived at Antioch, whither the news of his defeat had preceded him.

A third troop, composed, according to the authors of the time, of more than a hundred and fifty thousand pilgrims, set out from Constantinople under the orders of the count of Poictiers, the duke of Bavaria, and Hugh de Vermandois. They took possession of Philomelium and Samalia, and marched across devastated provinces towards the city of Stankon, where they expected to unite themselves with the army of the count de Nevers. It was before this city that the pilgrims heard of the disasters and defeat of the Christian armies that had preceded them. They advanced towards Heraclea, and were not long in meeting with the army of Kilidge Arslan, which was waiting for them in an advantageous position. As they had no longer anything to hope for except from their courage, they did not seek to avoid the enemy. A rivulet which separated the Christians from the infidels, was the signal and the theatre of battle. The Crusaders, pressed by thirst, rushed towards it in crowds. The Turks immediately discharged upon them a shower of javelins and arrows. The two armies were soon completely engaged; but the Christians fighting in a confined and marshy place, could neither draw up their forces nor make use of the lance or the sword. Their bravery and their efforts were of no avail against the skilful manœuvres of Kerboghâ and Kilidge Arslan. The Turks penetrated the Christian army everywhere; the carnage was horrible; scarcely a thousand of the Crusaders escaped from either death or slavery. The margravine of Austria disappeared amidst the tumult of the battle. Some say that she was crushed under the feet of the horses; whilst others assert that she fell into the hands of the enemy, and went to live and die in the harem of the sultan of Mossoul. The greater part of the women and young girls that followed the Christian army met with the same fate. The count of Vermandois, pierced by two arrows, fled across Lycaonia, and arrived with a feeble escort at the city of Tarsus, where he died of his wounds.

The duke of Bavaria and the count of Poictiers, after having wandered a long time in deserts and forests, arrived almost naked at Antioch, in which city were assembled all the Crusaders that had escaped after their defeat. The leaders, by gathering together the wrecks of their troops, were able to form an army of ten thousand men, with which they marched to Jerusalem. Whilst coasting the Sea of Syria, they took the city of Tortosa, which they gave up to Raymond, although they had accused him, only a few days before, of having been the cause of all their disasters. Upon their arrival in Palestine, they found new enemies to contend with. The duke of Burgundy and the count of Blois were killed in a battle fought near Ramla. Arpin, count de Berri, fell alive into the hands of the Saracens, and died in slavery. The count de Blandras, the count of Savoy, William, count of Poictiers, the count de Nevers, and the duke of Bavaria only led a small number of their soldiers back to Europe.

Such are the principal events of the first crusade, the commencement and the end of which were marked by the greatest disasters, and which deprived Europe of more than a million of men. When we reflect on the energies displayed and the forces employed in this expedition by the West, we are at first astonished that it did not succeed.

It has often been repeated, when speaking of this holy war, in which the East beheld an army of six hundred thousand men brought against it, "that Alexander conquered Asia with thirty thousand men." It is more than probable that the Greeks who wrote the life of Alexander have diminished the number of his forces in order to heighten the splendour of his victories; but, be that as it may, it must be admitted that the expedition of the Macedonian conqueror did not present the same dangers, or the same obstacles that the Crusaders had to encounter. The armies which left Greece for Asia had less to suffer from change of climate, or the length and difficulties of the voyage than those who came from the extremities of the West. The Macedonians, in their invasion of the East, had scarcely any nation to contend with but the Persians, an effeminate people, previously several times vanquished by the Greeks; whilst the Crusaders had to pass through a crowd of unknown, barbarous hordes, and when arrived in Asia, found, as enemies, several nations of conquerors.

The Greeks of Alexander's expedition did not go into Asia to introduce new laws, or change the manners and religion of the people; they even adopted something of the costumes and usages of the Persians, which very much facilitated their conquests. In the crusades, on the contrary, we behold two religions armed one against the other, which redoubled the hatred of the combatants, and forbade all approximation. As soon as the standard of Mahomet floated over a city, the Christians fled from it; whilst the cross of the Christians had the same effect upon the Mussulmans. As the greater part of the Mussulman cities which fell into the hands of the Christians were deserted, the latter were obliged to people the provinces they conquered, and exhaust their armies, to found, in some sort, colonies wherever their arms triumphed. If it be allowed that no wars are more sanguinary than religious wars, there are certainly none in which it is more difficult for a conqueror to extend or preserve his conquests. This is a very important observation, if we would appreciate the results of this crusade.

On all occasions where bravery alone was required, nothing can be comparable to the exploits of the Crusaders. When reduced to a small number of combatants, they triumphed no less over their enemies than when they consisted of vast armies. Forty thousand Christians obtained possession of Jerusalem, defended by a garrison of sixty thousand Saracens. There remained scarcely twenty thousand men under their standards, when they had to contend with all the forces of the East in the plains of Ascalon. If Alexander performed greater things, and particularly if he conquered a greater number of nations, it was because he commanded a disciplined army, of which he was the absolute leader. All his military and political operations were directed by one same mind and one same will. It was not thus in the army of the Crusaders, which was composed of many nations, and held within itself the fatal germs of license and disorder. The feudal anarchy with which Europe was then distracted followed the defenders of the cross into Asia, and that turbulent spirit of the knights, which constantly led them to have recourse to arms, was precisely that which checked and bounded their conquests.

When we think of their ever reviving discords, of the calamities which were the consequences of them, of that excess of bravery that made them commit so many faults, of that want of foresight which they almost always evinced on the eve of great dangers, one thing alone surprises us, and that is, that they did not entirely fail in their enterprise.

Philosophy may, with some justice, oppose its reasonings to the marvels of this war; but she will find in it an abundant source of profound and new observations. In it she will see man with his inexplicable contrasts; in it she will meet with the passions, with all that characterizes them, with all they possess that most plainly exhibits the human heart and mind. Reason, without doubt, must deplore the disorders, the excesses, and the delirium of the Crusaders; but such is human weakness, that we always interest ourselves in great events wherein man is fully developed.

The imagination of the most indifferent must be struck with the instances of heroism which the history of the crusades abounds in. If many of the scenes of this great epoch excite our indignation or our pity, how many of the events fill us with admiration and surprise! How many names, rendered illustrious by this war, are still the pride of families and nations! That which is perhaps most positive in the results of the first crusade, is the glory of our fathers,—that glory which is also a real good for a country; for great remembrances found the existence of nations as well as families, and are the most noble sources of patriotism.

In remotest antiquity, one of those passions which sometimes act upon a whole people, precipitated Greece upon Asia. This war, famous and rich in exploits, inflamed the imagination of the Greeks, and was for a great length of time celebrated in their temples and upon their stage. If great national remembrances inspire us with the same enthusiasm, if we entertain as strong a respect as the ancients for the memory of our ancestors, the conquest of the Holy Land must be for us as glorious and memorable an epoch as the war of Troy was for the people of Greece. These two wars, however different in their motives, present almost the same results to the enlightened observer; both offer grand lessons to policy and illustrious models to valour: both founded new states, new colonies, and established relations between distant nations. Both had a marked influence upon the civilization of the ages that followed them: both, in short, developed great passions and fine characters, and thus furnished the happiest subjects for the epic muse, who delights only in celebrating prodigies and wonders.

When comparing these two memorable wars, and the poetical masterpieces that have celebrated them, we cannot but think that the subject of the "Jerusalem Delivered" is more wonderful than that of the "Iliad." We may still further say, that the heroes of Tasso are more interesting than those of Homer, and their exploits less fabulous. The cause which armed the Greeks was much less important than that which actuated the Christians. The latter, in some sort, took up arms for the assistance of misfortune and oppressed weakness. They went to defend a religion able to make them sensible of ills that were endured far from them, and to make them find brothers in regions unknown to them. This character of sociability is not to be found in any belief of the ancients.

The Crusaders exhibited another spectacle with which antiquity was unacquainted—the union of religious humility with the love of glory. History shows us constantly these haughty heroes, the terror of Asia and the Mussulmans, bending their victorious brows to the dust, and marching from conquest to conquest, covered with the sack of penitence. The priests, who exhorted them in battle, only raised their courage by reproaching them with their sins. When they met with reverses, a thousand voices were raised among them to accuse their own misconduct; and when they were victorious, it was God alone that gave them the victory, and religion forbade their claiming glory from it.

The historian may be permitted to think that this difference between the heroes of the "Iliad" and those of the holy war is not sufficiently marked in the poem of "Jerusalem Delivered." Another reproach may likewise be addressed to the bard of Rinaldo and Godfrey; the ideas of magic and gallantry which he has too freely lavished upon his poem are not in accordance with the truth of history. Magic, which is nothing but a sort of degenerated superstition, and which only deals with small things, was but little known to the Crusaders. Their superstition, however gross, had something noble and grand in it, which associated them sufficiently with the spirit of the epopée, without the poet having anything to alter; their character and manners were grave and austere, and exceedingly well suited to the dignity of a religious epic. It was not till long after the first crusade that magic formed any part of the superstition of the Franks, or that their warlike manners abandoned the prominently epic character which distinguished them, to adopt the romantic character which they have preserved in all books of chivalry. It appears to us that we discover in Tasso much more of the manners of the times in which he lived than of those of the end of the eleventh century, the period of the events which form the subject of his poem.

But it does not enter into the plan or the object of this work to carry such observations further. After having spoken of the heroic deeds and of all that was wonderful in the first crusade, I will turn my attention to the immediate effects it produced upon Europe and Asia. We are sufficiently well acquainted with the evils by which it was followed; great disasters are the familiar subjects of history, but the slow and almost insensible progress of the good that may result from a great revolution, is much less easily perceived.

The first result of this crusade was to carry terror among the Mussulman nations, and to place it out of their power to undertake for a length of time any warlike enterprises against the West. Thanks to the victories of the Crusaders, the Greek empire extended its limits, and Constantinople, which was the road to the West for the Saracens, was rendered safe from their attacks. In this distant expedition Europe lost the flower of its population, but it was not, as Asia was, the theatre of a bloody and disastrous war; of a war in which nothing was respected, in which provinces and cities were, by turns, ravaged by the conquerors and the conquered. Whilst the warriors of Europe were shedding their blood on the plains of the East, the West remained in profound peace. Among Christian nations it was then considered a crime to take up arms for any other cause than that of Jesus Christ. This opinion contributed greatly to check the frightful brigandage that had prevailed, and to increase respect for *the truce of God*, which was, in the middle ages, the germ or the signal of the best institutions. Whatever were the reverses of the crusades, they were less deplorable than the civil wars and the scourges of feudal anarchy that had so long ravaged all the countries of the West.

This first crusade produced other advantages to Europe. The East, by the holy war, was in some sort laid open to the West, which, before, was but little acquainted with it; the Mediterranean became more frequented by European vessels, navigation made some progress, and commerce, particularly that of the Pisans and Genoese, must have been increased and enriched by the foundation of the kingdom of Jerusalem. A great part, it is true, of the gold and silver of Europe was carried into Asia by the Crusaders; but these treasures, heaped up and concealed by avarice and fear, had been long abstracted from circulation; the gold which was not carried away by the Crusaders circulated more freely, and Europe, with a less quantity of money, appeared all at once more rich than it had ever been.

We cannot perceive, whatever may have been asserted, that in the first crusade Europe received any great quantity of knowledge from the East. During the eleventh century, Asia had been the theatre of the most sanguinary revolutions. At this period the Saracens, but more particularly the Turks, cultivated neither the arts nor the sciences. The Crusaders had no other relation with them but a war of extermination. On another side, the Franks held the Greeks, among whom, besides, the arts and sciences were declining, in too much contempt to borrow any kind of instruction from them; nevertheless, as the events of the crusade had strongly affected the imagination of nations, this great and imposing spectacle was sufficient to give an impetus to the human mind in the West. Several writers undertook to trace the history of this memorable period. Raymond d'Agiles, Robert the monk of St. Remy, Tudebode, Foulcher de Chartres, Abbot Guibert, Baudry, the bishop of Dol, and Albert d'Aix, were contemporary historians, and most of them ocular witnesses of the conquests and exploits they have described. The histories they have left us are not destitute of merit, and some of them are even better than that which was written of the same kind among either the Greeks or the Arabs. These writers were animated in their labours by the same spirit of piety which governed the heroes of the cross. This spirit of piety caused them to take up the pen, and persuaded them that they wrote for the cause of God. They would have thought themselves wanting in their duty as Christians, if they had not employed their abilities in transmitting the events of the holy war to posterity. In whatever manner we judge of their motives, we cannot avoid being convinced that they have rendered great services to history, and that without them the heroic times of our annals would have remained without monuments.

The wonderful portion of the character of this first crusade likewise awakened the epic muse. Raoul de Caen, who, in his history, sometimes sounds the epic trumpet in order worthily to celebrate the "gestes" of Tancred, is not deficient in either warmth or fancy. The conquest of Jerusalem was during the twelfth century the subject of several works in verse. A Limousin knight, Geoffrey de la Tour, called the prior or abbot of the Vigeois, described very tolerably the events of these wars in a large volume all written in his maternal tongue, and in vulgar rhyme, in order that the people might understand it the better. This poem, written in verse, which was the fruit of the labour of twelve years, is lost. Many other similar works have doubtless shared the same fate; but that which remains suffices to prove that human intelligence began to expand at the commencement of the twelfth century.

Before this period, the science of legislation, which is the first and most important of all, had made but very little progress. Some cities of Italy and the provinces near the Pyrenees, where the Goths had encouraged the Roman laws, alone exhibited glimmerings of civilization. Among the rules and ordinances that Gaston de Béarn laid down before his departure for the Holy Land, are to be found many points and particulars which deserve to be preserved by history, because they exhibit the feeble beginnings of a legislation which time and fortunate circumstances would perfect. *Peace*, says this legislator of the eleventh century, *shall be observed at all times towards clerks, monks, travellers, and ladies and their suite.—If any one takes refuge in the abode of a lady, he shall enjoy security of person, on paying all loss or consequent injury. Let the peasant live in peace; let his cattle and agricultural instruments be exempt from seizure.* These benevolent dispositions were inspired by the spirit of chivalry, which had made some progress in the wars against the Saracens of Spain; they were particularly the works of the councils* which undertook to put a stop to private wars and the excess of feudal anarchy. The holy wars beyond the seas finished that which chivalry had begun, they perfected chivalry itself. The council of Clermont and the crusade that followed it only developed and consolidated all which preceding councils, all that the wisest lords and princes, had done for the cause of humanity.

Many of the princes of the crusades, such as the duke of Brittany and Robert count of Flanders, signalized their return by establishing wise regulations. A few salutary institutions began to displace the violent abuses of feudalism, and there might be seen, at least in some provinces, what a regime founded by the sword could exhibit of a moderate kind in its legislation.

It was in France that these changes were most obvious, because France had taken the greatest part in the crusade. Many nobles emancipated their serfs upon their following them in this expedition. Giraud and Giraudet Adhémar de Monthiel, who followed their brother, the bishop of Puy, to the holy war, to encourage and reward some of their vassals, by whom they were accompanied, granted them several fiefs by an act drawn up in the same year as the taking of Jerusalem. We might quote many similar acts made during the crusade and in the first year that followed it. Liberty awaited in

---

* All the ordinances of Gaston de Béarn are to be found in the decrees of the synod or council held in the diocese of Elne, in Roussillon, the 16th of May, 1027. These dispositions had for object the Truce of God. The council decreed that no unarmed clerk or monk should be attacked, nor any man who was going to church or coming from it, or was walking with women. At the council of Bourges in 1031, and in several others, these regulations were renewed; labourers, their cattle and mills, were placed under the safeguard of religion.

the West the small number that returned from the holy war, who seemed to acknowledge no other master but Jesus Christ.

In this crusade the nobility lost some portion of a power which they had abused, but they had more splendour and were held in greater honour. The king of France, although for a long time obnoxious to the censures of the Church, and although he did not distinguish himself by any great personal qualities, had a more tranquil and prosperous reign than his predecessors; he began to shake off the yoke of the great vassals of the crown, of whom several were ruined or perished in the holy war. We have often repeated that the crusade placed great wealth in the hands of the clergy; but we must likewise add, that the clergy composed the most enlightened part of the nation, and that this increase of prosperity was in the nature of things. After the first crusade, was seen that which is always to be observed in all nations that are progressing in civilization. Power had a tendency to centralize itself in the hands of him who protected liberty. Glory became the reward of all who were called upon to defend their country; consideration and riches took a direction towards that class from which intelligence was to be expected.

It is certain that knowledge arose in Europe among the clergy, and that they alone were able to consecrate in some way many of the salutary results of the crusades. As long as the clergy powerfully assisted the progress of civilization, they preserved their wealth; as soon as they went beyond civilization, they lost it. This is the course of things on earth. As long as institutions are favourable to society, society reveres them; when under some relations they are esteemed less useful, they lose their importance. Without any necessity for declamation, we must leave the ingratitude natural to nations to take its course, as we must their inconstancy, and to time; which are but too powerful in destroying instruments which society has employed with some advantage.

Many cities of Italy had arrived at a certain degree of civilization before the first crusade; but this civilization, born in the midst of a barbarous age, and spread amongst some isolated nations divided among themselves, had no power to attain maturity. For civilization to produce the salutary effects it is capable of, everything must at the same time, have a tendency to the same perfection. Knowledge, laws, morals, power, all must proceed together. This is what has happened in France; therefore must France one day become the model and centre of civilization in Europe. The holy wars contributed much to this happy revolution, which may be seen even in the first crusade.

THE DISCOVERY OF THE TRUE CROSS.

But the Crusaders soon turned their eyes from the treasures which victory had bestowed upon them to admire a conquest much more precious in their estimation ; this was the true cross, which had been borne away from Jerusalem by Cosroës and brought back again by Heraclius. The Christians shut up in the city had concealed it from the Saracens during the siege. The sight of it excited the most lively emotions in the pilgrims. "OF THIS THING," *says an old chronicle,* "THE CHRISTIANS WERE AS MUCH DELIGHTED AS IF THEY HAD SEEN THE BODY OF CHRIST HUNG THEREUPON." *It was borne in triumph through the streets of Jerusalem, and then replaced in the church of the Resurrection.*—BOOK IV.

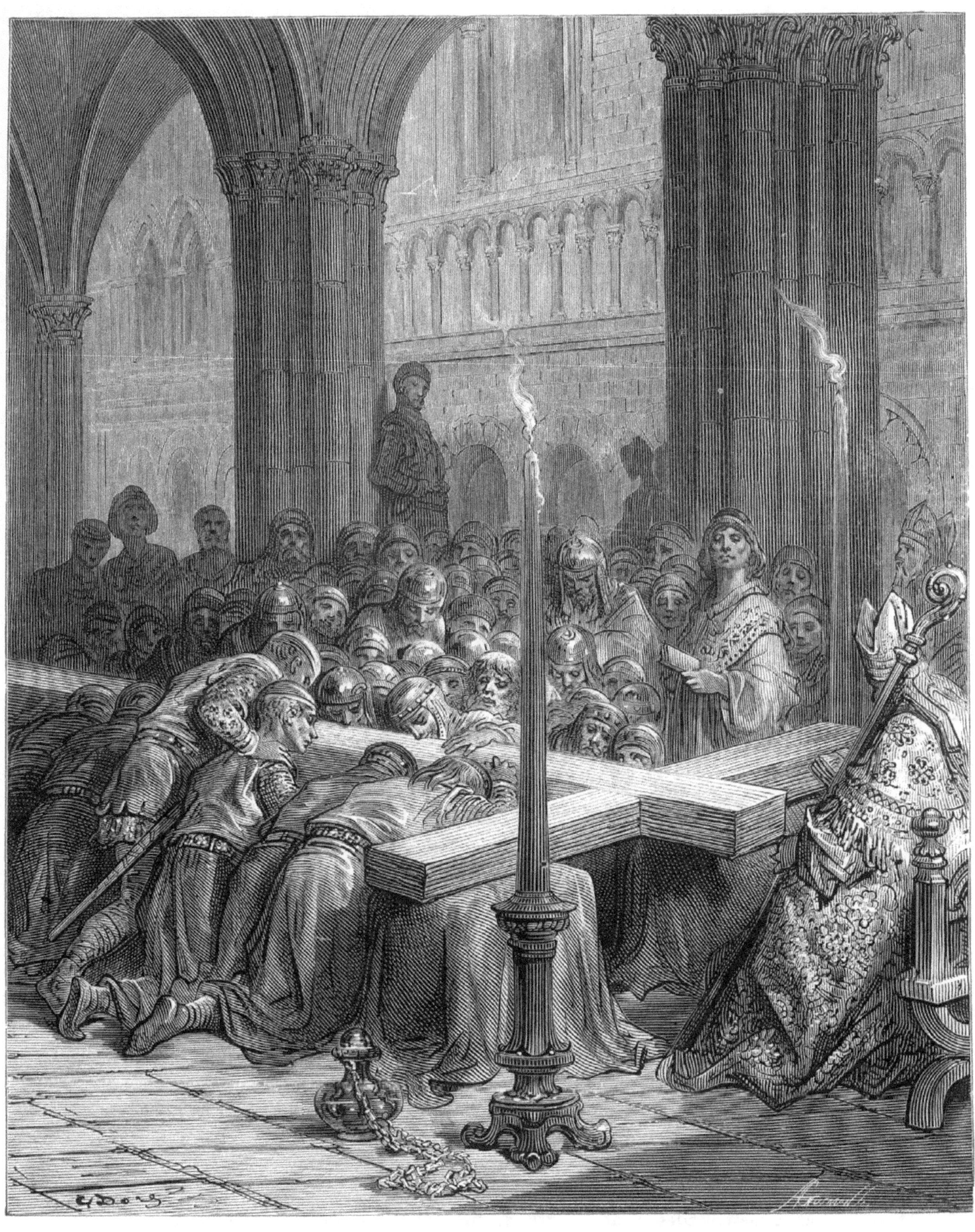

BOOK V.

HISTORY OF THE KINGDOM OF JERUSALEM.

A. D. 1099–1148.

Kingdom founded by the victories of the Crusaders—State of Palestine at that period—Political measures of Godfrey—Tiberias captured by Tancred—Siege of Arsur—Jerusalem visited by numerous pilgrims and distinguished Crusaders—Archbishop Daimbert elected patriarch of Jerusalem—"Assizes of Jerusalem"—Death of Godfrey—His brother Baldwin elected king—Carries on successful hostilities against the Infidels of Palestine, Egypt, &c.—Cæsarea and Arsur besieged and captured—City of Ramla taken by the Saracens—Hospitallers of St. John—Insidious policy of Alexius—Josselin de Courtenay—Baldwin taken prisoner—Bohémond, prince of Antioch, visits Italy, and returns with a large army against Alexius—His death—Release of Baldwin—Distresses of Antioch—Quarrels between Baldwin and the patriarch of Jerusalem—The Genoese and Pisan fleets assist the Crusaders—Siege and capture of Ptolemaïs—Armies of Egypt defeated—Tripoli, Biblies, Sarepta, Berytus, and Sidon taken by the Crusaders—Sigur, prince of Norway—The "true cross"—Death of Tancred—The Christians defeated—Palestine devastated—Death of Baldwin—Baldwin du Bourg elected king of Jerusalem—Taken prisoner—Eustache Grenier, regent—The Venetians destroy the fleet of the Saracens, and conquer Tyre—Release of Baldwin—Several cities of Egypt captured—The Ismaëlians—Zengui, prince of Mossoul—Dynasty of the Atabecks—Flourishing state of Antioch, Edessa, Tripoli, &c.—Knights of St. John and of the Holy Sepulchre—The Templars—Death of Baldwin du Bourg—Foulque of Anjou crowned king of Jerusalem—Raymond of Poictiers appointed governor of Antioch—The emperor of Constantinople attacks Antioch—Melisende, queen of Jerusalem—Baldwin III. ascends the throne—Disastrous retreat from Bosra—The country of Traconite—Conquests of Zengui—Death of Josselin de Courtenay—Noureddin, son of Zengui, captures Edessa, and threatens Jerusalem.

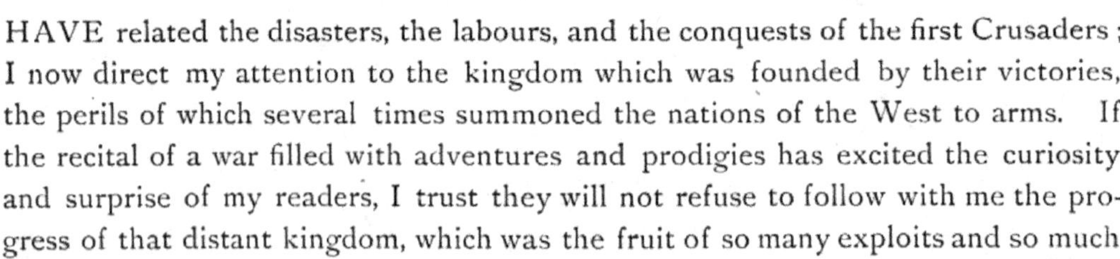

I HAVE related the disasters, the labours, and the conquests of the first Crusaders; I now direct my attention to the kingdom which was founded by their victories, the perils of which several times summoned the nations of the West to arms. If the recital of a war filled with adventures and prodigies has excited the curiosity and surprise of my readers, I trust they will not refuse to follow with me the progress of that distant kingdom, which was the fruit of so many exploits and so much glory, which cost so much blood and so many tears. After having beheld the countless crowds of pilgrims setting out for the deliverance of the Holy Land, who will not be astonished to see two or three hundred brave knights, the glorious remains of the Christian armies, suffice for the defence of the provinces and cities conquered by the united powers of the West? What spectacle can create more profound reflection in the minds of thinking and enlightened men, than that of a new people, cast, as it were by a tempest, on a foreign shore, in the midst of a country from which the arms, religion, and customs of numerous nations are unceasingly employed to expel them?

The country in which the Crusaders had just established themselves, and which the monuments of religion and history rendered so dear to the nations of the West, constituted the kingdoms of Judah and Israel of antiquity. When the Romans carried their arms into this country, its new masters added to the name which the Jews had given it that of Palestine, or the country of the Palestinians. It was bounded on the south and east by the deserts of Arabia and Idumea, on the west by the Mediterranean, and on the north by the mountains Libanus.

At the period of the crusades, as at the present time, a great part of the soil of Palestine, upon which rise the barren mountains of Sion, Hebron, Hebal, and Gelboëi, presented the aspect of a land upon which the curses of Heaven had fallen. This land, formerly promised to the elect people of God, had several times changed inhabitants. All the sects, all the dynasties of the Mussulmans, had disputed the possession of it sword in hand, and revolutions and wars had left numerous memorable ruins in its capital, and in the greater part of its provinces. The religious ideas of the Mussulmans and the Christians seemed alone to give importance to the conquest of Judea; history must, however, guard against the exaggeration with which certain travellers have spoken of the sterility of this unfortunate country. Amidst the calamities which, during many ages, desolated the provinces of Palestine, some traces of its ancient splendour may still be perceived. The shores of the Lake of Galilee and of the Jordan, some valleys watered by the Besor, the Arnou, and the Jaboc, and the plains contiguous to the sea which war had not ravaged, still recalled by their fertility the promises of Scripture. Palestine yet boasted some flourishing cities, and several of its ports offered a commodious asylum to the vessels of Asia and Europe.

In the condition of Palestine at that time, if the territory had been entirely subject to Godfrey, the new king might have equalled in power the greater part of the Mussulman princes of Asia; but the young kingdom of Jerusalem consisted but of the capital and about twenty cities or towns in its neighbourhood. Several of these cities were separated by places still occupied by the infidels. A fortress in the hands of the Christians was near to a fortress over which floated the standard of Mahomet. In the surrounding country dwelt Turks, Arabs, and Egyptians, who all united to make war upon the subjects of Godfrey. The latter were not free from alarm even in their cities, which were almost all badly garrisoned, and found themselves constantly exposed to the terrors and evils of war. The lands remained uncultivated, and all communications were interrupted. Amidst so many perils, several of the Latins abandoned the possessions which victory had bestowed upon them; and that the conquered country might not be left without inhabitants, the interest of property, or proprietorship, was called in to strengthen the wavering love for the new abode. Every man who had remained a year and a day in a house, or upon cultivated land, was recognised as the legitimate proprietor of it. All rights of possession were annulled by an absence of the same duration.

The first care of Godfrey was to repel the hostilities of the Saracens, and to extend the frontiers of the kingdom intrusted to his defence. By his orders Tancred entered into Galilee, and took possession of Tiberias, and several other cities situated in the neighbourhood of the Lake of Genesareth. As the reward of his labours, he obtained possession of the country he conquered, which in the end became a principality.

Tancred, master of a rich province, advanced into the territories of Damascus, whilst Godfrey, in a fortunate excursion, imposed tributes upon the emirs of Cæsarea, Ptolemaïs, and Ascalon, and brought to submission the Arabs dwelling on the left shores of the Jordan. He was returning victorious to Jerusalem, when the city of Asur, which had surrendered after the battle of Ascalon, refused to pay tribute, and shook off the yoke of the Christians. Godfrey resolved to lay siege to this rebel city; he collected his troops, marched them towards Asur, and proceeded to attack the town. Already had the rolling towers approached the ramparts, the rams had shaken the walls to their foundations, and the city was about to be carried, when the besieged employed a mode of defence worthy only of barbarians. Gerard of Avesnes, who had been left with them as an hostage by Godfrey, was fastened to the top of a very high mast which was attached to the very wall against which the efforts of the besiegers were principally directed. At the prospect of an inevitable and inglorious death, the unfortunate Christian knight uttered loud and painful cries, and conjured his friend Godfrey to save his life by a voluntary retreat. This cruel spectacle pierced the heart of Godfrey, but did not shake either his firmness or his courage. As he was sufficiently near to Gerard of Avesnes to make himself heard by him, he exhorted him to merit the crown of martyrdom by his resignation. "It is not in my power to save you," said he; "if my brother Eustace were in your place, I could not deliver him from death. Die, then, illustrious and brave knight, with the courage of a Christian hero; die for the safety of your brethren, and for the glory of Jesus Christ." These words of Godfrey gave Gerard of Avesnes the courage to die. He begged his old companions to offer at the holy sepulchre his horse and his arms, that prayers might be put up for the health of his soul. A short time after he died under a shower of darts and arrows launched by the hands of the Christians.

The soldiers of Godfrey, on witnessing the death of Gerard, burned with rage to revenge him, and redoubled their efforts to render themselves masters of the city. On their side, the besieged reproached the Christians with their barbarity, and defended themselves with vigour. The Greek fire consumed the towers and the machines of the besiegers; Godfrey had lost a great number of his soldiers, and despaired of reducing the city, which received succours by sea. As winter was approaching, he resolved at last to raise the siege and return to Jerusalem, deeply affected at having caused the death of Gerard of Avesnes without any advantage to the cause of the Christians.

During the siege of Asur several emirs from the mountains of Samaria came to visit Godfrey. They were struck with the greatest surprise when they found the king of the Christians without a guard, without splendour, sleeping on a straw pallet like the meanest of his soldiers. They were not less astonished when, at their request, he exhibited before them his extraordinary strength by cutting off the head of a camel at a single blow with his sword. The emirs, after having offered presents to Godfrey, returned to their own country, and related the wonders they had seen. Their recitals, which history has not disdained, contributed greatly to increase the fame of the king of Jerusalem.

When Godfrey reached his capital, he learnt the approach of a great number of pilgrims, the greater part of whom were Pisans and Genoese, led by the bishop of Ariana, and Daimbert, archbishop of Pisa. To the Christians arrived from the West were added Bohémond, prince of Antioch, Baldwin, count of Edessa, and Raymond, count of Thoulouse. These latter had come to visit the holy places, and to celebrate the epoch of the birth of Christ at Jerusalem.

Godfrey went out to meet the pilgrims as far as Bethlehem, with his knights and the clergy. "After they were come into the holy city," says an old chronicle, "the king received them and feasted them magnificently; and detained them in Judea during the winter, being much gratified with the presence of his brother Baldwin." Daimbert, archbishop of Pisa, had come into Palestine as legate from the Holy See. By means of presents and promises he got himself to be named patriarch of Jerusalem, in the place of Arnold de Rohés. This prelate, brought up in the school of Gregory VII., maintained with warmth the pretensions of the Holy See, and it was not long before his ambition introduced trouble among the Christians. In the places even where Christ had said that his kingdom was not of this world, he who called himself his vicar desired to reign with Godfrey, and demanded the sovereignty of a part of Jaffa, and of a quarter of Jerusalem in which the church of the Resurrection was built. After some debates, the pious Godfrey yielded to the imperious demands of Daimbert; and such was then the ascendancy of the Church and the clergy, that the new king was obliged to consent to a treaty by which the kingdom should belong to the patriarch, if Godfrey should die without children. Godfrey thus acknowledged himself the vassal of the sovereign pontiff, and received from the pope and his legate permission to reign over a country conquered by his arms. Bohémond and Baldwin consented at the same time to receive from the pope the investiture of their principalities. The prince of Antioch had refused to render homage to the king of Jerusalem, but he did not hesitate to acknowledge himself the vassal of a power which bestowed empires, and was able to send fresh armies into the East.

In the mean time the wise Godfrey, after having freed his territory from the incursions of the Mussulmans, and carried the terror of his arms beyond the Jordan, reflected that victory was not all that was required to found a state. His capital had been depopulated by the sword of the Crusaders; several other cities, like Jaffa, had lost the greater part of their inhabitants; and this new king reckoned among his subjects Armenians, Greeks, Jews, Arabs, renegades from all religions, and adventurers from all countries. The state confided to his care was like a place of passage, and had no other supporters or defenders but travellers and strangers. It was the rendezvous and the asylum of notorious sinners, who came thither to mitigate the anger of God, and of criminals, who thus eluded the justice of men. Both of these were equally dangerous when circumstances awakened their passions, or when fear and repentance gave way before new temptations. Godfrey, according to the spirit of feudal customs and the laws of war, had divided the conquered lands among the companions of his victories. The new lords of Jaffa, Tiberias, Ramla, and Naplouse, scarcely acknowledged the authority of a king. The clergy, encouraged by the patriarch, assumed the tone of masters, and the bishops exercised a temporal power equal to that of the barons. Some attributed the conquest of the kingdom to their valour, others to their prayers; every one claimed the reward of either his piety or his labours; and whilst the greater part aimed at domination, all insisted upon independence.

Godfrey undertook to rule so many conflicting pretensions, and to bring a tumultuous government into some regular form. In order that the execution of his project might have the greater solemnity, he chose the circumstance which had conducted the Latin princes to Jerusalem. After having accompanied them as far as Jericho, to celebrate with them the festival of the Epiphany, he returned to his capital, where he assembled the enlightened and pious men of the city, of whom he formed the states, or the assizes, of his kingdom. In this solemn assembly the first care was to regulate and determine the duties of the barons, the lords, and the common subjects, towards the king, and the duties of the king towards the lords and subjects. The king was to undertake to maintain the laws, to defend the Church, to protect widows and orphans, to watch over the safety of both people and lords, and to lead in war. The lord, who was the lieutenant of the prince, as regarded his vassals, was to guarantee them from insult, and to protect their property, their honour, and their rights. The first duty of the counts and barons towards the king was to serve him in council and fight. The first obligation of a subject or a vassal towards his prince or his lord, was to defend him or avenge him in every case of outrage, and to protect the honour of his wife, his daughter, or his sister; to follow him in all perils, and to surrender himself as hostage for him, if he fell into the hands of his enemies.

The king and his subjects, the great and the small vassals, mutually engaged their faith to each other. In the feudal hierarchy, every class had its privileges maintained by honour. Honour, that grand principle among knights, commanded all to repulse an injury inflicted upon a single one, and thus became, restrained within just limits, the security of public liberty.

War was the great affair in a kingdom founded by knights and barons; every one capable of bearing arms was reckoned as something in the state, and protected by the new legislation; all the rest, with the exception of the clergy, whose existence and privileges were held by divine right, were reckoned as nothing, and scarcely merited any attention from the legislators. The Assizes of Jerusalem did, indeed, deign to take notice of villains, slaves, peasants or cultivators, or captives taken in war; but they were only considered in the light of property, of which they wished to assure the enjoyment to its legitimate possessors. Those who had lost them could reclaim them as they could a falcon or a hound; the value of a falcon and a slave was the same; a war-horse was estimated at more than double the value of a peasant or a captive. The laws did not condescend to notice these unhappy classes, and left it to religion alone to protect them.

GODFREY IMPOSED TRIBUTES UPON EMIRS.

The first care of Godfrey was to repel the hostilities of the Saracens, and to extend the frontiers of the kingdom intrusted to his defence. By his orders Tancred entered into Galilee, took possession of Tiberias, and several other cities situated in the neighbourhood of the Lake of Genesareth. As a reward of his labours, he obtained possession of the country he conquered, which in the end became a principality.

Tancred, master of a rich province, advanced into the territories of Damascus, whilst Godfrey, in a fortunate excursion, imposed tributes upon the emirs of Cæsarea, Ptolemaïs, and Ascalon, and brought to submission the Arabs dwelling on the left shores of the Jordan. He was returning victorious to Jerusalem, when the city of Asur, which had surrendered after the battle of Ascalon, refused to pay tribute, and shook off the yoke of the Christians. Godfrey resolved to lay siege to this rebel city. —Book V.

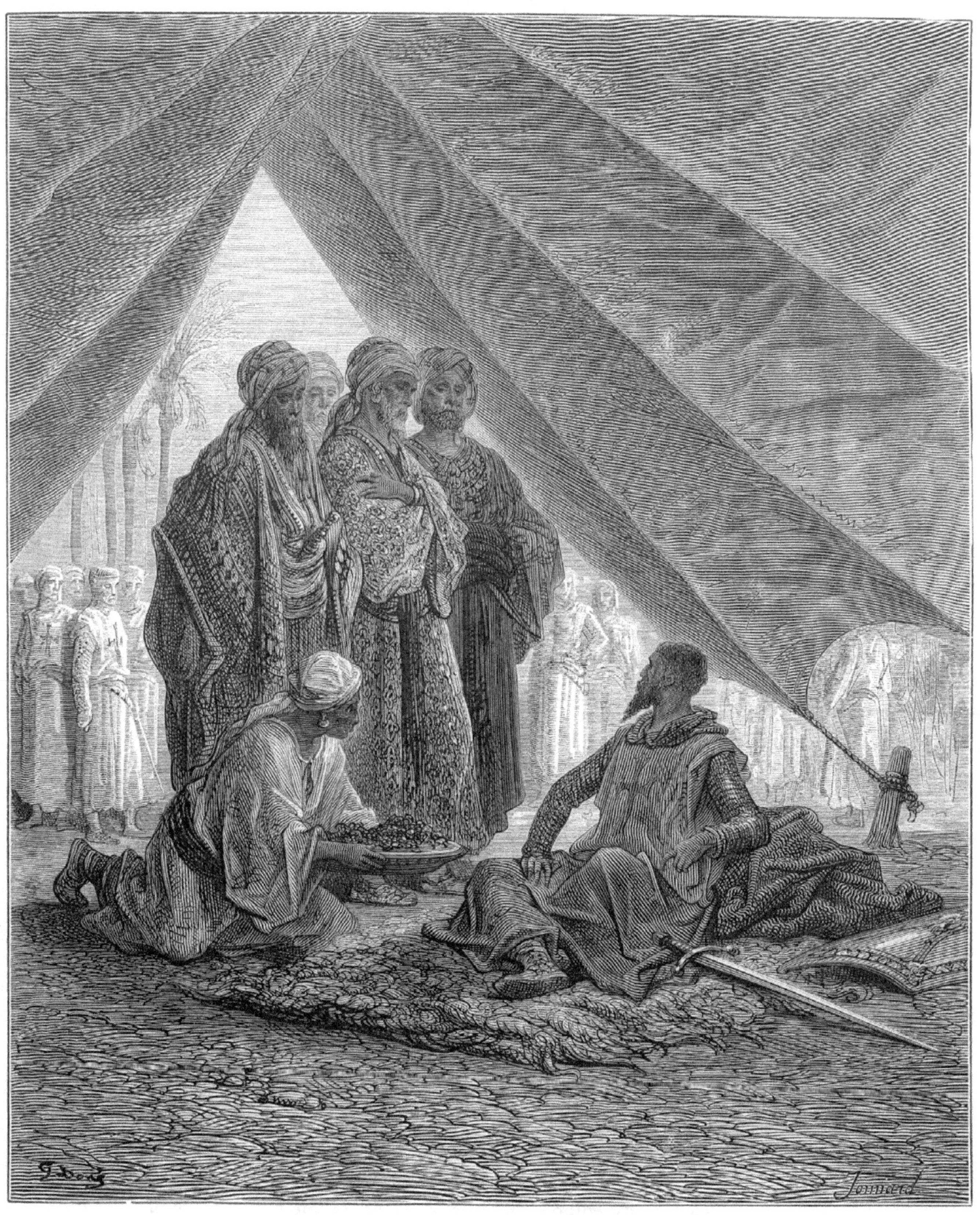

To watch over the execution of the constitutional laws of the state, and to decide in all disputes, two courts were instituted ; the one presided over by the king, and composed of the nobles, was to pronounce judgment upon differences among the great vassals ; the other, presided over by the viscount of Jerusalem, and formed of the principal inhabitants of each city, was to regulate the interests and the rights of the citizens and the common people. A third court was instituted, which was reserved for Oriental Christians ; the judges of it were born in Syria, spoke its language, and decided according to the laws and usages of the country. Thus all the citizens of the kingdom were judged by their peers, and enjoyed the benefits of an institution which has not been despised in ages much more enlightened.

The Franks, with their warlike character, were certain to evince disdain for the slow, and often uncertain, forms of justice ; they adopted, in their legislation made for the East, the ordeal by iron or fire, which had taken its birth among the nations of the North. Judicial combat was also admitted in criminal causes, and sometimes even in civil ones. Among a warlike people everything must present the image of war ; every action commenced against a baron or a knight was, in his eyes, an injury—an affront—that he ought to repulse sword in hand ; Christian knights were likewise persuaded that God would not allow innocence to succumb in an unequal combat, and victory appeared to them at once the triumph of human laws and divine justice.

Such dispositions still bespeak the barbarity of the most remote ages ; but a great number of other laws attest the wisdom of the legislators of the Holy Land : their code contained every institution that was reasonable in the feudal system. Palestine was then blessed by the revival of wise laws created for Europe, but which Europe had forgotten amidst the anarchy of civil wars ; many ameliorations made in feudal legislation in some of the states of the West, particularly in the cities of Italy, were consecrated in the new laws of Jerusalem.

It must be believed that in this circumstance religion sometimes mingled her useful inspirations with those of human sagacity ; justice and humanity assumed a more sacred character in the presence of the holy tomb. As all the subjects of Godfrey were called upon to defend the cause of God, the quality of a soldier of Jesus Christ might make the dignity of man respected. If it be true that the establishment of the commons, or a second court, was the work of the Crusaders, we cannot, with truth, assert that these wars contributed nothing towards the progress of civilization. The laws which they made, and in which may be plainly seen the first glimpses of regulated liberty, were a new spectacle for Asia ; they must likewise have been a subject of surprise and a means of instruction for Europe itself, where pilgrims related, on their return, the usages and customs established by the Franks in the Holy Land. This code of legislation, the best, or rather the least imperfect that had existed previous to that time, and which increased or was modified under other reigns, was deposited with great pomp in the church of the Resurrection, and took the name of the Assizes of Jerusalem, or Letters of the Holy Sepulchre.

After this ceremony, which was performed in the presence of all the pilgrims, the Latin princes then at Jerusalem returned to their own states ; Baldwin to Edessa, Bohémond to his principality of Antioch, and Raymond to Laodicea, of which he had rendered himself master, and which he governed in the name of the emperor of Constantinople. Scarcely had Tancred returned to his principality when he was attacked by all the forces of the sultan of Damascus. Godfrey, accompanied by his faithful knights and a great number of pilgrims eager to fight under his command, repaired immediately into Galilee, defeated the Saracens, and pursued them to the mountains of Libanus.

As he was returning from this expedition, the emir of Cæsarea came out to meet him, and presented to him an offering of some of the fruits of Palestine. Godfrey only accepted a single cedar-apple, and almost directly fell ill. This malady, which they did not hesitate to attribute to poison, created the most serious alarm among his followers. Godfrey with great difficulty reached Jaffa, whence he was conveyed to his capital, where he died, committing to the companions of his victories the charge of the glory of religion and of the kingdom of Jerusalem. His mortal remains were deposited within the enclosure of Calvary, near to the tomb of Christ, which he had delivered by his valour. His death was mourned by the Christians, of whom he was the father and the support, and by the Mussulmans, who had often experienced his justice and his clemency. History may say of him what the holy Scripture says of Judas Maccabeus: "It was he who increased the glory of his people, when, like a giant, he put on his arms in the fight, and his sword was the protection of the whole camp." Godfrey of Bouillon surpassed all the captains of his age in his skill in war; and if he had lived some time longer, would have merited a name among great kings. In the kingdom he founded he was constantly held up as a model for princes as well as warriors. His name still recalls the virtues of heroic times, and will live honoured amongst men as long as the remembrance of the crusades.

After the death of Godfrey great disputes arose upon the choice of his successor. The patriarch Daimbert endeavoured to avail himself of the rights conveyed by the promises of Godfrey, and claimed the throne of Jerusalem; but the barons would submit to no chief but one of their companions in arms. Garnier, count de Gray, took possession of the Tower of David and of the other fortresses of Jerusalem, in the name of Baldwin, count of Edessa. The patriarch invoked the authority of the Church to the assistance of his cause; and as Count Garnier died suddenly, the clergy of Jerusalem attributed his death to divine justice, which the impious projects of the barons and knights had offended. Daimbert wrote to Bohémond, prince of Antioch, and conjured him to come and defend what he called the rights of the Church and the cause of God. Jerusalem was filled with agitation and trouble; but whilst they were tumultuously deliberating, deputies from Antioch came to announce that their prince had been surprised in an expedition against the Turks, and was held prisoner by the infidels. This news spread consternation and grief among the Christians, and made them more sensible of the necessity for calling Baldwin to the throne, with whose valour they were so well acquainted.

Baldwin, to whom deputies had been sent, shed tears on learning the death of Godfrey, but soon consoled himself with the hope of obtaining a crown. The county of Edessa had become richer and more extensive than the mean kingdom of Jerusalem, several cities of which still belonged to the Saracens; but such was the active and enterprising spirit of Baldwin, that the prospect of a kingdom to be conquered appeared to him preferable to a country of which he was in peaceful possession. After having given up the county of Edessa to his cousin Baldwin du Bourg, he began his march with four hundred horsemen and a thousand foot. The emirs of Emessa and Damascus, informed of his intended march, laid wait for him in the narrow and difficult roads near the coast of the Sea of Phœnicia. Baldwin feigned to fly before the army of the infidels, and having drawn them into an open country, routed them, making a great many prisoners, whom he carried to Jerusalem. The knights, the barons, and a portion of the clergy came out to meet the conqueror. Baldwin made his triumphant entrance into the city in the midst of the acclamations of the whole Christian population, who flocked eagerly to see the brother of Godfrey. But whilst the inhabitants thus manifested their joy, the patriarch, with some of his partisans, protested against the election of the new king, and, feigning to believe that he was in safety nowhere but close to the tomb of Christ, retired in silence to Mount Sion, as if to seek an asylum there. Baldwin did not think it worth while to disturb the retreat of the patriarch, and, satisfied with having obtained the suffrages of the barons and knights, wished to assure to himself new titles to the crown, by gaining more victories over the Saracens. He marched from Jerusalem, followed by his bravest knights, and presented himself before Ascalon.

The season being too far advanced to lay regular siege to the city, he ravaged the enemy's country, penetrated into the mountains of Engaddi, surprised Segor, and seized a troop of brigands in a cavern which they had chosen as a place of retreat. In this campaign, which was little more than a pilgrimage, the soldiers of Baldwin passed along the shores of the Dead Sea, the sight of which recalled the memory of the punishment of Sodom; they visited the valley famous as the burial-place of the ancestors of Israel, and that in which it is believed Moses caused a stream of living water to spring from the side of a barren rock. The Christian soldiers were never weary of admiring these places, rendered sacred by scriptural remembrances. The historian Foulcher de Chartres, who accompanied Baldwin, displays in his recital the greatest enthusiasm, and tells us with lively joy, that he watered his horses at the miraculous fountain of the legislator of the Hebrews.

The little army of the Christians came back to Jerusalem loaded with booty. After Baldwin's return, the patriarch did not venture to say anything more about his pretensions, and consented to crown the successor of Godfrey with his own hands. The ceremony was performed with great solemnity at Bethlehem, in the presence of the barons, the bishops, and the principal people of the kingdom.

Tancred was not present at the coronation of the new king, for the two companions of Godfrey had not forgotten their ancient quarrel. Tancred had protested against the election of Baldwin, and refused to pay him homage. Baldwin, on his part, disputed Tancred's right to the principality of Galilee, and summoned him to appear before him as a contumacious vassal. The reply of Tancred was laconic, and full of proud contempt for his rival. "I do not know," said he, addressing the messengers of Baldwin, "that your master is king of Jerusalem." He did not deign to make any reply to a second summons. At length their mutual friends employed prayers and entreaties, to which Tancred reluctantly gave way. The two princes agreed to have an interview between Jerusalem and Jaffa, in which interview Tancred consented to forget past injuries, but would not renounce a principality which he held from Godfrey. The debates between the prince of Galilee and the king of Jerusalem were not terminated when messengers arrived from Antioch, conjuring Tancred to repair immediately to their city, to govern a state which had been without a head since the captivity of Bohémond. Tancred yielded to their entreaties, and immediately set out for Antioch, abandoning to Hugh de Saint Omer the city of Tiberias and the principality of Galilee.

These differences with Tancred did not impede Baldwin's wars against the infidels, or his endeavours to extend his young kingdom. Whilst Persia, Egypt, Syria, and Mesopotamia could bring numberless armies against the Christians, Baldwin could only muster under his standard a small body of warriors, to whom were added a few pilgrims from the West, the greater part without horses and very badly armed. His bravery and activity surmounted all obstacles, and carried him through all dangers. From the beginning of his reign, we see with surprise the kingdom of Jerusalem, disturbed in its infancy by discord, and only defended by a few knights, rise in the midst of formidable enemies, and carry terror amongst neighbours much more powerful than itself.

The king of Jerusalem took advantage of the arrival of a Genoese fleet, to punish the rebellion of the inhabitants of Arsur, and to lay siege to their city both by sea and land. On the third day the city fell into the hands of the Christians. A short time after, Baldwin besieged Cæsarea, a city built by Herod in honour of Cæsar. The siege was carried on with vigour; on the fifteenth day everything was ready for a general assault, and as soon as the trumpet had given the first signal, all the soldiers confessed and received absolution for their sins. The patriarch, clothed in white vestments, with a crucifix in his hand, led them to the foot of the ramparts;—the city was soon taken, and the inhabitants put to the sword. The Christians, particularly the Genoese, carried away by a thirst for pillage, and still more by vengeance and the fury of battle, stained their victory by horrible cruelties. The Mussulmans who escaped from the massacre of Cæsarea, carried terror into the cities of Ptolemaïs and Ascalon, and all the countries still under the domination of the Egyptians.

The caliph of Egypt, to revenge the death of his warriors, assembled an army, which advanced as far as the country round Ramla. Baldwin got together, in haste, a troop of three hundred knights and a thousand foot-soldiers, and marched to meet him. When he perceived the standards of the Egyptian army, ten times more numerous than that of the Christians, he represented to his soldiers that they were going to fight for the glory of Christianity; "if they fell, heaven would be open to them; if they triumphed, the fame of their victory would be spread throughout the Christian world. There could be no safety in flight; their home was beyond the seas; in the East there was no asylum for the conquered." After having thus animated his soldiers, Baldwin divided his troops into six battalions. The two first, on charging the enemy, were overwhelmed by numbers; two others, which followed, shared the same fate. Two bishops, who were with Baldwin, then advised him to implore the mercy of Heaven; and, at their desire, the king of Jerusalem alighted from his horse, fell on his knees, confessed, and received absolution. Springing to his feet, he resumed his arms, and rushed upon the enemy at the head of his two remaining battalions. The Christian warriors fought like lions, animated by their war-cry "*Victory or Death!*" Baldwin had attached a white kerchief to the point of his lance, and thus pointed out the road to carnage. The victory was for a length of time uncertain; but at last, says an historian, the will of God was declared in favour of the soldiers of Christ. The Egyptian army had lost its leader, and was entirely routed; five thousand infidels remaining on the field of battle.

The enemy fled in such complete disorder that they abandoned their tents and their baggage. As Baldwin was pursuing them his ear was struck by the plaintive cry of a woman. He checked his war-horse, and perceived a female Mussulman in the pains of childbirth. He threw his mantle to her to cover her, and ordered her to be placed on carpets laid upon the ground. By his commands, fruits and a skin of water were brought to this bed of pain, and a female camel furnished milk for the nourishment of the newly-born child. The mother was confided to the care of a slave, with orders to conduct her to her husband. The latter, who held a distinguished rank among the Mussulmans, shed tears of joy on beholding a wife whose death he was lamenting, and vowed never to forget the generous action of Baldwin.

Conqueror of the Saracens, the king of Jerusalem had sent back his troops, and was reposing at Jaffa, after the fatigues of the war, when he learnt that the Mussulman army had rallied, and was in full march to attack the Christians. Baldwin, whom victory had rendered rash, without assembling all his troops, went immediately to meet the enemy, at the head of two hundred knights, and a few pilgrims lately arrived from the West. Not at all dismayed by the number of the Saracens, he gave battle; but, at the first charge, the Christians were surrounded, and only sought a glorious death, fighting by the side of their leader. The king of Jerusalem, obliged to fly, concealed himself among the long dried grass and bushes which covered the plain. As the Saracens set fire to these, Baldwin with difficulty escaped being burnt alive; and, after many perils, was glad to take refuge in Ramla.

Night checked the pursuit of his enemies, but on the following day, the place which served him as an asylum was threatened with an immediate siege, and had no means of defence. Baldwin was a prey to the most distressing anxiety, when a stranger, who had by some means got into the city, demanded to speak instantly with the king of Jerusalem.—"It is gratitude," said he to him, "which brings me here. Thou hast been generous towards a wife who is most dear to me—thou hast restored her to me and her family, after having saved her life. I brave a thousand dangers to acquit myself

GERARD OF AVESNES EXPOSED ON THE WALLS OF ASUR.

Gerard of Avesnes, who had been left with them as an hostage by Godfrey, was fastened to the top of a very high mast which was attached to the very wall against which the efforts of the besiegers were principally directed. At the prospect of an inevitable and inglorious death, the unfortunate Christian knight uttered loud and painful cries, and conjured his friend Godfrey to save his life by a voluntary retreat. This spectacle pierced the heart of Godfrey, but did not shake either his firmness or his courage. As he was sufficiently near Gerard of Avesnes to make himself heard by him, he exhorted him to merit the crown of martyrdom by his resignation. "It is not in my power to save you," said he; "if my brother Eustace were in your place I would not deliver him from death. Die, then, illustrious and brave knight, with the courage of a Christian hero; die for the safety of your brethren, and for the glory of Jesus Christ." The words of Godfrey gave Gerard of Avesnes the courage to die. He begged his old companions to offer at the holy sepulchre his horse and his arms, that prayers might be put for the health of his soul.—BOOK V.

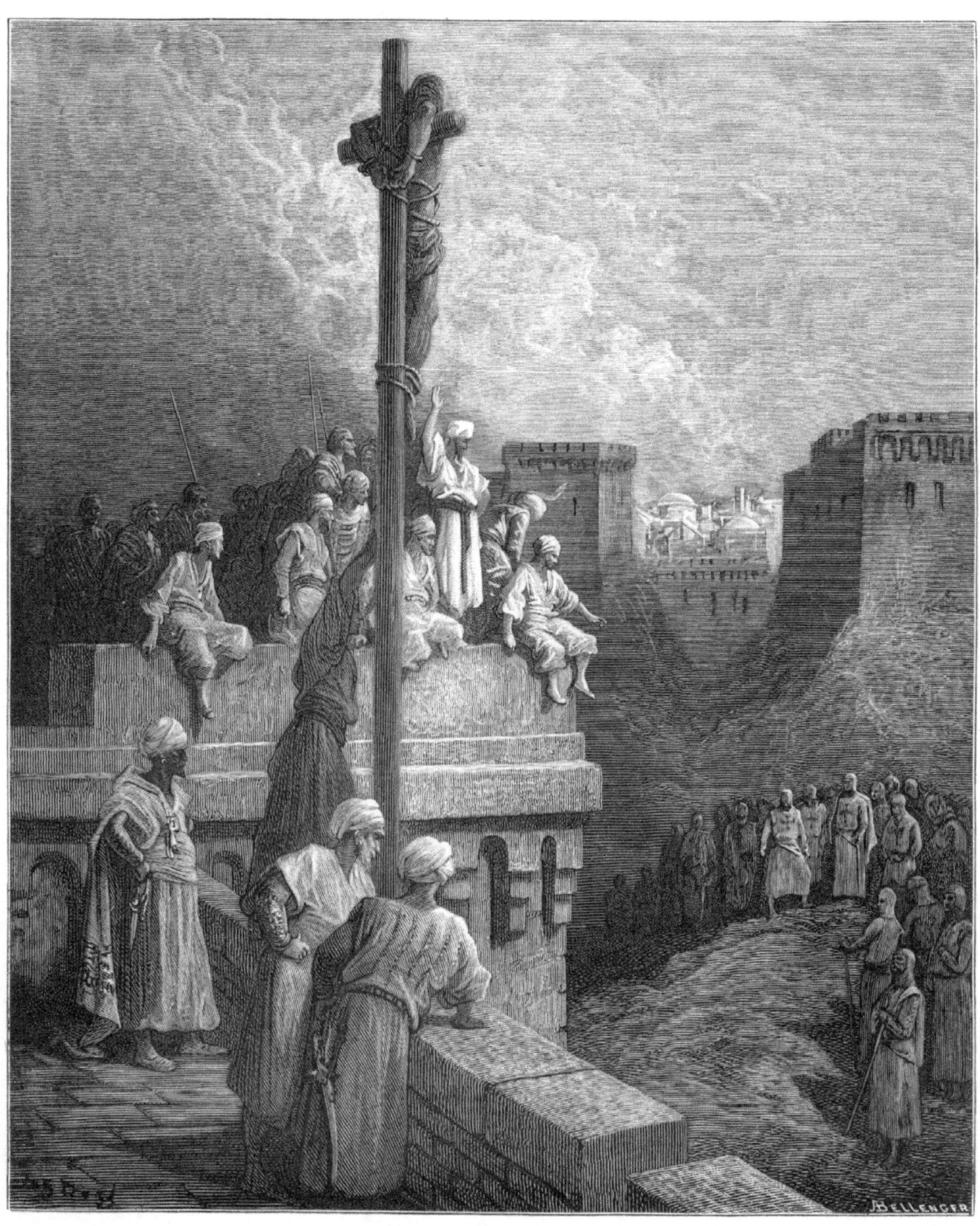

of so sacred a debt. The Saracens surround the city of thy retreat on all sides; to-morrow it will be taken, and not one of its inhabitants will escape death. I come to offer thee means of safety. I am acquainted with a path which is not guarded; hasten then, for time presses. Thou hast but to follow me; before the dawn of day thou wilt be among thy people."

Baldwin hesitated—he shed tears at the idea of what must be the fate of his companions in misfortune; but, at length, he yielded to the generosity of the Mussulman emir, and, accompanied by a weak escort, they both departed from the city, in the middle of a stormy night. On gaining the distance of a few leagues from Ramla, they separated with tears in their eyes; the emir rejoined the Mussulman army, and Baldwin succeeded in getting to the city of Arsur.

At break of day the Saracens advanced towards the ramparts of Ramla. They quickly gained possession of the city, and all they met with in the place were massacred. Some soldiers who escaped the Saracens' swords, carried the sad news to the neighbouring cities. It was the first defeat the Christians had experienced since their arrival in Palestine. As it was confidently said that Baldwin had been slain at the taking of Ramla, this loss added greatly to the general consternation. The great bell of Jerusalem announced the approach and invasion of the Saracens. The priests, the monks, the pilgrims, clothed in sackcloth and barefooted, went in procession through the streets of the holy city; women and children filled the churches, and with tears in their eyes and uplifted hands implored the mercy of Heaven. The bravest were beginning to despair of the safety of the kingdom, when Baldwin suddenly appeared among his people, says William of Tyre, like the morning star, and revived their hopes by his presence.

The king of Jerusalem assembled at Jaffa the wreck of his army; and the Christian cities sent him all their inhabitants capable of bearing arms. Several princes and knights, arrived from the West, likewise joined him. The Christians marched boldly forth to meet the Mussulmans, the patriarch of Jerusalem carrying through the ranks the wood of the holy cross. The war-cry of the Christian soldiers was:—"*Christ lives, Christ reigns, Christ commands.*" The two armies were soon in sight of each other on the plains of Jaffa, and instantly the trumpets sounded, and gave the signal of battle. Both sides fought with fury; the infidels surrounded the Christians, and pressed them so closely that they had scarcely room to wield their arms, and victory was on the point of being determined in favour of the Mussulmans, when Baldwin, snatching the white flag from the hands of his squire, and followed by a hundred and sixty knights, rushed into the very thickest ranks of the enemy. This act of bravery decided the fate of the battle, and the Christians regained their courage. The fight lasted during the whole day, but towards the approach of night, the Mussulmans fled in disorder, leaving dead upon the field the emir of Ascalon and four thousand of their bravest soldiers.

Baldwin, who, some few days before, had been believed to be dead, reëntered Jerusalem in triumph. He gave a great part of the booty to the hospitallers of St. John, whose office it was to entertain the poor and all pilgrims; and, to employ the expression of an old chronicle, he thus shared with God the spoils of the Saracens.

The Christians assembled in the churches rendered thanks to God for the deliverance of the kingdom; but this last victory could not dry all the tears which a first reverse had caused to flow, and funereal hymns were mingled with the songs of joy. In this campaign perished many of the princes and knights who had left Europe after the first crusade. Stephen, count of Chartres and Blois, and Stephen, duke of Burgundy, who had arrived in Palestine with the remains of an army dispersed by the Turks in Asia Minor, were killed under the walls of Ramla. As the Greeks were accused of having prepared the ruin of the armies sent to the assistance of the Latins, murmurs arose in all the Christian colonies against the emperor Alexius. This prince, constantly in dread of the powers of the

West, sent to congratulate the king of Jerusalem on his victories, and exerted himself to procure the liberty of the Christians who had fallen into the hands of the Egyptians and Turks. After having delivered or ransomed some Christian knights, he received them at Constantinople, loaded them with presents, and sent them back to their own country.

But whilst thus breaking the chains of a few captives, he was equipping fleets and raising armies to attack Antioch, and obtain possession of the cities on the coast of Syria which belonged to the Latins. He offered to pay the ransom of Bohémond, still a prisoner among the Turks, not for the purpose of setting him at liberty, but to have him brought to Constantinople, where he hoped to obtain from him a renunciation of his principality. Bohémond, who saw through the projects of Alexius, gained the good-will of the emir who detained him prisoner, promised him his alliance and support, and persuaded him to accept for his ransom, half the sum offered by the emperor of the Greeks. After a captivity of four years, he returned to Antioch, where he employed himself in repulsing the aggressions of Alexius. The fleets of the Pisans and the Genoese came to his relief, and several battles, both by sea and land, were fought with various success; the Latins and the Greeks, by turns, obtaining the advantage.

Whilst this war was being carried on between Alexius and Bohémond, the Franks neglected no opportunity of coming into collision with the infidels. Bohémond, Baldwin du Bourg, count of Edessa, and his cousin Josselin de Courtenay,* master of several cities on the banks of the Euphrates, united their forces to attack Charan, a flourishing city of Mesopotamia. The Christians, after a siege of several days, were on the point of entering the place, when the count of Edessa and the prince of Antioch disputed the possession of it. Whilst the debates kept the best leaders in the Christian tents, the Saracens of Mossoul and Aleppo came to the assistance of the city, and gave battle to the besiegers. A great number of Christians were slain in this conflict; and many fell into the hands of the infidels, who, in the intoxication of victory, insulted both the vanquished and the religion of Christ. History relates that the railleries of the Mussulmans inspired rage and despair among the army of the Christians, and that towards the end of the fight, one knight braved alone the victorious infidels, and rushed among the enemy's ranks, crying, "*Let all who are willing to sup with me in Paradise, follow me.*" This brave knight at first astonished the Saracens by his daring, but he soon fell, pierced with many wounds. The archbishop of Edessa, Josselin de Courtenay, and Baldwin du Bourg were loaded with irons, and taken to the prisons of Mossoul. The prince of Antioch and Tancred were alone able to escape the pursuit of the Mussulmans, with a small number of their soldiers. This defeat spread terror among all the Christians of the East. Bohémond, on his return to his capital, was menaced at the same time by the Greeks and the Saracens; and, as he had now neither allies nor auxiliaries, and was destitute of both men and money, he determined to go back into Europe, and to call upon the nations of the West to assist him.

After having spread abroad a report of his death, he embarked at Antioch, and, concealed in a coffin,† passed through the fleet of the Greeks, who rejoiced at his death, and heaped curses on his memory. On arriving in Italy, Bohémond went to throw himself at the feet of the sovereign pontiff; describing the misfortunes he had endured in defence of the holy religion, and invoking the vengeance of Heaven upon Alexius, whom he represented as the greatest scourge of the Christians. The pope welcomed him as a hero and a martyr; he praised his exploits, listened to his complaints, intrusted to

* See Gibbon for the interesting memoir of this noble family, whose name so frequently occurs in our own history, and is, I believe, still extant, in the Courtenays, earls of Devon.

† "Anna Comnena adds, that to complete the deceit, he was shut up with a dead cock; and wonders how the barbarian could endure the confinement and putrefaction."

him the standard of St. Peter, and permitted him, in the name of the Church, to raise in Europe an army to repair his misfortunes and avenge the cause of God.

Bohémond next went to France, where his adventures and exploits had made his name familiar to all classes. He presented himself at the court of Philip I., who received him with the greatest honours, and gave him his daughter Constance in marriage. Amidst the festivities of the court, he was by turns the most brilliant of knights and the most ardent of missionaries; he attracted general admiration by his skill in the tournaments, and preached war against the enemies of the Christians. He easily fired hearts already glowing with a love of military glory; and a great number of knights contended for the honour of accompanying him into the East. He crossed the Pyrenees and raised soldiers in Spain; he returned into Italy and met everywhere with the same eagerness to follow him. All preparations being completed, he embarked at Bari, and sailed towards the territories of the Greek emperor, where his threats and the fame of his expedition had already spread terror.

The prince of Antioch never ceased to animate by his speeches the ardour of his numerous companions; to some he represented the Greeks as the allies of the Mussulmans and the enemies of Christ; to others he spoke of the riches of Alexius, and promised them the spoils of the empire. He was on the point of realizing his brilliant hopes, when he was, all at once, abandoned by that fortune which had hitherto performed such prodigies in his favour.

The city of Durazzo, of which he had undertaken the siege, for a long time resisted all his efforts; disease, in the meanwhile, ravaging his army. The warriors who had followed him in the hopes of pillage, or from a desire to visit the Holy Land, deserted his standard; he was forced to make a disgraceful peace with the emperor he had endeavoured to dethrone, and come back to die in despair in the little principality of Tarentum, which he had abandoned for the conquest of the East.

The unfortunate issue of this crusade, which was directed entirely against the Greeks, became fatal to the Christians established in Syria, and deprived them of the succours they had reason to expect from the West. Tancred, who still governed Antioch, in the absence and after the death of Bohémond, was attacked several times by the Saracens of Aleppo, and only resisted them by displaying prodigies of valour. Josselin and Baldwin du Bourg did not return to their states till after five years of captivity. When Baldwin came back to Edessa he was so poor that he could not pay his common domestics; and an Armenian prince, whose daughter he had married, was obliged to redeem the beard of his son-in-law, which he had pledged for the means of paying his soldiers. The resources of the government of Antioch were not less exhausted than those of the county of Edessa. In the extremes of their misery, Tancred and Baldwin du Bourg had several disputes; each, by turns, called in the Saracens to defend his cause, and everything was in confusion on the banks of the Euphrates and the Orontes.

Neither was Jerusalem free from discord. Baldwin could not pay his soldiers, and demanded money of the patriarch, who was the depositary of the alms of the faithful. Daimbert at first refused to assist the king, who resolved to employ force to compel him: "Yes," said he to the patriarch, in a transport of anger, "I will bear away the treasures of the church and the holy sepulchre; I wish to save Jerusalem and the Christian people; when I have accomplished that noble project, I will restore the riches of the all-powerful God." Daimbert, intimidated by the menaces of Baldwin, consented to give up a part of his treasures; but as fast as the king of Jerusalem experienced new wants, he made fresh demands, to which the pontiff responded by an insulting refusal. He accused the king of profaning and plundering the sanctuary; whilst the king, on his part, accused Daimbert of betraying the cause of the Christians, and of dissipating in pleasures and festivities the treasures of Jesus Christ. The quarrels of Baldwin and the patriarch were renewed every year; both, in the end, often conveyed their complaints to the Holy See, which pronounced no decision likely to conciliate the angry parties. The death of Daimbert could alone put an end to these discussions, which spread scandal through the church of Christ, and by weakening the authority of the king, were likely to lead to the ruin of the kingdom.

Whilst the patriarch was unceasingly making complaints against Baldwin, the king seldom made any other reply than gaining new victories over the infidels; nothing being able to divert him from his purpose of every day aggrandizing his dominions. The prosperity and the safety of Jerusalem appeared closely connected with the conquest of the maritime cities of Syria and Palestine; it being by them alone that it could receive succour, or establish prompt and easy communications with the West. The maritime nations of Europe were interested in seconding, in this instance, the enterprises of the king of Jerusalem. The navigation of the Mediterranean, and the transporting of pilgrims to the Holy Land, were to them an inexhaustible source of riches; the ports of Syria would offer to them a commodious asylum for their vessels, and a safe entrepôt for their commerce.

From the period of the first crusades the Pisans and the Genoese had constantly sent vessels to the seas of the East; and their fleets had aided the Christians in several expeditions against the Mussulmans. A Genoese fleet had just arrived in the seas of Syria when Baldwin undertook the siege of Ptolemaïs. The Genoese were invited to assist in this conquest; but as religion was not the principle to bring them into action, they required, in return for their assistance and their labour, that they should have a third of the booty; they likewise stipulated to have a separate church for themselves, and a national factory and tribunal in the conquered city. Ptolemaïs was besieged by land and sea, and after a bloody resistance of twenty days, the inhabitants and the garrison proposed to surrender, and implored the clemency of the conquerors. The city opened its gates to the Christians, and the inhabitants prepared to depart, taking with them whatever they deemed most valuable; but the Genoese, at the sight of such a rich booty, paid no respect to the capitulation, and massacred without pity a disarmed and defenceless people. This barbarous conduct, which Baldwin could neither repress nor punish, excited the Mussulmans more than ever against the Christians.

At each fresh conquest of Baldwin's, a new army came from the banks of the Nile to impede the course of his victories; but the Egyptians had for a long time been accustomed to fly before the Franks, and they were never seconded in their expeditions by the Mussulmans of Syria, who were jealous of their appearance in their territories. A small number of Christian warriors, who could never have been taken for an army if they had not performed prodigies, were sufficient to put to the rout a multitude of soldiers who made a sortie from the walls of Ascalon. In consequence of this victory, several places which the Egyptians still held on the coasts of Syria, fell into the hands of the Christians.

Bertrand, son of Raymond de St. Gilles, arrived from Europe with the purpose of attacking the city of Tripoli. This city, taken at first by the Egyptians before the first crusade, and fallen again under the power of a Turkish commander, had, in order to defend itself against the Christians, once more recognised the authority of the caliph of Egypt. But this caliph thought more about punishing the rebellion of Tripoli than of providing for its defence. He had put the principal inhabitants in irons, had levied heavy tributes, and when the people implored his assistance against the enemies of Islamism, the caliph sent a vessel to demand a beautiful slave who was in the city, and whom he destined for his seraglio. The irritated people, instead of giving up the slave he demanded, sent him a piece of wood, saying, "*That he might make something out of that to amuse himself with.*" The inhabitants of Tripoli, then being without hope, surrendered to the Christians.

Raymond, count de St. Gilles and of Thoulouse, one of the companions of Godfrey, after having wandered for a long time about Asia, had died before this place, of which he had commenced the siege. In memory of his exploits in the first crusade, the rich territory of Tripoli was created a county, and became the inheritance of his family.

This territory was celebrated for its productions. Limpid streams rushing with impetuosity between the rocks of Libanus, flowed in many channels to water the numerous gardens of Tripoli. In the plains, and on the hills adjacent to the sea, grew in abundance wheat, the vine, the olive, and the white mulberry, whose leaves nourish the silkworm, which had been introduced by Justinian into the richest provinces of his empire. The city of Tripoli contained more than four thousand workmen, skilful in the manufactures of woollen stuffs, of silk, and of linen. A great part of these advantages was, no doubt, lost for the conquerors, who, during the siege, ravaged the country round, and on taking the city, carried fire and sword throughout the whole of it.

Tripoli contained other riches for which the Franks showed no less disdain than they had evinced for the productions of industry. A library established in this city, and celebrated through all the East, contained the monuments of the ancient literature of the Persians, the Arabians, the Egyptians, and the Greeks. A hundred copyists were there constantly employed in transcribing manuscripts. The cadi sent into all countries men authorized to purchase rare and precious books. After the taking of the city, a priest, attached to Count Bernard de St. Gilles, entered the room in which were collected a vast number of copies of the Koran, and as he declared the library of Tripoli contained only the impious books of Mahomet, it was given up to the flames. Some eastern authors have bitterly deplored this irreparable loss; but not one of our contemporary chronicles has spoken of it, and their silence plainly shows the profound indifference with which the Frank soldiers were witnesses of a fire which consumed a hundred thousand volumes.

Biblies, situated on the smiling and fertile shores of Phœnicia; Sarepta, where St. Jerome saw still in his day the tower of Isaiah; and Berytus, famous in the early ages of the Church for its school of eloquence, shared the fate of Tripoli, and became baronies bestowed upon Christian knights. After these conquests the Pisans, the Genoese, and several warriors who had followed Baldwin in his expeditions, returned into Europe; and the king of Jerusalem, abandoned by these useful allies, was obliged to employ the forces which remained in repulsing the invasions of the Saracens, who penetrated into Palestine, and even displayed their standards on Mount Sion. He had given up the idea of subduing the maritime cities which still belonged to the Egyptians, when Sigur, son of Magnus, king of Norway, arrived in the port of Jaffa. Sigur was accompanied by ten thousand Norwegians, who, three years before, had quitted the north of Europe for the purpose of visiting the Holy Land. Baldwin went to meet the prince of Norway, and conjured him to join with him in fighting for the safety and aggrandizement of the kingdom of Jesus Christ. Sigur acceded with joy to the prayer of the king, and required nothing as a recompense for his labour but a piece of wood from the true cross.

The patriarch of Jerusalem, in order to give additional value to that which the prince required, hesitated at first to grant it, and made with him a treaty at least as solemn as if it had concerned the possession of a kingdom. When they had both taken an oath to fulfil the conditions of the treaty, Sigur, accompanied by his warriors, entered Jerusalem in triumph. The inhabitants of Jerusalem beheld with surprise, mingled with their joy, the enormous battle-axes, the light hair, and lofty stature of the pilgrims from Norway; the presence of these redoubtable warriors was the sure presage of victory. It was resolved in a council to besiege the city of Sidon; Baldwin and Bertrand, count of Tripoli, attacked the ramparts of the place, whilst the fleet of Sigur blockaded the port, and directed its operations against the side next the sea. After a siege of six weeks the city surrendered to the Christians; the knights of Baldwin and the soldiers of Sigur performed during the siege prodigies of valour, and showed, after their victory, the humanity which always accompanies true bravery. After this conquest Sigur quitted Palestine, accompanied by the blessings of the Christian people. He embarked to return to Norway, carrying with him a piece of the true cross, a precious memorial of his pilgrimage, which he caused to be placed in a church of Drontheim, where it was for a long time the object of the veneration of the faithful.

Baldwin, on his return to his capital, learnt with grief that Gervais, count of Tiberias, had been surprised by the Turks, and led prisoner, together with his most faithful knights, to the city of Damascus. Mussulman deputies came to offer the king of Jerusalem the liberty of Gervais in exchange for Ptolemaïs, Jaffa, and some other cities taken by the Christians; a refusal, they added, would be followed by the death of Count Gervais. Baldwin offered to pay a considerable sum for the liberty of Gervais, whom he loved tenderly: "As for the cities you demand," said he to them, "I would not give them up to you for the sake of my own brother, nor for that of all the Christian princes together." On the return of the ambassadors Gervais and his knights were dragged to an open place in Damascus, and shot to death by the Saracens with arrows.

The Christians shed tears at the death of Count Gervais, but they soon had to weep for a much more painful loss. Tancred, who governed the principality of Antioch, died in an expedition against the infidels. He had raised high in the East the opinion of the heroic virtues of a French knight; never had weakness or misfortune implored his aid in vain. He gained a great many victories over the Saracens, but never fought for the ends of ambition. Nothing could shake his fidelity, nothing appeared impossible to his valour. He answered the ambassadors of Alexius, who required him to restore Antioch: "I would not give up the city which is confided to me even if the warriors who presented themselves to conquer it had bodies and bore arms of fire." Whilst he lived, Antioch had nothing to fear from the invasion of the infidels or the discord of the inhabitants. His death consigned the colony to disorder and confusion, it spread mourning through all the Christian states of the East, and was for them the signal of the greatest reverses.

The kingdom of Jerusalem had hitherto only had to contend against armies drawn from Egypt; the Turks of Syria, much more terrible in war than the Egyptians, had never united their forces to attack the Christians of Jerusalem.

The sultans of Damascus and Mossoul, with several emirs of Mesopotamia, assembled an army of thirty thousand fighting men, and penetrated through the mountains of Libanus into Galilee. During more than three months the banks of the Jordan and of the Lake of Genesareth were devastated by the horrors of war. The king of Jerusalem placed himself at the head of his knights to encounter this redoubtable enemy, and was defeated by the Saracens on the plains near Mount Tabor. Roger of Sicily, who had been governor of Antioch since the death of Tancred, and the counts of Tripoli and Edessa, came with their troops to the assistance of Baldwin. The Christian army, although it then mustered under its banners eleven thousand combatants, took up its encampment on the mountains, and did not dare to risk a battle. The Christians, intrenched upon the heights, beheld their fields ravaged and their cities burnt. All the banks of the Jordan seemed to be in flames; for a vast number of Saracens from Ascalon, Tyre, and other Mussulman cities, had taken advantage of the reverses of the Christians to lay waste many of the provinces of Palestine. The country of Sechem was invaded, and the city of Naplouse delivered up to pillage. Jerusalem, which was without defenders, shut its gates, and was in momentary fear of falling again into the power of the infidels.

The Turks, however, dreading the arrival of fresh pilgrims from the West, abandoned Galilee, and returned to Damascus and Mossoul. But other calamities soon followed those of war. Clouds of locusts from Arabia finished the devastation of the fields of Palestine. A horrible famine prevailed in the county of Edessa, the principality of Antioch, and all the Christian states. An earthquake was felt from Mount Taurus to the deserts of Idumea, by which several cities of Cilicia were reduced to heaps of ruins. At Samosata, an Armenian prince was swallowed up in his own palace; thirteen towers of the walls of Edessa, and the citadel of Aleppo, fell down with a fearful crash; the towers of the highest fortresses covered the earth with their remains, and the commanders, whether Mussulmans or Christians, fled with their soldiers to seek safety in deserts and forests. Antioch suffered more from the earthquake than any other city. The tower of the northern gate, many public edifices, and several churches were completely destroyed.

Great troubles always inspired the Christians with feelings of penitence. A crowd of men and women rushed to the church of St. Peter of Antioch, confessed their sins to the patriarch, and conjured him to appease the anger of Heaven. The shocks, nevertheless, were renewed during five months; the Christians abandoned the cities, and, a prey to terror, wandered among the mountains, which now were more thickly inhabited than the greatest cities. The few who remained in cities constantly formed religious processions, put on habits of mourning, and totally renounced pleasures of every kind. In the streets and the churches nothing was heard but lamentations and prayers; men swore to forgive all injuries, and were profuse in their charities. At length Heaven appeared to be appeased; the earthquake ceased its ravages, and the assembled Christians celebrated the mercy of God by a solemn festival.

Scarcely were the Christians delivered from these alarms than a new tempest threatened Syria and Palestine. Maudoud, prince or governor of Mossoul, had been killed by two Ismaëlians, as he was coming out of a mosque. As the prince of Mossoul was considered the most firm support of Islamism and the most redoubtable enemy of the Christians, the caliph and the sultan of Bagdad placed him in the rank of the martyrs, and resolved to revenge his death. They accused the Franks and the sultan of Damascus of the murder of a Mussulman prince. A numerous army set out from the banks of the Tigris, and advanced towards Syria, to punish at the same time both the Christian and Mussulman infidels. The warriors of Bagdad, united with those of Mossoul, penetrated as far as the lands of Aleppo, and carried destruction and death wherever they went. In this pressing danger the Saracens of Damascus and Mesopotamia did not hesitate to form an alliance with the Christian princes. The king of Jerusalem, the prince of Antioch, and the count of Tripoli united their troops with those of the Mussulmans. The Christians were full of zeal and ardour, and were eager for battle, but their new allies were not willing to give them the advantage of a victory, as they mistrusted the soldiers of Christ, and used every effort to avoid a decisive engagement, in which they dreaded the triumph of their auxiliaries as much as that of their foes. After having ravaged the territory of Aleppo, and the banks of the Euphrates and the Orontes, the warriors of Bagdad returned to their own country without trying their strength with their formidable adversaries. The Christians in this campaign did not illustrate their arms by any very brilliant exploits, but they kept up the division among the Saracens, and the discord of their enemies was more serviceable to them than a great victory.

The king of Jerusalem, no longer having the Turks of Bagdad or the Turks established in Syria to contend with, turned his attention towards Egypt, whose armies he had so frequently dispersed. He collected his chosen warriors, traversed the desert, carried the terror of his arms to the banks of the Nile, and surprised and pillaged the city of Pharamia, situated three days' journey from Cairo. The success of this expedition gave him room to hope that he should one day render himself master of a great kingdom, and he was returning triumphant and loaded with booty, to Jerusalem, when he fell sick at El-Arrich, on the confines of the desert which separates Egypt from Palestine. His life was soon despaired of, and the companions of his victories, assembled around him, could not conceal their deep sorrow. Baldwin endeavoured to console them by his discourses: "My dear companions," said he to them, "you who have suffered so many evils and braved so many perils, why do you allow yourselves to be overcome by grief? Remember that you are still in the territories of the Saracens, and that you stand in need of all your customary courage. Consider that you only lose in me a single man, and that you have among you several warriors who surpass me in skill. Think of nothing but of returning victorious to Jerusalem, and of defending the heritage of Christ. If I have fought a long time with you, and my many labours give me the right of addressing a prayer to you, I conjure you not to leave my bones in a foreign land, but to bury them near to the tomb of my brother Godfrey."

The king of Jerusalem then caused his servants to be assembled, and gave them orders for his sepulture. After having nominated Baldwin du Bourg as his successor, he expired, surrounded by his companions, who, though deeply grieved, endeavoured to conceal their tears, that the Saracens might not learn the great loss the Christians had experienced.

Baldwin lived and died in the midst of camps. During his reign, which lasted eighteen years, the inhabitants of Jerusalem were annually warned of the approach of the Saracens by the sound of the great bell; and they scarcely ever saw the wood of the true cross in the sanctuary, for this sacred relic always accompanied the armies to battle, and its presence not unfrequently was sufficient to give victory to the Christians.

During the time he occupied the throne of Jerusalem, the only means Baldwin had of keeping up his necessary army arose from the tenths of the produce of the cultivated lands, some taxes upon commerce, the booty obtained from enemies, and the ransom of prisoners. When peace lasted some months, or war was unsuccessful, the revenues of the state were diminished to half their usual amount, and could not meet the most necessary expenses. The forces of the kingdom were scarcely sufficient to defend it in the hour of danger. Baldwin could never undertake any great enterprise except when reinforcements arrived from the West; and when pilgrims who bore arms returned to their own country, he was often obliged to abandon an expedition which he had begun, and sometimes found himself without means of resistance, when exposed to the attacks of an enemy always eager to avenge his defeats.

The brother and successor of Godfrey was often on the point of losing his kingdom, and only preserved it by prodigies of valour. He lost several battles by his rashness and imprudence; but his wonderful activity always extricated him from whatever perils he chanced to fall into.

The historians of the times bestow warm eulogies upon the brilliant qualities of Baldwin. In the first crusade he made himself greatly hated for his ambitious and haughty character; but as soon as he had obtained what he desired and ascended a throne, he was at least equally admired for his generosity and clemency. When he became king of Jerusalem, he followed the example of Godfrey, and deserved in his turn to be held up as a model to his successors.

His extreme love for women sometimes drew upon him the severe censures of the clergy. To expiate his offences, in accordance with the opinions of the times, he richly endowed churches, particularly that of Bethlehem; and many other religious establishments owe their foundation to him. Amidst the tumult of camps, he added several articles to the code of his predecessor; but that which did most honour to his reign, was his constant anxiety to repeople Jerusalem. He offered an honourable asylum to all the Christians scattered over Arabia, Syria, and Egypt. Christians persecuted by Mussulmans came to him in crowds, with their wives, their children, and their wealth. Baldwin distributed amongst them lands and uninhabited houses, and Jerusalem began to be flourishing.

The last wishes of Baldwin were accomplished. The Christian army, preceded by the mortal

THE CRUSADERS MASSACRE THE INHABITANTS OF CÆSAREA.

A short time after, Baldwin besieged Cæsarea, a city built by Herod in honour of Cæsar. The siege was carried on with vigour; on the fifteenth day everything was ready for a general assault, and as soon as the trumpet had given the first signal, all the soldiers confessed and received absolution for their sins. The patriarch, clothed in white vestments, with a crucifix in his hand, led them to the foot of the ramparts;—the city was soon taken, and the inhabitants put to the sword.—BOOK V.

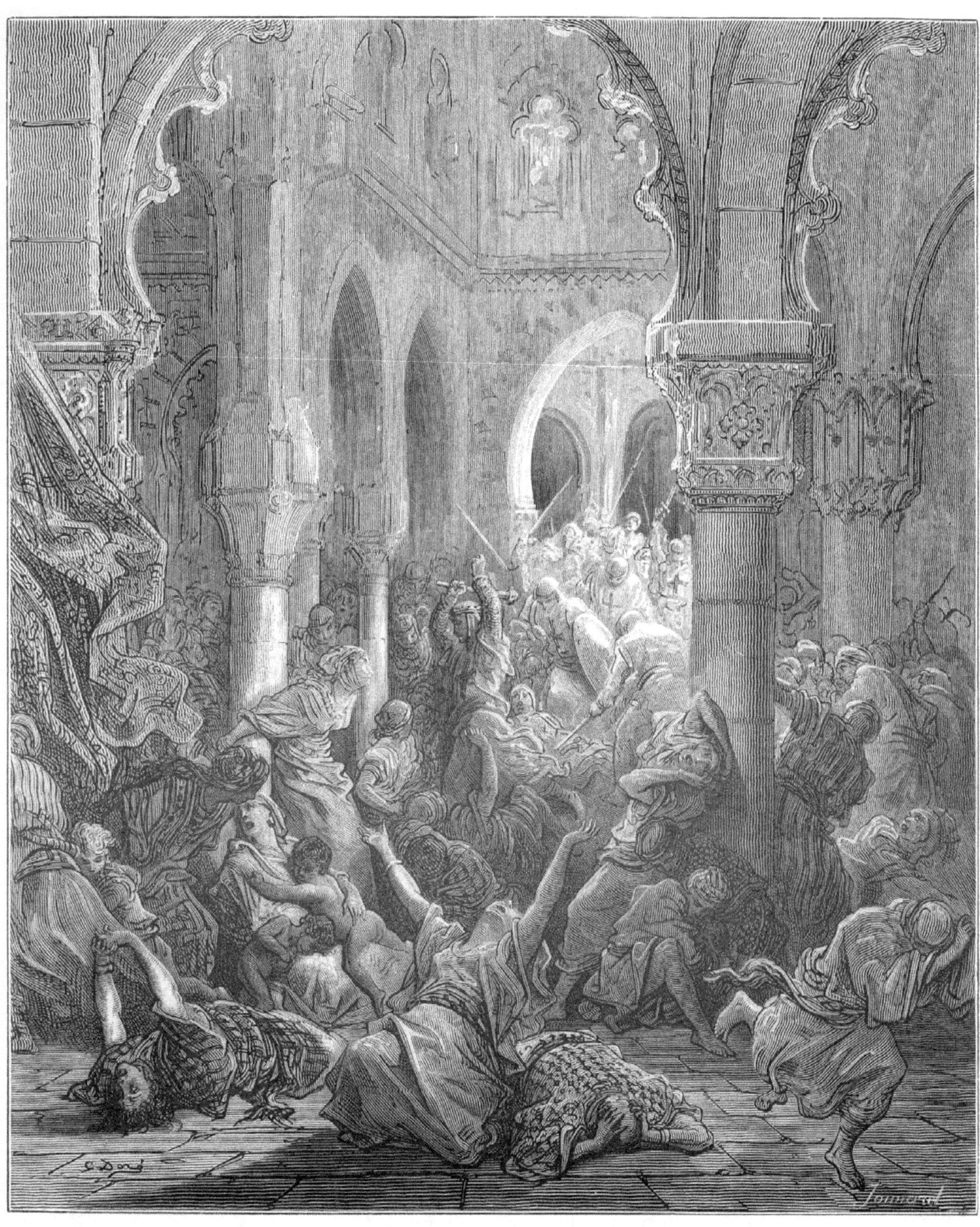

remains of its chief, returned to Jerusalem. Baldwin du Bourg, who came to the holy city to celebrate the festival of Easter and to visit the brother of Godfrey, arrived on Palm-Sunday at the hour in which the clergy and the people, according to ancient custom, go in procession to the Valley of Jehoshaphat. As he entered by the gate of Ephraim, the funeral train of Baldwin, accompanied by his warriors in mourning, entered by the gate of Damascus. At this sight melancholy cries were mingled with the hymns of the Christians. The Latins were deeply afflicted, the Syrians wept, and the Saracens, says Foulcher de Chartres, who were witnesses of this mournful spectacle, could not restrain their tears. In the midst of the sorrowing people, the count of Edessa accompanied the funereal convoy to the foot of Calvary, where Baldwin was buried close to Godfrey.

Although the late king had pointed out Baldwin du Bourg as his successor, the barons and the prelates met to elect a new prince. Several proposed to offer the crown to Eustace de Boulogne, the brother of Godfrey. Josselin de Courtenay, one of the first counts of the kingdom, declared himself in favour of Baldwin du Bourg. Josselin, on arriving in Asia, had been welcomed and loaded with favours by the count of Edessa, who gave him several cities on the Euphrates. Expelled afterwards ignominiously by his benefactor, who accused him of ingratitude, he had taken refuge in the kingdom of Jerusalem, in which he had obtained the principality of Tiberias. Whether he wished to make amends for old offences, or whether he hoped to obtain fresh benefits, he represented to the assembled barons, "that Baldwin du Bourg belonged to the family of the last king; that his piety, his wisdom, and courage were known to the entire East; and that no country on that side or beyond the sea could offer a prince more worthy of the confidence and love of the Christians. The benedictions of the inhabitants of Edessa pointed him out to the choice of the barons and knights, and Providence had opportunely sent him to Jerusalem to console the Christian people for the loss of Godfrey and Baldwin." This discourse united all the suffrages in favour of Baldwin du Bourg, who was crowned a few days after, and made over the county of Edessa to Josselin de Courtenay.

Scarcely was Baldwin du Bourg seated on the throne of Jerusalem than the principality of Antioch found itself again exposed to the horrors of war. The Mussulmans of Persia, Mesopotamia, and Syria, whom former defeats had not discouraged, swore to exterminate the Christian race, and marched towards the Orontes, conducted by Ylgazy, prince of Aleppo, the most ferocious of Islam warriors. The new prince of Antioch, Roger, had called to his assistance the king of Jerusalem, the counts of Edessa, and Tripoli; but, without waiting their arrival, he had the imprudence to give battle, with a result which imperilled all the Christian colonies. Before the combat, Ylgazy harangued his soldiers, and the cadi of Aleppo traversed the ranks, exciting, by the violence of his discourse, the fury of the barbarians. In the Christian camp the archbishop of Apamée recommended the Crusaders to confess and communicate, "in order that they might fortify themselves with the bread of heaven, and live or die as becomes the soldiers of Christ." Fortune was favouring the Crusaders, when they became demoralized at a tornado of wind which laid over the field of battle enormous black and sulphurous clouds. The Mussulmans understood this, and took advantage of the panic which they saw in the Christian ranks, charged again on their enemies, who fled. Roger in vain tried to arrest his fleeing soldiers, and was himself mortally wounded. After he fell, the Mussulmans pursued, killed, and captured. This battle took place near Arteria, in a place called the field of blood. The Mussulmans made a large number of prisoners, whom they massacred in presence of Gauthier, the chancellor, who was then given his life by Ylgazy, to go and tell the Christians the fate which awaited them in Palestine. Baldwin, accompanied by the count of Tripoli, hastened to the banks of the Orontes, attacked the victorious Mussulmans, and dispersed their army.

After this victory he returned to Jerusalem, when he learnt that Josselin de Courtenay had been made prisoner by the Turks. Baldwin flew to the defence of the county of Edessa, which was threatened with an invasion, and himself fell into the hands of the Mussulmans.

Old chronicles have celebrated the intrepid zeal of fifty Armenians, who swore to deliver two princes so much beloved by their subjects, and whose captivity spread desolation among the Christians of the East. Their efforts broke the chains of Josselin, but after having braved a thousand dangers without being able to release Baldwin du Bourg, they were themselves taken by the infidels. They all died amidst tortures, and received from Heaven alone, add the same chronicles, the reward of their generous devotion.

Josselin, escaped from his prison, repaired to Jerusalem, where he deposited in the church of the Holy Sepulchre the chains which he had borne among the Turks, and entreated prompt assistance for the deliverance of Baldwin. The mourning kingdom was menaced by the Saracens of Egypt, who, seeking to take advantage of the captivity of Baldwin, had assembled in the plains of Ascalon for the purpose of driving the Franks from Palestine. In this pressing danger the Christians of Jerusalem could pay attention to nothing but the defence of the kingdom. After the example of the inhabitants of Nineveh, they first sought to mitigate the anger of Heaven by penitence and prayer. A rigorous fast was commanded, during which women withheld the milk of their breasts from their children in the cradle, and the flocks even were driven to a distance from their pastures and deprived of their ordinary nourishment. War was proclaimed by the sound of the great bell of Jerusalem. The Christian army, which consisted of little more than three thousand combatants, was commanded by Eustache Grenier, count of Sidon, named regent of the kingdom in the absence of Baldwin. The patriarch of the holy city bore the true cross at the head of the army; he was followed, says Robert of the Mount, by Pontius, abbot of Cluni, carrying the lance with which the side of the Saviour was pierced, and by the Bishop of Bethlehem, who held in his hands a vase, in which the Christian priests boasted of having preserved the milk of the Virgin mother of God!*

The Christians met the army of the Saracens on the plains of Ascalon. The battle immediately began, and the Franks were at once surrounded by the Mussulmans, who reckoned forty thousand men beneath their standards. The defeat of the Christians appeared certain, when all at once, says the historian we have just now quoted, a light like to that of a thunderbolt darted through the air, and fell upon the army of the Mussulmans. This light, which the Christians considered as a miracle from Heaven, became the signal for the rout of the Saracens. The Mussulman warriors, still more superstitious than the Christians, were fascinated by a sudden terror, and no longer had either courage or strength to defend themselves. Seven thousand of them fell on the field of battle, and five thousand perished, swallowed up by the waves of the sea. The victorious Christians returned to Jerusalem, singing the praises of the God of armies.

The Christian knights thenceforth wept with less bitterness over the captivity of a king without whom they had been able to conquer the army of the Saracens; but the army of the Franks, employed in the defence of cities and frontiers constantly threatened by the enemy, could not leave the kingdom to make new conquests; and the warriors, who were detained in the Christian cities, after so great a victory, were deeply afflicted at their inaction, and appeared to place all their hopes in succours from the West. It was just at this time that a Venetian fleet arrived off the coast of Syria.

The Venetians, who for several centuries enjoyed the commerce of the East, and feared to break their profitable relations with the Mussulmans of Asia, had taken but very little interest in the first

* The account of this battle, and the preparations for it, are taken from Robert of the Mount (*Robertus de Monte, Appendice ad Sigebertum*). This author speaks of the fast the troops were ordered to undergo, as had been done at Nineveh: "Universo pecori pabula negabantur." He also speaks of the milk of the holy Virgin, carried in a vase:—"Episcopus Bethleemides ferens in pyxide lac sanctæ Mariæ virginis."

crusade, or in the events that had followed it. They waited the issue of this great enterprise, to take a part and associate themselves without peril with the victories of the Christians; but at length, jealous of the advantages that the Genoese and the Pisans had obtained in Syria, they wished likewise to have a share in the spoils of the Mussulmans, and prepared a formidable expedition against the infidels. Their fleet, whilst crossing the Mediterranean, fell in with that of the Genoese, which was returning from the East; they attacked it with fury, and forced it to fly in great disorder. After having stained the sea with the blood of Christians, the Venetians pursued their course towards the coasts of Palestine, where they met the fleet of the Saracens, just issuing from the ports of Egypt. A violent conflict ensued, in which all the Egyptian vessels were dispersed or destroyed, and covered the waves with their wrecks.

Whilst the Venetians were thus destroying the fleet of the Mussulmans, an army sent by the caliph of Cairo was beaten by the Christians under the walls of Jaffa. The doge of Venice, who commanded the Venetian fleet, entered the port of Ptolemaïs, and was conducted in triumph to Jerusalem. When celebrating the double victory, they resolved to profit by it, by following it up by an important expedition. In a council, held in presence of the regent of the kingdom and the doge of Venice, it was proposed to besiege either the city of Tyre or the city of Ascalon. As the opinions were divided, it was resolved to interrogate God, and to follow his will. Two strips of parchment, upon which had been written the names of Ascalon and Tyre, were deposited upon the altar of the Holy Sepulchre. In the sight of a numerous crowd of spectators, a young orphan advanced towards the altar, took one of the strips, and the chance fell upon the city of Tyre.

The Venetians, more devoted to the interests of their commerce and of their nation than to those of a Christian kingdom, demanded, before beginning the siege of Tyre, that they should enjoy a church, a street, a common oven, and a national tribunal in every city in Palestine. They further demanded other privileges and the possession of a third of the conquered city. The conquest of Tyre appeared to be so important, that the regent, the chancellor of the kingdom, and the great vassals of the crown accepted the conditions of the Venetians without hesitation: in a deed which history has preserved, they engaged not to acknowledge Baldwin du Bourg or any other prince who would refuse to subscribe to it.

When they had thus, by a treaty, shared the city they were about to conquer, they began their preparations for the siege. Towards the commencement of the spring, the Christian army set out from Jerusalem, and the Venetian fleet sailed from the port of Ptolemaïs. The historian of the kingdom of Jerusalem, who was for a long time archbishop of Tyre, stops here to describe the antique wonders of his metropolis. In his recital, at once religious and profane, he invokes by turns the testimony of Isaiah and of Virgil; after having spoken of the king, Hyram, and the tomb of Origen, he does not disdain to celebrate the memory of Cadmus, and the country of Dido. The good archbishop boasts above all of the industry and the commerce of Tyre; of the fertility of its territory, its dyes so celebrated in all antiquity, that sand which is changed into transparent vases, and those sugar-canes which, from that time, were sought for by every region of the universe. Tyre, in the time of Baldwin, was no longer that sumptuous city, whose rich merchants, according to Isaiah, were princes; but it was yet considered as the most populous and the most commercial of all the cities of Syria. It was built upon a delightful beach, which mountains sheltered from the blasts of the north; it had two large moles, which, like two arms, stretched out into the waves, to form a port to which no tempest could find access. Tyre, which had kept the victorious Alexander seven months and a half before its walls, was defended on one side by a stormy sea and steep rocks, and on the other by a triple wall surmounted by high towers.

The doge of Venice, with his fleet, entered the port and closed up all issue on the side of the sea. The patriarch of Jerusalem, the regent of the kingdom, and Pontius, count of Tripoli, commanded the army by land. In the early days of the siege, the Christians and the Mussulmans fought with obstinate ardour, and with equal success; but the divisions among the infidels soon came in to second the efforts of the Franks. The caliph of Egypt had yielded half of the place to the sultan of Damascus, to induce him to defend it against the Christians. The Turks and the Egyptians were divided among themselves, and would not fight together. The Franks profited by these divisions, and every day gained great advantages. After a siege of some months, the walls crumbled away before the machines of the Christians; provisions began to be short in the city, and the infidels were ready to capitulate, when discord arose to disunite the Christians in their turn, and was on the point of rendering useless the prodigies of valour, and the labours of the long siege.

The land army complained aloud of being obliged to support alone, both fighting and fatigue; the knights and their soldiers threatened to remain as motionless under their tents, as the Venetians did in their ships. To prevent the effect of their complaints, the doge of Venice came into the camp of the Christians, with his sailors armed with their oars, and declared that he was ready to mount the breach. From that time a generous emulation animated equally the zeal and courage of the land and sea forces. The Mussulmans, being without hope of succour, after a siege of five months and a half, were obliged to surrender. The standards of the king of Jerusalem and the doge of Venice waved over the walls of Tyre; the Christians made their triumphal entry into the city, whilst the inhabitants, according to the terms of the capitulation, went out with their wives and children.*

The day on which they received at Jerusalem the news of the conquest of Tyre, was a festival for the population of the holy city. To the sound of the bells the *Te Deum* was sung on bended knees; flags were hoisted on the towers and the ramparts of the city; branches of olive, and garlands of flowers were suspended in the streets and public places, and rich stuffs were hung upon the outsides of the houses, and upon the doors of the churches. Old men reminded their neighbours of the splendour of the kingdom of Judah, and young virgins repeated in chorus the psalms in which the prophets had celebrated the city of Tyre.

The doge of Venice, on his return to the holy city, was saluted by the acclamations of the people and the clergy. The barons and the principal inhabitants did all in their power to detain him in Palestine; they even went so far as to offer him the crown of Baldwin; some believing that that prince had died among the infidels, others only recognising a king when at the head of an army, or on the field of battle. The doge refused the crown they offered him; and, satisfied with the title of prince of Jerusalem, sailed with his victorious fleet back to Italy.

Whilst they were offering the throne of Jerusalem to a foreign prince, the captivity of Baldwin du Bourg was drawing to an end. The emir Balac,† who held him prisoner, after having conquered in a battle ten thousand Christians commanded by Josselin, besieged the citadel of a Mussulman city of Syria, and was preparing to succour the city of Tyre, when he was wounded by a javelin, and died regretted by the most ardent disciples of Mahomet. Baldwin was then enabled to purchase his liberty, and, after a captivity of eighteen months, appeared once again among the Christians. The king of Jerusalem had promised the Saracens a considerable sum as his ransom; but it was much more easy for him to fight and conquer his enemies than to fulfil such a promise. The Mussulmans, besides,

* Albert d'Aix finishes his history in the first year of the reign of Baldwin II., and Foulcher de Chartres terminates his after the siege of Tyre. We may consult for this reign many passages of Baronius, Robert of the Mount, Sanuti, and particularly William of Tyre and Bernardus Thesaurius.

† The emir Balac was a prince of the family of Ortoc, who possessed many places on the Euphrates, reigned in Aleppo and Mesopotamia, and could set on foot innumerable armies of Turcomans.

by ill-treating the hostages he had left with them,* furnished him with a pretext to attack them. When the infidels demanded of him the stipulated price of his liberty, he only replied by gaining victories over them. The Christian knights, who seemed to have forgotten him, now that they saw him once again in arms, returned thanks to Heaven for his deliverance, and came in troops to range themselves under his banners, and recognised with joy the authority of a prince who appeared only to have issued from his prison to lead them to new combats.

The Christian states at that period numbered as enemies the caliphs of Bagdad and Damascus, the emirs of Mossoul and Aleppo, and the descendants of Ortoc, who were masters of several places on the Euphrates. The Egyptians were weakened by their numerous defeats, and of all their ancient conquests on the coasts of Syria, only retained the city of Ascalon. But the garrison of this place, formed of the wrecks of several conquered armies, still threatened the territories of the Christians. Although the Egyptians had lost the cities of Tyre, Tripoli, and Ptolemaïs, they still continued masters at sea, and their fleets cruised without obstacle along the coasts of Syria, when the maritime nations of Europe did not happen to send succour to the Franks established in Palestine.

The Turks, accustomed to the military and pastoral life, did not aspire to the empire of the seas, but they never left the Christians at rest. They made themselves dreaded, not so much by their great armies, which were frequently nothing but confused and undisciplined multitudes, but by their continual, harassing incursions. Docile and patient, they endured hunger, thirst, and fatigue, better than they would face an enemy. Their knowledge of the country, their being accustomed to the climate, and the intelligence they kept up with the inhabitants, gave them, in all their warlike expeditions, a decided advantage over the Christians. Their soldiers surpassed the Franks in the arts of shooting with the bow, or hurling a javelin, as well as in horsemanship; and their leaders were practised, and excelled in all the stratagems of war. Their tactics consisted in wearing out their enemies, in preparing ambushes for them, or in drawing them into difficult positions, where they might triumph without fighting. The endless discord which prevailed among the Mussulman princes of Syria, and the revolutions which daily threatened their power, prevented them from following up, for any length of time, the same plan of defence or attack; but when in the enjoyment of a transient tranquillity, sometimes excited by a thirst for plunder, or sometimes animated by the prayers and the counsels of the caliph of Bagdad, they would burst like a sudden and unexpected storm over the territories of Antioch, Edessa, Tripoli, or the kingdom of Jerusalem. If the Mussulmans experienced a defeat, they retired with the hope of finding a more favourable opportunity; if they were conquerors, they ravaged the cities and the plains, and returned to their country, loaded with booty, singing these words: *"The Koran rejoices, and the Gospel is in tears."*

The hopes of booty every year attracted new hordes and tribes, which poured down from Mount Caucasus, Mount Taurus, from Koraçan and the banks of the Tigris. These tribes, for the most part wild and barbarous, mingled among the Mussulmans of Syria and Mesopotamia, and replaced in armies and cities the hosts which war had swept away. Among the tribes which had thus established themselves in Syria, history must not forget that of the *assassins* or Ismaëlians, whose sect had sprung up, towards the commencement of the eleventh century, in the mountains of Persia. A short time before the first crusade, they took possession of a part of Libanus, and founded a colony between Tripoli and Tortosa, which colony was governed by a chief whom the Franks called—*the Old Man, or the Lord of the Mountain.* The chief of the Ismaëlians only reigned over about twenty castles or towns, and scarcely more than sixty thousand subjects; but he had converted despotism into a species of worship,

* Edma, the daughter of Baldwin, still a child, was violated by the Mussulmans, to whom her father had given her as a hostage.

and his authority was without bounds. His subjects considered that he alone was the depositary of the laws of Mahomet, and that all who opposed his will merited death. The Old Man of the Mountains, according to the belief of the Ismaëlians, could distribute, at his pleasure, the delights of Paradise to his servants; that he who died in an act of obedience to his chief, ascended to heaven, whither the prophet of Mecca welcomed him, whilst he who died in his bed went through long probationary pains in the next world.

The Ismaëlians were divided into three classes: the people, the soldiers, and the *guards*. The people lived by the cultivation of the lands and by commerce; they were docile, laborious, sober, and patient: nothing could exceed the skill, strength, and courage of the soldiers, whose qualities were particularly valued in the defence or sieges of cities. The greater part of the Mussulman princes were very desirous of having them in their pay.

The most distinguished class was that of the *guards or fédaïs*. Nothing was neglected in their education. From their infancy their bodies were strengthened by constant and violent exercises, and their minds were cultivated by the study of the arts. They were taught the languages of Asia and Europe, in order that they might be sent into those countries to execute the orders of their master. All sorts of means were employed to inflame their imaginations and heighten their courage; during their sleep, which was provoked by intoxicating drinks, they were transported into delicious gardens, and awoke surrounded by the seductions of voluptuousness. It was there that the Old Man of the Mountains, by showing them the image of the joys of Paradise, inspired them with a blind obedience. In the midst of illusions which fascinated them, their master could order them to cast themselves from the height of a tower, to precipitate themselves into flames, or to pierce themselves with mortal wounds. When the Old Man of the Mountains had pointed out to them any one he wished to punish, they went, armed with a poniard, indifferently, to seek him in palaces or camps, and were impeded by neither obstacles nor dangers.

Princes often intrusted the charge of their revenge to the chief of the Ismaëlians, and looked to him for the death of their rivals or enemies. Powerful monarchs were his tributaries. The fears which he inspired, and the murders committed by his orders, heaped up his treasures. Surrounded by his intrepid soldiery, he sent death into distant regions; the terror of his name was spread everywhere, whilst he himself had nothing to fear from his enemies.

The Ismaëlians, as implacable sectarians, entertained a profound aversion for the Turks of Syria. Many of them were in the pay of the emirs and the sultans of that nation; but they sold their services at a very high price, and often took an active part in the bloody revolutions which precipitated from thrones the Mussulman dynasties of the East. They had less hatred for the Christians, because the latter fought against the Turks; nay, sometimes they became useful auxiliaries to the Franks. When Baldwin du Bourg was liberated, they proposed to deliver up Damascus to him, a great number of their warriors being in that city; but the plot being discovered, they miscarried in their enterprise, and six thousand Ismaëlians were slaughtered by the Mussulmans.

The Old Man of the Mountains commanded the death of the emir of Mossoul, who had defended the city of Damascus against the Christians. The murder of the Mussulman emir threw Syria into a state of excitement and trouble; but from the bosom of this disorder arose a new and formidable power. Zengui, son of Aksancar, one of the most skilful captains of his age, obtained the principality of Mossoul, got possession of Emessa and Aleppo, with several other cities of Syria, and founded the dynasty of the Atabecks, or governors of the prince, which was destined to dominate over the East, and render itself formidable to the Christians.*

* See, for the origin and the reign of Zengui, the *History of the Atabecks*, by Ben Latir.

Whilst this new power was rising in Syria, the Christian states of the East were at their highest point of prosperity. The county of Edessa, which contained a great portion of the rich provinces of Mesopotamia, had all the Armenian princes as its allies and auxiliaries. Several cities of Cœlesyria, Cilicia, and Lower Armenia constituted the principality of Antioch, the most extensive and the most flourishing of the Christian provinces.

The county of Tripoli comprised several places situated on the Sea of Phœnicia, from Margath to the river Adonis. This river, celebrated in both sacred and profane history, bounded on the north the kingdom of Jerusalem, which, towards the south, extended on the sea-coast as far as the gates of Ascalon, and towards the east, to the deserts of Arabia.

These four states formed a redoubtable confederacy. Europe beheld with pride these Christian colonies, which had cost her so much blood; she was afflicted at their reverses, and rejoiced at their progress. The safety of Christianity appeared identified with their preservation. The bravest of the Christians were always ready to devote themselves for the heritage of Christ; religion offered no recompense equal to that promised to their valour, and charity itself became warlike.

From the bosom of an hospital consecrated to the service of pilgrims and the poor, issued heroes armed against the infidels,—the humanity and the bravery of the knights of St. John* were equally conspicuous. Whilst some grew old in the offices of hospitality, others went forth to combat with the enemies of their faith. After the example of these pious knights, several men of gentle birth met near the place where the temple of Solomon had stood, and took an oath to protect and defend the pilgrims who repaired to Jerusalem. Their union gave birth to the order of the Templars, which, from its origin, was approved of by a council, and owed its statutes to St. Bernard.

These two orders were governed by the same principle that had given birth to the crusade, the union of the military spirit with the religious spirit. Retired from the world, they had no other country but Jerusalem, no other family but that of Jesus Christ. Wealth, evils, and dangers were all in common amongst them; one will, one spirit, directed all their actions and all their thoughts; all were united in one house, which appeared to be inhabited but by one man. They lived in great austerity, and the severer their discipline became, the stronger appeared the bonds by which it enchained their hearts and their wills. Arms formed their only decoration; precious ornaments were never seen in their houses or churches; but lances, bucklers, swords, and standards taken from the infidels abounded. At the cry of battle, says St. Bernard, they armed themselves with faith within and with steel without; they feared neither the number nor the fury of the barbarians, they were proud to conquer, happy to die for Jesus Christ, and believed that every victory came from God.

Religion had sanctified the perils and the violences of war. Every monastery of Palestine was a fortress, in which the din of arms was mingled with the voice of prayer. Humble cenobites sought glory in fight; the canons, instituted by Godfrey to pray near the holy tomb, after the example of the Hospitallers and the Templars, had clothed themselves with the casque and the cuirass, and, under the name of the Knights of the Holy Sepulchre, distinguished themselves amongst the soldiers of Christ.

The glory of these military orders was soon spread throughout the Christian world. Their renown penetrated even to the isles and the most remote nations of the West. All who had sins to expiate hastened to the holy city to share the labours of the Christian warriors. Crowds of men, who had devastated their own country, came to defend the kingdom of Jerusalem, and take part in the perils of the most firm defenders of the faith.

* The history of the knights of St. John has been written in Italian by Bosio, and translated into French by Boyssat. The history since written by the Abbé de Vertot has caused all that preceded it to be forgotten. The Templars, after their tragical end, had no historian of their exploits in the Holy Land but they have in our days found a very eloquent one in M. Raynouard.

There was not an illustrious family in Europe which did not send at least one knight to the military orders of Palestine. Princes even enrolled themselves in this holy militia, and laid aside the insignia of their dignity to assume the red coat of arms of the Hospitallers, or the white mantle of the knights of the Temple. In all the nations of the West castles and cities were bestowed upon them, which offered an asylum and succour to pilgrims, and became auxiliaries to the kingdom of Jerusalem. As monks, as soldiers of Christ, they were remembered in every will, and not unfrequently became the heirs of monarchs and princes.

The knights of St. John and of the Temple for a length of time were deserving of the greatest praises; more happy and more worthy of the benedictions of posterity would they have been, if, in the end, they had not allowed themselves to be corrupted by their success and their wealth; and if they had not frequently disturbed the welfare of the state of which their bravery was the support! These two orders were like a crusade that was unceasingly renewed, and preserved emulation in the Christian armies.

The military customs and manners of the Franks who were then engaged in Palestine, present an object worthy of fixing the attention of the historian and the philosopher, and may serve to explain the rapid rise and the following decline of the kingdom of Jerusalem. The spirit of honour which animated the warriors, and permitted them not to fly, even in an unequal fight, was the most active principle of their bravery, and with them took the place of discipline. To abandon a companion in danger, or to retire before an enemy, was an action infamous in the sight of God or man. In battle, their close ranks, their lofty stature, their war-horses, like themselves covered with steel, overturned, dispersed, or bore down the numerous battalions of the Saracens. In spite of the weight of their armour, nothing could exceed the rapidity with which they passed to places the most distant. They were to be seen fighting almost at the same time in Egypt, on the Euphrates, and on the Orontes; and only left these their customary theatres of victory to threaten the principality of Damascus, or some city of Arabia. In the midst of their exploits they recognized no other law but victory, abandoned and rejoined at pleasure the standards which led them to the enemy, and required nothing of their chief but the example of bravery.

As their militia had under its colours warriors of divers nations, the opposition of characters, the difference of manners and language kept alive amongst them a generous emulation; but sometimes, likewise, gave birth to discord. Very frequently chance, or some unexpected circumstance, decided an enterprise or the fate of a campaign. When the Christian knights believed themselves in a condition to fight an enemy, they went to seek him, without taking the least pains to conceal their march; confidence in their strength, in their arms, and, above all, in the protection of Heaven, made them neglect the stratagems and the artifices of war, and even the precautions most necessary to the safety of an army. Prudence in their chiefs frequently appeared to them an evidence of timidity or weakness, and many of their princes paid with their lives or their liberty for the vain glory of encountering useless perils in the Christian cause.

The Franks of Palestine saw scarcely any dangers or enemies except such as met them in the field of battle. Several important enterprises, which fortune alone seemed to direct, were necessary to assure the safety and the prosperity of the Christian states in Asia. The first of these enterprises was to lower the power of the caliphs of Egypt; the second, to conquer and preserve the maritime cities of Syria, in order to receive fleets and succour from the West; the third was to defend the frontiers, and oppose on all sides a barrier against the Turks and Saracens. Each of these great interests, or rather all of these interests united, constantly occupied the Franks established in Asia, without their having any other policy but that of circumstances, and without their employing, in order to

TWO HUNDRED KNIGHTS ATTACK TWENTY THOUSAND SARACENS.

Conqueror of the Saracens, the king of Jerusalem had sent back his troops, and was reposing at Jaffa, after the fatigues of the war, when he learnt that the Mussulman army had rallied, and was in full march to attack the Christians. Baldwin, whom victory had rendered rash, without assembling all his troops, went immediately to meet the enemy, at the head of two hundred knights, and a few pilgrims lately arrived from the West. Not at all dismayed by the number of the Saracens, he gave battle; but, at the first charge the Christians were surrounded, and only sought a glorious death, fighting by the side of their leader. The king of Jerusalem, obliged to fly, concealed himself among the long dried grass and bushes which covered the plain. As the Saracens set fire to these, Baldwin with difficulty escaped being burnt alive.—Book V.

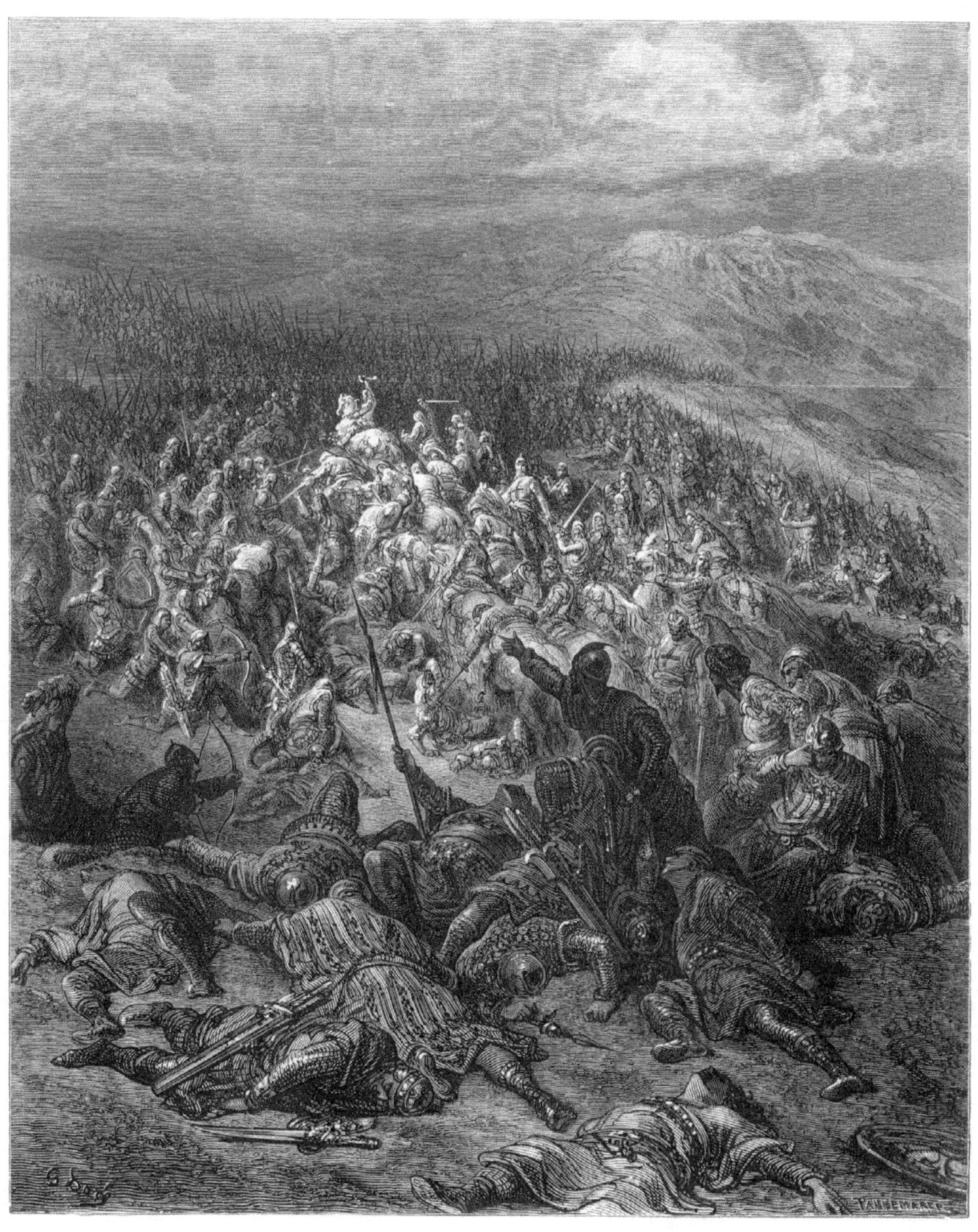

succeed, any other means but their swords. It is in this view we must admire their efforts, and find the bravery, which supplied the place of everything, wonderful.

Among the illustrious pilgrims who at this time repaired to Palestine, and took part in the labours of the Christian knights, history ought not to forget Foulque, count of Anjou. He was the son of Foulque le Rechin and Bertrade de Montfort, who became the wife of Philip I., and for whose sake the king of France had braved all the thunders of the Church. Foulque of Anjou could not be consoled for the death of his wife Eremberge, daughter of Elie, count of Maine. His grief led him into Palestine, where he maintained during a year a hundred men-at-arms, whom he led to battle. He united piety with valour, and attracted admiration by displaying all the qualities of a good prince. Baldwin, who had no male offspring, offered him his daughter Melisende in marriage, and promised to have him nominated his successor. Foulque accepted the proposition with joy, and became son-in-law to the king of Jerusalem.

From that time the two princes gave all their attention to promote the prosperity of the kingdom and to defend it against the Saracens. Their union served as a model to Christian princes, and lasted till the death of Baldwin, who, seeing his last hour approach, ordered himself to be carried to the spot where Christ had risen again, and died in the arms of his daughter and his son-in-law, to whom, with his latest breath, he recommended the glory of the Christians of the East.

Baldwin had a right mind, a lofty spirit, and unalterable mildness. Religion presided over his least actions and inspired all his thoughts; but he perhaps had more devotion than was suited to a prince or a warrior. He was constantly seen prostrated on the earth, and, if we may believe William of Tyre, his hands and knees were hardened by practices of piety. He passed eighteen years on the throne of Edessa, and twelve on that of Jerusalem; he was made prisoner twice, and remained seven years in the chains of the infidels. He had neither the faults nor the high qualities of his predecessor. His reign was rendered illustrious by conquests and victories in which he bore no part; but he was not the less regretted by the Christians, who loved to contemplate in him the last of the companions of Godfrey.

Under his reign the public manners began to decline: by his directions a council was assembled at Naplouse to check licentiousness, and punish offenders against order and morality. But the decrees of this council, deposited in the churches, only served to prove the existence of disorders among the Christians, and did not, in any way, stop the progress of corruption, which rapidly increased under the following reigns. Baldwin was more happy in the measures which he undertook to increase the number of his subjects and enrich his capital. An edict suppressed all duties upon grain and vegetables brought into the holy city by the Syrians. Baldwin, by this means, improved the trade and population of Jerusalem, and revived agriculture in the neighbouring provinces.

Foulque, count of Anjou, was crowned king of Jerusalem after the death of Baldwin. At his accession to the throne, discord disturbed the Christian states, and even threatened with speedy ruin the principality of Antioch. The son of Bohémond, who had recently assumed the reins of government, had been killed in a battle against the Turks of Asia Minor, and a daughter, whom he had had by Alise, sister of Melisende, was called to the inheritance of her father's throne; but the weakness of her sex and age did not permit her to make good her claim. Alise, her mother, wished to get possession of the royal seat, and in the prosecution of her projects did not scruple to avail herself of the aid of the Saracens. Another candidate appeared in Roger, king of Sicily, who, as a member of the family of Bohémond and Tancred, had pretensions to the principality of Antioch. The people, the clergy, and the nobility were divided into several factions.

The king of Jerusalem, as protector of the confederation of the Franks in Asia, determined to re-establish order, and took the road to Antioch with his barons and the knights of the Temple and St. John. The count of Tripoli, who had embraced the party of Alise, undertook to stop the king of Jerusalem on his passage. The powers of these two princes met; a battle ensued, and the plains of Phœnicia were stained with the blood of Christians shed in unnatural strife. Foulque of Anjou, after having routed the troops of the count of Tripoli, gained the banks of the Orontes, silenced the contending factions, and re-established peace. To perfect his work, he resolved to bestow the daughter of Bohémond on a husband able to defend her rights, who would merit the confidence of the Christian warriors. Syria presenting to him no prince or knight worthy of his choice, he turned his eyes towards the princes of Europe, and nominated Raymond of Poictiers governor of Antioch, as Baldwin II. had chosen him himself governor of Jerusalem. Thus Europe, which had found defenders for the Christian states of Asia, supplied them also with princes and kings. Raymond of Poictiers, brother of William, duke of Aquitaine, left France with the scrip and staff of a pilgrim, and came into Syria to espouse the daughter of Baldwin, and reign with her on the banks of the Orontes.

The troubles of Antioch had revived the pretensions of the emperors of Constantinople. John Comnenus, son and successor of Alexius, put himself at the head of an army, took possession of some places in Cilicia, and encamped before the walls of Antioch. After several conflicts, in which victory remained uncertain, negotiations were opened, which ended in the oath of obedience to the emperor being taken by Raymond of Poictiers. The two princes, united by a treaty, resolved to turn their arms against the Saracens. Their troops, which they commanded in person, attacked without success Aleppo and several other cities of Syria; the want of a good understanding, which accompanied the Greeks and Latins at all times, was sure to defeat their enterprises. The emperor returned with vexation to Antioch, of which he endeavoured to make himself master, but was compelled by a sedition to leave the city hastily. He then formed the project of visiting Jerusalem at the head of his army, with the intention, if the Latins are to be believed, of obtaining possession of Palestine. Foulque sent ambassadors to inform him that he could only be received in the holy city in the character of a simple pilgrim; whereupon John, who did not dare to complain, sent presents to Foulque of Anjou, and gave up, without much pain, his idea of a pilgrimage to Jerusalem. After a campaign, for which he had drawn out all the strength of the empire, he returned to his capital, having obtained nothing by his enterprise but the vain and hollow homage of the prince of Antioch.

Foulque of Anjou, after having re-established peace among his neighbours, found, on his return, that discord not only prevailed in his states, but had even made its way into his own house. Walter, count of Cæsarea, accused Hugh, count of Jaffa, of the crime of treason towards his king. This latter noble had drawn upon himself the hatred of the king and the principal people of the kingdom, some say by his pride and disobedience, and others by his guilty connection with the queen Melisende. When the barons had heard Walter of Cæsarea, they decided that a battle, *en champ clos*, should take place between the accused and the accuser; and as the count of Jaffa did not appear in the lists on the day nominated, he was declared guilty.

Hugh was descended from the famous lord of Puyset, who raised the standard of revolt against the king of France, and who, conquered in the end by Louis le Gros, despoiled of his possessions and banished his country, had taken refuge in Palestine, where his exploits had secured him the county of Jaffa, which he had transmitted to his son. Hugh possessed the turbulent and impetuous character of his father, and, like him, could neither pardon an injury nor submit to an act of authority. On learning that he was condemned without being heard, he set no bounds to his anger, but hastened immediately to Ascalon, to implore the aid of the infidels against the Christians. The Mussulmans, highly pleased with the division which had sprung up among their enemies, at once took the field, and ravaged the country as far as the city of Asur. Hugh, after having contracted a criminal alliance with the Saracens, shut himself up in Jaffa, where he was soon besieged by the king of Jerusalem.

The thirst of vengeance animated both parties; Foulque of Anjou had sworn to punish the treason of his vassal; and Hugh was equally determined to succeed, or bury himself under the ruins of Jaffa. Before the king's forces commenced the attack, the patriarch of Jerusalem interposed his mediation, and recalled to the minds of the Christian warriors the precepts of Gospel charity. Hugh at first rejected all mention of peace with indignation; but having been abandoned by his followers, he at last lent an unwilling ear to the pacific appeals of the patriarch, and consented to lay down his arms. The king of Jerusalem sent home his army, and the count of Jaffa agreed to quit the kingdom, into which he was not to return till after three years of exile. He was awaiting at Jerusalem the favourable moment for his departure, when an unexpected circumstance was on the point of renewing stifled quarrels. "It happened," says William of Tyre, "as the count was playing at dice in the street of the Furriers, before the shop of a merchant named Alpham, that a soldier, a Breton by nation, having drawn his sword, fell suddenly upon the said count, who, being attentive to his game, expected nothing less than such an attack, and with the first cut, without the least warning, dealt him such a blow with the said sword on the face as stretched him upon the ground." At the sight of such a tragical scene the people gathered round in crowds, anxiously inquiring the cause of it. The whole city was filled with rumours of various kinds; all mourned the fate of the count of Jaffa, and thought no more of his rebellion. They did not even hesitate to whisper complaints against the king, whom they accused of having himself directed the poniard of the assassin. The king, however, caused the murderer to be immediately arrested, and he was tried with the utmost rigour of the laws. He was ordered to have his limbs broken; and the king, whilst confirming the sentence, only added that the assassin of the count of Jaffa should not, as was usual, have his tongue cut out, in order that he might name his accomplices. The unhappy wretch expired, declaring that no one had induced him to commit the deed, but that he thought he should serve religion and his king by it. Every one was thus left free to form conjectures according to the feeling that animated him, or the party he had adopted. The count of Jaffa was not long in recovering from his wound; at the end of a few months he quitted Palestine, and went to Sicily, where he died before the time fixed for the end of his exile.

Queen Melisende entertained a deep resentment at all which had taken place; by which she proved that she was not a stranger to the origin of these fatal discords. "From the day on which the count left the kingdom," says William of Tyre, "all who had against him been informers to the king, and brought him into his ill graces, so incurred the indignation of the queen that they were not in too great safety of their persons, and even the king did not seem to be quite at his ease among the relations and favourites of the queen." The anger of the queen, however, yielded to time, and did not outlive the count of Jaffa. Foulque himself, whether it was that age had blunted his feelings, or that it appeared more prudent to him to efface the last traces of an unfortunate affair, repented of having compromised the honour of the queen, and neglected nothing that could make her forget the excess of his jealousy and the rigours he had employed.

Amidst these disagreeable events the king of Jerusalem had reason to congratulate himself at having no invasion of the Mussulmans to repel. The prince of Mossoul, Zengui, attacked some Christian fortresses, but he was soon diverted from his enterprises against the Franks by the project of uniting the principality of Damascus to his states. The Mussulman prince who reigned at Damascus could find no other means of resisting Zengui than by calling in the Christians to his help. The king of Jerusalem, after having received hostages and considerable sums of money, took the field at the head of his army, for the purpose of defending a Mussulman city; but Zengui, who feared to try his strength with the Franks, did not venture to attack Damascus. According to the conditions of the alliance with the Christians, the city of Paneas, or Cæsarea of Philippi, which had recently fallen into the hands of the Saracens, was to be given up to them. The warriors of Damascus and Jerusalem marched together to lay siege to that city, situated at the foot of Libanus, and near the sources of the Jordan. For the second time the standards of Christ and Mahomet were seen floating over one army and one camp. Cæsarea of Philippi capitulated after a siege of a few days, and was given up to the king of Jerusalem.

This conquest was the most important event that signalized the latter years of the reign of Foulque of Anjou. The king of Jerusalem, whilst hunting in the plain of Ptolemaïs, fell from his horse, and died of the fall, leaving no one to succeed him but two children of tender age. He was less regretted on account of his personal qualities than for the sad condition in which his death left the kingdom. William of Tyre, who praises the virtues of Foulque of Anjou, remarks, with a *naïveté* worthy of these remote times, that this prince had red hair, and yet he could not be reproached with any of the faults usually attributed to men of that colour. He was more than sixty years of age when he ascended the throne of Jerusalem; in the last years of his life his memory was so weakened that he did not know his own servants, and had not sufficient strength and activity to be the head of a kingdom surrounded by enemies. He employed himself more in building fortresses than in collecting armies, and in defending his frontiers than in making new conquests. Under his reign the military ardour of the Christians seemed to grow weaker, and was displaced by a spirit of discord, which brought about calamities much greater than those of war. At the period of the coronation of Foulque of Anjou, the Christian states were at the highest degree of their prosperity; towards the end of his reign they showed a tendency to decline.

Baldwin III., thirteen years of age, succeeded his father, and Queen Melisende became regent of the kingdom. Thus the reins of government fell from the weak and powerless hands of an old man into those of a woman and a child. Parties soon sprung up around the throne; the clergy, the knights, the barons, even the people took a dangerous part in affairs of state, and the authority of the prince, which hitherto had been but that of the general of an army, lost under the regency of Queen Melisende the consideration and splendour it had derived from victory. The government insensibly assumed the turbulent form of a republic, and in the political relations which the Christians held at this period with the Saracens, the latter believed that several chiefs were at the head of the kingdom of Jerusalem.

Baldwin did not wait for the period of his majority to be crowned king, being scarcely fourteen years old, when, in the presence of the barons and the clergy, he received the sword with which he was to defend religion and justice; the ring, the symbol of faith; the sceptre and the crown, marks of dignity and power; and the apple or globe, as an image of the earth and the kingdom he was called upon to govern. Young Baldwin already displayed courage above his age; in the very first days of his reign he achieved a glorious expedition beyond the Jordan, in which he gained possession of the Valley of Moses; but he had not experience enough to know what enemies he ought to attack or what allies he ought to defend. On his return from the expedition of the Jordan he undertook an unjust and unfortunate war, the presage of a sad future for the kingdom of Jerusalem.

An Armenian, who governed the city of Bosra in the name of the Sultan of Damascus, came to Jerusalem to offer to deliver up to the Christians the place which he commanded, and the barons and principal people were convoked to hear his proposals. The wiser part of the assembly referred to the alliance made with the Saracens of Damascus; the promises of an unknown soldier appeared to them

DEATH OF BALDWIN, KING OF JERUSALEM.

He collected his chosen warriors, traversed the desert, carried the terror of his arms to the banks of the Nile, and surprised and pillaged the city of Pharamia, situated three days' journey from Cairo. The success of this expedition gave him room to hope that he should one day render himself master of a great kingdom, and he was returning triumphant, and loaded with booty, to Jerusalem, when he fell sick at El-Arrich, on the confines of the desert which separates Egypt from Palestine. After having nominated Baldwin du Bourg as his successor, he expired, surrounded by his companions, who, though deeply grieved, endeavoured to conceal their tears, that the Saracens might not learn the great loss the Christians had experienced.—Book V.

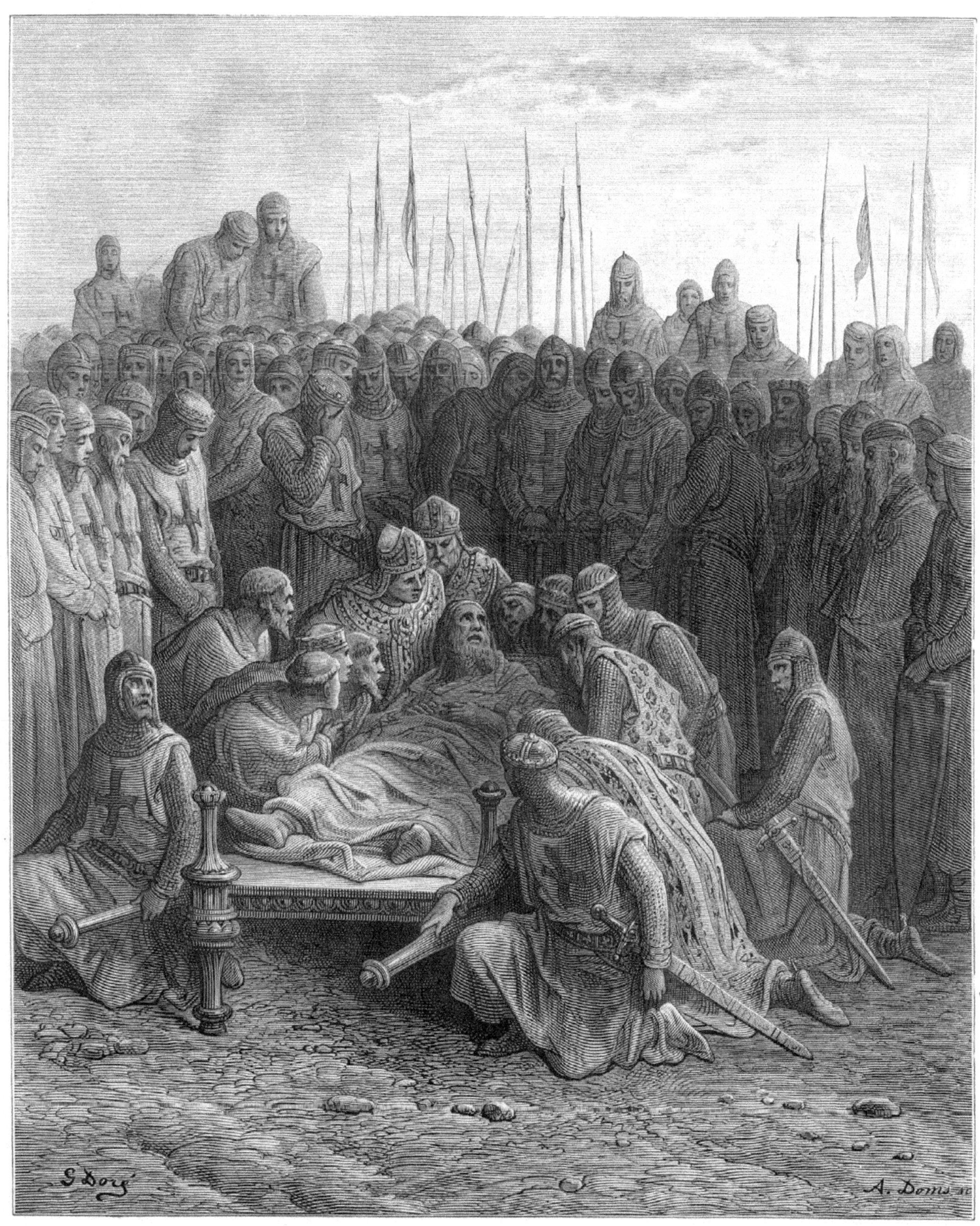
G. Doré
A. Doms

to have no security, and to inspire no confidence; they said the kingdom of Jerusalem did not want for enemies to combat, or conquests to attempt; it was their duty to attack the most formidable, and protect the others as useful auxiliaries. This advice, which was the most reasonable, was that which obtained the smallest number of suffrages. Wonders were related of the country they were about to conquer; Bosra was the capital of Upper Arabia, all the riches of that country appeared already to belong to the Christians, and all who opposed a conquest so brilliant and so easy were accused of treason. They deliberated in the midst of tumult, and the cries of a misled multitude smothered the voice of reason and prudence. The council of the barons and the principal people decided that an expedition, upon which so many hopes were built, should be undertaken.

The Christian army was soon on its march, and across the mountains of Libanus. When it arrived in the territory of Damascus, its first conflict was with the Saracens gathered together to oppose its passage. After sustaining several severe encounters, the Christians succeeded in gaining the country called Traconite, where they found nothing but plains burnt up by the ardent rays of the sun. The roads were difficult, and the locusts having fallen into the wells and cisterns, had poisoned all the waters. The inhabitants, concealed in subterranean caverns, laid ambushes in all directions for the Christian army; whilst the Mussulman archers, planted upon all the hills and acclivities, left the warriors of Jerusalem not a moment's repose. The misfortunes of the army (it is William of Tyre who speaks) increased every day, *and there was poured upon the Christians such a quantity, and as it were continually, of all sorts of arrows, that they appeared to descend upon them like hail or heavy rain upon houses covered with slates and tiles, men and beasts being stuck all over with them.* Nevertheless, the hope of winning a rich city sustained the courage of the Christian soldiers, and enabled them to brave all these perils. But when they arrived within sight of Bosra, it was announced to them that the wife of the Armenian commandant had called the garrison to arms, and that she was prepared to defend the city which her husband had promised to give up to the king of Jerusalem. This unexpected news at once spread consternation and discouragement through the Christian army. The knights and barons, struck with the misfortunes that threatened the Christian soldiers, pressed the king to abandon his army, and save his person and the cross of Christ. Young Baldwin rejected the advice of his faithful barons, and insisted upon sharing all their perils.

As soon as the order for retreat was given, the Mussulmans, with loud cries, set out in pursuit of the Christians. The soldiers of Jerusalem closed their ranks, and marched in silence, sword in hand, bearing away their wounded and dead. The Saracens, who could not shake or break through their enemy, and who, in their pursuit, found no trace of carnage, believed they were actually fighting against men of iron. The region which the Christians were traversing was covered with heath, thistles, and other plants dried by the heat of the summer. The Saracens set fire to these; the wind bore the flames and smoke towards the Christian army, and the Franks marched over a burning plain, with clouds of smoke, ashes, and dust floating over and around them. William of Tyre, in his history, compares them to smiths, to such a degree were their clothes and their faces blackened by the fire which devoured the plain. The knights, the soldiers, and the people who followed the army, gathered in a crowd around the bishop of Nazareth, who bore the wood of the true cross, and conjured him with tears to put an end by his prayers to calamities they were no longer able to bear.

The bishop of Nazareth, touched by their despair, raised the cross, imploring the mercy of Heaven,—and, at the moment the direction of the wind was changed. The flames and the smoke which desolated the Christians were immediately wafted against the Mussulmans. The Franks pursued their march, persuaded that God had wrought a miracle to save them. A knight, whom they had never before seen, mounted on a white horse, and bearing a red standard, preceded the Christian army, and conducted it out of danger. The people and the soldiers took him for an angel from heaven, and his miraculous presence re-animated their strength and their courage. At length the army of Baldwin, after having undergone all sorts of misery, returned to Jerusalem, where the inhabitants rejoiced at its arrival, singing these words from the Scriptures,—"*Let us give ourselves up to joy, for that people that was dead is resuscitated; it was lost, and behold here it is found again.*"

But whilst the inhabitants of Jèrusalem were rejoicing at the return of their warriors, the Christian states lost one of their most important places, and experienced an irreparable misfortune. Zengui, whom the caliph of Bagdad and all true Mussulmans considered as the buckler and the support of Islamism, extended his empire from Mossoul to the frontiers of Damascus, and was continuing without intermission the course of his victories and conquests. The Christians made no effort to stop the progress of so redoubtable a power. Zengui, who united with bravery all the resources of a skilful policy, left them in a deceitful security, and determined only to awaken them from their long sleep when he had it in his power to give a mortal blow to their empire. He knew, by experience, that nothing was more fatal to the Christians than too long a repose; the Franks, who owed everything to their arms, were almost always weakened by peace, and when not fighting against the Saracens, generally fell out among themselves.

The kingdom of Jerusalem had two formidable barriers, the principality of Antioch and the county of Edessa. Raymond of Poictiers defended the Orontes from the invasion of the Saracens, and old Josselin de Courtenay had been for a long time the terror of the infidels on the banks of the Euphrates; but he was recently dead. He had fought to his last breath, and even on his bed of death made his arms and his bravery respected.

Josselin was besieging a castle near Aleppo, when a tower fell down near him and covered him with its ruins. He was transported in a dying state to Edessa, and as he lay languishing on his bed, expecting nothing but death, it was announced to him that the sultan of Iconium had laid siege to one of his strong places; upon which he sent for his son and commanded him to go instantly and attack the enemy. Young Josselin hesitated, and represented to his father that he had not a sufficient number of troops to meet the Turks. The old warrior, who had never acknowledged the existence of obstacles, was determined before he died to leave an example to his son, and caused himself to be borne in a litter at the head of his soldiers. As they approached the besieged city, he was informed that the Turks had retired, whereupon he ordered his litter to stop, raised his eyes towards heaven as if to return thanks for the flight of the Saracens, and expired surrounded by his faithful warriors.

His mortal remains were transported to Edessa, the inhabitants of which city came out to meet and join the funeral procession, which presented a most affecting spectacle. Here were to be seen the mourning soldiers bearing the coffin of their chief; and there a whole people lamenting the loss of their support and defender, and celebrating the last victory of a Christian hero.

Old Josselin died deploring the fate of Edessa, about to be governed by a weak and pusillanimous prince; for from his childhood the son of Courtenay had been addicted to drunkenness and debauchery. In an age and a country in which these vices were sufficiently common, the excesses of young Josselin had frequently scandalized the Christian warriors. As soon as he was master, he quitted the city of Edessa, to take up his abode at Turbessel, a delicious retreat on the banks of the Euphrates. There, entirely abandoned to his vicious inclinations, he neglected the pay of his troops and the fortifications of his forts, equally heedless of the cares of government and the menaces of the Saracens.

Zengui had been for a length of time watching for a favourable opportunity of surprising the city of Edessa; as this conquest would not only flatter his pride and ambition, but would render him dearer to all the disciples of Mahomet. In order to retain Josselin in his fancied security, the prince of Mossoul feigned to make war against the Saracens; but at the moment he was supposed to be most busily engaged in an attack upon several Mussulman castles in the east of Mesopotamia, he appeared at the head of a formidable army before the walls of Edessa.* A great number of Curds and Turcomans, wandering and barbarous tribes, had joined his standard, attracted by the hopes of a rich booty. At the first signal given by Zengui, the city was surrounded on all sides; seven enormous wooden towers were raised higher than the ramparts; numbers of formidable machines unceasingly battered the walls, or hurled into the city stones, javelins, and inflammable matters; whilst the foundations of the towers of the fortifications were being undermined by the infidels. The walls, which were only supported by slight, ill-fixed posts, were falling to pieces, and, covering the earth with their ruins, seemed ready to offer an easy passage to the Mussulman soldiers.

When on the point to give the signal for destruction, the fierce Mussulmans stopped, and summoned the city to surrender. The sight of the death which threatened them did not at all weaken the courage of the inhabitants, and they answered that they would all perish sooner than give up a Christian city to the infidels. They exhorted each other to merit the crown of martyrdom: "Let us not fear," said they, "these stones launched against our towers and our houses; he who made the firmament, and created legions of angels, defends us against his enemies, or prepares us an abode in heaven." Animated by such discourses, the inhabitants of Edessa exerted themselves to destroy the towers and the works of the besiegers, the hopes of being succoured redoubling their zeal and courage. They expected, says an Armenian author, *assistance from a nation which they called the valiant*, and every day looked to see, from the height of their walls, the standards of the victorious Franks.

The hoped-for succours were vainly expected. When Josselin learnt the danger of his capital, he aroused himself from his sloth, and sent information of it to Raymond of Poictiers, and the queen regent of Jerusalem. But the prince of Antioch, who disliked Josselin, refused to assist Edessa, and the troops of Jerusalem, although set forward on their march, could not arrive in time. Josselin ought to have devoted himself to repair the consequences of his faults, but he had not the courage to seek death under the walls of a city he could not save, and whose defence he had neglected.

On the twenty-eighth day of the siege, several towers fell down with a horrible crash; and Zengui at once ordered his army to enter the place. To paint the frightful scenes of this last attack, I must borrow the words of a contemporary author:—"The moment at which the sun began to shine above the horizon, appeared like a night illumined by the fires of the storm. As soon as the ramparts and towers fell, all the city was filled with terror. Nevertheless the defenders of Edessa thought not, for a moment, of flight, but all joined in the cry of the brave, *conquer or die*. Some employed themselves in propping up the walls, whilst others boldly flew to meet the enemy; the clergy, clothed in helmet and cuirass, marching at their head. The bishops, bearing each a cross in his hands, bestowed their benedictions on the people and animated them to the fight."

The enemy advanced uttering frightful cries; even amidst the din of a general assault, the voices of the Saracen heralds-at-arms were heard encouraging the soldiers, and promising the pillage of the city to the conquerors. Then, to employ the expression of an Armenian poet, the pusillanimous were seen shedding torrents of tears, whilst the brave, heedless of the stroke of the sabre, rushed amidst the ranks of the Mussulmans.

Neither prodigies of valour, nor the last efforts of despair could save the city or its inhabitants. A great part of the Mussulman army was already in the place; and all who crossed the steps of the conquerors fell beneath the sword. Most of those who sought safety in the citadel, found death under

* Kemaleddin, an Arabian historian, and William of Tyre agree as to the principal circumstances of this siege.

its ramparts, and were trampled upon and stifled by the crowd. The city of Edessa presented, everywhere, the most lamentable scenes; some fell whilst flying, and died, crushed to death by the feet of the horses; whilst others, hastening to the succour of their friends and neighbours, were themselves slaughtered by the barbarians. Neither the weakness of a timid sex, nor age on the brink of the tomb; neither the cries of infants, nor the screams of young girls who sought safety in the arms, or beneath the garments of their parents, could abate the rage of the Saracens. They whom the sword had not yet reached, looked for nothing but death; some crept to the churches to await it, and died embracing the altars of Christ; whilst others, yielding to their despair, remained motionless in their houses, where they were massacred with their families.

The citadel soon surrendered; the soldiers who defended it only asking their lives; but, notwithstanding the capitulation, many were put to the sword. A great part of the priests who had survived the carnage were condemned to slavery; an Armenian patriarch was stripped of his vestments, dragged through the streets, and beaten with rods. Matthew of Edessa, one of the most celebrated historians of Armenia, fell under the sword of the Mussulmans. Hugh, a Latin archbishop, having endeavoured to escape, was, with all his clergy, slaughtered by the infidels. His treasures, which he carried with him, and which might have been usefully employed for the defence of the city, became the prey of the enemy. Pious historians impute the fall of Edessa to the avarice of this prelate, and appear to believe that he was punished in another world for having preferred his gold to the safety of his fellow-citizens.

When the Mussulmans had become masters of the citadel, their priests ascended the steeples of the churches to proclaim these words: "Oh Mahomet! prophet of heaven, we have gained a great victory in thy name; we have destroyed the people that worshipped *stone*, and torrents of blood have been shed to make thy law triumph." After this proclamation, the Saracens redoubled their excesses. The Gazis or conquerors satiated themselves with blood; the dead bodies were mutilated, and their heads sent to Bagdad, and even to Khorasan. All who remained alive in the city of Edessa were treated as a flock of animals, and sold in the public places. The Christians, loaded with chains, after having lost their property, their country, and their liberty, had the still further grief of seeing their religion, which was all they had left to console them in their misfortunes, made a subject of ridicule by the infidels. The churches were plundered of their ornaments, and the sanctuary became the scene of the most shocking debaucheries. Many of the faithful whom the horrors of war had spared, could not support the sight of such profanations, and died with despair.

Thus a city, whose citadel, ramparts, and position on two mountains, rendered one of the strongest places in Asia, fell into the power of the Mussulmans. The traditions of religion and history carry back its origin to the highest antiquity. Narses, in a pathetic elegy, deplores the fall of this celebrated city, and makes itself speak of its ancient splendour. "I was," says she, "as a queen in the midst of her court; sixty towns standing around me formed my train; my numerous children passed their days in pleasures; the fertility of my fields, the freshness of my limpid waters, and the beauty of my palaces were admired; my altars, loaded with treasures, shed their splendour afar, and appeared to be the abode of angels. I surpassed in magnificence the proudest cities of Asia, and I was as a celestial edifice built upon the bosom of the earth."

The conquest of Edessa exalted the pride of the Saracens. The caliph of Bagdad ordered that the barbarous destroyer of the Christians should be named in the public prayers of the Fridays, and that the whole Mussulman people should offer up thanks to Heaven for his victories. Zengui left some troops in the conquered city, and pursued the course of his triumphs; but fortune did not permit him to finish that which he had begun. He was besieging the castle of Schabar, in Mesopotamia,

YLGAZY GIVES GAUTHIER HIS LIFE.

The Mussulmans of Persia, Mesopotamia and Syria, whom former defeats had not discouraged, swore to exterminate the Christian race, and marched towards the Orontes, conducted by Ylgazy, prince of Aleppo, the most ferocious of Islam warriors. The new prince of Antioch, Roger, had called to his assistance the king of Jerusalem, the counts of Edessa and Tripoli, but without waiting their arrival he had the imprudence to give battle, with a result which imperilled all the Christian colonies. Fortune was favoring the Crusaders when they became demoralized at a tornado of wind, which laid over the field of battle enormous black and sulphurous clouds. The Mussulmans understood this, and took advantage of the panic, ... charged again on their enemies, who fled. Roger in vain tried to arrest his fleeing soldiers, and was himself mortally wounded. After he fell the Mussulmans pursued, killed and captured. This battle took place near Artesia, in a place called the field of blood. The Mussulmans made a large number of prisoners, whom they massacred in presence of Gauthier, the Chancellor, who was then given his life by Ylgazy, to go and tell the Christians the fate which awaited them in Palestine.—BOOK V.

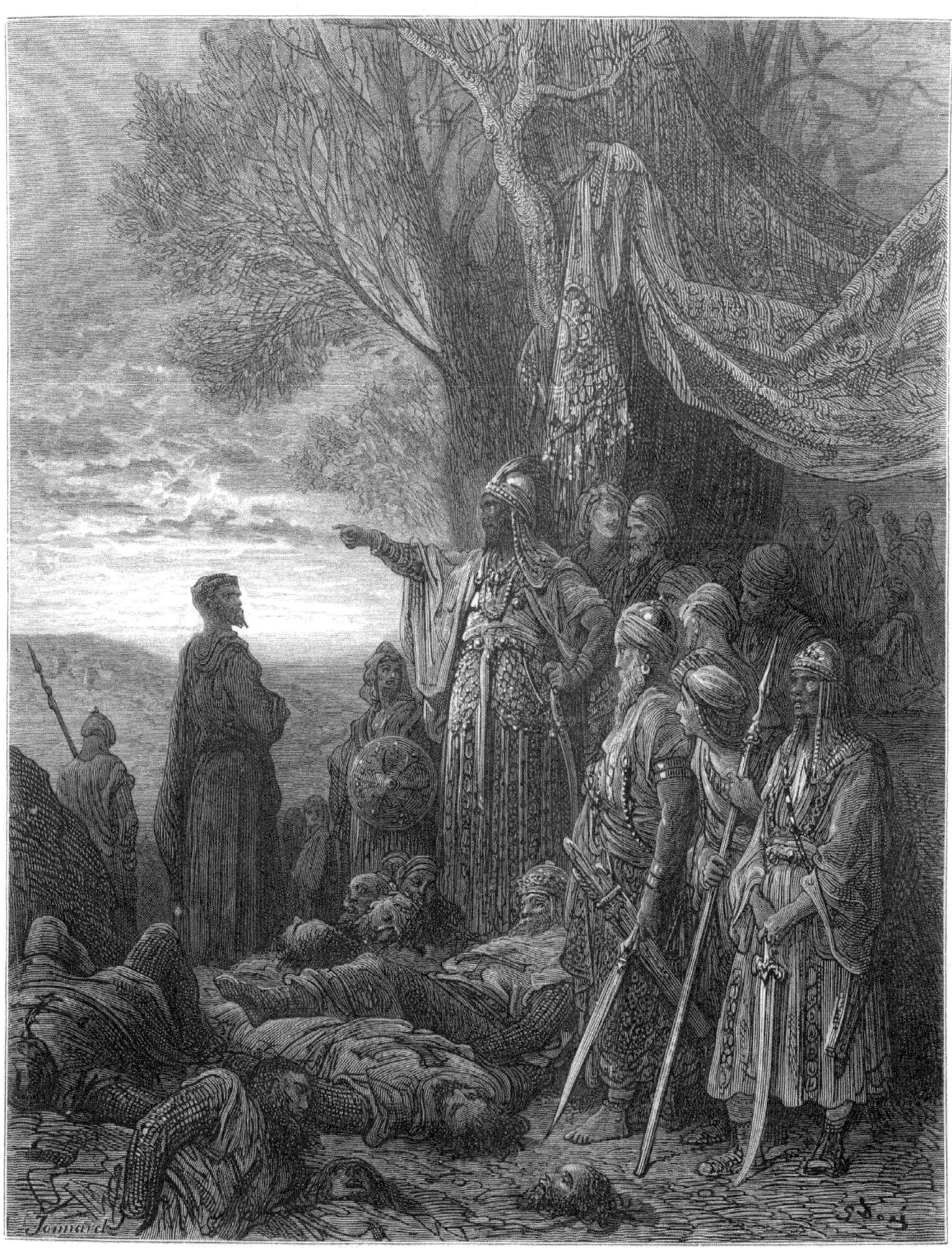

when he was assassinated by some slaves whom ill-treatment had irritated. The news of his death consoled the Christians for their defeats, and they expressed a joy as immoderate as if they had beheld the whole power of the Mussulmans fall at once. But this joy was of very short duration, for abundance of new enemies and new misfortunes soon followed to overwhelm them.

Josselin, who had taken advantage of the troubles which ensued upon the death of the prince of Mossoul to retake the city of Edessa, ill-guarded by the Mussulmans, found himself unexpectedly besieged by Noureddin, the second son of Zengui. Noureddin had received, as his share of the heritage of his father, the principality of Aleppo, and was eager to signalize his zeal against the Christians. Josselin and his companions, who had surprised the city of Edessa amidst the darkness of night, were wanting in machines of war to besiege and get possession of the citadel. When the city was invested by the prince of Aleppo, the Christian warriors who were placed between the garrison of the fortress and the Mussulman army, saw at once the danger of their position. As in desperate circumstances, a thousand resolutions are, by turns, formed and rejected; whilst they deliberated, the enemy pressed and threatened them. There soon remained no safety for them in a city which they had entered as conquerors; and, after having braved death to get possession of it, they decided upon facing equal perils to get out of it. The soldiers of Josselin, consisting of Christians who had gathered to the city, and of the small number of inhabitants who had survived the massacre of their brethren, had now nothing left but their endeavours to escape the barbarity of the Mussulmans. They made their preparations for flight in silence; the gates were opened in the middle of the night, and every one bearing away that which he esteemed most valuable, a weeping crowd pressed along the streets. Already a great number of these unhappy fugitives had passed the gates of the city, headed by the warriors commanded by Josselin, and had advanced into the plain where the Saracens were encamped, when the garrison of the citadel, warned by the tumult, made a *sortie*, and uniting themselves with the soldiers of Noureddin, who hastened towards the city, gained possession of the gates by which the Christians were issuing. Many severe conflicts were here maintained, of which darkness increased the horrors. The Christians succeeded in opening themselves a passage, and spread themselves about in the neighbouring fields. They who carried arms united in battalions, and endeavoured to pass through the camp of the enemy; whilst others, separated from the troop of warriors, went on at hazard, wandered about the plains, and everywhere found death following their footsteps. Whilst relating the events of this horrible night, William of Tyre cannot restrain his tears. "Oh disastrous night!" cries the historian Aboulfarage, "dawn of hell, day without pity, day of misfortune which arose upon the children of a city formerly worthy of envy!" In Edessa, out of Edessa, nothing was heard but cries of death. The warriors who had formed battalions, after having pierced through the army of the infidels, were pursued as far as the banks of the Euphrates, and the roads were strewed with their remains, their arms, and their baggage. Only a thousand of them succeeded in gaining the city of Samosata, which received them within its walls, and deplored their misfortunes, without being able to avenge them.

History relates that more than thirty thousand Christians were slaughtered by the soldiers of Zengui and Noureddin. Sixteen thousand were made prisoners, and dragged out their lives in misery and slavery. Noureddin in his vengeance did not spare either the ramparts or buildings of a rebel city; he razed the towers, the citadel, and the churches of Edessa to the ground. He banished all the Christians from it, and left nothing but a few mendicants to dwell amidst the ruins of their country.

Zengui had been considered as a saint, as a warrior beloved by Mahomet, for having conquered the city of Edessa; the blood-stained expedition of Noureddin rendered him dear to the Mussulmans, contributed much to the extension of his renown and his power, and already the Imans and the poets promised to his arms the much more glorious conquest of Jerusalem.

The inhabitants of Jerusalem and other Christian cities shed tears of despair on learning the fall and destruction of Edessa, sinister presages adding much to the terror which the news from the banks of the Euphrates inspired them with. Thunder fell upon the churches of the Holy Sepulchre and Mount Sion; a comet with shining hair was seen in the heavens, and spread general consternation; several other signs appeared, says William of Tyre, *contrary to custom, and out of time, indicative of future things.* As a crowning misfortune, Rodolphe, chancellor of Jerusalem, was taken by force to the siege of Tyre, and scandal prevailed in the sanctuary. All the faithful of the East were persuaded that Heaven had declared itself against them, and that horrible calamities were about to fall upon the Christian people.

BOOK VI.

THE SECOND CRUSADE.

A. D. 1142–1148.

Europe aroused to a second crusade by the impending dangers of Jerusalem and the Holy Land—The Abbot St. Bernard—Louis VII. of France—He destroys Vitri, repents, and determines on a crusade against the infidels—Pope Eugenius III. invokes the assistance of the faithful—Pons, abbot of Vèzelai—Preaching of St. Bernard—State of the Germanic empire—Conrad III. invokes a general diet at Spires, and engages in the crusade—Many distinguished personages take the cross—Enthusiasm of the Germans—Conrad and Louis VII. arrive at Constantinople—Hypocritical policy of the emperor, and treachery of the Greeks—Alarm created by an eclipse of the sun—The Crusaders defeated by the Turks—The oriflamme—Fatal blunder of Geoffrey de Rançon—Reported death of Louis VII.—Everard des Barres, grand master of the Templars—Perfidious policy of the Greeks—Sufferings of the Crusaders—Louis VII. arrives at Antioch with a small portion of his army—Eleanor of Guienne repudiated by her husband, Louis VII.—He proceeds to the Holy Land—Conrad arrives at Jerusalem—Baldwin III. urges on the war—The Crusaders besiege Damascus, and are repulsed—Ayoub, the father of Saladin—The Sclaves—Crusaders in Spain and Portugal—Suger, minister of France—Unfortunate results of this crusade—The conquests of Noureddin—The deaths of Raymond, Josselin, Suger, and St. Bernard.

THE Christian colonies, threatened by the Mussulmans, called upon the princes of Europe to assist them. The bishop of Gaballa in Syria, accompanied by a great number of priests and knights, repaired to Viterbo, where the sovereign pontiff then resided. The recitals of the Christian embassy not only caused tears to flow from the eyes of the chief of the faithful; the misfortunes of Edessa, and the impending dangers of Jerusalem excited universal commiseration and dread. Cries of alarm were raised throughout Europe. Forty-five years had passed away since the deliverance of the Holy Sepulchre, yet the minds of men were not at all changed, and eagerly, as at the first crusade, they flew to arms. In this instance it was principally the voice of St. Bernard that excited the nations and kings of Christendom to range themselves under the banners of the cross. Born of a noble family of Burgundy, St. Bernard, whilst yet in the dawn of manhood, had, with thirty relations and companions whom his discourses and his example influenced, secluded himself in the monastery of Citteaux. He was sent two years after to Clairvaux, a then unknown retreat, which he vivified with his presence, and rendered one of the most celebrated monasteries of Christendom. Many of the most learned doctors consulted the wisdom of the abbot of Clairvaux, and several councils bowed to his decisions. By the power of his eloquence alone he humbled the anti-pope Leo, and placed Innocent II. in the chair of St. Peter. Pope Innocent III. and Abbot Suger were his disciples. Prelates, princes, and monarchs glorified themselves in following his counsels, believing that God spoke by his mouth.

When the ambassadors from the East arrived in Europe, Louis VII. had just ascended the throne of France. The reign of this young monarch began under the most happy auspices. Most of the great vassals who had revolted against the royal authority had laid down their arms and renounced their pretensions. By a marriage with the daughter of William IX., Louis had added the duchy of

Aquitaine to his kingdom. France, in her enlarged condition, had nothing to fear from neighbouring states, and whilst civil wars were desolating both England and Germany, she flourished in peace under the administration of Suger.

Peace was not for a moment disturbed but by the unjust pretensions of the pope and by the intrigues of Thibaut, count of Champagne, who took advantage of the ascendancy he had over the clergy to direct the thunders of the Church against his sovereign. Louis resisted the attempts of the Holy See with firmness, and was determined to punish a rebellious and dangerous vassal. Urged on by a spirit of blind revenge, he carried fire and sword through the states of Thibaut; he besieged Vitri; was himself first in the assault, and put to the sword every inhabitant to be met with in the city. A great number of persons of all ages had taken refuge in a church, hoping to find the altar a secure asylum against the anger of a Christian prince; but Louis set fire to the church, and thirteen hundred people perished in the flames. An action so barbarous spread terror among the nation whom Louis was appointed to render happy; when he returned from this expedition to his capital, the people received him in melancholy silence; his ministers allowed him to read their regret in the dejection of their countenances; and St. Bernard, like another Ambrosius, boldly compelled him to hear the complaints of religion and outraged humanity.

In an eloquent letter, he represented to the monarch the country desolated, and pointed to the Church despised and trampled under foot. "I will fight for her," he said, "to the death; but instead of bucklers and swords, I will employ the arms which become me—*my tears and my prayers to God.*" At the voice of the holy abbot, Louis became sensible of his error; and the dread of the anger of Heaven made such a lively impression upon his mind, that he sank into a deep and alarming depression. He believed he saw the hand of God ready to strike him; he renounced all pleasures, and abandoned even the care of his authority, in order to devote himself to grief and tears. The abbot of Clairvaux, who had awakened his remorse, was obliged to calm his spirits and reanimate his courage, by representing to him the great mercy of God. The king of France recovered from his remorseless dejection; but as in the opinion of his age great crimes could only be absolved by a voyage to the Holy Land, his earnest desire to expiate the tragical death of the inhabitants of Vitri made him form the resolution of going to combat against the infidels.

Louis VII. convoked an assembly at Bourges, at which he made his project known to the principal nobility and the clergy. Godfrey, bishop of Langres, applauded his zeal, and in a pathetic discourse deplored the captivity of Edessa, and the dangers and disasters of the Eastern Christians. His eloquence moved his auditors; but the oracle of the assembly, he who held all hearts in his hand, had not yet spoken. Whether that he was yet not convinced of the utility of the crusade, or that he was desirous of giving it more solemnity, St. Bernard advised the king of France to consult the Holy See before he undertook anything. This advice was generally approved of. Louis sent ambassadors to Rome, and resolved to convoke a new assembly as soon as he should have received the answer of the sovereign pontiff.

Eugenius III., who then filled the chair of St. Peter, had already in several of his letters solicited the assistance of the faithful against the Saracens. The Holy See had never had stronger motives for the preaching of a crusade. A spirit of sedition and heresy was beginning to insinuate itself among the people, and even among the clergy of the West, threatening at the same time the power of the popes and the doctrines of the Church. Eugenius had to contend against the troubles excited by Arnold of Bressia; and nothing was talked of in the capital of the Christian world but rebuilding the Capitol, and substituting for the pontifical authority that of the consuls and tribunes of ancient Rome. In such a state of things, a great event like that of a crusade was likely to turn men's minds

LOUIS VII. RECEIVING THE CROSS FROM ST. BERNARD.

"Hasten then to expiate your sins by victories over the infidels, and let the deliverance of the holy places be the reward of your repentance. . . . If it were announced to you that the enemy had invaded your cities, your castles, and your lands, had ravished your wives and your daughters, and profaned your temples, which among you would not fly to arms? Illustrious knights, generous defenders of the cross, remember the example of your fathers who conquered Jerusalem, and whose names are inscribed in heaven; abandon then the things which perish to gather eternal palms, and conquer a kingdom which has no end." All the barons and knights applauded the eloquence of St. Bernard, and were persuaded that he had but uttered the will of God. Louis VII., deeply moved by the words he had heard, cast himself, in the presence of all the people, at the feet of St. Bernard, and demanded the cross.—BOOK VI.

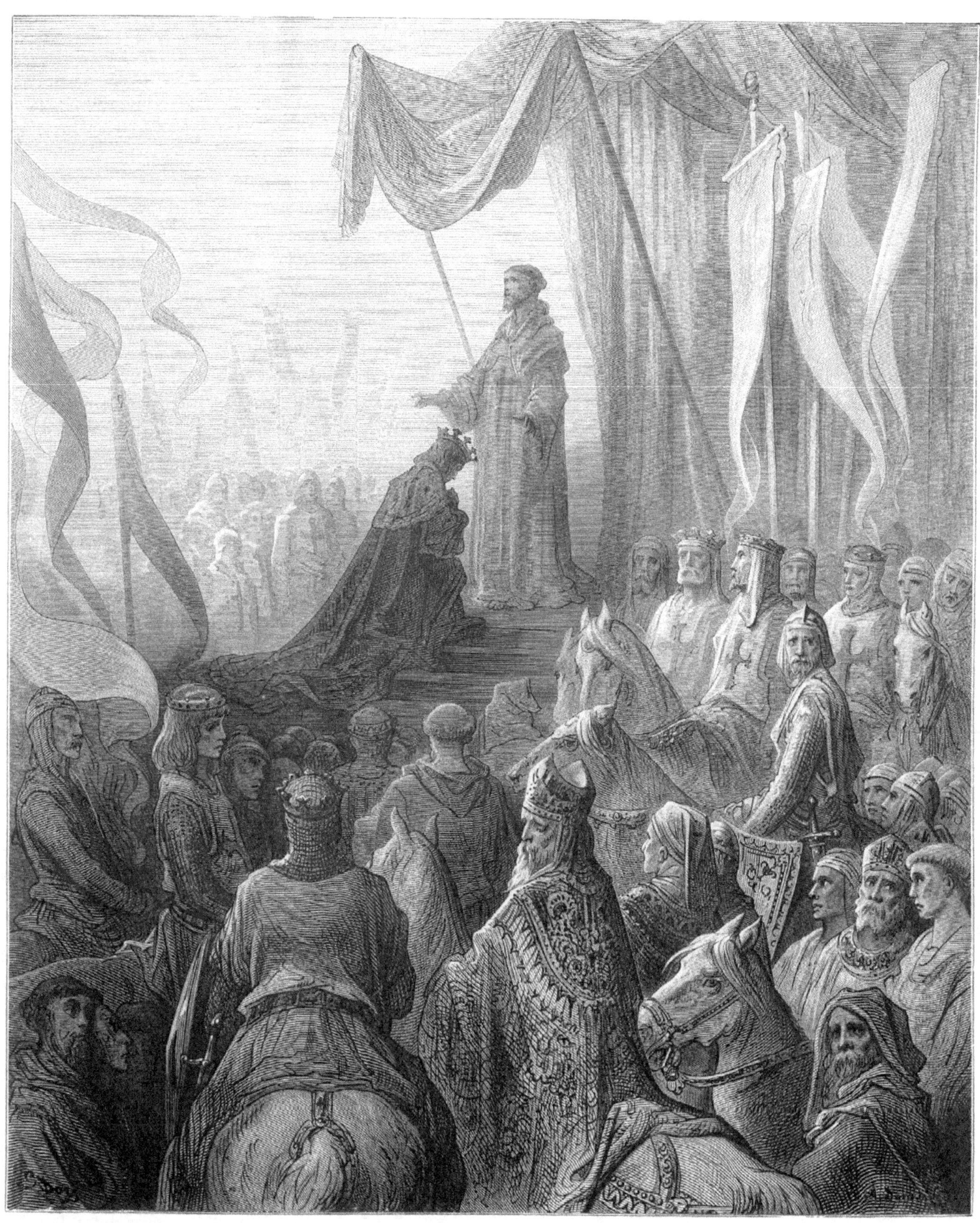

from dangerous novelties, and make them rally round the sanctuary. The sovereign pontiff could not avoid seeing in a holy war the double advantage of defending Jerusalem against the enterprises of the Saracens, and the Church and himself against the attacks of heretics and innovators. Eugenius congratulated the king of France on his pious determination, and by his letters again exhorted all Christians to assume the cross and take up arms, promising them the same privileges and the same rewards that Urban II. had granted to the warriors of the first crusade. Detained in Italy, where he was engaged in appeasing the troubles of Rome, he regretted not being able, as Urban had done, to cross the Alps, and reanimate the zeal of the faithful by his presence and his discourses; but he confided to St. Bernard the honourable mission of preaching the crusade in France and Germany.

After having received the approbation of the Holy See, Louis convoked a new assembly at Vèzelai, a little city of Burgundy; and the reputation of St. Bernard and the letters addressed by the pope to all Christendom, drew to this assembly a great number of nobles, knights, prelates, and men of all conditions. On the Palm-Sunday, after having invoked the Holy Ghost, all who had come to hear the abbot of Clairvaux repaired to the side of a hill just without the gates of the city. A large tribune was erected, in which the king in his royal robes, and St. Bernard in the humble costume of a cenobite, were saluted by the acclamations of an immense multitude. The orator of the crusade first read the letters of the sovereign pontiff, and then spoke to his auditors of the taking of Edessa by the Saracens, and of the desolation of the holy places. He showed them the universe plunged in terror on learning that God had begun to desert his beloved land; he represented to them the city of Sion as imploring their succour, Christ as ready to immolate himself a second time for them, and the heavenly Jerusalem opening all its gates to receive the glorious martyrs of the faith. "You cannot but know," said he to them, "we live in a period of chastisement and ruin; the enemy of mankind has caused the breath of corruption to fly over all regions; we behold nothing but unpunished wickedness. The laws of men or the laws of religion have no longer sufficient power to check depravity of manners and the triumph of the wicked. The demon of heresy has taken possession of the chair of truth, and God has sent forth his malediction upon his sanctuary. Oh, ye who listen to me! hasten then to appease the anger of Heaven, but no longer implore his goodness by vain complaints; clothe not yourselves in sackcloth, but cover yourselves with your impenetrable bucklers; the din of arms, the dangers, the labours, the fatigues of war are the penances that God now imposes on you. Hasten then to expiate your sins by victories over the infidels, and let the deliverance of the holy places be the reward of your repentance."

These words of the orator excited the greatest enthusiasm in the assembly of the faithful, and, like Urban at the council of Clermont, St. Bernard was interrupted by the repeated cries of "*It is the will of God! It is the will of God!*" Then raising his voice, as if he had been the interpreter of the will of Heaven, he promised them, in the name of God, success to their holy expedition, and thus continued his discourse:—

"If it were announced to you that the enemy had invaded your cities, your castles, and your lands, had ravished your wives and your daughters, and profaned your temples, which among you would not fly to arms? Well, then, all these calamities, and calamities still greater, have fallen upon your brethren, upon the family of Jesus Christ, which is yours. Why do you hesitate to repair so many evils—to revenge so many outrages? Will you allow the infidels to contemplate in peace the ravages they have committed on Christian people? Remember that their triumph will be a subject for grief to all ages, and an eternal opprobrium upon the generation that has endured it. Yes, the living God has charged me to announce to you that he will punish them who shall not have defended him against his enemies. Fly then to arms; let a holy rage animate you in the fight; and let the

Christian world resound with these words of the prophet, '*Cursed be he who does not stain his sword with blood!*' If the Lord calls you to the defence of his heritage, think not that his hand has lost its power. Could he not send twelve legions of angels, or breathe one word, and all his enemies would crumble away into dust? But God has considered the sons of men, to open for them the road to his mercy. His goodness has caused to dawn for you a day of safety, by calling on you to avenge his glory and his name. Christian warriors, he who gave his life for you, to-day demands yours in return. These are combats worthy of you, combats in which it is glorious to conquer, and advantageous to die. Illustrious knights, generous defenders of the cross, remember the example of your fathers who conquered Jerusalem, and whose names are inscribed in heaven; abandon then the things that perish to gather eternal palms, and conquer a kingdom which has no end."

All the barons and knights applauded the eloquence of St. Bernard, and were persuaded that he had but uttered the will of God. Louis VII., deeply moved by the words he had heard, cast himself, in the presence of all the people, at the feet of St. Bernard and demanded the cross. Clothed with this revered sign, he himself addressed the assembly of the faithful, to exhort them to follow his example. In his discourse he showed them the impious Philistine casting opprobrium upon the house of David, and reminded them of the holy determination which God himself had inspired in him. He invoked, in the name of the Christians of the East, the aid of that generous nation of which he was the chief; of that nation which would not endure shame when directed at itself or its allies, and which always carried terror amidst the enemies of its worship or its glory. At this discourse the whole auditory was melted in tears. The touching piety of the monarch persuaded all who had not been convinced by the eloquence of St. Bernard. The hill upon which this vast multitude was assembled, resounded for a length of time with the cries of "*It is the will of God! It is the will of God!*" and "*the Cross! the Cross!*" Eleanor of Guienne, who accompanied Louis, received, as his wife, the sign of the cross from the hands of the abbot of Clairvaux. Alphonso, count of St. Gilles de Thoulouse, Henry, son of Thibaut, count of Champagne, Thieri, count of Flanders, William of Nevers, Renaud, count de Tenniere, Yves, count de Soissons, William, count de Panthien, William, count de Varennes, Archanbaud de Bourbon, Enguerard de Coucy, Hugh de Lusignan, the count de Dreux, brother of the king, his uncle the count de Maurinne, and a crowd of barons and knights followed the example of Louis and Eleanor. Several bishops, among whom history remarks Simon, bishop of Noyon, Godfrey, bishop of Langres, Alain, bishop of Arras, and Arnold, bishop of Lisieux, threw themselves at the feet of St. Bernard, taking the oath to fight against the infidels. The crosses which the abbot of Clairvaux had brought were not sufficient for the great number who claimed them. He tore his vestments to make more, and several of those who surrounded him, in their turns, tore their clothes into strips in order to satisfy the impatience of all the faithful whom he had inflamed with a desire for the holy war.

To preserve the memory of this day, Pons, abbot of Vèzelai, founded upon the hill where the knights and barons had assembled, a church, which he dedicated to the holy cross.* The tribune, from the top of which St. Bernard had preached the crusade, remained there a long time the object of the veneration of the faithful.

After the assembly of Vèzelai, the abbot of Clairvaux continued to preach the crusade in the cities and neighbouring countries. France soon resounded with the fame of the miracles by which God seemed to authorize and consecrate, in some sort, his mission. He was everywhere considered as the messenger of Heaven, as another Moses, who was to conduct the people of God. All the Christians were persuaded that the success of the enterprise depended upon St. Bernard, and in an

* The pulpit from which St. Bernard preached the crusade remained in the church of Vèzelai until the period of the revolution of 1789.

assembly held at Chartres, in which were met several barons and princes, illustrious by their exploits, it was resolved by unanimous consent, to give him the command of the holy war. The Crusaders, they said, could never fail to be victorious under the laws of a leader to whom God appeared to have confided his omnipotence. The abbot of Clairvaux, who remembered the example of Peter the Hermit, refused the perilous employment with which they desired to honour him; he was even so much terrified by the pressing entreaties of the barons and knights, that he addressed himself to the pope, and conjured the sovereign pontiff not to abandon him to the fantasies of men.

The pope answered St. Bernard that he only need arm himself with the sword of the word of God, and content himself with sounding the evangelical trumpet to announce the war. The abbot of Clairvaux employed himself in nothing thereafter, but his mission; and he acquitted himself with so much zeal, and his preachings produced such an extraordinary, and I will venture to add, so unfortunate an effect, that they depopulated cities and countries. He wrote to Pope Eugenius: "*The villages and the castles are deserted; and there are none left but widows and orphans, whose husbands and parents are still living.*"

While St. Bernard was thus preaching the crusade in the provinces of France, a German monk, named Rodolphe, exhorted the people of the Rhine to massacre the Jews, whom he represented in his vehement discourses as the allies of the Saracens, and the most dangerous enemies of the Christian religion. The abbot of Clairvaux fearing the effect of these preachings, hastened into Germany to impose silence on this seditious apostle of the holy war. As the German monk had flattered the passions of the multitude, St. Bernard required all the ascendancy of his virtue and his fame to combat his doctrines. He ventured to raise his voice in the midst of an irritated people, and to make them feel that Christians ought not to persecute Jews, but pray to Heaven for their conversion; that it belonged to Christian piety to pardon the weak, and make war against the exalted and proud. The preacher of the crusade at length silenced the turbulent orator, and sent him back to his monastery, reminding him that the duty of monks was not to preach, but to weep · that they ought to consider *cities as prisons, and solitude as their paradise.*

This action of St. Bernard,* which was scarcely observed in his own barbarous age, and which has been turned into ridicule in ours, does honour to his character, and may excuse the extravagant zeal he displayed for a disastrous war. When he arrived in Germany, the Germanic empire was beginning to breathe after the long troubles that had followed the election of Lothaire. Conrad III., clothed with the purple, had just convoked a general diet at Spires. The abbot of Clairvaux repaired thither with the intention of preaching war against the Mussulmans, and peace among Christian princes. St. Bernard pressed the emperor, Conrad, several times to take up the cross; he at first exhorted him in private conferences, and afterwards renewed his exhortations in sermons preached in public. Conrad could not make up his mind to take the oath to go and fight against the infidels in Asia, alleging the recent troubles of the German empires. St. Bernard replied that the Holy See had placed him upon the imperial throne, and that the pope and the Church would support their work. "Whilst you shall defend his heritage, God himself will take care to defend yours; he will govern your people, and your reign will be the object of his love." The more hesitation the emperor felt, the warmer became the zeal and eloquence of St. Bernard to persuade him. One day as the orator of the crusade was saying mass before the princes and lords convoked at Spires, all at once he interrupted the service to preach the war against the infidels. Towards the end of his discourse, he trans-

* The Abbé Velly thus relates the same fact:—"Satisfied with the character of preacher and thaumaturge (performer of miracles), St. Bernard set out for Germany, where he put to silence another monk, who, without having the authority of the pope, dared to exhort the Christian nations to take up arms for the assistance of their brethren in Asia."

ported the imagination of his auditors to the day of judgment, and made them hear the trumpets which were to call all the nations of the earth before the tribunal of God. Jesus Christ, armed with his cross and surrounded by his angels, addressing himself to the emperor of Germany, recalled to him all the benefits with which he had loaded him, and reproached him with ingratitude. Conrad was so much affected by this vehement apostrophe, that he interrupted the speaker, and, with tears in his eyes, cried out: "*I know what I owe to Jesus Christ, and I swear to go wherever he shall call me.*" Then the nobles and the people who believed they had been witnesses of a miracle, threw themselves on their knees and returned thanks to God for his blessings. Conrad received from the hands of the abbot of Clairvaux the emblem of the Crusaders, together with a flag which was placed upon the altar, and which Heaven itself had blessed. A great number of barons and knights assumed the cross in imitation of Conrad, and the diet which had been assembled to deliberate upon the interests of the empire, was occupied entirely with the safety of the Christian colonies in Asia.

A new diet was convoked in Bavaria, where the letters of St. Bernard determined a great number of bishops and German nobles to take the cross. Ladislas, duke of Bohemia, Odoacer, marquis of Syria, Bernard, count of Carinthia, Amadeus, duke of Turin, and the marquis de Montferrat took the oath to go into the East to fight the Saracens. Among the prelates who enrolled themselves under the banners of the cross, history names the bishop of Passau, the bishop of Ratisbon, and the wise Otho of Frisingen, brother of the emperor, to whom posterity owes a relation of the principal events of this war.

The most dear interests, the most tender affections had no power to detain the knights and princes in their countries and homes. Frederick, nephew of the emperor, who had taken the cross, allowed himself not to be moved by the tears of his aged father, the duke of Suabia, who died with grief, in spite of the consolations of St. Bernard. A war-cry was heard from the Rhine to the Danube; Germany, although so long agitated by its own troubles, found in all parts warriors for the holy expedition. Men of all conditions obeyed the voice of the preacher of the holy war, and followed the example of kings and princes: a thing to be wondered at, says Otho of Frisingen, thieves and robbers were seen performing penance, and swearing to shed their blood for Jesus Christ. "Every reasonable man," adds the same historian, "a witness of the changes that were operated in them, plainly perceived the work of God, and was not the less astonished at it."

The Germans were so easily persuaded, that they came and listened to the abbot of Clairvaux, who preached to them in a language they did not understand, and returned convinced of the truth and holiness of the discourse. The sight of a preacher so much reverenced, appeared to bestow a marvellous sense upon every one of his words. The miracles which were attributed to him, and which were performed sometimes in private, sometimes in public, as Otho of Frisingen says, were like a divine language which warmed the most indifferent, and persuaded the most incredulous. Shepherds and labourers abandoned the fields to follow him into towns and cities; when he arrived in a city, all labours were suspended. The war against the infidels, and the prodigies by which God promised his protection to the soldiers of the cross, became the only business of men of all classes. Sometimes the abbot of Clairvaux assembled the clergy, and preached reform in their manners; sometimes he addressed the people and animated them against the Saracens.

St. Bernard visited all the cities of the Rhine, from Constance to Maestricht; in each city, say the ancient chronicles, he restored sight to the blind, hearing to the deaf, and cured the lame and the sick; they report thirty-six miracles performed in one day, at each prodigy the multitude crying out, "Jesus Christ, have mercy upon us! all the saints, succour us!" The disciples who followed the abbot of Clairvaux could not help regretting that the tumult which was constantly raised upon his passage, prevented their seeing several of his miracles. Every day an increasing crowd pressed around him. History relates that he was once on the point of being stifled by the multitude which followed his steps, and only owed his safety to the emperor of Germany, who took him in his arms, and drove back the people, who were impatient to see and touch him whom they regarded as the interpreter and messenger of God.

After having set Germany in a blaze with his preaching, and revived the zeal of the countries of Italy by his pathetic letters, St. Bernard returned to France, to announce the success of his mission. His absence had suspended everything, and that multitude of Crusaders, upon whom his eloquence had acted so powerfully, appeared to have neither chief, direction, nor rallying-point whilst he was not in the midst of them. The king of France and the nobles of the kingdom, assembled at Etampes, had formed no resolution; but the return of St. Bernard restored life to the councils of the princes and the barons, and made them resume with new ardour the enterprise of the holy war.

When he made, before the lords and prelates, the recital of his journey, and of the prodigies God had effected by his hand; when he spoke of the determination he had induced the emperor of Germany to form, a determination which he called the miracle of miracles, all hearts expanded with enthusiasm, and were filled with hope and joy.

At the same time several ambassadors appeared in the assembly of Etampes, to announce that their princes had determined to enrol themselves under the banners of the cross; and letters were read from distant countries, by which a great number of foreign lords and barons promised to join the French in their projected expedition against the Saracens. From that period no doubt was entertained of the happy results of the crusade; and the zeal which was displayed by all the nations of Europe was considered as a manifest expression of the will of Heaven.

Among the ambassadors who were present at the assembly of Etampes were some from Roger, king of Apulia and Sicily, who offered the Crusaders vessels and provisions, and promised to send his son with them to the Holy Land, if they determined to go by sea. The Sicilian deputies reminded the king of France and his barons of the perfidy of the Greeks towards the Franks in the first crusade. "You may," said they, "brave the forces of the most powerful nations, but nothing can secure you against the artifices and machinations of a deceitful and perfidious people." The assembly deliberated upon the offers of the king of Sicily, and upon the route it would be most advisable to take; the greater part of the barons, full of confidence in their arms and the protection of God, could not be brought to doubt the faith of the Greeks. The route by sea seemed to offer fewer wonders to their curiosity, and fewer perils for the exercise of their bravery; besides, the vessels which Roger could furnish would not nearly suffice to transport all whom religious zeal would lead to join the holy bands. It was therefore resolved that preference should be given to the route by land. The historian Odo de Deuil speaks with deep regret of this resolution, which proved so fatal to the Crusaders, and about which they had neglected to consult the Holy Ghost. The Sicilian deputies could not conceal their sorrow, and returned to their country predicting all the misfortunes that would ensue.

The assembly of Etampes appeared to act under a much better influence when it became necessary to choose the persons who should be intrusted with the government of the kingdom during the pilgrimage of Louis VII. When the barons and the prelates had deliberated upon this important choice, St. Bernard, who was their interpreter, addressed the king, and, pointing to Abbot Suger and the count de Nevers, said, "*Sire, there are two weapons, and they are enough.*" It was necessary that this choice of the assembly should obtain the approbation of the king and the suffrages of the people. The abbot of St. Denis had blessed France with a long peace, and had been the author of the glory of two reigns. He was opposed to the crusade; and what perfects his eulogy, he had preserved his popularity without sharing in the prevailing opinions. Suger advised the king not to abandon his subjects, and represented to him that his errors would be much better repaired by a wise administration of the kingdom God had placed him over, than by conquests in the East. He who could dare to give such advice as this, was more worthy than any other to represent his sovereign; but Suger at first refused an employment of which he plainly saw the burthen and the danger. The assembly would not make another choice; and the king himself had recourse to prayers and tears to induce his minister to take his place in the government of the kingdom. The pope, who arrived a short time after in France, ordered Suger to yield to the wishes of the monarch, the nobles, and the nation. The sovereign pontiff, in order to facilitate the honourable task which he imposed upon the abbot of St. Denis, launched, beforehand, the thunders of the Church against all who should make any attempts against the regal authority during the absence of the king.

The count de Nevers, who had likewise been pointed out by the assembly of the barons and bishops, declined, as the abbot of St. Denis had done, the dangerous charge which they offered him. When he was warmly pressed to accept the government of the kingdom, he declared that he had made a vow to enter into the order of St. Bruno. Such was the spirit of the age, that this intention was respected as the will of God; and whilst the assembly congratulated themselves upon inducing a monk to leave his cloister to govern a kingdom, they saw without astonishment a prince take an eternal farewell of the world, and bury himself in a monastery.

From this time preparations for departure were actively commenced, and all the provinces of France and Germany were in motion. The same motives which had armed the companions of Godfrey in the first expedition, inflamed the courage of the new Crusaders. The eastern war held out to their ambition the same hopes and the same advantages. The greater part of the people were animated by the never-forgotten remembrance of the conquest of Jerusalem. The relations that this conquest had established between Syria and Europe added still to the zeal and ardour of the soldiers of the cross; there was scarcely a family in the West that did not furnish a defender to the holy places, an inhabitant to the cities of Palestine. The Christian colonies in the East were to the Franks as a new country; warriors who assumed the cross appeared to be only arming themselves to defend another France, which was dear to all Christians, and which might be called the France of the East.

The example of two monarchs also necessarily influenced many warriors when ranging themselves under the banners of the crusade. Many of those turbulent nobles, who were then called *prædones*, must have had, as well as Louis VII., numerous guilty violences to expiate. The spirit of chivalry, which was every day making fresh progress, was not a less powerful principle with a nobility purely and enterely warlike. A great number of women, attracted by the example of Eleanor of Guienne, took up the cross, and armed themselves with sword and lance. A crowd of knights eagerly followed them; and indeed a species of shame seemed attached to all who did not go to fight the infidels. History relates that distaffs and spindles were sent to those who would not take arms, as an appropriate reproach for their cowardice. The troubadours and trouvères, whose songs were so much liked, and who employed themselves in singing the victories of knights over the Saracens, determined to follow into Asia the heroes and the dames they had celebrated in their verses. Queen Eleanor and Louis the Young took several troubadours and minstrels with them into the East, to alleviate the tediousness of a long journey.

And yet the enthusiasm of the Crusaders did not bear quite the same character as that of the first crusade. The world was not, in their eyes, filled with those prodigies which proclaim the especial will of Heaven; great phenomena of nature did not work upon the imagination of the pilgrims so vividly. God seemed to have delegated all his power to a single man, who led the people at his will by his eloquence and his miracles. Nobody was seen, nobody was heard, but St. Bernard; whereas in the time of Peter the Hermit orators everywhere abounded, and nature seemed charged by God himself to promote the crusade.

The only extraordinary occurrence of the time was the peace which prevailed throughout Europe. As at the approach of the first crusade, wars between individuals, civil troubles, and public outrage ceased all at once. The departure of the Crusaders was accompanied by less disorder than at the setting out of the first expedition; they neither showed the same imprudence in the choice of their leaders, nor the same impatience to march. France and Germany had not to suffer the depredations of an undisciplined multitude. The first crusade, some of the armies of which were commanded by princes and knights, and others by adventurers and monks, exhibited all the license and the tumultuous passions that are met with in unsettled republics. In the second holy war, which was led by two powerful princes, the more regular forms of a monarchy were preserved. The smaller vassals gathered around their lords, and the latter were obedient to the orders of the king of France or the emperor of Germany. Such good order in the outset of the holy enterprise appeared to promise certain victory, and could create no forethought of the disasters which awaited the Christian armies.

The city of Metz was the rendezvous of the French Crusaders, and Ratisbon that of the Germans. The roads which led to these cities were covered with pilgrims, marching under the banners of their lords. A great number of warriors also repaired to the ports of Flanders, England, and Italy, where fleets were prepared for the transport of provisions and arms, with Crusaders who were impatient to arrive in Asia.

As the routes to the East were now known, the pilgrims deceived themselves less with regard to the countries they had to pass through. The sovereign pontiff had advised the barons and knights not to take with them either dogs or birds for sport; they renounced the luxury of their castles, and contented themselves with their arms. They even had the precaution to take with them things that might be required in a distant journey; the Crusaders, but particularly the Germans, carried all sorts of instruments for throwing bridges, cutting down forests, and clearing roads.

The greatest difficulty was to find money to defray the expenses of the holy war. All whom infirmities or particular circumstances detained in Europe were anxious to assist, by their offerings, the enterprise of the crusade. According to the devotion of the times, the greater part of the rich who died without having seen Jerusalem, left by their will a sum for the promotion of pilgrimages to the East. All these pious gifts were, no doubt, considerable, but they could not suffice for the support of a large army. To procure the necessary money Louis VII. had recourse to loans, and levied imposts, which were regulated and approved of by the sovereign pontiff. St. Bernard and Peter the Venerable had exerted themselves with much courage against the persecution of the Jews; but the abbot of Cluny thought they ought to be punished in that which they held dearest, *their wealth, amassed by usury, and even by sacrilege.* He advised the king of France to take from the Jews the money necessary for the war against the Saracens. It is probable that the advice of Peter the Venerable was not disdained, and that the Jews furnished a considerable part of the expenses of the crusade. The clergy also, who had so much enriched themselves by the first crusade, were obliged to advance considerable sums for this expedition. The monastery of Fleury alone paid three hundred silver marks and a large sum in gold. In many other abbeys the vases and church ornaments were sold to purchase arms, and to pay the expenses of a war undertaken for the glory of Christ.

The lords and barons followed the example of the king of France. Some pledged or sold their lands, but the greater part made their vassals furnish means for their pilgrimage. The heavy taxes laid upon the people, and particularly the spoliation of the churches, excited many complaints, and began to cool the ardour for the crusade. "There was," says an ancient historian, "neither state, condition, age, nor sex, which was not forced to contribute to the equipment of the king and the princes going with him; whence followed the discontent of every one, and innumerable maledictions, as well directed against the king as the troops."

Nevertheless Louis VII. prepared for his undertaking by acts of devotion; he visited the hospitals, and caused prayers to be put up in all the churches for the success of the crusade. When his departure drew near, he went to St. Denis, to take the famous Oriflamme, which was borne before the kings of France in battle. The church of St. Denis was at that time decorated with great magnificence; among the historical monuments which were there collected, the portraits of Godfrey de Bouillon, Tancred, Raymond de St. Gilles, and the battles of Dorylæum, Antioch, and Ascalon, traced upon the windows of the choir, must have attracted the eyes and fixed the attention of Louis and his companions in arms. The king, prostrated on the tomb of the holy apostle of France, implored his protection and that of his pious ancestors, whose ashes reposed in the same place. The pope, who had come to St. Denis, placed anew the kingdom of France under the safeguard of religion, and presented to Louis VII. his scrip and staff, as the emblems of his pilgrimage. After this ceremony Louis set out, accompanied by Queen Eleanor and a great part of his court. He wept while he embraced Abbot Suger, who could not himself restrain his tears. The people, says a modern historian, who crowded his passage, after having followed him for a long distance with the most vociferous applauses, returned in melancholy silence to their homes as soon as he was out of sight. He left Metz at the head of a hundred thousand Crusaders, traversed Germany, and directed his march towards Constantinople, where he had appointed to meet the emperor of the West.

The emperor Conrad, after having caused his son Henry to be crowned, left Ratisbon in the beginning of spring. He was followed by an army so numerous, that, according to the report of Otho, of Frisingen, the waves were not sufficient to transport it, nor the fields spacious enough to contain all his battalions. He had sent ambassadors to announce his coming to Constantinople, and to demand permission to cross the territories of the Greek empire. Manuel Comnenus returned him a most friendly and flattering answer; but when the Germans arrived in Bulgaria and Thrace, they were not long in perceiving that they must not reckon upon the promises that had been made them.

At the time of the first crusade, Constantinople was in great dread of the Turks, which was of service to the Franks; but from that period the capital of the Greeks had experienced no alarms, and no longer feared the attacks of the Mussulmans. An opinion likewise had spread through all the provinces of the empire, that the warriors of the West entertained the project of taking possession of Constantinople. This report, probable in itself, and strengthened by the threats of the Crusaders, was very little calculated to reëstablish peace and harmony between people who despised each other reciprocally, and, perhaps with equal reason, exchanged accusations of violations of the faith of treaties.

Manuel Comnenus, whom Odo de Deuil will not even name, because, he says, his name is not written in the book of life, was the grandson of Alexius I., who reigned at the time of the first crusade. Faithful to the policy of his ancestor, more able, and above all more artful and hypocritical than he, he neglected no means to annoy and ruin the army of the Germans. In his councils the warriors of the West were considered as men of iron, whose eyes darted flames, and who shed torrents of blood with the same indifference as they would pour out the same quantity of water. At the same time that he sent them ambassadors, and furnished them with provisions, Manuel formed an alliance with the Turks, and fortified his capital. The Germans, in the course of their march, had often to repulse the perfidious attacks of the Greeks, and the latter had, more than once, cause to complain of the violence of the Crusaders. A relation of Conrad, who had remained sick in a monastery at Adrianople, was slain by the soldiers of Manuel; Frederick, duke of Suabia, gave the monastery in which this crime had been committed, up to the flames; and torrents of blood flowed to avenge an assassination.

Upon approaching Constantinople, the Germans had set up their tents in a rich valley watered by the river Melas. All at once a violent storm burst over the neighbouring mountains; the river, increased by the torrents, inundated the plain where the Christian army was celebrating the feast of the Assumption, and as if it had conspired with the Greeks, says a French historian, and as if it imitated their perfidy and treason, it carried away the horses and baggage, and brought desolation into the camp of the Crusaders. The Greeks afforded some succour to the German soldiers, but they saw with joy, in an event they affected to deplore, a presage of the defeats which threatened the armies of the Latins.

Constantinople, on the arrival of Conrad, presented the novel spectacle of two emperors who had inherited the wrecks of the empire of Augustus, and each of whom called himself the successor of Cæsar and Constantine. Their pretensions created some divisions; the emperor of the West had a valiant army to support his rights; he of the East did not dare to insist too openly upon his. He called in perfidy to his aid, and wounded vanity avenged itself in a manner as cowardly as it was cruel.

As soon as the Germans had passed the Bosphorus, they found themselves exposed to all sorts of treachery. All who straggled from the army were slain by the soldiers of Comnenus; the gates of all the cities on their route were closed; when they asked for provisions, they were obliged to put the money into the baskets which were lowered down from the walls, and after all, they frequently obtained nothing but insult and ridicule. The Greeks mixed lime with the flour they sold them; and when the Crusaders had anything for sale, they were paid in a false coin, which was refused when they became purchasers. Ambuscades awaited them throughout their route; the enemy was aware of their line of march, and as the height of perfidy, furnished them at Constantinople with faithless guides, who misled the army in the defiles of Mount Taurus, and delivered them up, worn out with fatigue, to famine and despair, or to the swords of the Mussulmans. The Germans, ill-treated by the Greeks, did not seek to revenge themselves, although it would have been easy to have done so, and, according to the ideas of the age, might have appeared glorious. This is the reason why Montesquieu says, *that the Germans were the best sort of people in the world.* The French, who came after them, showed themselves less patient, and were more respected. The emperor sent the principal lords of his court to the king of France, before whom they prostrated themselves, and only spoke to him on their knees. French haughtiness was more surprised than pleased at such homage, and only answered the flattery of the East by a disdainful silence. The two monarchs had an interview, in which they reciprocated the most tender caresses, and sought to surpass each other in magnificence. If Manuel on this occasion excelled his rival in the display of his riches, he showed less sincerity than Louis in the demonstrations of his friendship, for in the midst of the banquets which he gave to the Crusaders, the latter learnt that he preserved a close alliance with the sultan of Iconium, and that the Turks were fully informed of the plans of the French king.

This treachery irritated the French lords, and when the emperor required them to render him homage, as the leaders of the first crusade had done, it was proposed in the council that the only reply should be to take possession of Constantinople. "You have heard," said the bishop of Langres, "that the Greeks propose to you to recognise their empire, and submit to their laws: thus then weakness is to command strength, and cowardice bravery! What has this nation done? What have their ancestors done, that they should show so much pride? I will not speak to you of the snares and the ambushes that they have everywhere planted in your way; we have seen the priests of Byzantium mingling ridicule with outrage, purify with fire the altars at which our priests had sacrificed. They ask of us new oaths, which honour repudiates. Is it not time to revenge treasons, and repulse insults? Hitherto the Crusaders have suffered more from their perfidious friends than from their open enemies. Constantinople has long been a troublesome barrier between us and our brothers of the East. It is our duty at last to open a free road to Asia. The Greeks, you know, have allowed the sepulchre of Christ, and all the Christian cities of the East, to fall into the hands of the infidels. Constantinople, there is no doubt, will soon become a prey to Turks and barbarians, and by her cowardly weakness, she will one day open the barriers of the West. The emperors of Byzantium neither know how to defend their own provinces nor will they suffer others to do it for them. They have always impeded the generous efforts of the soldiers of the cross; even lately, this emperor, who declares himself your support, has endeavoured to dispute their conquests with the Latins, and ravish from them the principality of Antioch. His aim now is to deliver up the Christian armies to the Saracens. Let us hasten then to prevent our own ruin by effecting that of these traitors; let us not leave behind us a jealous and insolent city, which only seeks the means of destroying us; let us cast upon her the evils she prepares for us. If the Greeks accomplish their perfidious designs, it is of you the West will one day ask back its armies. Since the war we undertake is holy, is it not just that we should employ every means to succeed? Necessity, country, religion, all order you to do that which I propose to you. The aqueducts which supply the city with water are in our power, and offer an easy means of reducing the inhabitants. The soldiers of Manuel cannot stand against our battalions; a part of the walls and towers of Byzantium has crumbled away before our eyes, as by a species of miracle. It appears that God himself calls us into the city of Constantine, and he opens its gates to you as he opened the gates of Edessa, Antioch, and Jerusalem to your fathers."

When the bishop of Langres had ceased to speak, several knights and barons raised their voices in reply. The Christians, they said, were come into Asia to expiate their own sins, and not to punish the crimes of the Greeks. They had taken up arms to defend Jerusalem, and not to destroy Constantinople. It was true they must consider the Greeks as heretics, but it was not more just for them to massacre them than to massacre the Jews; when the Christian warriors assumed the cross, God did not put into their hands the sword of justice. In a word, the barons found much more policy than religion in that which they had heard, and could not conceive that it was right to undertake an enterprise which was not in accordance with the principles of honour. Neither had they faith in the misfortunes with which they were threatened, and relied upon Providence and their own valour to enable them to surmount all obstacles. The most fervent of the pilgrims dreaded any delay in the march of the Crusaders, and this fear increased their scruples; at length the loyalty of the knights, the general pious impatience to behold the sacred places, and perhaps also the presents and the seductions of Manuel, procured a triumph for the party advocating moderation.

The emperor was nevertheless alarmed at seeing a body of warriors, full of confidence and courage, thus deliberate so near to him on the conquest of his capital. The homage that the barons and knights paid him did not at all re-assure him as to their intentions. To hasten their departure, he caused a report to be spread that the Germans had gained great victories over the Turks, and that they had made themselves masters of Iconium. This succeeded even beyond Manuel's hopes.

When the Crusaders, impatient to pursue the Turks, were leaving Constantinople, they were surprised by an eclipse of the sun. A superstitious multitude saw in this phenomenon nothing but a fatal presage, and believed it to be either the warning of some great calamity, or of some new treachery on the part of Manuel; and the fears of the pilgrims were not long in being realized. Scarcely had they entered Bithynia when they were taught how to appreciate the false reports and perfidy of the Greeks. Louis, when encamped upon the shores of the Lake Ascanius, in the neighbourhood of Nice, received information of the complete defeat of the Germans. The sultan of Iconium, on the approach of the Christians of the West, had assembled all his forces, and at the same time solicited the aid of the other Mussulman powers to defend the passages of Asia Minor. Conrad, whom William of Tyre styles *vir simplex*, whom le Père Maimbourg compares to a victim crowned with flowers that is being led to slaughter, had advanced, on the faith of some unknown guides, into the mountains of Cappadocia. Impatient to be before the French, for whom he was to have waited, he marched on in perfect ignorance of the roads, and without provisions to feed the multitude which followed him. At a time that he entertained no suspicion of their vicinity, he was surprised by the Turks, who covered the summits of the mountains, and rushed down upon the exhausted and famished Christians. The Mussulmans were lightly armed, and performed their evolutions with the greatest rapidity. The Germans could scarcely move under the weight of their bucklers, corselets, and steel brassets; every day skirmishes were fought, in which the Christians had the disadvantage. Such as were more lightly armed, and bore sheep-skin bucklers, sometimes would rush among the enemy and put them to flight; but the Turks soon rallied upon the heights, and darted down again, like birds of prey, upon the terrified Christians. A crowd of pilgrims, whose arms only consisted of their scrip and staff, created the greatest trouble and confusion in the Christian army. The Mussulmans took advantage of their disorder, and never allowed their enemies a moment's repose. Despair and terror put an end to all discipline among the Crusaders; they no longer obeyed the orders of their leaders, but every one sought to insure his own safety by flight. At length the rout became general; the country was covered with fugitives, who wandered about at hazard, and found no asylum against the conquerors. Some perished with want, others fell beneath the swords of the Mussulmans; the women and children were carried off with the baggage, and formed a part of the enemy's booty. Conrad, who had scarcely saved the tenth part of his army, was himself wounded by two arrows, and only escaped the pursuit of the Saracens by a kind of miracle.

The news of this disaster threw the French into the greatest consternation. Louis, accompanied by his bravest warriors, flew to the assistance of Conrad. The two monarchs embraced in tears. Conrad related the particulars of his defeat, and complained the more bitterly of the perfidy of Manuel, from feeling the necessity of excusing his own imprudence. The two princes renewed their oath to repair together to Palestine, but the emperor of Germany did not keep his word. Whether he was ashamed of being without an army, whether he could not endure the haughtiness of the French, or that he dreaded their too just reproaches, he sent back the few troops he had left, and returned to Constantinople, where he was very well received, because he was no longer to be feared.

The French army, in the mean time, pursued its march, and, leaving Mount Olympus on its left, and Mount Ida on its right, passed through ancient Phrygia. The French, on their passage, passed Pergamus, Ephesus, and several other celebrated cities, which the Greeks had allowed to go to ruin. Winter was coming on, and the abundant rains and melted snows had swollen the rivers till they overflowed the country, and made the roads impracticable. The inhabitants of the mountains, a savage, wild people, fled away at the approach of the Christians, taking with them their flocks, and all that they possessed. The inhabitants of the cities shut their gates against the Crusaders, and refused provisions to all who had not full value to give in return. Whilst the French army was crossing Phrygia, Manuel sent ambassadors to the king of France, to inform him that the Turks were assembling in all parts, for the purpose of impeding his march. He offered the Crusaders an asylum in the cities of the empire; but this offer, accompanied by menaces, appeared to be only a snare, and Louis preferred braving the enmity of the Turks to trusting to the promises of the Greeks. The Christian army pursuing its march towards the frontiers of Phrygia, arrived at last at the banks of the Meander, towards the embouchure of the Lycus. The Turks, who had destroyed the army of the Germans, prepared to dispute the passage of the river with the French. Some were encamped on the mountains, others on the banks; the rains had swollen the Meander, and the passage was difficult and dangerous.

Animated by the speeches and the example of their king, no obstacle could stop the French. In vain the Turks showered their arrows upon them, or formed their battle-array on the banks; the French army crossed the river, broke through the ranks of the barbarians, slaughtered vast numbers of them, and pursued them to the foot of the mountains. The two shores of the Meander were covered with the bodies of the Turks: the historian Nicetas, who some years after saw their heaped-up bones, could not help saying, whilst praising the courage of the Franks, "that if such men did not take Constantinople, their moderation and patience were much to be admired."

After the battle they had fought with the Saracens, some pilgrims asserted that they had seen a knight, clothed in white, march at the head of the army, and give the signal for victory. Odo of Deuil, an ocular witness, speaks of this apparition, without giving faith to it, and satisfies himself with saying that the Christians would not have triumphed over the Turks without the protection and the will of God.

This victory gave great confidence to the Crusaders, and rendered their enemies more cautious. The Turks, whom it was impossible to pursue far in an unknown country, rallied again after the battle of the Meander. Less confident in their strength, and not daring to attack an army that had conquered them, they watched for a moment in which they might safely surprise them. The imprudence of a leader who commanded the French vanguard soon presented to them this opportunity. On quitting Laodicea, a city situated on the Lycus, the Crusaders had directed their course towards the mountains which separate Phrygia from Pisidia. These mountains offered nothing but narrow passages, in which they constantly marched between rocks and precipices. The French army was divided into two bodies, commanded every day by new leaders, who received their orders from the king.

Every evening they laid down in council the route they were to follow the next day, and appointed the place where the army was to encamp. One day when they had to cross one of the highest mountains, the order had been given to the vanguard to encamp on the heights, and to wait for the rest of the army, so that they might descend into the plain the next day in order of battle. Geoffrey de Rançon, lord of Taillebourg, this day commanded the first body of the French army, and bore the Oriflamme, or royal standard. He arrived early at the spot where he was to pass the night, which offered no retreat for his soldiers but woods, ravines, and barren rocks. At the foot of the mountain they beheld an extensive and commodious valley; the day was fine, and the troops were in a condition to march without fatigue several hours longer. The count de Maurienne, brother of the king, Queen Eleanor, and all the ladies of her suite, who had accompanied the vanguard, pressed Geoffrey de Rançon to descend into the plain. He had the weakness to comply with their wishes; but scarcely had he gained the valley, when the Turks took possession of the heights he had passed, and ranged themselves in order of battle.

During this time the rearguard of the army, in which was the king, advanced full of confidence and security; on seeing troops in the woods and on the rocks, they supposed them to be the French, and saluted them with cries of joy. They marched without order, the beasts of burden and the chariots were mingled with the battalions, and the greater part of the soldiers had left their arms with the baggage. The Turks, perfectly motionless, waited in silence till the Christian army should be enclosed

DESTRUCTION OF THE ARMY OF CONRAD III. OF GERMANY.

Conrad was followed by an army so numerous, that, according to the report of Otho, the waves were not sufficient to transport it, nor the fields spacious enough to contain all its battalions.... Impatient to be before the French, he marched on in perfect ignorance of the roads, and without provisions to feed the multitude which followed him.... he was surprised by the Turks who covered the summits of the mountains, and rushed down upon the exhausted and famished Christians. The Mussulmans were lightly armed, and performed their evolutions with the greatest rapidity. The Germans could scarcely move under the weight of their bucklers, corselets and steel brassets; such as were more lightly armed sometimes would rush among the enemy and put them to flight, but the Turks soon rallied on the heights, and darted down again like birds of prey, upon the terrified Christians. At length the rout became general, the country was covered with fugitives.... some perished with want, others fell beneath the swords of the Mussulmans; the women and children were carried off with the baggage, and formed a part of the enemy's booty. Conrad, who had scarcely saved a tenth part of his army, was wounded by two arrows, and only escaped the pursuit of the Saracens by a kind of miracle.—BOOK VI.

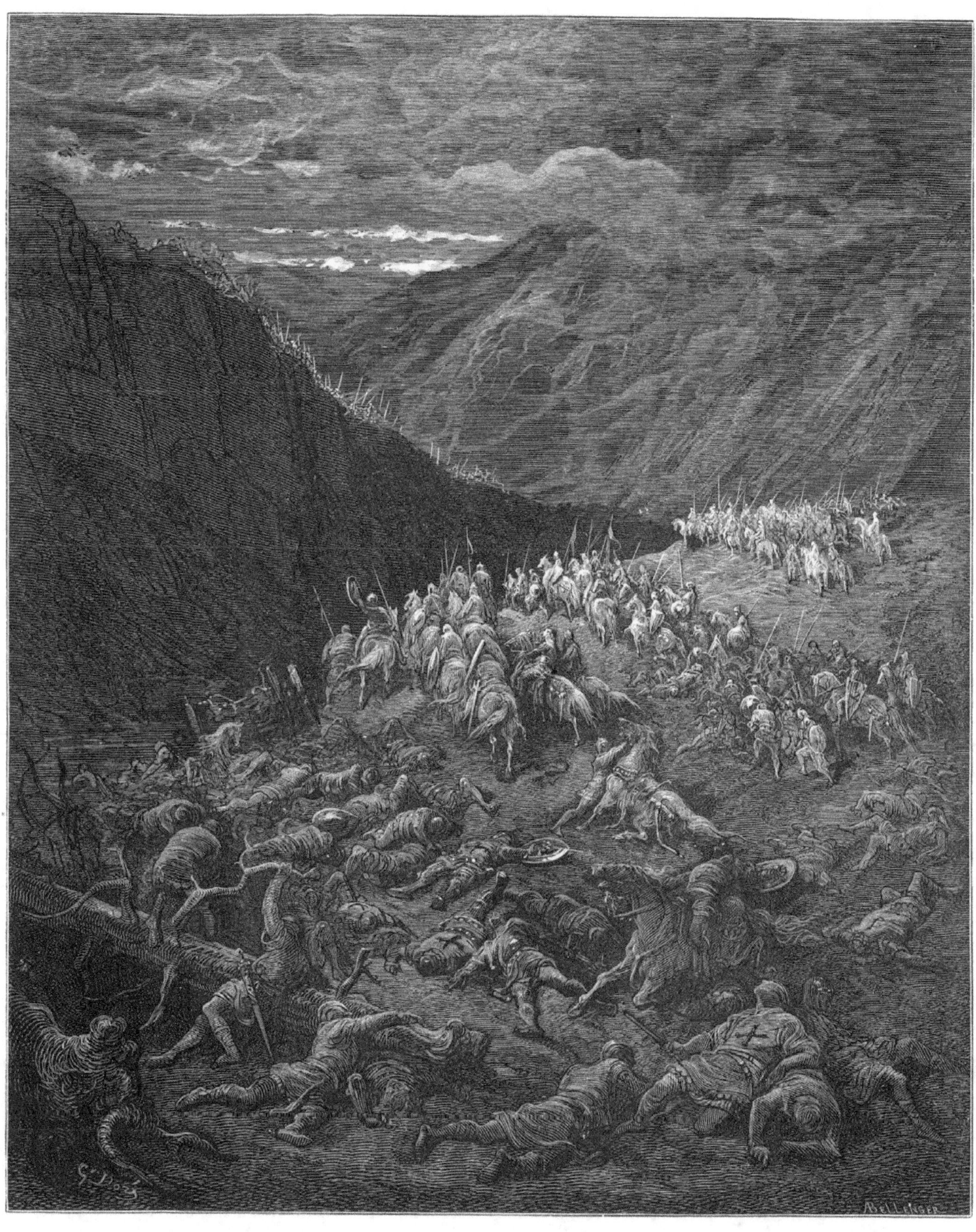

in the defiles, and when they thought themselves sure of victory, they moved forward uttering frightful cries, and, sword in hand, fell upon the unarmed Christians, who had no time to rally. The disorder and confusion of the French army cannot be described. "Above us," says an ocular witness, "steep rocks rose up to the clouds; beneath us precipices, dug by the torrent, descended to the infernal regions." The Crusaders were upon a narrow path, upon which men and horses could neither advance nor retreat; they dragged each other down into the abysses; whilst rocks, detached from the tops of the mountains, rolling down with horrible noise, crushed everything in their passage.

The cries of the wounded and the dying mingled with the confused roar of the torrents, the hissing of the arrows, and the neighing of the terrified horses. In this frightful tumult the leaders gave no orders, and the soldiers could neither fight nor fly. The bravest rallied around the king, and advanced towards the top of the mountain. Thirty of the principal nobles that accompanied Louis perished by his side, selling their lives dearly. The king remained almost alone on the field of battle, and took refuge upon a rock, whence he braved the attack of the infidels who pursued him. With his back against a tree, he singly resisted the efforts of several Saracens, who, taking him for a simple soldier, at length left him, to secure their share of the pillage. Although the night began to fall, the king expected to be attacked again, when the voices of some Frenchmen who had escaped the carnage, gave him the agreeable information that the Turks had retired. He mounted a stray horse, and, after a thousand perils, rejoined his vanguard, where all were lamenting his death.

After this defeat, in which the king had been exposed to such dangers, the report of his death was not only spread throughout the East, but reached Europe, where it filled the Christians, particularly the French, with grief and terror. William of Tyre, whilst relating the disastrous defeat of the Crusaders, expresses astonishment that God, always full of mercy, should have allowed so many illustrious warriors armed in his cause, to perish so miserably. The Crusaders who formed the vanguard of the army, whilst deploring the death of their brethren, raised their voices against Geoffrey de Rançon, and demanded that the loss of so much blood should be visited upon him. The king, however, had not sufficient firmness to punish an irreparable fault, and only so far yielded to the wishes of the barons and the soldiers as to give them as a leader an old warrior named Gilbert, whose skill and bravery were the boast of the whole army. Gilbert shared the command with Evrard des Barres, grand master of the Templars, who had come, with a great number of his knights, to meet the Christian army. Under these two leaders, whom the king himself obeyed, the Crusaders continued their march, and avenged their defeat several times upon the Mussulmans.

On their arrival in Pisidia the French had almost everywhere to defend themselves against the perfidy of the Greeks and the attacks of the Turks; but winter was even a more dangerous enemy than these to the Christian army. Torrents of rain fell every day; cold and humidity enervated the powers of the soldiers; and the greater part of the horses, being destitute of forage, perished, and only served to feed the army, which was without provisions. The clothes of the soldiers hung about them in rags; the Crusaders sold or abandoned their arms; the tents and baggage lay scattered on the roads, and the army dragged in its train a crowd of sick, and numbers of poor pilgrims, who made the air resound with their cries and lamentations. The king of France consoled them by his discourses, and relieved them by his charitable gifts; for in the midst of so many reverses God alone seemed to sustain his courage. "Never," says Odo of Deuil, "did he pass a single day without hearing mass, and without invoking the God of the Christians."

At last the Christians arrived before the walls of Attalia, situated on the coast of Pamphylia, at the mouth of the river Cestius. This city, inhabited by Greeks, was governed in the name of the emperor of Constantinople. As the inhabitants were mistrustful of the intentions of the Christian army, they refused to open their gates to them, and the Crusaders were obliged to encamp on the neighbouring plains, exposed to all the rigours of the season.

They could neither find provisions for themselves nor forage for their horses in a barren uncultivated country, constantly ravaged by the Turks. The Greeks refused to assist them in their distress, and sold them everything at its weight in gold. Famine, and the evils which the Christians had hitherto suffered, became still more insupportable to them when they lost all hope. Louis VII. having called a council, the chief men of the army represented to him that the Crusaders were without horses and without arms, they were not in a condition to give an enemy battle, nor could they support the fatigues of a long march. There remained, they added, no other resource for the Christians but to abandon themselves to the perils of the sea.* The king did not agree with their opinion, and wished that they should only embark the multitude of pilgrims that embarrassed the march of the army. "As for us," said he, "we will redouble our courage, and we will follow the route which our fathers, who conquered Antioch and Jerusalem, followed. Whilst anything remains to me, I will share it with my companions; and when I shall have nothing left, which of you will not undergo with me poverty and misery?" The barons, touched with this speech, swore to die with their king, but were not willing to die without glory. Animated by the example of Louis, they might triumph over the Turks, over their misfortunes, and the rigours of winter; but they were without defence against famine and the perfidy of the Greeks. They reproached Louis VII. with not having followed the counsels of the bishop of Langres, and with having pardoned enemies more cruel than the Mussulmans, more dangerous than the tempests or rocks of the ocean.

As at the end of this council, strong murmurs against the Greeks arose in the Christian army, the governor of Attalia became fearful of the effects of despair, and came to offer Louis vessels, in which to embark all the Crusaders. This proposition was accepted; but they had to wait for the promised vessels more than five weeks. In so long a delay the Crusaders consumed all the resources they had left, and many died of hunger and misery; the vessels which at length arrived in the ports of Attalia, were neither large enough nor sufficient in number to embark the whole Christian army. The Crusaders then perceived the abyss of evils into which they were about to fall; but such was their resignation, or rather the deplorable state of the army, that they committed no violence towards the Greeks, and did not even threaten a single city which refused to help them.

A crowd of poor pilgrims, among whom were barons and knights, appeared before the king, and spoke to him in these terms:—"We have not means wherewith to pay for our passage, and we cannot follow you into Syria; we remain here victims to misery and disease; when you shall have left us, we shall be exposed to greater perils; and being attacked by the Turks is the least of the misfortunes we have to dread. Remember that we are Franks, that we are Christians; give us leaders who may console us for your absence, and assist us to endure the fatigue, the hunger, and the death which await us." Louis, in order to reassure them, spoke to them in the most feeling terms, and distributed considerable sums amongst them. He was as liberal in his assistance, says Odo de Deuil, as if he had lost nothing, or wanted nothing for himself. He sent for the governor of Attalia, and gave him fifty silver marks to provide for the sick who remained in the city, and to conduct the land army as far as the coasts of Cilicia.

Louis VII. gave as leaders for all who could not embark, Thierri count of Flanders and Archambaud de Bourbon; he then went on board the fleet that had been prepared for him, accompanied by the queen Eleanor, the principal lords of his court, and all that remained of his cavalry. Whilst looking at the Crusaders whom he left at Attalia, the king of France could not refrain from tears; a mul-

* The Crusaders had then a march of forty days before them to arrive at Antioch by land. They might have reached it in three days by sea.

titude of pilgrims assembled upon the shore, followed with their eyes the vessel in which he had embarked, putting up vows for his voyage; and when they had lost sight of him, they thought of nothing but their own dangers, and sank into the deepest despondency.

On the day following the departure of Louis VII., the pilgrims, who were expecting the escort and the guides that had been promised them, saw the Turks come upon them, eager for murder and pillage. Archambaud and Thierri for a moment re-animated the courage of the Crusaders, and several times repulsed the infidels. But the Turks returned to the charge without ceasing; every day the Christians sustained fresh encounters without being able to compel their enemy to retreat. The Greeks would not consent to receive them into the city, and there remained to the Crusaders no means of safety. Despair stifled in their breasts even the sentiments of humanity; every one of these unfortunate wretches became insensible to the fate of his companions, and felt nothing but his own ills, saw nothing but his own dangers. The soldiers did not endeavour to rally or to succour each other; they no longer recognised or followed leaders; the leaders themselves were no longer guided by the spirit of religion, or governed by the love of glory. In the midst of the general desolation, Archambaud and Thierri, only anxious to avoid death, threw themselves on board a vessel which was going to join the fleet of Louis VII. The horrible disorder that then reigned among the miserable remains of the Christian army and the sick in the city of Attalia, is perfectly beyond description.

Two troops of pilgrims, one of three thousand and the other of four thousand, resolved to brave all dangers and march towards Cilicia. They had no boats to cross overflowing rivers; they had no arms with which to resist the Turks, and they almost all perished. Others who followed them shared the same fate, whilst the sick in the city of Attalia were ruthlessly massacred. It has been a painful task for the historian to record even a few details of these frightful disasters; and it is in this place we find the words of the old chronicles so applicable—"God alone knows the number of the martyrs whose blood flowed beneath the blade of the Turks, and even under the sword of the Greeks."

Many Christians, bewildered by despair, believed that the God who thus left them a prey to so many ills could not be the true God; three thousand of them embraced the faith of Mahomet and joined the Mussulmans, who took pity on their wretchedness. The Greeks were soon punished for their perfidious cruelty; pestilence uniting its ravages with those of war, left the city of Attalia almost without inhabitants, a very few weeks after the departure of Louis VII.

When Louis arrived in the principality of Antioch, the 19th of March, 1148, he had lost three-fourths of his army; but he was not the less warmly welcomed by Raymond of Poictiers. The French who accompanied him soon forgot, in the midst of pleasures, both the dangers of their voyage and the deplorable death of their companions.

Antioch could then boast of having within its walls the countess of Thoulouse, the countess of Blois, Sibylla of Flanders, Maurille countess de Roussy, Talquery duchess de Bouillon, and several other ladies celebrated for their birth or their beauty. The fêtes which Raymond gave them received additional splendour from the presence of Eleanor of Guienne. This young princess, daughter of William IX. and niece of the prince of Antioch, united the most seducing gifts of mind to the graces of her person. She had been much admired at Constantinople, and had found no rival in the court of Manuel. She was accused, and with some reason, of being more desirous of admiration than became a Christian queen. It was neither sincere piety nor an inclination to perform penance, that had led her to make a pilgrimage to Constantinople. The fatigues and dangers of the journey, the misfortunes of the Crusaders, the remembrance of the holy places, always present to the minds of true pilgrims, had not in the least abated her too lively taste for pleasures, or her strong inclination for gallantry.

Raymond of Poictiers, amidst the fêtes given to Queen Eleanor, did not forget the interests of his principality; he was anxious to weaken the power of Noureddin, the most formidable enemy of the Christian colonies, and ardently desired that the Crusaders would assist him in this enterprise. Caresses, prayers, presents, nothing was spared to engage them to prolong their sojourn in his states. The prince of Antioch addressed himself at first to the king of France, and proposed to him, in a council of the barons, to besiege the cities of Aleppo and Cæsarea, in Syria. This enterprise, which favoured his ambition, offered real advantages to all the Christian states of the East, which were threatened by the constantly increasing power of Noureddin; but Louis VII., who had been only brought into Asia by a spirit of devotion, answered Raymond that he could engage himself in no war before he had visited the holy places.

The prince of Antioch did not allow himself to be discouraged by this refusal; he employed every means to touch the heart of the queen, and resolved to make love subservient to his designs. William of Tyre, who has left us the portrait of Raymond, informs us that he was "*mild and affable of speech, exhibiting in his countenance and manner, I do not know what singular grace and behaviour of an excellent and magnanimous prince.*" He undertook to persuade Queen Eleanor to prolong her stay in the principality of Antioch. It was then the beginning of spring; the smiling banks of the Orontes, the groves of Daphne, and the beautiful skies of Syria, doubtless added their charms to the insinuating speeches of Raymond. The queen, seduced by the prayers of this prince, infatuated with the homage of a voluptuous and brilliant court, and, if historians may be believed, too much disposed to pleasures and indulgences unworthy of her, warmly solicited the king to delay his departure for the holy city. The king, in addition to an austere devotion, possessed a jealous and suspicious disposition; the motives therefore that made the queen desirous of remaining at Antioch strengthened his determination to go to Jerusalem. The instances of Eleanor filled his mind with suspicions, and rendered him still more inexorable; upon which Raymond, disappointed in his hopes, was loud in his complaints, and determined to be revenged. This prince, says William of Tyre, "*was impetuous in his will, and of so choleric a disposition, that when he was excited he listened to neither rhyme nor reason.*" He easily communicated his indignation to the mind of Eleanor, and this princess at once boldly formed the project of separating herself from Louis VII., and of dissolving their marriage, under the plea of relationship. Raymond, on his part, swore to employ force and violence to detain his niece in his dominions. At length the king of France, outraged both as a husband and a sovereign, resolved to precipitate his departure, and was obliged to carry off his own wife, and bear her into his camp by night.

The conduct of the queen must have scandalized both the infidels and the Christians of the East; and her example was likely to produce fatal effects in an army in which there were a great number of women. Among the crowd of knights, and even of Mussulmans, who during her abode at Antioch by turns were favoured by her partiality,* a young Turk is particularly mentioned, who received costly presents from her, and for whom she desired to abandon the king of France. In such affairs, ingeniously remarks Mézerai, "*more is frequently said than there is; but sometimes also there is more than is said.*" However that may be, Louis VII. could not forget his dishonour, and felt obliged some years after to repudiate Eleanor, who married Henry II., and bestowed the duchy of Guienne upon England, which was for France one of the most deplorable consequences of this second crusade.

The king and the barons of Jerusalem, who dreaded the stay of Louis VII. at Antioch, sent deputies to conjure him, in the name of Jesus Christ, to hasten his march towards the holy city. The king

---

* Some romancers, and even some historians, have advanced that Eleanor of Guienne was in love with Saladin, who founded the dynasty of the Ayoubites. Saladin, the son of Ayoub, was born the same year that Eleanor married Louis VII., and was scarcely ten years old at the time of the second crusade. Her *second* son, by Henry II. of England, became the great rival of Saladin in military glory.

of France yielded to their wishes, and crossed Syria and Phœnicia without stopping at the court of the count of Tripoli, who entertained the same projects as Raymond of Poictiers. His arrival in the Holy Land created the greatest enthusiasm, and re-animated the hopes of the Christians. The people, the princes, and the prelates of Jerusalem came out to meet him, bearing in their hands branches of olive, and singing the same words as the Saviour of the world was saluted with—"*Blessed be he who comes in the name of the Lord.*" The emperor of Germany, who had left Europe at the head of a powerful army, had just reached Jerusalem in the character of a simple pilgrim. The two monarchs embraced, wept over their misfortunes, and repairing together to the church of the Resurrection, adored the inscrutable decrees of Providence.

Baldwin III., who then reigned at Jerusalem, was a young prince of great hope, and being as impatient to extend his own renown as to enlarge his kingdom, he neglected no means to obtain the confidence of the Crusaders, and urge on the war against the Saracens. An assembly was convoked at Ptolemaïs, to deliberate upon the operations of this crusade. The emperor Conrad, the king of France, and the young king of Jerusalem repaired thither, accompanied by their barons and their knights. The leaders of the Christian armies and the heads of the Church deliberated together upon the subject of the holy war in the presence of Queen Melisende, the marchioness of Austria, and several other German and French ladies, who had followed the Crusaders into Asia. In this brilliant assembly the Christians were astonished at not seeing the queen, Eleanor of Guienne, and were thus reminded with regret of the sojourn at Antioch. The absence of Raymond of Antioch, and the counts of Edessa and Tripoli, who had not been invited to the meeting, must necessarily have created sad reflections, and given birth to presages upon the effects of discord among the Christians of the East.

The name of the unfortunate Josselin was scarcely mentioned in the council of the princes and barons; nothing was said of Edessa, the loss of which had raised the entire West to arms, nor of the conquest of Aleppo, which had been proposed by Raymond of Antioch. From the beginning of the reign of Baldwin, the princes and lords of Palestine had cherished a project for extending their conquests beyond Libanus, and gaining possession of Damascus. As the Christians, when they entered into a Mussulman province or city, divided amongst them the lands and the houses of the conquered, the people who dwelt on the barren mountains of Judea, the greater part of the warriors of Jerusalem, and even the clergy, all appeared to direct their wishes towards the territory of Damascus, which offered the rich booty to its captors of pleasant habitations, and fields covered with golden harvests. The hope of driving the Mussulmans from a fertile province, and enriching themselves with their spoils, made them even forgetful of the redoubtable power of Noureddin and the Attabecks. In the assembly at Ptolemaïs, it was resolved to commence the war by the siege of Damascus.

All the troops assembled in Galilee in the beginning of the spring, and advanced towards the source of the Jordan, commanded by the king of France, the emperor of Germany, and the king of Jerusalem, preceded by the patriarch of the holy city, bearing the true cross. The Christian army, to which were attached the knights of the Temple, and of St. John, in the early days of June set out from Melchisapar, a little city, memorable for the miraculous conversion of St. Paul, and crossing the chains of Libanus, encamped near the town of Dary, from whence they could see the city of Damascus.

Damascus is situated at the foot of the Anti-Libanus, forty-five leagues from Jerusalem; hills covered with trees and verdure arise in the neighbourhood of the city, and in its territory were several towns which have maintained a name in history. A river which falls impetuously from the mountains, rolls over a golden-coloured sand, and separating into several branches, waters the city, and bears freshness and fertility to the *valley of Abennefsage, or the valley of violets*, planted with all sorts of fruit-trees. The city of Damascus was celebrated in the remotest antiquity, having seen both the rise and fall of the city of Palmyra, whose ruins are still objects of curiosity and wonder in its neighbourhood. Ezekiel boasts of its delicious wines, its numerous workshops, and its wools of admirable tints; and several passages of Scripture represent Damascus as the abode of voluptuousness and delight. The beauty of its gardens, and the magnificence of its public edifices, many of which were built of marble of different colours, were much admired.

Damascus, after being conquered in turn by the Hebrews, the kings of Assyria, and the successors of Alexander, fell into the hands of the Romans. From the age of Augustus the preaching of St. Paul had filled it with Christians; but at the beginning of the Hegira it was attacked and taken by the lieutenants of Mahomet, and a great part of the inhabitants, who, after capitulation, endeavoured to seek an asylum in Constantinople, were pursued and massacred by the fierce conquerors, in the territories of Tripoli.

From this time, Damascus, which formed a government or a principality, had remained in the power of the Mussulmans. At the period of the second crusade, this principality, attacked by turns by the Franks, the Ortokides, and the Attabecks, and almost reduced to nothing but its capital, belonged to a Mussulman prince, who had no less occasion to defend himself against the ambition of the emirs than the invasion of foreign enemies. Noureddin, master of Aleppo and several other cities of Syria, had already made several attempts to gain possession of Damascus, and had by no means abandoned the hopes of uniting it to his other conquests, when the Christians formed the resolution of besieging it.

The city was defended by high walls on the east and the south; whilst on the west and the north it had no other defence but its numerous gardens, planted with trees, in all parts of which were raised palisades, walls of earth, and little towers, in which they could place archers. The Crusaders, when ready to begin the siege, resolved in a council to take possession of the gardens first, hoping to find therein water and abundance of fruits. But the enterprise was not without great difficulties; for the orchards, which extended to the foot of the Anti-Libanus, were like a vast forest, crossed by narrow paths, in which two men could scarcely walk abreast. The infidels had everywhere thrown up intrenchments, where they could, without danger to themselves, resist the attacks of the Crusaders. Nothing could, however, damp the bravery and ardour of the Christian army, which penetrated on several sides into the gardens. From the heights of the little towers, from the interior of the wall enclosures, and from the bosoms of the bushy trees, clouds of arrows and javelins were showered upon them. Every step taken by the Christians in these covered places was marked by a combat in which they could scarcely see their enemy. The infidels, however, attacked without intermission, were, in the end, obliged to abandon the positions they had occupied and fortified. The king of Jerusalem marched first at the head of his army and the knights of St. John and of the Temple; after the Christians of the East, advanced the French Crusaders, commanded by Louis VII.; whilst the emperor of Germany, who had got together the poor remains of his army, formed a body of reserve, to protect the besiegers from the surprises of the enemy.

The king of Jerusalem pursued the Mussulmans with ardour; his soldiers rushing with him into the midst of the enemy's ranks, comparing their leader to David, who, according to Josephus, had conquered a king of Damascus. The Saracens, after an obstinate resistance, united on the banks of the river which flows under its walls, to drive away with arrows and stones the crowd of Christians brought thither by fatigue and heat. The warriors commanded by Baldwin endeavoured several times to break through the army of the Mussulmans, but always met with an invincible resistance. It was then the emperor of Germany signalized his bravery by a deed of arms worthy of the heroes of the first crusade. Followed by a small number of his people, he passed through the French army, whom the difficulties of the situation almost prevented from fighting, and took his place in the vanguard of the Crusaders. Nothing could resist the impetuosity of his attack, all who opposed him falling beneath his arm; when a Saracen of gigantic stature, and completely clothed in armour, advanced to meet him, and defy him to the combat. The emperor at once accepted the challenge, and flew to meet the Mussulman warrior. At the sight of this singular combat, the two armies remained motionless, waiting in fear, till one of the champions had defeated the other, to re-commence the battle. The Saracen warrior was soon hurled from his horse, and Conrad, with one blow of his sword, dealt upon the shoulder of the Mussulman, divided his body into two parts. This prodigy of valour and strength redoubled the ardour of the Christians, and spread terror among the infidels. From this moment the Mussulmans began to seek safety within the walls of the city, and left the Crusaders masters of the banks of the river.

Eastern authors speak of the fright of the inhabitants of Damascus after the victory of the Christians. The Mussulmans prostrated themselves upon ashes during several days; they exposed in the middle of the great mosque, the Koran compiled by Omar; and women and children gathered around the sacred book to invoke the aid of Mahomet against their enemies. The besieged already contemplated abandoning the city; they placed in the streets, towards the entrance into the gardens, large posts, chains, and heaps of stones, in order to retard the march of the besiegers, and thus to afford them time to fly with their riches and their families by the north and south gates.

The Christians were so thoroughly persuaded they should shortly be masters of Damascus, that it became a question among the leaders, to whom the sovereignty of the city should be given. The greater part of the barons and lords who were in the Christian army, courted the favour of the king of France and the emperor of Germany, and all at once forgot the siege of the city, in their earnest endeavours to obtain the government of it. Thierri of Alsace, count of Flanders, who had been twice in Palestine before the crusade, and who had given up to his family all his possessions in Europe, solicited the principality more warmly than the others, and prevailed over his opponents and rivals. This preference gave birth to jealousy, and infused discouragement in the army; as long as the city they were about to conquer remained a bait for their ambition, the leaders showed themselves full of ardour and courage, but when they were without hope, some remained inactive, whilst others, no longer regarding the Christian glory as their own cause, sought every means to insure the failure of an enterprise from which they should reap no personal advantage.

The leaders of the besieged took advantage of these feelings to open negotiations with the Crusaders. Their threats, their promises and presents, succeeded in destroying what remained of the zeal and enthusiasm of the Christians. They addressed themselves particularly to the barons of Syria, and exhorted them to be on their guard against warriors come, as they said, from the West, to take possession of the Christian cities of Asia. They threatened to deliver up Damascus to the new master of the East, Noureddin, whom nothing could resist, and who would soon take possession of the kingdom of Jerusalem. The barons of Syria, whether deceived by these speeches, or that, in their hearts, they dreaded the successes of the Franks who had come to succour them, employed themselves only in retarding the operations of a siege they had themselves prosecuted with ardour; and, abusing the confidence of the Crusaders, they proposed a plan, which, being adopted too lightly, completed the ruin of all the hopes that had been built on this crusade.

In a council, the barons of Syria proposed to the leaders to change the mode of attack; the closeness of the gardens and the river, said they, prevented the placing of the machines of war in an advantageous manner; and the Christian army, in the position it occupied, might be surprised, and ran the risk of being surrounded by the enemy without the power of defending itself. It appeared to them, therefore, much more certain and safe to assault the city on the south and east sides.

Most of the chiefs possessed more valour than prudence, and the confidence which victory inspired made them think everything possible; besides, how could they mistrust the Christians of the East, for whom they had taken up arms, and who were their brothers? In addition to this, the fear of dragging out the siege to a great length made them adopt the advice of the barons of Syria. After having changed their points of attack, the Christian army, instead of finding easy access to the place, saw nothing before them but towers and impregnable ramparts. Scarcely had the Christians seated themselves in their new camp when the city of Damascus received within its walls a troop of twenty thousand Curds and Turcomans, determined to defend it. The besieged, whose courage was raised by the arrival of these auxiliaries, put on, says an Arabian historian, the buckler of victory, and made several sorties, in which they gained the advantage over the Christians. The Crusaders, on their part, made several assaults upon the city, and were always repulsed. Encamped upon an arid plain, they were destitute of water; all the adjacent country had been devastated by the infidels, and the corn that had escaped the ravages of war was concealed in caves and subterranean hiding-places, which they could not discover. The Christian army wanted provisions; then discord revived among them; nothing was spoken of in the camp but perfidy and treason; the Christians of Syria no longer united with the Christians of Europe in their attacks upon the city; they were soon informed that the sultans of Aleppo and Mossoul were coming with a numerous army; then they despaired of taking the city, and raised the siege. Thus the Christians, without having exercised their constancy, or tested their courage, abandoned, at the end of a few days, an enterprise, the preparations for which had cost so much to Europe, and raised such expectations in Asia. One of the circumstances of this siege the most worthy of remark is, that Ayoub, chief of the dynasty of the Ayoubites, commanded the troops of Damascus, and that he had with him his son, the young Saladin, who was destined one day to be so formidable to the Christians, and render himself master of Jerusalem. The eldest son of Ayoub having been killed in a sortie, the inhabitants of Damascus raised a tomb of marble to his memory, which was to be seen under the ramparts of the city many centuries after. An old Mussulman priest, who had passed more than forty years in a neighbouring cavern, was obliged to quit his retreat, and came into the city which the Christians were besieging. He regretted his solitude troubled by the din of war, and became ambitious of gathering the palm of martyrdom. In spite of the representations of his disciples, he advanced, unarmed, in the front of the Crusaders, found on the field of battle the death he desired, and was honoured as a saint by the people of Damascus.

If we may believe the Arabian historians, the Christian ecclesiastics who followed the army neglected no means of rekindling the enthusiasm of the soldiers of the cross. During a conflict under the walls of the city, a grey-headed Christian priest, mounted on a mule, and carrying a cross in his hands, advanced between the two armies, exhorting the Crusaders to redouble their bravery and ardour, and promising them, in the name of Jesus Christ, the conquest of Damascus. The Mussulmans directed all their arrows at him; the Christians pressed around to defend him; the combat became fierce and bloody; the priest fell at length pierced with many wounds, upon a heap of slain, and the Crusaders abandoned the field of battle.

The greater part of both Arabian and Latin authors describe the siege of Damascus in a contradictory manner, but all agree in attributing the retreat of the Christians to treachery. A Mussulman historian asserts that the king of Jerusalem received considerable sums from the inhabitants of Damascus, and that he was deceived by the besieged, who gave him pieces of lead covered with a thin coating of gold. Some Latin authors attribute the shameful raising of the siege to the covetousness of

SURPRISED BY THE TURKS.

On quitting Laodicea, a city situated on the Lycus, the Crusaders had directed their course towards the mountains which separate Phrygia from Pisidia. These mountains offered nothing but narrow passages, in which they constantly marched between rocks and precipices. The French army was divided into two bodies, commanded every day by new leaders, who received their orders from the king.

Every evening they laid down in council the route they were to follow the next day, and appointed the place where the army was to encamp. The count de Maurienne, brother of the king, Queen Eleanor, and all the ladies of her suite, who had accompanied the vanguard, pressed Geoffrey de Rançon to descend into the plain. He had the weakness to comply with their wishes; but scarcely had he gained the valley, than the Turks took possession of the heights he had passed, and ranged themselves in order of battle. . . . During this time the rearguard of the army, in which was the king, advanced full of confidence and security; on seeing troops in the woods and on the rocks, they supposed them to be the French, and saluted them with cries of joy. They marched without order, the beasts of burden and the chariots were mingled with the battalions, and the greater part of the soldiers had left their arms with the baggage. The Turks, perfectly motionless, waited in silence till the Christian army should be enclosed in the defiles.—Book VI.

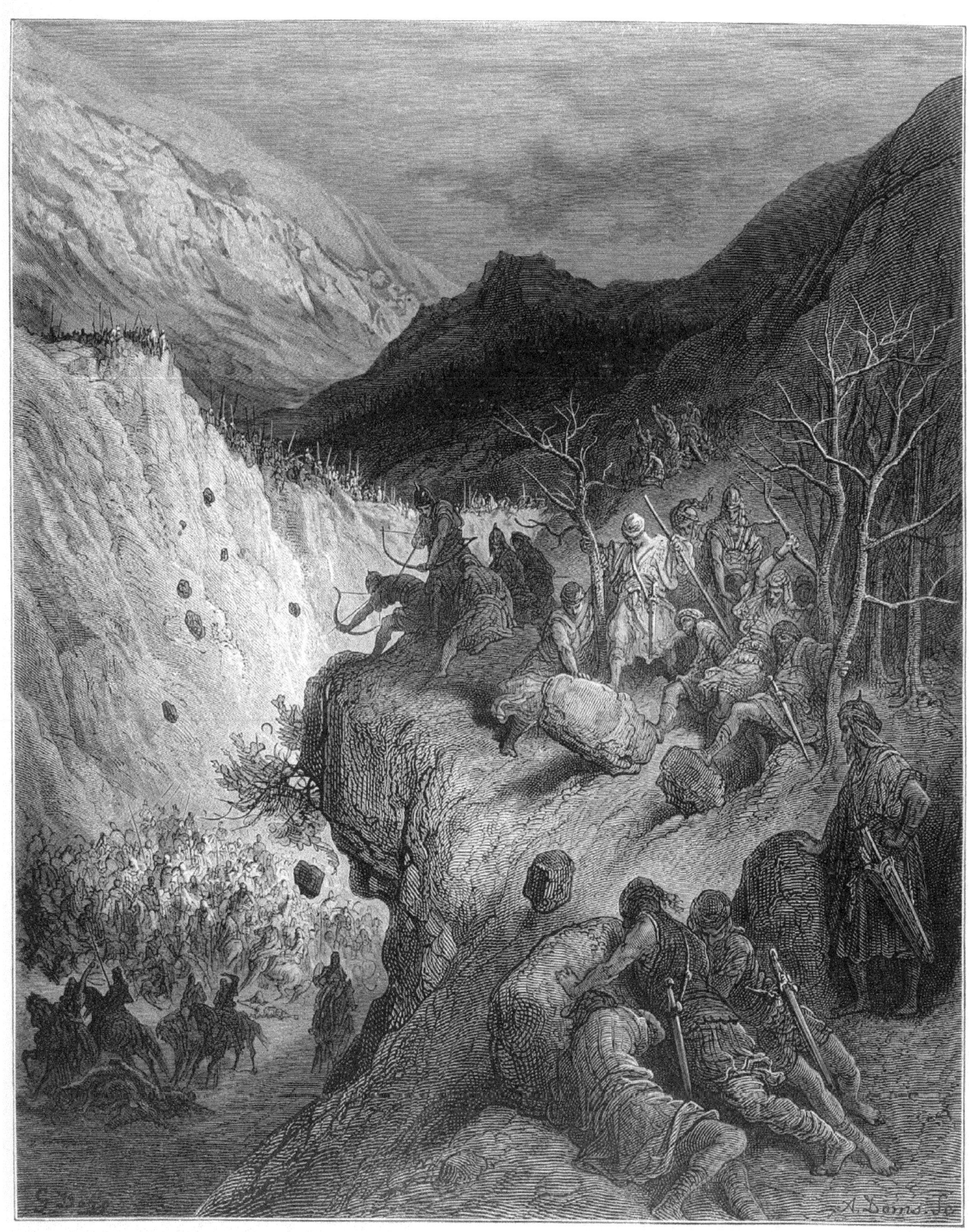

the Templars; others to Raymond of Antioch, who burned to revenge himself on the king of France. William of Tyre, whose opinion ought to have great weight, accuses the barons of Syria; but surely all must blame the ignorance and incapacity of the other chiefs of the crusade, who followed advice without examining it, and proved themselves incapable of remedying an evil they had not foreseen.

After so unfortunate an attempt, it was natural to despair of the success of this war. In the council of leaders the siege of Ascalon was proposed, but men's minds were soured, and their courage was depressed. The king of France and the emperor of Germany thought of returning into Europe, bearing back no other glory than that of having, the one defended his own life against some soldiers on a rock in Pamphylia, and the other of having cleft a giant in two under the walls of Damascus. "From that day," says William of Tyre, "the condition and state of the Oriental Latins began continually to proceed from bad to worse." The Mussulmans learnt no longer to dread the warriors and princes of the West. Full of confidence in their arms, they who had only thought of defending themselves, formed the project of attacking the Franks, and were excited to their enterprise by the hopes of sharing the spoils of an enemy who had invaded several of their provinces. Whilst the infidels thus regained their daring and their pride, and united against their enemies, discouragement took possession of the Christians, and the division which prevailed so fatally among them weakened every day their spirit and their power. "The Franks who returned into Europe" (we leave William of Tyre to speak) "could not forget the perfidies of the Oriental princes, and not only showed themselves more careless and tardy concerning the affairs of the kingdom of Jerusalem, but discouraged all those equally who had not been the voyage with them, so that they who heard speak of this crusade never after undertook the road of this peregrination with so much good-will or so much fervour."

This crusade was much more unfortunate than the first; no kind of glory mitigated or set off the reverses of the Christians. The leaders committed the same faults that Godfrey and his companions had committed; they neglected, as they had done, to found a colony in Asia Minor, and to possess themselves of cities which might protect the march of pilgrims into Syria. We admire the patience with which they endured the outrages and the perfidies of the Greeks; but this moderation, more religious than politic, only led them to their ruin. We must add that they entertained too low an opinion of the Turks, and did not take sufficient heed of the means necessary to contend with them. The Germans, in particular, were so full of confidence, that, according to the report of Nicetas, they would rather have thought of taking shovels and pick-axes with them than swords or lances, believing that they had nothing to do but to cut themselves a road across Asia Minor. By another singularity, the Crusaders, in this war, did not employ the cross-bow, which a council of the Lateran had condemned as too murderous, and the use of which was interdicted to the warriors of the West. The infantry was left almost without arms, and when the Crusaders had lost their cavalry, they had no defence against an enemy.

The Christian armies, as in the first crusade, dragged in their train a great number of children, women, and old men, who could do nothing towards victory, and yet always greatly augmented the disorder and despair consequent upon a defeat. With this multitude no discipline could be established; nor is it apparent that the leaders made any attempt to prevent the effects of license. Geoffrey de Rançon, whose imprudence caused the destruction of half the French army, and placed the king of France in the greatest peril, had no other punishment but his repentance, and thought he expiated his neglect of duty by prostrating himself at the tomb of Christ. That which was still more injurious to discipline was the depravity of manners in the Christian army, which must be principally attributed to the great number of women that had taken arms, and mixed in the ranks of the soldiery. In this crusade there was a troop of Amazons, commanded by a general whose dress was much more admired than her courage, and whose gilded boots procured her the name of *"the lady with the legs of gold."*

Another cause of the dissoluteness of manners was the extreme facility with which the most vicious men, even convicted malefactors, were admitted among the Crusaders. St. Bernard, who considered the crusade as a road to heaven, summoned the greatest sinners to take part in it, and rejoiced at seeing them thus enter into the way of eternal life. In a council of Rheims, of which the abbot of Clairvaux was the oracle, it was decreed that incendiaries should be punished by serving God one year either in Jerusalem or Spain. The ardent preacher of the holy war did not reflect that great sinners, enrolled under the banners of the cross, would be exposed to new temptations, and that during a long voyage it would be much more easy for them to corrupt their companions than to amend their own conduct. Disorders were unhappily tolerated by the leaders, who believed that Heaven was ever indulgent towards Crusaders, and did not wish to be more severe than it.

And yet the Christian army, amidst a most frightful state of morals, presented examples of an austere piety. Surrounded by the dangers of war, and harassed by the fatigues of a long pilgrimage, the king of France never neglected the most minute practices of religion. The greater part of the leaders took him for their model, and when in camp, paid more attention to religious processions than to military exercises; so that many warriors actually placed more confidence in their prayers than in their arms. In general, through the whole of this crusade, sufficient dependence was not placed on human means and human prudence,—everything was left to Providence, which seldom protects those who stray from the ways of reason and wisdom.

The first crusade had two distinctive characters,—piety and heroism; the second had scarcely any other principle but a piety which partook more of the devotion of the cloister than of a generous enthusiasm. The influence of the monks who had preached it, and who then meddled very much in temporal affairs, was but too evident through the whole of this crusade. The king of France in his misfortunes displayed nothing but the resignation of a martyr, and in the field of battle was only distinguished by the ardour and courage of a soldier. The emperor of Germany did not evince greater ability; he lost all by his mad presumption, and from having thought himself able to conquer the Turks without the assistance of the French. Both were limited in their views, and were greatly wanting in that energy which produces great actions. In the expedition which they directed, there was nothing elevated, everything seemed to keep down to the level of their character. In a word, this war developed neither heroic passions nor chivalric qualities. Camps had no great captains to admire or imitate; and the period we have described can boast of only two men of marked genius,—he who had roused the Western world by his eloquence, and the wise minister of Louis, who had to repair in France all the misfortunes of the crusade.

All the energies of this crusade were not directed against Asia. Several preachers, authorized by the Holy See, had exhorted the inhabitants of Saxony and Denmark to take up arms against some nations of the Baltic, still plunged in the darkness of paganism. This crusade was led by Henry of Saxony, several other princes, and a great number of bishops and archbishops. An army, composed of a hundred and fifty thousand Crusaders, attacked the barbarous and savage nation of the Sclaves, who unceasingly ravaged the sea-coasts, and made war upon the Christians. The Christian warriors wore upon their breasts a red cross, under which was a round figure, representing and symbolizing the earth, which ought to be obedient to the laws of Christ. Preachers of the gospel accompanied their march, and exhorted them to extend the limits of Christian Europe by their exploits. The Crusaders consigned to the flames several idolatrous temples, and destroyed the city of Malehon, in which the pagan priests were accustomed to assemble. In this holy war the Saxons treated a pagan people exactly as Charlemagne had treated their own ancestors; but they were not able to subdue the Sclaves. After a war of three years, the Saxon and Danish Crusaders grew weary of pursuing an enemy defended by the sea, and still further by their despair. They made proposals of peace; the Sclaves, on their part, promised to become converts to Christianity, and to respect Christian people.* They only made these promises to pacify their enemies; and when the latter laid down their arms, they returned to their idols and resumed their piracies.

Other Crusaders, to whom Christendom paid very little attention, prosecuted a more successful war on the banks of the Tagus. It was several centuries since Spain had been invaded by the Moors, and still two rival nations disputed empire and fought for territory in the names of Mahomet and Jesus Christ.† The Moors, often conquered by the Cid and his companions, had been driven from several provinces, and when the second crusade set out for the East, the Spaniards were besieging the city of Lisbon. The Christian army, small in numbers, was in daily expectation of reinforcements, when a fleet which was transporting to the East a great number of French Crusaders, entered the mouth of the Tagus. Alphonso, a prince of the house of Burgundy and grandson of King Robert, commanded the besieging army. He visited the Christian warriors, whom Heaven appeared to have sent to his assistance, and promised, as the reward of their co-operation, the conquest of a flourishing kingdom. He exhorted them to join him in combating those same Saracens whom they were going to seek in Asia through all the perils of the sea. "The God who had sent them would bless their army; noble pay and rich possessions would be the meed of their valour." Nothing more was necessary to persuade warriors who had made a vow to fight with the infidels and who were eager for adventures. They abandoned their vessels and joined the besiegers. The Moors opposed them with determined pertinacity, but at the end of four months Lisbon was taken and the garrison put to the sword. They afterwards besieged several other cities, which were wrested from the Saracens; Portugal submitted to the power of Alphonso, and he assumed the title of king. Amidst these conquests the Crusaders forgot the East, and, without incurring much danger, they founded a prosperous and splendid kingdom, which lasted much longer than that of Jerusalem.

We may judge by these crusades, undertaken at the same time, against nations of the north and others of the south, that the principle of holy wars began to assume a new character; Crusaders did not fight only for the possession of a sepulchre, but they took up arms to defend their religion wherever it might be attacked, and to make it triumphant among all nations that rejected its laws and refused its benefits. The diversity of interests which set the Crusaders in action, necessarily divided their forces, weakened their enthusiasm, and was sure to be injurious to the success of a holy war.

France, which then turned anxious looks towards Palestine, no longer demanded of God the deliverance of the holy places, but the return of a king over whose misfortunes they had wept. For a length of time, Suger, who was unable to sustain the royal authority, had endeavoured to recall his master by letters full of tenderness and devotion. Their interview, which proved an affecting spectacle for the French, alarmed the courtiers, who were desirous of awakening suspicions of the fidelity of the minister. A kingdom at peace and a flourishing people were the reply of Suger. The king praised his zeal, and bestowed upon him the title of *Father of his Country*. Suger enjoyed a great advantage, as he had been the only man of any consequence in Europe who had opposed the crusade.

---

* This crusade from the north is mentioned by Otto of Frisingen. Saxo the grammarian gives the most ample details in his thirteenth book. The reader may likewise consult the Latin *History of Germany*, by Kruntz. The *History of Denmark*, by Mallet, does not say a word of this war.

†Arnold, a Flemish preacher, on the publication of the second crusade, exhorted the nations of France and Germany to enrol themselves in this pious army; he followed the Crusaders who laid siege to Lisbon, under the command of Arnold count d'Arschot. Arnold sent an account of this siege to Milo, bishop of Terouane, in a letter published by Dom Martène, in the first volume of his great collection, upon two manuscripts. The relation of Arnold, an eye-witness, different from that of Robert of the Mount, is adopted by Fleury. The historian of Portugal, Manoel de Faria y Sousa, speaks also of this expedition of the Crusaders.

His wise foresight was everywhere the subject of praise, whilst all complaints were directed against St. Bernard. There was not a family in the kingdom that was not in mourning; and the same desolation reigned throughout Germany. So many widows and orphans had never been seen, and the glory of martyrdom, promised to all whose loss was regretted, had no power to dry their tears. The abbot of Clairvaux was accused of having sent Christians to die in the East, as if Europe had been without sepulchres; and the partisans of St. Bernard, who had seen his mission attested by his miracles, not knowing what to reply, were struck with stupor and astonishment. "God, in these latter days," said they among themselves, "has neither spared his people nor his name; the children of the Church have been given over to death in the desert, or massacred by the sword, or devoured by hunger; the contempt of the Lord has fallen even upon princes; God has left them to wander in unknown ways, and all sorts of pains and afflictions have been strewed upon their paths." So many evils resulting from a holy war, from a war undertaken in the name of God, confounded the Christians who had most applauded the crusade, and St. Bernard himself was astonished that God had been willing to judge the universe before the time, and without remembrance of his mercy. "What a disgrace is it for us," said he in an apology addressed to the pope, "for us who went everywhere announcing peace and happiness! Have we conducted ourselves rashly? Have our courses been adopted from fantasy? Have we not followed the orders of the head of the Church and those of the Lord? Why has not God regarded our fasts? Why has he appeared to know nothing of our humiliations? With what patience is he now listening to the sacrilegious and blasphemous voices of the nations of Arabia, who accuse him of having led his people into the desert that they might perish! All the world knows," added he, "that the judgments of the Lord are just; but this is so profound an abyss, that he may be called happy who is not disgraced by it." St. Bernard was so thoroughly persuaded that the unfortunate issue of the crusade would furnish the wicked with an excuse for insulting the Deity, that he congratulated himself that so many of the maledictions of men fell upon him, making him as a buckler to the living God. In his apology, he attributes the want of success in the holy war to the disorders and crimes of the Christians; he compares the Crusaders to the Hebrews, to whom Moses had promised, in the name of Heaven, a land of blessedness, and who all perished on their journey, because they had done a thousand things against God.

St. Bernard might have been answered that he ought to have foreseen the excesses and disorders of an undisciplined multitude, and that the brigands called upon to take up the cross were not the people of God. It appears to us, at the present time, that the partisans of the abbot of Clairvaux might have found better reasons for the justification of the holy war. The second crusade, although unfortunate, procured several advantages for Europe. The peace which reigned in the West, caused states to flourish, and repaired, in some sort, the disasters of a distant war. It was held shameful to carry arms in Europe, whilst the Crusaders were contending with the Saracens in the East. Religion itself watched over Germany, which had been so long troubled by civil wars. Conrad, a weak monarch without character, who had lost his army in Asia, was more powerful on his return from Palestine than he had been before he quitted his dominions. The king of France also found his authority increased, from having been defended during his absence by the thunders of the Church and the eloquence of St. Bernard. The crusade gave him a pretext for imposing taxes upon his people, and placed him at the head of a numerous army, where he accustomed the great vassals to consider him as their supreme head.

Still, if it is true that the divorce of Eleanor of Guienne was one of the consequences of the crusade, it must be admitted that the evils which resulted from this war were much greater for the French monarchy than any good it derived from it. The kingdom which then lost the province of Aquitaine,

LOUIS VII.

The bravest rallied around the king, and advanced toward the top of the mountain. Thirty of the principal nobles that accompanied Louis perished by his side, selling their lives dearly. The king remained almost alone on the field of battle, and took refuge upon a rock, whence he braved the attack of the infidels who pursued him. With his back against a tree, he singly resisted the efforts of several Saracens, who, taking him for a simple soldier, at length left him, to secure their share of the pillage. Although the night began to fall, the king expected to be attacked again, when the voices of some Frenchmen who had escaped the carnage, gave him the agreeable information that the Turks had retired. He mounted a stray horse, and, after a thousand perils, rejoined his vanguard, where all were lamenting his death.—BOOK VI.

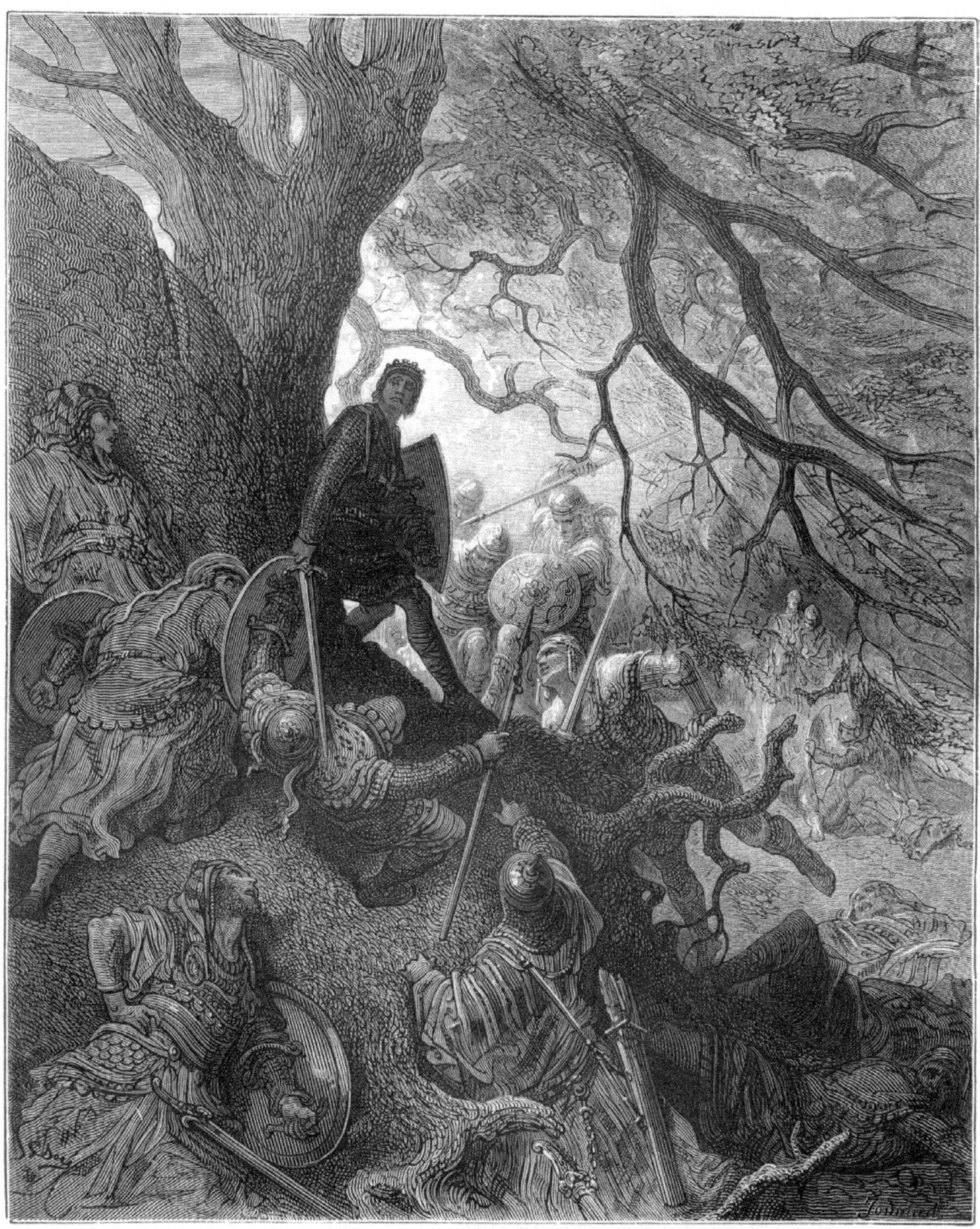

which fell into the hands of the English, was doomed to become the prey of the children that Eleanor had by her second marriage. A following age saw the descendants of these children crowned kings of France and England in the church of Notre Dame, at Paris, and the successors of Louis VII. found themselves almost reduced to seek an asylum in foreign lands.

Flattery undertook to console Louis the young, for the reverses he had experienced in Asia, and represented him, upon several medals,* as the conqueror of the East. He left Palestine with the project of returning thither; and in his journey to Rome, he promised the pope to place himself at the head of a new crusade.

And never did the Christian colonies stand in greater need of assistance. From the time the French quitted Palestine not a day passed without some new misfortune befalling the Christians established in Syria. A very short time after the siege of Damascus, Raymond of Poictiers lost his life in a battle against the Saracens, and his head was sent to the caliph of Bagdad. Josselin, after having lost the city of Edessa, himself fell into the hands of the infidels, and died in misery and despair in the prisons of Aleppo. Two emissaries of the Old Man of the Mountain assassinated Raymond II., count of Tripoli, under the walls of his capital, which was plunged into trouble and desolation. Two young Mussulman princes, of the family of Ortok, excited by their mother, believed that the moment was come to reconquer Jerusalem from the Christians. An army which they had assembled, came and pitched its camp on the Mount of Olives, and the holy city only owed its safety to the courage of some knights who induced the people to take arms. Noureddin had got possession of all the Christian cities of Mesopotamia, and several places in the principality of Antioch had opened their gates to him. Arrived on the shores of the sea, which he had never before seen, he bathed in its waves, as if to take possession of it; and, still accompanied by victory, he established the seat of his empire at Damascus, whence he menaced the city of Jerusalem.

The afflicting news of these occurrences created great sorrow among the Christians of the West, and the sovereign pontiff exhorted the faithful once again to take up the cross and arms; but neither the danger of the Christians beyond the sea, nor the exhortations of the pope, could change the opinion which the French had formed against distant wars. Louis VII. was obliged to renounce his intention of returning to the Holy Land. At this period a circumstance occurred which it is very difficult to give credit to. The abbot Suger, who had so strongly opposed the first expedition, formed the resolution of succouring Jerusalem; and in an assembly held at Chartres, exhorted the princes, barons, and bishops to enrol themselves under the banners of the holy war. As he was only answered by the silence of grief and astonishment, he formed the project of attempting an enterprise alone in which two monarchs had failed. Suger, at the age of seventy, resolved to raise an army, to maintain it at his own expense, and to lead it himself into Palestine. In accordance with the devotion of the time, he went to Tours, to visit the tomb of St. Martin, in order to obtain the protection of Heaven, and already ten thousand pilgrims had taken up arms, and were preparing to follow him into Asia, when death came to prevent the execution of his designs.

In his last moments Suger invoked the assistance and the prayers of St. Bernard, who sustained his courage, and exhorted him not to turn his thoughts from the heavenly Jerusalem, in which both of them hoped soon to meet; but in spite of the exhortations of his friend, the abbot of St. Denis regretted, when dying, not having been able to succour the holy city. St. Bernard was not long

* The legend of one of these medals is conceived in these terms:—

Regi invicto ab oriente reduci,
Frementes lætitia cives.

In another medal the Meander is represented, and a trophy raised upon its banks, with this inscription—

Turcis ad ripas Mæandri cæsis fugatis.

before he followed Suger to the tomb, bearing with him a deep regret at having preached an unfortunate war.

France lost in the same year two men who had greatly illustrated her, the one by talents and qualities useful to his country, the other by his eloquence and virtues dear to all Christians. At a time when general attention was given to the defence of the privileges of the Church, Suger defended the interests of royalty and the people; whilst eloquent preachers were animating the public zeal for holy wars which were always accompanied by disasters, the skilful minister of Louis VII. was preparing France, at a future day, to gather the salutary fruits of these great events. He was accused of having gone too deeply into the mundane affairs of his age; but politics never banished from his mind the precepts of the gospel. According to the judgment of his contemporaries, he lived at the court like a wise courtier, and in his cloister like a pious monk. If there is in the church of France, wrote St. Bernard to Pope Eugenius, any vase of price which would embellish the palace of the King of kings, it is doubtless the venerable abbot Suger. As abbot of St. Denis, he, perhaps, enjoyed more wealth than any monk ought to possess, since we see he proposed to maintain an army, but he always employed his treasures in the service of his country and the Church, and never had the state been so rich as under his administration. His whole life was a long series of prosperity, and of actions worthy of being remembered. He reformed the monks of his order without incurring their hatred; he created the happiness of the people without proving their ingratitude; and served kings, and yet obtained their friendship. Fortune favoured all his undertakings, and that there should be nothing unprosperous in his life, and that he might be reproached with no fault, he died when he was about to conduct an army to the East.

Suger and St. Bernard, united by religion and friendship, had a very different destiny; the first, born in a low condition, gave himself to the disposal of fortune, which carried him up to the highest dignities; the second, born in a more elevated rank, hastened to descend from it, and was nothing but by his genius. St. Bernard rendered few services to the state, but he defended religion with indefatigable zeal; and as *church* then took precedence of *country*, he was greater than the abbot Suger in the eyes of his contemporaries. Whilst he lived, the eyes of all Europe were fixed upon the abbot of Clairvaux; he was as a light placed in the midst of Christendom, every word he preached had the holy authority of the religion he taught. He stifled all schisms, silenced all impostors, and by his labours, merited in his age the title of *the last father of the Church*, as richly as the great Bossuet merited it in his.

St. Bernard may be reproached with having too frequently issued from his retreat, and with not having always been, as he himself expresses it, the disciple of oaks and beeches. He had a hand in most of the political events of his time, and interfered in all the affairs of the Holy See. Christians often asked who was the head of the Church; popes and princes sometimes murmured against his authority; but it must never be forgotten that he unceasingly preached moderation to kings, humanity to the people, and poverty to the clergy.

BOOK VII.

THE THIRD CRUSADE.

A. D. 1148–1188.

The religion of Mahomet—State of the East at the time of the third crusade—Dynasties of the Saracens and the Turks almost annihilated—Caliphs of Bagdad, the chiefs of Islamism—Heroic character of Noureddin—Capture of Ascalon by Baldwin III.—Baldwin's death—His brother Amaury elected his successor—Distracted state of Egypt—Warlike preparations against—Capture of Bilbeis by Baldwin—The Syrians invade Egypt—Baldwin marries the daughter of the emperor Manuel—Makes war on Egypt—Deposition and death of the caliph—The Fatimite dynasty extinguished—Extensive power of Noureddin, the sultan of Aleppo and Damascus—Saladin, the vizier of Egypt—Death of Noureddin—Empire of the Atabecks declines—Death of Amaury—The victories of Saladin in Syria—Baldwin IV., king of Jerusalem—The Mamelukes—Guy of Lusignan—Renaud de Chatillon—Raised to the throne of Antioch—His various military adventures—Rebellion of Guy de Lusignan—Distracted state of Jerusalem—Interview between Henry II. of England and Heraclius, patriarch of Constantinople—Philip Augustus, king of France—Deaths of Baldwin IV. and V.—Guy de Lusignan, the sovereign of Jerusalem—Sybilla, daughter of Amaury—The Templars defeated with great slaughter—Tiberias taken by Saladin—Disastrous defeat of the Christians—Capture of the "true cross"—Guy de Lusignan and many distinguished knights taken prisoners or slain—Saladin captures Ptolemaïs, Ascalon, Gaza, and numerous other cities in Palestine—He takes possession of Jerusalem—Sufferings of the Christians—The archbishop of Tyre preaches in support of the holy war—Henry II. of England, Richard I. and Philip of France determine on renewing the holy war—Persecution and massacre of the Jews—Archbishop Baldwin preaches the crusade in England—Frederick Barbarossa engages in the crusade—Miraculous vision—Contentions between the Greeks and the Latins—Andronicus of Constantinople dethroned—The Greeks defeated by Barbarossa—His victorious career—His death.

WE cannot help being convinced, whilst reading this history, that the religion of Mahomet, thoroughly warlike as it is in principle, does not endue its disciples with that obstinate bravery, that boundless devotedness, of which the Crusaders presented so many examples. The fanaticism of the Mussulmans required victory to keep up its power or its violence. Bred in a conviction of blind fatalism, they were accustomed to consider successes or reverses as simple decrees of Heaven; victorious, they were full of ardour and confidence; conquered, they were depressed, and without shame succumbed to an enemy, whom they believed to be the instrument of destiny. An ambition for renown seldom excited their courage, and even in the excesses of their warlike fervour, the fear of chastisements and punishments kept their faces towards the enemy more frequently than any generous love of glory. A chief, whom they themselves dreaded, was the only captain that could lead them to victory; and thus despotism became necessary to their valour.

After the conquest of the Christians, the dynasties of the Saracens and the Turks were dispersed and almost annihilated; the Seljoucides themselves had fallen back to the very extremities of Persia, and the people of Syria scarcely knew the names of those princes whose ancestors had reigned over Asia. Everything, even despotism, was destroyed in the East. The ambition of the emirs took advantage of the general disorder; slaves shared the spoils of their masters; provinces and cities became so many principalities, the uncertain and transient possession of which was a constant subject of dispute. The necessity for defending the Mussulman religion, whilst threatened by the Christians, had alone preserved the credit of the caliphs of Bagdad. They were still the chiefs of Islamism; their approbation seemed necessary for the preservation of the power of usurpers or conquerors; but their authority, which was nothing but a sacred phantom, commanded nothing but prayers and vain ceremonies, and inspired not the least fear. In this state of degradation their only employment seemed to be to consecrate the fruit of treachery and violence. It was not sufficient to bestow cities and employments which they had no power to refuse; all whom victory and license had favoured came to prostrate themselves before the vicars of the prophet; and crowds of emirs, viziers, and sultans, to borrow an Eastern expression, appeared to rise from the dust of their feet.

The Christians were not sufficiently aware of the state of Asia, which they might have conquered; and agreed so ill among themselves that they could never take advantage of the divisions which prevailed among their enemies. They seldom had, either in attack or defence, a well-sustained plan, and their impetuous bravery, directed generally by chance or passion, could only be compared to the tempest, whose fury rages or abates at the pleasure of the winds which reign over the horizon. Fortune, which had offered them such a brilliant opportunity for extending their empire, became, at last, adverse to them, and from the bosom of the chaos in which the East was plunged, arose a formidable power, which was destined to conquer and destroy them.

Noureddin, son of Zengui, who had obtained possession of Edessa before the second crusade, had inherited the conquests of his father, and added to them by his valour. He was bred among warriors who had sworn to shed their blood in the cause of the Prophet, and when he mounted the throne he revived the austere simplicity of the early caliphs. Noureddin, says an Arabian poet, united the most noble heroism with the profoundest humility. When he prayed in the temple, his subjects believed they saw a sanctuary in another sanctuary. He encouraged the sciences, cultivated letters, and, above all, applied himself to the maintenance of justice throughout his states. His people admired his clemency and moderation; and the Christians even were forced to praise his courage and his profane heroism. After the example of his father Zengui, he made himself the idol of his soldiers by his liberality; by taking charge of their families, he prevented their desire for the possession of lands, and thus accustomed them to consider the camp as their home and their country. In the midst of armies which he had himself formed, and which respected in him the avenger of the Prophet, he restrained the ambition of the emirs, and directed their efforts and their zeal towards one sole object, the triumph of Islamism. His victories, his fortune, his religious and political virtues drew upon him the attention of the entire East, and made the Mussulmans believe that the period of their deliverance had arrived.

Baldwin III., who undertook to stop the career of Noureddin, displayed great valour in several battles. The most important and the most fortunate of his expeditions was the taking of Ascalon, in which the Mussulmans always kept up a formidable garrison. This city, which is situated in a fertile plain, and which the Mussulmans call *the Spouse of Syria*, was succoured by an Egyptian fleet, and for a long time resisted all the efforts of the Christians. Rivers of blood flowed before its walls during several months; both Mussulmans and Christians fighting with fury, and neither giving nor receiving quarter. During the siege the knights of the Temple particularly distinguished themselves by their valour; the thirst for booty, far more than the love of glory, making them brave the greatest perils. The garrison and the inhabitants, exhausted by fatigue and pinched by famine, at length opened the gates of the city. Baldwin granted them a capitulation, permitted them to retire into Egypt with their families, and caused a *Te Deum* to be sung in the great mosque, which he consecrated to St. Paul.

After this victory the king of Jerusalem marched to encounter Noureddin, and compelled him to raise the sieges of both Paneas and Sidon. Baldwin was engaged in assisting the principality of Anti-

SALADIN.

Saladin was sprung from the people who inhabit the mountains situated beyond the Tigris. . . .Brought up at the court of Damascus, people saw in him nothing but a young dissipated soldier, without ambition ; . . . but he changed his conduct and reformed his manners; hitherto he had appeared fit only for the idleness and the obscurity of a seraglio; but, all at once, he came forth a new man, like one born for an empire. . . . . The Mussulmans, always governed by fear, were astonished that a sovereign could inspire them with so much love, and followed him with joy to battle. His generosity, his clemency, and particularly his respect for an oath, were often the subjects of admiration to the Christians, whom he rendered so miserable by his victories, and of whose power in Asia he had completed the overthrow.—Books VI. and VII.

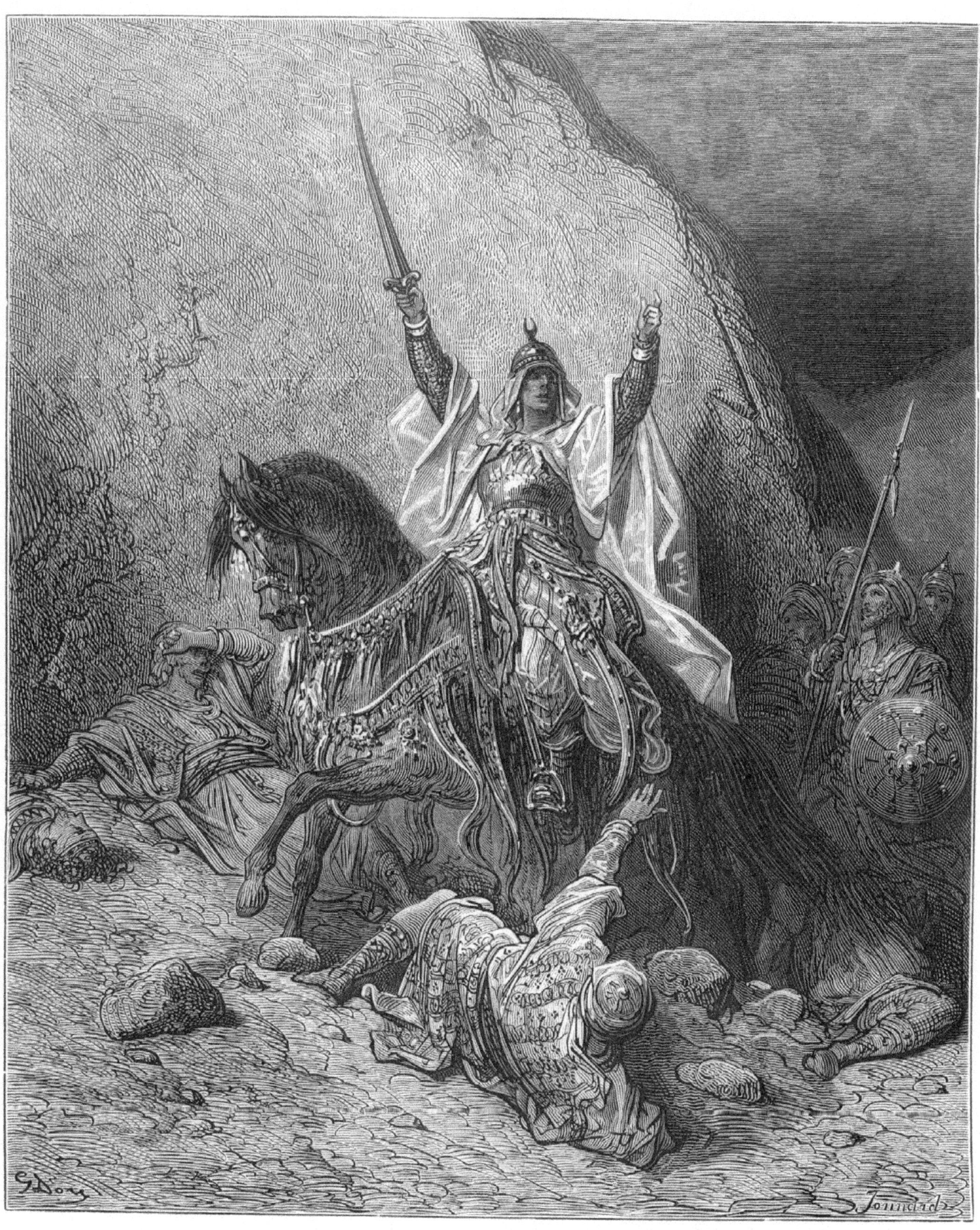

och, always disturbed by factions, always threatened by the Mussulmans, when he was poisoned by a Syrian physician. As soon as he became sensible of his danger, he set out for Jerusalem, and died in the city of Berouth. His remains were transported to the holy city, the clergy coming out to meet the funeral train. The people descended from the mountains to join the procession, and through the country and in the cities nothing was heard but lamentations. Noureddin himself, if we are to believe a Christian historian, was affected by the sorrow of the Franks. Some of his emirs advising him to take advantage of this melancholy occasion to enter Palestine, "God forbid," replied he, "that I should disturb the proper grief of a people who are weeping for the loss of so good a king, or fix upon such an opportunity to attack a kingdom which I have no reason to fear." Remarkable words, which at once denote two great men, and which further show what a serious loss the Christians had sustained.

As soon as the funeral ceremonies of Baldwin III. were over, warm debates arose upon the choice of a successor. The greater part of the barons and knights attached to the memory of Baldwin proposed to call to the throne his brother Amaury, count of Jaffa and Ascalon. This party was the most reasonable and the most conformable to the laws and interests of the kingdom; but the brother of Baldwin, by the haughtiness of his deportment, had made himself many enemies among the people, the clergy, and the army. He was reproached with an ambition and an avarice fatal to the interests of the Christians; and he was accused of not being restrained by honour, justice, or even the precepts of religion, in the execution of his projects. His partisans extolled his active and enterprising character, his bravery so often proved, and his great skill in war. Among the nobles of the kingdom who opposed his succession, and attributed to him ambitious views much to be dreaded, were several who themselves nourished aspiring projects, and allowed themselves to be seduced by the hope of ascending the throne. The conflicting parties were on the point of taking up arms to sustain their pretensions or their hopes, when the grand master of the Hospitallers exhorted the barons and knights to preserve the peace and the laws of the kingdom by crowning young Amaury. "The crown," said he to them, "which you refuse to place upon the head of a Christian prince will soon be upon that of Noureddin or the caliph of Egypt. If this misfortune should happen, you will become the slaves of the infidels, and the world will accuse you of having opened the gates of the holy city to the Saracens, as the traitor Judas gave up the Saviour of the world into the hands of his enemies." This speech, and the sight of the troops which Amaury had already collected to defend his rights, disarmed the factions which disturbed the kingdom. The brother of Baldwin was crowned in the Holy Sepulchre, and received the oaths of allegiance of those even who had openly declared themselves opposed to his claims.

As soon as Amaury had ascended the throne, he directed all his energies towards Egypt, now weakened by the victories of the Christians. The caliph of Cairo having refused to pay the tribute due to the conquerors of Ascalon, the new king of Jerusalem placed himself at the head of his army, traversed the desert, carried the terror of his arms to the banks of the Nile, and only returned to his kingdom when he had forced the Egyptians to purchase peace. The state in which Egypt was then placed was likely soon to recall the Christians thither; and happy would it have been for them if they had known how to profit by their advantages; and if their fruitless attempts had not served to favour the progress of a rival power.

Egypt was at that time the theatre of a civil war, occasioned by the ambition of two leaders who disputed the empire of it. For a length of time the caliphs of Cairo, like those of Bagdad, shut up in their seraglio, had borne no resemblance to the warrior from whom they derived their origin, who had said, whilst pointing to his soldiers and his sword, "*These are my family and my race.*" Enervated by effeminacy and pleasures, they had abandoned the government to their slaves, who adored them on their knees, and imposed laws upon them. They no longer exercised any real authority but in the mosques, and only preserved the disgraceful privilege of confirming the usurped power of the viziers, who corrupted the armies, disturbed the provinces, and in the field of battle quarrelled with each other for the right of reigning over both people and prince.

Each of the viziers, to secure the triumph of his cause, called in by turns the arms of the neighbouring powers. On the arrival of these dangerous auxiliaries, all was in confusion on the banks of the Nile. Blood flowed in all the provinces, sometimes shed by the executioners, sometimes by the soldiers; Egypt was at once desolated by its enemies, its allies, and its inhabitants.

Chaver, who, amidst these revolutions, had raised himself from the humble condition of a slave to the post of vizier, had been conquered and displaced by Dargan, one of the principal officers of the Egyptian militia. Obliged to fly and abandon Egypt, where his rival reigned, he went to seek an asylum at Damascus, imploring the assistance of Noureddin, and promising a considerable tribute if that prince would furnish him with troops to protect his return into Egypt. The sultan of Damascus yielded to the prayers of Chaver. To command the army which he resolved to send into Egypt, he selected Chirkou, the most skilful of his emirs, who having always shown himself cruel and implacable in his military expeditions, was likely to be without pity for the vanquished, and to take all advantage of the miseries of a civil war, for the benefit of his master. The vizier Dargan was not long in being warned of the projects of Chaver and the preparations of Noureddin. To resist the storm about to burst upon him, he implored the aid of the Christians of Palestine, and promised to give up his treasures to them if they succeeded in preserving his power.

Whilst the king of Jerusalem, seduced by this promise, was collecting an army, Chaver, accompanied by the troops of Noureddin, crossed the desert, and approached the banks of the Nile. Dargan, who came out to meet him with the Egyptian army, was conquered by the Syrians, and lost his life in the battle. The city of Cairo soon opened its gates to the conqueror. Chaver, whom the victory had delivered from his enemy, shed torrents of blood in the capital to insure his triumph, received amid the general consternation the congratulations of the caliph, and resumed the reins of government.

It was not long, however, before divisions arose between the general of Noureddin, who daily placed a more excessive price on his services, and the vizier, whom Chirkou accused of perfidy and ingratitude. Chaver desired in vain to send the Mussulmans back into Syria; they replied to him only by threats, and he was on the point of being besieged in Cairo by his own deliverers. All the Egyptians, particularly the people of the capital, were seized with trouble and consternation.

In the midst of so pressing a danger, the vizier Chaver placed his only hope in the Christian warriors, whose approach he had not long since so much dreaded. He made the king of Jerusalem the same promises that he had offered to Noureddin; and Amaury, who only wanted to enter Egypt, whatever might be the party that prevailed there, set out upon his march to defend Chaver with the very same army he had collected to fight against him. When arrived on the banks of the Nile, he united his troops with those of the vizier, and they sat down before the city of Bilbeis, into which Chirkou had retired. Noureddin's general resisted during three months all the attacks of the Christians and Egyptians; and when the king of Jerusalem proposed peace to him, he demanded payment of the expenses of the war. After some negotiations, in which he displayed great haughtiness, he marched out of Bilbeis still threatening the Christians, and led back his army to Damascus, loaded with the spoils of his enemies.

Chirkou had beheld the riches of Egypt, and become acquainted with the weakness of its government; the first advice he offered to Noureddin, after his arrival, therefore, was to endeavour to unite this rich country to his own empire. The sultan of Syria sent ambassadors to the caliph of Bagdad, not to ask aid of him, but to give a religious colour to his enterprise. During several centuries, the caliphs of Bagdad and Cairo had been divided by an implacable hatred; each of them boasting of being the vicar of the Prophet, and considering his rival as the enemy of God. In the mosques of Bagdad, they cursed the caliphs of Egypt and their sectarians; in those of Cairo, they devoted to the infernal powers, the Abassides and their partisans.

The caliph of Bagdad did not hesitate to comply with the wishes of Noureddin. Whilst the sultan of Syria was solely occupied by his endeavours to extend his empire, the vicar of the Prophet was only ambitious to preside alone over the Mussulman religion. He commanded the Imans to preach a war against the Fatimites, and promised the delights of Paradise to all who should take up arms in the holy expedition. At the call of the caliph, a great number of faithful Mussulmans flocked to the standard of Noureddin, and Chirkou, by the order of the sultan, prepared to return into Egypt, at the head of a powerful army.

The fame of these preparations spread throughout the East, particularly in Egypt, where it created the most serious alarms. Amaury, who had returned to his own states, received ambassadors from Chaver, soliciting his help and alliance against the enterprise of Noureddin. The states of the kingdom of Jerusalem were assembled at Naplouse, and the king there exposed to them the advantages of another expedition into Egypt. An impost was levied to carry on a war from which the greatest hopes were entertained, and the Christian army soon set out from Gaza to fight with the troops of Noureddin on the banks of the Nile.

In the mean time Chirkou was crossing the desert, where he encountered the greatest dangers. A violent tempest surprised him on his march; all at once the heavens were darkened, and the earth, which was strewed with the prostrate Syrians, became like a stormy sea. Immense waves of sand were lifted by the winds, and rising into whirlwinds or forming moving mountains, scattered, bore away, or swallowed up men and horses. In this tempest the Syrian army abandoned its baggage and lost its provisions and arms, and when Chirkou arrived on the banks of the Nile, he had no means of defence left except the remembrance of his former victories. He took great care to conceal the losses he had experienced, and the wreck of an army dispersed by a fearful tempest proved sufficient to throw all the cities of Egypt into consternation.

The vizier Chaver, frightened at the approach of the Syrians, sent ambassadors to the Christians, to promise them immense riches, and press them to hasten their march. On his side, the king of Jerusalem deputed to the caliph of Egypt, Hugh of Cæsarea, and Foulcher, a knight of the Temple, to obtain the ratification of the treaty of alliance with the Egyptians. Amaury's deputies were introduced into a palace in which no Christian had ever before been admitted. After having traversed several corridors filled with Moorish guards, and a vast number of apartments and courts in which glittered all the splendour of the East, they arrived in a hall, or rather a sanctuary, where the caliph awaited them, seated on a throne shining with gold and precious stones. Chaver, who conducted them, prostrated himself at the feet of his master, and supplicated him to accept the treaty of alliance with the king of Jerusalem. The prayer of the vizier was an imperious order, and the commander of the faithful, always docile to the will of the lowest of his slaves, made a sign of approbation, and stretched his uncovered hand out to the Christian deputies in presence of the officers of his court, whom so strange a spectacle filled with grief and surprise.

The army of the Franks was close to Cairo; but as the policy of Amaury was to lengthen the war, in order to prolong his stay in Egypt, he neglected opportunities of attacking the Syrians with advantage, and gave them time to recruit their strength. After having left them a long time in repose, he gave them battle in the isle of Maalle, and forced their intrenchments, but did not follow up his victory. Chirkou, in his retreat, endeavoured to reanimate the depressed courage of the soldiers of Noureddin, the latter not having yet forgotten the evils they had encountered in the passage over the desert. This calamity, still recent, together with the first victory of the Christians, destroyed the confidence they had in their arms and the protection of the Prophet. One of the lieutenants of Chirkou, upon witnessing their gloomy rage, cried out in the midst of the Mussulman army: "You who fear death or slavery, return into Syria; go and tell Noureddin that to repay him for the benefits with which he has loaded you, you abandon Egypt to the infidels, in order to shut yourselves up in your seraglios with women and children."

These words reanimated the zeal and fanaticism of the Syrian warriors. The Franks and the Egyptians who pursued the army of Chirkou, were conquered in a battle, and forced to abandon in disorder the hills of Baben,* where they had pitched their tents. The general of Noureddin took all possible advantage of his victory; he passed as a conqueror along the fertile banks of the Nile; penetrated, without encountering an obstacle, into lower Egypt; placed a garrison in Alexandria; and returned to lay siege to the city of Koutz, the capital of the Thebais. The ability with which Chirkou had disciplined his army, and planned the last battle he had fought with his enemies; his marches and his counter-marches in the plains and valleys of Egypt, from the tropic to the sea, announced the progress of the Mussulmans in military tactics, and warned the Christians beforehand of the enemy that was destined to put an end to their victories and conquests.

The Turks defended themselves during several months in Alexandria, against the seditions of the inhabitants and the numerous assaults of the Christians. They at length obtained an honourable capitulation, and as their army was becoming weaker every day by famine and fatigue, they retired a second time to Damascus, after exacting very dear payment for the transient tranquillity in which they left the people of Egypt.

After the retreat of the Syrians, the vizier Chaver hastened to send back the Christians, whose presence made him very uneasy. He engaged to pay the king of Jerusalem an annual tribute of a hundred thousand crowns in gold, and consented to receive a garrison in Cairo. He loaded the barons and knights with rich presents, and the soldiers even had a share in his bounties, proportionate to the fear the Franks inspired him with. The Christian warriors returned to Jerusalem, bearing with them riches which dazzled both people and nobles, and inspired them with other thoughts than that of defending the heritage of Christ.

As Amaury returned to his capital, the sight of his mountainous and sterile provinces, the poverty of his subjects, and the narrow limits of his kingdom, made him deeply regret having missed the opportunity of conquering a great empire. Soon after his return he married a niece of the Emperor Manuel; but whilst the people and his court gave themselves up to joy, and put up vows for the prosperity of his family and his kingdom, one single thought occupied him night and day, and haunted him even amongst the most sumptuous and brilliant festivities. The riches of the caliph of Cairo, the populousness and fertility of Egypt, its numerous fleets, and the commodiousness of its ports, presented themselves constantly to the mind of Amaury. His first endeavour was to make the marriage he had just contracted subservient to his projects, and he sent ambassadors to Constantinople, with instructions to induce Manuel to assist him in the conquest of Egypt. Manuel approved of the plans of the king of Jerusalem, and promised to send him fleets and share with him the glory and perils of a conquest which must so deeply interest the Christian world. Then Amaury hesitated no longer to declare his designs, and called together the barons and principal people of his kingdom.

* Near the castle of Toura, two leagues from Cairo, opposite ancient Memphis.

In this assembly, in which it was proposed to invade Egypt, the wisest, among whom was the grand master of the Templars, declared loudly and decidedly that the undertaking was unjust. "The Christians," said they, "ought not to set the Mussulmans the example of violating treaties. It perhaps would not be a difficult matter to obtain possession of Egypt, but it would not be so easy to keep it as to conquer it. Noureddin was the most formidable enemy of the Christians; it was against him they should bring all the united forces of the kingdom to bear. Egypt must belong to the power that should remain ruler of Syria, and it was not prudent or wise to endeavour to anticipate the favours of fortune, and send armies into a country of which they should only open the gates to the son of Zengui, as they had done in the instance of Damascus. They would sacrifice Christian cities, Jerusalem itself, to the hope of conquering a kingdom. Noureddin had already taken advantage of the king of Jerusalem's being engaged on the banks of the Nile, to get possession of several places which belonged to the Christians. Bohemond prince of Antioch, and Raymond count of Tripoli, had been made prisoners of war, and groaned in the chains of the Mussulmans, as victims of an ambition which had seduced the king of Jerusalem far from his kingdom and the Christian colonies of which he ought to be the support and defender."

The knights and barons who expressed themselves thus, added that the sight alone of Egypt would not fail to corrupt the Christian warriors, and enervate the courage and subdue the patriotism of the inhabitants and defenders of Palestine. These opinions, however prudent and just, had no effect upon the king of Jerusalem and the partisans of the war, among whom was conspicuous the grand master of the Hospitallers, who had exhausted the riches of his order by extravagant expenses, and had raised troops for whose pay he had assigned the treasures of Egypt. The greater part of the lords and knights, to whom fortune seemed to be waiting on the banks of the Nile in order to bestow upon them her favours, suffered themselves to be easily persuaded to the war, and found it very convenient to consider as an enemy the sovereign of a country which held out so rich a booty to them.

Whilst these preparations for the conquest of Egypt were in agitation in Jerusalem, the same projects occupied the emirs and the council of Noureddin. On his return from the banks of the Nile, Chirkou had announced to the sultan of Damascus, "that the government of Cairo wanted both officers and soldiers; and that revolutions, the cupidity of the Franks, and the presence of the Syrians, had weakened and ruined the empire of the Fatimites. The Egyptian people," added he, "accustomed to change masters, were neither attached to the caliph, whom they did not know, nor to the vizier, who brought upon them all sorts of calamities. They were ready to submit to the domination of a prince who should be powerful enough to protect them against both their enemies and the scourge of civil wars. The Christians were likewise aware how feeble this empire was, and it was to be dreaded that they would be the first. Such a favourable opportunity should not be neglected, or a conquest despised which fortune appeared to offer to the first power that should make its appearance in Egypt."

Thus the king of Jerusalem and the sultan of Damascus entertained the same views, and both made preparations for the same conquest. In the churches of the Christians, as in the mosques of the Mussulmans, prayers were put up for the success of a war about to be carried on on the banks of the Nile. As each of the two parties sought to give the best colour to their projects and proceedings, at Damascus it was asserted that the caliph of Egypt had made an impious alliance with the disciples of Christ, whilst at Jerusalem it was asserted that the vizier Chaver, in defiance of treaties, kept up a perfidious correspondence with Noureddin.

The Christians were the first to violate their treaties. Amaury set out at the head of a numerous army, and appeared in the character of an enemy before Belbeis, which place he had promised to the knights of St. John, as a reward for the ardour and zeal they had shown for his expedition. This city, situated on the right bank of the Nile, was besieged, taken by assault, and after being pillaged, consigned to the flames.

The misfortunes of Belbeis spread consternation throughout Egypt, and the people, irritated at the account of the cruelties practised by the Franks, took up arms and drove the Christian garrison out of Cairo. Chaver assembled troops in the provinces, fortified the capital, and set fire to the ancient city of Fostat, which burnt for more than six weeks. The caliph of Cairo again implored the assistance of Noureddin, and to excite his pity and prove his distress, he sent him in a letter the hair of the women of his seraglio. The sultan of Damascus attended with joy to the prayers of the caliph of Egypt, and as an army was ready to march, he gave orders to Chirkou to cross the desert and hasten to the banks of the Nile.

Whilst the Syrians were coming to the aid of Egypt, threatened by the Christians, Chaver employed every means in his power to stop the king of Jerusalem in his march, and suspend in his hands the thunderbolt ready to fall upon Egypt. Ambassadors were sent to implore the pity of Amaury, and to give some weight to their prayers, offered him two millions of crowns of gold. The offer of so enormous a sum, which Egypt, for so long a time devastated, could not possibly have furnished, seduced the king of the Christians, who was as much influenced by a love of gold as an ambition for conquests. He allowed himself to be thus deceived by the Mussulmans, to whom he himself had been wanting in faith; and whilst he was waiting for the treasures they had promised him, the Egyptians restored the fortifications of their cities, and assembled everywhere in arms. The Christians looked in vain for the fleets promised by Manuel, and soon, instead of welcoming auxiliaries, they learnt that Chirkou had arrived for the third time in Egypt at the head of a formidable army. Then Amaury opened his eyes, and set about repairing his error. He flew to meet the Syrians, and offer them battle; but their general avoided the encounter, and united his forces with those of the Egyptians. The evil was irreparable; the king of Jerusalem could not resist the two united armies, and ashamed of being deceived by those whom he had himself sought to deceive, he returned to his kingdom, and was pursued to the verge of the desert by the troops of Noureddin.

Before the enterprise, hopes of success had dazzled the minds of all; but when it had failed, they, as generally, perceived the injustice of it. The Christians all became aware of the evils with which Jerusalem was menaced, and reproached Amaury with not being able to preserve peace, or knowing how to make war. In the mean time Noureddin's general entered the capital of Egypt in triumph.

Chirkou hoisted his standard on the towers of Cairo, and Egypt, which thought it had received a liberator into its bosom, soon found that he was a master. Chaver paid with his life the evils he had inflicted upon his country; he was killed in the camp of Chirkou, and his authority became the reward of the conqueror. The caliph, who, in order to save himself, had demanded the head of his first minister, appointed the general of Noureddin as his successor, styling him in his letters, *the victorious prince*. It was thus that the degraded monarch of Egypt jested with his own favours by flattering a man he did not know, and for whose death he was, most likely, desirous; an image of blind fortune, who scatters at hazard good and evil, and views her favourites and her victims with equal indifference.

Some time after, the caliph of Cairo, always invisible in his palace, was deposed by the orders of Noureddin, and died peaceably without knowing that he had lost his empire. His treasures served to appease the murmurs of the people and the soldiery; the black flag of the Abassides displaced the green standard of the children of Ali, and the name of the caliph of Bagdad was heard of only in the mosques. The dynasty of the Fatimites, which reigned more than two centuries, and for which so much blood had been shed, was extinguished in a single day, and found not even one defender. From that time the Mussulmans had only one religion and one cause to defend; Egypt and Syria obeyed the same chief, and the richest provinces of the East were united under the powerful hand of Noureddin.

The sultan of Aleppo and Damascus had spread the terror of his arms from the banks of the Euphrates and the Tigris to the sources of the Nile; he had everywhere governors and armies; and posts of pigeons, which he had established, carried at the same time his orders into the principal cities of Egypt, Syria, and Mesopotamia. The justice of his laws and his victories over the Christians had created for him such a reputation for sanctity among the Mussulmans, that a shower of rain which fell in the midst of a drought, was considered by them as a miracle granted to his prayers. During the war of Egypt he had taken several fortresses belonging to the Franks; and the destruction of the Christian colonies was still the aim of all his labours and all his exploits. Full of confidence in the protection of Mahomet, the devout Noureddin employed his leisure in constructing, with his own hands, a pulpit, which he meant himself to place in the principal mosque of Jerusalem.

The sultan of Damascus was preparing to commence what the Mussulmans called a sacred war, and for the success of which public prayers had been offered up; but this glory was reserved for a young warrior brought up in armies, whose name was yet unknown in the East.

Saladin,* this young warrior, was sprung from the people who inhabit the mountains situated beyond the Tigris. His father Ayoub, and his uncle Chirkou, after the example of the warriors of their nation, who fight for pay under Mussulman powers, had left Kurdistan to serve in the troops of the sultan of Bagdad. They had both attained high military employments; but Chirkou, a violent and brutal man, having run through the body with his sword an officer of justice, the two brothers were obliged to take to flight, and came to offer their services to the Attabeks of Syria, whom they assisted in their wars against the Christians. The young Saladin, although he was brought up at the court of Damascus, under the eye of an ambitious father, did not at first appear to be eager for either fortune or glory. In his youth he was fond of dissipation and pleasures, and remained a long time a stranger to the cares of politics or the dangers and labours of war. Having followed his uncle Chirkou in his first expeditions to Egypt, he had distinguished himself by the defence of Alexandria; but he suffered so much, that when Noureddin commanded him to return to the banks of the Nile, he sought pretexts to avoid obedience. When the sultan repeated his orders, Saladin set out, as he himself said afterwards, with the despair of a man who is led to death. "Thus it is," says the historian Hamad Eddin, who was for a long time his secretary, "that men know not what they refuse or what they desire; but God, who knows all things, sports with their designs, which always terminate according to the views of Providence."

At the death of Chirkou, the caliph of Egypt, who trembled for his power, named Saladin to the post of vizier, because he thought him the least capable, by his talents or reputation, of usurping the supreme authority. The son of Ayoub deceived both the king and the army, who saw in him nothing but a young dissipated soldier, without ambition. But he changed his conduct and reformed his manners; hitherto he had appeared fit only for the idleness and the obscurity of a seraglio; but, all at once, he came forth a new man, like one born for empire. His gravity inspired the respect of the emirs; his liberality secured him the suffrages of the army; and the austerity of his devotion ren-

* Saladin has had many historians. Among the Arabian authors the most celebrated are Bohaddin, who has written his life; Omad-el-Cathed, secretary of the sultan, and author of the *Phatah;* Schahab-Eddin, author of the lives of Noureddin and Saladin, entitled *El Reudatains* (or the two gardens). Several particulars relative to the Mussulman hero are to be met with in Aboulfeda, who was of the family of Ayoub, and in several other Arabian writers quoted by D. Berthereau. There is a Life of Saladin in French, by Marin. In the National Library of France two manuscript Lives may likewise be consulted, one by the Abbé Renaudot, and the other by Galland, the translator of the *Thousand and One Nights.*

dered him dear to all true believers. A religious revolution which he brought about without trouble or the effusion of blood, made known his prudence and humanity, and showed that fortune destined him for extraordinary things. The caliph of Bagdad felicitated him publicly with having annihilated the sect of the Fatimites, and made him a present of a vest of honour. His name was celebrated by the poets, and mixed with those of Mahomet and Noureddin in the public prayers.

Saladin, master of Egypt, sent for his father Ayoub, and wished to associate him with himself in the government. When Ayoub arrived at Cairo, with all his family, he was compared to Jacob, and Saladin to the patriarch Joseph, whose name he bore. Aided by the counsels of his father, Saladin stifled all plots devised against him, and restrained the ambition and jealousy of the emirs.

In a council in which his son had spoken too openly of his projects, Ayoub, brought up among the intrigues of the courts of Asia, exclaimed with vehemence against all traitors, and swore he would cut off the head of even Saladin himself, if he received orders from the sultan of Damascus to do so. When left alone with his son, he reproached him with his indiscretion and imprudence. "I have spoken against you," added he, "before your rivals and enemies; but know that if Noureddin should come to attack you, I would be the first to take arms; if he required only the tribute of a sugar-cane from us, he should not obtain it of me." According to the advice of Ayoub, Saladin spoke only of his perfect submission to the commands of his master, and took honour to himself as being the lowest of the slaves of Noureddin, to whom he sent deputies and presents; but he could not destroy all his suspicions. Noureddin had determined upon going into Egypt himself, when death surprised him, and delivered Saladin from the uneasiness which a jealous and vindictive master naturally inspired.

At the death of Noureddin, the empire founded by the Attabeks declined towards its ruin. The sultan of the Attabeks only left a child to succeed him, the emirs already began to quarrel for the divisions of his power, and Syria was about to return to the chaos into which the fall of the Seljoucides had plunged it. The Mussulman nations, terrified at the evils before them, eagerly sought the yoke of Saladin, and recognised with joy for their master a warrior who was the only person capable of defending their religion or their dominions. Saladin inherited not only the power of Noureddin, but was anxious to follow up the projects of his predecessor, and nothing pleased his ambition more than the idea of pursuing the war against the Christians.

Amaury, instead of taking advantage of the troubles of Syria, was desirous of resuming his projects against Egypt; and requesting the aid of the emperor of Constantinople, the latter sent him a fleet and some troops. The Christians laid siege to Damietta; but the eternal divisions between the Greeks and Latins prevented the success of the enterprise. Amaury, entertaining still the hope of succeeding in his designs, sent ambassadors into Europe, thinking that the prospect of the conquest of Egypt would arm the knights of the West. As the deputies of Amaury returned without obtaining aid, he himself repaired to Constantinople to solicit fresh succours. He was received with magnificence; and great promises were made him; but he died without seeing them realized. Thus King Amaury, during the whole of his reign, had but one single thought, for which he exhausted all the resources of his kingdom. The obstinacy which he evinced for the execution of an unfortunate project, advanced the progress of the Mussulmans, and must have recalled to the Christians of the West the words which the prophets repeated to the Hebrews,—"*Children of Israel, direct neither your looks nor your steps towards Egypt.*"

Amaury, at his death, left a distressed kingdom, and as the governor of its states a son, thirteen years of age, sick and covered with leprosy. Raymond, count of Tripoli, and Milo de Plansy, lord of Carac and Montroyal, disputed the regency during the minority of young Baldwin. Milo, by his intrigues, obtained the suffrages of the barons, but was found, a short time after, pierced with several wounds inflicted by a sword, in one of the streets of Ptolemaïs; Raymond succeeded his rival, with whose death all Palestine accused him.

The father of the count of Tripoli had been killed by the Ismaëlians, and he himself had remained eight years in the chains of the infidels. The fourth in descent from the famous count de St. Gilles, he possessed the bravery, the activity, and the ambition of the hero from whom he drew his origin; but with them, that obstinacy of character, which, in difficult times, irritates the passions and provokes implacable hatreds. More impatient to reign over the Christians than to conquer the infidels, Raymond considered the right of commanding men as the only reward of the evils he had suffered; he demanded with haughtiness the recompense of his services and his long toils, and conceived that justice would triumph, and the safety of the kingdom be preserved, solely by his elevation.

If, amidst the disorders which continually agitated the Christian states, the new regent had had sufficient authority to direct the policy of the Franks, and make peace or war at his will, history might justly accuse him of having favoured the power of Saladin, and of having prepared the downfall of the kingdom of Jerusalem. After the death of Noureddin, the son of Ayoub had had to contend with the family of his old master, the emirs faithful to the dynasty of the Attabeks, and all who wished to profit by the troubles of Syria, and erect independent states for themselves. Prudence commanded the Christians to foment the discord which prevailed among the Saracens, and to ally themselves with every party which was opposed to Saladin. Instead of following this wholesome policy, and stirring up war in Syria, they determined upon renewing Amaury's unfortunate attempts upon Egypt. A Sicilian fleet having arrived in Palestine, aided by the Sicilians, the Christians laid siege to Alexandria, where all sorts of miseries combined to destroy their army. Frequently-repeated reverses conveyed no instruction to the Franks of the proper manner to make war with Saladin. As they were returning from their imprudent and unfortunate expedition, the Mussulman governor of the city of Emessa, then besieged by the new sultan of Damascus, solicited their alliance and support. The Christian warriors, after having placed a price upon their services which it was impossible the governor could pay, entered upon a campaign without an object, threatening those they pretended to defend, and ravaging at the same time the territories of their allies and their enemies. Nevertheless, their presence in Syria, and their transient alliance with the Mussulman princes, alarmed Saladin, who was making war against the son of Noureddin, shut up in the city of Aleppo. The sultan, resolving to keep them at a distance from the theatre of his conquests, made their leaders brilliant promises and rich presents, and soon succeeded in obtaining a truce, of which he took advantage to strengthen his power and extend the limits of his empire.

The Franks returned to Jerusalem, satisfied with having compelled Saladin to ask for peace. After having imprudently consented to a truce, they committed a second fault, which was to violate the treaty they had just signed, and that not to undertake an important enterprise, but to make an incursion into the territories of Damascus. They ravaged the country, and pillaged the towns and villages that they found without defence, whilst Saladin continued making useful conquests in Syria, and rendering himself sufficiently powerful to punish them for the infraction of their engagements.

The sultan of Cairo and Damascus soon assembled a formidable army and advanced towards Palestine. The whole country was in flames through which the Saracens passed; at their approach the Christians abandoned the cities and towns to take refuge in mountains and caverns. Baldwin IV., who had recently assumed the reins of government, placed himself at the head of the Franks; but fearing to measure himself with Saladin, he shut himself up in Ascalon, whence he contemplated with consternation his desolated provinces.

Everything appeared to presage the approaching fall of the kingdom, and Saladin was already distributing its cities among his emirs, when Providence, which at length took pity on the situation of the Christians, offered them an opportunity of repairing their misfortunes. The menaces of Saladin and the sight of the ravages he was committing exasperated the Christian soldiers. Baldwin led forth his army from Ascalon, and surprised the Mussulmans in the very same plains whereon Godfrey and the leaders of the first crusade gained their celebrated victory over the Egyptians. Saladin could not resist the impetuosity of their attack, and lost the battle after having defended himself valiantly in the midst of his Mamelukes, a new military force, which he had himself formed, and by which he was always surrounded in time of danger. Saladin saw all his army perish in this disastrous battle, which was never effaced from his memory, and which, as he said in a letter, "made the star of the family of Ayoub to pale." Mounted on a camel, and followed by a few officers, Saladin experienced the greatest dangers in his flight across the desert, and returned almost alone to Egypt, whence he had so recently set out at the head of a formidable army.

And yet the Christians did not reap much advantage from their victory; they laid siege in vain to the cities of Hemessa and Harem, whilst Saladin soon got together fresh troops in Egypt, and returned to threaten the kingdom of Jerusalem. The victory of Ascalon elated the Christians, and made them rash; Saladin, on the contrary, rendered more cautious by defeat, took advantage of every false step of his enemies, planned ambuscades, employed all the stratagems of war, and several times surprised and beat them on the banks of the Jordan, and in the vicinity of Paneas. Baldwin, who was very near falling into the hands of the Saracens, collected all the forces that were left in his dominions; but he could obtain no advantage over Saladin, and was obliged to sue for peace, which the state of his kingdom and his own infirmities rendered every day more necessary.

The leprosy by which he was attacked made alarming progress; he lost his sight, and was no longer able to undertake the cares of government. As he mistrusted most of the barons and leading men of his kingdom, he offered the government to Philip, count of Flanders, who was come into Asia to combat the infidels; but Philip preferred making war upon the Mussulmans to governing the Christians of Palestine.

The count of Tripoli was pointed out by the opinion of both the people and the nobles, as the only person capable of governing; but the suffrages of the people only augmented the suspicions of Baldwin, who had long dreaded the ambition of Raymond. Obliged to abandon a throne, the weak monarch trembled at the idea of placing on it a man who might soon make him forgotten; and he chose in preference a knight without name or glory, whose only title arose from his having espoused Sibylla, daughter of king Amaury, and widow of the Marquis of Montferrat, surnamed Long Sword. Guy of Lusignan did not justify the choice of Baldwin by his conduct, and disgusted every one by the excess of his pride. In this state of things, the interests of the Christian colonies required that the truce made with the Mussulmans should be strictly observed; but such was then the destiny of the kingdom of Jerusalem, that nobody had sufficient power or ascendancy to maintain peace, whilst the meanest of the barons or knights could, at his will, provoke war. The rashness and imprudence of one man again brought down upon Palestine the whole force of Saladin.

Old chronicles have related the romantic adventures and extraordinary fortune of Renaud de Chatillon. Born at Chatillon-sur-Indre, of obscure parents, he followed the army of Louis the Young into Asia, and enrolled himself in the troops of Raymond of Poictiers, prince of Antioch. Raymond having lost his life in battle, his widow Constance was solicited to select a new husband, who might be associated with her in the government. This princess passed by the most illustrious nobles and knights, for she had remarked the personal beauty and chivalric bravery of Renaud de Chatillon, and would accept of no other husband. By this marriage, which, according to William of Tyre, filled the

Christian barons with surprise, she all at once raised a young obscure man to the throne of Antioch.

Although Renaud de Chatillon had obtained the love of Constance, he could not conciliate the confidence and esteem of his new subjects. A formidable party was formed against him, at the head of which was the patriarch Amaury. Renaud, full of vexation and anger, cast into prison all who were opposed to him. By his orders the patriarch was led to the top of one of the towers of the citadel, and, with his bare head rubbed with honey, left in the heat of summer, during a whole day exposed to flies and insects. Renaud de Chatillon, after having filled the city of Ascalon with terror and mourning, was desirous of signalizing his reign by some warlike enterprise. Become the leader of an army in which he had been a soldier, he began by making war against the emperor of Constantinople, and armed several vessels, with which he ravaged the isle of Cyprus. The Greek emperor hastened to avenge the insult, and was soon with an army encamped within sight of Ascalon. Renaud not being master of a sufficient force with which to defend himself, had recourse to baseness to disarm the anger of his enemy, and came, with a cord round his neck, and torn vestments, to lay his sword at the feet of the emperor, who granted him peace. When the Greeks had resumed their way to Constantinople, Renaud turned his arms against the Saracens. He at once put to flight the army of Noureddin, who had advanced towards the territory of Antioch; but, led away by thirst for booty, he fell into an ambuscade, was made prisoner and conducted to Aleppo, where the Mussulmans detained him many years. At last some of his ancient companions succeeded in breaking his chains, and what is not unworthy of remark, the produce of the booty made in an incursion on the territories of Damascus was the price of his liberty.

When Renaud de Chatillon issued from his captivity, his wife Constance was no longer living, and the son of Raymond, arrived at the age of maturity, governed the principality of Antioch. Renaud repaired to Jerusalem, where the remembrance of his exploits and misfortunes, suffered in the cause of the Christians, secured him a welcome from the king and the barons. Having, in a second marriage, espoused the widow of Homfrey de Thourou, he became lord of Carac, and some castles situated on the confines of Arabia and Palestine. Renaud led into these cities and fortresses a great number of Templars, whom he associated with his fortunes. He had just established himself there, and had already begun to ravage the frontiers of Arabia, when the truce was concluded with Saladin. Nothing could induce Renaud de Chatillon to lay down his arms; every day he made fresh forays in the neighbourhood of Carac, and plundered the caravans of the Mussulman pilgrims on their way to Mecca. Heedless of the rights of nations or humanity, he imprisoned women and children, and massacred unarmed men.

Saladin complained to Baldwin of these infractions of treaties; but it was not in the power of the king of Jerusalem to give him the satisfaction he demanded. The sultan, irritated by the conduct of the Franks, seized fifteen hundred pilgrims, who were cast upon the shores of Egypt by a tempest, and threatened to detain them unless the Mussulman prisoners were promptly set at liberty. Neither the demands of Saladin nor the prayers of Baldwin, nor even the fate of the Christian captives, had the least effect upon Renaud de Chatillon and the Templars, so long accustomed to sport with all treaties made with the Mussulmans.

Thereupon Saladin again determined upon war, and set out a third time from the banks of the Nile, to enter Palestine at the head of an army. At the approach of danger, the Christians united their efforts to stop the progress of the Saracens. An assembly, formed of all classes of citizens, ordered a general contribution to be levied, the produce of which was employed in repairing the fortifications of the castles and cities, whilst all the barons and knights flew to arms. But the time was not yet come in which Saladin should invade the kingdom of Jerusalem. In each of his expeditions he appeared to try the strength of the Christians, and when he met with strong resistance, waited patiently for a more favourable moment. After having ravaged Galilee by his lieutenants, and commenced the siege of Berouth, he suddenly drew off his forces to go and make war upon the Attabeks, who were masters of Mossoul and several cities of Mesopotamia.

The Christians took no other advantage of his absence but to renew their incursions upon the territory of Damascus. Renaud de Chatillon made several expeditions to the shores of the Red Sea, and even conceived the daring project of going to the cities of Mecca and Medina, and plundering the Kaaba and the tomb of the Prophet. A troop of intrepid warriors set forward on their march under his orders; they surprised the Egyptian merchants who were bearing back the treasures of India, by way of the Red Sea; and, preceded by terror, advanced in triumph, into a country which had never before seen the Christians. Renaud and his companions had already reached the valley of Rabid, situated ten leagues from Medina, when they were surprised and attacked by a Mussulman army, which had been hastily despatched from Syria. After an obstinate and sanguinary combat, victory favoured the Saracens. Renaud escaped the pursuit of the conquerors as if by a miracle, and returned with a small number of his troops to the castle of Carac. Some of the prisoners were led into Egypt, where the sentence of the cadis condemned them to the death of the lowest criminals. Others were conveyed to Mecca, where their blood was shed with that of the victims immolated at the ceremony of the great Bayram.

These horrible executions did not satisfy the vengeance of Saladin. When he heard of the expedition of the Christians, which he considered a frightful sacrilege, his anger knew no bounds, and he swore upon the Koran to revenge the insult offered to the Mussulman religion. The sultan, whom the Christians already styled *the scourge of God,* re-entered Galilee with sword and flame, and advanced towards the castle of Carac, constantly repeating the oath he had taken of slaying Renaud with his own hand. The Mussulmans would have rendered themselves masters of the castle, but for the bravery of one knight, who alone maintained the drawbridge, and by a glorious death deprived Saladin of this conquest. A Christian army was soon upon the march to repel this attack of the Saracens. Saladin, despairing for the present of wreaking his revenge upon Renaud, laid waste the lands on the banks of the Jordan, in the very face of the Christian army, which did not dare to attack him. After having several times renewed his attempts upon the fortress of Carac, and given up to the flames Naplouse, Sebosto, and several other cities, he at length consented to a truce, and led back his army into Mesopotamia.

Saladin availed himself of the peace made with the Christians, to dissipate the troubles which had arisen in his states, and to pursue his conquests in Syria. At each truce he got possession of a city or a province; he extended his dominions, and thus placed under his control countries which became so many the more enemies for the Christians. The Franks, on the contrary, when war was suspended, gave themselves madly up to their internal divisions; peace with them gave birth to a thousand new factions, and the kingdom then found in its own bosom enemies much more dangerous than those against whom they had been at war.

The knights and barons, on their return to Jerusalem, accused Guy de Lusignan of having neglected the opportunity for conquering Saladin, and reproached him with having permitted the ravages exercised by the Mussulmans in the richest provinces of Palestine. Baldwin, who had yielded up the royal authority with great regret, listened to the complaints of the barons, and hastened to reascend a tottering throne. He undertook to dissolve the marriage with Sibylla, and cited Guy de Lusignan before the patriarch of Jerusalem and the nobles of the kingdom, in order to deprive him of the counties of Ascalon and Jaffa. As Guy did not appear on the day named, Baldwin, although infirm and blind, repaired to Antioch, and finding the gates shut, struck them several times with his hand without causing them to be opened. This unfortunate prince called upon Heaven to witness this insult, and returned to Jerusalem, swearing to revenge himself upon Guy de Lusignan. On his side, Guy no longer observed any measures, but took up arms to sustain his revolt. In this emergency, Baldwin could find no better means of punishing Guy than to oppose to him a regent and a new king. By his orders, Baldwin V., who was five years of age, and born of the first marriage of Sibylla with the son of the marquis de Montferrat, was crowned in the church of the Holy Sepulchre, in the presence of the nobles and the clergy. Raymond, count of Tripoli, less odious to Baldwin than Guy, obtained the regency and assumed the reins of government.

The kingdom of Jerusalem, which had proceeded rapidly to decay since the reign of Baldwin III., became now an object worthy of pity. The stormy passions, almost always inseparable from a feudal government, had long since weakened all the springs of authority. The royalty, for whose remains they were quarrelling, was nothing but a vain name; in the midst of the factions by which he was surrounded, a king of Jerusalem could neither revenge his own injuries, nor those of the Church or of Christ. Want of courage was the only crime he could punish without exciting the murmurs of the barons, because with them cowards found no defenders. Amaury had ignominiously hung twelve Templars, accused of having neglected the defence of a fortress; but he had not the power to receive an ambassador sent by the *Old Man of the Mountain*, in whom the hope of freeing himself from a tribute paid to the grand master of the Templars, had awakened a desire to become a Christian. When the ambassador was assassinated in Jerusalem by a Templar, Amaury had no authority to bring the murderer to judgment; deplorable weakness of a king who possesses not the first prerogative of royalty, that of maintaining justice and causing the rights of nations to be respected.

The kingdom was covered with strong castles, the commanders of which barely recognised the authority of the king. On the summit of every mountain upon which appeared threatening towers, in caverns even, which had been transformed into fortresses, barons commanded as masters, and made peace or war at their pleasure. The military orders, the only support of the state, were divided among themselves, and sometimes shed their blood in quarrels fatal to the cause of the Christians.

Discord reigned between the clergy and the knights of the Temple and St. John; the military orders were not subject to the jurisdiction of ecclesiastics, and the clergy, accustomed to dictate laws to princes, could not endure the haughty independence of a few warriors. Led away by the spirit of discord, the Hospitallers raised edifices in front of the church of the Resurrection, and often drowned the voices of the priests who celebrated the praises of God at the foot of his altars. Some of them even went so far as to pursue priests with arrow-shots into the very church of the Holy Sepulchre. As the only vengeance, the priests gathered together in bundles the arrows that had been shot at them, and placed them on an elevated spot on the Mount of Olives, that every one might be acquainted with the sacrilege.

These quarrels, which were every day renewed, were carried before the tribunal of the Holy See, whose decisions frequently only inflamed the minds of the disputants the more. The Church of Rome, very far from restoring peace to the Christians of the East, often cast amongst them fresh coals of discord. The schisms which troubled the West, more than once kindled war in the holy places, even upon the tomb of Christ.

Concord seldom prevailed long between the inhabitants of Palestine and the European warriors who came into Asia to combat the infidels. The Syrian barons employed the forces of their auxiliaries to carry out their own ambitious views; and the latter, by their pride and disdain, laid a high price upon their services. Almost always on the arrival of fresh pilgrims, a treaty was violated or a truce broken, in order to make incursions upon the territories of the Saracens; and not unfrequently, the Crusaders, without even seeing the enemy, abandoned Palestine to the perils of a war they had themselves provoked.

In the cities, particularly the maritime cities, several nations dwelt together, and disputed precedence and sovereignty, sword in hand. All who came to establish themselves in the Holy Land, brought with them and preserved the remembrances and prejudices of their native country. In the cities of Ascalon, Tyre, or Ptolemaïs, the inhabitants were much more interested in the glory and prosperity of Pisa, Genoa, and Venice, than in the safety of the kingdom of Jerusalem.

The greater part of the barons and knights displayed none of the heroic resignation of the early soldiers of the cross, in supporting fatigues or braving difficulties. Since the conquest of Egypt had been contemplated, war was only considered as a means of acquiring wealth; and the thirst for booty destroyed the principle of honour, the love of glory, and even all anxiety for the cause of Christ. The question was no longer what enemy was to be attacked, what ally was to be defended, but what city or province was to be delivered up to pillage. Discipline degenerated in the camp; the Christian warriors still displayed their natural bravery, but they neither knew how to obey nor to command, and anarchy reigned as completely in the army as throughout the kingdom. Many of the leaders abandoned their colours under the most perilous circumstances, and sold their inaction or their neutrality. Some, like the Templar Meslier and his companions, forgetful of their vows, ravaged the Christian provinces; whilst others, urged on by ambition or vengeance, allied themselves with the Saracens, and received in the service of the infidels the reward of their disgraceful apostasy.

Religion, which ought to have been the connecting tie between the Christians established in the Holy Land, and which alone could preserve among them sentiments of patriotism,—religion had lost all empire over their minds. War was still made in its name, but its laws were unpractised and unacknowledged. The conversion of the Maronites of Libanus, who rejoined the Church of Rome in the reign of Baldwin IV., was celebrated at Jerusalem as a victory gained over heresy, but it had not the effect of bringing back the Christians to the spirit of the Scriptures. Pious men who lived in a corrupted age, groaned under the depravity of manners which every day made such frightful progress. The respectable archbishop of Tyre trembles as he traces the history of this unhappy period, and fears lest truth should give to his recitals the colour of satire. "There is," says he, "scarcely one chaste woman to be found in the city of Jerusalem." The leaders of the Christian colonies, equally with the heads of the Church, themselves set the example of licentiousness. The Christians beheld a queen of Jerusalem, the widow of Baldwin III., keep up a criminal intercourse with Andronicus, and seek an abode among the Saracens with the companion of her debaucheries.* Bohémond, prince of Antioch, repudiated his wife Erina, to espouse a courtesan. The patriarch, disgusted with such a scandal, excommunicated young Bohémond, and placed an interdict upon his states; and thus the guilty amours of a Christian prince produced trouble and desolation throughout a whole nation. The sight even of the tomb of Christ was unable to inspire more holy thoughts. The patriarch Heraclius, who only owed his elevation to mundane and profane qualities, lavished the treasures due to pilgrims and the poor, upon infamous prostitutes, and the Christian people were often astonished to see the notorious Pâque de Rivery display, even in the sanctuary, ornaments purchased with the alms of the faithful.

A people thus degenerated could not possibly preserve the kingdom of Christ. The eyes of all were turned towards the West, and Heraclius, attended by the two grand masters of the Temple and

* This was the same Andronicus who afterwards ascended the throne of Constantinople, and became notorious for his cruelties.

St. John, were sent into Europe to solicit the prompt assistance of kings and their warriors. The king of France, Philip Augustus, received the Christian deputies with great honours; but as he had but recently ascended the throne, the interests of his kingdom would not permit him to go in person to the defence of Jerusalem. Henry II., king of England, appeared to be the last hope of the Christians; he had promised the pope to make the pilgrimage to the Holy Land, as an expiation of the murder of the archbishop of Canterbury, and Heraclius repaired to his court, presenting him with the keys and standard of the Holy Sepulchre, and pressing him to perform his promise. The bad reputation of the patriarch had preceded him into Europe, and very much weakened the effect of his words; he displayed, likewise, neither the meekness nor the charity of the Scriptures, and only irritated those whom he sought to persuade or convince. As the English monarch hesitated to fulfil his promises, alleging his advanced age and the welfare of his dominions, Heraclius loaded him with the most outrageous reproaches, threatening him with the anger of Heaven. The aged Henry appearing irritated by this language, the patriarch redoubled his insolence and pride. "You may," said he, on terminating his discourse, "treat me as you treated my brother Thomas, for it is quite indifferent to me whether I die in Syria by the hands of infidels, or perish here by the orders of you who are more wicked than a Saracen." Henry endeavoured to conceal his anger, and did not dare to punish the envoy of the Christians; he even treated him with great magnificence, but yet did not leave England. He contented himself with sending the Christians of Jerusalem a large sum of money, and exhorting his subjects to arm themselves for the defence of the Holy Land.

The zeal for crusades began at this time to abate, and several ambassadors returned to Jerusalem without having been able to arouse the enthusiasm of the western Christians. Nations, to be excited to active ardour for holy wars, required the example of princes or kings. The warriors of Europe paid little attention to the exhortations of the pope and Heraclius. The deputies returned into Palestine without having obtained the assistance they demanded; and their appearance produced discouragement and despair among all the Christians of the East.

The unfortunate king, Baldwin, had entirely lost the faculties of both mind and body; and, tormented by his sufferings, he every day drew nearer to the tomb, presenting but too faithful an image of the weakness and decline of his kingdom. Whilst the approach of death filled his palace with mourning, parties contended for a throne which tottered to its fall, and for a crown which the most wise compared to the crown of thorns of Christ. When he closed his eyes, the evils increased, and discord submitted to no restraint. The count of Tripoli wished to retain the reins of government as regent; whilst Sibylla was desirous of bestowing the sceptre upon her husband. In the midst of these dissensions Baldwin V., the weak and fragile hope of the kingdom, died suddenly. All who had aspired to his authority were accused of his death: unhappy period, in which such accusations could possibly be well founded, and in which a whole people could think of reproaching a queen with the murder of her own son!

Scarcely was Baldwin dead than his mother desired to reign in his place; and in order to satisfy the ambition of herself and Guy de Lusignan, she disdained no artifice and spared no perfidious promises. Whilst the count of Tripoli was gathering together at Naplouse the barons and principal men of the kingdom, the daughter of Amaury, by the advice of the patriarch and the grand master of the Templars, announced her intention of separating herself from her husband, and choosing a warrior able to defend the kingdom. When this report had circulated through Jerusalem, Sibylla ordered the gates of the city to be shut, and repaired to the church of the Holy Sepulchre. In the presence of the tomb of Christ, Heraclius took the oath of allegiance to her in the name of the clergy and the people, pronounced her divorce with a loud voice, and commanded her in the name of Heaven to bestow her hand and sceptre upon him she deemed most worthy of them. At these words Sibylla placed the crown upon the head of her husband, who was on his knees before her, saying it was not in the power of man to separate those whom God had united.

Whilst a part of the people and some of the barons, seduced by vain promises, applauded the choice of Sibylla, the partisans of Raymond were highly indignant at having been deceived by a woman. The coronation of Guy de Lusignan naturally alarmed all who thought that Jerusalem stood in less need of a king than of a defender. Baldwin of Ramla, one of the most skilful captains of his times, despaired of the safety of the kingdom, and retired into the principality of Antioch, repeating the threats of the prophets against Jerusalem. Geoffrey de Lusignan, when he heard of the elevation of his brother, could not forbear exclaiming: *"Well, if they have made a king of him, they would have made a god of me if they had known me."*

When that which had taken place at Jerusalem was announced to the barons assembled at Naplouse, most of them resolved to abandon Palestine; but the count of Tripoli detained them, advising them to name a new king, and bestow the crown upon Homfrey de Thorou, who had recently married Isabella, the second daughter of Amaury. He even promised to gain the support of Saladin for this election, and succeeded in persuading the assembly. Whilst they were yet deliberating, young Homfrey, terrified at the burden they wished to impose upon him, fled away secretly by night, and hastened to the capital to ask pardon of Queen Sibylla, protesting that he preferred ease and life to the throne of Jerusalem. This flight disconcerted all measures and changed all projects. Several barons, not knowing to what party it would be best to ally themselves, went and took the oath to Guy de Lusignan; whilst others, returning to their castles, awaited coming events. Raymond retired to his county of Tiberias, of which he had obtained the sovereignty.

The retreat and the murmurs of the enemies of Guy only increased his pride. The more he stood in need of mildness and moderation, the more haughtiness and severity he displayed. His disdainful manners drove from him the barons who had remained faithful to him. Stimulated by the grand master of the Templars, who was the declared enemy of the count of Tripoli, he made preparations to besiege the city of Tiberias; whilst Raymond, who was determined to defend himself, carried away by the excess of his anger, implored the aid of Saladin against the king of Jerusalem.

At the approach of the evils about to fall upon the kingdom, nothing was heard but complaints and seditious clamours; but neither the dangers of the Christian colonies, nor the aspect of the threatened holy places, could silence ambition or check revolt. The historian of the kingdom of Jerusalem here feels the pen fall from his hand, and stops, terrified at the events which are left for him to describe.

Amidst the general disorder and agitation, the superstitious minds of the Christians beheld nothing in the future but great calamities, and everything seemed to present sinister presages to their eyes. "The signs which were displayed in the heavens," says a contemporary chronicle, "allowed it to be plainly perceived that God held in abomination that which was going on. Impetuous winds, tempests, and storms arose on all sides; the light of the sun was obscured during several days, and hailstones as large as the eggs of a goose fell from heaven. The earth, equally agitated by frequent and horrible earthquakes, gave notice of coming ruin and destruction, with disasters and defeats in war which were soon to visit the kingdom. Neither could the sea confine itself within its bounds and limits, but announced to us, by its horrible floods or its unusually impetuous waves, the anger of God ready to fall upon us. Fire was seen blazing in the air like a house in flames; you would have sworn that all the elements and architecture of God were angry, and abhorred the excesses, wickednesses, dissoluteness, and offences of the human race."

GLORIOUS DEATH OF DE MAILLÉ, MARSHAL OF THE TEMPLE.

Above all the rest, nothing could equal the heroic valour of Jacques de Maillé, a knight of the Temple. Mounted on a white horse, he remained alone in the field of battle, and fought on, surrounded by heaps of slain. Although hemmed in on all sides, he refused to surrender. The horse which he rode, worn out with fatigue and exhausted by wounds, sunk under him, and dragged him with him; but the intrepid knight arose, lance in hand, covered with blood and dust, and bristling with arrows, and rushed upon the ranks of the Mussulmans, astonished at his audacity; at length he fell, covered with wounds, but fighting to the last. The Saracens took him for St. George, whom the Christians believed they saw descend from heaven to join their battalions. After his death the Turkish soldiers, whom an old historian calls THE CHILDREN OF BABYLON AND SODOM, *drew near with signs of respect to his body, slain by a thousand wounds; they wiped off the blood, they shared the rags of his clothes and the fragments of his arms, and, in their brutal excitement, evinced their admiration by actions which make modesty blush when speaking of them.*—BOOK VII.

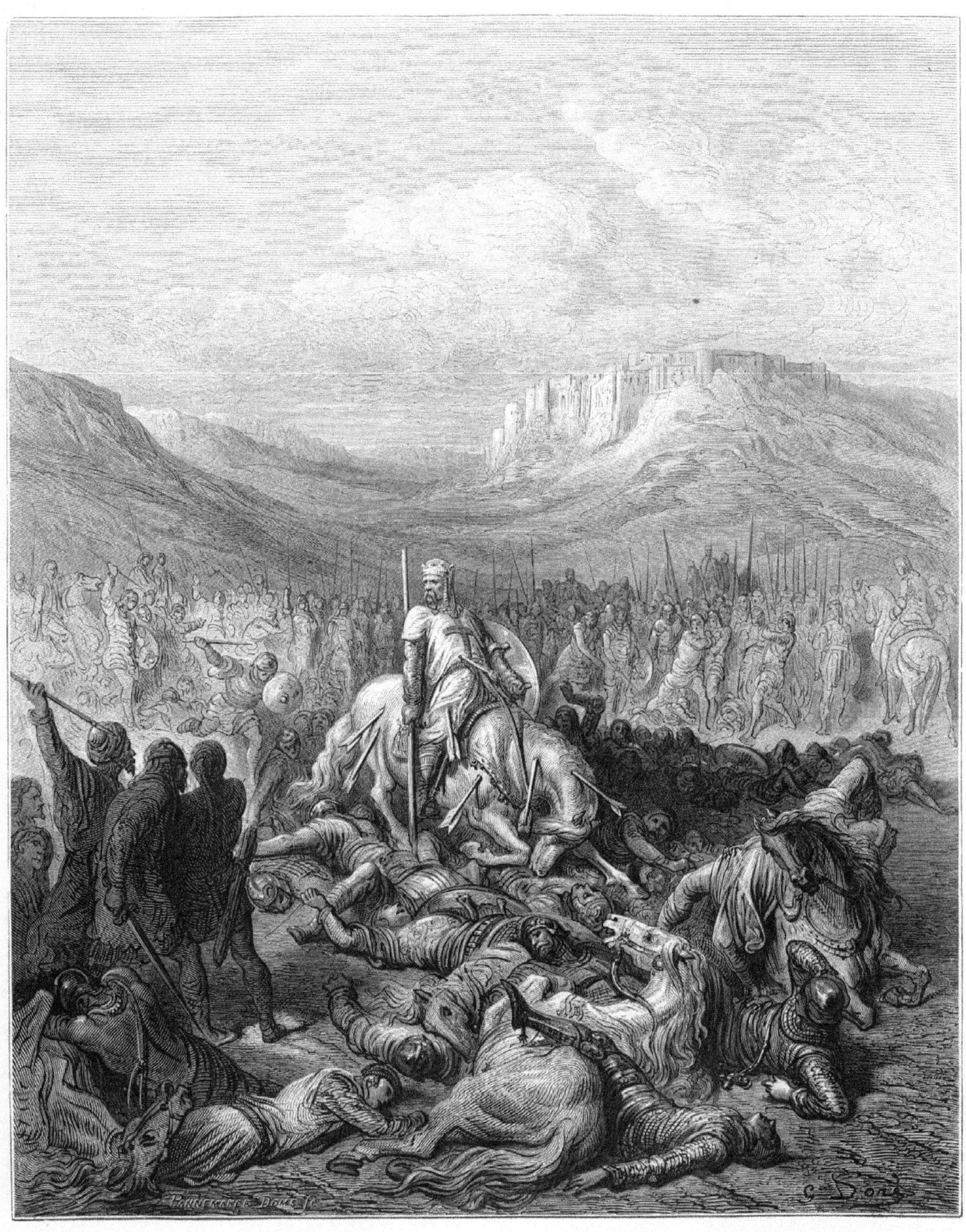

Such were the presages that struck the greater number of the Christians; but thinking men could perceive much more certain signs of the approaching fall of the kingdom of Jerusalem. Mossoul, Aleppo, and all the Mussulman cities of Syria and Mesopotamia, had submitted to the power of Saladin. The son of Ayoub had triumphed over the emirs and the scattered family of Noureddin. All the treasures of Egypt, all the forces of Asia, were in his hands; there remained only one conquest for him to make, and fortune, which had levelled all obstacles before him, soon furnished him with a pretext and an opportunity of giving the last blow to the power of the Christians.

The truce made with the king of Jerusalem was broken at the same time by both Christians and Mussulmans. Renaud de Chatillon continued his incursions upon the territories of the infidels, and only replied to the complaints of Saladin by new violations of treaties. A Mussulman army, which the sultan of Damascus had sent to the assistance of the count of Tripoli, advanced into the country of Galilee, whither five hundred knights of the Temple and St. John hastened to defend the Christian territory, and give battle to the Saracens. They were speedily overwhelmed by numbers, and almost all perished on the field of battle. Old chronicles, whilst celebrating the bravery of the Christian knights, relate prodigies which we have now great difficulty in believing. These indomitable heroes, after having exhausted their arrows, plucked from their own bodies such as had pierced them, and launched them back upon the enemy; pressed by fatigue and heat, they drank their own blood, and revived their strength by the very means which must weaken it; at length, after having broken their lances and swords, they rushed upon their enemies, fought body to body, rolling in the dust with the Mussulman warriors, and died threatening their conquerors. Above all the rest, nothing could equal the heroic valour of Jacques de Maillé, a knight of the Temple. Mounted on a white horse, he remained alone in the field of battle, and fought on, surrounded by heaps of slain. Although hemmed in on all sides, he refused to surrender. The horse which he rode, worn out with fatigue and exhausted by wounds, sunk under him, and dragged him with him; but the intrepid knight arose, lance in hand, covered with blood and dust, and bristling with arrows, and rushed upon the ranks of the Mussulmans, astonished at his audacity; at length he fell, covered with wounds, but fighting to the last. The Saracens took him for St. George, whom the Christians believed they saw descend from heaven to join their battalions. After his death the Turkish soldiers, whom an historian calls *the children of Babylon and Sodom*, drew near with signs of respect to his body, slain by a thousand wounds; they wiped off the blood, they shared the rags of his clothes and the fragments of his arms, and, in their brutal excitement, evinced their admiration by actions that make modesty blush when speaking of them.

The grand master of the Templars, with two of his knights, were all that escaped from the carnage. This battle was fought on the first of May, 1187. In the season, says an ancient chronicle, in which flowers and roses are gathered in the fields, the Christians of Nazareth found nothing but the traces of slaughter and the mangled bodies of their brethren. They buried them in the church of St. Mary, repeating these prophetic words: "*Daughters of Galilee, put on your garments of mourning; and you, daughters of Sion, weep over the ills that threaten the kings of Judah.*" The terror which this sanguinary defeat created for a moment appeased the discords of the Christians. The king consented to be reconciled to the count of Tripoli, whilst on his part Raymond resolved to forget his private injuries, and to use every effort to repair the misfortunes he had brought upon the kingdom. He repaired to Jerusalem, where Guy de Lusignan, coming forth to meet him, received him with marks of sincere affection. The two princes embraced before the people, and swore to fight in unison for the heritage of Christ.

After the rupture of the truce, Saladin employed himself in getting together a formidable army.

Turks, Arabs, Curds, and Egyptians flocked to his standard; he promised the spoils of the Christians to the Mussulman families that had been driven from Palestine; he distributed cities and provinces beforehand to his faithful emirs, and held out to all his soldiers the certainty of pillage or a glorious martyrdom. The caliph of Bagdad and all the imauns of Egypt, Syria, and Mesopotamia put up prayers for the triumph of his arms and the deliverance of Jerusalem. He crossed the Jordan, and advanced into Galilee at the head of eighty thousand horse.

In a council held at Jerusalem, Guy de Lusignan, the count of Tripoli, and the barons deliberated upon the measures most proper to be adopted to save the kingdom. The knights of the three military orders, the troops of the king and the nobles, the garrisons of cities, with all Christians able to bear arms, received orders to assemble on the plain of Sephouri. It was determined to employ in the prosecution of the war the treasures sent by Henry II., which were kept in the house of the Temple; and to associate the English monarch in the glory of this holy expedition, the arms of England were represented on the standards of the Christian army. The wood of the true cross, which had so often animated the Crusaders in fight, was exhibited to the people as a last means of safety, and carried in triumph to the place where the defenders of Jerusalem were assembled.

An army of fifty thousand fighting men had been collected on the plain of Sephouri, when the leaders learned that Saladin had carried the city of Tiberias by assault, and threatened the citadel, in which were shut up the women and children of the count of Tripoli. The Christians who had escaped from the sword of the Saracens, in the utmost terror, took refuge in the camp of Sephouri, conjuring the king and the chiefs to put an end to the ravages of the infidels. The barons assembled in the tent of Guy, and all at once exclaimed that it was necessary to march immediately against the enemy. Raymond then arose and demanded permission to speak. "I am about," said he, "to lay before you advice which will surprise you; but I offer it with the greater confidence from its being opposed to my personal interests. My desolated country, my cities in ashes, my subjects ready to submit to death or slavery, my wife exposed to the insults of the Mussulmans, all implore instant succour from me and you; but it is my duty to think of the safety of the Christian cities now left without garrisons. In this army assembled on the plain of Sephouri exists the only hope which the Christians of the East have left. You behold here all the soldiers of Christ, all the defenders of Jerusalem; if they perish, the infidels have no other foes to dread. Beware, then, of leading this multitude of men and horses into a dry and arid country, where the season, with thirst and hunger, must soon deliver them up without defence to the enemy. The number even of the Christian soldiers inspires me with more alarm than confidence. They present nothing but a confused troop of men got together in haste, and totally unable to support fatigue. The Mussulman archers are more skilful than our soldiers in casting javelins, and may harass us on our march, without our being able to defend ourselves; the cavalry of Saladin is more numerous and better trained than ours, and may attack us with advantage on the plains, across which we must pass. Abandon, then, I entreat you, Tiberias to the Mussulmans, and let us save an army which may yet repair our losses.

"I swear before God and before man, that I would willingly abandon the county of Tripoli, with all the lands I possess, to procure the safety of the city of Christ. Our only aim must be to destroy the power of Saladin, and at the same time to preserve some defenders for the kingdom of Jerusalem. If we go to meet the enemy and should be conquered, God himself will not be able to save the Christians, but will allow us to be delivered up to the infidels. If, on the contrary, the enemy come to offer themselves to our arms, all our losses will be repaired, and the evils that will fall upon me, will become for me a source of gratification, since I shall have suffered for the cause of Christ and the safety of his people."

The more generosity there was in this advice, the less sincere it was esteemed. The grand master of the Templars, blinded by his hatred for Raymond, interrupted him several times; he reminded the assembly of the alliance of the count of Tripoli with Saladin, and exclaimed aloud that he could plainly perceive *the wolf's skin under the fleece of the sheep.* When Raymond invoked the name of Christ, the grand master repeated with bitterness, that the name of *Mahomet* was better fitted to the mouth of a traitor. The count of Tripoli made not the least reply to the insulting words of the grand master, but finished his speech by these words, uttered with an accent of perfect conviction: "*I will submit to the punishment of death if these things do not fall out as I have said.*"

The council of the knights and barons adopted the opinion of Raymond; but when Guy was left alone in his tent, the grand master came to him, and infused into his mind the blackest suspicions of the conduct and secret designs of the count of Tripoli. The feeble Lusignan, who had already issued several contradictory orders, gave the command for marching to meet the enemy. For the first time, the king of Jerusalem was obeyed, and that was for the ruin of the Christians.

The undetermined conduct that Lusignan had exhibited, communicated itself to the other chiefs, and this want of a fixed purpose spread trouble and confusion throughout the army. The disheartened soldiers quitted the camp of Sephouri with reluctance, and saw nothing around them but presages of an approaching defeat. The Christian army advanced towards Tiberias, and were marching in silence across a plain, which modern travellers call the plain of Batouf, when they perceived the standards of Saladin.

The Mussulman army was encamped on the heights of Loubi, with the Lake of Tiberias in its rear; it covered the tops of the hills, and commanded all the defiles through which the Christians had to pass. The barons and knights then remembered the advice of Raymond, but they had lost the opportunity of following it, and the courage of the Christian soldiers alone could repair the errors of their leaders. The bold and desperate resolution was formed of cutting themselves a passage through the army of the enemy, so as to gain the banks of the Jordan. On the 4th of July, at break of day, the Christians began their march. From the moment they were in motion, the Mussulman archers unceasingly poured upon them showers of arrows. The army of the Franks was bravely enduring, on its march, the attacks of the Saracen archers, when Saladin descended into the plain at the head of his cavalry. Then the Christians were compelled to stop, and fight with the enemy that disputed their passage. The first shock was impetuous and terrible; but as the Franks had for many days been short of both provisions and water, and were oppressed by heat and thirst, they had less strength than courage, and fell more from lassitude than in consequence of their wounds. The bishops passed through the ranks, and endeavoured to revive the ardour of the soldiers by the images of religion.

The true cross, placed upon an elevated spot, for a moment reanimated them, and drew around it the most fervent and the most intrepid. Saladin himself said, in a letter, that the Christian soldiers fought around the cross with the greatest bravery, and that they seemed to consider it the strongest tie that bound them together, and as their impenetrable buckler. But the sight of a revered sign, and the passing ardour which it created, only served to increase the disorder of the fight. All the Mussulman forces united in one body to attack the Christians. The cavalry of Saladin poured down upon them several times with irresistible impetuosity, and penetrated through their ranks; victory was evidently about to incline to the side of the Saracens, when night put an end to the conflict. The Franks and the Saracens both remained on the plain where they had fought all day, and prepared to renew the battle on the morrow.

The Saracens were confident of victory. Saladin went through the ranks of his army, inflaming the courage of the Mussulman soldiers by his presence and his speeches. "To-morrow," said he, "is a festival for the true believers, for it is on Friday that Mussulmans offer up their prayers, and that Mahomet listens to the vows that are made to him." The Mussulmans replied to their leader by the loudest acclamations. Saladin then placed archers on the heights, ordered four hundred charges of arrows to be distributed, and disposed his troops in such a manner, that the Christian army should be surrounded from the very commencement of the contest. The Christian soldiers took advantage of the darkness to rally and close in their ranks; but their powers were exhausted. Sometimes they exhorted each other to brave death; and at others, raising their hands towards heaven, implored the All-Powerful to save them. They then uttered threats against the Saracens, who were near enough to hear them; but sad and sinister presentiments appeared to deprive them of all hopes of victory. In order to conceal their alarms, they made their camp resound during the whole night with the noise of drums and trumpets.

At last daylight appeared, and was the signal for the entire ruin of the Christian army. As soon as the Franks beheld the whole of the forces of Saladin, and found themselves surrounded on all sides, they were seized with surprise and terror. The two armies remained for a considerable time drawn up in sight of each other, Saladin waiting until the sun had completely illumined the horizon, to give the signal for attack. From dawn a strong wind had prevailed, which blew full in the faces of the Christians, and covered them with clouds of dust. When Saladin gave the fatal word, the Saracens rushed upon their enemies from all sides, uttering the most terrifying cries. To employ the expressions of Oriental writers,—"*It was then that the sons of Paradise and the children of fire fought out their terrible quarrel; the arrows sounded in the air like the noisy flight of birds; the water of swords* (sic), *the blood of arrows spouted out from the bosom of the* mêlée, *and covered the earth like the waters of rain.*" The Christians at first defended themselves valiantly, but Saladin having set fire to the dry grass that covered the plain, the flames surrounded their army, and scorched the feet of both men and horses.

Disorder began to prevail in their ranks, but they fought bravely still. Swords gleamed through the flames, and the Christian knights, rushing from masses of smoke and fire, precipitated themselves, lance in hand, upon their enemies. In their despair, they endeavoured to pierce through the battalions of the Saracens, but everywhere met with an invincible resistance. Again and again they returned to the charge, and as often were they repulsed. A prey to hunger and a consuming thirst, they saw nothing around them but burning rocks and the sparkling swords of their enemies. The mountain of Ettin arose on their left, and in it they endeavoured to find an asylum; but, hotly pursued by the Saracens, they were cast, some down precipices, and others into narrow ravines, where their bravery was of no avail.

The knights of the Temple and St. John performed prodigies of valour, and fought until the close of day, rallying around the wood of the true cross. This sacred standard was borne by the bishop of Ptolemaïs, who was killed in the heat of the battle. The bishop of Lidda, who took it up and endeavoured to fly, was stopped, and taken prisoner. A cry of despair arose from among the Franks when they saw the sign of their safety in the hands of the conqueror; even the most brave cast away their arms, and without attempting to fly, rushed upon the swords of the infidels. The field of battle became nothing but a scene of desolation; and the Christian warriors who had not been able to save the cross of Christ, no longer feared either death or slavery. The king of Jerusalem was made prisoner with his brother Geoffrey, the grand master of the Templars, Renaud de Chatillon, and all the most illustrious knights of Palestine. Raymond, who commanded the vanguard of the Christian army, after having fought valiantly, opened for himself a passage through the Saracens, and fled to Tripoli, where, a short time afterwards, he died of despair, accused by the Mussulmans of having violated treaties, and by the Christians of having betrayed both his religion and his country. Bohémond, prince of Antioch, Renaud of Sidon, the young count of Tiberias, and a small number of soldiers, accompanied Raymond in his flight, and were the only persons that escaped after this day, so fatal to the kingdom of Jerusalem.

The Oriental historians whilst describing the victory of the Saracens, have celebrated the bravery and firmness of the Frank knights, covered with their cuirasses, made with rings of steel. These brave warriors at first presented an impenetrable wall to the strokes of the Saracens; but when their horses sunk, exhausted by fatigue, or wounded by lances or javelins, Saladin met with very little more resistance, and the battle became a horrible carnage. An Arabian author, a secretary and companion of Saladin, who was present at this terrible conflict, has not been able to refrain from pitying the disasters of the vanquished. "I saw," says he, "the hills, the plains, the valleys covered with their dead bodies; I saw their colours abandoned and soiled with blood and dust; I saw their heads struck off, their members dispersed and their carcasses piled up like stones." After the battle, the cords of the tents were not sufficient to bind the prisoners; the Saracen soldiers drove them in crowds, like vile herds of cattle. The conquerors divided the captives amongst them, and the number was so great, that, according to an historian, a pair of shoes was exchanged for a Christian knight.

Saladin caused a tent to be erected in his camp, in which he received Guy de Lusignan, and the principal leaders of the Christian army, whom victory had placed in his hands. He treated the king of the Franks with kindness, and ordered him to be served with a drink cooled in snow. As the king, after having drunk, presented the cup to Renaud de Chatillon, who was next to him, the sultan stopped him, and said, "That traitor shall not drink in my presence, for I will show him no favour." Then addressing himself to Renaud, he made him the most severe reproaches for his violation of treaties, and threatened him with death if he did not embrace the religion of the prophet he had insulted. Renaud de Chatillon replied with noble firmness, and braved the menaces of Saladin, who struck him with his sabre. Some Mussulman soldiers, at the signal of their master, threw themselves upon the disarmed prisoner, and the head of a martyr of the cross fell at the feet of the king of Jerusalem.

On the following day the sultan ordered the knights of the Temple and St. John, who were among the prisoners, to be brought before him; and, as they were led past his throne, said, "I will deliver the earth of these two unclean races." The grand master of the Templars found favour before him, doubtless because his imprudent counsels had given up the Christian army to the swords of the Saracens. A great number of emirs and doctors of the law surrounded the throne of Saladin, and the sultan permitted each of them to slay a Christian knight. Some of them refused to shed blood, and turned their eyes away from so odious a spectacle; but others, arming themselves with swords, massacred knights bound with fetters, without pity, whilst Saladin sat on his throne, applauding the horrible execution. The knights received the palm of martyrdom with joy; most of the prisoners were anxious for death; and many among them, although not belonging to the military orders, cried aloud that they were Hospitallers or Templars, and, as if they feared they should want executioners, pressed before each other, in order to secure the fatal stroke from the hands of the infidels.

Saladin disgraced his victory by this barbarity; the fear with which the Christians inspired him, even after defeat, made him cruel. He became more humane and generous when he felt more assured of his victory and confident of his power. Two days were devoted by the Mussulmans to returning thanks to Heaven for the victory with which it had blessed their arms; and then Saladin gave his attention to all the advantages that might be obtained from it. As soon as he became master of the citadel of Tiberias, he sent the wife of Raymond to Tripoli; and was, with his army, very shortly under the ramparts of Ptolemaïs. This city, full of merchants, and which, at a later period, sustained the attacks of the most powerful armies of the West, during three years, did not stand out two days against Saladin. The inhabitants had liberty to retire with their most valuable property; and the churches were converted into mosques, in which thanks were offered up to Mahomet for the triumphs obtained over the Christian soldiers.

The terror which preceded his army opened to Saladin the gates of Naplouse, Jericho, Ramla, and a great number of other cities which were left almost without inhabitants. The cities of Cæsarea, Arsuf, Jaffa, and Berouth shared the fate of Ptolemaïs; the yellow standards of Saladin floated over their walls. On the sea-coast, the cities of Tyre, Tripoli, and Ascalon still remained in the hands of the Christians. Saladin attacked Tyre without success, and determined to wait for a more favourable opportunity to renew the siege. Ascalon presented itself to him as a conquest of much greater importance, as it would assure his communication with Egypt. This city was besieged by the Mussulmans, but it resisted, at first, with more firmness than Saladin had expected. When a breach was effected, the sultan proposed peace; but the inhabitants, with whom despair supplied the place of courage, sent back his messengers without granting them a hearing. The king of Jerusalem, whom Saladin led with him in triumph, then entreated the defenders of Ascalon not to compromise the safety of their families and the Christians of the city by a useless defence. After this appeal, the principal among them came to the tent of the sultan: "It is not for ourselves," said they, "that we are come to implore mercy, but for our wives and children. Of what importance is a perishable life to us? We look for a more solid blessing, and that death alone can procure us. God alone, the master of all events, has allowed you to obtain victories over the unhappy Christians; but you shall not enter into Ascalon unless you take pity on our families, and promise to restore the king of Jerusalem to liberty."

Saladin, touched by the heroism of the inhabitants of Ascalon, accepted the conditions proposed. Such devotedness merited the redemption of a prince of nobler character and more worthy of the love of his subjects than Guy de Lusignan. Saladin consented to liberate the captive monarch at the expiration of a year.

The moment was now come in which Jerusalem was again fated to fall into the power of the infidels; and all Mussulmans earnestly implored Mahomet for this crowning triumph for the arms of Saladin. After having taken Gaza, and several fortresses in the neighbourhood, the sultan drew his army together and marched towards the holy city. A queen in tears, the children of the warriors slain at the battle of Tiberias, a few fugitive soldiers, and some pilgrims recently arrived from the West were the only guardians of the Holy Sepulchre. A great number of Christian families which had left the devastated provinces of Palestine, filled the capital, and, very far from bringing it any assistance, only served to increase the general trouble and consternation.

When Saladin drew near to the holy city, he caused the principal inhabitants to be sent for, and said to them: "I acknowledge, as well as you, that Jerusalem is the house of God; I do not wish to profane its sanctity by the effusion of blood: abandon its walls and I will bestow upon you a part of my treasures; I will give you as much land as you will be able to cultivate." "We cannot," they replied, "yield the city in which our God died; still less can we give it up to you." Saladin, enraged by their refusal, swore upon the Koran to lay prostrate the towers and ramparts of Jerusalem, and to avenge the death of the Mussulmans slaughtered by the companions and soldiers of Godfrey of Bouillon.

At the moment in which Saladin was speaking to the deputies, an eclipse of the sun all at once left the heavens in utter darkness, and appeared to be a presage fatal for the Christians. Nevertheless, the inhabitants, encouraged by the clergy, prepared to defend the city, and chose as their commander Baleau d'Ibelin, who had been present at the battle of Tiberias. This old warrior, whose experience and virtues inspired confidence and respect, immediately set about repairing the fortifications, and training the new defenders of Jerusalem. As he was deficient in officers, he created fifty knights from amongst the citizens; and all the Christians able to bear arms, placed themselves under his command, and swore to shed their blood in the cause of Christ. They had no money to meet the expenses of the war, but all means of obtaining it seemed legitimate in a danger that threatened the city of God. They despoiled the churches, and the people, terrified at the approach of Saladin, beheld, without scandal, the precious metal which covered the chapel of the Holy Sepulchre converted into coin.

The standards of Saladin were soon seen floating over the heights of Emaüs, and the Mussulman army encamped on the same places on which Godfrey, Tancred, and the two Roberts had pitched their tents when they besieged the holy city. The besieged at first resisted boldly, and made frequent sorties, in which they bore in one hand a lance or a sword, and in the other a shovel filled with dust, which they cast upon the Saracens. A great number of Christians received the palm of martyrdom, and ascended, say the historians, to the heavenly Jerusalem—many Mussulmans fell beneath the swords of their enemies, and *went to dwell on the banks of the river which waters Paradise.*

Saladin, after being encamped for several days on the western side of the city, directed his operations towards the north, and caused the ramparts which extended from the gate of Jehoshaphat to that of St. Stephen to be undermined. The bravest of the citizens made a sortie, and endeavoured to destroy the machines and works of the besiegers, encouraging each other by repeating these words of Scripture: "*A single one of us shall make ten infidels fly, and ten of us shall put to flight ten thousand.*" They performed prodigies of valour, but they could not interrupt the progress of the siege. Repulsed by the Saracens, they were forced to return to the city, whither their appearance brought terror and discouragement. The towers and ramparts appeared ready to fall at the first signal for a general assault. Despair then took entire possession of the inhabitants, who saw no means of defence within their power but tears and prayers. The soldiers crowded to the churches instead of flying to arms; and not even the promise of a hundred pieces of gold could keep them on the tottering ramparts for one night. The clergy made processions through the streets, to invoke the protection of Heaven. Some struck their breasts with stones, whilst others tore their bodies with hair-cloth, crying aloud for *mercy!* Nothing was heard in Jerusalem but sobs and groans; "*but our Jesus Christ,*" says an old chronicle, "*would not hear them, for the luxury and impurity that were in the city would not allow either orisons or prayers to ascend before him.*" The despair of the inhabitants inspired them with the most contradictory projects at the same time; at one moment they formed the resolution of issuing in a body from the city, and seeking a glorious death in the ranks of the infidels; whilst, the next, they placed their last hope in the clemency of Saladin.

Amid the general trouble and agitation, the Greek and Syrian Christians, with the Melachite Christians, endured very unwillingly the authority of the Latins, and accused them of all the misfortunes of the war. A plot for giving up the city to the Mussulmans was discovered, which redoubled the general alarm, and made the principal inhabitants determine upon demanding a capitulation of Saladin. Accompanied by Baleau d'Ibelin, they went and proposed to the sultan to give up the place to him upon the conditions he had himself proposed before the siege. But Saladin remembered that he had sworn to take the city by assault, and put the inhabitants to the sword; and he sent back the deputies without giving them the least hope. Baleau d'Ibelin returned several times, renewing his supplications and his prayers, but always found Saladin inexorable. One day, whilst the Christian deputies were earnestly imploring him to accept their capitulation, turning towards the place, and pointing to his standards which floated over the walls,—"How can you ask me," said he, "to grant conditions to a city which is already taken?"

Nevertheless, the Saracens were repulsed; and Baleau, reanimated by the success the Christians had obtained, replied to the sultan: "You see that Jerusalem is not without defenders; if we can obtain no mercy from you, we will form a terrible resolution, and the fruits of our despair shall fill you with terror. These temples and palaces that you are so anxious to conquer, shall be totally destroyed; all the riches which excite the ambition and cupidity of the Saracens, shall become the prey of the flames. We will destroy the mosque of Omar; and the mysterious stone of Jacob, which is the object of your worship, shall be broken and pounded into dust. Jerusalem contains five thousand Mussulman prisoners; they shall all perish by the sword. We will, with our own hands, slay our wives and children, and thus spare them the shame of becoming your slaves. When the holy city shall be but a heap of ruins—one vast tomb—we will march out of it, followed by the angry manes of our friends and kindred; we will march out armed with sword and fire; and no one of us will ascend to Paradise without having consigned ten Mussulmans to hell. We shall thus obtain a glorious death, and shall die calling down upon your head the maledictions of the God of Jerusalem."

This spirited speech alarmed Saladin, and he invited the deputies to come again on the following day. He consulted with the doctors of the law, who decided that he might accept the capitulation proposed by the besieged, without violating his oath. The conditions were signed on the following day in the tent of the sultan, and thus Jerusalem again fell into the power of the infidels, after having been eighty-eight years under the domination of the Christians. The Latin historians had remarked that the Crusaders entered the city on a Friday, and at the same hour that Christ had submitted to death to expiate the crimes of the human race. The Saracens retook the city on a Friday, the anniversary of the day on which, according to their creed, Mahomet set out from Jerusalem to ascend into heaven. This circumstance, which might influence Saladin in his agreement to sign the capitulation, did not fail to add a new splendour to his triumph with the Mussulmans, and caused him to be regarded as the favourite of the Prophet.

All the warriors who were in Jerusalem when the capitulation was signed, obtained permission to retire to Tyre or Tripoli. The conqueror granted life to the inhabitants, and allowed them to purchase their liberty. All Christians, with the exception of the Greeks and Syrians, received orders to quit Jerusalem at the expiration of four days. The rate of ransom was fixed at ten pieces of gold for the men, five for the women, and two for the children. Such as could not purchase their liberty, remained in slavery.

These conditions had at first been received with joy by the Christians; but when they saw the day approach on which they were to leave Jerusalem, they experienced nothing but the most bitter grief at quitting the holy places. They watered the tomb of Christ with their tears, and regretted that they had not died to defend it; they visited Calvary and the churches they were never to see again, amidst groans and sighs; they embraced each other in the streets, weeping and lamenting over their fatal dissensions. Such as were unable to pay their ransom, and would only quit Jerusalem to become slaves to the Saracens, gave themselves up to all the excesses of despair. But such, in these deplorable moments, was their attachment to the religion whose precepts they had not always followed, that the insults offered to the sacred objects of their worship, afflicted them more than their own misfortunes.

At length the fatal day arrived on which the Christians were to quit Jerusalem. All the gates were shut except that of David, by which the people were to go out. Saladin, seated on an elevated throne, saw all the Christians pass before him. The patriarch, followed by the clergy, appeared the first, carrying the sacred vases, the ornaments of the church of the Holy Sepulchre, and treasures, of which God alone, says an Arabian author, knew the value. The queen of Jerusalem, accompanied by the barons and knights, came next. Saladin respected her grief, and addressed some words of kindness to her. The queen was followed by a great number of women, bearing their children in their arms, and uttering the most piercing cries. Many of them drew near to the throne of Saladin, and said to him: "You see at your feet the wives, the mothers, the daughters of the warriors you detain prisoners; we leave for ever our country which they have defended with glory; they helped to support our lives; in losing them, we have lost our last hope; if you deign to restore them to us, they will lessen the miseries of our exile, and we shall be no longer without help upon earth." Saladin was touched with their prayers, and promised to soften the misfortunes of so many bereaved families. He restored the children to their mothers, and the husbands to their wives, who were amongst the unredeemed captives. Several Christians had abandoned their most valuable goods, and bore upon their shoulders, some their parents weakened by age, and others their infirm or sick friends. Saladin was affected by this spectacle, and rewarded with gifts the virtue and piety of his enemies; he took pity upon all distresses, and allowed the Hospitallers to remain in the city to tend pilgrims, and assist such as were prevented from leaving Jerusalem by serious illness.

When the Saracens began the siege, the holy city contained more than a hundred thousand Christians. The greater part of them were able to purchase their own liberty; and Baleau d'Ibelin, who was the depositary of the treasures destined for the defence of the city, employed them in procuring the freedom of part of the inhabitants. Malec Adel, brother of the sultan, paid the ransom of two thousand captives. Saladin followed his example, by breaking the chains of a great number of poor and orphans. There only remained in bondage about fourteen thousand Christians, amongst whom there were four or five thousand children of tender age, who were insensible of their misfortunes, but whose fate the Christians the more deplored, from the certainty that these innocent victims of war would be brought up in the idolatry of Mahomet.

Many modern writers have compared the generous conduct of Saladin with the revolting scenes which accompanied the entrance of the first Crusaders into Jerusalem; but we must not forget that the Christians offered to capitulate, whilst the Mussulmans sustained a long siege with fanatical obstinacy; and that the companions of Godfrey, who were in an unknown land, in the midst of hostile nations, carried the city by assault, after braving numberless perils, and suffering all kinds of miseries. But we beg to observe that we do not make this observation to justify the Christians, or to weaken the praises history owes to Saladin, and which he even obtained from the people he had conquered.

After having done honour to misfortune and consoled humanity, Saladin gave his attention to his triumph. He entered Jerusalem preceded by his victorious standards. A great number of imauns, doctors of the law, and the ambassadors of many Mussulman princes, formed his train. By his orders all the churches, except that of the Holy Sepulchre, were converted into mosques. The sultan caused the walls and the vestibule of the mosque of Omar to be washed with rose-water, brought from Damascus, and with his own hands placed in it the pulpit constructed by Noureddin. On the first Friday which followed his entrance into Jerusalem, the people and the army assembled in the principal mosque, and the chief of the imauns, ascending the pulpit of the Prophet, returned thanks to God for the victories of Saladin. "Glory to God," said he, "who has caused Islamism to triumph, and who has broken the power of the infidels. Praise with me the Lord, who has restored to us Jerusalem, the dwelling of God, the abode of saints and prophets; it was from the bosom of this sacred dwelling that God caused his servant to travel during the darkness of night; it was to facilitate the conquest of Jerusalem by Joshua that God formerly arrested the course of the sun; and it is in this city, at the end of time, will assemble all the prophets of the earth." After having recapitulated the wonders and miracles of Jerusalem, the preacher of Islamism addressed himself to the soldiers of Saladin, and congratulated them with having braved so many perils, and having shed their blood to accomplish the will of Mahomet. "The soldiers of the prophet," added he, "the companions of Omar and Aboubeker, have appointed you places in their holy bands, and expect you amongst the elect of Islamism. Witnesses of your last triumph, the angels on the right hand of the Eternal have rejoiced; the hearts of the messengers of God have leaped with joy. Praise, then, with me the Lord; but yield not to the weaknesses of pride, and do not, above everything, believe that it was your swords of steel, with your horses, rapid as the wind, that have triumphed over the infidels. God is God; God alone is powerful; God alone has given you the victory; he orders you not to stop in a glorious career in which he himself leads you by the hand. *The holy war! the holy war!* that is the most pure of your adorations, the most noble of your duties. Cut down all the branches of impiety; cause Islamism to triumph everywhere; deliver the earth of the nations against which God is angry."

The chief of the imauns then prayed for the caliph of Bagdad, and terminated his prayer by naming Saladin. "O God!" cried he, "watch over the days of thy faithful servant, who is thy sharp sword, thy resplendent star, the defender of thy worship, the liberator of thy sacred dwelling. O God! let thy angels surround his empire, and prolong his days for the glory of thy name!"

Thus Jerusalem had changed its worship on changing its masters. Whilst the holy places resounded with the sacrilegious praises of the prophet, the Christians departed sadly, plunged in profound grief, and detesting the life which the Saracens had spared. Repulsed by their brethren of the East, who accused them of having given up the tomb of their God to the infidels, they wandered about Syria, without assistance and without asylum; many died of grief and hunger; the city of Tripoli shut its gates against them. Among this distracted multitude, one woman, urged by despair, cast her infant into the sea, cursing the Christians who refused them succour. They who directed their course to Egypt were less unfortunate, and touched the hearts of the Mussulmans; many embarked for Europe, whither they came to announce, with lamentations, that Jerusalem was in the hands of Saladin.

The loss of the holy city was generally attributed to the crimes of its inhabitants. Such was the policy of those times, that it explained everything by the corruption or the sanctity of the Christians; as if crime had not its moments of good fortune, and virtue its days of calamity. There is no doubt that the corruption of manners had weakened the springs of government, and enervated the courage of the people; but the never-ending discords of the Christians did not contribute less than their licentiousness and forgetfulness of scriptural morality, in producing the disasters of Jerusalem. When we reflect, likewise, that this weak kingdom, surrounded by enemies, was able to support itself, and defer its ruin for eighty-eight years, we are much less astonished at its fall than at the length of its duration. The kingdom of Jerusalem owed its preservation and splendour to the divisions of the Turks and Saracens, and the numerous supplies it received from Europe; it fell as soon as it was left to itself, and its enemies united to attack it.

As it was at that time, however, believed that the welfare of Christianity and the glory even of God were attached to the preservation of Jerusalem, the loss of the holy city created throughout Europe as much surprise as consternation. The news of this disaster was first brought into Italy; and Pope Urban III., who was then at Ferrara, died of grief. Christians forgot all the ills of their own country to weep over Jerusalem; it even superseded all other afflictions in private families. Priests carried from city to city images, representing the holy sepulchre trampled under the feet of horses, and Christ cast to the earth by Mahomet. Melancholy songs deplored the captivity of the king of Jerusalem and his knights, the fate of the virgins of the Lord abandoned to the insults of infidels, and the misfortunes of Christian children brought up in slavery and in the worship of false prophets.

Superstition, joined with despair, created a belief in the most sinister prodigies. On the day Saladin entered into the holy city, says Rigord, the monks of Argenteuil saw the moon descend from heaven upon the earth, and then re-ascend to heaven. In many churches, the crucifixes and images of the saints shed tears of blood in the presence of the faithful. A Christian knight had a dream, in which he saw an eagle flying over an army, holding in his claws seven javelins, and uttering in an intelligible voice, *Evil be to Jerusalem.*

Every one accused himself of having brought down the vengeance of Heaven by his own offences; and all the faithful sought to appease by penitence a God whom they believed to be irritated. "The Lord," said they among themselves, "has poured out the floods of his wrath, and the arrows of his anger are bathed in the blood of his servants. Let our whole life pass away in mourning, since we have heard a voice complaining on the mountain of Sion, and the children of the Lord are scattered." The sacred orators addressed God himself, and made the churches resound with their invocations and prayers. "O powerful God!" cried they, "thy hand has armed itself for the triumph of thy justice. Filled with tears, we come to implore thy goodness, in order that thou mayest remember thy people, and that thy mercies may exceed our miseries; deliver not over thy heritage to shame; and let the angels of peace obtain the fruits of penitence for Jerusalem."

The Christian world was for a moment changed. Whilst weeping for the loss of the tomb of Christ, people recalled the precepts of the holy Scriptures, and became all at once better. Luxury was banished from cities; injuries were forgotten, and alms were given abundantly. Christians slept upon ashes, clothed themselves in hair-cloth, and expiated their disorderly lives by fasting and mortification. The clergy set the example: the morals of the cloisters were reformed, and cardinals, condemning themselves to poverty, promised to repair to the Holy Land, supported on charity by the way.

These pious reformations did not last long; but men's minds were not the less prepared for a new crusade by them, and all Europe was soon roused by the voice of Gregory VIII., who exhorted the faithful to assume the cross and take up arms. The first care of the sovereign pontiff was to re-establish peace among Christian nations; and with that view he repaired to Pisa, to endeavour to terminate the angry disputes that had arisen between the Pisans and the Genoese. Gregory died without finishing the work he had begun, and left the direction of the crusade to his successor, Clement III., who, immediately after his accession to the pontifical throne, ordered prayers for the peace of the West and the deliverance of the land of the pilgrims.

William, archbishop of Tyre, had quitted the East to come into Europe to solicit the assistance of the Christian princes, and was charged by the pope to preach the holy war. William was more able and more eloquent than Heraclius, who had preceded him in this mission, and, further, more worthy by his virtues of being the interpreter of the Christians, and to speak in the name of Christ. After having awakened the zeal of the nations of Italy, he repaired to France, and was present at an assembly convoked near Gisors, by Henry II. of England, and Philip Augustus of France. On the arrival of William, these two kings, who were at war for the country of Vexin, laid down their arms. The bravest warriors of France and England, united by the dangers of their brothers of the East, came to the assembly whose object was the deliverance of the holy places. William was received with enthusiasm, and read with a loud voice, to the princes and knights, an account of the taking of Jerusalem by Saladin. After this reading, which drew tears from all the assembly, William exhorted the faithful to take the cross. "The mountain of Sion," said he, "still resounds with the words of Ezekiel: *O children of men, remember that day in which the king of Babylon triumphed over Jerusalem!* In one single day all the evils that the prophets announced fell upon the city of David and Solomon. That city, filled by all Christian nations, remains now alone, or rather is only inhabited by a sacrilegious people. The queen of nations, the capital of so many provinces, has paid the tribute imposed upon slaves. All her gates have been broken, and her guardians exposed with cattle in the markets of infidel cities. The Christian states of the East, which caused the religion of the cross to flourish in Asia, and formed the bulwark of the West against the invasions of the Saracens, are reduced to the cities of Tyre, Antioch and Tripoli. We have seen, according to the expression of Isaiah, the Lord extending his hand and its inflictions from the Euphrates to the torrent of Egypt. The inhabitants of forty cities have been driven from their homes, despoiled of their wealth, and are now wandering with their weeping families among the nations of Asia, *without finding a stone whereon to lay their heads*."

After having thus described the misfortunes of the Christians of the East, William reproached the warriors who listened to him, with not having come to the aid of their brethren, and with having allowed the heritage of Christ to be taken from them. He was astonished that they could entertain another thought, that they could seek any other glory than that of delivering the holy places; and addressing himself to the princes and knights: "To meet you here," said he, "I have traversed fields of carnage; nay, within sight even of this assembly I have seen preparations for war: what blood is it you have shed, what blood is it you are about to shed again? Why are you armed with these swords? You are fighting here for the banks of a river, for the limits of, a province, or for a transient renown, whilst infidels trample the banks of Siloë, whilst they invade the kingdom of God, and whilst the cross of Christ is dragged ignominiously through the streets of Bagdad. You shed torrents of blood for vain treaties, whilst the very Gospel, that solemn treaty between God and men, is being outraged! Have you forgotten the deeds of your fathers? A Christian kingdom was founded by them in the midst of Mussulman nations. A crowd of heroes, a crowd of princes born in your country, went to defend and govern it. If you have permitted their work to perish, come at least and deliver their tombs, which are in the power of the Saracens. Does your Europe no longer produce such warriors as Godfrey, Tancred, and their companions? The prophets and saints buried at Jerusalem, the churches transformed into mosques, the very stones of the sepulchres, all cry to you to avenge the glory of God and the death of your brethren. What! why, the blood of Naboth, the blood of Abel which arose towards heaven, found avengers, and shall the blood of Christ arise in vain against his enemies and his executioners?

"The East has beheld base Christians, whom avarice and fear have rendered the allies of Saladin; I do not suspect they will find imitators among you; but remember what Christ has said: *'He who is not for me is against me.'* If you do not defend the cause of God, what cause will you dare defend? If the King of heaven and earth find you not beneath his colours, where are the powers whose standards you will follow? Why then are the enemies of God no longer the enemies of all Christians? What will be the joy of the Saracens amidst their impious triumphs, when they shall be told that the West has no more warriors faithful to Christ, and that the princes and kings of Europe have learnt with indifference the disasters and captivity of Jerusalem?"

These reproaches made in the name of religion affected the hearts of the princes and knights deeply. Henry II. and Philip Augustus, to that time implacable enemies, embraced each other in tears, and put themselves forward the first to receive the cross. Richard, duke of Guienne, son of

DEATH OF FREDERICK OF GERMANY.

The leader of this formidable army had conquered several nations, and dictated laws to two empires, without having yet done anything towards the aim of his enterprise. After having crossed Mount Taurus, near Laurenda, he had resumed his march towards Syria at the beginning of spring, and was proceeding along the banks of the river Selef. Attracted by the freshness and limpidity of the waters, he wished to bathe; but, seized all at once by a mortal coldness, he was dragged out insensible, and soon after died, humbly bowing to the will of God, who would not allow him to behold the land he was going to defend. His death was more fatal to his army than the loss of a great battle; all the Germans wept for a chief who had so often led them to victory, and whose name alone was the terror of the Saracens. The bones of this unfortunate monarch were preserved for the purpose of being buried in that Jerusalem he had sworn to deliver, but in which he could not even obtain a tomb. William, who had been to preach the crusade in Europe, buried the remains of Frederick in the city of Tyre, and pronounced the funeral oration of the most powerful monarch of the Christians.

[Book VII.

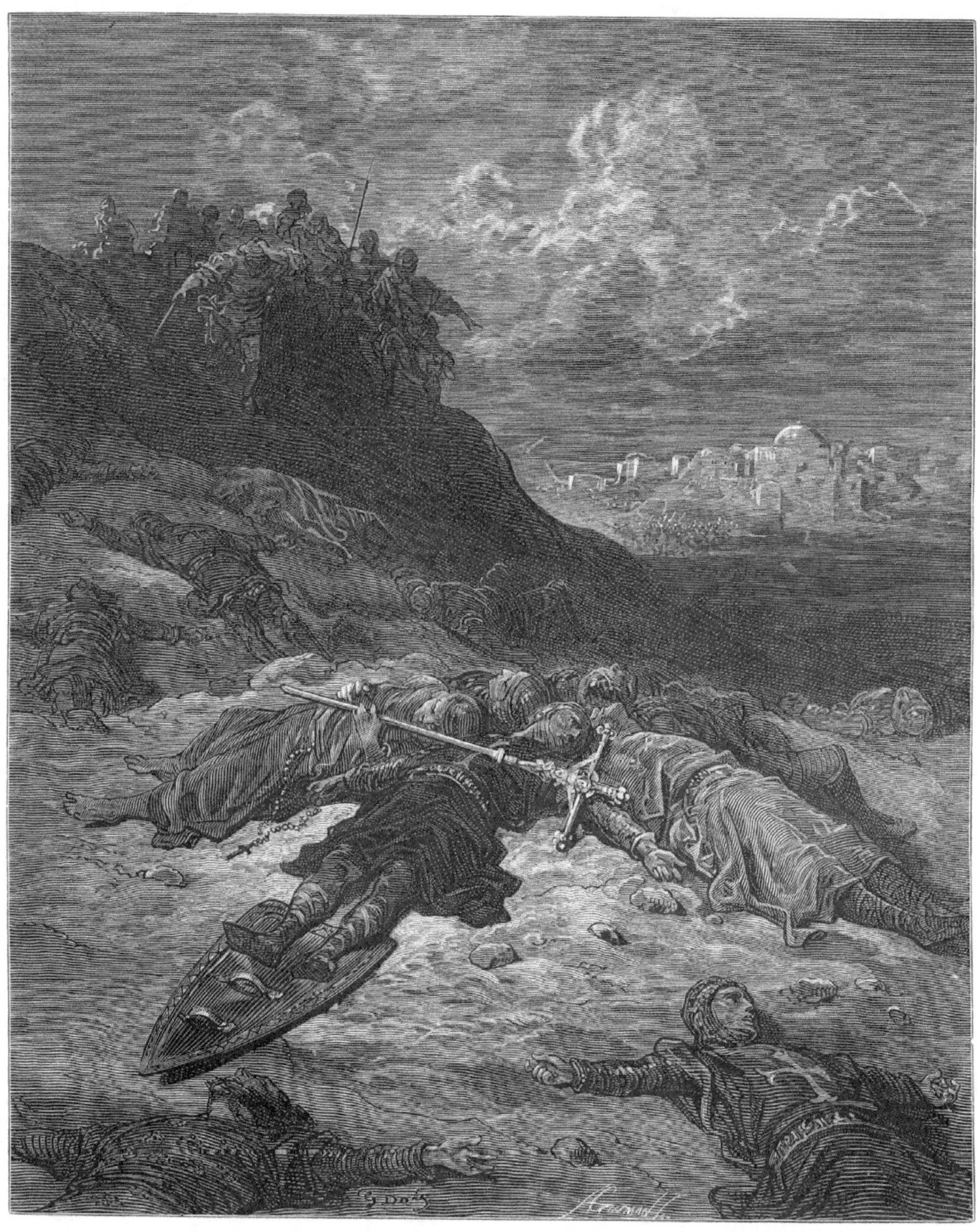

Henry, Philip, count of Flanders, Hugh, duke of Burgundy, Henry, count of Champagne, Thibaut, count of Blois, Retrou, count of Perche, the counts of Nevers, de Bar, Vendôme, Soissons, the two brothers Josselin and Matthew de Montmorency, with a crowd of barons and knights, together with several bishops of France and England, all took the oath to deliver the Holy Land. The whole assembly shouted the words "*the Cross! the Cross!*" and this war-cry soon resounded through all the provinces. The spot on which the faithful met was afterwards called the *sacred field*, and a church was built upon it to preserve the remembrance of the pious devotion of the Christian knights. As money was wanting to carry out the holy enterprise, it was resolved in the council of the princes and bishops that all who did not take the cross should pay a tenth part of their revenues and of the value of their property of all kinds. The terror which the arms of Saladin had inspired, caused the name of the *Saladin tithe* to be given to this tax. Excommunications were published against all such as refused to pay a debt so sacred. In vain the clergy, of whom Peter of Blois undertook the defence, alleged the liberty and independence of the Church, and pretended they could not be called on to assist the Crusaders otherwise than by their prayers; the ecclesiastics were told that they ought to set the example, that the clergy was not the Church, and that the wealth of the Church belonged to Christ. The orders of the Chartreux, of Citeaux and Fontevrault, with the hospital for lepers, were all that were exempt from a tribute raised for a cause which was believed to be that of all Christians.

In the two first crusades, the greater part of the villagers who had taken the cross, had done so to emancipate themselves from slavery. Some disorders naturally resulted from this; the country was deserted, the lands were uncultivated; in this crusade means were taken to set bounds to the too forward zeal of the labourers: all serfs who enrolled themselves for the holy war, without the permission of their lords, were condemned to pay the Saladin tithe, as if they had not taken the cross.*

Notwithstanding all this excitement, the peace which had been sworn to by the kings of France and England was not long held sacred. Richard, who was duke of Guienne, having had a quarrel with the count of Thoulouse, Henry took up arms to assist his son. Philip flew to the defence of his vassal; and Normandy, Berry, and Auvergne were soon in a blaze. The two monarchs, urged by the solicitations of the nobles and bishops, met for a moment in the sacred field in which they had laid down their arms, but they could not agree upon the conditions of the peace; and the elm-tree under which they held their conference, was cut down by the orders of Philip. Negotiations were renewed several times without putting a stop to the war. The king of France required that Richard should be crowned king of England, in the lifetime of his father, and that he should espouse Alice, a French princess, whom Henry detained in prison. The king of England, jealous of his authority, could not consent to accept these conditions; and would neither yield up his crown nor the sister of Philip, of whom he was enamoured. Richard, irritated by his father's refusal, threw himself into the party of Philip Augustus, and declared openly against Henry; on all sides they flew to arms, and the produce of the Saladin tithe was employed to carry on a sacrilegious war, which outraged both morality and nature.

This war was not a good augury for that which was about to be undertaken in Asia: the pope's legate excommunicated Richard, and threatened Philip with placing his kingdom under an interdict. Philip despised the menaces of the legate, and told him that the Holy See had no right to meddle with the quarrels of princes; Richard, still more violent, drew his sword, and was on the point of cutting down the legate. Peace seemed every day to be at a greater distance; in vain cries of indignation arose from the people; in vain the great vassals refused to take part in a quarrel which interested neither religion nor country. Henry, who consented to an interview, still haughtily rejected the con-

* "The noblest monument of a conqueror's fame and of the terror which he inspired, is the Saladin tenth."—*Gibbon.*—TRANS.

ditions that were proposed to him. He resisted for a long time both the prayers of his subjects and the counsels of the bishops; and the terror only with which the thunder of Heaven, which fell by his side during the conference, inspired him, could overcome his obstinacy. He at length accepted Philip's conditions, but soon repented of his acquiescence; and shortly after died of grief, leaving his maledictions to Richard, who had made open war against him, and to his youngest son, who had engaged in a conspiracy against him.

Richard accused himself of the death of his father, and, pressed by repentance, he remembered the vow he had made in the sacred field. Now become king of England, he began seriously his preparations for the holy expedition. He repaired to his kingdom, and convoked, near Northampton, an assembly of the barons and prelates, in which Baldwin, archbishop of Canterbury, preached the crusade. The preacher of the holy war then went through the provinces of England to raise the zeal and emulation of the faithful. Miraculous adventures attested the sanctity of his mission, and brought under the banners of the cross the wild and credulous inhabitants of Wales, and several other countries where the misfortunes of Jerusalem had never been heard of.

The enthusiasm of the English for this crusade, manifested itself at first by a violent persecution of the Jews, great numbers of whom were massacred in the cities of London and York. A vast many of these unfortunate people found no means of escape from their persecutors but in a self-inflicted death. These horrible scenes were renewed every crusade. When money was required for the holy expedition, it was perceived that the Jews were the depositaries of the general wealth; and the knowledge of the treasures accumulated in their hands, seemed to lead the people to remember that it was they who had crucified their God.

Richard did not take much pains to repress the misguided multitude, but availed himself of the persecution of the Jews to increase his own treasures. But neither the spoils of the Jews, nor the produce of the Saladin tithe, for the non-payment of which the English were threatened with imprisonment, at all satisfied the king of England. Richard alienated the domains of the crown, and put to sale all the great dignities of the kingdom; he would sell, he said, the city of London, if he could find a purchaser. He went afterwards into Normandy, where the "Estates" permitted him to exhaust that rich province, and gave him full means to support a war in which the whole people took so great an interest.

A great number of warriors assumed the cross in France and England, and the preparations for the crusade were finished amidst general fermentation. Many barons and lords, however, did not announce the period of their departure, and delayed, under various pretexts, the pilgrimage to which they had engaged themselves by oath. The celebrated Peter of Blois addressed a pathetic exhortation to them, in which he compared them to reapers who put off beginning their work until the harvest was finished. The orator of the holy war represented to them that strong and courageous men found a country everywhere, and that true pilgrims ought to resemble the birds of heaven. He recalled to their ambition the example of Abraham, who abandoned his home to elevate himself among the nations, who crossed the Jordan with a staff only, and returned followed by two troops of warriors. This exhortation revived the ardour for the crusade, which had evidently begun to cool. The monarchs of France and England had an interview at Nonancourt, where they agreed to proceed to Palestine by sea. They made, at the same time, several regulations to secure order and discipline in the armies they were about to lead into Asia. The laws of religion, and the penalties that they inflict, did not appear to them sufficient in this case. The justice of these barbarous ages was charged with the onerous task of suppressing the passions and vices of the Crusaders: whoever gave a blow, was to be plunged three times into the sea; he who struck with the sword, had his hand cut off; he who abused another, gave to the person he had offended as many ounces of silver as he had uttered invectives; when a man was convicted of theft, boiling pitch was poured upon his shaven head, it was then covered with feathers, and he was abandoned on the nearest shore; a murderer, bound to the corpse of his victim, was to be cast into the sea, or buried alive.

As the presence of women had occasioned many disorders in the first crusade, they were forbidden to go to the Holy Land. Gambling with dice, or other games of chance, together with profane swearing or blasphemy, were strictly forbidden among the Crusaders; and luxury of the table or in clothes was repressed by a law. The assembly of Nonancourt made many other regulations, and neglected nothing likely to bring back the soldiers of Christ to the simplicity and virtues of the Gospel.

Whenever princes, nobles, or knights set out for the holy war, they made their wills, as if they were certain never to return to Europe. When Philip came back to his capital, he declared his last will, and regulated, for the period of his absence, the administration of his kingdom, which he confided to Queen Adela, his mother, and his uncle, the Cardinal de Champagne. After having fulfilled the duties of a king, he laid down the sceptre, to take, at St. Denis, the staff and scrip of a pilgrim, and went to Vézelay, where he was to have another interview with Richard. The two kings again swore an eternal friendship, and both called down the thunders of the Church upon the head of him who should break his oaths. They separated full of friendship for each other; Richard hastened to embark at Marseilles, and Philip at Genoa. An English historian remarks that they were the only kings of France and England that ever fought together for the same cause; but this harmony, the work of extraordinary circumstances, was not likely to exist long between two princes acted upon by so many motives of rivalry. Both young, ardent, brave, and magnificent; Philip the greater king, Richard the greater captain; both animated by the same ambition and the same passion for glory. Desire for renown, much more than piety, drew them to the Holy Land: both haughty and prompt to revenge an injury, they acknowledged, in their various differences, no other arbitrator or judge but the sword: religion had not sufficient empire over their minds to humble their pride, and each would have thought himself degraded, if he had either demanded or accepted peace. To ascertain, at a glance, how little hope could be founded on the union of these two princes, it is only necessary to observe, that Philip, on ascending his throne, had shown himself to be the most inveterate enemy of England, and that Richard was the son of that Eleanor of Guienne, the first wife of Louis VII., who, after the second crusade, had quitted her husband, threatening France with her revenge.

After the conference of Gisors, the archbishop of Tyre repaired to Germany, to solicit Frederick Barbarossa to take the cross. This prince had signalized his valour in forty battles; a long and fortunate reign had rendered his name illustrious; but his age recognised no glory as true but that which was won in Asia. He wished to deserve the praises of his pious contemporaries, and took up arms for the deliverance of the Holy Land; he was, likewise, doubtless influenced by the scruples which his quarrels with the pope had left upon his conscience, and by his desire to perfect his reconciliation with the Holy See.

A general diet was assembled at Mayence. The nobles and prelates would not allow German to remain indifferent to a cause which had inflamed the zeal of the other nations of Europe Frederick, whose devotion they encouraged, descended from his throne, amidst general acclamations, and received the sign of the Crusaders from the hands of the archbishop of Tyre. His example was followed by his son, Frederick duke of Swabia; Leopold duke of Austria, and Berthold duke of Moravia; Herman, marquis of Baden, the count of Nassau, the bishops of Besançon, Munster, Osnaburg, and Passau, with a crowd of barons and knights, likewise swore to deliver the tomb of Christ.

The war against the infidels was preached in all the churches. Happy, said the sacred orators, are they who undertake this holy voyage; more happy are they who never return from it. Among the prodigies that appeared to announce the will of Heaven, the miraculous vision of a virgin of Lewenstein, is particularly mentioned. She had learnt the conquest of Jerusalem on the very day that the Saracens had entered the holy city, and rejoiced at this lamentable event, saying that it would furnish a means of salvation for the warriors of the West.

The multitude of those who presented themselves to receive the cross was so great, that means were obliged to be taken to repress their ardour. Frederick, who had followed his uncle Conrad in the second crusade, was aware of the disorders and misfortunes that might result from too great a number of followers. He refused to receive under his banners any who could not take with them three marks of silver; and rejected all such vagabonds and adventurers as had, in the other expeditions, committed so many excesses, and dishonoured the cause of the Christians by their brigandage.

Frederick, before his departure, sent ambassadors to the emperor of Constantinople, and the sultan of Iconium, to demand freedom of passage through their states; and wrote to Saladin, to declare war, if he did not restore to the Franks Jerusalem and the other Christian cities that had surrendered to his arms. The embassy addressed to Saladin, shows the spirit of chivalry in which Frederick entered upon this crusade. That which, without doubt, induced him to address the sultan of Iconium, was an opinion then spread through Europe, that the Mussulman prince had evinced a desire of embracing the Christian religion. Frederick left Ratisbon at the head of an army of a hundred thousand combatants, and crossed Hungary and Bulgaria, as the first Crusaders had done. He arrived in the provinces of the Greek empire before Richard and Philip had embarked for Palestine.

Isaac Angelus was then seated on the throne of Constantinople; this prince had only been brave on one single day, and his courage procured him an empire. Andronicus, the Nero of the Greeks, having been warned by soothsayers that he would be dethroned by one of his subjects, who bore the name of Isaac, desired to get rid of Isaac Angelus, and sent one of his officers to conduct him to prison. Isaac, animated by despair, instead of obeying, threw himself upon the minister of Andronicus, struck him to the earth, and running into the public streets, cried out: *"I have killed the devil! I have killed the devil!"* Upon the report of this event spreading through the city, the people assembled in crowds and proclaimed Isaac emperor. In vain Andronicus endeavoured to quiet the storm; he was seized by his own soldiers, and loaded with chains. Dragged through the streets by an infuriated multitude, he underwent in one day more torments than he had inflicted upon his enemies during all his reign, and Constantinople beheld a populace a hundred times more barbarous than all her tyrants.

It was amidst these bloody and disgusting scenes that Isaac was clothed with the imperial purple. He did not possess the savage character of Andronicus, but he was entirely incapable of defending the empire against its enemies. Instead of raising armies, he gathered together in his palace a troop of monks, who kept up his sense of security by their prayers, and turned his attention from the cares and duties of state by their visions and prophecies. The mutual hatred of the Greeks and Latins had increased under his reign and that of Andronicus. The Latins who inhabited Constantinople were driven from the city, their houses were given up to the flames, and a great number of them were put to death. They who escaped the carnage took refuge in the vessels and galleys, and made sanguinary reprisals on the islands and shores of the Hellespont. The monks who surrounded Isaac partook of the blind hatred entertained by the people for the Christians of the West, and dreaded their vengeance. They advised the successor of Andronicus to mistrust the emperor of Germany, and to betray him if he could not conquer him.

Faithful to their counsels, Isaac promised to entertain the Germans in his states, and at the same time formed an alliance with Saladin. He sent orders to his governors to harass the Crusaders, and even to attack them by open force. These imprudent hostilities exposed the weakness of the Greeks, and were of service to the Germans; for Frederick, after having put the troops of Isaac to flight, took every advantage of his victory. Isaac, constantly intoxicated by the incense of his courtiers, and seduced by the promises of the monks, only replied to the victories of Frederick by letters full of haughtiness and menaces; he refused to acknowledge him as emperor, and could see nothing but a vassal in a prince who was marching in triumph towards his capital. Whilst his subjects were from all parts flying before the Germans, he gave himself in his letters the titles of *most sublime, most powerful emperor, the angel of the whole earth;* and caused the ambassadors of Frederick to be imprisoned. The patriarch of Constantinople preached, by his orders, in the church of St. Sophia, the murder of the Latins.

Nevertheless, terror at length took possession of the heart of Isaac, and from that moment this prince altered the tone of his language, and became the most humble of suppliants. Frederick was now for him, *the most virtuous emperor of the Germans,* and he voluntarily granted him much more than he had before refused him. After having required hostages, he himself gave them, and fed during several months an army he had sworn to destroy. He endured without a murmur the violences which the Crusaders committed in their passage, and treated an army that laid waste his provinces as if they had saved his empire. The emperor of Germany received magnificent presents, and all the vessels of the Greek navy were employed in transporting the Crusaders into Asia.

The Germans embarked at Gallipoli, and crossed the Hellespont. The sight of the coasts of Asia, and the easy victories they had obtained over the Greeks, made them forget the obstacles and dangers of a long and painful march. They saw nothing in the regions they were about to traverse but laurels to be gathered and kingdoms to be destroyed or founded; but it was not long ere this brilliant prospect disappeared. Whilst they remained in the territories of Isaac, they had to suffer from the perfidy of the Greeks; and when they arrived among the Turks, they had fresh enemies to contend with. The sultan of Iconium, who had been as liberal of his promises as the emperor of Constantinople, did not prove at all more faithful to his word. When the Germans arrived on the banks of the Meander, near Laodicea, they found the Turks drawn up in order of battle upon the heights, and ready to surprise them in the defiles: the latter were, however, punished for the treachery of their master, and cut to pieces; their bodies covered the passages they had been charged to defend.

The Crusaders, ever persuaded that Heaven protected their arms, attributed this victory to miracles. Several knights declared, upon oath, that they had seen St. George and St. Victor, clothed in white, and armed with lances, fighting at the head of the Christians; but the celestial powers that had thus enabled the Germans to triumph over the arms of their enemies, did not destroy the obstacles which impeded the march of their victorious army. The Crusaders soon felt the want of provisions in a country ravaged at the same time by the conquerors and the conquered. Snow, rain, and the rigours of winter rendered their march exceedingly painful through a mountainous region, intersected by torrents that had overflowed their banks. Hunger and disease destroyed a great number of the soldiers. To remedy the evils which threatened his army with entire ruin, Frederick was obliged to attack Iconium, the very capital in which he had expected to find peace and all the provisions he stood in need of.

At the first signal the ramparts were scaled; Iconium was taken by assault and given up to pillage. The beaten sultan then fulfilled his promises, and this last victory restored abundance in the Christian army.

From this time the Germans spread terror in every country around them. The Armenians solicited their alliance, and the independent tribes of the Turcomans, on several occasions, felt the effects of their courage. During their triumphal march they attracted the admiration of the natives by their discipline; and the emirs, charged with announcing their arrival to Saladin, praised their indomitable valour in fight, and their heroic patience in the labours and fatigues of war.

The leader of this formidable army had conquered several nations, and dictated laws to two empires, without having yet done anything towards the aim of his enterprise. After having crossed Mount Taurus, near Laurenda, he had resumed his march towards Syria at the beginning of spring, and was proceeding along the banks of the river Selef.* Attracted by the freshness and limpidity of the waters, he wished to bathe; but, seized all at once by a mortal coldness, he was dragged out insensible, and soon after died, humbly bowing to the will of God, who would not allow him to behold the land he was going to defend. His death was more fatal to his army than the loss of a great battle; all the Germans wept for a chief who had so often led them to victory, and whose name alone was the terror of the Saracens. The bones of this unfortunate monarch were preserved for the purpose of being buried in that Jerusalem he had sworn to deliver, but in which he could not even obtain a tomb. William, who had been to preach the crusade in Europe, buried the remains of Frederick in the city of Tyre, and pronounced the funeral oration of the most powerful monarch of the Christians.

After the death of Frederick, grief weakened the courage of his soldiers; some deserted the banners of the crusade, whilst the others listlessly and sadly continued their march under the orders of Frederick, duke of Swabia, who reminded them of the virtues of his father, but was unable to lead them to victory. The contests they still had to maintain against the Saracens, together with hunger, fatigue and disease, reduced the army of the Germans to six or seven hundred horse, and about five thousand foot. This miserable wreck of a formidable army crossed Syria; and the report of their disasters having preceded them, their arrival must have created more terror than confidence among the Christians, who were then carrying on the siege of Ptolemaïs.

---

* The Arabian historian Omad relates that Frederick Barbarossa was drowned in endeavouring to cross the river on horseback; the force of the stream carried him towards a tree, against which he struck his head. He was dragged out of the water, adds Omad, and his soul being ready to quit his body, the angel of death took possession of it, and carried it to hell.

BOOK VIII.

SALADIN.

A. D. 1188–1192.

The conquests of Saladin—Conrad of Montferrat—Siege of Tyre—Marquis of Montferrat—The "Green Knight"—Siege of Tripoli—William, king of Sicily, engages in the holy war—Admiral Margaritt defends Tripoli—Capture of Tortosa—Heroic defence of Carac—Release of Guy de Lusignan—His siege of Ptolemaïs, and his numerous conflicts with Saladin—Description of Ptolemaïs—Karacoush, minister of Saladin—Conrad, marquis of Tyre, fits out a fleet for the Holy Land—Bravery of the Mamelukes—Death of André de Brienne—Defeat of the Crusaders at Ptolemaïs by Saladin—Death of Frederick, duke of Swabia, and of Sybilla, wife of Guy de Lusignan—Disputes about the succession to the kingdom of Jerusalem—Humphrey de Thorone—Conrad—Eleanor of Guienne—Philip of France arrives at Palestine—Cyprus captured by Richard I.—His marriage to Berengaria of Navarre—Jane, queen of Sicily—Isaac Comnenus—Disputes respecting the sovereignty of Jerusalem—Arrival of Richard I. before the walls of Ptolemaïs—His quarrels with Philip of France—Conflicts with Saladin—Ptolemaïs taken by the Christians—Guy de Chatillon, Josselin de Montmorency, and some of the bravest nobility of Europe, slain—The Mohammedans—Leopold, duke of Austria—Philip of France quits Palestine, and returns to France—Battle of Arsur—Ascalon destroyed by Saladin, and rebuilt by Richard I.—Richard marches on Jerusalem—Conrad assassinated—Treaty of peace between Richard and Saladin—Guy de Lusignan obtains the sovereignty of Cyprus—Palestine ceded to Henry, count of Champagne—Characters of Richard I. and of Saladin—Leopold of Austria detains Richard as a prisoner—Death of Saladin—Malek-Adel takes possession of Egypt.

WHILST the crusade was being preached in Europe, Saladin was following up the course of his victories. The battle of Tiberias and the taking of Jerusalem had created so general a terror, that the inhabitants of the Holy Land were persuaded it was useless to endeavour to resist the army of the Saracens. Amid this consternation, one city alone defied and checked all the united forces of the new conqueror of the East. Saladin was exceedingly anxious for the conquest of Tyre, and had twice collected both his fleets and his armies to attack it. But the inhabitants had sworn to die rather than surrender to the Mussulmans; which noble determination was the work of Conrad, who had recently arrived in the city, and appeared to have been sent by Heaven to save it.

Conrad, son of the marquis of Montferrat, bore a name renowned throughout the West, and the fame of his exploits had preceded him into Asia. In his earliest youth he had distinguished himself in the war of the Holy See against the emperor of Germany. A passion for glory and a love of adventure then led him to Constantinople, where he suppressed a sedition which threatened the imperial throne, and killed the leader of the rebels on the field of battle. The sister of Isaac Angelus and the title of Cæsar were the reward of his courage and his services; but his restless character would not allow him to enjoy his good fortune long. Whilst surrounded by peaceful grandeur, he was roused by the fame of the holy war, and, heedless of the tenderness of a bride, or the gratitude of an emperor, he hastened into Palestine. Conrad reached the coast of Phœnicia a few days after the battle of Tiberias. At the moment of his arrival, the city of Tyre had named deputies to demand a capitulation of Saladin; but his presence revived the courage of the besieged, and changed the face of everything. He caused himself to be made commander, he widened the ditches, and repaired the fortifications; and the inhabitants of Tyre, attacked by sea and land, becoming all at once invincible warriors under his orders, were able to contend with the fleets and armies of the Saracens.

The old marquis of Montferrat, the father of Conrad, who had left his peaceful states to visit the Holy Land, was present at the battle of Tiberias. Made prisoner by the Mussulmans, he languished in the prisons of Damascus, until his children might be able to deliver him or purchase his liberty.

Saladin sent for him to his army, and promised the brave Conrad to restore his father, and grant him rich possessions in Syria, if he would open the gates of Tyre to him. He threatened at the same time to place the old marquis before the front rank of the Saracens, and expose him to all the arrows of the besieged. Conrad haughtily replied that he despised the gifts of infidels, and that the life of his father was less dear to him than the cause of the Christians. He added that nothing should stop his exertions, and that if the Saracens were so barbarous as to sacrifice an old man who had surrendered himself upon the word of Saladin, he should take glory from being descended from a martyr. After this reply the Saracens renewed their attacks, and the Tyrians continued to defend themselves bravely. The Hospitallers, the Templars, and the bravest of the warriors that were still in Palestine, repaired to Tyre to take part in this glorious defence. Among the Franks who distinguished themselves by their valour, no one was more remarkable than a Spanish gentleman, known in history by the name of *the Green Knight.* Alone, say the old chronicles, he repulsed and dispersed whole battalions of the enemy; he fought several times in single combat, always overcoming the most intrepid of the Mussulmans, and creating in Saladin the strongest admiration for his courage and his feats of arms.

The city did not contain a single citizen that was not an active combatant; the children even were so many soldiers, and the women animated the warriors by their presence and their applause. On board the ships, under the walls, battles were continually fought; and the Saracens, on all occasions, again met with the Christian heroes that had so often inspired them with fear.

Saladin, despairing of taking Tyre, resolved to raise the siege, and attack Tripoli; but was not more successful in this new enterprise. William, king of Sicily, upon being informed of the disasters in Palestine, sent assistance to the Christians. Admiral Margaritt, whose talents and victories had procured for him the surname of *King of the Sea* and the *New Neptune,* arrived on the coast of Syria with fifty galleys, three hundred knights, and five hundred foot-soldiers. The Sicilian warriors hastened to the defence of Tripoli, and, commanded by the *Green Knight,* who had so eminently distinguished himself at the siege of Tyre, forced Saladin to abandon his undertaking.

The city and country of Tripoli, since the death of Raymond, had belonged to Bohémond, prince of Antioch. Saladin, exasperated by his double disappointment, laid waste the banks of the Orontes, and forced Bohémond to purchase a truce of eight months. The Mussulmans then took possession of Tortosa and some castles built on the heights of Libanus. The fortress of Carac, from which had issued the war so fatal to the Christians, defended itself during a whole year against a Mussulman army. The besieged, destitute of all succour, and a prey to every kind of evil and privation, carried resignation and bravery to perfect heroism. "Before they would surrender," says the continuator of William of Tyre, "they sold their wives and children to the Saracens, and there remained not an animal in the castle of which they could make food." They were at length, however, forced to yield to Saladin; the sultan granting them their lives and their liberty, and restoring to them their wives and children, whom a barbarous heroism had condemned to slavery.

Throughout his conquests, Saladin still kept Guy de Lusignan in chains; but when he became

THE SIEGE OF PTOLEMAÏS.

The roads of Galilee were covered with Mussulman soldiers coming from Damascus; and as Saladin looked daily for the arrival of a fleet from Egypt, which would make him master of the sea, he hoped soon to be able to triumph over the Christians, and deliver Ptolemaïs. A few days after the victory he had gained, a great number of vessels appeared upon the sea, directing their course towards the land. Both armies were filled with hope and joy, the Mussulmans believing them to be a fleet from the ports of Damietta and Alexandria, whilst the Crusaders confidently hoped them to be a Christian armament coming to their aid. The standard of the cross was soon seen floating from the masts of the vessels, which, whilst it excited the liveliest joy in the Christians, equally depressed the Mussulmans. Two fleets from Western ports entered the road of Ptolemaïs. The first bore the German Crusaders, commanded by the Duke of Gueldres and the Landgrave of Thuringia, and the other the warriors of Friesland and Denmark, who, after having fought the Saracens in Spain, came to defend the kingdom of Jerusalem. Conrad, Marquis of Tyre, could not remain idle while this war was going on; he armed vessels, raised troops, and united his forces with those of the Christian army.—Book VIII.

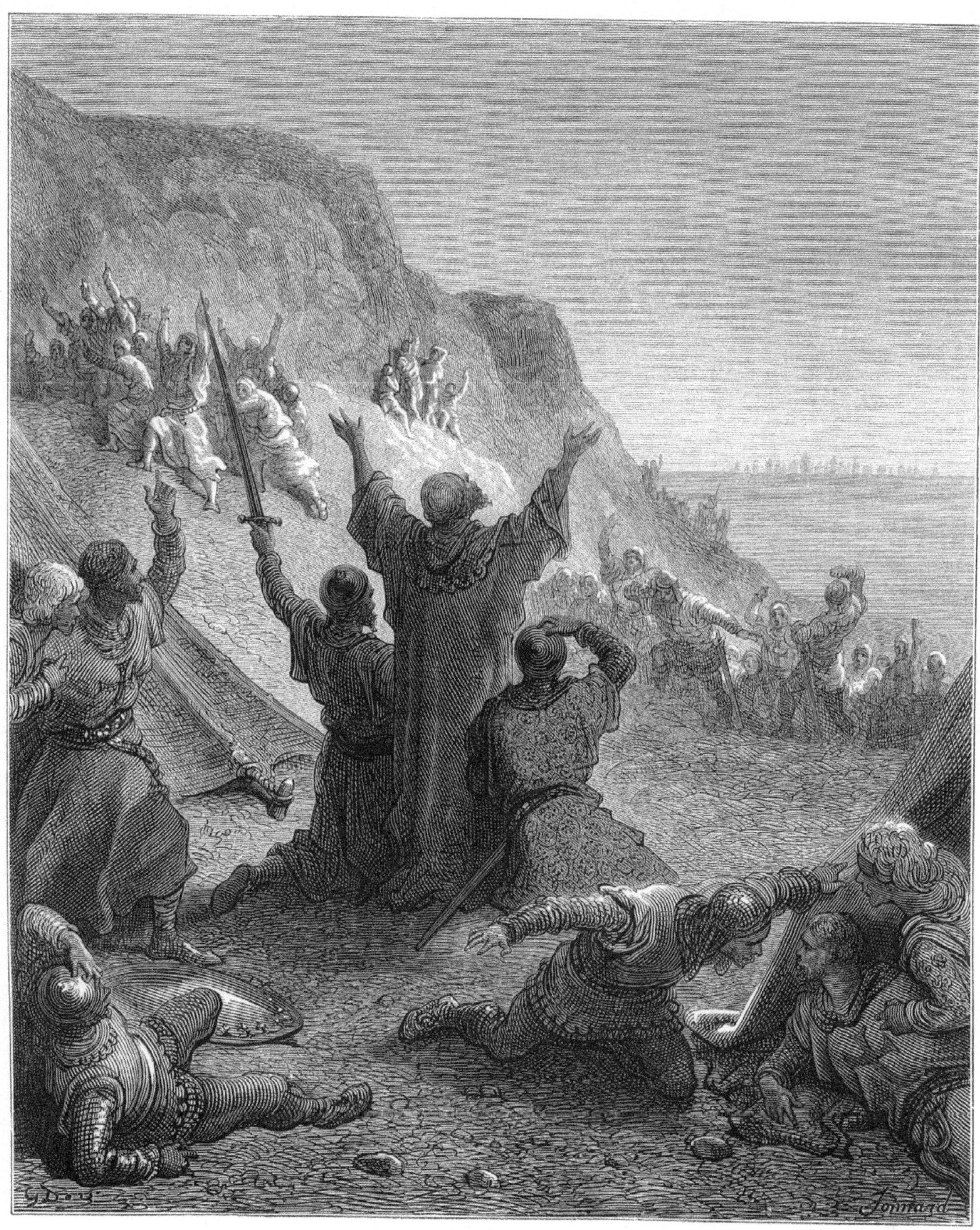

master of Carac and the greater part of Palestine, he at length set the unfortunate king of Jerusalem free, after having made him swear upon the Gospel to renounce his kingdom for ever, and to return to Europe. This promise, extorted by force, could not be regarded as binding in a war in which fanaticism set at nought the power of an oath, on the one side or the other. Saladin himself never entertained an idea that Guy would keep his word; and if he consented to liberate him, it was doubtless from the fear that a more able prince would be chosen in his place, and from the hope that his presence would bring discord among the Christians.

Guy was scarcely released from captivity, when he made his bishops annul the oath he had taken, and sought earnestly for an opportunity of reconstructing a throne upon which fortune had for a moment placed him. He presented himself in vain before Tyre; that city had given itself up to Conrad, and would not acknowledge as king a prince who had not been able to defend his own states. The king of Jerusalem wandered for a long time about his own kingdom, accompanied by a few faithful attendants, and at length resolved to undertake some enterprise that should draw attention, and unite under his banners the warriors who flocked from all parts of Europe to the assistance of the Holy Land.

Guy laid siege to Ptolemaïs, which had surrendered to Saladin a few days after the battle of Tiberias. This city, which historians call by turns *Acca, Accon,* and Acre, was built at the western extremity of a vast plain. The Mediterranean bathed its walls; it attracted, by the commodiousness of its port, the navigators of Europe and Asia, and deserved to reign over the seas with the city of Tyre, which was situated not far from it. Deep ditches surrounded the walls on the land side; and, at equal distances, formidable towers had been built, among which was conspicuous *The Cursed Tower*, which dominated over the city and the plain. A dyke, built of stone, closed the part towards the south, terminated by a fortress, erected upon an isolated rock in the midst of the waves.

The plain of Ptolemaïs is bounded on the north by Mount Saron, which the Latins called *Scala Tyrorum,*—the ladders of the Tyrians; on the east by the mountains of Galilee; and on the south by Mount Carmel, which stretches into the sea. The plain is intersected towards the city by two hills,—the *Turon,* or the Mountain of the Worshipper, and the Mahameria, or the Hill of the Prophet. Several rivers or torrents descend from Mount Saron or from the mountains of Galilee, and flow impetuously into the sea at a short distance from Ptolemaïs. The most considerable of these torrents is the Belus, which discharges itself to the south of the city. In the rainy season it overflows its banks, and forms around it marshes covered with rushes and reeds. The other torrents, whose beds in summer present nothing but an arid sand, overflow in winter like the Belus. During several months of the year a great part of the plain of Ptolemaïs is under water; and when summer comes to dry the long-flooded fields, the exhalations corrupt the air and spread around the germs of epidemic diseases.

Nevertheless, the plains of Ptolemaïs were fertile and smiling: groves and gardens covered the country near the city; some villages arose on the declivities of the mountains, and houses of pleasure dotted the hills. Religious and profane traditions had bestowed names upon several spots in the neighbourhood. A little hill reminded travellers of the tomb of Memnon; and upon Mount Carmel was pointed out the retreat of Eli and Pythagoras. Such were the places that were soon to become the theatre of a sanguinary war, and see assembled and fighting the armies of Europe and Asia.

Guy de Lusignan had but nine thousand men when he laid siege to Ptolemaïs; but the whole West was preparing to fly to the defence of the Holy Land. The army of the Christians soon became of sufficient magnitude to excite serious alarm among the Saracens. French, English, and Flemish warriors preceded Philip and Richard, under the command of Jacques d'Avesnes, one of the greatest captains of his time, and the bishop of Beauvais, brother to the count of Dreux. The Genoese, the Venetians, and the Pisans, with the greater part of the Crusaders from the provinces of Italy, arrived in Palestine under the orders of the archbishops of Pisa and Ravenna. The cries of alarm of the Christians of the East had resounded even to the north of Europe, where young warriors had taken up arms to combat the infidels. All the nations of the West furnished Jerusalem with defenders, and eighty thousand Crusaders attacked the ramparts of Ptolemaïs, whilst the powerful monarchs who had placed themselves at the head of the crusade, were still engaged in preparations for their departure.

Saladin, who had at first despised the Christians, now thought it prudent to gather his powers together to oppose them. After assembling his army at Damascus, he crossed Anti-Libanus, and the mountains of Galilee, and encamped at a short distance from Ptolemaïs. He pitched his tents and pavilions at the extremity of the plain, on the mountains of Casan, from whence he could overlook all the sea-coast. On one side his army extended from the river Belus, and on the other as far as *Mahumeria*, or the *Hill of the Mosque*. The sultan occupied all the elevated posts, and all the passages by which the Christians could pass out from the spot upon which they were encamped. Thus the besiegers were besieged, and the army before the walls of the city saw the banners of the Mussulmans floating around it.

The Christians made their intrenchments, dug wide ditches, and raised towers at proper distances around their camp, in order to repulse the attacks of Saladin or the garrison of Ptolemaïs. The Mussulman army had scarcely pitched its tents when it presented itself in battle array before the trenches of the Crusaders, and fought with them several combats, in which victory was doubtful. In one of these conflicts the sultan penetrated to the city, and after having ascertained from the top of the towers the position of the Crusaders, he joined the garrison in a sortie, and surprised, and drove them into their camp. By entering into Ptolemaïs, Saladin revived the courage of the inhabitants and troops; he arranged measures necessary for the providing of supplies, he left them some of his chosen warriors, and gave them for leaders the most intrepid of his emirs, Melchou, the faithful companion of his victories, and Karacoush,* whose capacity and bravery had been often tried during the conquest of Egypt. The sultan then returned to his camp, prepared to combat afresh the army of the Crusaders.

The roads of Galilee were covered with Mussulman soldiers coming from Damascus; and as Saladin looked daily for the arrival of a fleet from Egypt, which would make him master of the sea, he hoped soon to be able to triumph over the Christians, and deliver Ptolemaïs. A few days after the victory he had gained, a great number of vessels appeared upon the sea, directing their course towards the land. Both armies were filled with hope and joy, the Mussulmans believing them to be a fleet from the ports of Damietta and Alexandria, whilst the Crusaders confidently hoped them to be a Christian armament coming to their aid. The standard of the cross was soon seen floating from the masts of the vessels, which, whilst it excited the liveliest joy in the Christians, equally depressed the Mussulmans. Two fleets from western ports entered the Road of Ptolemaïs. The first bore the German Crusaders, commanded by the duke of Gueldres and the landgrave of Thuringia, and the other the warriors of Friesland and Denmark, who, after having fought the Saracens in Spain, came to defend the kingdom of Jerusalem. Conrad, marquis of Tyre, could not remain idle while this war was going on; he armed vessels, raised troops, and united his forces with those of the Christian army.

* Karacoush was the first minister of Saladin in Egypt. It was he who caused the well of Joseph to be dug, built the citadel, and began the inclosure of Cairo. Karacoush was short and hump-backed. His name is employed now in Egypt for a sort of Punchinello, who amuses the people in the streets, in whose mouth are placed abundance of obscenities.

The arrival of the new reinforcements restored the ardour of the Crusaders. The Christian knights, according to an Arabian historian, covered with their long cuirasses of steel, looked, from a distance, like serpents spread over the plain; when they flew to arms, they resembled birds of prey, and in the *mêlée*, they were as indomitable lions. In a council, several emirs proposed to Saladin to retire before an enemy as numerous, they said, as the sands of the sea, more violent than tempests, and more impetuous than torrents.

The Christians, encouraged by the reinforcements that continued to arrive daily, resolved to attack Saladin, and drive him beyond the mountains. They marched out from their intrenchments, and drew up in order of battle. Their army extended from the mouth of the Belus to the hill of Turon. The Crusaders, full of zeal and ardour, were commanded by many illustrious captains, among whom the grand master of the Templars, the marquis of Tyre, the counts of Blois, Bar, and Clermont, with de Brioude, and Guy and Gauche de Chatillon, were conspicuous. The clergy even appeared in arms; the archbishops of Ravenna, Pisa, Canterbury, Besançon, Nazareth, and Montréal; the bishops of Beauvais, Salisbury, Cambrai, Ptolemaïs, and Bethlehem, assumed the helmet and cuirass, and led warriors on to battle. The Christian army presented so redoubtable an aspect, and appeared so full of confidence, that a Christian knight cried out, in the height of his enthusiasm: *"Let God remain neuter, and the victory is ours!"*

The king of Jerusalem, who caused the book of the Evangelists to be borne before him, wrapped in a covering of silk, and supported by four knights, commanded the right wing; he had under his orders the French and the Hospitallers; his lines extended to the Belus. The Venetians, the Lombards, and the Syrians formed the left wing, which was flanked by the sea, and marched under the banners of Conrad. The centre of the army was occupied by the Germans, the Pisans, and the English, headed by the landgrave of Thuringia. The grand master of the Templars, with his knights, and the duke of Gueldres, with his soldiers, formed the body of reserve ready to hasten wherever danger or the chances of the day might call them. The guardianship of the camp was intrusted to Gerard d'Avesnes and Goeffrey de Lusignan.

When the Christian army was drawn up on the plain, the Saracens issued from their intrenchments, and prepared to sustain the shock of the Crusaders. Saladin placed himself with his Mamelukes in the centre; his nephew Teki-eddin Omar, one of his most skilful lieutenants, commanded the right wing, which extended to the sea at the north-east of Ptolemaïs; the princes of Mossoul and Sandjar commanded the left wing, bearing upon the river Belus. By this disposition, Saladin inclosed the Christians between the river Belus and the sea, and left them no means of retreat if fortune should favour his arms.

The archers and cavalry of the Christians commenced the conflict. At the first charge they broke the right wing of the Mussulmans, commanded by the nephew of Saladin. The cavalry and infantry of the marquis of Tyre advanced upon the field of battle, the Saracens giving way before them as they proceeded. Pursuing the enemy, who fled in disorder, the Christians ascended the hill of the Mosque, and planted their standards in the camp of the infidels. The count of Bar even penetrated to the tent of the sultan, which was given up to pillage. An Arabian historian, who followed the army, says of himself, that upon beholding the rout of the Mussulmans, he took to flight, and did not stop till he came to Tiberias. The terror was so great, that several Saracens fled as far as Damascus. Saladin remained almost alone upon the field of battle, and was several times in great danger.*

Followed by a few of his faithful Mamelukes, he endeavoured to rally his scattered forces, and at

* The author of the *Roudatains* says that one thousand Mussulman horsemen were all that maintained and recovered the battle. Saladin, adds the same author, remained alone upon the field, and angels defended him.

length succeeded in reviving their courage. No sooner had he the means of support, than he returned to the fight with characteristic energy, rushing down upon the Christians, whom he surprised in all the disorder of victory. The Mussulman cavalry now charged in their turn, and dispersed the cavalry of the Franks. The different bodies of the Christian army became soon separated from one another, and in vain endeavoured to rally in their flight. The grand master of the Templars then advanced with the reserve, to support the troops that fled, but he met the Mussulman cavalry in full career, that crushed everything in their passage. The reserve was broken at the first shock; they returned several times to the charge, but without being able to stand against the impetuosity of the Saracen horsemen. On all sides, victory was escaping from the hands of the Crusaders, terror pervaded the whole Christian army, and disorder and confusion reigned everywhere. Whilst the left wing was put to flight, and the body of reserve was making vain efforts to check the Mussulmans, the right wing and the centre were attacked not only by the princes of Aleppo, Mossoul, and Sandjar, with Teki-eddin Omar, but by the garrison of Ptolemaïs, which issued from the city in order of battle.

The Saracens made a most horrible slaughter; every part of the Christian army was broken and put to flight, and utter destruction threatened them if their camp should fall into the hands of the enemy. The conquerors proceeded at once to the attack of the intrenchments, but the height of the walls, the depth of the ditches, and the bravery of Geoffrey de Lusignan and Jacques d'Avesnes stopped the Mussulman cavalry, and preserved the last asylum of the Christian army.

During the contest, Saladin appears to have been everywhere at once: after having re-established the battle in his right wing, he returned to the centre, and thence passed to the left. Ten times he crossed the lines of the Christians, and himself directed every charge of his cavalry. The battle lasted during the whole day; in the evening, still many combats were kept up around the camp of the Christians, and night alone brought repose to the two armies. As the Mussulmans and Christians had by turns been victors, the loss was equal on both sides. The Crusaders had to deplore the death of several of their leaders; the grand master of the Templars, covered with wounds, was made prisoner on the field of battle, and led to the camp of the infidels. The emirs reproached him with having taken up arms against Saladin, who had generously broken his chains after the battle of Tiberias. He replied with haughty firmness, and received the palm of martyrdom. André de Brienne was cast from his horse whilst endeavouring to rally the Crusaders. He in vain implored assistance of his companions, whom fear rendered deaf to pity, and Erard de Brienne, whilst precipitating his flight, trampled under his horse's feet his brother, expiring on the field of battle.

The Latin historians attribute the defeat of the Crusaders to an unexpected accident, which threw the combatants into disorder. An Arabian horse, which had been taken from the enemy, escaping in the heat of the battle, was pursued by some soldiers, and it was believed they were flying before the Saracens. All at once a rumour prevailed that the Christian army was conquered and dispersed, and this news redoubled the tumult, and gave birth to general terror. Whole battalions, seized with a panic, abandoned their triumphant banners, and sought safety im a precipitate flight.

We only report this singular circumstance to show the spirit of the contemporary chronicles. The fate of the battle might be much better explained by saying that the Christian soldiers abandoned the fight for the sake of plunder; and that the greater part of the leaders, less skilful than brave, neither knew how to prevent or repair the reverses to which an undisciplined army must be exposed.

In the plain of Ptolemaïs, trod by two hundred thousand warriors, on the morrow was only to be seen, to employ an Oriental image, birds of prey and wolves attracted by the scent of carnage and death. The Christians did not dare to leave their intrenchments, and victory itself could not reassure Saladin, who had seen his whole army put to flight. The most frightful disorder prevailed in

THE SIEGE OF PTOLEMAÏS.

Baldwin had captured Ptolemaïs; Saladin recovered it from the Crusaders after two' days' siege; Saladin had captured and held prisoner Guy de Lusignan while he besieged Jerusalem and drove the Christians from it, then Saladin set free Guy, the ex-king of Jerusalem, after extracting an oath that he would renounce his kingdom and return to Europe. Guy immediately appeared at Tyre to reclaim his sovereignty, but was rejected; then he laid siege to Ptolemaïs. In the battles of this siege the Crusaders were generally successful in the morning, and at noon they would begin to rob the Saracens' camp, which was the signal for Saladin to make a sortie and repulse the careless, avaricious Christians. Bad weather, want, and disease reduced the Crusaders' camp to a pitiable condition, when Richard Cœur de Lion arrived, and he at first sided with one faction of the Crusaders, so that, when the French made an assault, Richard remained in his tent. Necessity healed these factions, and the final rallies were made. Moats were filled with bodies of the slain Crusaders, their battering rams and wooden towers were reduced to ashes, they dug under the ramparts, and the walls began to fall. "The tumultuous waves of the Franks," says an Arabian author, "rolled towards the place with the rapidity of a torrent; they mounted the half-ruined walls as wild goats ascend the steepest rocks, whilst the Saracens precipitated themselves upon the besiegers like stones detached from the summits of mountains." After sustaining a siege for nearly three years, Ptolemaïs capitulated.—Book VIII.

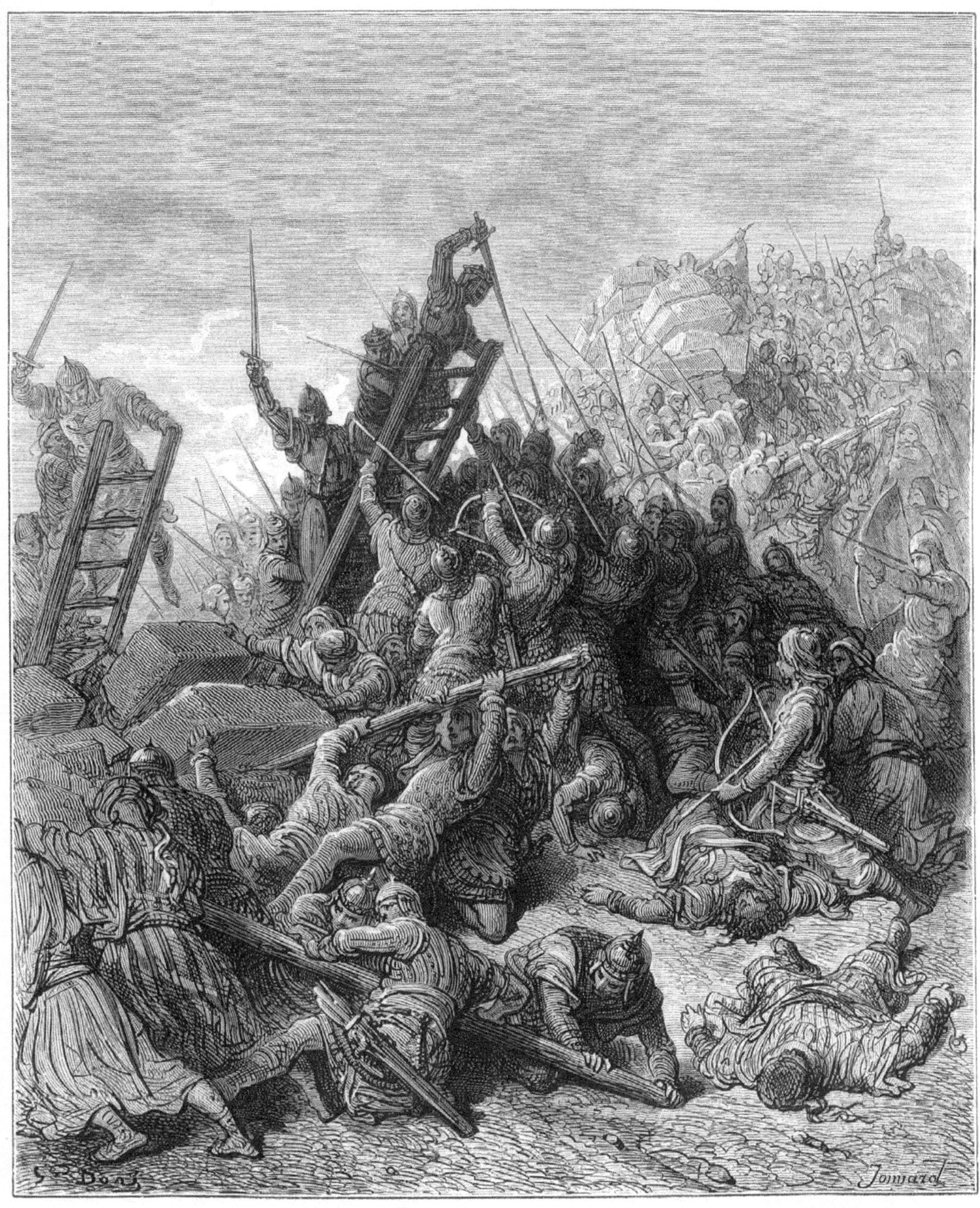

the camp of the Saracens; the slaves had pillaged it at the commencement of the battle, and had fled, carrying away the booty that escaped the hands of the Crusaders. Both the emirs and soldiers had lost their baggage; some pursued the fugitive slaves, whilst others addressed their complaints to Saladin. Amidst such confusion and tumult, it was impossible for the sultan to follow up the advantage he had gained, and as winter was approaching, and the Mussulmans were short of provisions, he abandoned the plain, and retired to the mountain Karouba.

The Christians, who now remained masters of the plain, extended their lines over the whole chain of hills that surrounded the city of Ptolemaïs; the marquis of Montferrat, with his troops, the Venetians, the Pisans, and the Crusaders commanded by the archbishop of Ravenna and the bishop of Pisa, encamped towards the north, and occupied ground from the sea to the road to Damascus. Near the camp of Conrad, the Hospitallers pitched their tents, in a valley which had belonged to them before the taking of Ptolemaïs by the Saracens. The Genoese occupied the hill which contemporary historians call Mount Musard. The French and English, who were in front of the Cursed Tower, were placed in the centre, under the orders of the counts of Dreux, Blois, and Clermont, and the archbishops of Besançon and Canterbury. Close to the camp of the French floated the banners of the Flemings, commanded by the bishop of Cambrai, and Raymond II., viscount de Turenne.

Guy de Lusignan encamped with his soldiers and knights upon the hill of Turon, which part of the camp served as citadel and head-quarters to the whole army. The king of Jerusalem had with him the queen Sibylla, his two brothers Geoffrey and Aimar, Humphrey de Theron, the husband of the second daughter of Amaury, the patriarch Heraclius, and the clergy of the holy city. The viscount de Chatellerault, who was of the same country as Guy de Lusignan, ranged himself under the standard of the king of Jerusalem. The knights of the Temple, and the troop of Jacques d'Avesnes, fixed their quarters between the hill of Turon and the Belus, and guarded the road that led from Ptolemaïs to Jerusalem. On the south of the Belus stood the tents of the Germans, the Danes, and the Frisons: these northern warriors, commanded by the landgrave of Thuringia and the duke of Gueldres, were placed along the shore of the Road of Ptolemaïs, and protected the disembarkation of the Christians who arrived from Europe by sea.

Such was the disposition of the Christian army before Ptolemaïs, and this order was preserved during the whole siege. The Christians dug ditches on the declivities of the hills whose heights they occupied; they raised high walls round their quarters, and their camps were so enclosed, says an Arabian historian, that the birds could scarcely find entrance. All the torrents which fell from the neighbouring mountains overflowed their banks, and covered the plain with their waters; and the Crusaders, having nothing to fear from surprise by the army of Saladin, prosecuted the siege without intermission. Their machines battered the walls night and day, and with each morning their assaults were renewed. The garrison, which opposed them with obstinate bravery, could not much longer defend itself without the aid of the Mussulman army. Every day pigeons bearing letters under their wings, and divers, who threw themselves into the sea, were sent to warn Saladin of the imminent dangers of Ptolemaïs.

At the approach of spring, several Mussulman princes of Mesopotamia and Syria came to range themselves and their troops under the standards of the sultan. Then Saladin quitted the mountain of Karouba, and his army descending towards the plain of Ptolemaïs, defiled in sight of the Christians, with colours spread and drums and trumpets sounding. The Crusaders had soon fresh contests to maintain. The ditches they had dug, to employ the expression of a Mussulman historian, became their own sepulchres, and were often filled with their dead bodies. The hopes they had fondly entertained of getting possession of the city, vanished at the sight of such formidable enemies. They had constructed during the winter three rolling towers, similar to those which Godfrey of Bouillon had erected at the taking of Jerusalem. These three towers arose above the walls of Ptolemaïs, and threatened the city with destruction. Whilst the Crusaders were engaged in repelling the attacks of Saladin, inflamed arrows and pots filled with burning naphtha were hurled on their machines, that were left unprotected at the foot of the ramparts. All at once the Christians saw flames arise in the air, and their wooden towers, seized upon by an unextinguishable fire, were consumed and reduced to ashes before their eyes, as if they had been struck by the lightning of heaven. So great was the terror spread among the Crusaders by this conflagration, that the landgrave of Thuringia quitted the siege and returned to Europe, believing that God no longer protected the cause of the Christians.

Saladin followed up his attacks so incessantly, that he left his enemy no repose. Every time that an assault was attempted on the city, the noise of drums and trumpets resounded from the ramparts to warn the Mussulman troops, who then flew to arms and attacked the camp of the Christians.

The Road of Ptolemaïs was often covered with vessels from Europe, and Mussulman vessels from the ports of Egypt and Syria. The latter brought supplies to the city, and the former to the Christian army. At a distance might be seen masts surmounted with the standards of the cross, and others bearing the banners of Mahomet, which seemed to mingle and float together. Several times the Franks and Saracens were spectators of the conflicts between their fleets laden with arms and provisions, that took place near the shore. At the sight of a naval combat the warriors of the cross and of Mahomet struck upon their shields, and announced by their cries their hopes and their fears. Sometimes even the two armies were so excited as to attack each other on the plain to assure the victory, or avenge the defeat of those who had fought upon the waves.

In the battles that took place sometimes on the banks of the Belus, and sometimes under the walls or at the foot of the hills, the Saracens often prepared ambushes, and did not disdain to have recourse to all the stratagems of war. The Christians, on the contrary, placed no confidence in anything but their valour and their own good swords. A car, upon which was raised a tower, surmounted by a cross and a white flag, served them as a rallying-point, and was their guiding star in battle. When the enemy gave way, the thirst for booty soon made every man quit the ranks; their chiefs, almost always without authority in the tumult of battle, became no more than simple soldiers in the *mêlée*, and had nothing to oppose to the enemy but their sword and lance. Saladin, more respected by his troops, commanded a disciplined army, and often profited by the disorder and confusion of the Christians to combat them with advantage and snatch a victory. Every battle began at sunrise, and the Christians were generally conquerors up to the middle of the day; but when even they had invaded and partly plundered the camp of the Mussulmans, and at evening returned home loaded with booty, they were almost sure to find their own camp had been broken into by the troops of Saladin or the garrison.

After the sultan's descent from the mountain of Karouba, an Egyptian fleet entered the port of Ptolemaïs. At the same time Saladin welcomed to his camp his brother Malec-Adel, who brought with him troops raised in Egypt. This double reinforcement revived the courage of the Mussulmans, but they did not long profit by these advantages, and the hope of conquering the Christians began to give way to the most serious alarms. A report was spread throughout the East that the emperor of Germany had quitted Europe at the head of a numerous army, and was advancing towards Syria. Saladin sent troops to meet such a formidable enemy, and several Mussulman princes quitted the sultan's army to defend their own states, which were menaced by the Crusaders coming from the West. Ambassadors were sent to the caliph of Bagdad, the princes of Africa and Asia, and to the Mussulman powers of Spain, to engage them to unite their efforts against the enemies of Islamism.

Whilst terror thus took possession of the Saracens, the Crusaders conceived fresh hopes, and redoubled their efforts to gain possession of Ptolemaïs before the arrival of the Germans. After several contests, they resolved to make one last attempt to drive the Mussulman army beyond the mountains. Marching from their camp, they presented themselves in order of battle before the Saracens. The Mussulman historians compare their multitude to that which will assemble at the last day in the valley of Jehoshaphat.

At the first signal, the two armies approached, mingled, and soon appeared nothing but one horrible, contending mass. Arrows hissed through the air, lances crossed, and the rapid blows of sabres and swords resounded from the bucklers and steel casques. The Christian knights seemed animated with an invincible ardour. The Templars and Hospitallers carried death wherever they directed their course; Syrians and Franks, foot-soldiers and horsemen, contended for the prize of valour, and rushed together to meet peril and find victory or death. The Mussulman army could not resist their impetuosity, and at the first charge retired in disorder. The plains and hills were covered with Saracen warriors, who fled, throwing away their arms. Victory remained with the Christians; but soon the thirst of booty led them to abandon their ranks, and the face of the battle was changed. The Mussulmans had time to rally, and returned to surprise the conquerors, who were pillaging the tent and camp of the sultan. All at once the Christians were surrounded on every side; and having laid down their arms in their eagerness for booty, could not defend themselves, but were seized by a terror like that with which they had inspired their enemies. The Mussulmans, irritated by their defeat, immolated to their vengeance every Christian that fell in their way. Such of the Crusaders as were most greedy of plunder, lost their lives, together with the spoils with which they were loaded, and were slaughtered without defence in the very tents they had invaded. "The enemies of God," says Bohaheddin, "dared to enter into the camp of the lions of Islamism; but they experienced the terrible effects of divine wrath. They fell beneath the sword of the Mussulmans as leaves fall in autumn, under the gusts of the tempest. The earth was covered with their bodies, heaped one upon another, like lopped branches which fill the valleys and hills in a forest that has been cut down." Another Arabian historian speaks thus of this bloody battle:—"The Christians fell under the swords of the conquerors, as the wicked will fall into the abode of fire at the last day. Nine ranks of dead covered the ground between the hill and the sea, and each rank was of a thousand warriors."

Whilst the Christians were being conquered and dispersed, the garrison of Ptolemaïs made a sortie; and, penetrating into their camp, carried off a great number of women and children that were left without defence. The Crusaders, whom night saved from destruction, returned to their camp, deploring their double defeat. The sight of their plundered tents and the losses they had experienced, quite depressed their courage; and the death of Frederick Barbarossa, with the disasters of the German army, of which they were soon informed, appeared to fill up their cup of wretchedness. The despair of the leaders was so great that they determined to return to Europe, and, in order to secure their departure, were seeking to obtain a disgraceful peace of Saladin, when a fleet arrived in the Road of Ptolemaïs, and landed a great number of French, English, and Italians, commanded by Henry, count of Champagne.

Once more hope was restored to the Crusaders; the Christians were again masters of the sea, and might, in their turn, make Saladin tremble, who had believed he had nothing more to dread from them. They renewed their attacks upon the city with spirit. The count of Champagne, who had restored abundance to the camp, caused to be constructed, at great expense, rams of a prodigious size, with two enormous towers composed of wood, steel, iron, and brass. These machines are said to have cost fifteen hundred pieces of gold. Whilst these formidable auxiliaries menaced the ramparts, the

Christians mounted several times to the assault, and were, more than once, on the point of planting the standard of the cross on the walls of the infidels.

But the besieged continued to repulse them, and the Mussulmans shut up in the city supported the horrors of a long siege with heroic firmness. The emirs Karacoush and Melchoub were unremitting in their endeavours to keep up the courage of their soldiers. Vigilant, present everywhere, sometimes employing force, and as often stratagem, they allowed no opportunity of surprising the Christians to escape, or to render their attacks abortive. The Mussulmans burnt all the machines of the besiegers, and made several sorties, in which they drove the Christians to the security of their camp.

The garrison received daily reinforcements and provisions by sea; sometimes barks stole along the shore, and got into Ptolemaïs under the favour of night; at others, vessels from Berytus, manned by apostate Christians, hoisted the white flag with a red cross, and thus deceived the vigilance of the besiegers. The Crusaders, to prevent all communication by sea, resolved to get possession of the Tower of the Spies, which overlooked and dominated the port of Ptolemaïs. A vessel, upon which was placed a wooden tower, advanced towards the fort they wished to attack, whilst a bark filled with combustible matters, to which fire had been set, was launched into the port among the Mussulman fleet. Everything seemed to promise success to this attempt, when, all at once, the wind changed, and drove the blazing fire-ship full upon the wooden tower, which was rapidly consumed by the flames. The duke of Austria, who commanded this perilous expedition, followed by several of the bravest of his warriors, had mounted the tower of the infidels sword in hand; but at the sight of the conflagration which was devouring the vessel he came on, he cast himself into the sea, covered with his own blood and that of the Saracens, and gained the shore almost alone.

Whilst the duke of Austria attacked the tower, the army left their camp to make an assault upon the city. The besiegers performed prodigies of valour without success, and were obliged to return in haste to defend their own tents, undergoing fire and pillage by the army of Saladin.

It was amidst this double defeat that Frederick, duke of Swabia, arrived under the walls of Ptolemaïs with five thousand men, the deplorable remains of a numerous army. When the Christians in Syria had heard of the preparations of the Germans, their invincible powers were the theme of every tongue, and the Crusaders before Ptolemaïs were animated by the most sanguine expectations; but when they arrived, and related the disasters they had undergone, their presence spread mourning and depression throughout the army.

Frederick wished to signalize his arrival by an attack upon the Saracens. "The Christians," say the Arabian writers, "issued from their camp like ants swarming to their prey, and covered the valleys and hills." They attacked the advanced post of the Mussulman army, encamped upon the heights of Aiadhiat, not far from the mountains of Galilee. Saladin, whom a serious illness prevented from mounting on horseback, caused himself to be carried to Mount Karouba, from whence he could overlook all that went on, and issue his orders. The Christians renewed their attacks several times without producing any effect upon their enemies; and after having fought the whole day, they renounced the hope of a triumph, and returned to their camp, where the famine, which was beginning to be severely felt, allowed them nothing wherewith to recruit their exhausted strength.

Every leader of this multitude of Crusaders was obliged to feed the troops that he commanded, and they at no time were possessed of more than provisions for one week. When a Christian fleet arrived, they enjoyed abundance; but when no vessels appeared for a time, they were destitute of the commonest necessaries of life. As winter approached, and the sea became more stormy, want was necessarily proportionately increased.

When the Crusaders made incursions upon neighbouring lands to procure provisions, they fought

RICHARD CŒUR DE LION IN REPRISAL MASSACRES CAPTIVES.

The capitulation remained unexecuted: Saladin, under various pretexts, deferring the completion of the conditions. Richard, irritated by a delay which appeared to him a breach of faith, revenged himself upon the prisoners that were in his hands. Without pity for disarmed enemies, or for the Christians he exposed to sanguinary reprisals, he massacred five thousand Mussulmans before the city they had so valiantly defended, and within sight of Saladin, who shared the disgrace of this barbarity by thus abandoning his bravest and most faithful warriors.—Book VIII.

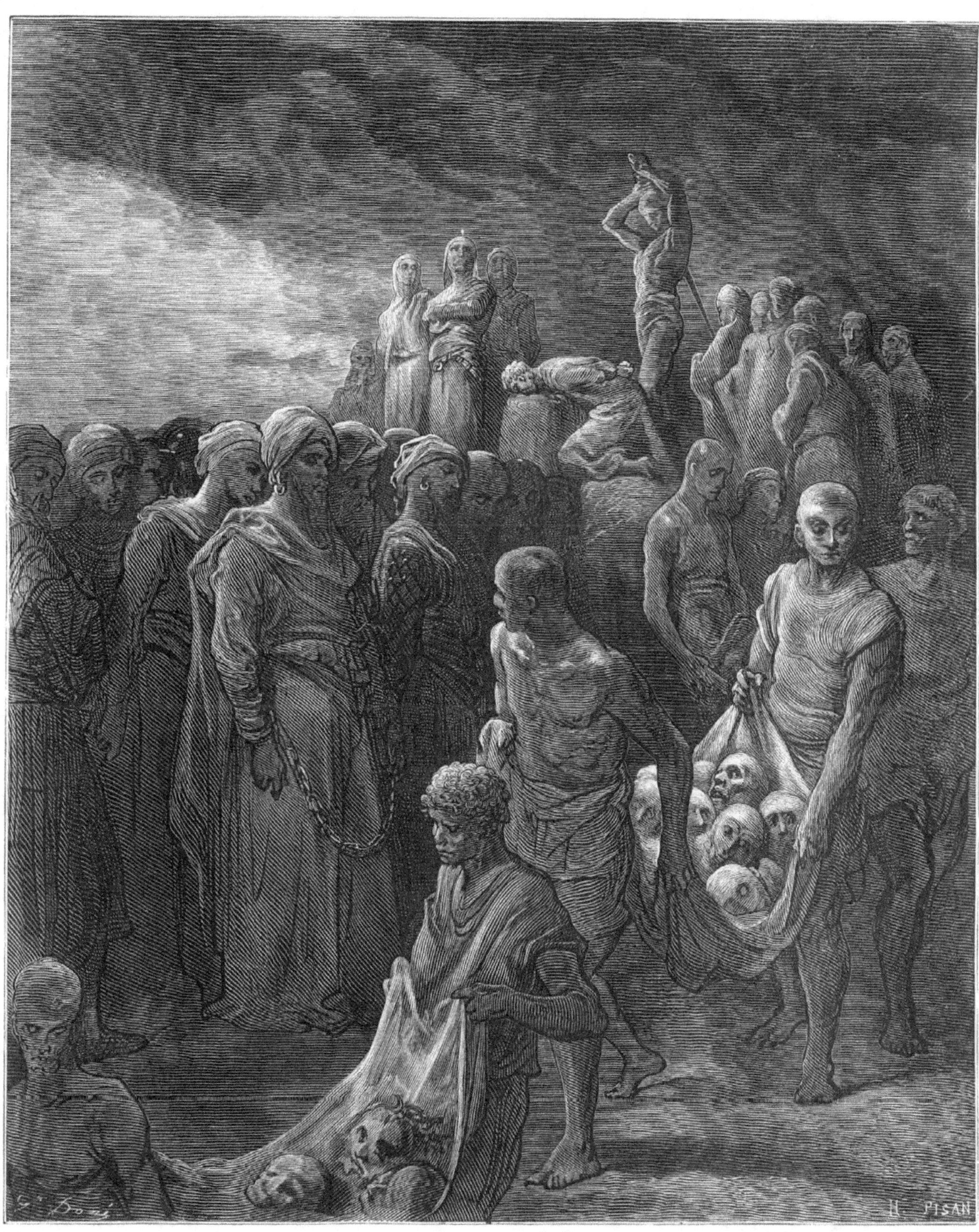

amidst the ambuscades of the Saracens. Animated by despair, they several times attacked the enemy in their intrenchments, but were always repulsed. At length famine began to make frightful ravages in the Christian army; a measure of flour, that weighed two hundred and fifty pounds, was sold for ninety-six crowns, a sum so exorbitant that not even princes could pay it. The leaders insisted upon fixing the prices of all provisions brought to the camp; the venders then hid them in the earth, and the scarcity was increased by the very measures adopted to lessen it. The Crusaders were obliged to feed upon their horses; next they devoured leather, harness, and old skins, which were sold for their weight in gold. Many Christians, driven from their camp by famine, took refuge in that of Saladin; some embraced Islamism to obtain relief in their misery; whilst others, going on board Mussulman vessels, and braving the perils of the sea, went to pillage the isle of Cyprus and the coasts of Syria.

During the rainy season the waters covered the plains, and the Crusaders remained crowded together on the hills. The carcasses left on the banks of the rivers, or cast into the torrents, exhaled a pestilential odour, and contagious diseases were very soon added to the horrors of famine. The camp was filled with mourning and funeral rites; from two to three hundred pilgrims were buried daily. Several of the most illustrious leaders found in contagion the death they had so often braved in the field of battle. Frederick, duke of Swabia, died in his tent, after having escaped all the perils of war. His unhappy companions in arms gave tears to his memory, and, despairing of the cause of the Christians, for which they had suffered so much, returned to the West.

To complete their misfortune, Sibylla, the wife of Guy de Lusignan, died, with her two children, and her death gave rise to fresh discord. Isabella, second daughter of Amaury, and sister to Queen Sibylla, was heir to the throne of Jerusalem; consequently Humphrey de Thoron, the husband of this princess, immediately asserted her rights. On the other side, Guy de Lusignan could not consent to abandon his, and maintained that the character of king was indelible; no one had the right to deprive him of a crown he had once worn. Amidst these disputes, Conrad, already master of Tyre, was all at once seized with the ambition of reigning over Jerusalem and Palestine; he succeeded in gaining the love of Isabella, induced the council of bishops to dissolve the marriage of Humphrey, and, although himself married to the sister of the Emperor Isaac, espoused the sister and heiress of Baldwin, determined to defend with the sword the rights which this new union gave him.

The Christians, though plunged in such horrible misery, and at the same time constantly menaced by Saladin, were entirely engaged by the pretensions of the two rival princes. Humphrey, who defended his rights very weakly, was in great dread of the threats of Conrad, and was wise enough not to regret a sceptre which he must win, or a wife who had abandoned him. He renounced all his claims, and would have been happy if his docility had restored unanimity; but there remained still two kings for an invaded, or rather a nominal kingdom, and the two factions divided the army. Some were touched by the misfortunes of Guy, and declared themselves his partisans; whilst others, admiring the bravery of Conrad, thought the kingdom should fall to him who was most capable of defending it. Guy was reproached with having fostered the power of Saladin; the Marquis of Tyre, on the contrary, was praised for having preserved the only two cities that remained in the power of the Franks; he alone, they added, could furnish the Christians with provisions, and put an end to the famine which was consuming them.

Not one of the Crusaders was ignorant of this quarrel. Dissension spread from the leaders to the soldiers; they heaped abuse upon each other, and were even ready to cut the throats of their comrades to determine who should possess a broken sceptre and the vain title of king. The bishops at length calmed the fury of these differences, and persuaded the rivals to refer the matter to the judgment of Richard and Philip.

These two princes, who had embarked at Genoa and Marseilles, met at Messina. Sicily was then at war with Germany for the succession of William II. Constance, the heir of William, had married the Emperor Henry VI., and had charged him with the duty of proclaiming her rights, and defending her inheritance; but Tancred, natural brother of Constance, who had obtained the love of the nobility of Sicily, had usurped the throne of his sister, and maintained himself upon it by force of arms, against the efforts of the Germans.

This prince, not firmly settled on his throne, was much alarmed at the approach of the Crusaders. He feared in Philip an ally of the emperor of Germany, and in Richard, the brother of Queen Jane, the widow of William, whom he had ill-treated, and still detained in prison. Being totally unable to contend with them, he attempted to conciliate them by his submission and attentions: he at first succeeded with Philip beyond his expectations, but had much more trouble in appeasing Richard, who, immediately after his arrival, haughtily demanded the liberty of Jane, and took possession of the two forts which commanded Messina. The English soon got embroiled with the subjects of Tancred, and the banners of England were seen floating over the capital itself. By this act of violence and authority Richard gave great umbrage to Philip, whose vassal he was. The king gave orders that Richard's standards should be removed; and the impetuous Cœur de Lion was forced to comply, though trembling with rage. This submission, although it was accompanied with menaces, seemed to appease Philip, and put an end to the quarrel; but from that time Richard became friendly with Tancred, who endeavoured to create suspicions of the loyalty of the king of France, and to secure peace to himself, sowed dissension among the Crusaders.

The two kings by turns accused each other of breach of faith and perfidy, and the French and English took part in the hatred of their monarchs. Among these divisions, Philip pressed Richard to espouse the princess Alice, who had been promised to him in marriage; but the face of circumstances had changed, and the king of England refused with contempt a sister of the king of France, whom he had himself earnestly sought, and for whom he had made war against his own father.

Eleanor of Guienne, who had only ceased to be queen of the French to become their implacable enemy, had for a long time endeavoured to dissuade Richard from this marriage. In order to complete her work, and create an eternal division between the two kings, she brought with her into Sicily, Berengaria, the daughter of Don Sancho of Navarre, with the view of marrying her to the king of England. The report of her arrival augmented the suspicions of Philip, and was a fresh source of complaints on his part. War was upon the point of breaking out, but some wise and pious men succeeded in soothing these angry spirits; the two kings formed a new alliance bound by new oaths, and discord was for a moment quelled. But a friendship which required to be sworn to so often, and a peace which every day demanded a fresh treaty, were very little to be relied on.

Richard, who had just been making war upon Christians, all at once became a prey to repentance and penitence; he assembled the bishops that had accompanied him in a chapel, presented himself before them in his shirt, confessed his sins, and listened to their reproofs with the docility of the humblest of the faithful. Some time after this whimsical ceremony, his mind being naturally inclined to superstition, he took a fancy to hear Abbot Joachim, who lived in retirement in the mountains of Calabria, and passed for a prophet.

In a voyage to Jerusalem, this solitary had, it was said, received from Jesus Christ the faculty of explaining the Apocalypse, and to read in it, as in a faithful history, all that was to take place on earth. On the invitation of the king of England, he quitted his retreat, and repaired to Messina, preceded by the fame of his visions and miracles. The austerity of his morals, the singularity of his behaviour, with the mystical obscurity of his discourses, at once procured him the confidence and veneration of the Crusaders. He was questioned upon the issue of the war they were about to make in Palestine; and he predicted that Jerusalem would be delivered seven years after its conquest by Saladin. "Why, then," said Richard, "are we come so soon?" "Your arrival," replied Joachim, "is very necessary; God will give you the victory over his enemies, and will render your name celebrated above all the princes of the earth."

This speech, which did not at all flatter the passions or impatience of the Crusaders, could only minister to the self-love of Richard. Philip was very little affected by a prediction which was afterwards also falsified by the event; and was only the more anxious to encounter Saladin, the redoubtable conqueror, in whom Joachim saw one of the seven heads of the Apocalypse. As soon as spring rendered the sea navigable, Philip embarked for Palestine. He was received there as an angel of the Lord, and his presence reanimated the valour and hopes of the Christians, who had during two years unsuccessfully besieged Ptolemaïs. The French fixed their quarters within bow-shot of the enemy, and, as soon as they had pitched their tents, proceeded to the assault. They might have rendered themselves masters of the city; but Philip, inspired by a chivalric spirit, rather than by a wise policy, was desirous that Richard should be present at this first conquest. This generous consideration proved fatal to the enterprises of the Christians, and gave time to the Saracens to receive reinforcements.

Saladin had passed the winter on the mountain of Karouba, and fatigue, frequent combats, want, and disease had greatly reduced his army. He himself likewise was weakened by a complaint which the physicians could not cure, and which, on many occasions, prevented him from accompanying his warriors to the field of battle. When he heard of the arrival of the two powerful Christian monarchs he once more, by his ambassadors, called upon the Mussulman nations for assistance. In all the mosques prayers were put up for the triumph of his arms and the deliverance of Islamism; and in every Mussulman city the Imauns exhorted the true believers to hasten to the war.

"Numberless legions of Christians," said they, "are come from countries situated beyond Constantinople, to bear away from us conquests that gave such joy to the Koran, and to dispute with us a land upon which the companions of Omar planted the standard of the Prophet. Spare neither your lives nor your treasures to oppose them. Your marches against the infidels, your perils, your wounds, all, even to the passage of the torrent, is written in the book of God. Thirst, hunger, fatigue, death itself will become for you treasures in heaven, and will open to you the gardens and delicious bowers of Paradise. In whatever place you may be, death must overtake you; neither your mansions nor your lofty towers can defend you against his darts. Some among you have said, Let us not go to seek for battles during the heats of summer, or the rigours of winter; but hell will be more terrible than the rigours of winter or the heats of summer. Go, then, and bravely fight your enemies in a war undertaken for religion. Victory or Paradise awaits you; fear God more than the infidels; it is Saladin who calls you to his banners; and Saladin is the friend of the Prophet, as the Prophet is the friend of God. If you do not obey, your families will be driven from Syria, and God will plant in your places other nations better than you. Jerusalem, the sister of Medina and Mecca, will fall again into the power of idolaters, who give a son, a companion, an equal to the Most High, and wish to extinguish the knowledge of God. Arm yourselves then with the buckler of victory; disperse the children of fire, the sons of hell, whom the sea has vomited upon your shores, and remember these words of the Koran: *'He who shall abandon his dwelling to defend the holy religion, shall meet with abundance and a great number of companions.'* "

Animated by such discourses, the Mussulmans flew to arms, and from all parts flocked to the camp of Saladin, whom they looked upon as the arm of victory, and the beloved son of the Prophet

Whilst this was going on Richard was retarded in his march by interests quite foreign to the crusade. At the moment that his rival was waiting for him to take a city from the Saracens, and was willing to share even glory with him, he made himself master of a kingdom, and kept it for himself.

On leaving the port of Messina, the English fleet was dispersed by a violent tempest; three vessels were wrecked upon the coast of Cyprus, and the unfortunate crews, who escaped, were ill-treated by the inhabitants and cast into prison. A ship, on board of which were Berengaria of Navarre, and Jane, queen of Sicily, upon presenting itself before Limisso, was forbidden to enter the port. A short time after, Richard arrived with his fleet, which he had succeeded in getting together again, and himself met with an insolent refusal. Isaac, of the family of Comnenus, who, during the troubles of Constantinople, had got possession of the isle of Cyprus, and governed it with the ostentatious title of emperor, dared to threaten the king of England.

His menaces became the signal for war; and both sides were eager for the conflict. Isaac could not resist the first shock of the English; his troops were beaten and dispersed; his cities opened their gates to the conqueror, and the emperor of Cyprus himself fell into the hands of Richard, who, to insult his vanity and avarice, caused him to be bound with chains of silver. The king of England, after having delivered the inhabitants of Cyprus from a master whom they called a tyrant, made them repay this service with the half of their property, and took possession of the island, which was erected into a kingdom, and remained nearly three hundred years under the domination of the Latins.

It was on this island, in the bosom of victory, and in the vicinity of the ancient Amathus, that Richard celebrated his marriage with Berengaria of Navarre. He then set out for Palestine, dragging after him Isaac, loaded with chains, and the daughter of that unfortunate prince, in whom, it is said, the new queen found a dangerous rival.

The Franks celebrated the arrival of Richard with *feux de joie*, lighted up throughout the camp. When the English had united their forces with those of the Christian army, Ptolemaïs saw beneath its walls all that Europe could boast of as illustrious captains and valiant warriors. The tents of the Franks covered a vast plain, and their army presented a most majestic and terrible aspect. A spectator, on beholding on the coast of the sea the towers of Ptolemaïs, and the camp of the Christians, in which they had built houses and traced streets, traversed unceasingly by an immense crowd, might have supposed he saw two rival cities which were at war with each other. Each nation had its leader and its separate quarter, and so many languages were spoken by the Crusaders, that the Mussulmans could not find interpreters enough to enable them to understand all the prisoners. In this confused multitude, each people had a different character, different manners, and different arms; but, at the signal for battle, all were animated by the same zeal and the same ardour; the presence of the two monarchs had re-established discipline, and Ptolemaïs could not have prolonged its resistance, if discord, that eternal enemy of the Christians. had not entered their camp with Richard.

The debates relative to the succession to the throne of Jerusalem were renewed on the arrival of the English. Philip declared for Conrad, which was quite enough to determine Richard to give his voice for Guy de Lusignan. The Christian army was filled with troubles, and again divided into two factions: on one side were the French, the Germans, the Templars, and the Genoese; on the other, the English, the Pisans, and the knights of the Hospital. The two parties, ready to break into open war, no longer united their efforts or their arms against the Saracens; whenever the king of France, at the head of his warriors, proceeded to the assault, the king of England remained in his tent in a state of sullen repose. The besieged had never more than one of the monarchs to contend with at once, and the Christian army, after it had received such powerful auxiliaries, became much less redoubtable to the Saracens.

Amidst the disputes which divided the Crusaders, both kings fell dangerously ill, and their hatred and suspicion were so great, that each accused the other of having made an attempt upon his life. As Saladin sent them refreshments and physicians, and as they addressed frequent messages to him, each party reproached the monarch who was opposed to him with keeping up an impious understanding with the Saracens.

The perils of the army, however, with the glory of religion and the interests of the crusade, for a moment stifled the voice of faction, and induced the Crusaders to unite against the common enemy. After long debates, it was decided that Guy de Lusignan should retain the title of king during his life, and that Conrad and his descendants should succeed to the kingdom of Jerusalem. It was at the same time agreed that when one of the two monarchs should attack the city, the other should watch over the safety of the camp, and keep the army of Saladin in check. This agreement re-established harmony; and the Christian warriors, who had been upon the point of taking arms against each other, now only contended for the glory of conquering the infidels.

The siege was resumed with fresh ardour, but the Mussulmans had employed the time wasted by the Christians in vain disputes, in strengthening the city. When the besiegers appeared before the walls, they met with a resistance entirely unexpected, whilst the army of Saladin continued indefatigable and unceasing in its attacks. At the earliest break of day, the drums and trumpets constantly sounded the signal for battle, both from the walls of Ptolemaïs and the camp of the sultan. Saladin animated his troops by his presence; whilst his brother, Malec-Adel, offered an example of bravery to the emirs. Many great battles were fought at the foot of the hills on which the Christians were encamped, and twice the Crusaders gave a general assault; but on both occasions were obliged to return hastily to their tents, to defend them against Saladin.

In one of these attacks, a Christian knight singly defended one of the gates of the camp against a host of Saracens. The Arabian writers compare this knight to a demon animated by all the fires of hell. An enormous cuirass entirely covered him; arrows, stones, lance-thrusts, made no impression on him; all who approached him were slain, and he alone, though stuck all over with javelins and surrounded by enemies, appeared to have nothing to fear. No weapons or force being able to prevail, the Greek fire was at length employed, which being poured upon his head, devoured by flames, he perished like one of the enormous machines that the besieged had burnt under the walls of the city.

Every day the Crusaders redoubled their efforts, and by turns repulsed the army of Saladin, or made assaults upon Ptolemaïs. In one of these assaults, they filled up a part of the ditches of the city with the carcasses of their dead horses and the bodies of their companions who had fallen beneath the swords of the enemy, or been swept away by disease. The Saracens raised up these horrid masses heaped up under their walls, and cast them back again in fragments upon the banks of the ditches, where the sword and lance were for ever immolating fresh victims. Neither the spectacle of death, nor obstacles, nor fatigue affected the Christians. When their wooden towers and their battering-rams were reduced to ashes, they dug into the earth, and by subterranean ways advanced under the foundations of the ramparts. Every day they employed some fresh means or some new machine to subdue the place.. An Arabian historian relates that they raised near their camp a hill of earth of a prodigious height, and that by constantly throwing the earth up before them, they brought this mountain close to the city. It had advanced within half a bow-shot, when the Mussulmans issued from their gates, and precipitated themselves in front of this enormous mass, which grew nearer and nearer, and already threatened their walls. Armed with swords, pickaxes, and shovels, they attacked the troops employed in forwarding it, using every effort to remove it back towards the plain; but were only able to arrest its progress by digging vast and deep ditches in its passage.

Among all the Christian warriors, the French distinguished themselves greatly, and directed their efforts principally against the Cursed Tower, which was erected at the eastern side of the city. A great part of the walls began to fall, and must soon offer a passage to the besieging army. War, famine, and disease had weakened the garrison; the city had not soldiers enough left to defend the ramparts and move about the machines employed against those of the Christians. The place not only stood in need of provisions, but of warlike munitions and Greek fire. The warriors who had gone through so much, began to feel discouragement, and the people loudly murmured against Saladin and the emirs. In this extremity, the commander of the garrison came and proposed a capitulation to Philip Augustus, who swore by the God of the Christians that he would not spare a single inhabitant of Ptolemaïs, if the Mussulmans did not restore all the cities that had fallen into their power since the battle of Tiberias.

The chief of the emirs, irritated by the refusal of Philip, retired, saying that he and his companions would rather bury themselves beneath the ruins of the city, than listen to such terms, and that they would defend Ptolemaïs *as a lion defends his blood-stained lair*. On his return into the place, the commander of the Saracens communicated his courage, or rather his despair, to every heart. When the Christians resumed their assaults, they were repulsed with a vigour that astonished them. "The tumultuous waves of the Franks," says an Arabian author, "rolled towards the place with the rapidity of a torrent; they mounted the half-ruined walls as wild goats ascend the steepest rocks, whilst the Saracens precipitated themselves upon the besiegers like stones detached from the summits of mountains."

In one general assault, a Florentine knight of the family of Bonaguisi, followed by some of his men, fought his way into one of the towers of the infidels, and got possession of the Mussulman banner that floated from it. Overpowered by numbers, and forced to retreat, he returned to the camp, bearing the flag he had carried off from the Saracens. In the same assault, Alberic Clement, the first marshal of France of whom history makes mention, scaled the ramparts, and, sword in hand, penetrated into the city, where he found a glorious death. Stephen, count of Blois, and several knights were burnt by the Greek fire, the boiling oil, the melted lead, and heated sand which the besieged poured down upon all who approached the walls.

The obstinate ardour of the Mussulmans was sustained during several days; but as they received no succour, many emirs, at length despairing of the safety of Ptolemaïs, threw themselves, by night, into a bark, to seek an asylum in the camp of Saladin, preferring to encounter the anger of the sultan, to perishing by the sword of the Christians. This desertion, and the contemplation of their ruined towers, filled the Mussulmans with terror. Whilst pigeons and divers constantly announced to Saladin the horrible distresses of the besieged, the latter came to the resolution of leaving the city by night, and braving every peril to join the Saracen army. But their project being discovered by the Christians, they blocked up and guarded every passage by which the enemy could possibly escape. The emirs, the soldiers, and the inhabitants then became convinced that they had no hope but in the mercy of Philip Augustus, and promised, if he would grant them liberty and life, to cause to be given up to the Christians sixteen hundred prisoners, and the wood of the true cross. By the capitulation they engaged to pay two hundred thousand pieces of gold to the leaders of the Christian army, and the garrison, with the entire population of Ptolemaïs, were to remain in the power of the conquerors till the execution of the treaty.

A Mussulman soldier was sent from the city to announce to Saladin that the garrison was forced to capitulate. The sultan, who was preparing to make a last effort to save the place, learnt the news with deep regret. He assembled his council, to know if they approved of the capitulation; but scarcely were the principal emirs met in his tent, when they beheld the standards of the Crusaders floating over the walls and towers of Ptolemaïs.

Such was the conclusion of this famous siege, which lasted nearly three years, and in which the Crusaders shed more blood and exhibited more bravery than ought to have sufficed for the subjugation of the whole of Asia. More than a hundred skirmishes and nine great battles were fought before the walls of the city; several flourishing armies came to recruit armies nearly annihilated, and were in their turn replaced by fresh armies. The bravest nobility of Europe perished in this siege, swept away by the sword or disease. Among the illustrious victims of this war, history points out Philip, count of Flanders, Guy de Chatillon, Bernard de St. Vallery, Vautrier de Mory, Raoul de Fougères, Eudes de Gonesse, Renaud de Maguy, Geoffroi d'Aumale, viscount de Châtellerault, Josselin de Montmorency, and Raoul de Marle; the archbishops of Besançon and Canterbury; with many other ecclesiastics and knights whose piety and exploits were the admiration of Europe.

In this war both parties were animated by religion; each side boasted of its miracles, its saints, and its prophets. Bishops and imauns equally promised the soldiers remission of their sins and the crown of martyrdom. Whilst the king of Jerusalem caused the book of the Evangelists to be borne before him, Saladin would often pause on the field of battle to offer up a prayer or read a chapter from the Koran.* The Franks and the Saracens mutually accused each other of ignorance of the true God and of outraging him by their ceremonies. The Christians rushed upon their enemies crying, "*It is the will of God! It is the will of God!*" and the Saracens answered by their war-cry, "*Islam! Islam!*"

Fanaticism frequently augmented the fury of slaughter. The Mussulmans from the height of their towers insulted the religious ceremonies of the Christians. They raised crosses on their ramparts, beat them with rods, covered them with dust, mud, and filth, and broke them into a thousand pieces before the eyes of the besiegers. At this spectacle the Christians swore to avenge their outraged worship, and menaced the Saracens with the destruction of every Mahomedan pulpit. In the heat of this religious animosity, the Mussulmans often massacred disarmed captives; and in more than one battle they burnt their† Christian prisoners in the very field of conflict. The Crusaders but too closely imitated the barbarity of their enemies; funeral piles, lighted up by fanatical rage, were often extinguished in rivers of blood.

The Mussulman and Christian warriors provoked each other during single combats, and were as lavish of abuse as the heroes of Homer. Heroines often appeared in the *mêlée*, and disputed the prize of strength and courage with the bravest of the Saracens.‡ Children came from the city to fight with the children of the Christians in the presence of the two armies.

But sometimes the furies of war gave place to the amenities of peace, and Franks and Saracens would for a moment forget the hatred that had led them to take up arms. During the course of the siege several tournaments were held in the plain of Ptolemaïs, to which the Mussulmans were invited. The champions of the two parties harangued each other before entering the lists; the conqueror was borne in triumph, and the conquered ransomed like a prisoner of war. In these warlike festivities, which brought the two nations together, the Franks often danced to the sound of Arabian instruments, and their minstrels afterwards played or sang to the dancing of the Saracens.

Most of the Mussulman emirs, after the example of Saladin, affected an austere simplicity in

* Saladin had a copy of the *Koran*, compiled by Omar, always carried with his army.

† "One of our people," says Omad, "having been made prisoner, was burnt, and the flames accompanied him to his place of everlasting repose; we took a Christian, we burnt him, and the flames that devoured him mingled with the fires of hell."

‡ A combat of children is related by Omad of Ispahan; and the same author speaks of the Christian heroines who mingled in the fight. He adds, that the young women fought, and the old women animated them by their cries.

their vestments and manners. An Arabian author compares the sultan, in his court, surrounded by his sons and brothers, to the star of night, which sheds a sombre light amidst the other stars. The principal leaders of the crusade did not entertain the same love of simplicity, but endeavoured to excel each other in splendour and magnificence. As in the first crusade, the princes and barons were followed into Asia by their hunting and fishing appointments, and the luxuries of their palaces and castles. When Philip Augustus arrived before Ptolemaïs, all eyes were for a moment turned upon the falcons he had brought with him. One of these having escaped from the hands of his keeper, perched upon the ramparts of the city, and the whole Christian army was excited by endeavours to recapture the fugitive bird. As it was caught by the Mussulmans, and carried to Saladin, Philip sent an ambassador to the sultan to recover it, offering a sum of gold that would have been quite sufficient for the ransom of many Christian warriors.

The misery which so often visited the Crusaders, did not at all prevent a great number of them from indulging in excesses of license and debauchery. All the vices of Europe and Asia were met together on one spot. If an Arabian author may be believed, at the very moment in which the Franks were a prey to famine and contagious diseases, a troop of three hundred women from Cyprus and the neighbouring islands arrived in the camp. These three hundred women, whose presence in the Christian army was a scandal in the eyes of the Saracens, prostituted themselves among the soldiers of the cross, and stood in no need of employing the enchantments of the Armida of Tasso to corrupt them.

Nevertheless, the clergy were unremitting in their exhortations to the pilgrims to lead them back to the morals of the Gospel. Churches, surmounted by wooden steeples, were erected in the camp, in which the faithful were every day called together. Not unfrequently the Saracens took advantage of the moment at which the soldiers left their intrenchments unguarded to attend mass, and made flying but annoying incursions. Amidst general corruption, the siege of Ptolemaïs presented many subjects of edification. In the camp, or in the field of battle, charity hovered constantly around the Christian soldier, to soothe his misery, to watch his sick pallet, or dress his wounds. During the siege the warriors from the North were in the greatest distress, and could gain little assistance from other nations. Some pilgrims from Lubeck and Bremen came to their aid, formed tents of the sails of their vessels to shelter their poor countrymen, and ministered to their wants and tended their diseases. Forty German nobles took part in this generous enterprise, and their association was the origin of the hospitable and military order of the Teutonic knights.

When the Crusaders entered Ptolemaïs, they shared the sovereignty of it amongst them, each nation taking possession of one of the quarters of the city, which had soon as many masters as it had had enemies. The king of Jerusalem was the only leader that obtained nothing in the division of the first reconquered place of his kingdom.

The capitulation remained unexecuted; Saladin, under various pretexts, deferring the completion of the conditions. Richard, irritated by a delay which appeared to him a breach of faith, revenged himself upon the prisoners that were in his hands. Without pity for disarmed enemies, or for the Christians he exposed to sanguinary reprisals, he massacred five thousand Mussulmans before the city they had so valiantly defended, and within sight of Saladin, who shared the disgrace of this barbarity by thus abandoning his bravest and most faithful warriors.

This action, which excited the regret of the whole Christian army, sufficiently exposed the character of Richard, and showed what was to be dreaded from his violence; a barbarous and implacable enemy could not become a generous rival. On the day of the surrender of Ptolemaïs, he committed a gross outrage upon Leopold, duke of Austria, by ordering the standard of that prince, which had been planted on one of the towers, to be cast into the ditch.

CRUSADERS SURROUNDED BY SALADIN'S ARMY.

In this army were Bedouin Arabs armed with arrows and round shields; Scythians with long hair mounted on strong fleet horses and armed with javelins; Ethiopians painted with white and red; after these came several other phalanxes with lances decorated with flags of all sorts of colors. These barbarians advanced against the Crusaders with the rapidity of light, the earth trembling under their feet, and the noise of their clarions and cymbals would have drowned the reverberations of thunder. They had among them men whose only occupation was to make horrible howls, not only to frighten the enemy, but to warm to the work of carnage the Mussulman warriors, chase fear from their hearts, and give them the courage of the drunkenness of victory. Their battalions animated thus, now precipitated themselves on the Crusaders, new battalions followed the first, and these were followed by others. Soon the Mussulman army, as an Arabian historian writes, surrounded the Christians "as the eyelashes surround the eye."—BOOK VIII.

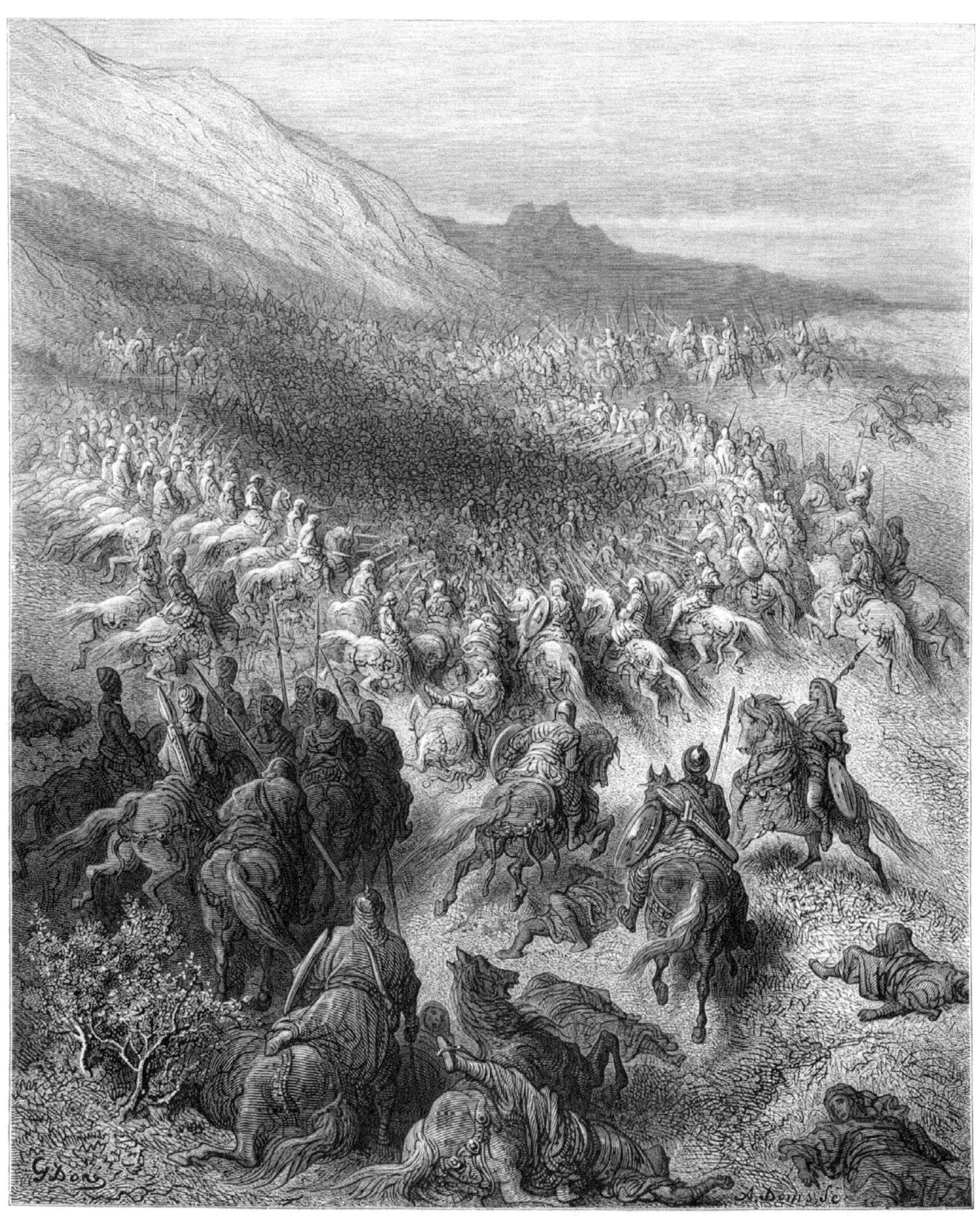
G. Doré

Leopold dissembled his resentment, but swore to avenge this insult whenever he should find an opportunity. Richard, for ever carried away by his violent and imperious character, desired to command as a master, and alone dictate laws for the whole army of the Crusaders. He endeavoured to corrupt the troops of Philip by largesses ; he set a price upon infidelity and treason ; and Philip, fearing to compromise the dignity of a king and the interests of the crusade by punishing the outrages and perfidy of his rival, resolved to return to France, where fortune offered him more than one opportunity of usefully revenging himself upon the king of England.

Philip quitted Palestine, leaving in the army ten thousand foot and five hundred horse, under the command of the duke of Burgundy. On his arrival at Tyre, from which port he embarked, he received a solemn embassy from Saladin, who sent him magnificent presents, and complimented him as the most powerful monarch of the West. He soon arrived in Italy, where the holy pontiff praised his devotion, and bestowed upon him the palms of pilgrimage. Welcomed on his return tc his kingdom by the benedictions of his people, he carried back the sacred oriflamme to the church of St. Denis, and returned thanks to the apostles of France for having protected his life and the glory of his arms amidst the greatest perils.

When Philip left Palestine, Richard remained at the head of an army of a hundred thousand Crusaders. After having repaired the walls of Ptolemaïs, and allowed his soldiers some little repose, he passed the Belus, crossed Mount Carmel, and marched towards Cæsarea. A fleet from Ptolemaïs kept close to the shore, and transported the provisions, machines of war, and baggage of the Christian army. Saladin, whom Arabian writers often compare to a lioness that has lost her young, upon receiving intelligence of the march of the Crusaders, gathered together his army, and set out in pursuit of them ; sometimes getting in advance and attacking their van, at others harassing their flanks, and seizing every soldier that ventured to stray from the main body. Although Cæsarea was only twelve leagues from Ptolemaïs, the Crusaders could not accomplish the distance in less than six days. All the Christians, who were unable to keep up with the army, and fell into the power of Saladin, were put to death by his orders, and their bodies left upon the shore, as an expiation of the massacre of the garrison of Ptolemaïs.

Richard, who found that perils and obstacles multiplied in his route, desired an interview with Malek-Adel, and proposed to make peace, if the Mussulmans would restore the city of Jerusalem to the Christians. Malek-Adel replied that the last of the soldiers of Saladin would perish, rather than renounce conquests made in the name of Islamism. Richard, irritated by this refusal, swore that he would obtain by victory that which he could not obtain from Saladin, and gave orders for the army to pursue their march.

The Crusaders advanced towards the city of Arsur, marching over a long but narrow plain, intersected by torrents, ravines, and marshes, and covered in many places with fragments of rocks, marine plants, and reeds. They had the sea on their right, and on the left rose the steep mountains of Naplouse, defended by the inhabitants of the country and the troops of Saladin. At every passage of a torrent, at every dune or hillock of sand, at every village, a fresh contest had to be sustained, whilst the Mussulman archers, placed upon the heights, annoyed them unceasingly with their arrows. Richard's army marched in order of battle ; the cavalry being placed in the centre, whilst the foot, closing their ranks, presented an impenetrable wall to the enemy, and braved their constantly renewed attacks.

The army of the sultan got in advance of the Crusaders, and laid waste everything in their way ; exhausting their efforts and ingenuity to retard, or entirely stop their march. Across the plain of Arsur flowed a torrent which cast itself into the sea near the ramparts of the city ; and not far from this torrent, a wood of oaks, which historians call the forest of Sarun, and which is believed to be the forest celebrated by Tasso, extended along the declivities of the mountains of Naplouse: it was upon this spot Saladin awaited the Crusaders to offer them a decisive battle.

A part of his army covered the heights, whilst the remainder encamped upon the banks of the torrent of Arsur. The Christians soon arrived in face of their enemy, and drew up in order of battle. The Danes, Flemings, and Tuscans, commanded by Jacques d'Avesnes, formed the van. Richard marched in the centre, at the head of the English, Normans, Gascons, the Syrian troops, and those of the count of Champagne: the rear-guard was composed of French and Germans, under the orders of the duke of Burgundy and Leopold of Austria. Whilst the archers were showering their arrows from a distance, Saladin passed through the ranks and roused the courage of his soldiers, who replied to him with cries of *Allah ac bar!*—God is powerful. In this army were Bedouin Arabs armed with arrows and round shields; Scythians with long hair mounted on strong fleet horses and armed with javelins; Ethiopians painted with white and red; after these came several other phalanxes with lances decorated with flags of all sorts of colors. These barbarians advanced against the Crusaders with the rapidity of light, the earth trembling under their feet, and the noise of their clarions and cymbals would have drowned the reverberations of thunder. They had among them men whose only occupation was to make horrible howls, not only to frighten the enemy, but to warm to the work of carnage the Mussulman warriors, chase fear from their hearts, and give them the courage of the drunkenness of victory. Their battalions animated thus, now precipitated themselves on the Crusaders, new battalions followed the first, and these were followed by others. Soon the Mussulman army, as an Arabian historian writes, surrounded the Christians "as the eyelashes surround the eye."

Profound silence prevailed in the Christian army; the black cuirasses of the Crusaders seeming to darken the horizon, whilst sixty thousand swords gleamed out from amidst clouds of dust. All at once the Christian infantry opened their ranks, and the cavalry rushed forward towards the enemy, drawn up on the banks of the torrent of Arsur. Jacques d'Avesnes, who commanded them, penetrated twice into the closely-pressed ranks of the Saracens, and twice was compelled to retreat in disorder. At the third charge his leg was severed by the stroke of a sabre, but he still pursued the infidels, when the arm with which he fought was struck off at a blow. The Christian hero fell amidst the enemy, calling aloud upon Richard, and conjuring him to avenge his death.

The king of England advanced with the main body, sweeping away the crowd of Saracens that opposed his passage, and pursuing them to the other side of the torrent; but whilst he yielded to his ardour, and advanced before the Christian army, the chosen troops of the Mussulmans descended from the mountains of Naplouse, and poured down upon the rear of the Christians. Richard was forced to retrace his steps to support the French and Germans, who were beginning to give way. The plain in which the battle was fought, could scarcely contain all the combatants. The Christians and Mussulmans closed, and attacked each other man to man; the foot fought pell-mell with the horse, exhorting each other to brave death. The cries of rage, despair, and agony were mingled with the clashing of swords, lances, and shields. The two armies, confounded and mixed together, became nothing but one horrible spectacle. If we believe the somewhat improbable account of an English historian,* Richard and Saladin met in the *mêlée*, and rushed upon each other sword in hand, and the two armies instantly became motionless, leaving to their great leaders the honour of deciding the fate of the battle. This singular circumstance, which poetry might envy history, is not mentioned by Arabian writers.† The battle lasted almost during the whole day. Towards evening the Mussul-

* Arabian historians say nothing of the single combat between Richard and Saladin. English historians alone mention it.

† I cannot attach much consequence to the silence of the Arabian writers on this subject, neither can I think, with our author, such a *rencontre* so im-

mans were broken on all sides, and retreated in disorder into the forest of Saron, whither the fear of an ambuscade prevented the Christians from pursuing them, and destroying the wreck of their army.

The battle of Arsur was one of the most celebrated of this war; in it the Mussulmans lost a great number of their bravest emirs, and particularly regretted a chief of Saladin's Mamelukes, whose heroic courage is highly celebrated by their historians. No Saracen warrior was more prompt to meet danger, and he was always the first to fly to the assistance of his companions, though he himself needed aid from no man. His horse being slain, this brave emir was encumbered with the weight of his iron armour, and received several mortal wounds. Many Mussulman soldiers hastened to his relief, *but he was already amongst the inhabitants of heaven!*

The Christians wept for the death of Jacques d'Avesnes, who had so often shown them the path to victory. In this glorious day the loss of the Crusaders was much less than that of the Mussulmans; their leaders and soldiers displayed a degree of skill that they had never evinced before. The Saracen cavalry, superior to that of the Crusaders, had not room to perform their usual evolutions with advantage in so confined a field. They attacked the Christians several times with great impetuosity, but the Crusaders withstood them with immovable firmness, and constantly rallied around their great standard, which floated from the summit of a rolling tower. A remarkable circumstance of this battle is, that it was principally gained by the infantry, a force which, although held in contempt in the first crusade, had learnt to be redoubtable under the walls of Ptolemaïs.

Richard, who had conquered the Saracens, was not wise enough to profit by their defeat; instead of pursuing the enemy, or marching straight to Jerusalem, he led his army to Jaffa, the ramparts of which Saladin had demolished, and which the Mussulmans had abandoned. He occupied himself with repairing the fortifications, and sent for the Queen Berengaria, Jane, the widow of the king of Sicily, and the daughter of Isaac. Surrounded by a brilliant court, he forgot, in the intoxication of pleasure and festivities, the conquest of Jerusalem, for which he had come into Asia. During this fatal repose, he was on the point of losing with his life and liberty the fruit of all his victories. Being one day hunting in the forest of Saron, overcome by heat or fatigue, he alighted from his horse and fell asleep under a tree. All at once he was aroused by the cries of those who accompanied him,—a troop of Saracens was close upon them! He sprang upon his horse, and prepared to defend himself; but was near sinking beneath the force of numbers, when a knight of his suite, named *William Pourcelet*, cried out in the Arabic tongue, "*I am the king; spare my life.*" At these words, this generous warrior was surrounded by the Mussulmans, who made him prisoner and conducted him to Saladin. The king of England, thus saved by the heroism of a French knight, escaped the pursuit of the enemy, and returned to Jaffa, where his army learnt with terror the danger they had been in of losing their leader.

Richard formed the project of besieging Ascalon; and Saladin being doubtful of his power to defend that city, resolved to destroy it. In vain the inhabitants came to implore his pity; in the space of a few days the strongest and most flourishing city of Syria was consumed by fire, and remained nothing but a heap of ruins.

The demolition of Ascalon excited great sorrow among the Mussulmans; and the king of England, who had entertained hopes of rendering himself master of the place, was as much afflicted as if he had lost one of his conquests. This city, which had cost the Christians and Mussulmans so much blood, opened at once to the Crusaders the gates of Palestine and Egypt. Richard undertook to rebuild the ramparts that the Mussulmans had destroyed, and led his army into the plain, covered by the ruins of Ascalon.

probable in such a *mêlée*. The principal argument against it is, that Saladin survived the battle. Richard was at least twelve years younger than Saladin, and in the full vigour of a large, powerful frame, whilst Saladin was weakened by toil and disease.—TRANS.

It was a curious spectacle to behold thirty thousand warriors from the West employed in rebuilding the walls of a city of Syria. The Crusaders, as the Hebrews have been described to us whilst erecting the temple of Jerusalem, were obliged to work with the sword in one hand and the tools of masonry in the other. Saladin might have disturbed their labours; but he preferred giving his army a little repose, and recruiting its numbers; persuaded that the divisions that existed among his enemies would soon work to his advantage. The Christian army obeyed Richard very unwillingly. Leopold of Austria, accused by the king of England of remaining idle with his Germans, contented himself with replying *that he was neither a carpenter nor a mason.* The greater part of the knights who were thus employed in moving stones and digging ditches, were exceedingly indignant, and said aloud that they did not come into Asia to rebuild Ascalon, but to conquer Jerusalem.

Whilst the Christian army was in this dissatisfied state, the marquis of Tyre, who had been ill-treated by Richard, courted the alliance of the sultan, and promised to restore Ptolemaïs to him, if the Mussulmans would agree to protect him against his enemies. The king of England, warned of this perfidious negotiation, became only anxious to defeat the projects of Conrad, and himself made propositions to Saladin. He renewed the promise he had made to Malek-Adel to return into Europe if Jerusalem and the wood of the true cross were restored to the Christians. "Jerusalem," replied Saladin, "never belonged to you; we cannot without a crime abandon it to you, for in it were accomplished the mysteries of our religion." As to the wood of the true cross, Saladin considered it as an object of scandal, as an insult to divinity. He had refused to give it up to the king of Georgia or the emperor of Constantinople, both of whom had offered him considerable sums for it. "All the advantages to be procured by peace," said he, "cannot bring me to restore this disgraceful monument of their idolatry to the Christians."

Richard, who really considered the restitution of the true cross of very little importance, did not reiterate his demand; but as he was desirous of peace, he made other proposals, in which he adroitly interested the ambition of Malek-Adel, the brother of the sultan. The widow of William of Sicily, the sister of Richard, was offered in marriage to the Mussulman prince; under the auspices of Saladin and Richard, they might reign together over Mussulmans and Christians, and govern the kingdom of Jerusalem. The historian Omad was charged by Malek-Adel with the task of communicating this proposition to Saladin, who appeared to adopt it without repugnance. The project of this singular union created great surprise among the imauns and doctors of the law; and the Christian bishops, when they were informed of it, expressed the strongest indignation, and threatened both Jane and Richard with the thunders of the Church.

The execution of this plan appeared impossible in the midst of a religious war; and everything leads us to believe that Saladin only affected to give it attention that he might gain time to fortify Jerusalem, which the Christians still demanded of him. Skilful workmen from Aleppo were, by his orders, employed in widening the ditches and repairing the walls. Among the Mussulman workmen were two thousand Christian prisoners, condemned to rebuild the fortresses occupied by the infidels. Saladin encouraged the labours by his presence and his example, animating the zeal of the people and soldiers by frequently reminding them of the victories of the Mussulmans, and of the massacre of their brethren slaughtered before Ptolemaïs.

The conquest of the holy city was the object of the war,—the great reward promised to the labours of the Crusaders; and they at length earnestly pressed Richard to march towards Jerusalem. He was obliged to yield to their impatience, and led them as far as Bethonopolis, situated between Ascalon and the capital of Palestine. At the approach of the Franks, Saladin ordered all the country through which their army must pass to be laid waste. By the commands of the sultan the ramparts of Ramla and Lidda, with the fortress of Nitro, were demolished. All the routes which led to Jerusalem were guarded by Mussulman cavalry, who unceasingly harassed the Christians, and prevented their receiving provisions from Ptolemaïs or other maritime cities.

In proportion with their approximation to Jerusalem, the enthusiasm and ardour of the Crusaders increased; but Richard and most of the leaders did not at all partake of the impatience of the soldiers. The Christian army was only one day's march from the sea-coast, and yet want of provisions began to be sensibly felt. If in the plains of Ptolemaïs, where the Crusaders could look for provisions to the Mediterranean, they had experienced all the horrors of famine, what miseries had they not reason to expect under the walls of Jerusalem? Mussulman troops were encamped in the plains of Jericho and Hébron, and in the country of Naplouse, and had the power at all times to throw succour into Jerusalem, if that city were besieged by the Christians. Winter, besides, was beginning to create a dread of contagious diseases; the leaders of the army were divided among themselves, and even the sight of danger could scarcely bring them to act in concert. All these circumstances produced doubt and irresolution in the minds of Richard and the most prudent of the barons and knights.

Richard entertained hopes that Saladin would come and offer him battle, and that a victory would at once throw open the gates of Jerusalem to him; but the sultan, who had proved the strength and bravery of the Christians at Arsur, was not willing to expose his conquests to the hazard of a battle. Richard, on his part, dreaded the perils and fatigues of a protracted siege, and suddenly led back his army to the plains of Ascalon.

The multitude of the Crusaders, who were ignorant of or did not appreciate the motives of the king of England, only obeyed him with murmurs, and most of the leaders, declared enemies of Richard, mingled their complaints with those of the soldiers. Several dissatisfied Crusaders deserted the standards which no longer pointed out to them the road to Jerusalem.

Whilst the army was marching despondingly back to the plains of Ascalon, the Genoese and Pisans, continually at variance, broke into open war within the walls of Ptolemaïs. Conrad took part with the Genoese, whilst the king of England as eagerly defended the Pisans, and terminated this civil war by forcing Conrad and the Genoese to retreat to the city of Tyre.

Amidst these sanguinary disputes, Conrad, who had an ambassador at the court of Saladin, unable longer to endure the authority of Richard, entered into an alliance with the Mussulmans. Saladin, by treaty, abandoned to the marquis of Tyre all the cities the latter might take from the Christians, and promised to aid him in his conquests, only reserving the booty for the Mussulman soldiers. This treaty, dictated by hatred to Richard, was the signal for the death of Conrad; a very short time afterwards the marquis of Tyre perished by an unknown hand.

English authors assert that Conrad had had quarrels with the chief of the Ismaëlians, and that he was assassinated by the orders of this redoubtable enemy. Two young slaves left the voluptuous gardens, in which their master had brought them up, to execute his vengeance. They arrived at Tyre, and, in order to conceal their purpose the better, received baptism. They engaged themselves in the service of Conrad, and remained six months about his person, apparently only occupied in offering up prayers to the God of the Christians. One day, as the marquis was coming from dining with the bishop of Beauvais, the two Ismaëlians attacked him, and wounded him mortally. Whilst the people congregated tumultuously, one of the assassins fled into a neighbouring church, into which, likewise, the bleeding marquis was borne. The Ismaëlian, who had concealed himself, suddenly rushed through the crowd, and again falling upon Conrad, struck him repeatedly with his dagger, till he was quite dead. The two assassins were seized, and both died amidst tortures, without uttering a single groan, or naming the person who had employed them to take away the life of the marquis of Tyre.

The continuator of Tabary says that Saladin had offered the Old Man of the Mountains ten thousand pieces of gold if he would cause the marquis of Tyre and the king of England to be assassinated; but the prince of the mountain, adds the same historian, did not think proper to deliver Saladin entirely from his war with the Franks, and only performed half of that which had been required of him. The Christians did not attribute the death of Conrad to Saladin, but many among them accused Richard of it. A short time after the murder, a letter was published, in which the lord of the mountain avowed himself to be the author of the assassination; but this letter bore no character of authenticity about it. The savage lord of the mountain could not write, and could have no interest in making the apology of a Christian prince. The king of England himself strengthened the public suspicions by taking possession of Tyre, and giving the widow of Conrad in marriage to his nephew, the count of Champagne. However it may be, this accusation, which was accredited among the Christians, announced plainly the idea they entertained of the character of Richard. The account of the death of Conrad soon reached Europe, and Philip Augustus, dreading the same fate, no longer appeared in public without being surrounded by a guard. The court of France accused Richard of the blackest attempts; but it is probable that Philip, on this occasion, showed more fear than he really felt, in order to render his rival the more odious, and to arm against him the hatred of the pope, and the indignation of all the princes of Christendom.

After the death of Conrad, Richard had no rivals to suspect, or enemies to fight with among the Christians; the opinion even that was entertained of his character, only served to augment his authority, by creating a dread of his hatred or vengeance. He took advantage of a moment, in which Saladin disbanded part of his army, to get possession of the castle of Darcum, built upon the confines of Palestine, towards Egypt. He undertook several other enterprises, which spread terror and surprise among the Saracens; and, all at once, to satisfy the wishes of the Crusaders, marched towards Jerusalem, in which city Saladin had shut himself up with all the troops he could gather together. At the approach of the Christians, the sultan convoked his emirs, and made them swear, on the stone of Jacob, to be buried beneath the ruins of the city rather than yield it up to the soldiers of Richard.

The Christian army encamped at the foot of the mountains of Judea, all the passes of which were guarded by the troops of Saladin and the Saracen peasants of Naplouse and Hebron. As Richard drew near to Jerusalem, his aversion to the idea of allowing the duke of Austria and the duke of Burgundy to share in such a glorious conquest increased; whilst they were not at all willing to assist the king of England in an enterprise that would so much augment his pride and renown. Every time that he proposed to proceed against the holy city, the zeal of the leaders of the army appeared to cool; and when Richard sought to defer the conquest, most of them endeavoured to arouse the enthusiasm of the Crusaders, and repeated the oath they had taken to deliver the tomb of Christ. Thus the proximity to Jerusalem, which ought to have united the Christians more firmly, only served to increase their divisions, and spread trouble, disorder, and discouragement through the whole army.

The Christians were but a few leagues from Jerusalem, and the council assembled to determine what steps must be taken. Many of the leaders thought that they ought at once to besiege the city, and spoke of the consternation of the Mussulmans. The soldiers of Saladin, said they, had not forgotten the evils of Ptolemaïs, and trembled at the idea of again shutting themselves within the ramparts of a city. Fugitives from Jerusalem had informed them that the presence even of Saladin could not keep up the spirits of the soldiers, and that all the inhabitants, seized with terror, were upon the point of flying to Damascus.

They who maintained an opposite opinion, among whom was Richard, thought that the reports spread regarding the disposition of the Mussulmans were but a snare of Saladin's, by which he hoped to lure the Crusaders into places in which he could destroy them without fighting. "At the moment in which we are speaking," said they, "the Mussulman cavalry surround the plain on which our army is encamped. It is difficult and dangerous to advance across the mountains of Judea. The roads, bordered by precipices, are, in many places, cut through the solid rock, and are dominated by steep heights, from which ill-armed peasants will be sufficient to crush, or at least to stop the columns of the Christians. How are we to transport through such narrow passes our baggage, our machines, or our munitions of war? If our bravery should succeed in surmounting all these difficulties, will it be easy to keep up our communications with the coast? If we are conquered, how shall we make our retreat, pursued by the army of Saladin?"

Opinions continued to be divided: the king of England wished to retreat to Ascalon; whilst the dukes of Austria and Burgundy warmly maintained that they ought to march towards Jerusalem. Twenty-four knights were selected to determine upon the course that was to be adopted, and the Christian army awaited their decision with an impatience mingled with fear. After having deliberated for some time, the twenty-four knights concluded that the army could not pursue its march without danger, and that the most prudent plan would be to retreat towards the sea-coast. Richard, after having given the order for retreat, whether he was sincerely afflicted, or whether he wished to regain the confidence and esteem of the Crusaders, turned towards Jerusalem with his eyes filled with tears, and covering his face with his buckler, declared himself unworthy to behold a city that he could not conquer.

The Crusaders once more turned their backs upon Jerusalem, which they had sworn so often and so solemnly to deliver, the soldiers totally unable to comprehend the policy or intentions of their leaders. Richard, who had led the Christian army towards the holy city, might at least be accused of want of determination of purpose. The uncertainty of his plans completed the destruction of the confidence which his skill and great military talents had created; and the despair of the Crusaders put an end to the fear of a chief they no longer loved. Discord broke out with fresh fury; such as remained partisans of Richard, reproached his enemies with misleading the spirit of the army; but all parties mutually accused each other of favouring the cause of the infidels. As is generally the case in unsuccessful wars, perfidy and treachery were the subjects most current among the Crusaders.

The most violent complaints were uttered against Richard, who replied to his enemies in a strain of high-minded bravery, worthy of an Amadis or a Roland. At the head of a weak detachment, he took a convoy of seven thousand camels on the way to Jerusalem; on another occasion, going on board a vessel with a few knights, he landed at Jaffa, where the banners of Saladin floated over the towers and ramparts; he pursued the conquerors sword in hand, and forced them to abandon their temporary conquest. A few days after, the king of England, with a troop of his chosen knights, attacked a body of seven thousand Mussulman horse; he rushed in amongst them, and with a stroke of his sabre struck dead at his feet the leader of the Saracens, who all appeared stupefied and motionless with surprise and fear.

But all these perils and all this glory were lost for the cause of the Christians. Richard became every day more odious to his associates; the duke of Burgundy with the French retired discontented to Ptolemaïs; the Germans, commanded by the duke of Austria, quitted Palestine, and Richard remained alone with the English. Hitherto the king of England, as he himself told the ambassadors of Saladin, had taken but little interest in the deliverance of the holy places, and had only performed such prodigies of valour to increase his fame in the Christian world. A desire to efface the glory of

Philip, much more than a zeal for religion, governed him in his contests with the Saracens; he underwent the labours of the holy war in the hope that his exploits in Palestine would assist him in triumphing over his rivals and enemies beyond the seas; but as he began to fear being left without an army, and dreaded the enterprises of Philip, and the plots of his brother John, against his European states, he determined to resume his negotiations with Saladin. The various thoughts that harassed his mind, the shame of not having conquered Jerusalem, the fear of losing his own kingdom, made him adopt and reject resolutions of the most opposite nature. At one time he determined upon returning to Europe without making peace at all—first he supplicated, then he menaced Saladin, and endeavoured to frighten him, by spreading a report that the pope was about to arrive in Palestine with an army of two hundred thousand Crusaders.

Winter had not yet passed away, and the passage of the Mediterranean was not without danger. "The sea is stormy," wrote he one day to Saladin, "but I will brave its tempests, and return to Europe if you are disposed to make peace. But if you still desire war, I will brave all its perils, and will lay siege to Jerusalem." Saladin was encamped in the vicinity of Ramla, and called his emirs together to deliberate upon the proposals of Richard. "Up to this period," said he, "we have fought with glory, and the cause of Islamism has triumphed by our arms. I fear that death may surprise me during a peace, and may prevent my terminating the good work we have begun. Since God gives us victory, he commands us to continue the war, and we ought to obey his will." Most of the emirs applauded the courage and firmness of Saladin, but they represented to him, "that the cities were without defence, and the provinces were devastated; the fatigues of war had weakened the Mussulman army; the horses wanted forage, and provisions for the soldiers were dearer than gold." "If we reduce the Franks to despair," added they, "they may still overcome us, and wrest all our victories from our hands. It is wise to observe the maxim of the Koran, which orders us to grant peace to our enemies when they ask it. Peace will give us time to fortify our cities, to recruit our forces, and resume the war with advantage; when the Franks, always faithless in treaties, will offer us fresh pretexts for attacking them."

Saladin plainly perceived by this speech of his emirs, that the greater part of the Saracen warriors were beginning to lose the ardour and zeal they had evinced for the cause of Islamism. The sultan was abandoned by several of his auxiliaries, and dreaded the appearance of division in his own empire. The armies were close to each other, and the dust which arose from the two camps, says an Arabian author, mingled in the air and formed but one cloud. Neither the Christians nor the Mussulmans showed the least impatience to go beyond the boundaries of their ramparts and ditches, and both being equally tired of the war, it became the interest of the two leaders to make peace. The disposition of the minds of the combatants, with the impossibility of pursuing any warlike enterprises, at length led to the adoption of a truce for three years and eight months.

It was determined that Jerusalem should be open to the devotion of the Christians, and that they should hold all the seacoast from Java to Tyre. The Saracens and the Christians had both claims upon Ascalon, which was considered as the key to Egypt, and which the Arabs called the *spouse of Syria*. To terminate these disputes, it was agreed that this city should be again demolished. It is not unworthy of remark, that not a word was said about the true cross, which had been the subject of the first negotiations, and for which Richard had sent several ambassadors to Saladin. The principal leaders of the two armies swore, on the one side upon the Koran, and on the other upon the Gospel, to observe the conditions of the treaty. Royal majesty assumed something more imposing and august than even the sanctity of an oath, for the sultan and the king of England contented themselves with giving their word and touching the hands of the ambassadors.

RICHARD CŒUR DE LION AND SALADIN AT THE BATTLE OF ARSUR.

Profound silence prevailed in the Christian army; the black cuirasses of the Crusaders seeming to darken the horizon, while sixty thousand swords gleamed out from amidst clouds of dust. All at once the Christian infantry opened their ranks, and the cavalry rushed forward towards the enemy, drawn up on the banks of the torrent of Arsur. The king of England advanced with the main body, sweeping away the crowd of Saracens that opposed his passage, and pursuing them to the other side of the torrent; but whilst he yielded to his ardour, and advanced before the Christian army, the chosen troops of the Mussulmans descended from the mountains of Naplouse, and poured down upon the rear of the Christians. Richard was forced to retrace his steps to support the French and Germans, who were beginning to give way. The plain in which the battle was fought could scarcely contain all the combatants. The Christians and Mussulmans closed, and attacked each other man to man; the foot fought pell-mell with the horse, exhorting each other to brave death. The cries of rage, despair, and agony were mingled with the clashing of swords, lances, and shields. The two armies, confounded and mixed together, became nothing but one horrible spectacle.—Book VIII.

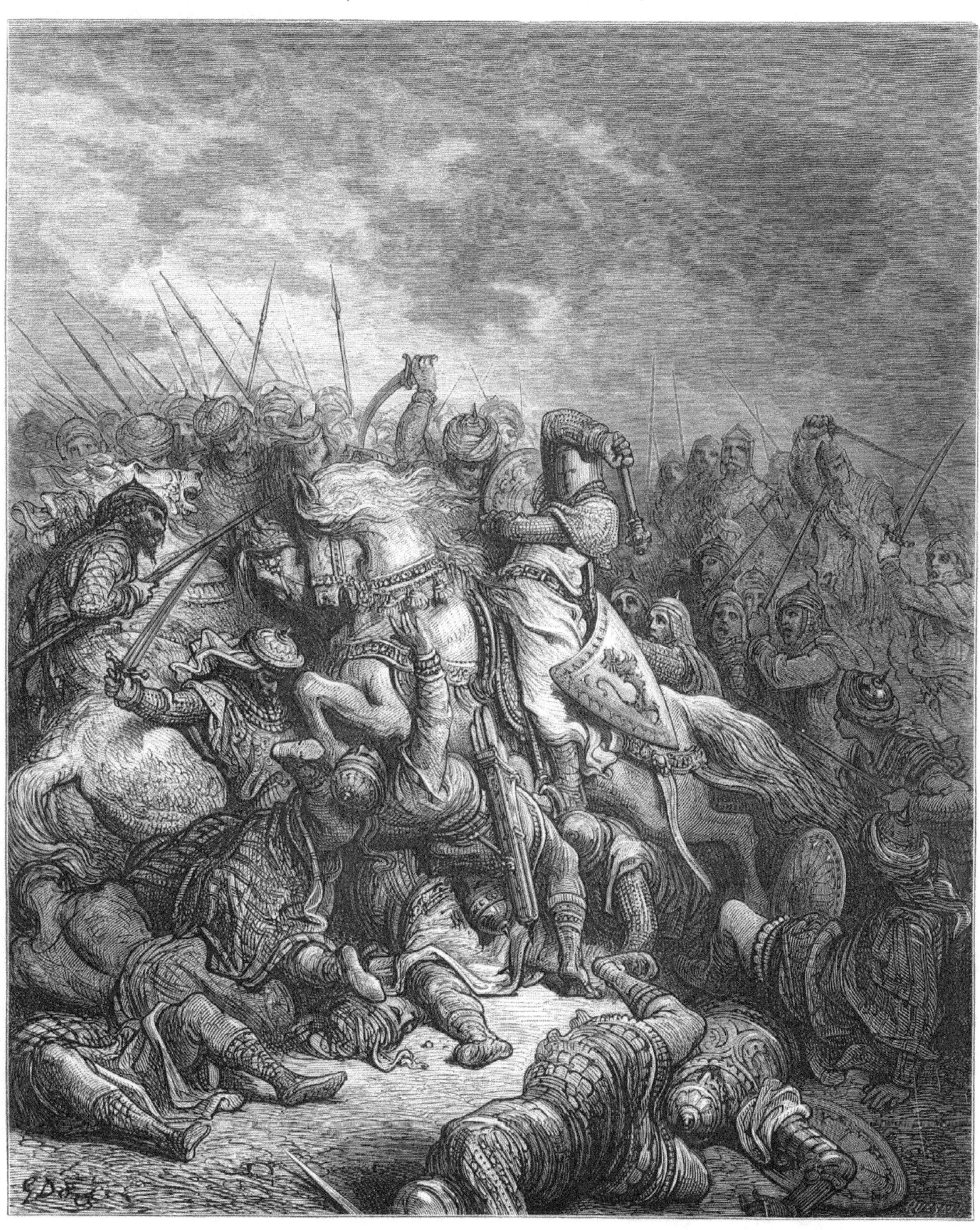

All the Mussulman and Christian princes of Syria were invited to sign the treaty concluded between Richard and Saladin. Among those who were called upon to be guarantees of the peace, neither the prince of Antioch, who had taken little share in the war, nor the chief of the Ismaëlians, the enemy of both Christians and Mussulmans, was forgotten. Guy de Lusignan alone was not named in the treaty. This prince enjoyed a momentary importance from the dissensions he had given birth to, and sunk into oblivion as soon as fresh subjects of discord arose among the Crusaders. Despoiled of his kingdom, he obtained that of Cyprus, a far more real possession, but for which he was obliged to pay the Templars, to whom Richard had sold it. Palestine was ceded to Henry, count of Champagne, the new husband of that Isabella who appeared to be promised to all the pretenders to the crown of Jerusalem, and who, by a singular destiny, had married three kings, without being able to ascend a throne.

The conclusion of the peace was celebrated by tournaments and festivities, in which the Mussulmans and Christians laid aside the fanaticism and hatred which had led them to shed so much blood. Most of the warriors of the West, by the invitation of Saladin, visited the holy places they had been unable to deliver, and then embarked for Europe. At the moment of departure, the French lost the duke of Burgundy, who fell sick and died in the city of Tyre, as he was preparing to leave Palestine.

Thus finished this third crusade, in which all the western powers in arms obtained no greater advantages than the taking of Ptolemaïs and the demolition of Ascalon; in it Germany lost, without glory, one of the greatest of its emperors and the finest of its armies. If we may believe Arabian authors, six hundred thousand Crusaders appeared before Ptolemaïs, and scarcely one hundred thousand of these warriors saw their native country again. Europe had the greater reason to deplore the losses of this war, from the fact of her armies having been so much better composed than in preceding expeditions; criminals, adventurers, and vagabonds, had been strictly excluded from the ranks. All that the West could boast of the most noble and illustrious of its warriors had taken up arms.

The Crusaders that contended with Saladin were better armed and better disciplined than any that preceded them in Palestine; the foot-soldiers employed the cross-bow, which had been neglected or prohibited in the second crusade. Their cuirasses, and their bucklers covered with thick leather, defied the arrows of the Saracens; and on the field of battle, soldiers were often seen bristling with arrows and darts, whom the Arabs compared to porcupines, still keeping their ranks and fighting bravely. The Saracens had likewise made some progress in the art of war, and began to resume the use of the lance, which they did not employ when the first Crusaders arrived in Syria. The Mussulman armies were not confused multitudes; they remained longer under their banners, and fought with less disorder. The Curds and Turks surpassed the Franks in the art of attacking and defending cities and castles. The Mussulmans had, besides, more than one advantage over the Crusaders; they made war upon their own territories and in their own climate; they were under the command of one single leader, who communicated the same spirit to all, and only presented to them one cause to defend.

In this crusade the Franks appeared to be more polished than they had been till that time. Great monarchs making war against each other without ceasing to give evidences of mutual esteem and generous feeling, was a new spectacle for the world. Subjects followed the example of their princes, and lost beneath the tent much of their barbarism. The Crusaders were sometimes admitted to the table of Saladin, and emirs received at that of Richard. By thus mingling together, Saracens and Christians might make a happy exchange of usages, manners, knowledge, and even virtues.

The Christians, rather more enlightened than during the first crusades, stood in less need of excitement from the visions of fanaticism. The passion for glory was for them almost as powerful a principle as religious enthusiasm. Chivalry also made great progress in this crusade; it was held in such honour, and the title of KNIGHT was so glorious, even in the eyes of the infidels, that Saladin did not disdain to be decorated with it.

The sentiment of honour, and the humanity which is inseparable from it, often dried tears that the disasters of war had caused to flow; tender and virtuous passions associated themselves in the minds of heroes with the austere maxims of religion and the sanguinary images of battle. Amidst the corruption of camps, love, by inspiring the knights and troubadours who had taken the cross with noble and delicate sentiments, preserved them from the seductions of gross debauchery. More than one warrior, animated by the remembrance of beauty, caused his bravery to be greatly admired, whilst fighting against the Saracens. It was in this crusade that the Châtelain de Coucy fell, mortally wounded, by the side of King Richard. In a song, which is still extant, he had bid adieu to France, saying that he went to the Holy Land to obtain three things of inestimable value to a knight,—*Paradise, glory, and the love of his mistress.* A chronicle of the middle ages relates, that after he had received a mortal wound and was about to breathe his last sigh, the faithful Châtelain first confessed himself to the legate of the Pope, and then charged his squire to bear his heart to the lady de Fayel. The last commands of Coucy, and the horrible banquet that a cruel husband caused to be served up to the victim of his jealousy, show at once what chivalry could inspire of the most touching kind, and that which the manners of the twelfth century could exhibit of the most barbarous. The troubadours celebrated in their songs the chivalric love of the noble Châtelain, and the despair of the beautiful De Vergy, when she learnt she had eaten the heart of her faithful knight. If we may believe old chronicles, the lord de Fayel, pursued by remorse and the opinion of his contemporaries, was obliged to go to the Holy Land, to expiate his crime and the death of his unfortunate wife.

In this crusade, in which so many knights rendered themselves illustrious, two men acquired an immortal glory, one by a useless bravery, and qualities more brilliant than solid, the other by real successes and virtues that might have served as models to Christians. The name of Richard remained during a century the terror of the East, and the Saracens and Turks celebrated him in their proverbs a long time after the crusades. He cultivated letters, and merited a place among the troubadours; but the arts did not at all soften his character; it was his ferocity as well as his courage that procured him the surname of Cœur de Lion. Carried away by the inconstancy of his inclinations, he often changed his projects, his affections, and his principles of action; he sometimes braved religion, and very often devoted himself to its service. Sometimes incredulous, as often superstitious; measureless in his hatred as in his friendship, he was extravagant in everything, and only showed himself constant in his love for war. The passions which animated him scarcely ever permitted his ambition to have an aim or a determinate object. His imprudence, his presumption, and the unsteadiness of his plans, made him lose the fruits of his exploits. In a word, the hero of this crusade is more calculated to excite surprise than to create esteem, and appears to belong less to history than to the romances of chivalry.

With less rashness and bravery than Richard, Saladin possessed a more firm character, one far better calculated to carry on a religious war. He paid more attention to the results of his enterprises; more master of himself, he was more fit to command others. When mounting the throne of the Atabeks, Saladin obeyed rather his destiny than his inclinations; but when once firmly seated, he was governed by only two passions,—that of reigning, and that of securing the triumph of the Koran. On all other subjects he was moderate, and when a kingdom or the glory of the prophet was not in question, the son of Ayoub was admired as the most just and mild of Mussulmans. We may add that the stern devotion and ardent fanaticism that made him take up arms against the Christians, only rendered him cruel and barbarous in one single instance. He displayed the virtues of peace amidst the horrors of war. "From the bosom of camps," says an Oriental poet, "*he covered the nations with the wings of his justice, and poured upon his cities the plenteous showers of his liberality.*" The Mussulmans, always governed by fear, were astonished that a sovereign could inspire them with so much love, and followed him with joy to battle. His generosity, his clemency, and particularly his respect for an oath, were often the subjects of admiration to the Christians, whom he rendered so miserable by his victories, and of whose power in Asia he had completed the overthrow.

The third crusade, which was so glorious for Saladin, was not entirely without advantages for Europe. Many Crusaders on the way to Palestine, stopped in Spain, and by their victories over the Moors, prepared the deliverance of the kingdoms situated beyond the Pyrenees. A great number of Germans, as in the second crusade, prevailed upon by the solicitations of the pope, made war upon the barbarous inhabitants of the shores of the Baltic, and thus, by useful exploits, extended the limits of the Christian republic in the West. As in this war the greater part of the Crusaders went to Palestine by sea, the art of navigation made a sensible advance; the maritime nations of Europe acquired an accession of prosperity, their fleets became more formidable, and they were able, with glory, to dispute the empire of the sea with the Saracens.

In several states of Europe, commerce, and the spirit of the holy wars contributed to the enfranchisement of the lower classes. Many serfs, upon becoming free, took up arms. It was not one of the least interesting spectacles of this crusade, to see the standards of several cities of France and Germany floating in the Christian army amongst the banners of lords and barons.

This crusade was particularly beneficial to France, from which it banished both civil and foreign wars. By prolonging the absence of the great vassals and the enemies of the kingdom, it weakened their power, and gave Philip Augustus authority to levy imposts, even upon the clergy. It afforded him an opportunity of surrounding his throne with a faithful guard, to keep up regular armies, and prepare, though at a distance, that victory of Bovines which proved so fatal to the enemies of France.

A long captivity awaited Richard on his return to Europe. The vessel in which he embarked was shipwrecked on the coast of Italy, and fearing to pass through France, he took the route of Germany, concealed under the habit of a simple pilgrim. His liberality betrayed the monarch, and as he had enemies everywhere, he was seized by the soldiers of the duke of Austria. Leopold had not sufficient generosity to forget the outrages received from Richard at the siege of Ptolemaïs, and detained him prisoner. It was not known in Europe what had become of King Richard, when a gentleman of Arras, named Blondel, set out in search of his master, and traversed Germany in the dress and with the lyre of a minstrel. On his arrival before a castle, in which, it was said, languished an illustrious captive, Blondel began to sing the first couplet of a song which he had composed in conjunction with Richard. From the top of a high tower a voice answered him, and sang the second couplet. Then the faithful troubadour returned into England to announce that he had discovered the prison of the king. The duke of Austria, terrified at this discovery, did not dare to detain longer his redoubtable captive in his own hands, and gave him up to the emperor of Germany. Henry VI., who had likewise insults to revenge, was rejoiced to get Richard in his power, and kept him in chains, as if he had made him a prisoner in the field of battle. The hero of the crusade, who had filled the world with his renown, was cast into a dark dungeon, and remained a long time a victim to the vengeance of his enemies—and they were Christian princes.

He was brought before the German diet, assembled at Worms, where he was accused of all the crimes that hatred and envy could invent. But the spectacle of a king in chains was so affecting, that no one durst condemn Richard, and when he offered his justification, the bishops and nobles melted into tears, and besought Henry to treat him with less injustice and rigour.

Queen Eleanor implored all the powers of Europe for the release of her son. The complaints and tears of a mother touched the heart of Celestine, who had recently ascended the chair of St. Peter. The pope several times demanded the liberty of the king of England, and even excommunicated the duke of Austria and the emperor; but the thunders of the Church had so often been launched against the thrones of Germany, that they no longer inspired fear. Henry braved the anathemas of the Holy See; the captivity of Richard lasted another year; and he only obtained his liberty after engaging to pay a considerable ransom. His kingdom, which he had ruined at his departure for the Holy Land, exhausted itself to hasten his return; and England gave up even her sacred vases to break the chains of her monarch. He was received with enthusiasm by the English; his adventures, which drew tears, obliterated the remembrance of his cruelties, and Europe only recollected his exploits and his misfortunes.

After the truce made with Richard, Saladin retired to Damascus, where he enjoyed his glory but one year. The Orientals celebrate the edifying manner in which he died, distributing his alms or benevolences to Mussulmans and Christians alike. Before he expired he ordered one of his officers to carry his shroud through the streets of his capital, and to cry with a loud voice: *"Behold all that Saladin, who overcame the East, bears away of his conquests."*

Scarcely had he ceased to breathe, when nothing remained but a vain remembrance of his laws and his victories; his death was attended by that which so frequently happens in Oriental monarchies, where nothing is regulated concerning the succession; where victory appears to be the most legitimate title, and where a too numerous offspring await the death of the prince in fear, servitude, and in ignorance of the affairs of the state.

Saladin only left behind him slaves intimidated by his glory and his boundless power, who divided his authority among them, but could not support the weight of it. Twelve of his sons and relatives succeeded him and disputed the sovereignty. Malek-Adel, the brother of the sultan, and companion in his exploits, profited by the inexperience of his nephews, and took possession of Egypt and Mesopotamia. The most powerful of the emirs followed his example, and shared the cities and provinces amongst them. Asia then beheld that empire fall to decay, which, raised for the ruin of the Christians, had, in its growth and progress, twice roused all the nations of the West to arms.

RICHARD CŒUR DE LION DELIVERING JAFFA.

Richard, who had conquered the Saracens, was not wise enough to profit by their defeat; instead of pursuing the enemy, or marching straight to Jerusalem, he led his army to Jaffa, the ramparts of which Saladin had demolished, and which the Mussulmans had abandoned. He occupied himself with repairing the fortifications, and sent for Queen Berengaria, Jane, the widow of the king of Sicily, and the daughter of Isaac. Surrounded by a brilliant court, he forgot, in the intoxication of pleasure and festivities, the conquest of Jerusalem for which he had come to Asia.

At the head of a weak detachment, he took a convoy of seven thousand camels on the way to Jerusalem; on another occasion, going on board a vessel with a few knights, he landed at Jaffa, where the banner of Saladin floated over the towers and ramparts; he pursued the conquerors sword in hand, and forced them to abandon their temporary conquest. A few days after, the king of England, with a troop of his chosen knights, attacked a body of seven thousand Mussulman horse; he rushed in amongst them, and with a stroke of his sabre struck dead at his feet the leader of the Saracens, who all appeared stupefied and motionless with surprise and fear.—Book VIII.

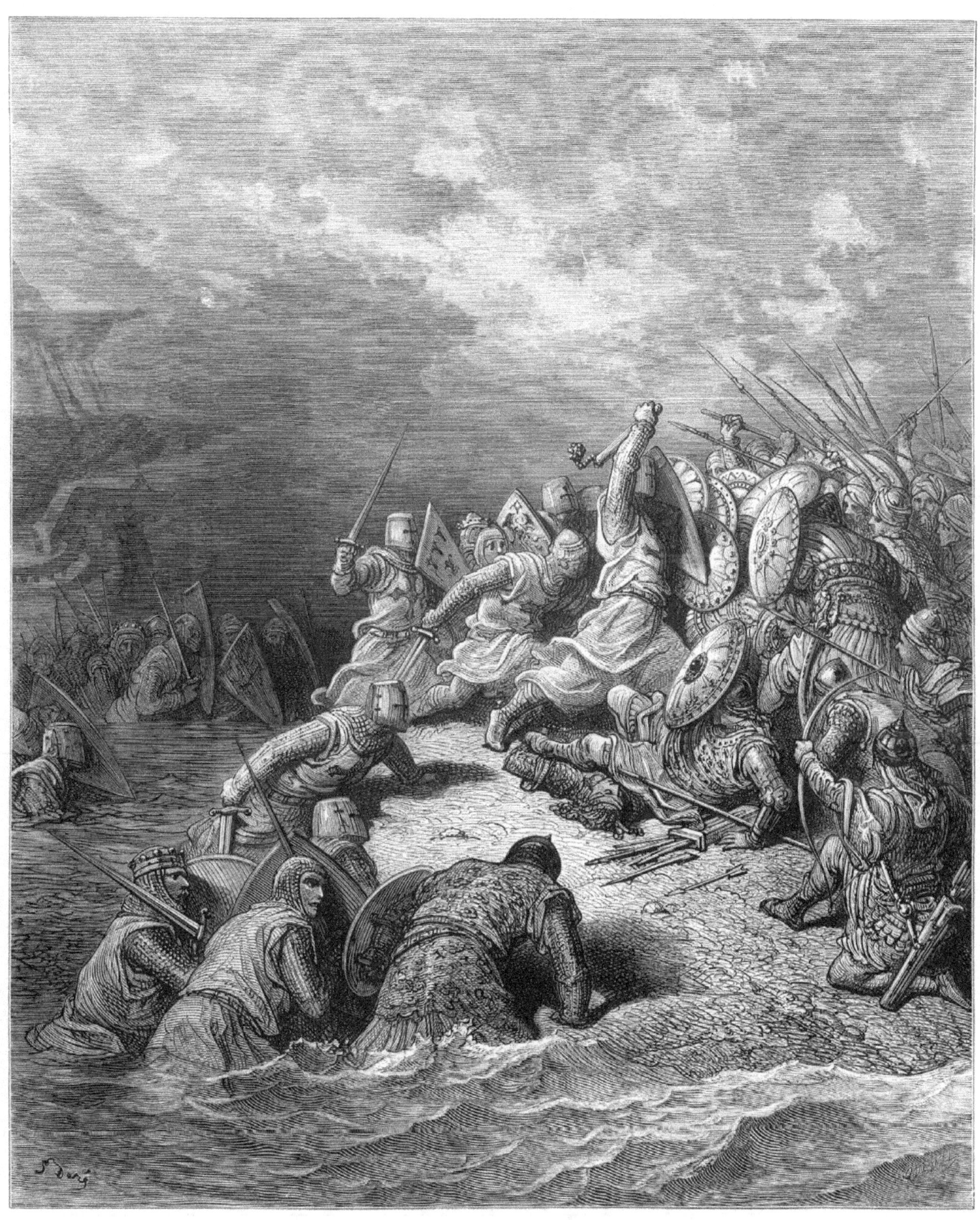

BOOK IX.

THE FOURTH CRUSADE.

A. D. 1195–1198.

The empire of Saladin divided among his successors—The civil wars thence arising—Dynasty of the Ayoubites—Extensive empire of Afdhal, son of Saladin—His civil contests—Alaziz, sultan of Egypt, takes arms against his brother—Nazr-Allah, vizier of the sultan Afdhal—Malek-Adel—Civil commotions of Palestine—Agitated state of the Christian colonies—Bohémond III. governor of Antioch, taken prisoner—Hospitallers and Templars—Pope Celestine III. instigates the fourth crusade—Henry VI., emperor of Germany, engages to assist—Diet of Worms—Hostilities at Ptolemaïs—Death of Henry of Champagne—Jaffa captured by the Mussulmans—Siege and battle of Berytus—Malek-Adel defeated—Fallandus, the Sicilian historian—Henry VI. of Germany conquers Naples and Sicily—Progress of his arms in Palestine—The Saracens defeated—Death of Henry VI.—Massacre of the garrison of Jaffa—St. Martin—Causes of the failure of this crusade, and its mischievous consequences—Cruel character of Henry VI.

WHEN we cast a retrospective glance over the periods we have described, we congratulate ourselves upon not having lived in those times of war and trouble; but when we look around us, and reflect upon the age of which we form a part, we fear we have little reason to boast over the epochs commonly termed barbarous. During twenty-five years a revolution, born of opinions unknown to past ages, has pervaded cities, agitated nations, and shaken thrones. This revolution has for auxiliaries war and victory; it strengthens itself with all the obstacles that are opposed to it; it is for ever born again from itself, and when we believe we can perceive the end of its ravages, it re-appears more terrible and menacing than ever. At the moment in which I resume the account of the Crusades,* the spirit of sedition and revolt, the fanaticism of modern doctrines, which seemed to slumber, all at once awake, and again threaten the world with universal disorder; nations which tremble for their liberty and their laws, are aroused, and spring up in arms; a coalition of all kings and of all nations, a general crusade is formed, not to defend the tomb of Christ, but to preserve that which Europe possesses of its ancient civilization. It is amidst the rumours of a new revolution, of a formidable war, that I am about to describe the revolutions and wars that disturbed the East and the West in the middle ages. May I, whilst deploring the calamities of my country, profit by the events of which I am a witness, and by the frightful spectacle which is before my eyes, to paint with greater truth the passions and the troubles of a remote age, and revive in the hearts of my contemporaries a love of concord and peace.

The death of Saladin was followed by that which almost always is to be observed in the dynasties of the East,—a reign of agitation and trouble succeeding a reign of strength and absolute power. In these dynasties, which have no other support but victory, and the all-powerful will of a single man,

* The author wrote the history of the fourth, fifth, and sixth crusades during the last usurpation of Buonaparte.

as long as the sovereign, surrounded by his soldiers, commands, he is tremblingly obeyed; but as soon as he has closed his eyes, his people precipitate themselves towards license with the same ardour that they had yielded to servitude; and passions, long restrained by the presence of the despot, only blaze forth with the greater violence when there remains nothing of him but a vain remembrance.

Saladin gave no directions respecting the order of succession, and by this want of foresight prepared the ruin of his empire. One of his sons, Almélik-Alazoz, Emad-eddin Otsman, who commanded in Egypt, caused himself to be proclaimed sultan of Cairo; another, Alemélek Almansour, Nassir-eddin Mohammed, took possession of the sovereignty of Aleppo, and a third of the principality of Amath, Almélek Aladel Seïf-eddin Aben-beer Mohammed. Malek-Adel, the brother of Saladin, assumed the throne of Mesopotamia, and the countries in the neighbourhood of the Euphrates. The principal emirs, and all the princes of the race of the Ayoubites, made themselves masters of the cities and provinces of which they held the command.

Afdhal, eldest son of Saladin, was proclaimed sultan of Damascus. Master of Syria, and of the capital of a vast empire, sovereign of Jerusalem and Palestine, he appeared to have preserved something of the power of his father; but all fell into disorder and confusion. The emirs, the old companions of the victories of Saladin, endured with reluctance the authority of the young sultan. Several refused to take the oath of obedience,* drawn up by the cadis of Damascus; others consented to take it, but on condition that their fiefs should be secured to them, or that new ones should be bestowed upon them. Far from labouring to reduce the power of this haughty soldiery, Afdhal neglected the duties of his throne for the pleasures of debauchery, to which he gave himself up entirely, abandoning the welfare of his empire to a vizier, the historian Nasr-allah, who rendered him odious to the Mussulmans. The army demanded the dismissal of the vizier, whom they accused of having usurped the authority of the prince; the vizier, on his part, advised his master to banish the seditious emirs. The weak sultan, who only saw with the eyes of his minister, annoyed by the presence and complaints of a discontented army, dismissed from his service a great number of soldiers and emirs, who went among all the neighbouring princes, complaining of his ingratitude, and accusing him of forgetting, in the bosom of idleness and effeminacy, the holy laws of the prophet and the glory of Saladin.

The greater number of them, who went into Egypt, exhorted Alaziz to take arms against his brother. The sultan of Cairo gave ear to their advice, and under the pretence of avenging the glory of his father, conceived the project of possessing himself of Damascus. He assembled his forces, and marched into Syria at the head of an army. At the approach of danger, Afdhal invoked assistance from the princes that reigned over the countries of Amath and Aleppo. Soon a formidable war blazed forth, into which was dragged the whole of the family of the Ayoubites. Alaziz laid siege to Damascus. The hopes of an easy conquest animated his emirs, and made them believe that they were fighting in a just cause; but as they at first had but little success, and as victory seemed every day to fly further from their banners, the war began to appear to them unjust. At first they murmured; then they revolted from Alaziz, and at length rejoined the troops of Syria. The sultan of Cairo, upon being thus abandoned, was obliged to raise the siege disgracefully, and return into Egypt. The sultans of Damascus and Aleppo pursued him across the desert, with the design of attacking him in his capital. Afdhal, at the head of a victorious army, soon carried terror to the banks of the Nile.

* This is the text of the oath, as it has been preserved by an historian:—"I, such a one, devote myself entirely from this moment to the service of the sultan Elmélek Alnaser Salak-eddin, as long as he shall live. I swear to consecrate my life, my property, my sword, and my powers to the defence of his empire, and to be always obedient to his orders. I swear to observe the same engagements after him to his son and heir Almélek Alafdhal. I swear to submit myself to him, to fight for his empire and states with my life, my wealth, my sword, and my troops. I swear to obey him in everything; I devote myself to him inwardly and outwardly, and I take God for a witness of this engagement."

Alaziz was about to be dethroned, and Egypt to be conquered by the Syrians, if the brother of Saladin, guided by a policy, whose motive might be easily divined, had not opposed the authority of his counsels to the arms of the conqueror, and re-established peace in the family of the Ayoubites.

The princes and emirs respected the experience of Malek-Adel, and allowed him to be the arbitrator of their differences. The warriors of Syria and Egypt, accustomed to see him in camps, looked upon him as their leader, and followed him with joy to battle; whilst nations, that he had often astonished by his exploits, invoked his name in their reverses and dangers. The Mussulmans now perceived with surprise that he had been in a manner exiled in Mesopotamia, and that an empire, founded by his valour, was abandoned to young princes who bore no name among warriors: he himself grew secretly indignant at not having received due recompense for his labours, and was aware of all that the old soldiers, he had so often led to victory, might one day do to further his ambitious views. It was important to his designs that too much of the empire should not be in the same hands, and that the provinces should remain for some time longer shared by two rival powers. The peace which he had brought about could not be of long duration, and the discord, ever on the point of breaking out among his nephews, must soon offer him an opportunity of reaping the rich harvest of the vast heritage of Saladin.

Afdhal, warned by the dangers he had run, resolved to change his conduct. Hitherto he had scandalized all faithful Mussulmans by his intemperance in the use of wine. Aboulfeda, who was descended from the family of Saladin, says, in his history, that the sultan of Damascus, during the early years of his reign, passed his life amidst banquets and indulgence, taking delight in nothing but listening to songs and composing verses. On his return from Egypt, Afdhal exhibited an entire alteration in his manners; but he only fell from one excess into another; he was now constantly at prayers, or employed in the most minute practices of the Mussulman religion; but, in his excessive devotion, as in his dissipated life, he was perfectly inattentive to the duties of a monarch, and submitted himself, without reserve, to the counsels of the same vizier who had already nearly cost him his dominions. "Then," says Aboulfeda, "complaints against him were heard from all quarters, and tongues that had been loud in his praise became silent."

Alaziz thought this opportunity favourable for again taking up arms against his brother; and Malek-Adel, persuaded that war was most likely to minister to his ambition, no longer advocated peace, but placed himself at the head of the army of Egypt. Having intimidated by his threats, or won by his presents, the principal emirs of Afdhal, he at once took possession of Damascus in the name of Alaziz, and soon governed as sovereign the richest provinces of Syria.

Every day fresh quarrels broke out among the emirs and princes; all those who had fought with Saladin, thought the moment was come at which to put forth and establish their pretensions; and the princes who still remained of the family of Noureddin began to entertain hopes of regaining the provinces wrested from the unfortunate Attabeks by the son of Ayoub. All the East was in a state of fermentation. Bloody divisions desolated Persia, a prey to the various claims of the feeble remains of the race of the Seljoucides. The empire of the Carismians, which conquest was every day extending, threatened at the same time the capital of Corosan and the city of Bagdad, in which the pontiff of the Mussulman religion lived in perpetual fear. For a long time the caliphs had been unable to take any active part in the events that changed the face of Syria; and the only authority they possessed was exercised in consecrating the victories of the triumphant party, whoever that might be. Afdhal, driven from Damascus, called in vain upon the caliph of Bagdad for protection; all that shadow of power could afford him was a recommendation to exercise patience, and an assurance "*that his enemies would have to render an account to God of what they had done.*"

Among the rivalries that convulsed the Mussulman states, Malek-Adel met with no obstruction to his projects; the troubles and disorders which his usurpation gave birth to, even the wars undertaken against him, all contributed to the consolidation and extension of his unjustly-obtained power. It became evident that he must soon unite under his sway the greater part of the provinces conquered by Saladin. Thus was verified, for the second time within a few years, the observation of an Arabian historian, who expressed himself in the following words when speaking of the succession of Noureddin: "*The greater part of the founders of empires have not been able to leave them to their posterity.*" This instability of power is not a thing to be wondered at in countries where success renders everything legitimate, where the caprices of fortune are frequently laws, and where the most formidable enemies of an empire founded by arms, are the very men whose bravery has assisted in raising it. The historian we have quoted, deplores the revolutions of military despotism, without duly searching for the natural causes of them; and can explain so many changes only by referring to the justice of God, always ready to punish, at least in their children, all who have employed violence or shed the blood of man to attain empire.

Such were the revolutions which, during many years, agitated the Mussulman states of Syria and Egypt. The fourth crusade, which we are about to describe, and in which the Christians might have greatly profited by the troubles of the East, only served to reunite the scattered members of the empire of Saladin. Malek-Adel owed the progress of his power not only to the divisions of the Mussulmans, but to the spirit of discord that reigned among the Christians.

After the departure of the king of England, as was always the case at the termination of every crusade, the Christian colonies, surrounded by perils, advanced more rapidly to their fall. Henry of Champagne, charged with the government of Palestine, disdained the title of king, as he was impatient to return to Europe, and looked upon his kingdom as a place of exile. The three military orders, detained in Asia by their vows, constituted the principal strength of a state which but lately had had all the warriors of Europe for its defenders. Guy of Lusignan retired to Cyprus, took no more interest in the fate of Jerusalem, and had full occupation in keeping himself on his new throne, shaken by the continual revolts of the Greeks and threatened by the emperors of Constantinople.

Bohémond III., grandson of Raymond of Poictiers, and descended, in the female line, from the celebrated Bohémond, one of the heroes of the first crusade, governed the principality of Antioch and the county of Tripoli. Amidst the misfortunes that afflicted the Christian colonies, the sole aim of this prince was the extension of his dominions, and every means appeared to him good and just that could forward his designs. Bohémond pretended to have claims to the principality of Armenia; and employed by turns force and stratagem to get possession of it. After several useless attempts, he succeeded in decoying into his capital Rupin of the Mountain, one of the princes of Armenia, and detained him prisoner. Livon, the brother of Rupin, determined to take signal vengeance for such an outrage; and, under the pretence of treating for peace, invited Bohémond to repair to the frontiers of Armenia. The two princes engaged by oath to come without escort or train to the place of conference; but each formed a secret design of laying a snare for his adversary. The Armenian prince, better seconded by either his genius or fortune, remained conqueror in this disgraceful contest. Bohémond was surprised, loaded with chains, and carried away to a fortress of Lesser Armenia. The war was instantly renewed with fury; the people of both Armenia and Antioch rushed to arms, and the countries and cities of the two principalities were speedily by turns invaded and ravaged. At length peace became desirable, and after some disputes upon the conditions, the prince of Antioch was sent back to his states, and Rupin of the Mountain was restored to the nations of Armenia. By an agreement entered into by the two princes, Alice, the daughter of Rupin, married the eldest son of Bohémond.

DANDOLO, DOGE OF VENICE, PREACHING THE CRUSADE.

Nobody was more skilful in seizing a favourable opportunity, or of taking advantage of the least circumstance for the furtherance of his designs. At the age of ninety, the doge of Venice exhibited no symptoms of senility but virtue and experience. Everything that could save his country aroused his activity and inflamed his courage; with the spirit of calculation and economy which distinguished his compatriots, Dandolo mingled passions the most generous, and threw an air of grandeur over all the enterprises of a trading people. Dandolo praised with warmth an enterprise that appeared glorious to him, and in which the interests of his country were not opposed to those of religion. The deputies required vessels to transport four thousand five hundred knights and twenty thousand foot, with provisions for the Christian army for nine months. Dandolo promised, in the name of the republic, to furnish the necessary provisions and vessels, on condition that the Crusaders should engage to pay the Venetians the sum of eighty-five thousand silver marks. As he was not willing that the people of Venice should be unconnected with the expedition of the French Crusaders, Dandolo proposed to the deputies to arm, at the expense of the republic, fifty galleys, and demanded for his country half the conquests that might be made in the East.—Book X.

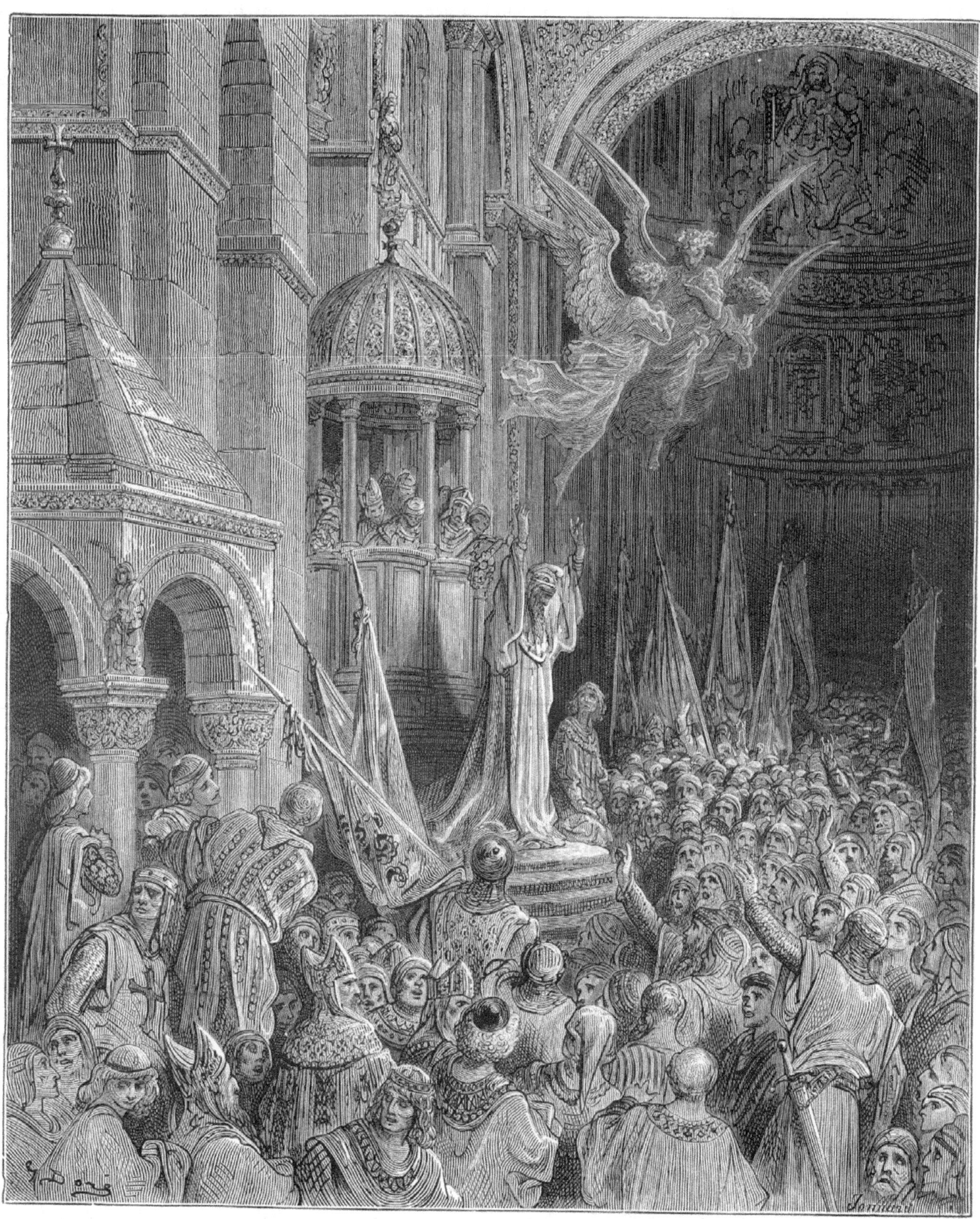

This union promised to be the pledge of a durable peace; but the germ of so many divisions still subsisted; the two parties retained a strong feeling of the outrage they had received; and every treaty of peace becoming a fresh subject of discussion, war was always ready to be rekindled.

In another direction, ambition and jealousy set at variance the orders of the Temple and St. John. At the period of the third crusade, the Hospitallers and the Templars were as powerful as sovereign princes; they possessed in Asia and Europe villages, cities, and even provinces.* The two orders, rivalling each other in power and glory, attended far less to the defence of the holy places than to the augmentation of their own renown and riches. Every one of their immense possessions, every one of their prerogatives, the renown of the knights, the credit of the leaders, all, even to the trophies of their valour, were for them subjects of rivalry, and, at length, this spirit of discord and jealousy produced an open war. A French gentleman, established in Palestine, possessed, as a vassal of the Hospitallers, the castle of Margat, situated towards the frontiers of Arabia. The Templars pretended that this castle belonged to them, and took possession of it by main force. Robert,—that was the name of the gentleman,—carried his complaints to the Hospitallers, who immediately flew to arms and drove the Templars from the castle. From that time the knights of the two orders never met without provoking each other to the combat; most of the Franks and Christians always taking a part in the quarrel, some for the order of St. John, others for that of the Temple. The king of Jerusalem and the most prudent of the barons made many useless attempts to restore peace; and several Christian princes endeavoured in vain to reconcile the two rival orders. The pope himself had much difficulty in getting his sacred mediation to be accepted; and it was only after long debates that the Holy See, sometimes armed with evangelical thunders, sometimes employing the paternal language of the head of the Church, terminated, by its wisdom and supreme ascendancy, a contest which the knights themselves would have preferred deciding with sword and lance.

During these fatal divisions none thought of defending themselves against the general enemy, the Saracens. One of the most melancholy consequences of the spirit of faction is, that it always leads to a lamentable indifference for the common cause. The more violently the parties attacked each other, the less perception they seemed to have of the dangers that threatened the Christian colonies; neither the knights of the Temple or of St. John, nor the Christians of Antioch or Ptolemaïs, ever thought of asking for succour against the infidels; and history does not say that one person was sent from the East to make Europe aware of the griefs of Sion.

The situation of the Christians in Palestine was besides so uncertain and perilous, that the wisest could form no idea of coming events, or dare to adopt a resolution. If they appealed afresh to the warriors of the West, they broke the truce made with Saladin, and exposed themselves to all the resentment of the infidels; if they respected treaties, the truce might be broken by the Mussulmans, ever ready to profit by the calamities which fell upon the Christians. In this state of things, it appeared difficult to foresee a new crusade, which was neither called for by the wishes of the Christians of Asia, nor promoted by the interests of Europe. In fact, when we cast our eyes over the Christian colonies of the East, as they are described to us in these unhappy times, and see the spirit of ambition and discord displacing in all hearts the holy spirit of the Gospel, we cannot wonder that Christendom took so little interest in their fate. Again, when contemporary history represents to us these colonies a prey to license and division, and destitute of everything that could render them flourishing, we can scarcely believe that the West was again likely to lavish its wealth and its blood to support and defend them. But the great name of Jerusalem still produced a powerful effect upon the minds of all; the

* The Hospitallers then possessed within the limits of Christendom *nineteen thousand manors;* the Templars had only *nine thousand.* A manor in the middle ages *was the labour of one plough.*

remembrance of the first crusade still aroused the enthusiasm of Christians; and the veneration for the holy places, which appeared to grow weaker in the kingdom of Christ itself, was yet cherished beyond the seas and in the principal countries of the West.

Celestine III. had, by his exhortations, encouraged the warriors of the third crusade; and, at the age of ninety, pursued with zeal all the projects of his predecessors; ardently wishing that the last days of his pontificate should be illustrated by the conquest of Jerusalem. After the return of Richard, the news of the death of Saladin had spread joy throughout the West, and revived the hopes of the Christians. Celestine wrote to all the faithful to inform them that the most formidable enemy of Christendom had ceased to live; and, without regarding the truce made by Richard Cœur de Lion, he ordered his bishops and archbishops to preach a new crusade in their dioceses.* The sovereign pontiff promised all who would take the cross the same privileges and the same advantages as in the preceding crusades. The profanation of the holy places; the oppression under which the faithful of the East groaned; the ever-increasing insolence and audacity of the Saracens—such were the motives by which he supported his holy exhortations. He addressed himself particularly to the bishops of England, and commanded them to use every persuasion to induce Richard again to take up arms against the infidels.

Richard, although returned, had never laid aside the cross, the symbol of pilgrimage; and it might be supposed he still intended to repair again to the Holy Land; but, scarcely escaped from an unjust captivity, taught by his own experience how great were the difficulties and perils of a distant enterprise, his thoughts and time were engrossed by his endeavours to remedy his losses, to defend or aggrandize his states, and to be on his guard against the insidious attempts of Philip Augustus. His knights and barons, whom he himself exhorted to resume the cross, professed, as he did, a warm devotion for the cause of Jerusalem; but they could not make up their minds to return to a country which had been to them a place of suffering and exile.

Although the appearance of the preachers of the crusade everywhere inspired respect, they had no better success in France, where, only a few years before, a hundred thousand warriors had been roused by the summons to defend the holy places. If the fear of the enterprises of Philip was sufficient to detain Richard in the West, the dread of the vindictive and jealous disposition of Richard exercised the same influence over Philip. The greater number of his knights and nobles followed his example, and contented themselves with shedding tears over the fate of Jerusalem. The enthusiasm for the crusade was communicated to only a small number of warriors, amongst whom history names the count de Montfort, who afterwards conducted the cruel war against the Albigeois.

From the commencement of the crusades, Germany had never ceased to send its warriors to the defence of the Holy Land. It deplored the recent loss of its armies, destroyed or dispersed in Asia Minor, and the death of the Emperor Frederick, who had gained nothing but a grave in the plains of the East; but the remembrance of so great a disaster did not extinguish in all hearts the zeal for the cause of Jerusalem. Henry VI., who occupied the imperial throne, had not partaken, as the kings of France and England had, the perils and reverses of the last expedition. Unpleasant remembrances or fears of his enemies in Europe could have no effect in preventing him from joining in a new enterprise, or deter him from a holy pilgrimage which so many illustrious examples seemed to point out as a sacred duty.

Although this prince had been excommunicated by the Holy See, only the preceding year, the

* We possess two letters written by Celestine to Hubert, archbishop of Canterbury, to engage him to preach the crusade. The pope commands the archbishop to employ ecclesiastical censures against those who, after taking the cross, delayed their departure for the Holy Land; and to require such as could not possibly set out, to send, at their own expense, one or two men to fight against the infidels.

Pope sent an embassy to him, charged with the duty of recalling to his mind the example of his father Frederick, and urging him to assume the cross. Henry, who sought every occasion to conciliate the head of the Church, and who likewise entertained vast projects in which a new crusade might be very serviceable, received the envoy of Celestine with great honours.

Of all the princes of the middle ages, no one evinced more ambition than Henry VI.; his imagination, say historians, was filled with the glory of the Cæsars, and he wished to be able to say with Alexander, *all that my desires can embrace belongs to me.* Tancred, a natural son of William II., king of Sicily, chosen by the Sicilian nobility to succeed his father, was recently deceased; and the emperor, who had espoused Constance, the heiress of a throne founded by Norman Crusaders, and desirous of establishing his claims, judged that the time was come to carry out his designs and achieve his conquests. The expedition of which the Holy See desired him to be the leader, was exceedingly favourable to his ambitious projects; when, promising to defend Jerusalem, he only thought of the conquest of Sicily; and the conquest of Sicily had no value in his estimation but as opening the road to Greece and Constantinople. At the same time that he professed entire submission to the will of the head of the Church, he endeavoured to form an alliance with the republics of Genoa and Venice, promising them the spoils of the conquered; but in his mind he nourished the hope that he should one day overthrow the Italian republics and lower the authority of the Holy See, and upon their remains revive, for himself and his family, the empire of Augustus and Constantine.

Such was the prince to whom Celestine sent an embassy, and whom he wished to persuade into a holy war. After having announced his intention of taking the cross, Henry convoked a general diet at Worms, in which he himself exhorted the faithful to take up arms for the defence of the holy places. Since Louis VII., king of France, who harangued his subjects to induce them to join in the crusade, Henry was the only monarch that had mingled his voice with that of the preachers of the holy war, to make his subjects acquainted with the sufferings and complaints of the Church of Jerusalem. His eloquence, celebrated by the historians of his time, but above all, the spectacle presented of a great emperor himself preaching a holy war against the infidels, made a profound impression upon the multitude of his auditors. After this solemn address, the most illustrious of the prelates assembled at Worms ascended the evangelical pulpit to keep up the rapidly increasing enthusiasm of the faithful; during eight hours nothing was heard but the groans of Sion and the city of God. Henry, surrounded by his court, assumed the symbol of the Crusaders; a great number of German nobles followed his example, some to please God, *and others to please the emperor.* Among those who took the oath to combat the Saracens, history names Henry duke of Saxony; Otho marquis of Brandenburgh; Henry count palatine of the Rhine; Herman landgrave of Thuringia; Henry duke of Brabant; Albert count of Apsburg; Adolphus count of Schwemburg; Henry count of Pappenhein, marshal of the empire; the duke of Bavaria; Frederick, son of Leopold, duke of Austria; Conrad marquis of Moravia; Valeran de Limbourg; and the bishops of Wurtzburg, Bremen, Verdun, Habbastadt, Passau, and Ratisbon.

The crusade was preached in all the provinces of Germany, and the letters of the emperor and the pope kindled the zeal of the Christian warriors everywhere; never had an enterprise against the infidels been undertaken under more favourable auspices. As Germany undertook the crusade almost singly, the glory of the German nations seemed as much interested in this war as religion itself. Henry was to command the holy expedition; and the Crusaders, full of confidence and hope, were preparing to follow him to the East. But Henry entertained other views; several nobles of his court, some who penetrated his secret designs, and others who believed they offered him prudent advice, conjured him to remain in the West, and direct the crusade from the bosom of his dominions;

and Henry, after a slight resistance, yielded to their prayers, and gave his whole attention to the hastening of the departure of the Crusaders.

The emperor of Germany placed himself at the head of forty thousand men and took the route for Italy, where everything was prepared for the conquest of Sicily; the remainder of the Crusaders were divided into two armies, which, proceeding by different roads, were to meet in Syria. The first, commanded by the duke of Saxony and the duke of Brabant, embarked at ports of the German Ocean and the Baltic; the second crossed the Danube, and directed its march towards Constantinople, whence the fleet of the Greek emperor Isaac was to transport it to Ptolemaïs. To this army, commanded by the archbishop of Mayence and Valeran de Limbourg, were joined the Hungarians, who accompanied their queen Margaret, sister to Philip Augustus. The queen of Hungary, after having lost Bela her husband, had made a vow to live only for Christ, and to end her days in the Holy Land.

The Crusaders under the command of the archbishop of Mayence and Valeran de Limbourg, were the first to arrive in Palestine. Scarcely were they landed when they expressed their desire and resolution to begin the war against the infidels. The Christians, who were then at peace with the Saracens, hesitated to break the truce signed by Richard, and were, further, unwilling to give the signal for hostilities before they could open the campaign with some hopes of success. Henry of Champagne and the barons of Palestine represented to the German Crusaders the danger to which an imprudent rupture would expose the Christians of the East, and conjured them to wait for the army of the dukes of Saxony and Brabant. But the Germans, full of confidence in their own strength, were indignant at having obstacles thrown in the way of their valour by vain scruples and chimerical alarms; they were astonished that the Christians of Palestine should thus refuse the assistance sent to them by Providence itself, and added, in a tone of anger and contempt, that warriors of the West were not accustomed to defer the hour of battle, and that the pope had not induced them to take up arms and the cross to remain in a state of shameful inactivity. The barons and knights of the Holy Land could not listen to such injurious speeches without indignation, and replied to the German Crusaders that they had neither solicited nor wished for their arrival; that they were better acquainted than the northern warriors of Europe with what was advantageous to the kingdom of Jerusalem; that they had without any foreign succour braved the greatest perils, and that when the proper moment should arrive they knew how to prove their valour otherwise than by words. Amidst such warm debates the minds of both parties became daily more exasperated, and the most cruel discord thus prevailed among the Christians before war was declared against the infidels.

All at once the German Crusaders marched out in arms from Ptolemaïs, and commenced hostilities by ravaging the lands of the Saracens. At the first signal of war the Mussulmans gathered together their forces; and the danger that threatened them putting an end to their discord, from the banks of the Nile and from the remotest parts of Syria crowded hosts of warriors but lately armed against each other, but who now, assembled under the same banners, acknowledged no other enemies but the Christians.

Malek-Adel, towards whom all Mussulmans turned their eyes when the defence of Islamism was the question, marched from Damascus at the head of an army and repaired to Jerusalem, where all the emirs of the adjoining provinces came to take his orders. The Mussulman army, after dispersing the Christians who had advanced towards the mountains of Naplouse, laid siege to Jaffa.

In the third crusade much importance had been attached to the conservation of this city. Richard Cœur de Lion had fortified it at great expense, and when that prince returned to Europe he left a numerous garrison in it. Of all the maritime places, Jaffa was nearest to the city which was the object of the wishes of the faithful; if it remained in the hands of the Christians, a road was always open for them to Jerusalem, and the means of laying siege to that place were rendered more easy; but if it fell into the power of the Mussulmans, it gave them proportionate advantages for the defence of the holy city.

When it was known at Ptolemaïs that the city of Jaffa was threatened, Henry of Champagne, with his barons and knights, immediately took arms to defend it, and joined the German Crusaders, giving all their energies to the prosecution of a war which they found could now no longer be deferred or avoided. The three military orders, with the troops of the kingdom, were about to set forward on their march, when a tragical accident once more plunged the Christians in grief, and retarded the effects of the happy harmony which had been re-established at the approach of peril. Henry of Champagne, leaning against a window of his palace, at which he had placed himself to see his army defile from the city, the window all at once gave way, and in its fall precipitated him with it. The unfortunate prince expired in sight of his soldiers, who, instead of following him to battle, accompanied him to his grave, and lost several days in celebrating his funeral obsequies. The Christians of Ptolemaïs were still weeping the death of their king, when the misfortune they dreaded increased their grief and consternation; the garrison of Jaffa having attempted a sortie, had fallen into an ambuscade, and all the warriors that composed it were either killed or taken prisoners. The Mussulmans entered the city almost without resistance, and twenty thousand Christians were put to the sword.

These disasters had been foreseen by all who had dreaded the breaking of the truce; but the barons and knights of Palestine lost no time in vain regrets, or in the utterance of useless complaints, and looked with eager impatience for the arrival of the Crusaders who had set out from the ports of the Ocean and the Baltic. These troops had stopped on the coast of Portugal, where they had defeated the Moors, and taken from them the city of Silves. Proud of their triumph over the infidels, they landed at Ptolemaïs at the moment the people were lamenting the loss of Jaffa and crowding to the churches to implore the mercy of Heaven.

The arrival of the new Crusaders restored hope and joy to the Christians, and they resolved to lose no time, but to march at once against the infidels. The army left Ptolemaïs and advanced towards the coast of Syria, whilst a numerous fleet kept along shore, loaded with provisions and warlike stores. The Crusaders, without seeking the army of Malek-Adel, laid siege to Berytus.

The city of Berytus, at an equal distance between Jerusalem and Tripoli, by the commodiousness of its port, its large population, and its commerce, had become the rival of Ptolemaïs and Tyre. The Mussulman provinces of Syria acknowledged it as their capital, and it was in Berytus that the emirs, who contended for the lordship of the neighbouring cities, came to display the pomp of their coronations. After the taking of Jerusalem, Saladin was here saluted sovereign of the city of God, and crowned sultan of Damascus and Cairo. The pirates, who infested the seas, brought to this city all the spoils of the Christians; the Mussulman warriors there deposited the riches acquired by conquest or brigandage; and the Frank captives, made in late wars, were crowded together in the prisons of Berytus; so that the Christians had powerful motives for endeavouring to get possession of this place, and the Mussulmans had no less urgent ones for defending it.

Malek-Adel, after having destroyed the fortifications of Jaffa, advanced with his army as far as the mountains of Anti-Libanus, on the route to Damascus; but on hearing of the march and determination of the Crusaders, he crossed the mountains on his left, and drew near to the coast: the two armies met on the plain watered by the river Eleuthera, between Tyre and Sidon. The trumpets soon sounded to battle; the army of the Saracens, which covered an immense space, endeavoured at first to surround the Franks, and then to get between them and the coast; their cavalry precipitated itself by turns on the flanks, the van, and the rear of the Christians. The Christians closed their battalions, and on all sides presented impenetrable ranks. Whilst their enemies showered arrows and darts upon them, their lances and swords were bathed in the blood of the Saracens. They fought with different arms, but with the same bravery and fury. The victory remained for a long time uncertain; the Christians were several times on the point of losing the battle; but their obstinate valour at length triumphed over all the resistance of the Mussulmans, and the sea-coast, the banks of the river Eleuthera, and the declivities of the mountains were covered with dead. The Saracens lost a great many of their emirs. Malek-Adel, who displayed, during the whole of this day, the skill of a great captain, was wounded on the field of battle, and only owed his safety to flight. All his army was dispersed; some fled towards Jerusalem, whilst others hurried along the road to Damascus, whither the news of this bloody defeat carried consternation and despair.

In consequence of this victory, all the cities on the coast of Syria, which still belonged to the Mussulmans, fell into the power of the Christians; the Saracens abandoned Sidon, Laodicea, and Giblet. When the Christian fleet and army appeared before Berytus, the garrison was surprised, and did not venture to offer any resistance. This city contained, say historians, more provisions than would have sufficed for the inhabitants during three years; two large vessels, add the same chronicles, could not have contained the bows, arrows, and machines of war that were found in the city of Berytus. In this conquest immense riches fell into the hands of the victors, but the most precious reward of their triumph doubtless was the deliverance of nine thousand captives, impatient to resume their arms, and avenge the outrages of their long captivity. The prince of Antioch, who had joined the Christian army, sent a dove to his capital to announce to all the inhabitants of the principality the miraculous victory gained by the soldiers of the cross. In all the Christian cities thanks were offered up to the God of armies. The historians, who have transmitted to us the account of these glorious events, in order to paint the transports of the Christian people, content themselves with repeating these words of holy writ: "*Then Sion leaped with joy, and the children of Judah were filled with delight.*"

Whilst the Crusaders were thus pursuing their triumphs in Syria, the emperor Henry VI. took advantage of all the means and all the powers that the crusade had placed in his hands, to achieve the conquest of the kingdoms of Naples and Sicily. Although, in the course of his victories, he unceasingly invoked religion, humanity, and justice, he only listened to the dictates of his ambition; and, tormented by the sentiment of an implacable revenge, he was neither touched by the misery of the conquered, nor the submission of his enemies. All who had shown any respect or any fidelity for the family of Tancred, were cast by his orders into dungeons, or perished in horrible tortures, which he himself had invented. The army he led but too well seconded his gloomy and savage policy; the peace which the conquerors boasted of having restored to the people of Sicily, caused them more evils, and made more victims than war itself. Falcandus, who died some years before this expedition, had deplored beforehand, in his history, the misfortunes that were about to desolate his country. He already saw the most flourishing cities and the rich country of Sicily laid waste by the irruption of the barbarians. "Oh! unfortunate Sicilians," cried he, "it would be less frightful for you still to endure the tyrants of old Syracuse, than to live under the empire of this savage nation, which advances to invade your territory, and plunge you into all the horrors of misery and slavery."

Nevertheless, these pitiless soldiers wore the crosses of pilgrims; and their emperor, although not yet relieved from his excommunication, arrogated to himself glory as the first of the soldiers of Christ. Henry VI. was considered as the head of the crusade, and supreme arbiter of the affairs of the East. The king of Cyprus offered to become his vassal; Livon, prince of Armenia, begged the title of king of him. The emperor of Germany having no more enemies to dread in the West, gave his whole attention to the war against the Saracens, and, in a letter addressed to all the nobles, magistrates, and bishops of his empire, exhorted them to hasten the departure of the Crusaders. The emperor undertook to keep up an army of fifty thousand men for one year, and promised to pay thirty ounces of gold to every one that should remain under his banners till the end of the holy war. A great number of warriors, seduced by this promise, entered into an engagement to cross the sea, and fight against the infidels. Henry had no further need of them for his own conquests, and therefore pressed their departure for the East. Conrad, bishop of Hildesheim, chancellor of the empire, whose counsels in the wars of Sicily had but too well aided the ambition and barbarous policy of his master, was charged with the task of leading the third army of the Crusaders into Syria.

The arrival of so powerful a reinforcement in Palestine rekindled the zeal and enthusiasm of the Christians, and it might be expected that they would signalize their arms by some great enterprise. The victory they had recently gained in the plains of Tyre, the taking of Berytus, Sidon, and Giblet, had struck the Mussulmans with terror. Some of the leaders of the Christian army proposed to march against Jerusalem. "That city," said they, "cannot resist our victorious arms; her governor is a nephew of Saladin, who endures with impatience the authority of the sultan of Damascus, and has often appeared disposed to listen to the propositions of the Christians." Most of the barons did not, however, partake in this hope, and placed no confidence in the words of the Mussulmans. It was well known that the infidels, after the departure of Richard Cœur de Lion, had very considerably augmented the fortifications of Jerusalem; that a triple wall, and ditches of great depth, must render this conquest more perilous, and particularly more difficult, than in the time of Godfrey of Bouillon. Winter was approaching; the Christian army might be overtaken by the rainy season, and forced to raise the siege in face of the army of the Saracens. These considerations determined the Crusaders to put off the attack of the holy city to the following year.

It is not impertinent to remark here, that in the Christian armies they were constantly talking about Jerusalem, but that the leaders as constantly directed their efforts and their arms to the acquisition of other conquests. The holy city, situated far from the sea, contained within its walls no other treasures but religious relics and monuments. The maritime cities of Asia could boast of more worldly wealth, and held out far greater advantages to the conquerors; they afforded, likewise, more easy communication with Europe; and if the conquest of Jerusalem sometimes tempted the piety and devotion of the pilgrims, that of cities bordering upon the sea constantly kept awake the ambition of the maritime and warlike nations of the West.

All the sea-coast from Antioch to Ascalon belonged to the Christians; the Mussulmans having only been able to keep possession of Thoron. The garrison of this fortress frequently made incursions into the neighbouring countries, and by continual hostilities, intercepted the communication between the Christian cities. The Crusaders resolved that before they set out for Jerusalem, they would lay siege to the castle of Thoron. This fortress, built by Hugh de Saint-Omer, in the reign of Baldwin II., was situated at some leagues from Tyre, on the summit of a mountain, between the chain of Libanus and the sea. It was only accessible across steep rocks, and by a narrow way bordered by precipices. The Christian army had no machines sufficiently lofty to reach the heights of the walls, and arrows or stones hurled from the foot of the mountain, could not injure the besieged; whilst beams and fragments of rock precipitated from the ramparts made dreadful havoc among the besiegers. In the early attacks, the Saracens ridiculed the vain efforts of their enemies, and witnessed, almost without danger to themselves, prodigies of valour, and the most murderous inventions of the art of sieges, exercised ineffectually against their walls. But the almost insurmountable difficulties that might have been supposed likely to arrest the progress of the Christians, only redoubled their ardour and courage. They every day made fresh attacks, each day seeming to increase their efforts, and their obstinate bravery was seconded by newly-invented machines of war. With incredible labour, they dug out the earth, and made themselves a way across the rocks; whilst some Saxons, who had worked in the mines of Rammesberg, were employed in opening the flank of the mountain. The Crusaders at length reached the bottom of the ramparts of the fortress; the walls, the foundations of which they demolished, began to shake in various parts, without being struck by the ram, and their fall, which seemed delayed by a miracle, filled the besieged with dread.

The Mussulmans now losing all hope of defending themselves, proposed to capitulate; but such was the disorder of the Christian army, with its multitude of leaders, that not one of them durst take upon himself to listen to the proposals of the infidels. Henry, palatine of the Rhine, and the dukes of Saxony and Brabant, who enjoyed great consideration among the Germans, could enforce obedience from none but their own soldiers. Conrad, chancellor of the empire, who represented the emperor of Germany, might have been able to exercise beneficial power; but, weakened by disease, without experience in war, always shut up in his tent, he awaited the issue of the contest, and did not even deign to be present at the councils of the princes and barons. When the besieged had come to the determination to capitulate, they remained several days without knowing to which prince it would be most proper to address themselves, and when their deputies came to the Christian camp, their propositions were heard in a general assembly, in which the spirit of rivalry, short-sighted zeal, and blind enthusiasm held much greater empire than reason and prudence.

The Saracens, in their speech, confined themselves to imploring the clemency of their conquerors; they promised to abandon the fort with all their wealth, and only asked life and liberty as the price of their submission. The suppliant attitude of the Saracens must have touched the pride of the Christian warriors; religion and policy united to procure a favourable answer to the proposals that were made to them, and the greater part of the leaders were disposed to sign the capitulation. But some of the most ardent could not see without indignation that it was wished to obtain by treaty that which they must soon gain by force of arms. "It is necessary," said they, "that all our enemies should be struck with terror; and if the garrison of this place perish by the sword, the affrighted Saracens will not dare to wait for us either in Jerusalem or the other cities still in their possession."

As their advice was not adopted, these ardent and inconsiderate soldiers resolved to employ every means to interrupt the negotiation, and whilst re-conducting the deputies to the fortress, said to them: "*Defend yourselves, for if you surrender to the Christians, you will all perish in tortures.*" In addition to this, they addressed the Christian soldiers, and informed them, with accents of anger and grief, that a disgraceful peace was about to be concluded with the enemies of Christ. At the same time, such of the leaders as inclined towards peace, spread themselves through the camp, and represented to the army that it was useless, and perhaps dangerous, to purchase by new contests that which fortune, or rather Providence itself, offered to the Crusaders. Among the Christian warriors, some yielded to the counsels of moderation, others were unwilling to trust to anything but the sword; such as preferred victory to peace, ran to arms, and they who accepted the capitulation, retired to their tents. The camp, in which some remained in inaction and repose, whilst others prepared for battle, presented, at the same time, an image of peace and war: but in this diversity of opinions, amidst so strange a spectacle as the army then presented, it was easy to foresee that they would very soon be unable either to treat with enemies or fight them.

The capitulation was, notwithstanding, ratified by the principal chiefs and by the chancellor of the empire. The hostages the Saracens were to send were looked for in the camp, and the Crusaders fancied they could see the gates of the castle of Thoron thrown open to them; but despair had all at once changed the resolutions of the Saracens. When the deputies to the Christian camp reported to their companions in arms what they had seen and what they had heard; when they told them of the menaces that had been made to them, and of the divisions that existed among the enemies, the besieged forgot that their walls were in ruins, that they wanted both arms and provisions; that they had to defend themselves against a victorious army; and they swore rather to die than treat with the Crusaders. Instead of sending hostages, they appeared in arms upon the ramparts, and provoked the besiegers to renew the contest. The Christians resumed the labours of the siege, and recommenced their attacks; but their courage grew weaker every day, whilst, in the same proportion, despair seemed to increase the bravery of the Mussulmans. The besieged laboured without intermission in repairing their machines and rebuilding their walls; sometimes the Christians were attacked in the subterranean passages they had dug, and perished, buried under masses of loosened earth; whilst arrows and stones were constantly showered upon them from the ramparts. Frequently the Saracens succeeded in surprising some of their enemies, whom they carried alive into the place, and then slaughtered without mercy; the heads of these unfortunate prisoners were exposed upon the walls, and afterwards hurled by the machines into the camp of the Christians. The Crusaders appeared to have sunk into a sort of dejection or apathy; some still fought and remembered their oaths; but others remained indifferent spectators of the dangers and death of their brethren. Many added the scandal of the most depraved morals to their indifference for the cause of God. There might be seen, says an historian, men who had quitted their wives to follow Christ, forgetting all at once the most sacred duties, and attaching themselves to vile prostitutes; in fact, the vices and disorders of the Crusaders were so disgraceful, that the authors of the old chronicles blush whilst they retrace the picture of them. Arnold of Lubec, after having described the corruption that reigned in the camp of the Christians, appears to ask pardon of his reader; and, that he may not be accused of writing a satire, he takes care to add that he does not recall such odious remembrances to confound the pride of men, but to warn sinners, and touch, if possible, the hearts of his brothers in Christ.

Fame soon brought to the ears of the Christians that the kingdoms of Aleppo and Damascus were in arms, that Egypt had assembled an army, and that Malek-Adel, followed by a numberless multitude of warriors, was advancing by forced marches, impatient to avenge his late defeat.

At this news, the leaders of the crusade resolved to raise the siege of Thoron; and to conceal their retreat from the enemy, they did not blush to deceive their own soldiers. On the day of the Purification of the Virgin, whilst the Christians were engaged in the offices of devotion, the camp was informed, by sound of trumpet, that it was intended to make a general assault on the morrow. The whole army passed the night in preparations for the fight; but, at break of day, they learnt that Conrad and most of the leaders had quitted the army and taken the road to Tyre. The men assembled in groups round their tents to ascertain the truth, and made inquiries of each other with the greatest inquietude. The blackest forebodings took possession of the minds of the Crusaders; as if they had been conquered in a great battle, their only thought was flight. Nothing had been prepared for the retreat, no order had been given; no man saw anything but his own danger, or listened to any advice but that suggested by his fear; some loaded themselves with everything valuable they possessed, whilst others abandoned even their arms. The sick and wounded dragged themselves along with pain in the steps of their companions; such as could not walk were abandoned in the camp. The confusion was general; the soldiers marched *pêle-mêle* with the baggage; they knew not what route to take, and many lost themselves in the mountains; nothing was heard but cries and groans, and, as if Heaven wished to denote its anger at this disorder, a frightful tempest came on; fierce lightning rent the clouds, the thunder rolled in awful peals, and torrents of rain inundated the country. In their tumultuous flight, not one of the Crusaders ventured to turn his eyes to that fortress which, but a few days before, had offered to surrender to their arms: their terror was not abated till they beheld the walls of Tyre.

The army being at last re-assembled, it became a general inquiry, "What was the cause of the disorder they had experienced?" Then a new delirium took possession of the Christians; mistrust and mutual hatred succeeded to the panic terror of which they had been the victims; the most grave suspicions were attached to actions the most simple, and gave an odious meaning to words perfectly innocent. The Crusaders reproached each other, as with wrongs and proofs of treachery, with all the evils they had suffered or feared to suffer. The measures that an improvident zeal had counselled, as well as those that had been dictated by necessity and prudence, were the work of perfidy without example. The holy places, which so lately the Crusaders had contemplated with apparent indifference, now occupied their every thought; and the most fervent reproached the leaders with introducing none but profane views into a holy war; with having sacrificed the cause of God to their own ambition, and with having abandoned the soldiers of Christ to the fury of the Saracens. The same Crusaders proclaimed loudly, that God had been unfavourable to the Christians, because those whom he had appointed to lead the defenders of the cross, disdained the conquest of Jerusalem. Our readers may remember that after the siege of Damascus, in the second crusade, some Templars and Germans were accused of avarice, and of having sacrificed the zeal and bravery of the Christian warriors. Accusations quite as serious were renewed on this occasion, and with equal bitterness. If we are to believe the old chronicles, Malek-Adel had promised several leaders of the Christian army a great number of pieces of gold to engage them to raise the siege of Thoron; and the same chronicles add, that when the Mussulman prince paid them the sum agreed, he gave them nothing but false gold,—a worthy price of their cupidity and treachery. The Arabian historians give no sanction to these odious accusations; but such was the spirit of animosity which then reigned among the Christian warriors, that they were judged with more severity by their brethren and companions in arms than by their enemies.

At length the rage of discord was carried so far that the Germans and the Syrian Christians would not remain under the same colours; the former retired to the city of Jaffa, the ramparts of which they restored, and the latter returned to Ptolemaïs. Malek-Adel, willing to profit by these divisions, marched towards Jaffa, and offered the Germans battle. A severe conflict took place at a short distance from the city. The duke of Saxony and the duke of Brabant both perished in the *mêlée*. The Crusaders lost a great number of their bravest warriors; but the victory was in their favour. After a triumph which was due to their arms alone, the pride of the Germans knew no bounds; and they treated the Christians of Palestine with the greatest contempt. "We have," said they, "crossed the seas to defend their country; and, far from taking any part in our labours, these warriors, without either gratitude or courage, abandoned us in the hour of peril." The Christians of Palestine, on their side, reproached the Germans with having come into the East, not to fight, but to command; not to assist their brethren, but to impose a yoke upon them more insupportable than that of the Saracens. "The Crusaders," added they, "only quitted the West to make a pleasurable military progress into Syria; they there found peace, but they left war behind them; like those birds of passage that announce the season of storms and tempests."

In these fatal divisions nobody had sufficient credit and power to restrain angry spirits, or reconcile discordant opinions. The sceptre of Jerusalem was in the hands of a woman; the throne of Godfrey, so often shaken, was destitute of support: the empire of religion and law was every day fading away, and violence alone possessed the privilege of making itself respected. Necessity and force were the only powers that commanded obedience; whilst the license and corruption that prevailed among the people, still called *the people of God*, made such frightful progress, that we are tempted to accuse contemporary authors and ocular witnesses of employing great exaggeration in their recitals.

In this state of decline, amidst such shameful disorders, the most wise and prudent of the prelates and barons thought the best step they could adopt would be to give an able and worthy leader to the Christian colonies, and they entreated Isabella, the widow of Henry of Champagne, to take a new husband, who might consent to be their sovereign. Isabella, by three marriages, had already given Palestine three kings. They proposed to her Amaury, who had recently succeeded Guy de Lusignan in the kingdom of Cyprus. An Arabian historian says that Amaury was *a wise and prudent man, who loved God and respected humanity*. He did not fear to reign, amidst war, troubles, and factions, over the poor remains of the unfortunate kingdom of Jerusalem, and came to share with Isabella the vain honours of royalty. Their marriage was celebrated at Ptolemaïs, with more pomp, say historians, than the posture of affairs warranted. Although this marriage might not remedy all the evils under which the Christians laboured, it at least afforded them the consolatory hope that their discords would be appeased, and that the colonies of the Franks, when better governed, might gather some fruit from so many victories gained over the infidels. But news which arrived from the West, soon spread fresh grief through the kingdom, and put an end to the barren exploits of the holy war. Amidst the festivities which followed the marriage and coronation of Amaury, the death of the emperor Henry VI. was announced. The election of a new head of the empire would most probably produce a violent contest in Germany; and every one of the German princes or nobles then in Palestine, naturally turned his attention to that which he had to hope or fear in the events preparing in Europe: they determined to return immediately into the West.

The Count de Montfort and several other French knights had but recently arrived in the Holy Land, and earnestly entreated the German princes to defer their return. The Pope likewise, on receiving intelligence of the death of Henry VI., wrote to the leaders of the Crusaders, to implore them to finish their good work, and not to abandon the cause of Christ; but neither the prayers of the count de Montfort nor the exhortations of the pope could detain the Germans, impatient to return to their country. Of so many princes who had left the West to secure a triumph to the cause of God, the queen of Hungary alone was faithful to her vows, and remained with her knights in Palestine. On quitting Syria, the Germans contented themselves with leaving a garrison in Jaffa. A short time after their departure, whilst celebrating the feast of St. Martin with every excess of drunkenness and debauchery, this garrison was surprised and massacred by the Saracens.* Winter was approaching; neither party could keep the field; discord reigned equally among Christians and Mussulmans; and both sides were desirous of peace, because they were incapable of carrying on the war. The count de Montfort concluded with the Saracens a truce for three years. Thus terminated this crusade, which only lasted a few months, and was really nothing but a pilgrimage for the warriors of the West.

* Fuller, an English historian, speaks of this disaster at great length. As his work is scarce, I will translate the passage from it relative to this crusade, in which the impartial reader will find the gross misrepresentations of a violent enemy of the Crusaders. "In this war," says he, "we may contemplate an episcopal army which might have served for a synod; or, more truly, it offers us a picture of the *Church militant*. Many captains returned home secretly, and when the soldiers wanted to fight, the officers went away: what remained of this army fortified themselves in Jaffa. The feast of St. Martin, that great saint of Germany, fell at this time. This holy man, a German by birth, and bishop of Tours in France, distinguished himself eminently by his charity. The Germans changed his charity for the poor into excess for themselves, observing the 11th of November in such a manner that it ought no longer to be called a saint's day, but a day of festivity. Drunkenness reduced them to such a state, that the Turks, falling upon them, killed more than twenty thousand of them. This day, which the Germans write in red letters in their calendars, takes its colour from their own blood, and as their camp was a slaughter-house, the Turks were their butchers. We may compare them to the oxen of St. Martin, which differ little from droves of drunkards."—*Nicol. Fuller*, b. ii. chap. xvi. p. 133.

The victories of the Crusaders rendered the Christians masters of all the coasts of Syria; but their precipitate departure destroyed the fruits of their conquests. The cities they had obtained were left without defenders, and almost without inhabitants.

This fourth crusade, in which all the powers of the West miscarried in an attempt upon a little fortress of Syria, and which presents us with the strange spectacle of a holy war directed by an excommunicated monarch, furnishes the historian with fewer great events and a smaller number of great misfortunes than the preceding expeditions. The Christian armies, which made but a transient visit to the East, experieneed neither the famine nor the diseases that had proved so fatal to the former enterprises. The foresight and attention of the emperor of Germany, who had become master of Sicily, provided for all the wants of the Crusaders, whose exploits were intended to assist his ambitious projects, and whom he considered as his own soldiers.

The German warriors that composed the Christian armies had not the requisite qualities to secure the advantages of victory. Always ready to throw themselves blindly into danger; quite ignorant that it is possible to ally prudence with courage; listening to nothing but the violence of their own passions, and recognising no law but their own will; obedient to leaders of their own nation, and despising all others; full of an indomitable pride, which made them disdain the help of their allies and the lessons of experience, such men could neither make peace nor war.

When we compare these new Crusaders with the companions of Richard or Godfrey, we find in them the same ardour for fight, the same indifference for danger; but we find them very deficient in that enthusiasm which animated the first soldiers of the cross at the sight of the holy places. Jerusalem, which had never ceased to be open to the devotion of the faithful, no longer beheld within its walls that crowd of pilgrims which, at the commencement of the holy wars, repaired thither from all parts of the West. The pope and the leaders of the Christian army forbade Crusaders to enter the holy city without having conquered it; and they, who did not always prove so docile, obeyed the prohibition without pain. More than a hundred thousand warriors that had left Europe for the purpose of delivering Jerusalem, returned to their homes without having entertained perhaps one thought of visiting the tomb of Christ, for which they had taken up arms. The thirty ounces of gold promised by the emperor to all who should cross the sea to fight the infidels, very much increased the number of the Crusaders; this was not the case in former expeditions, in which the crowd of soldiers of the cross was influenced principally by religious motives. More religion than politics had entered into the other holy wars; in this crusade, although it had been directly promoted by the head of the Church, and was to a considerable extent directed by bishops, we may safely say there was more of politics than religion. Pride, ambition, jealousy, the most disgraceful passions of the human heart, did not make an effort, as in the preceding expeditions, to cover themselves with a religious veil. The archbishop of Mayence, the bishop of Hildesheim, with most of the other ecclesiastics who took the cross, attracted no admiration for either their wisdom or piety, or distinguished themselves by any personal quality. Conrad, the chancellor of the empire, on his return to Europe, was followed by the suspicions which had been attached to his conduct during the holy war; and when, a long time after, he was slain by several gentlemen of Wurtzburg, who conspired against him, the people considered his tragical death as a punishment from Heaven.

Henry VI., who had preached the crusade, only viewed this distant expedition as a means and an opportunity for increasing his power and extending his empire; whilst the West put up prayers for the success of a holy war, of which he was the life and soul, he prosecuted an impious war, desolated a Christian people for the purpose of subjecting them to his laws, and threatened the empire of Greece. The son of Tancred was deprived of his sight, and cast into prison, and the daughters of the king of Sicily were carried away into captivity. Henry's barbarities were so excessive, that he irritated his neighbours, and created enemies in his own family. When he died, a report prevailed in Europe that he had been poisoned; the nations that he had rendered miserable could not believe that so many cruelties could remain unpunished, and they asserted that Providence had employed the wife of the emperor to be his executioner, and to avenge all the calamities he had inflicted upon the kingdoms of Naples and Sicily. At the approach of death, Henry remembered that he had persecuted Richard; that he had detained a prince of the Crusaders in chains, in spite of the solicitations of the father of the faithful; and he hastened to send ambassadors to the king of England, charged with the task of making him a solemn reparation for so great an outrage. After his death, as he had been excommunicated, it was thought necessary to address the sovereign pontiff to obtain permission to bury him in the Holy Land; and the pope coolly replied, that they were at liberty to bury him among Christians, but before they did so, they must offer up man prayers to mitigate the anger of God.

In taking possession of the beautiful and rich territories of Italy by perfidy and violence, Henry prepared for that unfortunate country a series of revolutions, to be renewed from age to age. The odious war he had made against the family of Tancred, naturally gave birth to other wars injurious to his own family. In removing so far from Germany with his armies, Henry afforded opportunity for the formation of powerful parties, which, at his death, disputed the imperial sceptre with some success, and at length gave rise to a war in which the principal states of Europe were involved. Thus, whilst the other holy wars had contributed to maintain or establish public peace in Europe, this fourth crusade produced divisions among the states of Christendom, without at all diminishing the power of the Saracens, and only served to introduce trouble and confusion into many kingdoms of the West.

BOOK X

THE FIFTH CRUSADE

A. D. 1198 TO 1204

BOOK X.

THE FIFTH CRUSADE.

A.D. 1198–1204.

Rousseau's opinion of the Crusaders—Enthusiasm and valour of the Christian troops—Causes which led to the fifth crusade—Instigated by Pope Innocent III.—His quarrel with Philip of France—Death of Richard I. of England—Preaching of Foulkes in favour of the crusade—Thibault IV., count of Champagne, engages in the crusade—Louis, count of Chartres—Preaching of Martin Litz—Villehardouin, marshal of Champagne—Baldwin, count of Flanders—Commercial greatness of Venice—Dandolo, the doge of Venice—He engages to assist the Crusaders—Gauthier de Brienne—Sums advanced by Venice—Death and character of Thibault—Count de Bar—Death of Eude III., duke of Burgundy—Boniface, marquis of Montferrat, elected commander of the crusade—Famine in Egypt and Europe—Death of Foulkes—Pecuniary exactions of Venice—Revolt of the city of Zara—Dandolo's address to the Venetians in favour of the Crusaders—Isaac, emperor of Constantinople, dethroned—Siege of Zara—The Abbot de Cernay—Quarrels between the Venetians and the French Crusaders—Address of Philip of Swabia to the French Barons—Policy of Malek-Adel—Reproaches of Innocent III. against the Crusaders at Zara—Character of the Emperor Alexius—Capture of Corfu—Conquests of the younger Alexius, son of Isaac—Description of Constantinople—Besieged by the Crusaders—The Varangians—Speeches of Rossi and Conon de Bethune—Capture of Constantinople—Alexius dethroned—Isaac and his son Alexius restored to the sovereignty—The Crusaders become the allies of the Greeks, and the protectors of the Greek empire—Their communications with the pope.

CHRISTIAN TROOPS, says J. J. Rousseau in his "Contrat Social," "*are, as they say, excellent; I deny it; show me such; for my part, I know no Christian troops.*" The events we have just related, and those we are about to make known, will, there is no doubt, suffice to refute this strange paradox of J. J. Rousseau. The author of the "Social Contract" does not dissemble, it is true, the objections that may be made to him from the history of the crusades; but, ever faithful to his system, and taking no account of historical truths, he answers, that "*the Crusaders, far from being Christians, were citizens of the Church; that they fought for their spiritual country, which the Church had rendered temporal nobody knows how.*" Strange abuse of reasoning, which confounds the sense of words, and refuses the title of Christians to those who fought in the name of Christ! In representing the Crusaders as citizens of the Church, Rousseau doubtless meant to say that the popes were the origin of the crusades, and that the soldiers of the cross defended the temporal power of the popes. We at once reply that the crusades owed their birth and growth to the religious and warlike enthusiasm that animated the nations of the West in the twelfth century, and that without this enthusiasm, which was not the work of the heads of the Church, the preachings of the Holy See would not have been able to collect a single army under the banners of the cross. We may further add that, during the holy wars, the sovereign pontiffs were frequently driven from Rome and despoiled of their states, and that they did not summon the Crusaders to the defence of the power or *temporal country* of the Church. Not only were the Crusaders not always the blind instruments of the Holy See, but they sometimes resisted the will of the popes, and yet in their camps were no less models of valour united with Christian piety. No doubt, the leaders were often seduced by ambition, the love of glory, and a passion for war; but religion, well or ill understood, acted upon the greater number; the Christian religion which they defended, or believed they defended, by inspiring them with a desire for the blessings of heaven and a contempt for life, elevated them above all perils, and enabled them to brave death on every occasion. Here is the whole truth; but this truth is too simple for such as disdain common routes, and cannot form a judgment upon human affairs without displaying all the parade of a proud and austere philosophy. For ourselves, who are persuaded that true philosophy consists in studying the human heart and the spirit of societies, not in vain theories, but in the faithful history of past ages; we will not refute brilliant sophisms by long arguments; but to show in all its splendour the valour of *Christian soldiers,* we will content ourselves with pursuing our recital, and making known with impartiality the labours, the reverses, and the victories of the soldiers of the cross.*

The departure of the German Crusaders plunged the eastern Christians into grief and consternation; the colonies, when left to their own resources, were only protected by the truce concluded between the count de Montfort and Malek-Adel. The infidels had too great a superiority over their enemies to respect, for any length of time, a treaty which they considered as an obstacle to the progress of their power. The Christians, threatened by new perils, again turned their eyes to the West. The bishop of Ptolemaïs, accompanied by several knights, embarked for Europe, in order to solicit the aid of the faithful. The vessel in which he embarked had scarcely quitted the port, when it was swallowed up by the waves, and the bishop and every person of his suite perished. Other ships, that set sail a short time afterwards, were surprised by the tempest, and forced to return to the port of Tripoli; so that the prayers and complaints of the Christians of Palestine could not reach the ears of their brethren of the West. Nevertheless, the afflicting news of the situation of the feeble kingdom of Jerusalem soon became generally known; some pilgrims, escaping from the perils of the sea, described, on their return, the triumphs and threats of the Saracens; but in the state of Europe at that moment, nothing could be more difficult than to induce nations to undertake a new crusade. The death of the Emperor Henry VI. divided the princes and prelates of Germany, and Philip Augustus was still at war with Richard of England. One of the sons of Bela, king of Hungary, who pretended to take the cross, only assembled an army to agitate the kingdom, and get possession of the crown. Amidst the fierce contentions that disturbed Europe, the Christian people seemed to have forgotten the tomb of Christ; a single man was touched with the misfortunes of the faithful of the East, and was not without hope of alleviating them.

Innocent III., at the age of thirty-three, had recently gained the suffrages of the conclave. At a period of life in which the passions are generally masters, devoted to the most austere retirement, constantly occupied with the study of holy books, and ready at all times to confound new heresies by the force of reason, the successor of St. Peter shed tears on being informed of his elevation; but when seated on the pontifical throne, Innocent all at once exhibited a new character; the same man, who had appeared to dread the splendour of a lofty position, became most eager, by any means, to increase his power, and displayed all the ambition and inflexible obstinacy of Gregory VII. His youth, which promised him a long reign; his ardour in the defence of justice and truth; his eloquence, his knowledge, his virtues, which drew upon him the respect of the faithful, all united to give birth to the hope that he would assure the triumph of religion; and that he would one day accomplish the projects of his predecessors.

* Our excellent author has conceived a kind of parental affection for the crusades, which makes him blind to their defects. If we speak of the *spirit* of Christianity, certainly the philosopher of Geneva has the advantage of him, as his own pages show. Divested of their mundane motives, the crusades were little else than "a savage fanaticism." There was, at least, as much religious merit in the Mussulmans, who fought to defend their faith. A philosopher may deduce beneficial results from the crusades, particularly to Europe; but he will be much puzzled to prove that that which we now consider a truly Christian spirit, influenced many of the warriors that carried them out, or the churchmen that promoted them. The Inquisition and the crusade against the Albigeois were of the same age, and the principal agents in them equally prostituted the name of religion in their horrors.—TRANS.

As the power of the pope was founded upon the progress of the faith and the holy enthusiasm of the Christians, Innocent gave his first attention to the suppression of the dangerous innovations and imprudent doctrines that began to corrupt his age and menace the sanctuary; he particularly endeavoured to re-animate the ardour for the crusades: and, to master the minds of kings and nations, to rally all Christians, and make them concur in the triumph of the Church, he spoke to them of the captivity of Jerusalem; he pointed to the tomb of Christ, and the holy places profaned by the presence and the domination of infidels.

In a letter addressed to the bishops, the clergy, the nobles, and people of France, England, Hungary, and Sicily, the sovereign pontiff made known the will, the menaces, and the promises of God. "Since the lamentable loss of Jerusalem," said he, "the Holy See has never ceased to cry towards Heaven, and to exhort the faithful to avenge the injury done to Christ, thus banished from his heritage. Formerly Uriah would not enter into his house, or see his wife, whilst the ark of the Lord was in the camp; but now our princes, in this public calamity, abandon themselves to illegitimate amours; immerse themselves in voluptuousness; abuse the blessings that God has given them; and pursue each other with implacable hatred; only thinking of revenging their own personal injuries, they never consider that our enemies insult us, saying: '*Where is your God, who cannot deliver himself out of our hands? We have profaned your sanctuary, and the places in which you pretend your superstition had its birth; we have crushed the arms of the French, the English, the Germans, and subdued a second time the proud Spaniards: what remains then for us to do? to drive out those you have left in Syria, and to penetrate into the West to efface for ever both your name and your memory.*'" Assuming then a more paternal tone: "Prove," cried Innocent, "that you have not lost your courage; be prodigal, in the cause of God, of all you have received from him; if, on an occasion so pressing, you refuse to serve Christ, what excuse will you be able to offer at his terrible tribunal? If God died for man, shall man fear to die for his God? Will he refuse to give up his transitory life and the perishable goods of this world for him who lays before us the treasures of eternity?"

Prelates were at the same time sent through all the countries of Europe, to preach peace among princes, and exhort them to unite against the common enemies of God. These prelates, clothed in the full confidence of the Holy See, were to engage cities and nobles to equip, at their own expense, for the Holy Land, a certain number of warriors, to serve there during two years at least. They promised remission of sins, and the special protection of the Church to all that would take up the cross and arms, or would contribute to the equipment and support of the soldiers of Christ. To receive the pious tribute of the faithful, boxes were placed in all the churches. At the tribunal of penitence, the priests were ordered to command all sinners to concur in the holy enterprise; no error could find grace before God, without the sincere will of participating in the crusade; zeal for the deliverance of the holy places appeared to be at that time the only virtue the pope required of Christians, and even charity itself lost some of its value, if not exercised in promoting the crusades. As the Church of Rome was reproached with imposing upon the people *burdens to which she only applied the tip of her own finger*, the pope exhorted the heads of the clergy, and the clergy themselves, to set an example of devotedness and sacrifices. Innocent ordered his gold and silver plate to be melted to defray the expenses of the holy war, and would allow none but vessels of wood and clay to be seen on his table whilst the crusade lasted.

The sovereign pontiff was so satisfied of the zeal and piety of the Christians, that he wrote to the patriarch and king of Jerusalem, to announce to them the coming succours from the West. He neglected nothing that could augment the numbers of the soldiers of Christ; he addressed himself to the emperor of Constantinople, and reproached him with indifference for the deliverance of the holy places. The emperor Alexius endeavoured, in his answer, to show his zeal for the cause of religion; but he added that the time of deliverance was not yet arrived, and that he feared to oppose himself to the will of God, irritated by the sins of the Christians. The Greek prince adroitly reminded him of the ravages committed in the territories of the empire by the soldiers of Frederick, and conjured the pope to direct his reproofs against those who, feigning to labor for Jesus Christ, acted against the will of Heaven. In his correspondence with Alexius, Innocent III. did not at all conceal his pretensions to universal empire, and spoke in the character of sovereign arbiter of the kings of the East and West. He applied to himself these words addressed to Jeremiah: "I have placed thee over the nations and over the kingdoms, to pull up and scatter, to edify and to plant." When speaking of the power of the popes and that of the princes, he compared the one to the sun, which lights the universe during the day, and the other to the moon, which lights the earth during the night.

The pretensions that Innocent put forth, and the haughtiness with which he sought to establish them, were, no doubt, injurious to the effect of his exhortations, and must have weakened the zeal of the Christian princes whom he wished to persuade to undertake the crusade. The princes and bishops of Germany were divided between Otho of Saxony and Philip of Swabia; the sovereign pontiff pronounced strongly for Otho, and threatened with the thunders of the Church all who assisted the opposite party. In the dissensions occasioned by this momentous affair, some availed themselves of the opportunity to gain the favour of the pope, and others to secure themselves from the effects of his anger; but all Germany being engaged in the quarrel, nobody took the cross.

One of the pope's legates, Peter of Capua, succeeded in re-establishing peace between Richard Cœur de Lion and Philip Augustus. Richard, who was desirous of conciliating the good-will of the Holy See, constantly promised to equip a fleet and collect an army to go and make war against the infidels. He proclaimed a tournament in his capital, in the midst of which he called upon the barons and knights to follow him into the East; but all these demonstrations, the sincerity of which was very suspicious, remained unproductive. It was not long before war again broke out between France and England; and Richard, who on all occasions repeated his vow of combating the infidels, was killed in a petty quarrel with Christians.

Philip Augustus repudiated Ingeburge, daughter of the king of Denmark, to marry Agnes de Meranie. The sovereign pontiff, in a letter addressed to the faithful, strongly censured princes who gave themselves up to illegitimate amours; he ordered Philip Augustus to take back Ingeburge, and as Philip refused to obey, the kingdom of France was placed under an interdict. During several months all religious ceremonies were suspended; the pulpits of the Gospel ceased to give forth the holy word; church bells and the voice of prayer were silenced; Christian burial was refused to the dead; the sanctuary was closed against the faithful; a long mourning veil seemed to hang over cities and plains, from which the Christian religion was banished, and which might almost be fancied to be invaded by the Saracens. Although such as took the cross were exempt from the interdict, the spectacle which France presented discouraged and saddened its inhabitants. Philip Augustus, irritated against the pope, showed very little disposition to revive their zeal; and the clergy, whose influence might have had a powerful effect, had less reason to deplore the captivity of Jerusalem than the unhappy state of the kingdom.

At length a curé of Neuilly-sur-Maine began to fill France with the fame of his eloquence and his miracles. Foulques had at first led a very dissipated life, but, touched with sincere repentance, he was not satisfied with expiating his irregularities by penitence, but became desirous of bringing back all sinners to the paths of salvation, and travelled through the provinces endeavouring to awaken in the people a contempt for the things of this life. God, to try him, permitted that, in his early sermons, Foulques should be exposed to the ridicule of his auditors; but the truths he uttered soon obtained a marvellous ascendancy over all that came to hear him. Bishops invited him to preach in their dioceses; he received everywhere extraordinary honours, and both people and clergy flocked out to meet him, as if he had been an envoy of God. Foulques, says the chronicle of St. Victor, had nothing remarkable in his vestments or manner of living; *he travelled on horseback, and ate that which was given to him.* He preached sometimes in churches, at others in public places, and not unfrequently amidst the excitement of tournaments. His eloquence was simple and natural; safe, by his ignorance, from the bad taste of his age, he neither astonished his auditors by the vain subtleties of the schools, nor by an absurd mixture of passages from the Scriptures and profane quotations from antiquity. His words, from being unadorned by the erudition then so much admired, were the more persuasive, and found their way more directly to the heart. The most learned preachers ranked themselves among his disciples, and declared that the Holy Ghost spoke by his mouth. Animated by that faith which performs prodigies, he enchained at his pleasure the passions of the multitude, and caused to resound, even in the palaces of princes, the *thunders of evangelical denunciations.** At his voice, all that had enriched themselves by fraud, brigandage, or usury, hastened to restore that which they had unjustly acquired; libertines confessed their sins, and devoted themselves to the austerities of penitence; prostitutes, following the example of Madeline, deplored the scandal of their lives, cut off their hair, exchanged their gaudy apparel for hair-cloth and mean garments, and made vows to sleep upon ashes and die in retirement. In short, the eloquence of Foulques of Neuilly effected such miracles, that contemporaries speak of him as of another St. Paul, sent for the conversion of his age. One of them even goes so far as to say that he dares not relate all he knows of him, fearing the incredulity of men.

Innocent III. cast his eyes upon Foulques of Neuilly, and confided to him the mission that, fifty years before, had been given to St. Bernard. The new preacher of the crusade himself assumed the cross at a general chapter of the order of Citeaux. At the sound of his voice, the zeal for the holy war, which had appeared extinct, blazed out again in all parts. In every city he passed through, the people crowded to listen to him; and all who were in a condition to bear arms, took the oath to combat the infidels.

Several holy orators were associated with Foulques of Neuilly; Martin Litz, of the order of Citeaux, in the diocese of Bâle, and on the banks of the Rhine; Herloin, a monk of St. Denis, took his cause through the still wild countries of Bretagne and the lower Poitou; and Eustace, abbot of Flay, crossed the sea twice, to awaken the enthusiasm and holy ardour of the provinces of England.

These pious orators were not all endowed with the same eloquence; but all were animated by the most ardent zeal. The profanation of the holy places, the evils suffered by the Eastern Christians, and the remembrance of Jerusalem, imparted the most lively interest to their discourses, and touched all hearts. Such was the spirit spread through Europe, that simply to mention the name of Christ, or to speak of the city of God, held in captivity by the infidels, melted auditors to tears, and gave birth to transports of enthusiasm. The people everywhere evinced the same piety and the same feelings; but the cause of Christ still wanted the example and courage of princes and nobles. As a celebrated tournament had been proclaimed in Champagne, at which the boldest warriors of France, Germany, and Flanders were expected to be present, Foulques repaired to the castle of Ecry-sur-Aisne, which was the rendezvous of the knights. His eloquence procured attention to the complaints

* If we may believe contemporary chronicles, Foulques addressed Richard Cœur de Lion, and said to him,—"You have three daughters to dispose of in marriage, Avarice, Pride, and Luxury." "Well," replied Richard, "I give my pride to the Templars, my avarice to the monks of Citeaux, and my luxury to the bishops." This anecdote is quoted by Rigord.

of Sion, even amidst the profane and violent amusements of chivalry; when Foulques spoke of Jerusalem, knights and barons neglected their jousts, the shivering of lances, or high feats of árms; they became insensible of the presence of *dames* and *demoiselles*, who accorded the prizes to valour; and turned a deaf ear to the gay minstrels who celebrated *la prouesse achetée et vendue au fer et à l'acier*. All took the oath to fight against the infidels; and it must have been surprising to see numerous defenders of the cross come forth from these warlike festivals that were so severely reprehended by the Church.

Among the princes and lords who enrolled themselves .n the crusade, the most conspicuous were Thibault IV., count of Champagne, and Louis, count of Chartres and Blois, both relations of the kings of France and England. The father of Thibault had followed Louis VII. to the second crusade, and his elder brother had been king of Jerusalem. Two thousand five hundred knights owed him homage and military service, and the nobility of Champagne excelled in all the noble exercises of arms. The marriage of Thibault with the heiress of Navarre brought to his standard a great number of warriors from the countries bordering on the Pyrenees. Louis, count of Chartres and Blois, reckoned among his ancestors one of the most illustrious chiefs of the first crusade, and was master of a province abounding in warriors of name. After the example of these two princes, the following distinguished leaders took the cross:—The count of St. Paul, the counts Gauthier and Jean de Brienne, Manassès de l'Isle, Renard de Dampièrre, Mathieu de Montmorency, Hugh and Robert de Boves, d'Amiens, Renaud de Boulogne, Geoffrey de Perche, Renaud de Montmirail, Simon de Montfort, who had just signed a treaty with the Saracens, but was no less ready on that account to take an oath to fight against them; and Geoffrey de Villehardouin, marshal of Champagne, who has left us an account of this crusade in the unadorned language of his time.

Among the ecclesiastics, history names Nivelon de Chérisi, bishop of Soissons; Garnier, bishop of Langres; the abbot of Looz, and the abbot of Veaux-de-Cernai. The bishop of Langres, who had been the object of the censures of the pope, expected to find in the pilgrimage to the Holy Land, an opportunity of reconciling himself with the Holy See. The abbot of Looz and the abbot of Veaux-de-Cernai were both remarkable for their piety and learning; the former full of wisdom and moderation, the latter animated by a holy enthusiasm and an ardent zeal, which afterwards he but too strongly displayed against the Albigeois and the partisans of the count of Thoulouse.

When the knights and barons returned to their homes, bearing a red cross upon their baldrics and their coats of mail, they aroused by their presence the enthusiasm of their vassals and brothers in arms. The nobility of Flanders, after the example of those of Champagne, were anxious to prove their zeal for the recovery of the holy places. Baldwin, who had taken the part of Richard against Philip Augustus, sought beneath the standard of the cross an asylum against the anger of the king of France, and swore, in the church of St. Donatien of Bruges, to go into Asia to combat the Saracens. Mary, countess of Flanders, sister of Thibault, count of Champagne, would not live separated from her husband; and although she was still in the flower of her youth, and was several months advanced in her pregnancy, took an oath to follow the Crusaders beyond the seas, and to quit a home she was doomed never to see again. The example of Baldwin was followed by his two brothers, Eustace and Henry, count of Sarbuck; by Canon de Bethune, whose piety and eloquence were held in high estimation, and by Jacques d'Avesnes, son of him who, under the same name, had made himself so famous in the third crusade. Most of the knights and barons of Flanders and Hainault also took the oath to share the labours and perils of the holy war.

The principal leaders first met at Soissons, and afterwards at Compiègne. In their assembly, they gave the command of the expedition to Thibault, count of Champagne. It was decided also that the Crusaders should repair to the East by sea; and, in consequence of this determination, six deputies were sent to Venice, in order to obtain from the republic the vessels required to transport the men and horses.

The Venetians were at that period in the highest state of their greatness and prosperity. Amidst the convulsions that had preceded and followed the fall of the Roman power, these industrious people had taken refuge in the islands that border the extremity of the Adriatic Gulf; and, placed upon the waves, had directed all their views to the empire of the sea, of which the barbarians took no heed. Venice was at first under the dominion of the emperors of Constantinople; but, in proportion with the decline of the Greek empire, the republic acquired territory, strength, and splendour, which necessarily produced independence. From the tenth century, palaces of marble had replaced the humble huts of fishermen, scattered over the island of the Rialto. The cities of Istria and Dalmatia obeyed the sovereigns of the Adriatic Sea. The republic, become formidable to the most powerful monarch, was able, at the least signal, to arm a fleet of a hundred galleys, which it employed successively against the Greeks, the Saracens, and the Normans. The power of Venice was respected by all the nations of the West; and the republics of Genoa and Pisa in vain contended with her for the domination of the seas. The Venetians remembered with pride these words of Pope Alexander III., when the republic had protested against the emperor of Germany, who presented a ring to the doge, saying, "*Espouse the sea with this ring, that posterity may know that the Venetians have acquired the empire of the waves, and that the sea has been subjected to them as a woman is to her husband.*"

The fleets of the Venetians constantly visited the ports of Greece and Asia; they transported pilgrims to Palestine, and returned laden with the rich merchandise of the East. The Venetians entered into the crusades with less eagerness and enthusiasm than other Christian nations, but knew well how to profit by them for their own interests; whilst the warriors of Christendom were fighting for glory, for kingdoms, or for the tomb of Christ, the merchants of Venice fought for counting-houses, stores, and commercial privileges; and avarice often made them undertake that which other nations could not have been able to effect but by an excess of religious zeal. The republic, which owed all its prosperity to its commercial relations, sought without scruple the friendship and protection of the Mussulman powers of Syria and Egypt; and often, even when all Europe was arming against the infidels, the Venetians were accused of supplying the enemies of the Christian nations with both arms and provisions.

When the deputies of the Crusaders arrived at Venice, the republic had for doge Dandolo, so celebrated in its annals. Dandolo had for a length of time served his country in important missions, and in the command of its fleets and armies; now, placed at the head of its government, he watched over its liberties and the operations of its laws. His labours in war and peace, his useful regulations of the money currency, with his administration of justice and public security, deservedly procured him the esteem and gratitude of his fellow-citizens. He had acquired the power of mastering, by words, the passions of the multitude, even in the stormy disputes of a republic.

Nobody was more skilful in seizing a favourable opportunity, or in taking advantage of the least circumstance for the furtherance of his designs. At the age of ninety, the doge of Venice exhibited no symptoms of senility but virtue and experience. Everything that could save his country aroused his activity and inflamed his courage; with the spirit of calculation and economy which distinguished his compatriots, Dandolo mingled passions the most generous, and threw an air of grandeur over all the enterprises of a trading people. His patriotism, always sustained by the love of glory, appeared to possess something of that sentiment of honour, and that chivalric greatness of soul which formed the predominant characteristic of his age.

Dandolo praised with warmth an enterprise that appeared glorious to him, and in which the interests of his country were not opposed to those of religion. The deputies required vessels to transport four thousand five hundred knights and twenty thousand foot, with provisions for the Christian army for nine months. Dandolo promised, in the name of the republic, to furnish the necessary provisions and vessels, on condition that the Crusaders should engage to pay the Venetians the sum of eighty-five thousand silver marks. As he was not willing that the people of Venice should be unconnected with the expedition of the French Crusaders, Dandolo proposed to the deputies to arm, at the expense of the republic, fifty galleys, and demanded for his country half of the conquests that might be made in the East.

The deputies accepted without hesitation the more interested than generous proposals of the doge. The conditions of the treaty were first examined in the doge's council,* composed of six patricians; it was afterwards ratified in two other councils, and at last presented for the sanction of the people, who then exercised supreme power.

A general assembly was convoked in the church of St. Mark, and when the mass of the Holy Ghost had been celebrated, the marshal of Champagne, accompanied by the other deputies, arose, and addressing the people of Venice, pronounced a discourse, the simple and unaffected expressions of which paint, better than we possibly can, the spirit and feelings of the heroic periods of our history. "The lords and barons of France, the most high and the most powerful, have sent us to you to pray you, in the name of God, to take pity on Jerusalem, which the Turks hold in bondage; they cry to you for mercy, and supplicate you to accompany them to avenge the disgrace of Jesus Christ. They have made choice of you, because they know that no people that be upon the sea have so great power as your nation. They have commanded us to throw ourselves at your feet, and not to rise until you shall have granted our request, until you shall have had pity on the Holy Land beyond the seas." At these words the deputies were moved to tears, and feeling it no degradation to humble themselves in the cause of Christ, they fell upon their knees and held up their hands in a supplicating manner towards the assembly of the people. The strong emotion of the barons and knights communicated itself to the Venetians, and ten thousand voices replied as one, "*We grant your request.*" The doge, ascending the tribunal, praised highly the earnestness and loyalty of the French barons, and spoke with enthusiasm of the honour God conferred upon the people of Venice in choosing them from amongst all other nations, to partake in the glory of the most noble of enterprises, and associate them with the most valiant of warriors. He then read the treaty entered into with the Crusaders, and conjured his assembled fellow-citizens to give their consent to it in the forms ordained by the laws of the republic. Then the people arose, and cried with an unanimous shout, "*We consent to it.*" All the inhabitants of Venice were present at this meeting; an immense multitude covered the place of St. Mark and filled the neighbouring streets. Religious enthusiasm, love of country, surprise and joy were manifested by acclamations so loud and general, that it might be said, according to the expression of the marshal of Champagne, "*that the world was about to engage in one common conflict.*"

On the morrow of this memorable day, the deputies of the barons repaired to the palace of St. Mark, and swore on their swords and the Gospel, to fulfil all the engagements they had made. The preamble of the treaty recalled the faults and the misfortunes of the princes who had to that time undertaken the deliverance of the Holy Land, and praised the wisdom and prudence of the French lords and knights, who neglected nothing to assure the success of an enterprise full of difficulties and

* The Venetians undertook, in the treaty, to distribute to each individual of the army of the Crusaders, six setiers of bread, corn, wheat, or vegetables, and half a pitcher (*demi-cruche*) of wine; for each horse three bushels, Venetian measure, and water in sufficient quantities. We are not able to value the six setiers of corn, or the half-pitcher of wine, having no means of ascertaining the Venetian measures.

perils. The deputies were charged to endeavour to cause the conditions they had sworn to to be adopted by their brothers in arms, the barons and knights, by *the whole of their nation*, and *if possible, by their sovereign lord the king of France.* The treaty was written on parchment and sent immediately to Rome, to receive the approbation of the pope; and, full of confidence in the future, as well as in the alliance they had contracted, the French knights and the patricians of Venice exchanged the most touching protestations of friendship. The doge lent the barons the sum of ten thousand silver marks, and the latter swore never to forget the services the republic had rendered to Jesus Christ. "There were then shed," says Villehardouin, "many tears of tenderness and joy."

The government of Venice was a new spectacle for the French nobles; deliberations of the people were perfectly unknown to them, and must have struck them with astonishment. On the other side, the embassy of the knights and barons could not fail to flatter the pride of the Venetians; the latter felicitated themselves upon being thus acknowledged as the greatest maritime nation, and, never separating their glory from their commercial interests, rejoiced at having made so advantageous a bargain. The knights, on the contrary, only thought of honour and the cause of Christ; and although the treaty was ruinous to the Crusaders, they bore back the news to their companions in arms with the greatest joy and satisfaction.*

The preference given to the Venetians by the Crusaders naturally excited the jealousy of the other maritime powers of Italy; thus the French deputies, upon going to Pisa and Genoa to solicit the aid of the two republics in the name of Jesus Christ, met with a cold reception and a perfect indifference for the deliverance of the holy places.

The account of what had taken place at Venice, and the presence of the barons, did not fail, however, to arouse the enthusiasm of the inhabitants of Lombardy and Piedmont; a great number of them took the cross and arms, and promised to follow Boniface, marquis of Montferrat, to the Holy Land.

The marshal of Champagne, whilst crossing Mount Cenis, met Gauthier de Brienne, who had taken the cross at the castle of Ecry, and was on his way to Apulia. He had married one of the daughters of Tancred, last king of Sicily. Followed by sixty knights of Champagne, he was going to endeavour to make good the claims of his wife, and conquer the kingdom founded by the Norman knights. The marshal Villehardouin and Gauthier de Brienne congratulated each other upon the brilliant prospects of their expeditions, and promised to meet again in the plains of Egypt and Syria. Thus the future presented nothing to the knights of the cross but victories and trophies; and the hope of conquering distant kingdoms redoubled their ardour.

When the deputies arrived in Champagne, they found Thibault dangerously ill. The prince was so delighted at learning the success of their embassy, that, heedless of the disease that had confined him to his bed, he insisted upon putting on his armour and mounting on horseback; but "this was great pity and misfortune," says Villehardouin; "for the malady increased, and gathered such strength, that he declared his will, took leave of his friends, and got no more on horseback." Thibault, the model and hope of the Christian knights, died in the flower of his age, deeply regretted by his

* The author of the *History of the Republics of Italy* recapitulates thus the sum that was due to the Venetians by the Crusaders:—

For four thousand five hundred horses, at four marks per horse	18,000
For the knights, at two marks per knight	9,000
For twenty thousand foot-soldiers, at two marks per soldier	40,000
For two squires per horse, nine thousand squires	18,000
Total marks	85,000

Eighty-five thousand marks of silver are equal to $850,000.

vassals and companions in arms. He deplored before the barons the rigorous destiny that condemned him thus to die without glory, at the moment that he was about to gather the palms of victory or of martyrdom in the plains of the East; he exhorted them to perform the vow he had made to God to deliver Jerusalem, and left them all his treasures to be employed in this holy enterprise. An epitaph in Latin verse, which still exists, celebrates the virtues and pious zeal of Count Thibault, recalls the preparations for his pilgrimage, and terminates by saying, that this young prince *found the heavenly Jerusalem, when about to seek the earthly Jerusalem.*

After the death of the count of Champagne, the barons and kn ghts who had taken the cross assembled to choose another leader, and their election fell upon the count de Bar and the duke of Burgundy. The count de Bar refused to take the command of the Christian army. Eudes III., duke of Burgundy, still mourned the death of his father, who had died in Palestine after the third crusade, and could not be induced to quit his duchy to undertake the pilgrimage to the East. The refusal of these two princes was a subject of scandal for the soldiers of the cross; and contemporary history informs us that they afterwards repented of the indifference they had evinced for the cause of Christ. The duke of Burgundy, who died within a few years, was desirous of taking the cross on his bed of death, and, to expiate his fault, sent several of his warriors into Palestine.

The knights and barons then offered the command to Boniface marquis of Montferrat. Boniface belonged to a family of Christian heroes; his brother Conrad had rendered himself famous by the defence of Tyre, and he himself had already fought many times against the infidels: he did not hesitate in complying with the wishes of the Crusaders. He came to Soissons, where he received the cross from the hands of the curé of Neuilly, and was proclaimed leader of the crusade in the church of Notre Dame, in the presence of the clergy and the people.

Two years had passed away since the sovereign pontiff had ordered the bishops to preach the crusade in their dioceses. The situation of the Christians of the East became every day more deplorable; the kings of Jerusalem and Armenia, the patriarchs of Antioch and the holy city, and the grand masters of the military orders, addressed day after day their complaints and lamentations to the Holy See. Touched by their prayers, Innocent again exhorted the faithful, and conjured the Crusaders to hasten their departure; warmly censuring the indifference of those who, after having taken the cross, appeared to be forgetful of their vow. The Christian father, above all, reproached the ecclesiastics with their tardiness in paying the fortieth part of their revenues, destined to the expenses of the holy war; "and you and we," said he, "and all persons supported by the goods of the Church, ought we not all to fear that the inhabitants of Nineveh should appear against us at the day of judgment, and pronounce our condemnation? for they were made penitent by the preaching of Jonas; and you, not only you have not rent your hearts, you have not even opened your hands to succour Christ in his poverty, and repulse the opprobrium with which the infidels load him." The epoch of a holy war being for Christians a season of penitence, the sovereign pontiff proscribed, in his letters, sumptuousness in living, splendour in dress, and public amusements; and although the new crusade had been first preached at the tournament of Ecry, tournaments were in the number of diversions and spectacles forbidden to all Christians by the holy father during the space of five years.

To reanimate the courage and confidence of those who had taken the cross, Innocent told them of the new divisions that had sprung up among the Mussulman princes, and of the scourges with which God had recently afflicted Egypt. "God," cried the pontiff, "has struck the country of Babylon with the rod of his power; the Nile, that river of Paradise, which fertilizes the land of the Egyptians, has not had its accustomed course. This chastisement has given them up to death, and prepared the triumph of their enemies." The letters of the pope had the desired effect. The marquis of Montferrat went into France, towards the autumn of the year 1201, and the whole winter was devoted to preparations for the holy war. These preparations were unaccompanied by disorder, and the princes and barons refused to receive under their banners any but disciplined soldiers and men accustomed to the use of the lance and the sword. Some voices were raised against the Jews, whom they desired to force to contribute to the expenses of the holy war, but the pope took them under his protection, and threatened all who made attempts upon their lives or liberty with excommunication. The pope was satisfied with liberating the Crusaders from the usurious debts which they owed to the Jews. At that period all interest upon money lent was considered usury.

Before they left their homes, the Crusaders had to deplore the loss of the holy orator who had awakened their zeal and animated their courage. Foulques fell sick, and died in his parish of Neuilly. Some time before, loud murmurs had been heard respecting his conduct, and his words had ceased to exercise their accustomed power over the minds of his auditors. Foulques had received considerable sums of money destined for the expenses of the holy war, and as he was accused of appropriating these to his own use, the more money he amassed, says James of Vitri, the more consideration and credit he lost. The suspicions attached to his conduct were not, however, generally credited. The marshal of Champagne informs us, in his history, that the knights and barons were deeply affected by the death of the curé of Neuilly. Foulques was buried in the church of his parish with great pomp; his tomb, a monument of the piety of his contemporaries, attracted even in the last century, the respect and veneration of the faithful.

With the earliest days of spring the Crusaders prepared to quit their homes, "and knew," says Villehardouin, "that many tears were shed at their parting, and at taking leave of their relations and friends." The count of Flanders, the counts of Blois and St. Paul, followed by a great number of Flemish warriors and their vassals; the marshal of Champagne, accompanied by several Champenois knights, advanced across Burgundy, and passed the Alps to repair to Venice. The Marquis Boniface soon joined them, bringing with him the Crusaders of Lombardy, Piedmont, Savoy, and the countries situated between the Alps and the Rhone. Venice also received within its walls the warriors from the banks of the Rhine, some under the command of the bishop of Halberstadt, and others under that of Martin-Litz, who had persuaded them to take arms, and still continued to animate them by the example of his virtues and piety.

When the Crusaders reached Venice, the fleet that was to transport them into Asia was ready to set sail: they were at first received with every demonstration of joy; but amidst the festivities that followed their arrival, the Venetians called upon the barons to redeem their word, and pay the sum agreed upon for transporting the Christian army; and then it was that, with deep grief, the barons became aware of the absence of a great number of their companions in arms. Jean de Nesle, châtelain of Bruges, and Thierri, son of Philip, count of Flanders, had promised Baldwin to bring to him, at Venice, Marguerite, his wife, and a chosen band of Flemish warriors; they did not keep their appointment, for having embarked upon the ocean, they had directed their course to Palestine. Renaud de Dampierre, to whom Thibault, count of Champagne, had left all his treasures to be employed in the voyage to the Holy Land, had embarked with a great number of Champenois knights at the port of Bari. The bishop of Autun, Gilles, count of Ferez, and several other leaders, after having sworn upon the Gospel to join the other Crusaders, had set out from Marseilles, and others from Genoa. Thus half the Crusaders did not come to Venice, which had been agreed upon as the general rendezvous of the Christian army: "by which," says Villehardouin, "they received great shame, and many misadventures afterwards befell them in consequence of it."

This breach of faith might prove very injurious to the enterprise; but what most grieved the princes and barons assembled at Venice, was the impossibility of fulfilling their engagements with the republic without the concurrence of their unfaithful companions. They sent messengers into all parts to warn the Crusaders that had set out, and to implore them to join the main army; but whether most of the pilgrims were dissatisfied with the agreement entered into with the Venetians, or whether it appeared to them more convenient and safe to embark at ports in their own vicinity, a very small number of them could be prevailed upon to repair to Venice. Those who were already in that city, were neither sufficiently numerous nor sufficiently rich to pay the promised amount, or fulfil the engagements made in their names. Although the Venetians were more interested in the crusade than the French knights, as they possessed a part of the cities of Tyre and Ptolemaïs, which they were going to defend, they were unwilling to make any sacrifice, and the barons, on their side, were too proud to ask any favour, or to solicit the Venetians to change or moderate the conditions of the treaty. Each of the Crusaders was required to pay the price of his passage. The rich paid for the poor; soldiers as well as knights being eager to give all the money they possessed, persuaded, they said, that God was powerful enough to return it to them a hundred-fold, when it should please him. The count of Flanders, the counts of Blois and St. Paul, the marquis of Montferrat, and several other leaders despoiled themselves of their plate, their jewels, and everything they had that was most valuable, and only retained their horses and arms. Notwithstanding this noble sacrifice, the Crusaders still were indebted to the republic a sum of fifty thousand silver marks. The doge then assembled the people, and represented to them that it was not honourable to employ too much rigour; and proposed to demand of the Crusaders the assistance of their army for the republic, until they could discharge their debt.

The city of Zara had been for a length of time under the dominion of the Venetians; but thinking the government of a king less insupportable than that of a republic, it had given itself up to the king of Hungary, and, under the protection of a new master, braved the authority and menaces of Venice. After having obtained the approbation of the people, Dandolo proposed to the Crusaders to assist the republic in subduing a revolted city, and promised to put off the entire execution of the treaty until God, by their common conquests, should have given them the means of fulfilling their promises. This proposition was received with much joy by the greater part of the Crusaders, who could not support the idea of being unable to keep their word; the barons and knights deemed it prudent to conciliate the Venetians, who were so serviceable to them in carrying out their enterprise, and thought they did but little to pay their debts by an affair in which they should expend nothing but their blood.

Some murmurs, however, arose in the Christian army; many of the Crusaders recollected the oath they had taken to fight the infidels, and could not make up their minds to turn their arms against a Christian people. The pope had sent the Cardinal Peter of Capua to Venice, to deter the pilgrims from an enterprise which he termed sacrilegious. "The king of Hungary had taken the cross, and by doing so had placed himself under the especial protection of the Church; and to attack a city belonging to him was to declare themselves enemies of the Church itself." Henry Dandolo braved menaces and reproaches that he deemed to be unjust. "The privileges of the Crusaders," said he, "could not screen the guilty from the severity of laws divine and human. Crusades were not undertaken to promote the ambition of kings or protect rebellious nations. The pope had not the power to enchain the authority of sovereigns, or turn the Crusaders aside from a legitimate enterprise; from a war made against revolted subjects, against pirates whose brigandage perilled the freedom of the seas, and jeopardized the safety of pilgrims on their way to the Holy Land."

To complete his conquest over all scruples, and dissipate all fears, the doge resolved to associate himself with the perils and labours of the crusade, and to engage his fellow-citizens to declare themselves the companions in arms of the Crusaders. The people being solemnly convoked, Dandolo ascended the pulpit of St. Mark, and demanded of the assembled Venetians permission to take the cross. "Seigneurs," said he to them, "you have made an engagement to concur in the most glorious of enterprises; the warriors with whom you have contracted a holy alliance, surpass all other men in piety and valour. For myself, you see that I am laden with years, and have need of repose; but the glory that is promised to us restores me courage and strength to brave all the perils, to support all the labours of war. I feel by the ardour that leads me on, by the zeal which animates me, that nobody will merit your confidence, nobody will conduct you so well as the man you have chosen as head of your republic. If you will permit me to fight for Jesus Christ, and allow my son to perform the duties you have confided to me, I will go and live or die with you and the pilgrims."

At this discourse his whole auditory was much affected, and the people loudly applauded the resolution of the doge. Dandolo descended from the tribunal, and was led in triumph to the foot of the altar, where the cross was attached to his ducal cap. A great number of Venetians followed his example, and swore to die for the deliverance of the holy places. By this skilful policy, the doge completely won the Crusaders, and placed himself, in a manner, at the head of the crusade. He soon found himself sufficiently powerful to deny the authority of the cardinal of Capua, who spoke in the name of the pope, and pretended to have a right to direct the holy war, in his character of legate of the Holy See. Dandolo told the envoy of Innocent, that the Christian army stood in no need of leaders to conduct it, and that the legates of the sovereign pontiff ought to content themselves with edifying the Crusaders by their examples and discourses.

This bold, free language very much astonished the French barons, accustomed to respect the will of the Holy See; but the doge, by taking the cross, had inspired them with a confidence nothing could shake. The cross of the pilgrims was, for the Venetians and French, a pledge of alliance, a sacred tie, which united all their interests, and made of them, in a manner, but one same nation. From that time no one listened to those who spoke in the name of the Holy See, or persisted in raising scruples in the minds of the Crusaders. The barons and knights showed the same zeal and ardour for the expedition against Zara as the Venetians themselves. The army of the Crusaders was ready to embark, when there happened, says Villehardouin, "a great wonder, an unhoped-for circumstance, the strangest that ever was heard of."

Isaac, emperor of Constantinople, had been dethroned by his brother Alexius. Abandoned by all his friends, deprived of sight, and loaded with irons, this unhappy prince languished in a dungeon. The son of Isaac, named also Alexius, who shared the captivity of his father, having deceived the vigilance of his guards and broken his chains, had fled into the West, in the hope that the princes and kings would one day undertake his defence, and declare war against the usurper of the imperial throne. Philip of Swabia, who had married Irene, the daughter of Isaac, received the young prince kindly; but he was not then in a position to undertake anything in his favour, being fully engaged in defending himself against the arms of Otho and the menaces of the Holy See. Young Alexius next in vain threw himself at the feet of the pope, to implore his assistance. Whether the pontiff saw in the son of Isaac only the brother-in-law of Philip of Swabia, then considered an enemy to the court of Rome, or whether all his attention was directed towards the East, he gave no ear to the complaints of Alexius, and seemed to dread countenancing a war against Greece. The fugitive prince had in vain solicited most of the Christian monarchs, when he was advised to address himself to the Crusaders, the noblest warriors of the West. The arrival of his ambassadors created a lively sensation at Venice; the knights and barons were impressed with generous pity by the account of his misfortunes; they had never defended a more glorious cause. To avenge injured innocence, to remedy a great calamity, stirred the spirit of Dandolo; and the proud republicans, whose head he was, feelingly deplored the fate of a fugitive emperor. They had not forgotten that the usurper preferred to an alliance with them one with the Genoese and Pisans; it appeared to them that the cause of Alexius was their own, and that their vessels ought to bear him back to the ports of Greece and Byzantium.

Nevertheless, as everything was prepared for the conquest of Zara, the decision of this business was deferred to a more favourable opportunity; and the fleet, with the Crusaders on board, set sail amidst the sounds of martial music and the acclamation of the whole population of Venice. Never had a fleet so numerous or so magnificently equipped been seen in the Adriatic Gulf. The sea was covered with four hundred and eighty ships; the number of the combatants, horse and foot, amounted to forty thousand men. After having subdued Trieste and some other maritime cities of Istria that had shaken off the yoke of Venice, the Crusaders arrived before Zara on the 10th day of November, 1202, the eve of St. Martin. Zara, situated on the eastern side of the Adriatic Gulf, sixty leagues from Venice, and five leagues north of Jadera, an ancient Roman colony, was a rich and populous city, fortified by high walls, and surrounded by a sea studded with rocks. The king of Hungary had sent troops to defend it, and the inhabitants had sworn to bury themselves beneath the ruins of the place rather than surrender to the Venetians. At the sight of the ramparts of the city, the Crusaders perceived all the difficulty of the enterprise, and the party opposed to this war again ventured to murmur. The leaders, however, gave the signal for the assault. As soon as the chains of the port were broken, and the machines began to make the walls shake, the inhabitants forgot the resolution they had formed of dying in defence of their ramparts, and, filled with dread, sent deputies to the doge, who promised to pardon them on account of their repentance. But the deputies charged with the petition for peace, met with several Crusaders among the besiegers, who said to them, "Why did you surrender? you have nothing to fear from the French?" These imprudent words rekindled the war; the deputies, on their return, announced to the inhabitants that all the Crusaders were not their enemies, and that Zara would preserve its liberty if the people and soldiers were willing to defend it. The party of the malcontents, whose object was to divide the army, seized this opportunity for reviving their complaints; the most ardent amongst them, insinuating themselves into the tents of the soldiers, and endeavouring to disgust them with a war which they termed impious.

Guy, abbot of Vaux de Cernai, of the order of Citeaux, made himself conspicuous by his endeavours to secure the failure of the enterprise against Zara; everything that could divert the march of the Crusaders from the route to the holy places, was, in his eyes, an attack upon religion. The most brilliant exploits, if not performed in the cause of Christ, could command neither his esteem nor his approbation. The abbot of Cernai was deficient in neither subtlety nor eloquence, and knew how to employ both prayers and menaces effectively; he had that influence over the pilgrims that an inflexible mind and an ardent, obstinate character always obtains over the multitude. In a council, he arose, and forbade the Crusaders to draw their swords against Christians, and was about to read a letter from the pope, when he was interrupted by threats and cries.

Amidst the tumult which followed in the council and the army, the abbot of Cernai would have been in danger of his life, if the count de Montfort, who partook his sentiments, had not drawn his sword in his defence. The barons and knights could not, however, forget the promise they had made to fight for the republic of Venice; nor could they think of laying down their arms in presence of an enemy that had promised to surrender, and who now defied their attacks. The greater the efforts of the count de Montfort and the abbot of Cernai to interrupt the war, the more they conceived their honour and glory to be engaged to continue the siege they had begun. Whilst the malcontents were giving vent to their scruples and complaints, the bravest of the army proceeded to the assault. The besieged, whose hopes were built upon the divisions among their enemies, placed crosses upon the walls, persuaded that this revered sign would protect them more effectually than their machines of war; but they were not long in finding that there was no safety for them except in submission. On the fifth day of the siege, without having offered their enemies any serious resistance, they opened their gates, and only obtained from the conqueror liberty and life. The city was given up to pillage, and the booty divided between the Venetians and the French.

One of the results of this conquest was a fresh quarrel in the victorious army, in which more blood flowed than had been shed during the siege. The season being too far advanced to allow the fleet to put to sea, the doge proposed to the Crusaders to winter at Zara. The two nations occupied different quarters of the city; but as the Venetians had chosen the handsomest and most commodious houses, the French loudly proclaimed their dissatisfaction. After a few complaints and many threats, they had recourse to arms, and every street became the theatre of a conflict; the inhabitants of Zara beheld with delight the sanguinary disputes of their conquerors. The partisans of the abbot of Cernai applauded in secret the deplorable consequences of a war they had condemned; whilst the doge of Venice and the barons employed every effort to separate the combatants. Their prayers and threats at first had no effect in appeasing this horrible tumult, which was prolonged to the middle of the night. On the morrow, all the passions that divided the army were near breaking out with increased fury. Whilst interring their dead, the French and Venetians renewed their disputes and menaces. The leaders were, for more than a week, in despair of being able to calm the irritated spirits of their followers, and reunite the soldiers of the two nations. Scarcely was order re-established when a letter was received from the pope, who disapproved of the capture of Zara, ordered the Crusaders to renounce the booty they had made in a Christian city, and to engage themselves, by a solemn vow, to repair the injuries they had inflicted. Innocent reproached the Venetians bitterly with having seduced the soldiers of Christ into this impious and sacrilegious war. This letter from the pope was received with respect by the French, with disdain by the Crusaders of Venice. The latter openly refused to bow to the decisions of the Holy See; and to secure the fruits of their victory, began to demolish the ramparts of Zara. The French barons could not endure the idea of having incurred the anger of the pope, and sent deputies to Rome to endeavour to mitigate the displeasure of his holiness, and solicit their pardon, alleging that they had only obeyed the law of necessity. The greater part of them, though fully determined to retain all they had obtained, promised the pope to restore their spoils: they undertook, by a solemn act, addressed to all Christians, to repair the wrongs they had done, and to merit by their conduct pardon for past errors. Their submission, far more than their promises, disarmed the anger of the pope, who replied to them with mildness, and commanded the leaders to salute the knights and pilgrims, giving them absolution and his benediction, as to his children. He exhorted them, in his letter, to set out for Syria, *without turning to the right or the left;* and permitting them to cross the sea with the Venetians, whom he had just excommunicated,* *but only from necessity, and with bitterness of heart.* If the Venetians persisted in their disobedience, the sovereign pontiff advised the barons, when they arrived in Palestine, to separate themselves from a people reproved of God, for fear of bringing a malediction upon the Christian

* The pope adds, whilst speaking of the Venetians: "Excommunicated as they are, they still remained tied by their promises; and you are not the less authorized to require the performance of them; it is further a maxim of right, that in passing over the land of a heretic or an excommunicated person, you may buy or receive necessary things from him. Moreover, excommunication denounced against the father of a family, does not prevent his household from communicating with him."

army, as formerly Achan had brought down the divine wrath upon the Israelites. Innocent promised the Crusaders to protect them in their expedition, and to watch over their wants during the perils of the holy war. "In order that you may not want provisions," said he to them, "we will write to the emperor of Constantinople to furnish you with them, as he has promised; if that be refused to you which is refused to none, it will not be unjust, if, after the example of many holy persons, you take provisions wherever you may find them; for it will be known that you are devoted to the cause of Christ, to whom all the world belongs."* These counsels and these promises, which so completely reveal to us the spirit of the thirteenth century and the policy of the Holy See, were received by the knights and barons as evidence of the paternal goodness of the sovereign pontiff: but the face of things was about again to change; and fortune, which sported with the decisions of the pope as well as those of the pilgrims, was not long in giving an entirely new direction to the events of the crusade.

Ambassadors from Philip of Swabia, brother-in-law of young Alexius, arrived at Zara, and addressed the council of the lords and barons, assembled in the palace of the doge of Venice. "Seigneurs," said they, "the puissant king of the Romans sends us to recommend to you the young prince Alexius, and to place him in your hands, under the safeguard of God. We do not come for the purpose of turning you aside from your holy enterprise, but to offer you an easy and a certain means of accomplishing your noble designs. We know that you have only taken up arms for the love of Christ and of justice; we come, therefore, to propose to you to assist those who are oppressed by unjust tyranny, and to secure at once the triumph of the laws of religion and humanity: we propose to you to turn your victorious arms towards the capital of Greece, which groans under the rod of an usurper, and to assure yourselves for ever of the conquest of Jerusalem by that of Constantinople. You know, as well as we do, how many evils our fathers, the companions of Godfrey, Conrad, and Louis the Young, suffered from having left behind them a powerful empire, the conquest and submission of which would have become a source of victories to their arms. What have you not now to dread from this Alexius, more cruel and more perfidious than his predecessors, who has gained a throne by parricide, who has, at once, betrayed the laws of religion and nature, and whose only means of escaping from the punishment due to his crime is by allying himself with the Saracens? We will not tell you how easy a matter it would be to wrest the empire from the hands of a tyrant hated by his subjects, for your valour loves obstacles and delights in dangers; nor will we spread before your eyes the riches of Byzantium and Greece, for your generous souls aim at nothing in this conquest, but the glory of your arms and the cause of Jesus Christ.

"If you overturn the power of the usurper in order that the legitimate sovereign may reign, the son of Isaac promises, under the faith of oaths the most inviolable, to maintain, during a year, both your fleet and your army, and to pay you two hundred thousand silver marks towards the expenses of the war. He will accompany you in person in the conquest of Syria or Egypt; and if you think proper, will furnish ten thousand men, as his portion of the armament; and, moreover, will maintain, during the whole of his life, five hundred knights in the Holy Land. But that which must weigh above all other considerations, with warriors and Christian heroes, is that Alexius is willing to swear, on the holy Gospel, to put an end to the heresy which now defiles the empire of the East, and to subject the Greek Church to the Church of Rome. So many advantages being attached to the enterprise proposed to you, we feel confident you will listen to our prayers. We see in Holy Writ that

---

* This permission to live by pillage, even in a friendly country, is remarkable, particularly as the pope pretends to authorize it by examples from Scripture.—*Fleury, Hist. Eccl.* book lxxv.

Innocent, in giving the Crusaders permission to take provisions wherever they may find them, adds, "Provided it be with the fear of God, without doing injury to any person, and with a resolution to make restitution."

God sometimes employed men the most simple and the most obscure to make known his will to his chosen people; on this occasion, it is a young prince he has appointed the instrument of his designs; it is Alexius that Providence has commissioned to lead you in the way of the Lord, and to point out to you the road you must follow to render certain the triumph of the armies of Jesus Christ."

This discourse made a strong impression upon a great number of the knights and barons, but it did not command the suffrages of the whole assembly. The doge and the lords dismissed the ambassadors, telling them they would deliberate upon the proposals of Alexius. Warm debates then ensued in the council; those that had been averse to the siege of Zara, among whom the abbot of Vaux de Cernai was still conspicuous, opposed the expedition to Constantinople with great vehemence; they were indignant that the interests of God should be placed in the balance against those of Alexius; they added that this Isaac, whose cause they were called upon to defend, was himself an usurper, elevated by a revolution to the throne of the Comnenas; that he had been, during the third crusade, the most cruel enemy of the Christians, the most faithful ally of the Turks; as for the rest, the nations of Greece, accustomed to the change of masters, supported the usurpation of Alexius without murmuring, and the Latins had not quitted their homes to avenge the injuries of a people that really did not call upon them for aid.

The same orators further said, that Philip of Swabia exhorted the Crusaders to assist Alexius, but was content himself with making speeches and sending ambassadors; they warned the Christians not to trust to the promises of a young prince, who engaged to furnish armies, and had not a single soldier; who offered treasures, and possessed nothing; who, besides, had been brought up amongst the Greeks, and would, most likely, some day turn his arms against his benefactors. "If you are so sensible to misfortune," added they, "and impatient to defend the cause of justice and humanity, listen to the groans of our brethren in Palestine, who are menaced by the Saracens, and who have no earthly hope but in your courage." They moreover told the Crusaders, that if they wished for easy victories and brilliant conquests, they had but to turn their eyes towards Egypt, the population of which was at that moment devoured by a horrible famine, and which the seven plagues of Scripture yielded up to the arms of the Christians almost without defence.

The Venetians, who had cause of complaint against the emperor of Constantinople, were not at all affected by these arguments, and appeared much more inclined to make war upon the Greeks than the infidels; they were anxious to destroy the warehouses of their rivals the Pisans, now established in Greece, and to see their ships crossing the straits of the Bosphorus in triumph. Their doge nourished a keen resentment on account of some personal offence; and to inflame the minds of his compatriots, he magnified all the wrongs inflicted by the Greeks on his own country and the Christians of the West.

If ancient chronicles may be believed, Dandolo was impelled by another motive, which he did not avow before the Crusaders. The sultan of Damascus, made aware of a Christian army being assembled at Venice, and terrified at the crusade that was preparing, had sent a considerable treasure to the republic, to engage it to divert the Crusaders from an expedition into the East. Whether we yield faith to this account, or whether we consider it as a fable invented by hatred and party spirit, such assertions, collected by contemporaries, at least prove that violent suspicions were then entertained against the Venetians by the dissatisfied Crusaders, and particularly by the Christians of Syria, justly irritated at not being assisted by the soldiers of the cross. Nevertheless, we feel bound to add that the majority of the French Crusaders stood in no need of being stimulated by the example or speeches of the doge, to undertake a war against the Greek empire. Even those who opposed the new expedition the most strongly, as well as all the other Crusaders, entertained an inveterate hatred and a sovereign contempt for the Greeks; and the discussions had only the more inflamed the general mind against a nation considered inimical to the Christians.

Several ecclesiastics, having at their head the abbot of Looz, a personage remarkable for his piety and the purity of his manners, did not accord in opinion with the abbot of Vaux de Cernai, and maintained that there was much danger in leading an army into a country devastated by famine; that Greece presented much greater advantages to the Crusaders than Egypt, and that there could be no doubt that the conquest of Constantinople was the most certain means of securing to the Christians the possession of Jerusalem. These ecclesiastics were particularly fascinated by the hope of one day seeing the Greek Church united to that of Rome, and they constantly announced in their discourses the approaching period of concord and peace among all Christian people.

Many knights contemplated with satisfaction the prospect of the union of the two churches, likely to be brought about by their arms; but they yielded further to motives not less powerful over their minds; they had sworn to defend innocence and the rights of the oppressed, and they believed they performed their duty in embracing the cause of Alexius. Some of them, without doubt, who had heard of the vast wealth of Byzantium, might believe that they should not return from such a brilliant undertaking empty handed; but such was the spirit of the lords and knights, that by far the greater number were attracted by the mere prospect of the perils, and still more by the wonders of the enterprise. After a long deliberation, it was decided in the council of the Crusaders that the proposals of Alexius should be accepted, and that the Christian army should embark for Constantinople at the commencement of spring.

Before the siege of Zara, the report of the armament of the Crusaders, and of an expedition against Greece, had reached the court of Byzantium. The usurper of the throne of Isaac immediately sought for means to avert the storm about to fall upon his states, and hastened to send ambassadors to the pope, whom he considered the arbiter of peace and war in the West. These ambassadors were ordered to declare to the sovereign pontiff that the prince who reigned at Constantinople was the only legitimate emperor; that the son of Isaac had no right to the empire; that an expedition against Greece would be an unjust enterprise, dangerous, and adverse to the great designs of the crusade. The pope, in his reply, did not at all seek to calm the fears of the usurper, but told his envoys that young Alexius had numerous partisans among the Crusaders, because he had made a promise to succour the Holy Land in person, and to put an end to the rebellion of the Greek Church. The pope did not approve of the expedition against Constantinople; but, by speaking in the way he did, he thought that the sovereign who then reigned over Greece might be induced to make the same promises as the fugitive prince, and would be more able to fulfil them; he conceived a hope that they might treat advantageously, without having recourse to the sword, and that the debates concerning the empire of the East would be referred to his supreme tribunal. But the elder Alexius, whether he was persuaded that he had sufficiently interested the pope in his cause, or whether he deemed it most prudent not to appear alarmed, or, in short, whether the prospect of a distant danger could not remove his habitual indolence, sent no more ambassadors, and made not the least exertion to prepare against the invasion of the warriors of the West.

In another direction, the king of Jerusalem and the Christians of Palestine never ceased to give vent to their complaints, and to implore the assistance that the head of the Church had promised them. The pope, much affected by their prayers, and always zealous for the crusade he had preached, renewed his efforts to direct the arms of the Crusaders against the Saracens. He sent the cardinals, Peter of Capua, and Siffred, into Palestine, as legates of the Holy See, to revive the courage of the Christians, and announce to them the approaching departure of the army of Crusaders; but when he learnt that the leaders had determined upon attacking the empire of Constantinople, he poured upon them the most bitter reprimands, and reproached them with *looking behind them*, as Lot's wife had done. "Let none among you," said he, "flatter himself that he may be allowed to invade or plunder the lands of the Greeks, under the pretence that the empire is not sufficiently submissive, or that the emperor has usurped the throne of his brother; whatever crime he may have committed, it is not for you to constitute yourself the judge of it: you did not assume the cross to avenge the injuries of princes, but that of God."

Innocent finished his letter without bestowing his benediction upon the Crusaders; and, to frighten them from their new enterprise, threatened them with the maledictions of Heaven. The barons and knights received the remonstrances of the sovereign pontiff with respect; but did not at all waver in the resolution they had formed.

Then the opponents of the expedition to Constantinople renewed their complaints, and employed no sort of moderation in their discourses. The abbot of Vaux de Cernai, the abbot Martin Litz, one of the preachers of the crusade, the count de Montfort, and a great number of knights employed every effort to shake the determination of the army; and when they found they could not succeed, resolved to leave them, some to return to their homes, and others to take the route to Palestine. Those who abandoned their colours, and those who remained in the camp, mutually accused each other with betraying the cause of Christ. Five hundred soldiers having thrown themselves on board a vessel, were shipwrecked and all swallowed up by the waves; many others, in crossing Illyria, were massacred by the savage inhabitants of that country. These perished cursing the ambition and errors which had turned the Christian army aside from the true object of the crusade; whilst those who remained faithful to their standards, deplored the tragical death of their companions, saying among themselves: "*The mercy of the Lord has remained with us; evil be to them who stray from the way of the Lord.*"

The knights and barons regretted in secret that they had not been able to obtain the approbation of the pope, but were persuaded that, by means of victories, they should justify their conduct in the eyes of the Holy See; and that the father of the faithful would recognise in their conquests the expression of the will of Heaven.

The Crusaders were upon the point of embarking, when young Alexius himself arrived at Zara. His presence created a fresh enthusiasm for his cause; he was received amidst the sounds of trumpets and clarions, and presented to the army by the marquis of Montferrat, whose elder brothers had been connected by marriage and the dignity of Cæsar, with the imperial family of Constantinople. The barons hailed young Alexius as emperor, with the greater joy, that they hoped his future grandeur would be the work of their hands. Alexius took arms to break the chains of his father, and they admired in him a most touching model of Christian piety: he was about to combat usurpation, to punish injustice, and stifle heresy, and they looked upon him as an envoy of Providence. The misfortunes of princes destined to reign affect us more sensibly than those of other men; in the camp of the Crusaders, the soldiers talked over the story of Alexius among themselves, and they pitied his youth, and deplored his exile and the captivity of Isaac. Alexius, accompanied by the princes and barons, went constantly among the soldiery, and replied by demonstrations of the warmest gratitude to the generous interest the Crusaders evinced in his favour.

Animated by sentiments which misfortune inspires, and which not unfrequently terminate with it, the young prince was lavish of vows and protestations, and promised even more than he had done by his envoys, without thinking that he placed himself under the necessity of failing in his word, and drawing upon himself, one day, the reproaches of his liberators.

The Crusaders, however, renewed every day their vow to place young Alexius on the throne of Constantinople; and Italy and the whole West rung with the fame of their preparations. The emperor of Byzantium appeared to be the only person ignorant of the war declared against his usurped power, and slept upon a throne ready to crumble from under him.

The emperor Alexius, like the greater part of his predecessors, was a prince without virtues or character; when he deposed his brother, he allowed the crime to be committed by his courtiers, and when he was upon the throne he abandoned to them the charge of his authority. He was lavish of the treasures of the state, to secure pardon and oblivion for his usurpation; and, to repair his finances, he sold justice, ruined his subjects, and plundered the merchant ships that traded between Ramisa and Constantinople. The usurper scattered dignities and honours with such profusion, that no one thought himself honoured by them, and there remained in his hands no true reward for merit. Alexius had associated his wife Euphrosyne with himself in the sovereign authority, and she filled the empire with her intrigues, and scandalized the court by the laxity of her morals. Under his reign the empire had been several times menaced by the Bulgarians and the Turks; Alexius occasionally visited the army, but he never faced the enemy. Whilst the Bulgarians were ravaging his frontiers, he employed himself in levelling hills, and tracing gardens on the shores of the Propontis. Abandoned to a shameful effeminacy, he disbanded a part of his army; and fearing to be disturbed in his pleasures by the din of arms, he sold the sacred vases, and plundered the tombs of the Greek emperors, to purchase peace of the emperor of Germany, who had become master of Sicily. The empire had no navy left; the ministers had sold the rigging and equipments of the vessels, and the woods, that might have furnished timber for new ships, were reserved for the pleasures of the prince, and guarded as strictly, says Nicetas, as those formerly consecrated to the gods.

Such numbers of conspiracies never were heard of; under a prince who was rarely visible, the government appeared to be in a state of interregnum; the imperial throne was as an empty seat, which every ambitious man aspired to occupy. Devotedness, probity, bravery, were no longer held in esteem by courtiers or citizens. Nothing was deemed worthy of public approbation or reward but the invention of a new pleasure or the fabrication of a fresh impost. Amidst this general depravity, the provinces knew nothing of the emperor but by the exaction of taxes; and the army, without discipline and without pay, had no leaders capable of commanding it. Everything announced an approaching revolution in the empire; and the peril was the greater from no one having the courage to foresee it. The subjects of Alexius never dreamt of obtruding truth upon the imperial ear; birds, taught to repeat satires, alone interrupted the silence of the people, and published from the roofs of houses, and in the high streets, the scandals of the court and the disgrace of the empire.

The Greeks, at the same time superstitious and corrupt, still preserved some remembrances of ancient Greece and old Rome; but these remembrances, instead of creating a noble, emulative pride, only nourished in their hearts a puerile vanity, and their history, of which they were so vain, only served to render more striking their own degradation and their empire's too evident decay. The voice of patriotism was never heard, and no influence was obeyed but that of the monks placed at the head of affairs of all kinds, who attracted and preserved the confidence of both people and prince by frivolous predictions and senseless visions. The Greeks wasted their time in vain disputes, which enervated their character, increased their ignorance, and stifled their patriotism. At the moment the fleet of the Crusaders was about to set sail, Constantinople was in a state of ferment with discussing the question whether the body of Jesus Christ, in the Eucharist, is corruptible or incorruptible; each opinion had its partisans, whose defeats or triumphs were, by turns, loudly proclaimed—and the threatened empire remained without defenders.

The Venetians and French left Zara, and the isle of Corfu was appointed as the place of meeting for the whole fleet. When they landed on the shores of Macedon, the inhabitants of Duras brought young Alexius the keys of the city, and acknowledged him as their master. The people of Corfu were not tardy in following this example, and received the Crusaders as liberators: the acclamations of the Greek people, in the passage of the Latins, was a happy augury for the success of their expedition.

The island of Corfu, the country of the Phœnicians, so celebrated by the shipwreck of Ulysses and by the gardens of Alcinoüs, afforded the Crusaders pasturage and abundance of provisions. The fertility of the island induced the leaders to remain there several weeks; but so long a repose did not fail to produce evil consequences in an army supported by enthusiasm, to which no time for reflection should have been allowed, and, amidst indulgence and idleness, the complaints and murmurs of the siege of Zara broke out again.

They learnt that Gauthier de Brienne had conquered Apulia and the kingdom of Naples. This conquest, effected in a few months, by sixty knights, inflamed the imagination of the Crusaders, and furnished the malcontents with a fresh opportunity for blaming the expedition to Constantinople, the preparations for which were immense, the perils evident, and the success uncertain. "Whilst we are going," said they, "to exhaust the resources of the West in a useless enterprise, in a distant war, Gauthier de Brienne has made himself master of a rich kingdom, and is preparing to fulfil the promises he has entered into with us to deliver the Holy Land; why should we not demand vessels of him? why should we not set out for Palestine with him?" These speeches prevailed over a great number of the knights, who were ready to separate themselves from the army.

The chief malcontents had already assembled in a secluded valley to deliberate upon the means of executing their project, when the leaders of the army were warned of their plot, and immediately united all their efforts to prevent the fatal consequences of it. The doge of Venice, the count of Flanders, the counts of Blois and St. Paul, the marquis of Montferrat, and several bishops clothed in mourning habits, with crosses borne before them, repaired to the valley in which the malcontents were met. As soon as they, from a distance, perceived their unfaithful companions, who were deliberating on horseback, they alighted, and advanced towards the place of assembly in a suppliant manner. The instigators of the desertion, seeing the leaders and prelates of the army coming thus towards them, suspended their deliberations, and themselves dismounted from their horses. The parties approached each other; the princes, counts, and bishops threw themselves at the feet of the malcontents, and, bursting into tears, swore to remain thus prostrated till the warriors who wished to abandon them, had renewed the oath to follow the army of the Christians, and to remain faithful to the standard of the holy war. "When the others saw," says Villehardouin, an ocular witness, "when they saw their liege lords, their dearest relations and friends, thus cast themselves at their feet, and, so to say, cry to them for mercy, they were moved with great pity, and their hearts were so softened, they could not refrain from weeping, and they told them that they would consider of it together (*Qu'ils s'en aviseraient par ensemble*)." After having retired for a moment to deliberate, they came back to their leaders, and promised to remain with the army until the beginning of autumn, on condition that the barons and lords would swear upon the Gospel to furnish them at that period with vessels to convey them to Syria. The two parties engaged themselves by oath to perform the conditions of the treaty, and returned together to the camp, where nothing now was spoken of but the expedition to Constantinople.

The fleet of the Crusaders quitted the island of Corfu under the most happy auspices; the historians who have described its progress through that archipelago, so full of remembrances of antiquity, have not been able to refrain from employing the language of poetry. The wind was favourable, and the sky pure and serene; a profound calm reigned over the waves; three hundred vessels of all sizes, with their colours floating from their sterns, covered an immense space; the helmets and cuirasses of thirty thousand warriors reflected the rays of the sun; now were heard sounding over the waters the hymns of the priests, invoking the blessings of Heaven; and then the voices of the soldiers, soothing the leisure of the voyage with warlike songs; and the braying of trumpets and neighing of horses, mingled with the dashing of oars, resounded from the coasts of the Peloponnesus, which presented themselves to the eyes of the pilgrims. The Crusaders doubled Cape Matapan, known formerly as Tenara, and passed before the heights of Malea, without dread of the rocks so much feared by ancient navigators. Near Cape Malea they met two vessels returning from Palestine, in which were many Flemish pilgrims. At sight of the Venetian fleet, a soldier on board one of the two ships, slipped down a rope, and bade adieu to his companions, saying: "*I leave you all I have on board, for I am going with people who intend to conquer kingdoms.*"

The Crusaders landed at several islands they fell in with on their passage; the inhabitants of Andros and Negropont came out to meet Alexius, and acknowledged him as their emperor. It was the period of harvest, and the land presented, everywhere, a spectacle of the richest abundance. The enjoyment of a beautiful climate, the satisfaction at the submission of the Greeks, so many riches, so many wonders, so many unknown regions, all daily increased the enthusiasm of the Crusaders. At length the fleet arrived at the entrance of the Bosphorus, and cast anchor in the port of St. Stephen, three leagues from the capital of the Greek empire.

Then the city of Constantinople, of which they were about to effect the conquest, broke full upon the view of the Crusaders; bathed on the south by the waves of the Propontis, on the east by the Bosphorus, and on the north by the gulf that serves as its port, it presented a spectacle at once magnificent and formidable. A double enclosure of walls surrounded it in a circumference of more than seven leagues; a vast number of splendid buildings, whose roofs towered above the ramparts, appeared to proclaim the queen of cities. The shores of the Bosphorus to the Euxine and to the Hellespont, resembled an immense faubourg, or one continued line of gardens. The cities of Chalcedon and Scutari, built on the Asiatic shore, and Galata, placed at the extremity of the gulf, appeared in the distance, and crowned the immense and magnificent picture which lay before the warlike hosts of the Crusaders.

Constantinople, situated between Europe and Asia, between the Archipelago and the Black Sea, joins together the two seas and the two continents. In the times of its splendour, it held at its pleasure the gates of commerce open or shut; its port, which received the vessels of all the nations of the world, deserved to be termed by the Greeks, *the golden horn*, or *the horn of abundance*. Like ancient Rome, Constantinople extended over seven ascents, and, like the city of Romulus, it sometimes bore the name of the city of the seven hills; in the times of the crusades, its walls and its towers were compared to those of Babylon; its deep ditches were converted at will into a large and rapid lake, and the city could, at the least signal, be surrounded by waters, and separated from the continent.

The monarch who founded it reigned over all the known nations of the world, and in the execution of his designs he had the advantage of making the arts and sciences of Greece concur with the genius and power of the Romans. Not content with employing the beautiful marbles of the isles of the Archipelago, he caused materials to be transported from the extremities of Europe and Asia; all the cities of the Roman empire, Athens, and Rome itself, were spoiled of their ornaments to embellish the new city of the Cæsars. Several of the successors of Constantine had repaired the edifices that were crumbling into ruins, and had erected fresh monuments in Constantinople, which in its temples, upon its public places, and around the walls, everywhere recalled the memory of twenty glorious reigns. The city was divided into fourteen quarters; it had thirty-two gates; it contained within its bosom circuses of immense extent, five hundred churches, among which St. Sophia claimed attention as one of the wonders of the world; and five palaces, which themselves looked like cities in the midst of the great city. More fortunate than its rival Rome, the city of Constantine had never beheld the barbarians within its walls; it preserved with its language the depository of the masterpieces of antiquity, and the accumulated riches of the East and the West.

It would be difficult to paint the enthusiasm, the fear, the surprise that took possession of the minds of the Crusaders at the aspect of Constantinople. The leaders landed, and passed one night in the abbey of St. Stephen. This night was employed in anxious deliberation upon what they had to do; at one time they resolved to land upon the isles; then they determined to make a descent upon the continent. In the very same instant they drew back in terror and gave themselves up to a wild joy; they could not come to any fixed determination, but changed their plans and their projects a thousand times. At daybreak Dandolo, Boniface, Baldwin, and the count de Blois ordered all the standards of the army to be unfurled; the escutcheons and coats of arms of the counts and knights were ranged along the vessels, to display the military pomp of the West and recall to the warriors the valour of their ancestors. The signal was given to the fleet, which entered into the canal, and, driven on by a favourable wind, passed close to the walls of Constantinople. An immense population, who only the day before were ignorant of the arrival of the Latins, crowded the ramparts and covered the shore. The warriors of the West, clad in complete armour,* stood erect upon the decks of their vessels; some stones and arrows were launched from the towers and fell upon the ships: "there was no heart," says Villehardouin, "so bold as not to be moved; for never was so great an affair undertaken." Every warrior turned his eye towards his sword, thinking the time was come in which to make use of it. The Crusaders fancied that in the crowd of spectators they beheld the defenders of Constantinople; but the capital of the empire was only defended by the memory of its past glory, and by the respect of the nations ignorant of its weakness. Of true soldiers the imperial army only mustered two thousand Pisans, who despised the Greeks, and the troop of Varangians, mercenary soldiers from the northern parts of Europe, with whose origin and country the Greeks themselves were scarcely acquainted.

The Crusaders made a descent upon the Asiatic shore of the Bosphorus, pillaged the city of Chalcedon, and established themselves in the palace and gardens in which the emperor Alexius had so long forgotten his own dangers and those of his empire. At the approach of the Venetian fleet, this prince had retreated to Constantinople, where, like the last king of Babylon he continued to live amidst pleasures and festivities, without reflecting that he had been judged, and that his hour was nearly come. His courtiers, in the intoxication of the banquet, celebrated his power and proclaimed him invincible; amidst the pomp that surrounded him, and which appeared to him a rampart against the attacks of his enemies, he, in his speeches, insulted the simplicity of the Latins, and believed he had conquered them because he had called them barbarians.

When he saw the Crusaders masters of his palace and gardens, he began to entertain some degree of fear, and sent an Italian named Rossi, with orders to salute the lords and barons. "The emperor my master," said the envoy of Alexius, "knows that you are the most puissant and most noble princes among those who do not wear crowns; but he is astonished that you should have come to bring war into a Christian empire. Rumour proclaims that your design is to deliver the Holy

---

* Nicetas, speaking of the Crusaders, says they were almost all as tall as their spears.

Land from the yoke of the Saracens; the emperor applauds your zeal, and solicits the honour of being associated with your enterprise; he is ready to assist you with all his power. But if you do not quit his states, he shall feel obliged to direct against you the forces he would willingly have employed in your cause and in that of Christ. Accept, then, the generous offers that he makes to you by me; but do not believe that this pacific language is dictated by fear. The emperor Alexius reigns over Greece by the love of his people as well as by the will of God; with one single word he could gather around him innumerable armies, disperse your fleet and your battalions, and close against you for ever the routes to the East."

The envoy of the emperor thus terminated his speech without naming either Isaac or young Alexius. Conon de Béthune, who answered for the leaders of the army, was astonished that the brother of Isaac should dare to speak as master of the empire, and that he had not thought fit to attempt to justify a parricide which had roused the indignation of all Christian nations. "Go and tell your master," said the orator of the Crusaders, addressing the emperor's envoy, "go and tell him, that the earth we tread upon does not belong to him, but that it is the heritage of the prince you see seated amongst us. If he be desirous of knowing the motive that brings us hither, let him ask his own conscience, and remember the crimes he has committed. A usurper is the enemy of all princes; a tyrant is the enemy of the whole human race. He who sent you has but one means of escaping the justice of Heaven and of men; that is, to restore to his brother and his nephew the throne he has wrested from them, and implore the pity of those same princes towards whom he has been so merciless. In that case we promise to add our prayers to his supplications, and to procure for him, with his pardon, the means of passing his life in a repose far preferable to the splendour of an usurped sovereignty; but if he is not willing to act justly, if he is inaccessible to repentance, tell him we disdain his threats as we do his promises, and that we have no time to waste in listening to ambassadors." This vehement reply was an actual declaration of war, and left the emperor no hope of either seducing or intimidating the Crusaders. The lords and barons were, however, astonished that the Greeks took no notice of young Alexius, and that the cause they came to promote found no partisans in the city of Constantinople. They resolved to ascertain the inclinations of the people. A galley, on board of which was the son of Isaac, was brought close to the walls of the capital; Boniface and Dandolo held up the young prince, whilst a herald-at-arms repeated in a loud voice these words:—"*Behold the heir of the throne; acknowledge your sovereign; have pity on him and on yourselves.*" The Greeks assembled on the ramparts remained motionless; some answered by insulting language, others maintained a sullen silence. Whilst the Crusaders were thus making a last attempt to preserve peace, the most horrible tumult reigned in the interior of the city. The presence of the Latins irritated the multitude; they assembled in the public places; they excited each other to vengeance; the people ran to the quarter of the Franks, demolished several houses, and gave the rest up to pillage. A great number of Latins, threatened with loss of life, immediately sought an asylum in the camp of the Crusaders. Their presence, their accounts, their complaints, fired the easily kindled indignation of the knights and barons. From that moment the leaders saw no hopes but in the chance of war and in the protection of the Heaven that had confided to their hands the cause of innocence and misfortune.

Eighty knights succeeded in putting to flight a numerous body of troops that the emperor had sent across the Bosphorus. "The Greek commanders," says Nicetas, "were more timid than deer, and did not dare to resist men whom they called *exterminating angels, statues of bronze*, which spread around terror and death." The Crusaders, however, had great cause to fear that the Greeks, recovered from their first panic, might become aware of the small number of their enemies, and succeed in overwhelming them by their multitudes; they resolved, therefore, to take advantage of the fear they had inspired, and gave their whole attention to forward the preparations for attacking enemies that had provided nothing for their defence.

The Christian army assembled at Chrisopolis (Scutari), and beheld full in front of them the capital of the Greek empire. After having put to flight some troops sent out to follow their march or skirmish with them, the leaders mounted on horseback and deliberated in full assembly, on the plan of action best to be pursued. They decided that the army should cross the canal of the Bosphorus, and encamp under the walls of Constantinople. "Then," says Villehardouin, "the bishops and the clergy addressed their remonstrances to all those of the camp, exhorting them to confess themselves, and make their testaments, for they did not know the hour at which it might please God to call them, and do his will by them; which they did very willingly, and with great zeal and devotion." When all was ready, and the Crusaders had invoked the protection of Heaven by their prayers, the signal for departure was given; the war-horses, saddled and covered with their long caparisons, were embarked in the flat-bottomed boats; the knights stood erect near their horses, helm on head and lance in hand; the remainder of the troops went on board the large ships, each of which was towed by a galley. The army of the Greeks, commanded by the emperor in person, was drawn up in battle array on the opposite shore, and appeared disposed to dispute the passage of the Crusaders. All at once the vessels heaved their anchors to the sounds of trumpets and clarions. Every soldier, with his eyes fixed on Constantinople, swore to conquer or die. On approaching the shore, the barons and knights cast themselves into the sea, fully armed, and contended for the honour of first gaining the strand occupied by the Greeks. The archers and foot-soldiers followed the example of the knights; in less than an hour the whole army was on the other side of the Bosphorus, and looked about in vain for an enemy over a plain they had so recently seen covered with arms and warriors. The army of Alexius took to flight; and, if we may believe a letter of the count de St. Pol, the swiftest arrows of the Latins could scarcely overtake a few of the fugitives. The Crusaders, following up their advantage, found the camp of the Greeks abandoned, and plundered the tents of the emperor, without meeting with one of his soldiers.

Night surprised them in the midst of their bloodless victory; and on the morrow they resolved to attack the fortress of Galata, which, erected upon a hill, commanded the port of Constantinople. From break of day the Greeks rushed in crowds to anticipate and surprise the Latins. At the first shock, Jacques d'Avesnes was wounded grievously, and placed *hors de combat;* the sight of his wound highly incensed the Flemish warriors, who precipitated themselves with fury into the *mêlée.* The Greeks were not able to withstand the impetuous attack of their enemies, and took to flight in great disorder; some, hoping to find an asylum in the ships in the port, perished in the waves, whilst others fled bewildered to the citadel, into which the conquerors entered with the conquered. Whilst the French thus got possession of Galata, the Venetian fleet, which was drawn up in line of battle before Scutari, turned its prows towards the port of Constantinople. The entrance of the gulf was defended by an enormous chain of iron, and by twenty galleys, which constituted the whole navy of the empire. The resistance of the Greeks was obstinate; but a vessel of extraordinary size, assisted by a favourable wind, struck the extended chain violently in its passage, and divided it with enormous shears of steel, which opened and shut by the operation of a machine. The galleys of the Greeks were soon taken, or dispersed in fragments on the face of the waters, and the whole of the Venetian fleet rode in triumph into the port: it was then the Greeks were able to perceive what they had to dread from the invincible courage of these barbarians, who had till that period been the object of their contempt.

The French, masters of Galata, divided their army into six great battles or divisions. Baldwin, who had under his orders a great number of archers and crossbow-men, led the van. The rear was composed of Lombards, Germans, and Franks, from countries near the Alps, commanded by the marquis of Montferrat. The other four divisions, in which were ranged the Crusaders from Champagne, Burgundy, and the banks of the Seine and the Loire, had at their head Henry, brother of Baldwin, the counts of St. Pol and Blois, and Matthew de Montmorenci.

This army advanced towards the west of the city, without meeting with a single foe in its passage, and encamped between the gate of Blachernæ and the tower of Bohémond.

The Greeks, in a single battle, had lost the empire of the sea, and had no longer the power to defend the approach to their capital. The Venetian fleet cast anchor near the mouth of the river Barbysses. The Venetians, masters of the port, were secure from all surprise, and had no cause to fear being overpowered by numbers. If the whole army had been united on board the fleet, there is very little doubt it would have more easily triumphed over the efforts and multitudes of the Greeks, and it was the advice of the doge that such should be the plan; but the knights and barons could not be prevailed upon to fight on an element with which they were unacquainted; and they answered (we quote Villehardouin), that they could not act so well upon the sea as they could upon the land, where they could have their horses and their arms. Their army, which did not muster twenty thousand men under its banners, attacked without fear a city, which, according to the account of some historians, contained a million of inhabitants, and more than two hundred thousand men able to bear arms.

Before they began the assault, the Crusaders deemed it proper once more to invite the Greeks to make peace, by receiving the son of Isaac as emperor; and several barons drew near to the walls, crying with a loud voice that there was still time to listen to justice. Young Alexius was surrounded by the Latin leaders, and his presence among them explained sufficiently clearly the meaning of the words addressed to the inhabitants of Constantinople. Their only reply was hurling stones and javelins at the Crusaders; the people of Byzantium had been persuaded that young Alexius came for the purpose of changing the manners, religion, and laws of Greece.

History ought to add here, that since the intrigues of ambition and the caprices of fortune had enjoyed the privilege of bestowing masters upon them, the Greeks beheld with indifference the successions of power or the changes of their princes; the Greek nations had not forgotten that it was a revolution that lifted the family of Isaac to the imperial throne. With the impressions this family had left in their minds, the misfortunes and prayers of Alexius did not move them sufficiently to declare in his favour, or take arms to support his cause; since they were obliged to choose between two new princes, he who was reigning amongst them appeared preferable to him who implored their aid.

From that time the attention and efforts of the Crusaders were solely directed to the prosecution of their perilous enterprise. Their camp, placed between the gate of Blachernæ and the castle of Bohémond, occupied but a very small space before walls many leagues in extent. Every day the Greeks made sorties; the country round was covered with the soldiers of the enemy; the army of the besiegers appeared to be themselves besieged by troops that were unceasingly renewed. Day and night the Crusaders were under arms, and had neither time to take their food nor refresh themselves by sleep. They had only provisions for three weeks, and could look for safety to nothing but a speedy victory; nevertheless, they continued to fill up the ditches, and make their approaches to the ramparts. Balistas, catapultas, rams, everything that could carry destruction and death into the city, were employed to second the bravery and indefatigable ardour of the besiegers; without cessation, enormous masses fell with fearful crash from the tops of the walls; and such was the surprising power of the machines of war then in use, that the houses and palaces of Constantinople were often shaken to their foundations by stones launched from the camp of the Latins.*

After ten days of labour and fighting, the Crusaders determined to storm the city. On the morning of the 17th of July, 1203, the trumpets and clarions sounded the signal; the count of Flanders, who commanded the attack, passed through the ranks, and directed the attention of his knights to the ramparts of Constantinople, *as the road which would conduct them to an eternal glory.* The army was immediately in motion, and every machine was directed against the walls. One tower, which had fallen in with a great crash, appeared to offer a passage to the troops of Baldwin. Ladders were planted, and the most intrepid contended for the honour of entering first into the city; but, this time, numbers prevailed over valour. A host of Greeks, encouraged by the presence of the Varangians and Pisans, hastened to the rampart, and overturned the ladders. Fifteen Frank warriors, braving stones, beams, and torrents of Greek fire, alone were able to maintain themselves on the walls, and yielded only after fighting with desperate valour. Two of these intrepid warriors were led to the emperor, who watched the fight from the windows of the palace of Blachernæ. Alexius had ceased to despise the Latins; and, in his fright, he had such an idea of their courage, that the sight of the two prisoners appeared to him a victory.

At the same time the Venetians attacked the city by sea. Dandolo ranged his fleet in two lines; the galleys were in the first rank, manned by archers, and laden with machines of war; behind the galleys advanced the large vessels, upon which were constructed towers exceeding the loftiest of the walls of Constantinople in height. At daybreak the contest began between the city and the fleet; the Greeks, armed with the Greek fire, the Venetians, covered with their armour, the ramparts and the vessels charged with a thousand destructive instruments, cast from one to the other, by turns, terror, fire, and death. The incessant dashing of the oars, the shocks of the vessels against each other, the cries of the sailors and combatants, the hissing of the stones, javelins, and arrows, the Greek fire darting along the sea, seizing on the ships and boiling upon the waves, presented altogether a spectacle a thousand times more fearful than that of a tempest. Amidst this horrible tumult, Henry Dandolo was heard: standing erect in his galley, he excited his troops, and, with a terrible voice, threatened to hang every man that did not land. The orders of the intrepid doge were soon executed. The men of his galley took him in their arms and bore him swiftly to the shore, the standard of St. Mark floating over him. At sight of this, the efforts of the crews of the other galleys were redoubled, all struck the shore, and the soldiers rushed forward to follow their venerable leader. The vessels, which had hitherto remained motionless, now advanced and placed themselves between the galleys, so that the whole fleet was extended in a single line before the walls of Constantinople, and presented to the terrified Greeks a formidable rampart raised upon the waters. The floating towers lowered their draw-bridges upon the ramparts of the city, and whilst, at the foot of the walls, ten thousand arms planted ladders and battered with rams, on the summit a fearful conflict was maintained with sword and lance.

All at once the standard of St. Mark appeared upon one of the towers, planted by an invisible hand; upon seeing this the Venetians uttered a loud shout of joy, persuaded that their patron saint fought at their head; their courage proportionately increased with the terror and despair of their enemies; the most intrepid cast themselves on to the walls, and soon twenty-five towers were in their possession. They pursued the Greeks into the city; but fearing to fall into some ambush or be overwhelmed by the people, crowds of whom filled the streets and covered the public places, they set fire

* Nevertheless the superb palaces were ruined by the stones of an extraordinary size that the besiegers launched with their machines, and they were themselves terrified by the heavy masses that the Romans rolled upon them from the walls.—*Nicetas*, *Hist. of Alexius Comnenus*, book iii.

to the houses as they came to them on their passage. The conflagration extended rapidly, and drove before it the terrified and trembling multitude. Whilst the flames, preceding the conquerors, spread devastation on their path, and the greatest disorder prevailed in Constantinople, Alexius, pressed by the cries of the people, mounted on horseback, and ordered a sortie of the troops, by three different gates, to attack the French, who were less fortunate in this day's fight than the Venetians.

The army conducted by the emperor was composed of sixty battalions; clothed in all the marks of imperial dignity, Alexius rode along the ranks, animated his soldiers, and promised them victory. At his approach, the Crusaders abandoned the ramparts, and drew up in line of battle before their camp. Villehardouin admits that the bravest knights were, for a moment, seized with fear. Dandolo, who saw the danger in which the French were placed, abandoned his victory, and flew to their aid. But all the Crusaders united could not have resisted the imperial army, if the Greeks, but more particularly their leaders, had shown a spark of courage. The troops of Alexius would not advance nearer than within bow-shot, and contented themselves with showering a multitude of arrows from a safe distance. The son-in-law of the emperor, Lascaris, of whose courage the Greeks and even the Latins boast, demanded with loud cries that the Crusaders should be attacked in their intrenchments; but he could not prevail upon Alexius, surrounded by base courtiers who endeavoured to communicate their own alarms to him, and assured him that he had done enough for his glory in showing himself to his enemies. The emperor, without having fought, ordered a retreat to be sounded, and his numerous troops, who still bore the name of Romans, and before whom the eagles of Rome were carried, returned with him into Constantinople.

Every quarter of the capital resounded with lamentations and groans; the Greeks were more terrified at the cowardice of their defenders, than by the bravery of their enemies; the people accused the army, and the army accused Alexius. The emperor, mistrusting the Greeks and dreading the Latins, now only thought of saving his own life: he abandoned his family, his friends, his capital; he embarked secretly in the darkness of night, and fled to seek a retreat in some obscure corner of his empire.

When daylight informed the Greeks that they had no longer an emperor, the disorder and excitement of the city became excessive; the people assembled in the streets, and freely discussed the errors and deficiencies of their leaders, the infamy of the favourites, and their own misfortunes. Now Alexius had abandoned his power, they remembered the crime of his usurpation, and a thousand voices were raised to invoke the anger of Heaven upon his head. Amidst the confusion and tumult, the wisest were at a loss what part to take, when the courtiers rushed to the prison in which Isaac languished, broke his chains, and led him in triumph to the palace of Blachernæ. Although blind, he was placed upon the throne, and, whilst he believed himself to be still in the hands of his executioners, his ears were saluted with the unexpected accents of flattery; on seeing him again clothed in the imperial purple, the courtiers for the first time became affected by misfortunes he no longer endured. All denied having been partisans of Alexius, and related what vows they had put up for his cause. They next sought out the wife of Isaac, whom they had forgotten, and who had lived in a retreat to which no one knew or had inquired the road during the preceding reign.

Euphrosyne, the wife of the fugitive emperor, was accused of having endeavoured to take advantage of the troubles of Constantinople, to clothe one of her favourites with the purple. She was cast into a dungeon, and reproached with all the evils that had fallen on her country, but most particularly with the lengthened miseries of Isaac. Such as had been loaded with favours by this princess, were conspicuous among her accusers, and pretended to make a merit of their ingratitude.

In political troubles, every change is, in the eyes of the people, a means of safety; they felicitated themselves upon this new revolution in Constantinople; hope revived in all hearts, and Isaac was saluted by the multitude with cries of joy and congratulation. Rumour soon carried to the camp all that had taken place in the city. At this news the council of the barons and knights was assembled in the tent of the marquis of Montferrat, and they returned thanks to Providence, which, in delivering Constantinople, had, at the same time, delivered them from the greatest dangers. But when they recollected having seen only on the preceding day the emperor Alexius surrounded by an innumerable army, they could scarcely give faith to the miracle of his flight.

The camp was, however, soon crowded with a multitude of Greeks, who came to relate the wonders of which they had been witnesses. Many of the courtiers who had not been able to attract the attention of Isaac, flocked to young Alexius, in the hope of securing his first favours; they returned warm thanks to Heaven for having listened to the ardent vows they had put up for his return, and conjured him, in the name of his country and the empire, to come and share the honours and the power of his father. But all these testimonies could not persuade the Latins, so accustomed were they to mistrust the Greeks. The barons kept their army in the strictest order, and always prepared for battle, and then sent Matthew of Montmorenci, Geoffrey de Villehardouin, and two Venetian nobles to Constantinople to ascertain the truth.

The deputies were directed to congratulate Isaac, if he had recovered his throne, and to require of him the ratification of the treaty made with his son. On arriving in Constantinople, they were conducted to the palace of Blachernæ between two ranks of soldiers, who, the day before, had formed the body-guard of Alexius, and who had just taken the oath to defend Isaac. The emperor received the deputies on a throne sparkling with gold and precious stones, and surrounded by all the splendour of Eastern courts. "This is the manner," said Villehardouin, addressing Isaac, "in which the Crusaders have fulfilled their promises; it now remains with you to perform those that have been made in your name. Your son, who is with the lords and barons, implores you to ratify the treaty he has concluded, and commands us to say that he will not return to your palace until you have sworn to perform all he has promised us." Alexius had engaged to pay the Crusaders two hundred thousand silver marks, to furnish their army with provisions for a year, to take an active part in the perils and labours of the holy war, and to reduce the Greek Church to submission to that of Rome. When Isaac heard the conditions of the treaty, he could not forbear from expressing his surprise, and pointing out to the deputies how difficult it must be to perform such promises; but he could deny nothing to his liberators, and thanked the Crusaders for not requiring more: "*You have served us so well,*" added he, "*that if we were even to give you the whole empire, you would have merited it.*" The deputies praised the frankness and good faith of Isaac, and carried back to the camp the imperial patents, to which was affixed the seal of gold that confirmed the treaty made with Alexius.

The lords and barons immediately mounted on horseback, and conducted young Alexius into Constantinople. The son of Isaac rode between the count of Flanders and the doge of Venice, followed by all the knights, clad in complete armour. The people, who so lately had preserved a sullen silence on beholding him, now crowded around him on his passage, and saluted him with loud acclamations; the Latin clergy accompanied the son of Isaac, and those of the Greek Church sent out their magnificent *cortège* to meet him. The entrance of the young prince into the capital was a day of festivity for both the Greeks and the Latins; in all the churches thanks were offered up to Heaven; hymns of public rejoicing resounded everywhere; but it was particularly in the palace of Blachernæ, so long the abode of mourning and fear, that the greatest transports of joy were manifested. A father, blind, and immured during eight years in a dungeon, clasping in his arms a son to whom he owed the restoration of his liberty and crown, presented a new spectacle that must have penetrated every heart with lively emotions. The crowd of spectators recalled to their minds the long calamities of these two princes; and the remembrance of so many evils past, appeared to them a pledge for the blessings that Heaven had in store for the empire.

The emperor, reunited to his son, again thanked the Crusaders for the services they had rendered him, and conjured the leaders to establish themselves with their army on the other side of the Gulf of Chrysoceras. He feared that their abode in the city might give birth to some quarrel between the Greeks and the Latins, too long divided. The barons yielded to the prayer of Isaac and Alexius, and the army of the Crusaders took up their quarters in the faubourg of Galata; where, in abundance and repose, they forgot the labours, perils, and fatigues of the war. The Pisans, who had defended Constantinople against the Crusaders, made peace with the Venetians; all discords were appeased, and no spirit of jealousy or rivalry divided the Franks. The Greeks came constantly to the camp of the Latins, bringing provisions and merchandise of all kinds. The warriors of the West often visited the capital, and were never tired of contemplating the palaces of the emperors, the numerous edifices, the master-pieces of art, the monuments consecrated to religion, and, above all, the relics of saints, which, according to the marshal of Champagne, were in greater abundance in Constantinople than in any other place in the world.

A few days after his entrance into Constantinople, Alexius was crowned in the church of St. Sophia, and admitted to a partition of the sovereign power with his father. The barons assisted at his coronation, and offered up sincere wishes for the happiness of his reign. Alexius hastened to discharge a part of the sum promised to the Crusaders. The greatest harmony prevailed between the people of Byzantium and the warriors of the West; the Greeks appeared to have forgotten their defeats, the Latins their victories. The subjects of Isaac and Alexius mingled with the Latins without mistrust, and the simplicity of the Franks was no longer the subject of their raillery. The Crusaders, on their side, confided in the good faith of the Greeks. Peace reigned in the capital, and seemed to be the work of their hands. They respected the two princes they had placed upon the throne, and the emperors retained an affectionate gratitude for their liberators.

The Crusaders, having become the allies of the Greeks, and the protectors of a great empire, had now no other enemies to contend with but the Saracens; and they turned their minds to the fulfilment of the oath they had made on taking the cross; but, ever faithful to the laws of chivalry, the barons and knights deemed it right to declare war before beginning it. Heralds-at-arms were sent to the sultan of Cairo and Damascus, to announce to him, in the name of Jesus Christ, in the name of the emperor of Constantinople, and in the names of the princes and nobles of the West, that he would soon experience the valour of the Christian nations, if he persisted in holding under his laws the Holy Land and the places consecrated by the presence of the Saviour.

The leaders of the crusade announced the wonderful success of their enterprise to all the princes and nations of Christendom. Whilst addressing the emperor of Germany, they conjured him to take part in the crusade, and come and place himself at the head of the Christian knights. The account of their exploits excited the enthusiasm of the faithful; the news, when carried into Syria, spread terror among the Saracens, and revived the hopes of the king of Jerusalem and the defenders of the Holy Land: so much glorious success ought to have satisfied the pride and valour of the Crusaders; but, whilst the world resounded with their glory, and trembled at the fame of their arms, the knights and barons believed they had achieved nothing for their own renown, or for the cause of God, until they had obtained the approbation of the Holy See. The marquis of Montferrat, the count of Flanders, the count of St. Pol, and the principal leaders of the army, when writing to the pope, represented to him that the success of their enterprise was not the work of men, but the work of God. These warriors, filled with haughty pride, who had just conquered an empire; who, according to Nicetas, boasted of *fearing nothing but the falling of the heavens*, thus bent their victorious brows before the tribunal of the sovereign pontiff, and protested at the feet of Innocent, that no mundane view had directed their arms, and that he must only contemplate in them the instruments Providence had employed in accomplishing its designs.

Young Alexius, in concert with the leaders of the crusades, wrote at the same time to the pope, to justify his conduct and that of his liberators. "We avow," said he, "that the principal cause that induced the pilgrims to assist us, was that we had promised, with an oath, to recognise the Roman pontiff as our ecclesiastical head, and the successor of St. Peter." Innocent III., in replying to the new emperor of Constantinople, praised his intentions and his zeal, and pressed him to accomplish his promises; but the excuses of the Crusaders were not able to appease the resentment which the pope retained on account of their disobedience to the counsels and commands of the Holy See. In his answer, he did not salute them with his usual benediction, fearing that they were again fallen under excommunication, by attacking the Greek emperor in spite of his prohibition. If the emperor of Constantinople, said he to them, does not make haste to do that which he has promised, it will appear that neither his intentions nor yours have been sincere, and *that you have added this second sin to that you have already committed.* The pope gave the Crusaders fresh advice; but neither his counsels nor his threats produced any better effect than they had done at the siege of Zara: Providence was preparing in secret, events that exceeded the foresight of the Crusaders, or even that of the Holy See, and which would once again change the aim and object of the holy war.

BOOK XI.

FROM THE RESTORATION OF ISAAC TO THE DEATH OF BALDWIN.

A. D. 1198-1204.

Character of the Greeks—Position of Alexius the younger—His proposals to the Crusaders—Disputes between the Greeks and the Latins on articles of faith—Contentions with the Bulgarians—Conflagration of Constantinople—Imbecility and bigotry of the emperor Isaac—Statue of Minerva destroyed—Insurrectionary spirit in Constantinople—Famine in Egypt—Contests between the Greeks and the Latins—Greek fire—Treachery of Mourzouffle—He murders young Alexius, and ascends the throne—Character of Alexius—Mourzouffle's contests with the Latins—Is dethroned—Death of Isaac—Lascaris chosen Emperor—Abandons the city—Constantinople taken possession of, and plundered by the Latins—Destruction of the works of art—Statues of Bellerophon, Hercules, and Helen, destroyed—Reverence for relics and images—Fanaticism of Martin Litz—Fragment of the "true cross"—Virtues of Dandolo, the doge of Venice—Baldwin, count of Flanders, elected emperor of Constantinople—The conquered lands distributed among the Crusaders—Thomas Morasini elected patriarch of Constantinople—Correspondence between Baldwin and the pope—Death of Marguerite of Flanders, wife of Baldwin—Conquests of Leo Sguerre—Michael Angelus Comnenus gains the kingdom of Epirus—Lascaris proclaimed emperor at Nice—Mourzouffle captured and executed—Column of Theodosius—Quarrels between Boniface, marquis of Montferrat, and Baldwin—Boniface invades Greece—The Greeks rebel against the domination of the Latins—Victories of the Bulgarians—Defeat and Massacre of the Latins—Bravery of Henry of Hainault—Incidents of Baldwin's life—Death of Dandolo—Boniface is slain—Characters of the Greeks and the Franks—Their different historians—Disputes respecting the sovereignty of Cyprus—Death of Gauthier de Brienne—Policy of Innocent III.—Knowledge of Greek diffused in the West—Refinement of the Venetians, and commercial greatness of Venice.

WHEN war and revolutions have shaken an empire to its foundation, evils arise against which no human wisdom can provide. It is then that princes, called to the throne, are more to be pitied than their subjects, and that their power is more likely to excite commiseration than to awaken the ambition or hatred of other men. The people, in the extreme of misery, know not what bounds to put to their hopes, and always demand of the future more than the future can possibly bring. When they continue to suffer irreparable misfortunes, they blame their leaders, by whose influence they expected all sorts of prosperity; the murmurs of unjust hatred soon succeed to the acclamations of an irreflective enthusiasm, and, not unfrequently, virtue itself is accused of having caused evils which are the effects of revolt, war, or bad fortune.

Nations themselves, when they have succumbed, and have forever lost their political existence, are not judged with less severity or injustice than princes or monarchs: after the fall of an empire, the terrible axiom *væ victis*, receives its application even in the judgment of posterity. Generations, quite equally with contemporaries, allow themselves to be dazzled by victory, and entertain nothing but contempt for conquered nations. We shall endeavour, whilst speaking of the Greeks and their princes, to guard against the prejudices that history has transmitted to us, and when we shall pronounce a severe judgment upon the character and people of Greece, our opinion will be always founded upon authentic traditions and the testimony of the historians of Byzantium.

Whilst young Alexius had nothing to do but make promises and give hopes, he was gratified by the flattering benedictions of both Greeks and Crusaders; but when the time arrived for him to perform all he had promised, he met with nothing but enemies and obstacles. In the position in which his return had placed him, it was extremely difficult for him to preserve at the same time the confidence of his liberators and the love of his subjects. If, in order to fulfil his engagements, the young emperor undertook to unite the Greek Church with the Church of Rome; if, to pay that which he owed to the Crusaders, he oppressed his people with taxes, he must expect to hear violent murmurs arise throughout his empire. If, on the contrary, he respected the religion of Greece, if he lightened the excessive weight of the imposts, the treaties would remain unexecuted, and the throne he had so recently ascended might be overturned by the arms of the Latins.

Dreading every day to see the fires of either revolt or war kindled, obliged to choose between two perils, after having long and earnestly deliberated, he did not dare to confide his destiny to the equivocal valour of the Greeks, and conjured the barons to become a second time his liberators. He repaired to the tent of the count of Flanders, and spoke as follows to the assembled leaders of the crusade. "You have restored to me life, honour, and empire, and I have only one thing to desire: that is, to be able to perform all the promises I have made you. But if you abandon me now, in order to go into Syria, it will be impossible for me to find the money, the troops, or the vessels I have undertaken to furnish. The people of Constantinople have received me with joy; but the frequency of revolutions has caused them to lose the habits of submission and obedience. The laws of their country, the majesty of the throne, no longer inspire them with respect; a spirit of faction reigns in the capital, and throughout the too-long agitated provinces. I conjure you then, in the name of your own glory, in the name of your own interests, to finish your work, and render firm the power you have reëstablished. Winter is approaching, the navigation is perilous, and the rains will not permit you to commence the war in Syria; wait then till the spring, when the sea will present fewer dangers, and war greater success and glory; you will then have all Greece as auxiliaries in your enterprises; I shall myself be able to keep the oaths that chain me to your cause, and accompany you with an army worthy of an emperor." At the conclusion of his speech, Alexius promised to furnish all that the army would require, and to make such suitable arrangements with the doge, that the Venetian fleet might remain at the disposal of the Crusaders during their abode at Constantinople, and to the end of their expedition.

A council was called to deliberate upon the proposals of the young emperor: those who had been desirous of separating themselves from the army at Zara and Corfu, represented to the assembly that they had, until that time, fought for the glory and profane interests of princes of the earth, but that the time was now come for them to fight for religion and for Jesus Christ. They were indignant at new obstacles being raised to retard the holy enterprise. This opinion was warmly combated by the doge of Venice and the barons who had embarked their glory in the expedition against Constantinople, and could not make up their minds to lose the fruit of all their labours. "Shall we," said they, "allow a young prince, whose cause we have brought to a triumphant issue, to be delivered over to his enemies, who are as ours, and an enterprise so gloriously begun, become for us a source of shame and repentance? Shall we allow the heresy that our arms have stifled in humbled Greece, to reconstruct its impure altars, and be again a subject of scandal for the Christian church? Shall we leave the Greeks the dangerous faculty of declaring against us, and allying themselves with the Saracens, to war with the soldiers of Christ?" To these weighty motives the princes and lords did not disdain to add supplication and prayers; at length their opinion triumphed over an obstinate opposition, and the council decided that the departure of the army should be deferred until the festival of the Easter of the following year.

Alexius, in concert with Isaac, thanked the Crusaders for their favourable determination, and neglected nothing that could prove his gratitude to them. For the purpose of paying the sums he had promised, he exhausted his treasury, increased the imposts, and even melted the images of the saints and the sacred vases. Upon seeing the churches despoiled of the sacred images, the people of Constantinople were struck with surprise and terror, and yet had not the courage to utter their complaints aloud. Nicetas reproaches his compatriots bitterly with having remained quiet spectators of such sacrilege, and accuses them of having, by their cowardly indifference, drawn upon the empire the anger of Heaven. The most fervent of the Greeks deplored, as Nicetas did, the violation of their holy places; but scenes much more grievous were soon to be brought before their eyes.

The leaders of the army, influenced by the councils of the Latin clergy and by the fear of the pontiff of Rome, required that the patriarch, the priests, and the monks of Constantinople should abjure the errors that separated them from the Romish church; and neither the clergy, nor the people, nor the emperor, attempted to resist this demand, although it alarmed every conscience and alienated all hearts. The patriarch, from the pulpit of St. Sophia, declared, in his own name, and in the name of the emperor and the Christian people of the East, that he acknowledged *Innocent, third of that name, as the successor of St. Peter, first vicar of Jesus Christ upon earth, pastor of the faithful flock.* The Greeks who were present at this ceremony believed they beheld the abomination of desolation in the holy place, and if they afterwards pardoned the patriarch the commission of such a scandal, it was from the strange persuasion in which they were, that the head of their church was deceiving the Latins, and that the imposture of his words redeemed in some sort the crime of blasphemy and the shame of perjury.

The Greeks persisted in believing that the Holy Ghost does not proceed from the Son, and quoted in support of their belief, the Creed of Nice; the discipline of their church differed in some points from that of the Church of Rome; in the early days of the schism it might have been easy to effect a reunion, but now the disputes of theologians had too much exasperated men's minds.* The hatred of the Greeks and the Latins appeared but too likely to separate the two creeds for ever. The law that was imposed upon the Greeks only served to promote the growth of their invincible resistance. Such among them as scarcely knew what the subject was of the long debates that had sprung up between Byzantium and Rome, showed no less fanaticism and opposition than all the others; whilst such as had no religion at all adopted with warmth the opinions of the theologians, and appeared all at once disposed to die for a cause which till that time had inspired them with nothing but indifference. The Greek people, in a word, who believed themselves to be superior to all other nations of the earth, repulsed with contempt all knowledge that came from the West, and could not consent to recognise the superiority of the Latins. The Crusaders, who had changed the emperors and conquered the empire, were astonished at not being able to change men's hearts likewise; but, persuaded that everything must in the end yield to their arms, they employed, in subduing minds and opinions, a rigour which only augmented the hatred of the vanquished, and prepared the fall of the emperors whom victory had replaced upon the throne.

In the mean time, the usurper Alexius, on flying from Constantinople, had found a retreat in the province of Thrace; several cities opened their gates to him, and a few partisans assembled under his banner. The son of Isaac resolved to seek the rebels and give them battle. Henry of Hainault, the count of St. Pol, and many knights, accompanied him in this expedition. At their approach, the

* The Greeks and Latins were divided on three principal points; first, the addition made by the Latin Church to the creed of Constantinople, to declare that the Holy Ghost proceeds from the Father; 2nd, the refusal on the part of the Greeks to acknowledge the primacy of the pope; 3rdly, the pretension of the Greeks that it is not possible to consecrate in the Eucharist with unleavened bread. Photius began the schism; the patriarch Cerularius established it; this latter wished to be acknowledged as the head of the universal Church instead of the pope. L'Abbé Fleury, in his *Histoire Ecclésiastique*, thinks that the schism of the Greeks only really began at the period the Latins were masters of Constantinople.

usurper, shut up in Adrianople, quickly abandoned the city, and fled away towards Mount Hemus. All the rebels who had the courage to await them, were either conquered or dispersed. But young Alexius and the Crusaders had a much more formidable enemy to contend with : this was the nation of the Bulgarians. These wild and ferocious people, obedient to the laws of Constantinople at the time of the first crusade, had taken advantage of the troubles of the empire to shake off the yoke of its rulers. The leader of the Bulgarians, Joannices, an implacable enemy of the Greeks, had embraced the faith of the Church of Rome, and declared himself a vassal of the sovereign pontiff, to obtain from him the title of king. He concealed under the veil of a new religion the most vindictive hatred and aspiring ambition, and employed the support and credit of the court of Rome to make war against the masters of Byzantium. Joannices made frequent incursions into the countries adjoining his own territories, and threatened the richest provinces of the empire with invasion. If young Alexius had been guided by prudent counsels, he would have taken advantage of the presence of the Crusaders to intimidate the Bulgarians, and compel them to remain on the other side of Mount Hemus: this expedition might have deservedly obtained him the confidence and esteem of the Greeks, and assured the repose of several provinces ; but whether he was not seconded by the Crusaders, or that he did not perceive the advantages of such an enterprise, he contented himself with threatening Joannices ; and, without having made either peace or war, after receiving the oaths of the cities of Thrace, his sole wish was to return to Constantinople.

The capital of the empire, which had already undergone so many evils, had just experienced a fresh calamity. Some Flemish soldiers, encouraged by the Latins established in Constantinople, had provoked and insulted the Jews in their synagogue, and the people had taken up the defence of the latter against the aggressors. Both sides had recourse to arms, and in the tumult of fight, chance, or malevolence, set fire to some neighbouring houses. The conflagration extended on all sides, during the night and the following day, with a rapidity and violence that nothing could stop or confine ; the flames meeting from several points, rolled on with the swiftness of a torrent, consuming, as if of straw, galleries, columns, temples, and palaces. From the bosom of this frightful mass of fire issued fragments of burning matter, which, falling upon distant houses, reduced them to ashes. The flames, at first impelled by a north wind, were afterwards driven back, by a strong change, from the south, and poured upon places that had appeared secure from danger. The conflagration began at the synagogue, near the sea, on the eastern side of the city, and extended its ravages as far as the church of St. Sophia, on the western side, traversing a space of two leagues, and in its course including the port, where many ships were consumed upon the waters.

During eight days the fearful element continued the destruction ; the crash of houses and towers falling on all sides, and the roaring of the winds and flames mingling with the cries of a ruined and distracted multitude. The crowds of inhabitants rushed over and against each other in the streets, flying before the closely-pursuing fire, some bearing their goods and most valuable effects, others dragging along the sick and the aged. Such as perished in the conflagration were the least unfortunate, for multitudes of others, weeping the death of their relations and friends, and the loss of their whole worldly property, many of them wounded, some half-burnt, wandered about bewildered among the ruins, or were huddled together in the public places, without any means of subsistence, or the hope of finding an asylum.

The Crusaders viewed the progress of this horrible disaster from the heights of Galata, and deplored the calamities of Constantinople. A great number of knights lent their most earnest endeavour to subdue the raging element, and lamented that they had to contend with an enemy against which valour was powerless. The princes and barons sent a deputation to the emperor Isaac, to

THE EMPEROR ALEXIUS POISONED AND STRANGLED BY MOURZOUFLE.

Mourzoufle then presented himself before Alexius: he employed every means to aggravate the alarm of the young prince, and, under the pretext of providing for his safety, drew him into a secluded apartment, where his creatures, under his direction, loaded him with irons, and cast him into a dungeon. Coming forth, he boldly informed the people what he had done for the salvation of the empire; and the throne, from which he had dragged his master, benefactor, and friend, appeared but a just recompense for the devotedness of his services; he was carried in triumph to the church of St. Sophia, and crowned emperor amidst the acclamations of the people. Scarcely was Mourzoufle clothed with the imperial purple, than he resolved to possess the fruit of his crime in security; dreading the caprice of both fortune and the people, he repaired to the prison of Alexius, forced him to swallow an empoisoned draught, and because death did not keep pace with his impatience, strangled him with his own hands.

BOOK XI.

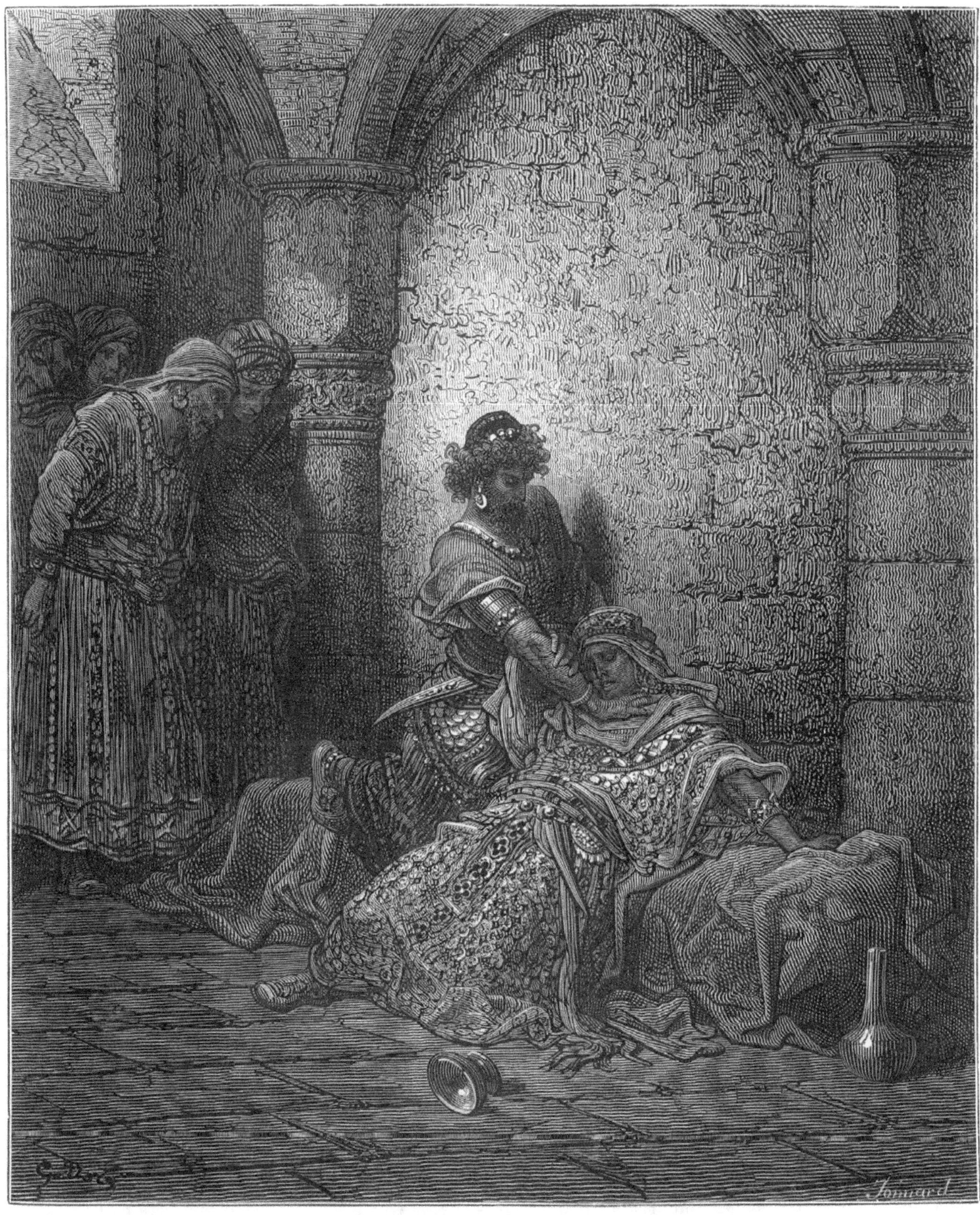

assure him how sincerely they participated in his sorrow, and to declare that they would punish the authors of the conflagration with the utmost severity, if they should prove to be among their soldiers. The protestations and assistance which they promptly and earnestly offered to the victims, could neither console nor appease the Greeks, who, whilst contemplating the ruins and misfortunes of their capital, accused the two emperors, and threw out horrible implications against the Latins.

The families of the Franks established at Constantinople, who, in spite of persecutions, had remained in the city, became again subject to the ill-treatment of the people; and, forced to seek an asylum without the walls, they took refuge in the faubourg of Galata. Their groans and complaints revived all the animosity of the Crusaders against the Greeks. Thus everything contributed to inflame the hatred of two nations, whom such great misfortunes ought to have more closely united, and to rekindle discords that were doomed to bring in their train new and incurable calamities.

When Alexius re-entered Constantinople in triumph, the people received him with moody silence; the Crusaders alone applauded victories he had gained over Greeks; and his triumph, which contrasted so keenly with the public calamities, and his laurels, gathered in a civil war, only served to render him more odious to the inhabitants of his capital. He was obliged, more than ever, to throw himself into the arms of the Latins; he passed his days and nights in their camp; he took part in their warlike games, and associated himself with their gross orgies. Amidst the intoxication of banquets, the Frank warriors treated Alexius with insolent familiarity, and more than once they pulled off his jewelled diadem to place on his head the woollen cap worn by Venetian sailors. The Greeks, who took great pride in the magnificence of their sovereigns, only conceived the stronger contempt for a prince, who, after abjuring his religion, degraded the imperial dignity, and did not blush to adopt the manners of nations that were only known at Constantinople under the name of barbarians.

Nicetas, whose opinions are not wanting in moderation, never speaks of this prince but with a sort of anger and violence. According to the historian of Byzantium, "Alexius had a countenance resembling that of the exterminating angel; he was a true incendiary; and far from being afflicted by the burning of his capital, he would have wished to see the whole city reduced to ashes." Isaac himself accused his son of having pernicious inclinations, and of corrupting himself daily by an intercourse with the wicked; he was indignant that the name of Alexius should be proclaimed at court and in public ceremonies, whilst that of Isaac was rarely mentioned. In his blind anger, he loaded the young emperor with imprecations; but, governed by a vain jealousy, much more than by any proper sentiment of dignity, whilst he applauded the hatred of the people for Alexius, he evaded the duties of a sovereign, and did nothing to merit the esteem of men of worth. Isaac lived retired in his palace, surrounded by monks and astrologers, who, whilst kissing his hands still scarred with the irons of his captivity, celebrated his power, made him believe that he would deliver Jerusalem, that he would plant his throne upon Mount Libanus, and would reign over the whole universe. Full of confidence in an image of the Virgin which he always carried with him, and boasting of being acquainted, by means of astrology, with all the secrets of policy, he could yet imagine, to prevent sedition, nothing more effective than to have transported from the hippodrome to his palace, the statue of the wild boar of Calydon, which was considered the symbol of revolt and the image of an infuriated people.

The people of Constantinople, no less superstitious than Isaac, whilst deploring the evils of their country, laid the blame upon both marble and brass. A statue of Minerva which decorated the Square of Constantine, had its eyes and arms turned towards the West; it was believed that she had called in the barbarians, and the statue was torn down and dashed to pieces by an exasperated mob:*

* Nicetas gives a sufficiently long description of this statue of Pallas.—See the *History of Isaac Angelus*, chap. iii. This statue was thirty feet high; its eyes, says the Greek historian, were turned towards the south, so that those who were ignorant of the science of angles considered she was looking towards the West, and that she invited the nations from the north of Europe to come to the shores of the Bosphorus.

"cruel blindness of the Greeks," cries an historical *bel esprit,* Nicetas, "who took arms against themselves, and could not endure in their city the image of a goddess who presides over prudence and valour!"

Whilst the capital of the empire was thus agitated by popular commotions, the ministers of Alexius and Isaac were busied in levying taxes for the payment of the sums promised to the Latins. Extravagance, abuses of power, and numerous instances of injustice, added still further to the public calamities; loud complaints were proclaimed by every class of the citizens. It was at first intended to lay the principal burden of the imposts upon the people; but the people, says Nicetas, arose like a sea agitated by the winds. Extraordinary taxes were then, by necessity, laid upon the richer citizens, and the churches continued to be plundered of their gold and silver ornaments. All the treasures they could collect were not sufficient to satisfy the insatiable desires of the Latins, who began to ravage the country, and pillage the houses and monasteries of the Propontis.

The hostilities and violence of the Crusaders excited the indignation of the people to a greater degree than they moved that of the patricians and the great. In the course of so many revolutions, it is astonishing to find that the spirit of patriotism so frequently revives amongst the multitude, when it is extinct in the more elevated classes. In a corrupt nation, so long as revolutions have not broken forth, and the day of peril and destruction is not arrived, the riches of the citizens is a sure pledge of their devotedness and patriotism; but this pledge is no longer the same at the height of danger, when society finds itself in antagonism with all the enemies of its existence and its repose; a fortune, the loss of which is dreaded, is often the cause of shameful transactions with the party of the conquerors; it enervates more than it fortifies moral courage. Amidst the greatest perils, the multitude, who have nothing to lose, sometimes preserve generous passions that skilful policy may direct with advantage. Unfortunately, the same multitude scarcely ever obey anything but a blind instinct; and in moments of crisis, become a dangerous instrument in the hands of the ambitious, who abuse the names of liberty and patriotism. It is then that a nation has no less to complain of those who are not willing to save her, than of those who do not dare defend her; and that she perishes, the victim at once of culpable indifference and senseless ardour.

The people of Constantinople, irritated against the enemies of the empire, and urged on by a spirit of faction, complained at first of their leaders; and, soon passing from complaint to revolt, they rushed in a crowd to the palace of the emperors, reproached them with having abandoned the cause of God and the cause of their country, and demanded, with loud cries, avengers and arms.

Among those who encouraged the multitude, a young prince of the illustrious family of Ducas was conspicuous. He bore the name of Alexius, a name which must always be associated with the history of the misfortunes of the empire: in addition, he had obtained the surname of *Mourzoufle,* a Greek word, signifying that his two eyebrows met together. Mourzoufle concealed a subtle spirit beneath that severe and stern air that the vulgar never fail to take for an indication of frankness. The words patriotism and liberty, which always seduce the people; the words glory and religion, which recall noble sentiments, were for ever in his mouth, and only served to veil the machinations of his ambition. Amidst a timid and pusillanimous court, surrounded by princes, who, according to the expression of Nicetas, *had greater fear of making war against the Crusaders, than stags would have in attacking a lion,* Mourzoufle was not deficient in bravery, and his reputation for courage was quite sufficient to draw upon him the eyes of the whole capital. As he possessed a strong voice, a haughty look, and an imperious tone, he was pronounced fit to command. The more vehemently he declaimed against tyranny, the more ardent were the wishes of the multitude that he should be clothed with great power. The hatred that he affected to entertain for foreigners, gave birth to the hope that he would one day defend the empire, and caused him to be considered the future liberator of Constantinople.

Skilful in seizing every available chance, and in following all parties, after having rendered criminal services to the usurper, Mourzoufle gathered the reward of them under the reign that followed the usurpation; and he who was everywhere accused of having been the gaoler and executioner of Isaac, became the favourite of young Alexius. He neglected no means of pleasing the multitude, in order to render himself necessary to the prince; and knew how to brave, on fit occasions, the hatred of the courtiers, to augment his credit among the people. He was not tardy in taking advantage of this double influence to sow the seeds of new troubles, and bring about the triumph of his ambition.

His counsels persuaded young Alexius, that it was necessary for him to break with the Latins, and prove himself ungrateful to his liberators, to obtain the confidence of the Greeks; he inflamed the minds of the people, and to make a rupture certain, he himself took up arms. His friends and some men of the people followed his example, and, led by Mourzoufle, a numerous troop rushed from the city, in the hope of surprising the Latins; but the multitude, always ready to declaim against the warriors of the West, did not dare to face them. Mourzoufle, abandoned on the field of battle, had nearly fallen into the hands of the Crusaders. This imprudent action, that might have been expected to ruin him, only tended to increase his power and influence; he might be accused of having risked the safety of the empire by provoking a war without the means of sustaining it; but the people boasted of the heroism of a young prince, who had dared to brave the warlike hosts of the Franks; and even they who had deserted him in the fight, celebrated his valour, and swore, as he did, to exterminate the enemies of their country.

The frenzy of the Greeks was at its height; and, on their side, the Latins loudly expressed their dissatisfaction. In the faubourg of Galata, inhabited by the French and Venetians, as well as within the walls of Constantinople, nothing was heard but cries for war, and nobody durst speak of peace. At this period a deputation from the Christians of Palestine arrived in the camp of the Crusaders. The deputies, the principal of whom was Martin Litz, were clothed in mourning vestments, which, with the sadness of their aspect, made it sufficiently plain that they came to announce fresh misfortunes. Their accounts drew tears from all the pilgrims.

In the year that preceded the expedition to Constantinople the Flemish and Champenois Crusaders, who had embarked at the ports of Bruges and Marseilles, landed at Ptolemaïs. At the same time came many English warriors, commanded by the earls of Northumberland, Norwich, and Salisbury; and a great number of pilgrims from Lower Brittany, who had chosen for leader the monk Hélain, one of the preachers of the crusade. These Crusaders, when united with those who had quitted the Christian army after the siege of Zara, became impatient to attack the Saracens, and as the king of Jerusalem was averse to breaking the truce made with the infidels, the greater part of them left Palestine, to fight under the banners of the prince of Antioch, who was at war with the prince of Armenia. Having refused to take guides, they were surprised and dispersed by a body of Saracens, sent against them by the sultan of Aleppo; the few that escaped from the carnage, among whom history names two seigneurs de Neuilly, Bernard de Montmirail, and Renard de Dampierre, remained in the chains of the infidels. Hélain, the monk, had the grief to see the bravest of the Breton Crusaders perish on the field of battle, and returned almost alone to Ptolemaïs, to announce the bloody defeat of the soldiers of the cross. A horrible famine had, during two years, desolated Egypt, and extended its ravages into Syria. Contagious diseases followed the famine; the plague swept away the inhabitants of the Holy Land; more than two thousand Christians had received the rights of sepulture in the city of Ptolemaïs, in one single day!

The deputies from the Holy Land, after rendering their melancholy account, invoked by tears and groans the prompt assistance of the army of the Crusaders; but the barons and knights could not abandon the enterprise they had begun; they promised the envoys from Palestine that they would turn their arms towards Syria, as soon as they had subdued the Greeks; and, pointing towards the walls of Constantinople, said: "*This is the road to salvation; this is the way to Jerusalem.*"

Alexius was bound to pay the Latins the sums he had promised; if he was faithful to his word, he had to apprehend a revolt of the Greeks; if he did not fulfil his engagements, he dreaded the arms of the Crusaders. Terrified by the general agitation that prevailed, and restrained by a double fear, the two emperors remained inactive in their palace, without daring to seek for peace, or prepare for war.

The Crusaders, dissatisfied with the conduct of Alexius, deputed several barons and knights to demand of him peremptorily whether he would be their friend or their enemy. The deputies, on entering Constantinople, heard nothing throughout their passage but the insults and threats of an irritated populace. Received in the palace of Blachernæ, amidst the pomp of the throne and the court, they addressed the emperor Alexius, and expressed the complaints of their companions in arms in these terms: "We are sent by the French barons and the doge of Venice to recall to your mind the treaty that you and your father have sworn to upon the Gospel, and to require you to fulfil your promises as we have fulfilled ours. If you do us justice, we shall only have to forget the past, and give due praise to your good faith; if you are not true to your oaths, the Crusaders will no longer remember they have been your friends and allies, they will have recourse to no more prayers, but to their own good swords. They have felt it their duty to lay their complaints before you, and to warn you of their intentions, for the warriors of the West hold treachery in horror, and never make war without having declared it; we offer you our friendship, which has placed you upon the throne, or our hatred, which is able to remove you from it; we bring you war with all its calamities, or peace with all its blessings: it is for you to choose, and to deliberate upon the part you have to take."

These complaints of the Crusaders were expressed with so little respect, that they must have been highly offensive to the ears of the emperors. In this palace, which constantly resounded with the acclamations of a servile court, the sovereigns of Byzantium had never listened to language so insolent and haughty. The emperor Alexius, to whom this menacing tone appeared to reveal his own helplessness and the unhappy state of his empire, could not restrain his indignation; the courtiers fully partook of the anger of their masters, and were desirous of punishing the insolent orator of the Latins on the spot; but the deputies left the palace of Blachernæ, and hastened to regain the camp of the Crusaders.

The council of Isaac and Alexius breathed nothing but vengeance; and, on the return of the deputies, war was decided on in the council of the barons. The Latins determined to attack Constantinople; nothing could equal the hatred and fury of the Greeks; but fury and hatred cannot supply the place of courage: not daring to meet their enemy in the open field, they resolved to burn the fleet of the Venetians. The Greeks, on this occasion, had again recourse to that Greek fire, which had, more than once, served them instead of courage, and saved their capital. This terrible fire, skilfully hurled or directed, devoured vessels, soldiers, and their arms; like the bolt of Heaven, nothing could prevent its explosion, or arrest its ravages; the waves of the sea, so far from extinguishing it, redoubled its activity. Seventeen ships, charged with the Greek fire and combustible matter, were carried by a favourable wind towards the port in which the Venetian vessels lay at anchor. To assure the success of this attempt, the Greeks took advantage of the darkness of night; and the port, the gulf, and the faubourg of Galata, were, all at once, illumined by a threatening and sinister light. At the aspect of the danger, the trumpets sounded the alarm in the camp of the Latins; the French flew to arms and prepared for the fight, whilst the Venetians cast themselves into their barks, and went out to meet vessels bearing within their sides destruction and fire.

The crowd of Greeks assembled on the shore applauded the spectacle, and enjoyed the terror of the Crusaders. Many of them embarked in small boats, and rowed out upon the sea, darting arrows and endeavouring to carry disorder among the Venetians. The Crusaders encouraged each other; they rushed in crowds to encounter the danger, some raising plaintive and piercing cries towards Heaven, and others uttering horrible imprecations against the Greeks: on the walls of Constantinople, clapping of hands and cries of joy resounded, and were redoubled as the vessels covered with flames drew nearer. Villehardouin, an ocular witness, says that amidst this frightful tumult, nature appeared to be in confusion, and the sea about to swallow up the earth. Nevertheless, the Venetians, by the means of strong arms and numberless oars, succeeded in turning the course of the fire-ships wide of the port, and they were carried by the current beyond the canal. The Crusaders, in battle array, standing on their vessels or dispersed among the barks, rendered thanks to God for having preserved them from so great a disaster; whilst the Greeks beheld with terror their fire-ships consuming away upon the waters of the Propontis, without having effected the least injury.

The irritated Latins could not pardon the perfidy and ingratitude of the emperor Alexius: "It was not enough for him to have failed in his engagements and broken his oaths, he endeavoured to burn the fleet that had borne him triumphantly to the heart of his empire: the time was now come to repress the enterprises of traitors by the sword, and to punish base enemies, who were acquainted with no other arms but treachery and deceit; and, like the vilest brigands, only ventured to deal their blows in the darkness and silence of night." Alexius, terrified at these threats, could think of no other resource than that of imploring the clemency of the Crusaders. He offered them fresh oaths and fresh promises, and threw the blame of the hostilities upon the fury of the people, which he had not the power to restrain. He conjured his friends, his allies, his liberators, to come and defend a throne ready to fall to pieces beneath him, and proposed to give up his own palace to them.

Mourzoufle was directed to convey to the Latins the supplications and offers of the emperor, and, seizing the opportunity to augment the alarms and discontent of the multitude, he caused the report to be spread that he was going to deliver Constantinople up to the barbarians of the West. On learning this, the people assembled tumultuously in the streets and public places; the report became general that the enemies were already in the city, and all joined in the cry that to prevent the greatest calamities, not a moment was to be lost; the empire required a master who was able to defend and protect it.

Whilst the young prince, seized with terror, shut himself up in his palace, the crowd of insurgents flocked to the church of St. Sophia to choose a new emperor.

Since the imperial dynasties had become the playthings of the caprice of the multitude, and of the ambition of conspirators, the Greeks made the changing of their sovereigns quite a sport, without reflecting that one revolution produces other revolutions; and, to avoid present calamities, rushed headlong into new ones. The most prudent of the clergy and the patricians presented themselves at the church of St. Sophia, and earnestly endeavoured to prevent the evils with which the country was threatened. But it was in vain they explained to their excited auditory that by changing their master they were sure to overthrow both the throne and the empire. "When they asked my opinion," says the historian Nicetas, "I was careful not to consent to the deposition of Isaac and Alexius, because I felt assured that the man they would elect in their place would not be the most able. But the people," adds the same historian, "whose only motive of action is passion,—the people, who twenty years before had killed Andronicus and crowned Isaac, could not endure their own work and live under princes whom they themselves had chosen." The multitude reproached their sovereign with their misery, which was the bitter fruit of the war; and with the weakness of their government, which was but the result of general corruption. The victories of the Latins, the inefficiency of the laws, the caprices of fortune, the very will of Heaven, all were gathered into one great accusation to be brought against those who governed the empire. The distracted crowd looked to a revolution foı everything; a change of emperors appeared to them the only remedy for the ills under which they groaned. They pressed, they solicited the patricians and senators,—they scarcely knew the names of the men they wished to choose as masters; but any other than Isaac, any other than Alexius, must merit the esteem and love of the Greeks. To be the wearer of a purple robe, was quite enough to entitle a man to ascend the throne of Constantine. Some excused themselves on account of age, others from alleged incapacity. The people, sword in hand, required them to accept the sovereign authority. At length, after three days of stormy debate, an imprudent young man, named Canabus, allowed himself to be prevailed upon by the prayers and threats of the people. A phantom of an emperor was crowned in the church of St. Sophia, and proclaimed in Constantinople. Mourzoufle was no stranger to this popular revolution. Several historians have thought that he promoted the election of an obscure man, to test the peril in some sort, and to become acquainted with the power and will of the people, in order, one day, to profit by it himself.

Alexius, made aware of this revolution, trembled in the recesses of his deserted palace; he had no hope but in the Latins; he solicited, by messages, the support of the barons; he implored the pity of the marquis of Montferrat; who, touched by his prayers, entered Constantinople by night, and came, at the head of a chosen troop, to defend the throne and the lives of the emperors. Mourzoufle, who dreaded the presence of the Latins, flew to Alexius, to convince him that they were the most dangerous enemies he had, and told him that all would inevitably be lost if the Franks once appeared in arms in the palace.

When Boniface presented himself before the palace of Blachernæ, he found all the doors closed; Alexius caused him to be informed that he was no longer at liberty to receive him, and conjured him to leave Constantinople with his soldiers. The sight of the warriors of the West had spread terror throughout the city; their retreat revived both the courage and fury of the people. A thousand different rumours prevailed at once; the public places resounded with complaints and imprecations; from moment to moment the crowd became more numerous and the tumult increased. Amidst all this confusion and disorder, Mourzoufle never lost sight of the prosecution of his designs; by promises and caresses he won over the imperial guard, whilst his friends pervaded the capital, exciting the fury and rage of the multitude by their speeches and insinuations. An immense crowd soon assembled before the palace of Blachernæ, uttering seditious cries. Mourzoufle then presented himself before Alexius: he employed every means to aggravate the alarm of the young prince, and, under the pretext of providing for his safety, drew him into a secluded apartment, where his creatures, under his direction, loaded him with irons and cast him into a dungeon. Coming forth, he boldly informed the people what he had done for the salvation of the empire; and the throne, from which he had dragged his master, benefactor, and friend, appeared but a just recompense for the devotedness of his services: he was carried in triumph to the church of St. Sophia, and crowned emperor amidst the acclamations of the people. Scarcely was Mourzoufle clothed with the imperial purple, than he resolved to possess the fruit of his crime in security; dreading the caprice of both fortune and the people, he repaired to the prison of Alexius, forced him to swallow an empoisoned draught, and because death did not keep pace with his impatience, strangled him with his own hands.

Thus perished, after a reign of six months and a few days, the emperor Alexius, whom one revolution had placed upon a throne, and who disappeared amidst the storms of another, without having tasted any of the sweets of supreme rank, and without an opportunity of proving whether he was worthy of it. This young prince, placed in a most difficult situation, had not the power, and perhaps not the will, to rouse the Greeks to oppose the Crusaders. On the other side, he had not the tact to employ the support of the Latins so as to keep the Greeks within the bounds of obedience; directed by perfidious counsels, ever vacillating between patriotism and gratitude, fearing by turns to alienate his unhappy subjects, or to irritate his formidable allies, he perished, the victim of his own weakness and irresolution. Isaac Angelus, on learning the tragical end of his son, died of terror and despair; thus sparing Mourzoufle another parricide, of which he was not the less suspected to be guilty. History makes no more mention of Canabus; the confusion was so great that the Greeks were ignorant of the fate of a man whom but a few days before they had elevated to the rank of their sovereign; four emperors had been dragged violently from the throne since the arrival of the Latins, and fortune reserved the same fate for Mourzoufle.

In order to profit by the crime that had ministered to his ambitious views, the murderer of Alexius formed the project of committing another, and to bring about by treachery the death of all the principal leaders of the army of the Crusaders. An officer, sent to the camp of the Latins, was directed to say that he came on the part of the emperor Alexius, of whose death they were ignorant, to engage the doge of Venice and the French nobles to come to the palace of Blachernæ, where all the sums promised by the treaties, should be placed in their hands. The barons at first agreed to accept the invitation of the emperor, and prepared to set out with great joy; but Dandolo, who, according to Nicetas, deservedly obtained the name of the *Prudent of the Prudent*, awakened their mistrust, and pointed out strong reasons for fearing a fresh perfidy of the Greeks. It was not long before they were fully informed of the death of Isaac, the murder of Alexius, and all the crimes of Mourzoufle. At this news the indignation of the Crusaders was strong and general; knights had difficulty in crediting such baseness; every fresh account made them tremble with horror; they forgot the wrongs of Alexius towards themselves, deplored his unfortunate end, and swore to avenge him. In the council, the leaders loudly exclaimed that an implacable war must be made against Mourzoufle, and that the nation that had crowned treachery and parricide should be punished. The prelates and ecclesiastics, more animated than all the others, invoked at once the thunders of religion and earthly war against the usurper of the imperial throne, and against the Greeks, untrue to their sovereign, untrue to God himself. Above all, they could not pardon the subjects of Mourzoufle, for willingly remaining plunged in the darkness of heresy, and escaping, by an impious revolt, from the domination of the Holy See. They promised all the indulgences of the sovereign pontiff and all the riches of Greece to the warriors called upon to avenge the cause of God and men.

Whilst the Crusaders thus breathed nothing but war against the emperor and people of Constantinople, Mourzoufle was preparing to repel their attacks; he earnestly endeavoured to attach the inhabitants of the capital to his cause; he reproached the great with their indifference and effeminacy, and laid before them the example of the multitude; to increase his popularity and fill his treasury, he persecuted the courtiers of Alexius and Isaac, and confiscated the property of all those who had enriched themselves in public offices. The usurper at the same time set about reëstablishing discipline among the troops, and augmenting the fortifications of the city; he no longer indulged in pleasures or allowed himself repose; as he was accused of the greatest crimes, he had not only to contend for empire, but for impunity; remorse doubled his activity, excited his bravery, and proved to him that he could have no safety but in victory. He was constantly seen parading the streets, with his sword by his side, and an iron club in his hand, animating the courage of the people and the soldiers.

The Greeks, however, contented themselves with declaiming against the Crusaders. After having made another attempt to burn the fleet of the Venetians, they shut themselves up within their walls, and supported with patience the insults and menaces of the Latins. The Crusaders appeared to have nothing to fear but famine; as they began to feel the want of provisions, Henry of Hainault, brother of the count of Flanders, undertook, in order to obtain supplies for the army, an expedition to the shores of the Euxine Sea; and, followed by several knights, laid siege to Philea. The city of Philea was the ancient Philopolis, celebrated in the heroic ages of antiquity for the palace in which were received Jason and the Argonauts, who, like the French knights, had left their country, to seek distant adventures and perils. Henry of Hainault, after a short resistance from the inhabitants, made himself master of the city, in which he met with a considerable booty, and found provisions in abundance; the latter he transported by sea to the army.

Mourzoufle, being informed of this excursion, marched out, by night, with a numerous body of troops, and placed himself in ambush on the route which Henry of Hainault would take on his return to the camp. The Greeks attacked the Crusaders unexpectedly, in the full persuasion that their victory would be an easy one; but the Frank warriors, without displaying the least alarm, closed in their ranks, and made so firm and good a resistance, that the ambuscaders themselves were very quickly obliged to fly. Mourzoufle was upon the point of falling into the hands of his enemies, and only owed his safety to the swiftness of his horse; he left behind on the field of battle, his buckler, his arms, and the standard of the Virgin, which the emperors were accustomed to have borne before them in all great perils. The loss of this ancient and revered banner was a source of great regret to the Greeks. The Latins, on their part, when they saw the standard and image of the patroness of Byzantium floating amongst their victorious ranks, were persuaded that the mother of God had abandoned the Greeks, and declared herself favourable to their cause.

After this defeat, the Greeks became convinced that there existed no other means of safety for them but the fortification of their capital; it was much more easy for them to find workmen than soldiers, and a hundred thousand men laboured day and night at the reparation of the walls. The subjects of Mourzoufle appeared satisfied that their ramparts would defend them, and handled the implements of masonry without repugnance, in the hope that they would prevent the necessity for their wielding the sword or lance.

Mourzoufle had learnt to dread the courage of his enemies, and as strongly doubted the valour of his subjects; therefore, before risking any fresh warlike attempts, he determined to sue for peace, and demanded an interview with the leaders of the Crusaders. The lords and barons refused with horror to have an interview with the usurper of the throne, the murderer, the executioner of Alexius; but the love of peace, and the cause of humanity, induced the doge of Venice to consent to listen to the proposals of Mourzoufle. Henry Dandolo repaired in his galley to the point of the gulf, and the usurper, mounted on horseback, approached him as near as possible. The conference was long and animated. The doge required Mourzoufle to pay immediately fifty centenaries of gold, to aid the Crusaders in their expedition to Syria, and again to swear obedience to the Romish church. After a long altercation, Mourzoufle promised to give the Latins the money and assistance they demanded; but he could not consent to submit to the yoke of the Church of Rome.* The doge, astonished that,

* Dandolo demanded of Mourzoufle fifty centenaries of gold, which have been valued at 50,000 pounds' weight of gold, or 48,000,000 of francs (about $10,000,000). Nicetas alone speaks of this interview, of which Villehardouin and other historians make no mention.

MOURZOUFLE PARLEYING WITH DANDOLO.

Henry Dandolo repaired in his galley to the point of the gulf, and the usurper, mounted on horseback, approached him as near as possible. The conference was long and animated. The doge required Mourzoufle to pay immediately fifty centenaries of gold, to aid the Crusaders in their expedition to Syria, and again to swear obedience to the Romish church. After a long altercation, Mourzoufle promised to give the Latins the money and assistance they demanded; but he would not consent to submit to the yoke of the Church of Rome. The doge, astonished that, after having outraged all the laws of Heaven and nature, he should attach so much importance to religious opinions, casting a glance of contempt at Mourzoufle, asked him if the Greek religion excused treachery and parricide? The usurper, although much irritated, dissembled his anger, and was endeavouring to justify his conduct, when the conference was interrupted by some Latin horsemen.—Book XI.

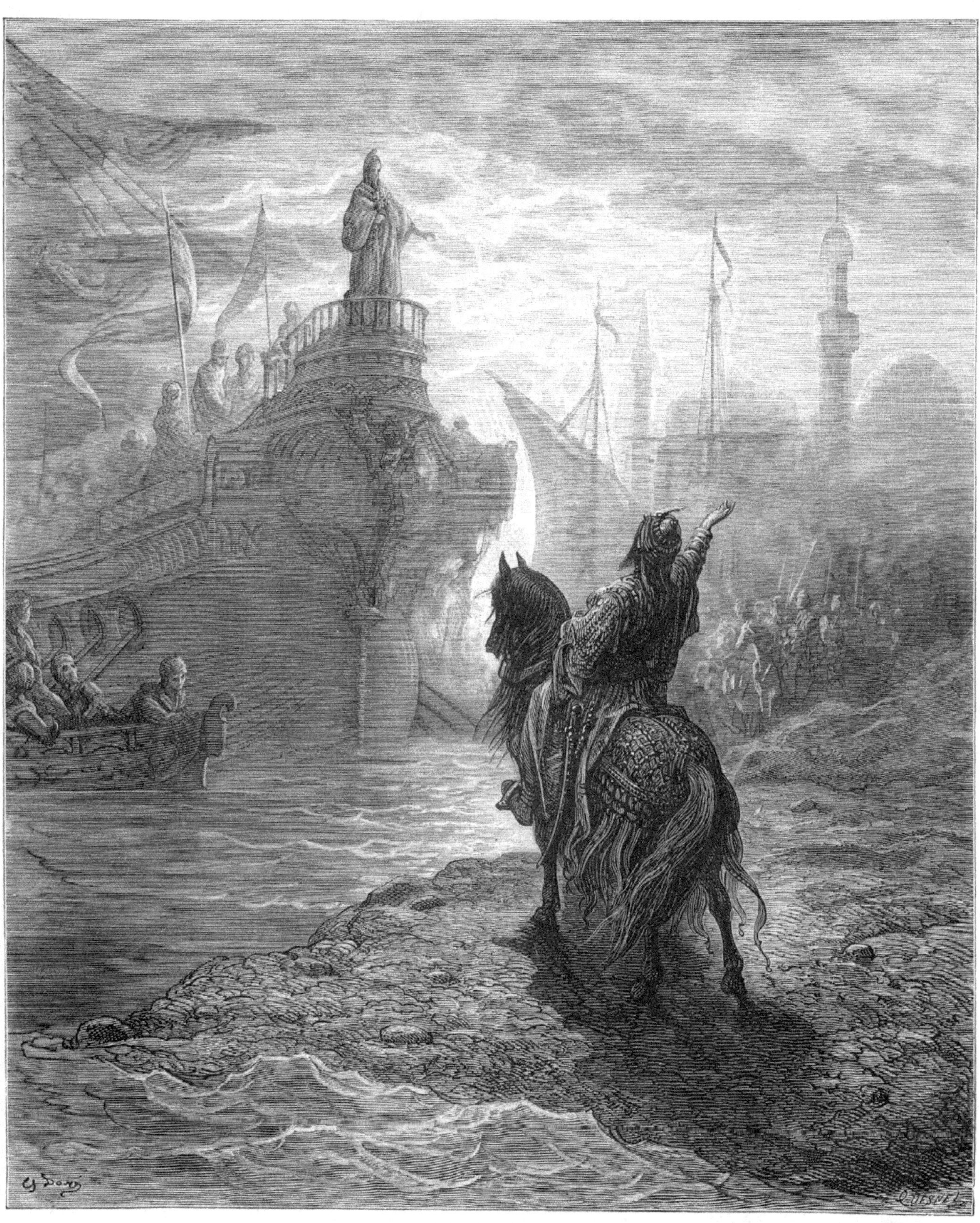

after having outraged all the laws of Heaven and nature, he should attach so much importance to religious opinions, casting a glance of contempt at Mourzoufle, asked him, if the Greek religion excused treachery and parricide? The usurper, although much irritated, dissembled his anger, and was endeavouring to justify his conduct, when the conference was interrupted by some Latin horsemen.

Mourzoufle, on his return to Constantinople, convinced that he must prepare for war, set earnestly about his task, and determined to die with arms in his hand. By his orders, the walls and towers that defended the city on the side of the port were elevated many feet. He constructed upon the walls galleries of several stages, from which the soldiers might launch arrows and javelins, and employ balistas and other machines of war; at the top of each tower was placed a drawbridge, which, when lowered upon the vessels, might afford the besieged a means of pursuing their enemies, even to their own fleet.

The Crusaders, although supported by their natural bravery, could not view all these preparations with indifference. The most intrepid could not help feeling some inquietude on comparing the small number of the Franks with the imperial army and the population of Constantinople; all the resources they had till that time found in their alliance with the emperors were about to fail them, without their having any hope of supplying their place but by some miraculous victory: for they had no succour to look for from the West. Every day war became more dangerous, and peace more difficult; the time was gone by for retreat. In this situation, such were the spirit and character of the heroes of this crusade, that they drew fresh strength from the very circumstances that would appear likely to have depressed them, and filled them with dread; the greater the danger, the more courage and firmness they displayed; menaced on all sides, expecting to meet with no asylum on either sea or land, there remained no other part to take but that of besieging a city from which they could not retire with safety: thus nothing could overcome their invincible bravery.

On viewing the towers that the Greeks considered as a certain means of safety, the leaders assembled in their camp, and shared amongst them the spoils of the empire and the capital, of which they entertained no doubt of achieving the conquest. It was decided in the council of the princes, barons, and knights, that a new emperor should be nominated instead of Mourzoufle, and that this emperor should be chosen from the victorious army of the Latins. The chief of the new empire should possess by right a fourth of the conquest, with the two palaces of Blachernæ and Bucoleon. The cities and lands of the empire, as well as the booty they should obtain in the capital, were to be distributed among the Franks and Venetians, with the condition of rendering homage to the emperor. In the same council regulations were made to assign the proportions of the Latin clergy, and of the lords and barons. They regulated, according to the feudal laws, the rights and duties of the emperors and subjects, of the great and small vassals. Thus Constantinople, under the dominion of the Greeks, beheld before its walls a small band of warriors, who, helm on head, and sword in hand, abolished in her walls the legislation of Greece, and imposed upon her beforehand the laws of the West. By this act of legislation, which they derived from Europe, the knights and barons appeared to take possession of the empire; and, whilst making war against the inhabitants of Constantinople, might imagine that they were already fighting for the safety and glory of their own country.

In the first siege of Byzantium, the French had been desirous of attacking the city by land, but experience had taught them to appreciate properly the wiser counsels of the Venetians. They determined, with an unanimous voice, to direct all their efforts to an attack by sea. They conveyed into the vessels the arms, provisions, and appointments of all kinds; and the whole army embarked on Thursday, the 8th day of April, 1204. On the morrow, with the first rays of the sun, the fleet which bore the knights and their horses, the pilgrims and all they possessed, the tents, the machines of the

Crusaders, *and the destinies of a great empire*, heaved anchor, and crossed the breadth of the gulf. The ships and galleys, arranged in line, covered the sea for the space of half a league. The sight of the towers and ramparts, bristling with arms and soldiers, and covered with murderous machines and long tubes of brass, from which poured the Greek fire, did not in the least intimidate the warriors of the West. The Greeks had trembled with fright at seeing the fleet of the Crusaders in motion; but as they could look for no safety but in resistance, they appeared disposed to brave all perils in defence of their property and their families.

Mourzoufle had pitched his tents in the part of the city ravaged by the fire; his army was encamped amidst ruins, and his soldiers had nothing beneath their eyes but melancholy pictures, the sight of which he thought must necessarily excite them to vengeance. From the summit of one of the seven hills, the emperor was able to view the contest, to send succours where he saw they were wanted, and to reanimate at every moment the courage of those who defended the walls and towers.

At the first signal, the Greeks put all their machines in full operation, and endeavoured to defend the approach to the ramparts; but several ships soon gained the shore; the ladders are planted, and the walls shake beneath the continuous blows of the rams. The attack and defence proceed with equal fury. The Greeks fight with advantage from the tops of their elevated towers; the Crusaders, everywhere overpowered by numbers, cannot open themselves a passage, and find death at the foot of the ramparts they burn to surmount. The ardour for fight, itself, produced disorder among the assailants, and confusion in their fleet. The Latins faced all perils, and sustained the impetuous shock of the Greeks till the third hour of the evening: "It was then," says the marshal of Champagne, "that fortune and our sins decreed that we should be repulsed." The leaders, dreading the destruction of their fleet and army, ordered the retreat to be sounded. When the Greeks saw the Crusaders drawing off they believed that their capital was saved; the people of Byzantium flocked to the churches to return thanks to Heaven for so great a victory, and, by the excess of their transports, proved how great the fear had been with which the Latins had inspired them.

On the evening of the same day, the doge and barons assembled in a church near the sea, to deliberate upon their future proceedings; they spoke with deep grief of the check they had sustained, and expatiated strongly upon the necessity of promptly retrieving their defeat. "The Crusaders were still the same men that had already surmounted the ramparts of Byzantium; the Greeks were still the same frivolous, pusillanimous nation, that could oppose no other arms but those of cunning to those of valour. The soldiers of Mourzoufle had been able to resist for one day; but they would soon remember that the Latins had conquered them many times; the recollections of the past were sufficient to revive the confidence of the one party, and to fill the others with terror. Besides, it was well known that the Greeks only contended for the triumph of usurpation and parricide; whilst the Crusaders fought for the triumph of humanity and justice. God would recognize his true servants, and would protect his own cause."

These discourses could not reassure all the Crusaders, and many proposed to change the point of attack, and make a new assault on the side of the Propontis. The Venetians did not agree with this opinion, and dreaded lest the fleet should be drawn away by the currents of the sea. Some of the leaders despaired of the success of the enterprise; and, in their despair, would have been very willing, says an eye-witness, "that the winds and the waves should carry them away beyond the Archipelago." The advice of the Venetians was, however, adopted; and the council decided that the attack upon Constantinople should be renewed on the same side, and at the same point at which the army had been repulsed. Two days were employed in repairing the vessels and machines; and on the third day, the 12th of April, the trumpets once more sounded the signal for battle. The fleet got into motion, and advanced in good order towards the ramparts of Constantinople. The Greeks, who were still rejoicing over their first advantage, could scarcely believe the approach of the Latins to be reality, and their surprise was by no means free from terror. On the other side, the Crusaders, who had met with a resistance they had not at all expected, advanced with precaution towards the ramparts, at the foot of which they had fought in vain. To inflame the ardour and emulation of the soldiers, the leaders of the Latins had proclaimed, by a herald-at-arms, that he that should plant the first banner of the cross upon a tower of the city, should receive a hundred and fifty silver marks.

The combat soon commenced, and was as quickly general; the defence was no less vigorous than the attack: beams, stones, javelins were hurled from one side to the other, crossed or met in mid-air, and fell with a loud noise on the ramparts and the ships; the whole shore resounded with the cries of the combatants and the clashing of swords and lances. In the fleet, the vessels were joined together, and proceeded two by two, in order that upon each point of attack, the number of the assailants might correspond with that of the besieged. The drawbridges are soon let down, and are covered with intrepid warriors, who threaten the invasion of the most lofty towers. The soldiers mount in file, and gain the battlements; the opponents seek, attack, and repulse each other in a thousand different places. Some, on the point of seizing victory, are overthrown by a mass of stone: others are consumed by the Greek fire; but they who are repulsed, again return to the charge, and the leaders everywhere set an example by mounting to the assault like common soldiers.

The sun had run half his course, and prodigies of valour had not been able to triumph over the resistance of the besieged, when a strong breeze from the north arose, and brought two ships that fought together close under the walls. The bishop of Troie and the bishop of Soissons were on board of these two vessels, called the *Pilgrim* and the *Paradise*. Scarcely were the drawbridges lowered, than two Frank warriors were seen upon one of the towers of the city. These two warriors, one of whom was a Frenchman, named D'Urboise, and the other a Venetian, Pietro Alberti, drew after them a crowd of their companions, and the Greeks were massacred or took to flight. In the confusion of the *mêlée*, the brave Alberti was slain by a Frenchman, who mistook him for a Greek, and who, on discovering his mistake, attempted to kill himself in despair. The Crusaders, excited by the fight, scarcely perceived this sad and tragical scene, but pursued the flying, disordered enemy.

The banners of the bishops of Troie and Soissons were planted on the top of the towers, and attracted the eager eyes of the whole army. This sight inflames those who are still on board the vessels; on all sides they press, they rush forward, they fly to the escalade. The Franks obtain possession of four towers: terror prevails among the Greeks, and the few who resist are slaughtered at every point they endeavour to defend; three of the gates of the city fall to pieces beneath the strokes of the rams; the horsemen issue from the ships with their horses, and the whole army of the Crusaders precipitates itself at once into the city. A horseman (Pierre Bacheux), who preceded his fellows, advanced almost alone to the hill upon which Mourzoufle was encamped, and the Greeks, in their fright, took him for a giant. Nicetas himself says that his helmet appeared as large as a tower; the soldiers of the emperor could not stand against the appearance of a single Frank horseman. Mourzoufle, abandoned by his troops, fled: the Crusaders took possession of the imperial tents, continued their victorious course into the city, and put to the sword every Greek they met with. "*It was a horrible spectacle*," says Villehardouin, "*to see women and young children running distractedly here and there, trembling and half dead with fright, lamenting piteously, and begging for mercy.*"

The Crusaders set fire to the quarter they had invaded, and the flames, driven by the wind, announced to the other extremities of the city the presence of an irritated conqueror. Terror and despair prevailed in every street of Constantinople. Some Greek soldiers retired to the palace, whilst others, to escape recognition, threw away both their clothes and their arms. The people and the clergy took refuge in the churches, and the more wealthy inhabitants, in all parts, endeavoured to conceal their most valuable property by burying it in the earth. Many rushed out of the city, without at all knowing whither to direct their steps.

Whilst all were flying before them, the Crusaders were in a state of astonishment at their own victory. At the approach of night, they dreaded an ambuscade, and did not venture to pursue the conquered enemy further; the Venetians encamped within sight of their vessels; the count of Flanders, by a happy augury, occupied the imperial tents, and the marquis of Montferrat advanced towards the palace of Blachernæ. The Latins entertained no idea that the conflict was ended, and kept careful watch under the ramparts they had invaded and won.

Mourzoufle went through many quarters of the city, endeavouring to rally the soldiers: he spoke to them of glory, he invoked the name of their country, he promised rich rewards for valour: but the voice of patriotism was no longer listened to, and neither the love of glory nor the hopes of reward could affect men whose whole thoughts were engaged in the means of saving their lives. Mourzoufle no longer inspired either respect or confidence, and the people, in reply to his exhortations, reproached him with his parricide, and attributed to him all the calamities of the war. When he found himself without hope, it became necessary to endeavour to escape both the pursuit of the conquerors and the resentment of the conquered, and he embarked secretly on the Propontis, with the purpose of seeking an army, or rather an asylum, in the mountains of Thrace. When his flight became known in Constantinople, his name was loaded with maledictions, and, as if it was necessary that an emperor should be present at the fall of the empire, a distracted crowd flocked to the church of St. Sophia, to choose a new master.

Theodore Ducas and Theodore Lascaris solicited the suffrages of the assembly, and contended for a throne that no longer existed. Lascaris was chosen emperor, but he did not dare to assume the imperial crown. This prince possessed both firmness and spirit; the Greeks even boasted of his skill in war, and he undertook to reanimate their courage and arouse their patriotism. "The Latins," said he, "are few, and advance with trembling caution into a city that has still numberless defenders; the Crusaders are afraid to leave their ships at any distance, as they know they are their only refuge in case of defeat: pressed by the approach of danger, they have called in the assistance of fire as their faithful auxiliary, and conceal their fears behind a rampart of flames and a heap of ruins. The warriors of the West neither fight for religion, nor their country, nor their property, nor the honour of their families. The Greeks, on the contrary, defend all they hold most dear, and must carry to the contest every sentiment that can increase the courage and inflame the zeal of citizens. If you are still Romans," added Lascaris, "the victory is easy; twenty thousand barbarians have shut themselves up within your walls; fortune has given them up to our arms." The new emperor then addressed the soldiers and the imperial guards; he represented to them that their safety was inseparably connected with that of Constantinople, that the enemy would never pardon being driven back by them several times from the ramparts of the capital; that in victory they would find all the advantages of fortune, all the pleasures of life: whilst in flight, neither land nor sea could afford them an asylum, and that shame, misery, and death itself would follow their footsteps everywhere. Lascaris did not neglect to flatter the pride, and endeavour to kindle the zeal of the patricians. He reminded them of the heroes of ancient Rome, and presented to their valour the great examples of history. "It was to their arms Providence had confided the safety of the imperial city; if, contrary to all hopes, the country should be subdued, they could have but few regrets in abandoning life, and would find perhaps some glory in dying on the same day on which the old empire of the Cæsars should be doomed to fall."

The soldiers only replied to his speech by demanding their pay; the people listened to Lascaris with more surprise than confidence, and the patricians preserved a gloomy silence, sensible to no other feeling but a profound despair. The trumpets of the Crusaders were soon heard, and at this signal, terror seized even the bravest; there was no longer any idea of disputing the victory with the Latins. Lascaris, left alone, was himself obliged to abandon a city which he could find no one to assist him in defending. Thus Constantinople, that had beheld two emperors in one night, was once again without a master, and presented the image of a vessel without a rudder, dashed about by the winds, and ready to perish amidst the howling of the tempest. The conflagration begun by the Latins, extended to several other quarters, and consumed, by the admission of the barons, more houses than three of the greatest cities of either France or Germany contained. The fire continued its ravages during the whole night, and before day the Crusaders prepared, by the light of its flames, to follow up their victory. Ranged in order of battle, they were advancing with precaution and mistrust, when their ears were saluted with supplicating voices that filled the air with lamentations and prayers. Women, children, and old men, preceded by the clergy, bearing crosses and images of saints, came in procession, to throw themselves at the feet of the conquerors. The leaders allowed their hearts to be touched by the cries and entreaties of this weeping crowd, and a herald-at-arms was ordered to pass through the ranks, and proclaim the laws of clemency; the soldiers were commanded to spare the lives of the inhabitants, and to respect the honour of women and maidens. The Latin clergy joined their exhortations with those of the leaders of the army, and threatened with the vengeance of the Church all who should abuse victory by outraging humanity.

In the mean time the Crusaders advanced amidst the braying of trumpets and the noise of clarions, and their banners were soon planted in the principal quarters of the city. When Boniface entered the palace of Bucoleon, which was supposed to be occupied by the imperial guard, he was surprised to find a great number of women, of the first families of the empire, whose only defence was their groans and tears. Marguerite, daughter of the king of Hungary, and wife of Isaac, and Agnes, daughter of a king of France, the wife of two emperors, threw themselves at the feet of the barons, and emplored their mercy. The marquis of Montferrat respected their misfortunes, and placed them under the protection of a guard. Whilst Boniface occupied the palace of Bocoleon, Henry of Hainault took possession of that of Blachernæ; these two palaces, filled with immense riches, were reserved from pillage, and were exempted from the lamentable scenes which, during several days, desolated the city of Constantinople.

The Crusaders, impatient to gather the treasures they had shared beforehand, spread themselves through all the quarters of the capital, and carried off, without pity or consideration, everything that offered itself to their avidity. The houses of the poorest citizens were no more respected than the mansions of the rich. The Greeks, plundered of their property, ill-treated by the conquerors, and turned out of their homes, implored the humanity of the counts and barons, and pressed around the marquis of Montferrat, crying, "*Holy king marquis, have pity upon us!*" Boniface was touched by their prayers, and endeavoured to recall the Crusaders to some sentiments of moderation; but the license of the soldiers increased with the sight of booty; the most dissolute and most undisciplined gave the signal, and marched at their head, and their example lead on all the rest: the intoxication of victory had no longer any restraint,—it was sensible to neither fear nor pity. There was nothing so difficult, says Nicetas, as to soften the fierce temper, appease the anger, or gain the affections of these barbarians. Their bile was so heated, that it only required a word to set it in a blaze; it was a ridiculous undertaking to attempt to render them tractable, a folly to speak reason to them.

When the Crusaders discontinued the slaughter, they had recourse to every kind of outrage and violence to plunder the conquered; no spot in Constantinople was free from brutal search. In spite of the frequently-repeated prohibitions of their leaders and priests, they respected neither the modesty of women nor the sanctity of churches. Some soldiers and followers of the army plundered the tombs and coffins of the emperors; the body of Justinian, which ages had spared, and which presented itself to their eyes in a fresh and undecayed state, could not repel their sacrilegious hands, or make them respect the peace of the grave; in every temple where a rag of silk shone, or a particle of gold glittered, their greedy fingers were stretched out to clutch them. The altar of the Virgin, which decorated the church of St. Sophia, and which was admired as a masterpiece of art, was beaten to pieces, and the veil of the sanctuary was torn to rags. The conquerors played at dice upon the marble tables which represented the apostles, and got drunk out of the cups reserved for divine service. Horses and mules led into the sanctuary, bent beneath the weight of the spoils, and, pierced by sword-points, stained with their blood and their ordure the vestibule of St. Sophia. A prostitute girl, whom Nicetas calls the follower of demons, the priestess of furies, mounted the patriarchal pulpit, sang an immodest song, and danced in the church, amidst a crowd of soldiers, as if to insult the ceremonies of religion.

The Greeks could not behold these impious scenes without trembling with horror. Nicetas, whilst deploring the misfortunes of the empire and the Greek Church, declaims with vehemence against the barbarous race of the Franks. "Here," says he, "is what was promised by that golden gorget, that haughty bearing, those elevated eyebrows, that closely-shaven beard, that hand so ready to shed blood, those nostrils breathing anger, that proud eye, that cruel disposition, that prompt and hurried utterance." The historian of Byzantium reproaches the Crusaders with having surpassed the Saracens in barbarity, and reminds them of the example of the soldiers of Saladin, who, when masters of Jerusalem, neither violated the modesty of matrons and virgins, nor filled the sepulchre of the Saviour with bloody carcasses, nor subjected Christians to fire, sword, hunger, or nakedness.

The country on the shores of the Bosphorus offered a no less deplorable spectacle than the capital. Villages, churches, country-houses were all devastated and given over to pillage. A distracted crowd covered the roads, and wandered about at hazard, pursued by fear, bending under fatigue, and uttering cries of despair. Senators, patricians, the offspring of a family of emperors, strayed homeless about, covered with rags, seeking for any miserable asylum. When the church of St. Sophia was pillaged, the patriarch fled away, imploring the charity of passengers; all the rich fell into indigence, and inspired nothing but contempt; the most illustrious nobility, the highest dignities, the splendour of talents or virtues, possessed nothing to create respect or attract admiration. Misery, like inevitable death, effaced all distinctions, and confounded all ranks; the dregs of the people completed the spoliation of the fugitives, at the same time insulting their misfortunes. A senseless multitude rejoiced at the public evils, applauded the degradation of the noble and the rich, and called these disastrous days, days of justice and equality.

Nicetas describes his misfortune and his own deplorable adventures; the house he had inhabited under the reign of the emperors was consumed by the flames of the second conflagration: having retired with his family to another house, built near the church of St. Sophia, he soon found himself in danger in this last asylum, and only owed his safety to devoted friendship and gratitude. A Venetian merchant, whom he had saved from the fury of the Greeks before the flight of Alexius, was desirous, in his turn, of saving his benefactor; he armed himself with a sword and a lance, assumed the dress of a soldier of the cross, and as he spoke the languages of the West, he defended the entrance of the house of Nicetas, saying it was his, the price of his blood, shed in fight. This vigilant sentinel at first repulsed all aggressors, and braved a thousand perils; a model of fidelity and virtue, amidst the horrid disorders that desolated Constantinople.

The turbulent crowd of soldiers that filled the streets and penetrated everywhere, became indignant that a single house should be thus exempt from their brutal searches. The despairing Venetian at length came to Nicetas, and told him that it was totally out of his power to defend him any longer. "If you remain here," said he, "to-morrow, perhaps, you will be loaded with chains, and your family become a prey to all the violences of the conquerors. Follow me, and I will conduct you out of the gates of Constantinople." Nicetas, with his wife and children, followed the faithful Venetian: their liberator, in armour, marched at their head, and led them as if they were prisoners

This unfortunate family proceeded, filled with fear, meeting at every step soldiers greedy of pillage, who ill-treated the Greeks they plundered, and threatened every woman with insult. Nicetas, and some of his friends who had come to join him, carried their children in their arms, the only wealth that Heaven had left them; and defended alone by the pity which their despair and misery inspired. They walked together, placing their wives and daughters in the centre, after having advised the youngest to blacken their faces with earth. In spite of this precaution, the beauty of one young girl attracted the attention of a soldier, and she was borne away from the arms of her father, weighed down by age and infirmities. Nicetas, touched by the tears of the old man, flew after the ravisher, and addressing himself to all the warriors he met, he implored their pity, and conjured them, in the name of Heaven, the protector of virtue, in the name of their own families, to snatch a daughter from dishonour, to save a father from despair. The Frank warriors were affected by his prayer, and the unfortunate father soon saw his daughter restored to him, the only hope of his exile, the last consolation of his grey hairs. Nicetas and his companions in trouble encountered still further dangers, but at length got safely out of Constantinople by the Golden Gate, happy at being able to quit a country so lately the object of all their affections. The generous Venetian received their blessings, and in return prayed Heaven to protect them in their exile.

Nicetas, with tears, embraced his liberator, whom he never had the good fortune to see again; then casting a look upon Constantinople, upon his unhappy country, he addressed to it these touching complaints, which express the griefs of his exile, and which he himself has transmitted to us:—"O Queen of Cities, what power has been able to separate us from thee! What consolation shall we find on issuing from thy walls, as naked as we issued from the bosom of our mothers! Become the sport of strangers, the companions of wild animals that inhabit the forests, we shall never again visit thy august domes, and can only fly with terror around thee, like sparrows round the spot where their nest has been destroyed."

Nicetas arrived with his family at Cylindria, and afterwards retired to Nice, where he employed himself in retracing the history of the misfortunes of his country.

Constantinople did not cease to be the theatre of the frightful deeds of violence that war brings in its train. Amidst the sanguinary sports of victory, the Latins, to insult the effeminate manners of the Greeks, clothed themselves in long flowing robes, painted of various colours; they fastened to the heads of their horses linen hoods with their silken cords, in which the Orientals dress themselves; whilst others paraded the streets carrying in their hands, instead of a sword, some paper and an inkhorn; thus ridiculing the conquered, whom they termed scribes and copyers.

The Greeks had on all occasions insulted the ignorance of the Latins; the knights, without seeking to retort upon their enemies for their affronts, esteemed nothing but the trophies of valour and the labours of war, and hold in contempt the quiet occupations of peace. With these dispositions it was not likely they should spare the monuments that decorated the public places, the palaces, or the edifices of Byzantium. Constantinople, which to this period had stood erect amidst the ruins of several empires, had collected within its walls the scattered relics of the arts, and was proud to exhibit the masterpieces that had been saved from the destruction of barbarous ages. The bronze, in which breathed the genius of antiquity, was cast into the furnace, and converted into money, to satisfy the greedy soldiers. The heroes and gods of the Nile, those of ancient Greece and of ancient Rome, the masterpieces of Praxiteles, Phidias, and the most celebrated artists, fell beneath the strokes of the conquerors.

Nicetas, who deplores the loss of these monuments, has left us a description, from which the history of art may derive some advantage. The historian of Byzantium informs us that in the Place of Constantine stood, before the siege, the statue of Juno, and that of Paris offering to Venus the prize of beauty, or the apple of discord. The statue of Juno, which had formerly adorned the temple of the goddess at Samos, was of so colossal a size, that when it was destroyed by the Crusaders, eight harnessed oxen were required to drag the gigantic head to the palace of Bucoleon. In the same place was erected an obelisk of a square form, which astonished the spectator by the multitude and variety of the objects it presented to his view. On the sides of this obelisk the artist had represented, in basso-relievo, all sorts of birds saluting the return of the sun, villagers employed in their rustic labours, shepherds playing on their pipes, sheep bleating, lambs bounding on the grass; further on, a tranquil sea and fishes of a thousand sorts, some taken alive, others breaking the nets and regaining their deep retreats; at the back of the landscape naked cupids playing and throwing apples at each other; at the top of the obelisk, which terminated in a pyramidal form, was the figure of a woman that turned with the least breath of air, which was called *the attendant of the winds.*

An equestrian statue* ornamented the place of Mount Taurus; the horse appeared to throw up the dust with his feet, and outspeed the winds in his course. As the horseman had his arm extended towards the sun, some supposed it to represent Joshua, commanding the star of day to stand still, on the plains of Gabaon; others believed the artist meant to describe Bellerophon mounted on Pegasus.

A colossal statue of Hercules, attributed to Lysippus, was one of the ornaments of the Hippodrome; the demigod had neither his bow nor his club; he was seated on a bed of osier; his left knee bent, sustained his elbow; his head reclining on his left hand; his pensive looks and air expressing the vexation and sorrow caused by the jealousy of Eurystheus. The shoulders and chest of Hercules were broad, his hair was curled, and his limbs were large and muscular; his leg alone exceeded in height the stature of an ordinary man. The skin of the Nemean lion, exhibited over the shoulders of the son of Alcmena, the erected mane and the head of the animal, which might be fancied still to roar and terrify the passers by, who stopped to contemplate the statue.

Not far from the terrible Hercules, was a group of an ass and its driver, which Augustus placed in his colony of Nicopolis, to perpetuate the remembrance of a singular circumstance that had foretold the victory of Actium to him. Near this were the hyena or she-wolf that suckled Romulus and Remus, a monument from the old nations of the West; the sphinx, with the face of a woman, dragging frightful animals behind her; the crocodile, an inhabitant of the Nile, with his tail covered with horrible scales; a man fighting with a lion; an elephant with his supple trunk; and the antique Scylla,

* The Bellerophon. This statue is that of Theodosius, showing a trophy placed upon a neighbouring column; it was thus the Pacificator was represented: *fuit a Deo pacificatoris habitus.* Nicestas says that in his left hand he held a globe. The statues of the other emperors of Constantinople present a similar sign, to which a cross is attached. The people believed that under the hoof of the left fore foot, was the figure of a Venetian or a Bulgarian, or of a man of some other country which had no intercourse with the Romans. The statue being destroyed by the Latins, it was said that the figure of a Bulgarian was found concealed in the hoof, crossed by a nail and incrusted in lead. This statue came from Antioch in Syria. At the quadrilateral base was a basso-relievo, in which the populace, ever superstitious, fancied they beheld the prediction of the fall of the empire. They even said that the Russians there represented would accomplish the prediction.

showing before, the features of a woman, with large breasts and a deformed figure; and behind, such monsters as those that pursued Ulysses and his companions. In the same place was an eagle clutching a serpent in his talons, and bearing it away towards the azure vault; the bronze beautifully exhibited the pain of the reptile, and the haughty fierceness of the bird of Jupiter. When the sun shone on the horizon, the extended wings of the king of the air denoted, by lines skilfully traced, the twelve hours of the day.

All who, in that gross age, preserved any taste for the arts, admired the figure of a young woman, her hair plaited on her brow, and gathered into a knot behind, placed upon a column of the Circus; this young woman, as if by enchantment, bore in her right hand a horseman, whose horse she held by one foot; the horseman covered with his cuirass, and the spirited, neighing steed, seemed listening to the warlike trumpet, and to breathe nothing but eagerness for the fight. Near the eastern boundary of the Circus were represented in bronze, the charioteers who had gained prizes, and whose triumphs, in times gone by, had often divided the empire into two factions; they appeared standing in their chariots, running in the lists, pulling and loosening by turns the reins of their coursers, and encouraging them by gesture and voice. Not far from this, upon a basis of stone, were several Egyptian animals, the aspic, the basilisk, and the crocodile, all engaged in mortal combat,—an image of the war made by the wicked on each other; the hideous forms of these animals, the rage and pain expressed throughout their bodies, the livid poison which seemed to exhale with their bites, altogether inspired a feeling of disgust and terror. Another masterpiece, made to charm the sight, ought, at least, to have touched and disarmed the conquerors. Among the statues described by Nicetas, none is more conspicuous than a Helen with her charming smile and her voluptuous attitude; a Helen, with perfect regularity of features, her hair floating at the pleasure of the winds, her eyes full of languor, her lips, which even in the bronze were rosy; her arms, of which even the same bronze showed the whiteness; Helen, in short, with all her beauty, and such as she appeared before the old men of Ilium, who were ravished at her presence.

Constantinople contained many other splendid objects of art, which preceding ages had admired; almost all such as were of bronze were condemned to perish, the Crusaders seeing in these monuments nothing but the metal of which they were composed. "That which antiquity had judged," says Nicetas, "of inestimable value, became, all at once, a common matter; and that which had cost immense sums, was changed by the Latins into pieces of coin of very little value!" The statues of marble held out less temptation for the cupidity of the conquerors, and received no other injuries than such as were inseparable from the tumult and disorders of war.

The Greeks, who appeared so proud of their knowledge, themselves neglected the fine arts. The sciences of Greece, the profane wisdom of the Academy and the Lyceum, had given place among them to the debates of scholastic theology; they passed by the Hippodrome with indifference; and held nothing in reverence but relics and images of saints. These religious treasures, preserved with care in the churches and palaces of Byzantium, had, during several ages, attracted the attention of the Christian world; in the days that followed the conquest, they tempted the pious cupidity of the Crusaders. Whilst the greater part of the warriors bore away the gold, the jewels, the carpets, and the rich stuffs of the East, the more devout of the pilgrims, particularly the ecclesiastics, collected a booty much more innocent and appropriate to the soldiers of Christ. Many braved the prohibitions of their leaders and their superiors, and did not disdain to employ by turns supplications and menaces, stratagem or violence, to procure relics that were the objects of their respect and veneration. Contemporary history relates several examples of this, which serve to make us acquainted with the spirit of the pilgrim conquerors of Byzantium. Martin Litz, abbot of Paris, in the diocese of Bâle.

entered into a church that had been given up to pillage, and penetrated, without being observed, into a retired place, where numerous relics were deposited, under the guardianship of a Greek monk. This Greek monk was then at prayers, with his hands raised supplicatingly towards heaven. His old age, his white hairs, his fervent piety, and the grief impressed upon his brow, were calculated to inspire both respect and pity; but Martin, approaching the venerable guardian of the treasures with an angry manner, exclaimed in a threatening tone, "Miserable old man, if thou dost not instantly conduct me to the place where thy relics are hidden, prepare to die on the spot!" The monk, terrified by this menace, immediately and tremblingly arose, and pointed to a large iron coffer, into which the pious abbot eagerly plunged both his hands, and seized everything precious that he could grasp. Delighted with this conquest, he ran to conceal his treasures on board a vessel, and contrived, by a holy fraud, to keep them for several days from the knowledge of the leaders and prelates of the army, who had strictly ordered the pilgrims to bring to an appointed place all the relics that fell into their hands.

Martin Litz, at first, returned to the Christians of Palestine, who had sent him to Constantinople; and, a short time after, came back to Europe, loaded with spoils obtained from the clergy of Byzantium. Among the relics he exhibited on his return, were, a piece of the true cross, the bones of St. John the Baptist, and an arm of St. James. The miraculous translation of this treasure is celebrated with much pomp by the monk Gunther, in whom it created more surprise and joy than the conquest of a great empire. If we may credit the account of the German monk, angels descended from heaven to watch over the relics of Martin Litz. On the route of the holy abbot, the tempests of the ocean were silent, pirates were struck motionless, and robbers, those pests of travellers, stopped short, seized with respect and fear. At length Martin Litz was received in triumph at Bâle, and the treasures he had preserved through so many perils, were distributed among the principal churches of the diocese.

Another priest, named Galon de Dampierre, of the diocese of Langres, less adroit or less fortunate than Martin Litz, had not been able to obtain any share of the spoils of the churches; he went and threw himself at the feet of the pope's legate, and implored him, with tears in his eyes, to permit him to carry back to his country the head of St. Mames. A third ecclesiastic of Picardy, having found the head of St. George, and the head of St. John the Baptist, concealed among the ruins, hastened to quit Constantinople, and, laden with such a rich prize, presented to the cathedral of Amiens, his country, the inestimable relics of which Providence had made him the possessor.

The princes and barons did not despise these holy spoils. Dandolo, receiving as his share* a piece of the true cross, which the emperor Constantine was accustomed to have borne before him to battle, made a present of it to the republic of Venice. Baldwin kept for himself the crown of thorns of Christ, and several other relics found in the palace of Bucoleon. He sent Philip Augustus, king of France, a portion of the true cross, a foot in length; some of the hair of Jesus Christ, when an infant; and the linen in which the Man-God was enveloped in the stable in which he was born.

The Greek priests and monks, thus plundered by the conquerors, parted with tears from the remains of the saints that had been confided to their keeping, and which every day cured the sick, made the lame to walk, restored sight to the blind, and strength to the paralytic. These holy spoils, that the devotion of the faithful had gathered together from all the countries of the East, went to

---

* We have spoken in the early part of the work of the true cross which the kings of Jerusalem caused to be borne before them in battle, and which was taken by Saladin at the battle of Tiberias; Saladin refused to deliver it up to Richard, as many of the Crusaders must have known. How then could the true cross be found at Constantinople? The Greeks, however, were not very nice with respect to the authenticity of their relics, and the Christians of the West on this point yielded very easy faith to them.

illustrate the churches of France and Italy, and were received by the Christians of the West as the most glorious trophies of the victories God had enabled the Crusaders to obtain.

Constantinople fell into the power of the Latins on the 10th of April, towards the end of Lent. The marshal of Champagne, after relating some of the scenes we have described, says with great simplicity, "Thus passed the splendid festivities of Easter." The clergy called the Crusaders to penitence; the voice of religion made itself heard in hearts hardened by victory; the soldiers crowded to the churches they had devastated, and celebrated the sufferings and death of Christ upon the wrecks of his own altars.

This solemn epoch without doubt inspired some generous sentiments; all the Latins were not deaf to the language of the charity of the Gospel. We feel bound here to admit that the greater part of the knights and ecclesiastics protected the liberty and lives of the citizens, and the honour of matrons and virgins; but such was the spirit that then possessed the warriors, that all the Crusaders allowed themselves to be overcome by the thirst for booty; and the leaders, equally with the soldiers, exercised, without hesitation or scruple, the right which their victory had given them of plundering the conquered. It was agreed that all the spoils should be deposited in three churches, selected for the purpose; and the leaders commanded the Crusaders to bring, in common, the whole of the booty, and threatened with death and excommunication all who should abstract anything from the prize of the valour, and the recompense due to the labours of the whole army. Many soldiers, and even some knights, allowed themselves to be led away by avarice, and retained valuable objects that fell into their hands. "Which," says the marshal of Champagne, "made the Lord to begin to love them less." The justice of the counts and barons was inflexible towards the guilty; the count of St. Pol ordered one of his knights, who had withheld something from the common stock or booty, to be hung, with his escutcheon suspended from his neck. Thus the Greeks, plundered by violence, might be present at the punishment of some of the ravishers of their property, and might contemplate with surprise the regulations of stern equity mingled with the disorders of victory and pillage. After the festival of Easter, the Crusaders shared the captured riches; the fourth part of the spoil was set aside for him who should be chosen emperor, and the rest was divided among the French and the Venetians. The French Crusaders, who had conquered Zara, to the sole advantage of the Venetians, were not the less called upon to pay the fifty thousand silver marks they owed to the republic; the amount was deducted beforehand from the portion of the booty that belonged to them. In the division that was made among the warriors of Lombardy, Germany, and France, each knight had a part equal to that of two horsemen, and every horseman one equal to that of two foot-soldiers. All the plunder of the Greeks only yielded* four hundred thousand silver marks; but although this sum far exceeded the revenues of all the kingdoms of the West, it did not by any means represent the value of the riches accumulated in Byzantium. If the princes and barons, upon making themselves masters of the city, had been satisfied with imposing a tribute upon the inhabitants, they might have received a much larger sum; but this pacific manner of obtaining wealth agreed neither with their character nor the humour they were in. History asserts that the Venetians, in this circumstance, offered them some very prudent advice, and made propositions that were rejected

* One edition of Villehardouin makes the plunder of Constantinople amount to five hundred thousand silver marks, equivalent to twenty-four millions; if we add to this sum the fifty thousand marks due to the Venetians, and deducted before the division, and the part which they had in the division itself, we shall find the total amount of booty fifty millions four hundred thousand francs (about $10,500,000). As much, says the modern historian who supplies us with this note, perhaps, was appropriated secretly by individuals. The three fires which had consumed more than half the city had destroyed at least as much of its riches, and in the profusion that followed the pillage, the most precious effects had lost so much of their value, that the advantage of the Latins probably was not equivalent to a quarter of what they had cost the Greeks. Thus we may suppose that Constantinople, before the attack, contained 600,000,000 of wealth ($125,000,000).

with scorn. The Frank warriors could not condescend to submit the advantages of victory to commercial calculations; the produce of pillage was always, in their eyes, the most worthy fruit of conquest, and the most noble reward of valour.

When they had thus shared the rich plunder of the eastern empire, the Crusaders gave way to the most extravagant joy, without perceiving that they had committed a great fault in exhausting a country which was about to become their own; they did not reflect that the ruin of the conquered might one day bring on that of the conquerors, and that they might become as poor as the Greeks they had just despoiled. Without regrets, as without foresight, hoping everything from their own good swords, they set about electing a leader who should reign over a people in mourning and a desolated city. The imperial purple had still the same splendour in their eyes, and the throne, though shaken by their arms, was still the object of their ambition. Six electors were chosen from among the Venetian nobles, and six others from among the French ecclesiastics, to give a master to Constantinople; the twelve electors assembled in the palace of Bucoleon, and swore, upon the Gospel, to crown only merit and virtue.

Three of the principal leaders of the crusade had equal claims to the suffrages of the electors. If the purple was to be the reward of experience, of ability in council, and of services rendered to the cause of the Latins, Henry Dandolo, who had been the moving spirit, the very soul of the enterprise, certainly had the first claim to it. The marquis of Montferrat, likewise, had titles worthy of great consideration; the Latins had chosen him for their leader, and the Greeks already acknowledged him as their master. His bravery, proved in a thousand fights, promised a firm and generous support to a throne that must rise from amidst ruins. His prudence and moderation might give the Latins and the people of Greece reason to hope that, when once raised to empire, he would repair the evils of war. The claims of Baldwin to the imperial crown were not less cogent than those of his concurrents. The count of Flanders was related to the most powerful monarchs of the West, and was descended, in the female line, from Charlemagne. He was much beloved by his soldiers, whose dangers he was always ready to share; he had deservedly obtained the esteem of the Greeks, who, even amidst the disorders of conquest, celebrated him as the champion of chastity and honour. Baldwin was the protector of the weak, the friend of the poor; he loved justice, and had no dread of truth. His youth, which he had already illustrated by brilliant exploits and solid virtues, gave the subjects of the new empire hopes of a long and happy reign; the rank he held among the warriors, his piety, his intelligence, his love of study and learned men, rendered him worthy of ascending the throne of Augustus and Constantine.

The electors at first turned their attention towards the venerable Dandolo; but the republicans of Venice trembled at the idea of seeing an emperor among their fellow-citizens: "What shall we not have to dread," said they, "from a Venetian become master of Greece, and of part of the East? Shall we be subject to his laws, or will he remain subject to the laws of our country? Under his reign, and under that of his successors, who will assure us that Venice, the Queen of the Seas, will not become one of the cities of this empire?" The Venetians, whilst speaking thus, bestowed just eulogiums upon the virtue and character of Dandolo; they added, that their doge, who was approaching the end of a life filled with great actions, had nothing left him but to finish his days with glory, and that he himself would find it more glorious to be the head of a victorious republic, than the sovereign of a conquered nation. "What Roman," cried they, "would have been willing to lay down the title of citizen of Rome, to become king of Carthage?"

On terminating their speeches, the Venetians conjured the assembly to elect an emperor from among the other leaders of the army. After this, the choice of the electors could only be directed

ENTRY OF THE CRUSADERS INTO CONSTANTINOPLE.

The banners of the bishops of Troie and Soissons were planted on the top of the towers, and attracted the eager eyes of the whole army. This sight inflames those who are still on board the vessels; on all sides they press, they rush forward, they fly to the escalade. The Franks obtain possession of four towers; terror prevails among the Greeks, and the few who resist are slaughtered at every point they endeavour to defend; three gates fall to pieces beneath the strokes of the rams; the horsemen issue from the ships with their horses, and the whole army of the Crusaders precipitates itself at once into the city. A horseman (Pierre Bacheux), who preceded his fellows, advanced almost alone to the hill upon which Mourzoufle was encamped, and the Greeks, in their fright, took him for a giant. Nicetas himself says that his helmet appeared as large as a tower; the soldiers of the emperor could not stand against a single Frank horseman. Mourzoufle, abandoned by his troops, fled; the Crusaders took possession of the imperial tents, continued their victorious course into the city, and put to the sword every Greek they met with. "IT WAS A HORRIBLE SPECTACLE," *says Villehardouin,* "TO SEE WOMEN AND YOUNG CHILDREN RUNNING DISTRACTEDLY HERE AND THERE, TREMBLING AND HALF DEAD WITH FRIGHT, LAMENTING PITEOUSLY AND BEGGING FOR MERCY." *The Crusaders set fire to the quarter they had invaded, and the flames, driven by the wind, announced to the other extremities of the city the presence of an irritated conqueror.*—BOOK XI.

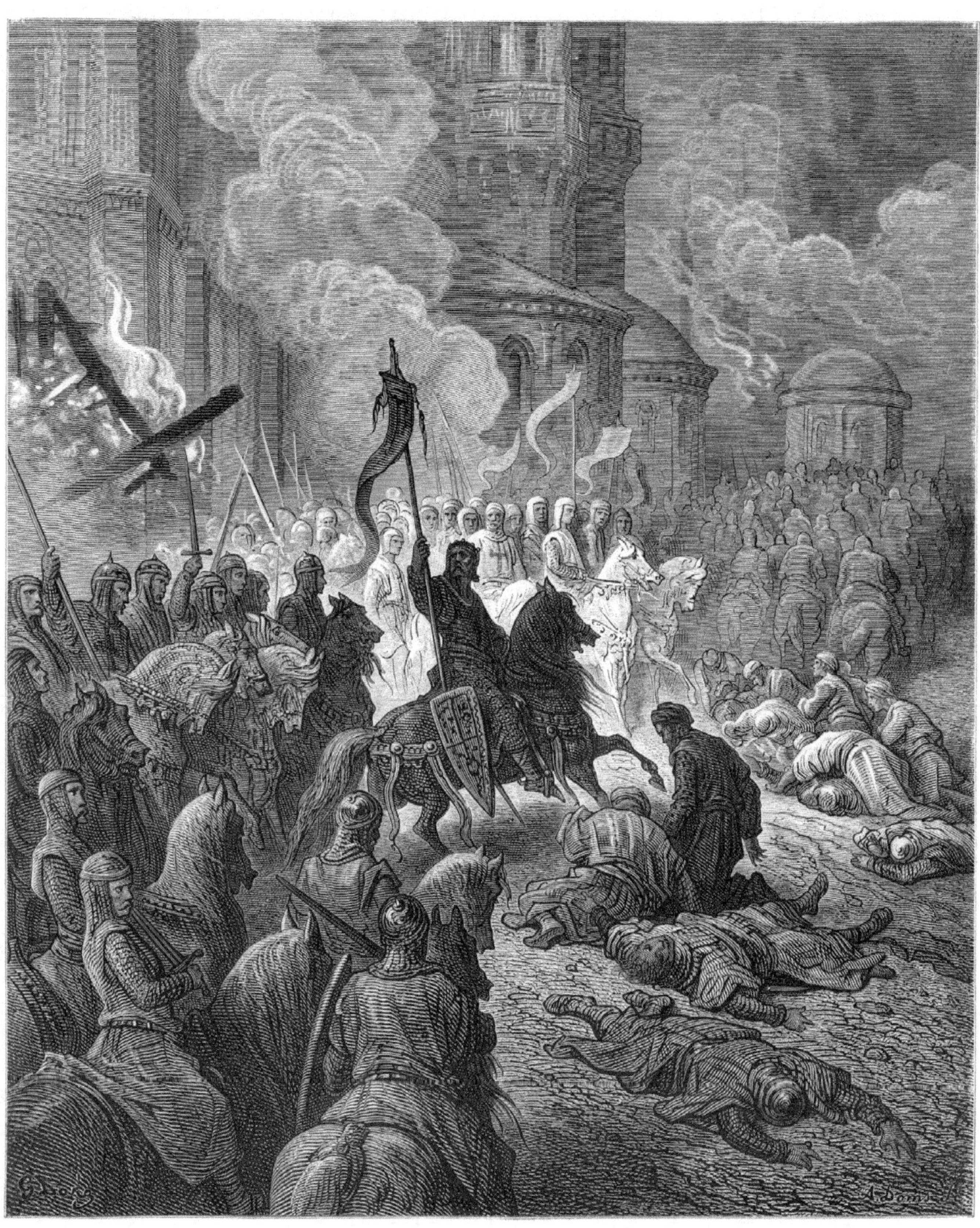

towards the count of Flanders and the marquis of Montferrat; the most wise dreading that the one of the two concurrents who should not obtain the empire, would be sure to give vent to his dissatisfaction, and would desire the fall of the throne occupied by his rival. They still remembered the violent debates which, in the first crusade, had followed the election of Godfrey of Bouillon; and the troubles excited in the young kingdom of Jerusalem, by the jealous ambition of Raymond de St. Gilles. To prevent the effects of such a fatal discord, it was judged best to decree, at once, that the prince that should gain the suffrages for the imperial throne, should yield to the other, under the condition of fealty and homage, the property of the island of Candia, and all the lands of the empire situated on the other side of the Bosphorus. After this decision, the assembly turned their whole attention to the election of an emperor. Their choice was for a long time uncertain. The marquis of Montferrat at first appeared to have the majority of the suffrages; but the Venetians were fearful of seeing upon the throne of Constantinople a prince who had any possessions in the neighbourhood of their territories, and represented to the assembly that the election of Baldwin would be much more advantageous to the Crusaders, particularly as it would interest the warlike nations of the Flemings and French in the glory and support of the new empire. The interests and jealousies of policy, and, without doubt, also wisdom and equity, at length united all voices in favor of the count of Flanders.

The Crusaders, assembled before the palace of Bucoleon, awaited with impatience the decision of the electors. At the hour of midnight, the bishop of Soissons came forward under the vestibule, and pronounced, in a loud voice, these words: "This hour of the night, which witnessed the birth of a Saviour of the world, gives birth to a new empire, under the protection of the Omnipotent. You have for emperor, Baldwin, count of Flanders and Hainault." Loud cries of joy arose from among the Venetians and the French. The people of Constantinople, who had so often changed masters, received, without repugnance, the new one just given to them, and mingled their acclamations with those of the Latins. Baldwin was elevated upon a buckler, and borne in triumph to the church of St. Sophia. The marquis of Montferrat followed in the train of his rival; the generous submission of which he presented an example, was much admired by his companions in arms, and his presence drew scarcely less attention than the warlike pomp that surrounded the new emperor.

The ceremony of the coronation was postponed till the fourth Sunday after Easter. In the mean time the marriage of the marquis of Montferrat with Margaret of Hungary, the widow of Isaac, was celebrated with much splendour. Constantinople beheld within its walls the festivities and spectacles of the West, and, for the first time, the Greeks heard in their churches the prayers and hymns of the Latins. On the day appointed for the coronation of the emperor, Baldwin repaired to St. Sophia, accompanied by the barons and the clergy. Whilst divine service was being performed, the emperor ascended a throne of gold, and received the purple from the hands of the pope's legate, who performed the functions of patriarch. Two knights carried before him the *laticlavici tunica* of the Roman consuls, and the imperial sword, once again in the hands of warriors and heroes. The head of the clergy, standing before the altar, pronounced, in the Greek language, these words: "*He is worthy of reigning;*" and all persons present repeated in chorus, "*he is worthy! he is worthy!*" The Crusaders shouting their boisterous acclamations, the knights clad in armour, the crowd of miserable Greeks, the sanctuary despoiled of its ancient ornaments, and decked with foreign pomp, presented altogether a spectacle solemn and melancholy—all the evils of war amidst the trophies of victory. Surrounded by the ruins of an empire, reflective spectators could not fail to remark among the ceremonies of this day, that in which, according to the custom of the Greeks, were presented to Baldwin a little vase filled with dust and bones, and a lock of lighted flax, as symbols of the shortness of life, and the nothingness of human grandeur.

Before the ceremony of his coronation, the new emperor distributed the principal dignities of the empire among his companions in arms. Villehardouin, marshal of Champagne, obtained the title of marshal of Romania; the count de St. Pol, the dignity of constable; the charges of master of the wardrobe, great cupbearer and butler, were given to Canon de Bethune, Macaire de St. Ménéhoult, and Miles de Brabant. The doge of Venice, created despot or prince of Romania, had the right of wearing purple buskins, a privilege, among the Greeks, reserved for members of the imperial family. Henry Dandolo represented the republic of Venice at Constantinople; half the city was under his dominion and recognised his laws; he raised himself, by the dignity of his character as well as by his exploits, above all the princes and all the nobles of the court of Baldwin; he alone was exempt from paying fealty and homage to the emperor for the lands he was to possess.

The barons began to be impatient to share the cities and provinces of the empire. In a council composed of twelve of the patricians of Venice and twelve French knights, all the conquered lands were divided between the two nations. Bithynia, Romania or Thrace, Thessalonica, all Greece from Thermopylæ to Cape Sunium, with the larger isles of the Archipelago, fell to the share and under the dominion of the French. The Venetians obtained the Cyclades and the Sporades, in the Archipelago; the isles and the oriental coast of the Adriatic Gulf; the coasts of the Propontis and the Euxine Sea; the banks of the Hebrus and the Vardas; the cities of Cypsedes, Didymatica, and Adrianople; the maritime countries of Thessalonica, &c. &c. Such was at first the distribution of the territories of the empire. But circumstances that could not be foreseen, the diversity of interests, the rivalries of ambition, all the chances of fortune and of war, soon produced great changes in this division of dominions. History would in vain endeavour to follow the conquerors into the provinces allotted to them; it would be more easy to mark the banks of an overflowing torrent, or to trace the path of the storm, than to fix the state of the uncertain and transitory possessions of the conquerors of Byzantium.

The lands situated beyond the Bosphorus were erected into a kingdom, and, with the island of Candia, given to the marquis of Montferrat. Boniface exchanged them for the province of Thessalonica, and sold the island of Candia to the republic of Venice for thirty pounds weight of gold. The provinces of Asia were abandoned to the count of Blois, who assumed the title of duke of Nice and Bithynia. In the distribution of the cities and lands of the empire, every one of the lords and barons had obtained domains proportionate with the rank and services of the new possessor. When they heard speak of so many countries of which they scarcely knew the names, the warriors of the West were astonished at their conquests, and believed that the greater part of the universe was promised to their ambition. In the intoxication of their joy, they declared themselves masters of all the provinces that had formed the empire of Constantine. They cast lots for the countries of the Medes and Parthians, and the kingdoms that were under the domination of the Turks and Saracens; several barons expressed a great desire to reign at Alexandria; others disputed for the palace of the sultans of Iconium; some knights exchanged that which had been assigned to them for new possessions, whilst others complained of their share and demanded an augmentation of territory. With the money which arose from the plunder of the capital, the conquerors purchased the provinces of the empire; they sold, they played at dice, for whole cities and their inhabitants. Constantinople was during several days a market, in which seas and their islands, nations and their wealth, were trafficked for; in which the Roman world was put up to sale, and found purchasers among the obscure crowd of the Crusaders.

Whilst the barons were thus distributing cities and kingdoms, the ambition of the Latin clergy was by no means idle, but was busy in invading the property of the Greek Church. All the churches of Constantinople were divided between the French and the Venetians; they named priests of the two nations, to minister in the temples torn from the conquered; and no other religious ceremonies were celebrated within the walls of the city but those of the West. The leaders of the crusade had agreed among themselves, that if the emperor of Constantinople should be chosen from the French, the patriarch should be a Venetian. According to this convention, which had preceded the conquest, Thomas Morosini was elevated to the chair of St. Sophia; priests and Latin bishops were, at the same time, sent into the other conquered cities, and took possession of the wealth and the privileges of the Greek clergy. Thus the Romish worship associated itself with the victories of the Crusaders, and made its empire acknowledged wherever the banners of the conquerors floated.

Nothing now opposed the arms of the Crusaders; all trembled before them; fame wafted everywhere the accounts of their exploits and their power; but, on casting a glance into the future, the leaders had great reason to fear that the retreat or death of their warriors would leave the empire they had founded destitute of defenders. The population, weakened and dispersed, were not sufficient for either the cultivation of the lands or the work of the cities. In this conjuncture, the counts and barons, who always expected with fear the judgments of the head of the Church, redoubled their submission to the sovereign pontiff, and sought his support, in the hope that the Holy See would bring the West to pronounce in their favour, and that at the voice of the father of the faithful, a great number of French, Italians, and Germans would come to people and defend the new empire.

After his coronation, Baldwin wrote to the pope, to announce to him the extraordinary victories by which it had pleased God to crown the zeal of the soldiers of the cross. The new emperor, who assumed the title of knight of the Holy See, recalled to the mind of the sovereign pontiff the perfidies and the long revolt of the Greeks. "We have brought under your laws," said he, "that city, which, in hatred for the Holy See, would scarcely hear the name of the prince of the apostles, and did not afford a single church to him who received from the Lord the supremacy over all churches." Baldwin, in his letter, invited the vicar of Jesus Christ to imitate the example of his predecessors, John, Agapetus, and Leo, who visited in person the Church of Byzantium. To complete the justification of the pilgrims who had made themselves masters of the Greek empire, the emperor invoked the testimony of all the Christians of the East. "When we entered into this capital," added he, "many inhabitants of the Holy Land, who were there, expressed greater joy than any others, and asserted aloud that we had rendered God a more agreeable service than if we had retaken Jerusalem."

The marquis of Montferrat at the same time addressed a letter to the sovereign pontiff, in which he protested his humble obedience to all the decisions of the Holy See. "As for me," said the king of Thessalonica, "who only took up the cross for the expiation of my sins, and not to obtain an opportunity of sinning with more license under the pretext of religion, I submit myself blindly to your will. If you judge that my presence in Romania may be useful, I will die there, contending against your enemies and those of Christ: if you think, on the contrary, I ought to abandon these rich countries, pay no regard to the wealth or dignities I possess there, I am ready to return to the West; for I am not willing to do anything that will draw upon me the anger of the sovereign judge."

The doge of Venice, who till that time had braved with so much haughtiness the threats and thunders of the Church, acknowledged the sovereign authority of the pope, and joined his protestations with those of Baldwin and Boniface. To disarm the anger of Innocent, they represented to him that the conquest of Constantinople had prepared the deliverance of Jerusalem, and boasted of the wealth of a country which the Crusaders had at length brought under the laws of the Holy See. In all their letters to the pope or the faithful of the West, the conquerors of Byzantium spoke of the

Greek empire as of a new land of promise, which awaited the servants of God and the soldiers of Christ.

Innocent had been for a long time irritated by the disobedience of the Crusaders; in his reply, he reproached with bitterness the victorious army of the Latins for having preferred the riches of the earth to those of heaven; he reprimanded the leaders for having exposed to the outrages of the soldiers and followers of the army, the honour of matrons and maidens, and virgins consecrated to the Lord; for having ruined Constantinople, plundered *both great and small*, violated the sanctuary, and put forth a sacrilegious hand upon the treasures of the churches. Nevertheless, the father of the faithful would not take upon him to fathom the judgments of God; he was satisfied to believe that the Greeks had been justly punished for their faults, and that the Crusaders were recompensed as the instruments of Providence, as the avengers of divine justice. "Dread," said he, "the anger of the Lord; hope with fear that he will pardon the past, if you govern the nations with equity; if you are faithful to the Holy See, and, above everything, if you entertain a firm resolution to accomplish your vow for the deliverance of the Holy Land."

Notwithstanding this outward show of anger, the sovereign pontiff was gratified to the depths of his heart by the prayers and submission of the heroes and princes whose exploits made the Eastern world tremble. Cardinal Peter of Capua had given absolution to the Venetians excommunicated after the siege of Zara. Innocent at first blamed the indulgence of his legate, but finished by confirming the pardon granted to Dandolo and his compatriots. The pope approved the election of Baldwin, who took the title of knight of the Holy See, and consented to recognise an empire to which he was to give laws. The more submissive the Crusaders showed themselves to his authority, the more plainly it appeared to him that their conquests must concern the glory of God and that of the vicar of Christ upon earth. He wrote to the bishops of France, that God had been willing to console the Church by the conversion of heretics; that Providence had humbled the Greeks, an impious, proud, and rebellious people; and again placed the empire in the hands of the Latins, a pious, humble, and submissive nation. The sovereign pontiff invited, in the name of the emperor Baldwin, the French of both sexes and all conditions, to repair to Greece to receive lands and riches proportioned to their merit and their quality. He promised the indulgences of the crusade to all the faithful, who, sharing the glory of the Crusaders, should go to defend and promote the prosperity of the new empire of the East.

The pope did not, however, lose sight of the Syrian expedition, and appeared persuaded that succours sent to Constantinople must contribute to the deliverance of the holy places. The king of Jerusalem implored more earnestly than ever, both by letters and ambassadors, the effective protection of the Holy See, as well as that of the princes of the East.

The new emperor of Byzantium did not renounce the hope of assisting the Christian colonies of Syria; and to raise the courage of his brethren of the Holy Land, he sent to Ptolemaïs the chain of the port and the gates of Constantinople. When these trophies reached Palestine, scarcity, famine, and all the evils of an unfortunate war ravaged both cities and plains. At the news of approaching aid, the people of Ptolemaïs passed at once from excessive grief and despondency to all the transports of joy. Fame, whilst publishing the miraculous conquests of the companions of Baldwin and Boniface, carried the hope of safety into all the Christian cities of Syria, and spread terror among the Mussulmans. The sultan of Damascus had recently concluded a truce with the Christians, and trembled lest it should be broken, when, all at once, he owed his safety to the very event that had caused his alarms.

The greater part of the defenders of the Holy Land, who had experienced nothing but the evils of war, became desirous of partaking of the glory and the good fortune of the French and Venetians. They even who had quitted the victorious army at Zara, who had so severely blamed the expedition to Constantinople, believed that the will of God called them to the shores of the Bosphorus, and they abandoned the Holy Land. The legate of the pope, Peter of Capua, was drawn away by the example of the other Crusaders, and went to animate with his presence the zeal of the Latin clergy, who were labouring for the conversion of the Greeks; the knights of St. John and the Temple also directed their course towards Greece, where glory and rich domains were the reward of valour; and the king of Jerusalem was left almost alone at Ptolemaïs, without means of making the truce he had entered into with the infidels respected.

Baldwin warmly welcomed the defenders of the Holy Land; but the joy he experienced at their arrival was much troubled by the intelligence of the death of his wife, Marguerite of Flanders. This princess had embarked in the fleet of John de Nesle, in the belief that she should meet her husband in Palestine; sinking under the fatigue of a long voyage, and perhaps the pains of disappointment, she fell sick at Ptolemaïs, and died at the moment she learnt that Baldwin had been crowned emperor of Constantinople. The vessel destined to convey the new empress to the shores of the Bosphorus only brought back her mortal remains. Baldwin, amidst his knights, wept for the loss of a princess he had loved tenderly, and who, by her virtues and the graces of her youth, he had hoped would be the ornament and example of the court of Byzantium. He caused her to be buried with great pomp in the same church in which, but a few days before, he had received the imperial crown. Thus the people of Constantinople witnessed, almost at the same time, the coronation of an emperor and the funeral of an empress;—days of joy and triumph mingled with days of mourning. This contrast of the pageantry of death and the pomps of victory and of a throne, appeared to offer a faithful image of the glory of conquerers, and the future destiny of the empire.

The emperor and his barons, with all the succours they had received from the East, had scarcely twenty thousand men to defend their conquests, and restrain the people of the capital and the provinces. The sultan of Iconium and the king of the Bulgarians had long threatened to invade the lands contiguous to their states, and they thought that the dissensions and subsequent fall of the Greek empire presented a favourable opportunity for the outbreak of their jealousy and ambition. The nations of Greece were conquered without being subdued. As in the disorder which accompanied the conquest of Byzantium, no other right had been acknowledged but that of force and the sword, all the Greeks, who had still arms in their hands, were desirous of forming a principality or a kingdom. On all sides new states and empires sprang up from the bosom of the ruins, and already threatened that which the Crusaders had so recently established.

A grandson of Andronicus founded in a Greek province of Asia Minor the principality of Trebizonde; Leo Sgurre, master of the little city of Napoli, had extended his dominions by injustice and violence, and, to employ a comparison offered by Nicetas, he had grown greater, like the torrent that swells in the storm and is enlarged by the waters of the tempest. A barbarous conqueror, a fierce and cruel tyrant, he reigned, or rather he spread terror, over Argos and the isthmus of Corinth. Michael-Angelus Comnenus, employing the arms of treachery, gained the kingdom of Epirus, and subdued to his laws a wild and warlike people. Theodore Lascaris, who, like Æneas, had fled from his burning country, collected some troops in Bithynia, and caused himself to be proclaimed emperor at Nice, whence his family was destined at a future day to return in triumph to Constantinople.

If despair had imparted any degree of courage to the two fugitive emperors, they might have obtained a share of their own spoils, and preserved a remnant of power; but they had not profited by the lessons of misfortune. Mourzoufle, who had completed all the crimes begun by Alexius, did not hesitate to place himself in the power of his unfortunate rival, whose daughter he had married: the wicked sometimes take upon themselves the duty of punishing one another. Alexius, after having loaded Mourzoufle with caresses, inveigled him into his house, and caused his eyes to be put out. In this condition, Mourzoufle, abandoned by his followers, for whom he was now nothing but an object of disgust, went to conceal his existence and his misery in Asia; but on his road fell into the hands of the Latins. Being led to Constantinople, and condemned to expiate his crimes by an ignominious death, he was precipitated from the top of a column raised by the emperor Theodosius in the Place of Taurus. The multitude of Greeks that had offered the purple to Mourzoufle were present at his tragical end, and appeared terrified at a punishment that was much more new to them than the crimes for which it was inflicted. After the execution, the crowd contemplated with surprise a basso-relievo on the column of Theodosius, which represented a king falling from a very elevated place, and a city stormed by sea. In these times of troubles and calamities, presages were discovered everywhere. Everything, even to marble and stone, appeared to have told of the misfortunes of Constantinople. Nicetas was astonished that such great misfortunes had not been announced by a shower of blood, or some sinister prodigies; the most enlightened Greeks explained the fall of the empire of Constantine by the verses of poets and sibyls, or by the prophecies of the Scriptures; the common people read the death of tyrants and their own miseries in the looks of statues, and upon the columns that remained standing in the capital.

The perfidy and cruelty of Alexius did not remain long unpunished; the usurper was obliged to wander from city to city, and, not unfrequently, to conceal the imperial purple under the garb of a mendicant. For a considerable time he only owed his safety to the contempt in which he was held by the conquerors. After having long strayed about in a state of destitution, he was given up to the marquis of Montferrat, who sent him a prisoner into Italy; escaping thence, he again passed into Asia, and found an asylum with the sultan of Iconium. Alexius could not be satisfied to live in peace in his retreat, but joined the Turks in an attack upon his son-in-law Lascaris, whom he could not pardon for having saved a wreck of the empire, and reigning over Bithynia. As the Turks were beaten, the fugitive prince fell at length into the hands of the emperor of Nice, who compelled him to retire to a monastery, where he died, forgotten by both Greeks and Latins.

Thus four emperors were immolated to ambition and vengeance:—a deplorable spectacle, and most worthy of pity! Amidst the convulsions and fall of an empire, we behold princes of the same family quarrelling for a phantom of authority, snatch from each other by turns both the sceptre and life, surpass the populace in fury, and leave them no crime, no parricide, to commit.

If we could believe Nicetas, Alexius was a model of mildness and moderation; he never made a woman put on mourning for her husband, he never caused a citizen to weep for the loss of his fortune. This eulogy of Nicetas throws a far greater light upon the nature of the government than upon the qualities of the monarch. If it be true that we ought to be thankful to despotism for every ill that it has not committed, we must not forget that Alexius only obtained the throne by infamous means; that he did not redeem his parricide by any public virtue; and that the crime of his usurpation gave birth to a thousand other crimes, brought about a horrible revolution, and caused the ruin of a nation. Nicetas treats Mourzoufle with much more severity; but some modern historians, dazzled by a few actions of bravery, have undertaken to justify a prince who sacrificed everything to his ambition. They have not hesitated to point out to us in a cruel, unscrupulous tyrant, a model and a martyr of the patriotic virtues, as if love of country was the same thing as a boundless love of power, and could possibly ally itself with treachery and parricide.

Whilst the Greek princes were thus making war against each other, and quarrelling for the wrecks of the empire, the French counts and barons quitted the capital to go and take possession of the cities and provinces that had fallen to their share. Many of them were obliged to conquer, sword in hand, the lands that had been assigned to them. The marquis of Montferrat set out on his march to visit the kingdom of Thessalonica, and receive the homage of his new subjects. The emperor Baldwin, followed by his brother Henry of Hainault, and a great number of knights, made a progress through Thrace and Romania, and everywhere on his passage, was saluted by the noisy acclamations of a people always more skilful in flattering their conquerors than in combating their enemies. When he arrived at Adrianople, where he was received in triumph, the new emperor announced his intention of pursuing his march as far as Thessalonica. This unexpected resolution surprised the marquis of Montferrat, who entertained the desire of going alone to his own kingdom. Boniface promised to be faithful to the emperor, to be always ready to employ his forces against the enemies of the empire; but he feared the presence of Baldwin's army in his cities, already exhausted by war. A serious quarrel broke out between the two princes. The marquis of Montferrat accused the emperor of wishing to get possession of his states; Baldwin fancied he could perceive in the resistance of Boniface the secret design of denying the sovereignty of the head of the empire. Both loved justice, and were not wanting in moderation; but now one had become king of Thessalonica, and the other emperor of Constantinople, they had courtiers, who endeavoured to exasperate their quarrel and inflame their animosity. Some told Boniface that Baldwin was entirely in the wrong, and that he abused a power that ought to have been the reward of virtues very different from his. Others reproached the emperor with being too generous to his enemies, and, in the excess of their flattery, said he was guilty of only one fault, and that was of having too long spared an unfaithful vassal. In spite of all the representations of the marquis of Montferrat, Baldwin led his army into the kingdom of Thessalonica. Boniface considered this obstinacy of the emperor as a flagrant outrage, and swore to take vengeance with his sword. Impelled by passion, he departed suddenly with several knights who had declared in his favour, and got possession of Didymatica, a city belonging to the emperor.

The marquis of Montferrat took with him his wife, Mary of Hungary, the widow of Isaac; and the presence of this princess, with the hopes of keeping up the division among the Latins, drew many Greeks to the banner of Boniface. He declared to them that he fought for their cause, and clothed in the imperial purple a young prince, the son of Isaac and Mary of Hungary. Dragging in his train this phantom of an emperor, around whom the principal inhabitants from all parts of Romania rallied, he resumed the road to Adrianople, and made preparations for besieging that city. Boniface, daily becoming more irritated, would listen to neither the counsels nor the prayers of his companions in arms; and discord was about to cause the blood of the Latins to flow, if the doge of Venice, the count of Blois, and the barons that remained at Constantinople, had not earnestly employed their authority and credit to prevent the misfortunes with which the new empire was threatened. Deeply afflicted by what they learnt, they sent deputies to the emperor and the marquis of Montferrat. The marshal of Champagne, the envoy to Boniface, reproached him, in plain terms, with having forgotten the glory and honour of the Crusaders, of whom he had been the leader; with compromising, to gratify a vain pride, the cause of Christ and the safety of the empire, and preparing days of triumph and joy for the Greeks, the Bulgarians, and the Saracens. The marquis of Montferrat was touched by the reproaches of Villehardouin, who was his friend, and who spoke in the name of all the Crusaders. He promised to put an end to the war, and to submit his quarrel with Baldwin to the judgment of the counts and barons.

In the meanwhile Baldwin had taken possession of Thessalonica. As soon as he heard of the hostilities of the marquis of Montferrat, he hastily marched back to Adrianople. He was brooding over projects of vengeance, and threatening to repel force by force, and oppose war to war, when he met the deputies, who came in the name of the leaders of the crusade, to speak to him of peace, and recall to his heart the sentiments of justice and humanity. A knight of the train of the count of Blois addressed a speech to the emperor, that Villehardouin has preserved, in which our readers will be pleased, without doubt, to meet with a picture of the noble frankness of the conquerors of Byzantium. "Sire," said he, "the doge of Venice, the Count Louis of Blois, my very honoured lord, and all the barons who are at Constantinople, salute you as their sovereign, and make complaint to God and you against those who, by their evil counsels, have created fatal discords. You did, certes, very wrong to lend an ear to these perfidious counsellors, for they are our enemies and yours. You know that the Marquis Boniface has submitted his quarrel to the judgment of the barons; the lords and princes hope that you will do as he has done, and that you will not hold out against justice. They have sworn, and we are charged to declare so in their name, not to suffer any longer the scandal of a war kindled between Crusaders."

Baldwin did not at first answer this speech, and appeared surprised at such language; but they spoke to him thus in the name of the doge of Venice, whose old age he respected, and whom he loved tenderly; in the name of the counts and barons, without whose help he could not hope to preserve his empire, and, at length, he listened to the united voices of reason and friendship. He promised to lay down his arms, and repair to Constantinople, to adjust the quarrel between him and the marquis of Montferrat. On his arrival, the counts and barons spared neither complaints nor prayers and they found him docile to all their counsels. The marquis of Montferrat, who very shortly followed him, entered the capital with a degree of mistrust; he was accompanied by a hundred knights, with their men-at-arms; but the welcome he received from Baldwin and the other leaders completely appeased all his resentments, and dissipated all his misgivings. From that time the re-establishment of harmony and peace became the sincere object of the Crusaders. The doge of Venice, the counts and barons, with the most respected of the knights, who reminded the masters of the new empire of the redoubtable institution of the PEERS of the West, gave judgment in the quarrel that was submitted to them, and pronounced, without appeal, between the king of Thessalonica and the emperor of Constantinople. The two princes swore never to listen again to perfidious counsels, and embraced in presence of the army, who rejoiced at the return of concord, as they would have done at a great victory obtained over the enemies of the empire. "Great evil might they have done," says Villehardouin, "who excited this discord; for if God had not taken pity on the Crusaders, they were in danger of losing their conquests, and Christianity might have perished."

As soon as peace was re-established, the knights and barons again quitted the capital to pass through the provinces, and subdue such as were refractory. The count of Blois, who had obtained Bithynia, sent his knights across the Bosphorus; the troops of the Crusaders gained several advantages over those of Lascaris. Penamenia, Lopada, Nicomedia, and some other cities, opened their gates to the conquerors, after a feeble resistance. The Latins brought under their dominion all the coasts of the Propontis and the Bosphorus, as far as the ancient Eolis. Henry of Hainault was not idle in this new war; whilst the warriors of the count of Blois were pushing their conquests towards Nice, he led his men-at-arms into Phrygia, unfurled his triumphant banners in the plains where Troy once stood, fought at the same time both Greeks and Turks, in the fields which had been trod by the armies of Xerxes and Alexander, and took possession of all the country that extends from the Hellespont to Mount Ida.

At the same time the marquis of Montferrat, now the peaceable master of Thessalonica, undertook the conquest of Greece. He advanced into Thessaly, passed the chain of mountains of Olympus and Ossa, and took possession of Larissa. Boniface and his knights, without fear and without danger, passed through the narrow straits of Thermopylæ, and penetrated into Bœotia and Attica. They put to flight Leo Sgurre, who was the scourge of a vast province; and their exploits might have reminded the Greeks of those heroes of the early ages who travelled about the world fighting monsters and subduing tyrants. As all the Greeks, for so long a time oppressed, sighed for a change, the heroes of the crusades were everywhere received as liberators. Whilst Boniface was becoming possessed of the beautiful countries of Greece, Geoffrey de Villehardouin, nephew of the marshal of Champagne, established the authority of the Latins in the Peloponnesus. After having driven the troops of Michael Comnenus to the mountains of Epirus, he occupied, without fighting, Coronea and Patras, and met with no resistance except in the canton of Lacedæmonia. The conquered lands and cities were given to the barons, who rendered fealty and homage to the king of Thessalonica and the emperor of Constantinople. Greece then beheld lords of Argos and Corinth, grand sieurs of Thebes, dukes of Athens, and princes of Achaia. French knights dictated laws in the city of Agamemnon, in the city of Minerva, in the country of Lycurgus, and in that of Epaminondas. Strange destiny of the warriors of this crusade, who had quitted the West to conquer the city and lands of Jesus Christ, and whom fortune had conducted into places filled with the remembrances of the gods of Homer and the glory of profane antiquity!

The Crusaders were not allowed to felicitate themselves long upon their conquests. Possessors of an empire much more difficult to be preserved than invaded, they had not the ability to master fortune, who soon took from them all that victory had bestowed. They exercised their power with violence, and conciliated neither their subjects nor their neighbours. Joannice, king of the Bulgarians, had sent an ambassador to Baldwin, with offers of friendship; Baldwin replied with much haughtiness, and threatened to compel Joannice to descend from his usurped throne. When despoiling the Greeks of their property, the Crusaders shut out from themselves every source of prosperity, and reduced men to whom they left nothing but life, to despair. To fill up the measure of their imprudence, they received into their armies the Greeks, whom they loaded with contempt, and who became their implacable enemies. Not content with reigning over cities, they were desirous of subjugating hearts to their will, and awakened fanaticism. Unjust persecutions exasperated the minds of the Greek priests, who declaimed with vehemence against tyranny, and who, reduced to misery, were listened to as oracles and revered as martyrs.

The new empire of the Latins, into which the feudal laws had been introduced, was divided into a thousand principalities or lordships, and was nothing but a species of republic, governed with great difficulty. The Venetians had their particular jurisdiction, and the greater part of the cities were regulated by turns by the legislation of Venice and the code of feudalism. The lords and barons had among themselves opposite interests and rivalries, which, every day, were likely to bring on discord and civil war. The Latin ecclesiastics, who had shared the spoils of the Greek Church, did not at all conciliate peace by their example, but carried the scandals of their dissensions even into the sanctuary. It was their constant wish and endeavour to exalt the laws and authority of the court of Rome over those of the emperors. Many of them had usurped the fiefs of the barons, and as the fiefs they possessed were exempted from military service, the empire thus became weakened in its natural defences.

The delicious climate and the riches of Greece, with the long sojourn at Constantinople, enervated the courage of the conquerors, and fostered corruption among the soldiers of the cross. The nations in the end ceased to respect the power and the laws of those whose morals and manners they despised. As the Latins had separated, some to go into Greece, and others into Asia Minor, the Greeks, who no longer beheld great armies, and who had sometimes resisted their enemies with advantage, began to fancy that the warriors of the West were not invincible.

In their despair, the conquered people resolved to have recourse to arms; and, looking around them to find enemies for the Crusaders, they implored the alliance and protection of the king of the Bulgarians. There was formed a widely-extended conspiracy, into which all entered to whom slavery was no longer tolerable. All at once the storm burst forth by the massacre of the Latins; a war-cry arose from Mount Hemus to the Hellespont; the Crusaders, dispersed in the various cities and countries, were surprised by a furious and pitiless enemy. The Venetians and French, who guarded Adrianople and Didymatica, were not able to resist the multitude of the Greeks; some were slaughtered in the streets; others retired in disorder, and, in their flight, beheld with grief their banners torn down from the towers, and replaced by the standards of the Bulgarians. The roads were covered with fugitive warriors, who found no asylum in a country which lately trembled at the fame of their arms.

Every city besieged by the Greeks was ignorant of the fate of the other cities confided to the defence of the Latins; communications were interrupted; sinister rumours prevailed in the provinces, which represented the capital in flames, all the cities given up to pillage, and all the armies of the Franks dispersed or annihilated. The old chronicles, whilst speaking of the barbarity of the Greeks, also describe the terror that took possession of some of the barons and knights. The sense of danger appears to have stifled in their hearts every other feeling. In the hour of peril, crusaders abandoned their companions in arms, brothers abandoned brothers. An old knight, Robert de Trils, who, in spite of his grey hairs, had insisted upon following his son to the crusade, was besieged by the Greeks in Philippolis; the city was surrounded by enemies, and Robert had but slender hopes of safety. Even in such circumstances, his prayers and tears could not prevail upon either his son or his son-in-law to remain with him. Villehardouin informs us that these recreant warriors were slain in their flight; for God would not save those who had refused to succour their own father.

When the report of these disasters reached Constantinople, Baldwin assembled the counts and barons; it was determined to apply the promptest remedy to so many evils, and to put into action all the energies of the empire to stop the progress of the revolt. The Crusaders who were engaged in warlike expeditions on the other side of the Bosphorus, received orders to abandon their conquests, and to return immediately to the standards of the main army. Baldwin waited for them several days, but as he was impatient to begin the war, and wished to astonish the enemy by the promptitude of his proceedings, he set out at the head of the knights that remained in the capital, and, five days after his departure, appeared before the walls of Adrianople.

The leaders of the crusade, accustomed to brave all obstacles, were never checked or restrained by the small number of their own soldiers, or the multitude of their enemies. The capital of Thrace, surrounded by impregnable ramparts, was defended by a hundred thousand Greeks, in whom thirst of vengeance supplied the want of courage. Baldwin mustered scarcely eight thousand men around his banners. The doge of Venice soon arrived with eight thousand Venetians. The Latin fugitives came from all parts to join this small army. The Crusaders pitched their tents, and prepared to lay siege to the city. Their preparations proceeded but slowly, and provisions were beginning to fail them, when the report reached them of the march of the king of the Bulgarians. Joannice, the leader of a barbarous people, himself more barbarous than his subjects, was advancing with a formidable army. He concealed his ambitious projects and his desire for vengeance under an appearance of religious zeal, and caused a standard of St. Peter, which he had received from the pope, to be borne before him. This new ally of the Greeks boasted of being a leader of a holy enterprise, and threatened to exterminate the Franks, whom he accused of having assumed the cross for the purpose of ravaging the provinces and pillaging the cities of Christians.

The king of the Bulgarians was preceded in his march by a numerous troop of Tartars and Comans, whom the hopes of pillage had drawn from the mountains and forests near the banks of the Danube and the Borysthenes. The Comans, more ferocious than the nations of Mount Hemus, drank, it was said, the blood of their captives, and sacrificed Christians on the altars of their idols. Like the warriors of Scythia, accustomed to fight whilst flying, the Tartar horsemen received orders from Joannice to provoke the enemy, even in their camp, and to endeavour to draw the heavy cavalry of the Franks into an ambuscade. The barons were aware of this danger, and forbade the Crusaders to quit their tents, or go beyond their intrenchments. But such was the character of the French warriors, that prudence, in their eyes, deprived valour of all its lustre, and it appeared disgraceful to shun the fight in the presence and amidst the scoffs of an enemy.

Scarcely had the Tartars appeared near the camp, when the sight of them made even the leaders themselves forget the orders they had issued only the night before. The emperor and the count of Blois flew to meet the enemy, put them to flight, and pursued them with ardour for the space of two leagues. But all at once the Tartars rallied, and in their turn charged the Christians. The latter, who believed they had gained a victory, were obliged to defend themselves in a country with which they were unacquainted. Their squadrons, exhausted by fatigue, were surprised and surrounded by the army of Joannice; pressed on all sides, they made useless efforts to recover their line of battle, but had no power either to fly, or resist the barbarians.

The count of Blois endeavoured to retrieve his fatal imprudence by prodigies of valour; when seriously wounded he was thrown from his horse amidst the enemy's ranks, one of his knights raised him up, and wished to draw him out of the *mêlée:* "No," cried this brave prince, "leave me to fight and die. God forbid I should ever be reproached with having fled from battle." As he finished these words, the count of Blois fell, covered with wounds, and his faithful squire died by his side.

The emperor Baldwin still disputed the victory; the bravest of his knights and barons followed him into the *mêlée*, and a horrible carnage marked their progress through the ranks of the barbarians. Peter bishop of Bethlehem, Stephen count of Perche, Renaud de Montmirail, Mathieu de Valencourt, Robert de Ronçai, and a crowd of lords and valiant warriors lost their lives in defending their sovereign. Baldwin remained almost alone on the field of battle, and still continued fighting bravely; but at length, overpowered by numbers, he fell into the hands of the Bulgarians, who loaded him with chains. The wreck of the army retired in the greatest disorder, and only owed their safety to the prudent bravery of the doge of Venice and the marshal of Champagne, who had been left to guard the camp.

In the night that followed the battle, the Crusaders raised the siege of Adrianople, and retook the route to the capital, amidst a thousand dangers. The Bulgarians and the Comans, proud of their victory, pursued without intermission the army they had conquered; this army, which had lost half of its numbers, was in great want of provisions, and had great difficulty in dragging along the wounded and the baggage. The Crusaders were plunged in a melancholy silence, their despair was evident in their actions and on their countenances. At Rodosto they met Henry of Hainault, and several other knights, who were on their way from the provinces of Asia, to join the army of Adrianople. The retreating leaders related with tears their defeat and the captivity of Baldwin. All these warriors, who knew not what it was to be conquered, expressed at once their astonishment and their grief; they mingled their lamentations and tears, and raised their hands and eyes towards heaven, to implore the divine mercy. The Crusaders who returned from the shores of the Bosphorus, addressed the marshal of Romania, and weeping, said to him: "Order us where the greatest danger exists, for we no longer wish to live: are we not sufficiently unfortunate in not having come in time to succour our emperor?" Thus the knights of the cross, though pursued by a victorious enemy, were still strangers to fear; the grief caused by the remembrance of their defeat scarcely allowed them to be sensible of the perils by which they were threatened.

All the Crusaders, however, did not exhibit this noble degree of courage; many knights whom Villehardouin is not willing to name, that he may not dishonour their memory, abandoned the banners of the army and fled to Constantinople; they related the disasters of the Crusaders, and, to excuse their desertion, drew a lamentable picture of the misfortunes that threatened the empire. All the Franks were seized with grief and terror, on learning they had no longer an emperor. The Greeks that inhabited the capital, applauded in secret the triumph of the Bulgarians, and their ill-concealed joy still further increased the alarms of the Latins. A great number of knights, overcome by so many reverses, saw no safety but in flight, and embarked hastily on board some Venetian vessels. In vain the legate of the pope and several leaders of the army endeavoured to detain them, threatening them with the anger of God and the contempt of men: they renounced their own glory; they abandoned an empire founded by their arms, and went to announce the captivity of Baldwin in the cities of the West, where the rejoicings for the first victories of the Crusaders were still being celebrated.

In the mean time, Joannice continued his pursuit of the conquered army. The Greeks, united with the Bulgarians, took possession of all the provinces, and left the Latins no repose. Among the disasters of which contemporary history has left us a deplorable account, we must not forget the massacre of twenty thousand Armenians. This numerous colony had left the banks of the Euphrates, and established themselves in the province of Natolia. After the conquest of Constantinople, they declared for the Latins, and when the latter experienced their reverses, finding themselves menaced and pursued by the Greeks, they crossed the Bosphorus, and followed Henry of Hainault, who was marching towards Adrianople. The Armenians took with them their flocks and their families: they drew, in carriages, all that they possessed that was most valuable, and had great difficulty, on their march across the mountains of Thrace, in keeping up with the army of the Crusaders. These unfortunate people were surprised by the Tartars, and, to a man, perished beneath the swords of a pitiless conqueror. The Franks wept at the defeat and destruction of the Armenians, without being able to avenge them: they had nothing but enemies throughout the vast provinces of the empire. Beyond the Bosphorus, they only preserved the castle of Peges: on the European side, only Rodosto and Selembria. Their conquests in ancient Greece were not yet threatened by the Bulgarians; but these distant possessions only served to divide their forces. Henry of Hainault, who took the title of regent, performed prodigies of valour in endeavouring to retake some of the cities of Thrace; and lost, in various combats, a great number of the warriors that remained under his banners.

The bishop of Soissons and some other Crusaders, invested with the confidence of their unfortunate companions in arms, were sent into Italy, France, and the county of Flanders, to solicit the assistance of the knights and barons; but the succour they hoped for could only arrive slowly, and the enemy continued to make rapid progress. The army of the Bulgarians, like a violent tempest, advanced on all sides; it desolated the shores of the Hellespont, extended its ravages into the kingdom of Thessalonica, repassed Mount Hemus, and returned, more numerous and more formidable than ever, to the banks of the Hebrus. The Latin empire had no other defenders but a few warriors divided among the various cities and fortresses, and every day war and desertion diminished the numbers and strength of the unfortunate conquerors of Byzantium. Five hundred knights, picked warriors of the army of the Crusaders, were attacked before the walls of Rusium, and cut to pieces by a countless multitude of Bulgarians and Comans. This defeat was not less fatal than the battle of Adrianople; the hordes of Mount Hemus and the Borysthenes carried terror everywhere. On their passage, the country was in flames, and the cities afforded neither refuge nor means of defence. The land was covered with soldiers, who slaughtered all who came in their way; the sea was covered with pirates, who threatened every coast with their brigandage. Constantinople expected every day to see the standards of the victorious Joannice beneath its walls, and only owed its safety to the excess of evils that desolated all the provinces of the empire.

The king of the Bulgarians did not spare his allies any more than his enemies; he burnt and demolished all the cities that fell into his hands. He ruined the inhabitants, dragged them in his train like captives, and made them undergo, in addition to the calamities of war, all the outrages of a jealous and barbarous tyranny. The Greeks, who had solicited his assistance, were at last reduced to implore the aid of the Latins against the implacable fury of their allies. The Crusaders accepted with joy the alliance with the Greeks, whom they never ought to have repulsed, and re-entered into Adrianople. Didymatica, and most of the cities of Romania, shook off the intolerable yoke of the Bulgarians, and submitted to the Latins. The Greeks, whom Joannice had urged on to despair, showed some bravery, and became useful auxiliaries to the Latins; and the new empire might have hoped for a return of days of prosperity and glory, if so many calamities could possibly have been repaired by a few transient successes. But all the provinces were strewed with ruins, and the cities and countries were without inhabitants. The hordes of Mount Hemus, whether victorious or conquered, still continued their predatory habits. They easily recovered from their losses; the losses of the Franks became every day more irreparable. The leader of the Bulgarians sought out everywhere the foes of the new empire; and, being abandoned by the Greeks of Romania, he formed an alliance with Lascaris, the implacable enemy of the Latins.

The pope in vain exhorted the nations of France and Italy to take up arms for the assistance of the conquerors of Byzantium; he could not awaken their enthusiasm for a cause that presented to its defenders nothing but certain evils, and dangers without glory.

Amidst the perils that continued to multiply, the Crusaders remained perfectly ignorant of the fate of Baldwin; sometimes it was said that he had broken his bonds, and had been seen wandering in the forests of Servia;* sometimes that he had died of grief in prison; sometimes that he had been massacred in the midst of a banquet by the king of the Bulgarians; that his mutilated members had been cast out upon the rocks, and that his skull, enchased in gold, served as a cup for his barbarous conqueror. Several messengers, sent by Henry of Hainault, traveled through the cities of Bulgaria to learn the fate of Baldwin; but returned to Constantinople, without having been able to ascertain anything. A year after the battle of Adrianople, the pope, at the solicitation of the Crusaders, conjured Joannice to restore to the Latins of Byzantium the head of their new empire. The king of the Bulgarians contented himself with replying, that Baldwin had paid the tribute of nature, and that his

* Among the romantic accounts that were circulated concerning Baldwin, we must not omit the following:—The emperor was kept close prisoner at Terenova, where the wife of Joannice became desperately in love with him, and proposed to him to escape with her. Baldwin rejected this proposal, and the wife of Joannice, irritated by his disdain and refusal, accused him to her husband of having entertained an adulterous passion. The barbarous Joannice caused his unfortunate captive to be massacred at a banquet, and his body was cast on to the rocks, a prey to vultures and wild beasts.

But people could not be convinced that he was dead. A hermit had retired to the forest of Glançon, on the Hainault side, and the people of the neighbourhood became persuaded that this hermit was Count Baldwin. The solitary at first answered with frankness, and refused the homage they wished to render him. They persisted, and at length he was induced to play a part, and gave himself out for Baldwin. At first he had a great many partisans; but the king of France, Louis VIII., having invited him to his court, he was confounded by the questions that were put to him: he took to flight, and was arrested in Burgundy by Erard de Chastenai, a Burgundian gentleman, whose family still exists. Jane countess of Flanders caused the impostor to be hung in the great square of Lisle.

deliverance was no longer in the power of mortals. This answer destroyed all hopes of again seeing the imprisoned monarch, and the Latins no longer entertained a doubt of the death of their emperor. Henry of Hainault received the deplorable heritage of his brother with tears and deep regret, and succeeded to the empire amidst general mourning and sorrow. To complete their misfortunes, the Latins had to weep for the loss of Dandolo, who finished his glorious career at Constantinople, and whose last looks must have perceived the rapid decline of an empire he had founded.* The greater part of the Crusaders had either perished in battle, or returned to the West. Boniface, in an expedition against the Bulgarians of Rhodope, received a mortal wound, and his head was carried in triumph to the fierce Joannice, who had already immolated a monarch to his ambition and vengeance. The succession of Boniface gave birth to serious disputes among the Crusaders; and the kingdom of Thessalonica, which had exhibited some splendour during its short existence, disappeared amidst the confusion and the storms of a civil and a foreign war. In the brother and successor of Baldwin were united the civil and military virtues; but he could scarcely hope to restore a power so shaken on all sides.

I have not the courage to pursue this history, and describe the Latins in the extremes of their abasement and misery. On commencing my narration, I said: "*Evil to the conquered;*" on terminating it, I cannot refrain from saying: "*Evil to the conquerors.*"

An old empire which moulders away, a new empire ready to sink into ruins, such are the pictures that this crusade presents to us; never did any epoch offer greater exploits for admiration, or greater troubles for commiseration. Amidst these glorious and tragical scenes, the imagination is excited in the most lively manner, and passes, without ceasing, from surprise to surprise. We are at first astonished at seeing an army of thirty thousand men embark to conquer a country which might reckon upon many millions of defenders; a tempest, an epidemic disease, want of provisions, disunion among the leaders, an indecisive battle, all, or any of these, might have ruined the army of the Crusaders, and brought about the failure of their enterprise. By an unheard of good fortune, nothing that they had to dread happened to them. They triumphed over all dangers, and surmounted all obstacles: without having any party among the Greeks, they obtained possession of their capital and the provinces; and, at the moment when they saw their standards triumphant all around them, it was that their fortune deserted them, and their ruin began. A great lesson is this, given to nations by Providence, which sometimes employs conquerors to chastise both people and princes, and then, at its pleasure, destroys the instrument of its justice! There is no doubt that that Providence, which protects empires, will not permit great states to be subverted with impunity; and to deter those who wish to conquer everything by force of arms, it has decreed that victory shall sometimes bear none but very bitter fruits.

The Greeks, a degenerate nation, honoured their misfortunes by no virtue; they had neither sufficient courage to prevent the reverses of war, nor sufficient resignation to support them. When reduced to despair, they showed some little valor; but that valor was imprudent and blind; it precipitated them into new calamities, and procured them masters much more barbarous than those whose yoke they were so eager to shake off. They had no leader able to govern or guide them; no sentiment of patriotism strong enough to rally them: deplorable example of a nation left to itself, which has lost its morals, and has no confidence in its laws or its government!

The Franks had just the same advantages over their enemies that the barbarians of the north

* Dandolo was magnificently buried in the church of St. Sophia, and his mausoleum existed till the destruction of the Greek empire. Mahomet II. caused it to be demolished, when he changed the church of St. Sophia into a mosque. A Venetian painter, who worked during several years in the court of Mahomet, on returning to his own country obtained from the sultan the cuirass, the helmet, the spurs, and the toga of Dandolo, which he presented to the family of this great man.

had over the Romans of the Lower Empire. In this terrible conflict, simplicity of manners, the energy of a new people for civilization, the ardour for pillage, and the pride of victory, were sure to prevail over the love of luxury, habits formed amidst corruption, and vanity which attaches importance to the most frivolous things, and only preserves a gaudy resemblance of true grandeur.

The events we have recorded are, doubtless, sufficient to make us acquainted with the manners and intellectual faculties of the Greeks and Latins. Two historians, however, who have served us as guides, may add by their style even, and the character of their works, to the idea that we form of the genius of the two races.

The Greek Nicetas makes long lamentations over the misfortunes of the vanquished; he deplores with bitterness the loss of the monuments, the statues, the riches which ministered to the luxury of his compatriots. His accounts, full of exaggeration and hyperboles, sprinkled all over with passages from the Scriptures and profane authors, depart almost always from the noble simplicity of history, and only exhibit a vain affectation of learning. Nicetas, in the excess of his vanity, hesitates to pronounce the names even of the Franks, and fancies he inflicts a punishment upon them by preserving silence as to their exploits; when he describes the misfortunes of the empire, he can only weep and lament; but whilst lamenting, he is still anxious to please, and appears much more interested about his book than his country.

The marquis of Champagne does not pique himself upon his erudition, but even seems proud of his ignorance. It has been said that he could not write, and he himself confesses that he dictated his history. His narration, void of all spirit of research, but lively and animated, constantly recalls the language and the noble frankness of a *preux chevalier*. Villehardouin particularly excels in the speeches of his heroes, and delights in praising the bravery of his companions: if he never names the Grecian warriors, it is because he did not know them, and did not wish to know them. The marshal of Champagne is not affected by the evils of war, and only elevates his style to paint traits of heroism; the enthusiam of victory alone can draw tears from him. When the Latins experienced great reverses, he cannot weep, he is silent; and it may be plainly seen he has laid down his book to go and fight.

There is another contemporary historian, whose character may likewise assist us in forming a judgment upon the age in which he lived and the events he has related. Gunther, a monk of the order of Citeaux, who wrote under the dictation of Martin Litz, expatiates upon the preachings of the crusade, and on the virtues of his abbot, who placed himself at the head of the Crusaders of the diocese of Bâle. When the Christian army directs its course towards the capital of the Greek empire, Gunther remembers the orders of the pope, and becomes silent; if he affords us a few words upon the second siege of Constantinople, he cannot conceal the terror which this rash enterprise creates in him. In his recital, the valour of the Crusaders scarcely obtains a modest eulogy; the imagination of the historian is only struck by the difficulties and perils of the expedition; filled with the most sinister presentiments, he constantly repeats that there is no hope of success for the Latins. When they are triumphant, his fear is changed all at once into admiration. The monk Gunther celebrates with enthusiasm the unhoped-for success of the conquerors of Byzantium, among whom he never loses sight of his abbot, Martin Litz, loaded with the pious spoils of Greece.

When reading the three histories contemporary with the expedition to Constantinople, we plainly perceive that the first belongs to a Greek brought up at the court of Byzantium, the second to a French knight, and the third to a monk. If the two first historians, by their manner of writing and the sentiments they express, give us a just idea of the Greek nation and the heroes of the West, the last may also explain to us the opinions and the character of the greater part of those Crusaders, who were constantly threatening to quit the army after it had left Venice, and who, perhaps, were only so mindful of the oath they had made to go to the Holy Land, because the name alone of Constantinople filled them with terror. There were, as may be plainly seen, but very few of these timid Crusaders in the Christian army, and even these were governed by the general spirit that animated the knights and barons. Other crusades had been preached in councils, this crusade was proclaimed at tournaments; thus the greater parts of the Crusaders proved more faithful to the virtues and laws of chivalry than to the will of the Holy See. These warriors, so proud and so brave, were full of respect for the authority and judgment of the pope; but, governed by honour, placed between their first vows and their word given to the Venetians, they often swore to deliver Jerusalem, and were led, without thinking of it, to the walls of Constantinople. Armed to avenge the cause of Christ, they became subservient to the ambition of Venice, to which republic they esteemed themselves bound by gratitude, and overturned the throne of Constantinople to pay a debt of fifty thousand silver marks.

The chivalric spirit, one of the peculiar characteristics of this war, and of the age in which it was undertaken, kept up in the hearts of the Crusaders ambition and the love of glory. In the early days of chivalry, knights declared themselves the champions of beauty and innocence; at first they were appealed to for justice against injuries and robberies; but soon princes and princesses, deprived of their rights by force, came to demand of them the restitution of provinces and kingdoms. The champions of misfortune and beauty then became illustrious liberators and true conquerors.

At the same time that a young prince came to implore the Crusaders to assist him in replacing his father upon the throne of Constantinople, a young princess, the daughter of Isaac, king of Cyprus, despoiled by Richard Cœur de Lion, repaired to Marseilles, to solicit the support of the Crusaders, who were embarking for Palestine. She married a Flemish knight, and charged him with the task of recovering her father's kingdom. This Flemish knight, whose name history does not mention, but who belonged to the family of Count Baldwin, when he arrived in the East, addressed himself to the king of Jerusalem, and demanded the kingdom of Cyprus of him; he was supported in his demand by the châtelain of Bruges, and the greater part of his companions who had taken the cross. Amaury, who had received from the pope and the emperor of Germany, the title of king of Cyprus, far from yielding to such pretentions, ordered the Flemish knight, John of Nesle, and their companions, to quit his dominions. The knights who had embraced the cause of the daughter of Isaac, abandoned the idea of retaking the kingdom of Cyprus, and without stopping in the Holy Land, turned their steps towards the banks of the Euphrates and the Orontes, to seek for other countries to conquer.

Before there was a question of attacking Constantinople, we have seen a daughter of Tancred, the last king of Sicily, espouse a French knight, and transfer to him the charge of avenging her family and establishing her claims to the kingdom founded by the Norman knights. Gauthier de Brienne, after his marriage, set out for Italy, furnished with a thousand *livres tournois*, and accompanied by sixty knights. Having received at Rome the benediction of the pope, he declared war against the Germans, then masters of Apulia and Sicily; got possession of the principal fortresses, and appeared likely to enjoy the fruits of his victories in peace, when he was surprised in his tent, and fell, covered with wounds, into the hands of his enemies. He was offered his liberty upon the condition of renouncing his claim to the crown of Sicily; but he preferred the title of king to freedom, and allowed himself to die with hunger rather than abandon his rights to a kingdom which victory had bestowed upon him.

This spirit of conquest, which appeared so general among the knights, might favour the expedition to Constantinople; but it was injurious to the holy war, by turning the Crusaders aside from the essential object of the crusade. The heroes of this war did nothing for the deliverance of Jerusalem, of which they constantly spoke in their letters to the pope. The conquest of Byzantium, very far from being, as the knights believed, the road to the land of Christ, was but a new obstacle to the taking of the holy city; their imprudent exploits placed the Christian colonies in greater peril, and only ended in completely subverting, without replacing it, a power which might have served as a barrier against the Saracens.

The Venetians skilfully took advantage of this disposition of the French knights; Venice succeeded in stifling the voice of the sovereign pontiff, who often gave the Crusaders counsels dictated by the spirit of the gospel. The republic had the greatest influence over the events of this war, and over the minds of the barons and knights, who allowed themselves to be governed by turns by the sentiments of honor and by a desire to win rich dominions, and thus exhibited throughout their conduct an inconsistent mixture of generosity and avarice.

The inclination to enrich themselves by victory had, particularly, no longer any bounds when the Crusaders had once beheld Constantinople; ambition took the place in their hearts of every generous sentiment, and left nothing of that enthusiasm which had been the moving principle of other crusades. No prodigy, no miraculous apparition came to second or stimulate the valour of knights to whom it was quite sufficient to point out the wealth of Greece. In preceding crusades, the bishops and ecclesiastics promised the combatants indulgences of the Church and eternal life; but in this war, as the Crusaders had incurred the displeasure of the head of the faithful, they could not be supported in their perils by the hope of martyrdom; and the leaders who were acquainted with the spirit that animated their followers, contented themselves with offering a sum of money to the soldier that should first mount the ramparts of Constantinople. When they had pillaged the city, knights, barons, and soldiers exclaimed, in the intoxication of their joy,—*Never was so rich a booty seen since the creation of the world!*

We have remarked that, in the conquest of the provinces, every knight wished to obtain a principality; every count, every lord, wished for a kingdom; the clergy themselves were not exempt from this ambition, and often complained to the pope of not having been favoured in the division of the spoils of the Greek empire.

To recapitulate, in a few words, our opinion of the events and consequences of this crusade, we must say that the spirit of chivalry and the spirit of conquest at first gave birth to wonders; but that they did not suffice to maintain the Crusaders in their possessions. This conquering spirit, carried to the most blind excess, did not allow them to reflect that among the greatest triumphs, there is a point at which victory and force themselves are powerless, if prudence and wisdom do not come to the assistance of valour.

The Franks, their ancestors, who set out from the North to invade the richest provinces of the Roman empire, were better seconded by fortune, but more particularly by their own genius. Respecting the usages of the countries that submitted to their arms, they only beheld in the conquered, fellow-citizens and supporters of their own power; they did not create a foreign nation in the midst of the nations they had desolated by their victories. The Crusaders, on the contrary, evinced a profound contempt for the Greeks, whose alliance and support they ought to have been anxious to seek; they wished to reform manners and alter opinions,—a much more difficult task than the conquest of an empire,—and only met with enemies in a country that might have furnished them with useful allies.

We may add that the policy of the Holy See, which at first undertook to divert the Latin warriors from the expedition to Constantinople, became, in the end, one of the greatest obstacles to the preservation of their conquests. The counts and barons, who reproached themselves with having failed in obedience to the sovereign pontiff, at length followed scrupulously his instructions to procure by their arms the submission of the Greek Church, the only condition on which the holy father would pardon a war commenced in opposition to his commands. To obtain his forgiveness and approbation, they employed violence against schism and heresy, and lost their conquest by endeavouring to justify it in the eyes of the sovereign pontiff. The pope himself did not obtain that which he so ardently desired. The union of the Greek and Roman churches could not possibly be effected amidst the terrors of victory and the evils of war; the arms of the conquerors had less power than the anathemas of the Church, to bring back the Greeks to the worship of the Latins. Violence only served to irritate men's minds, and consummated the rupture, instead of putting an end to it. The remembrance of persecutions and outrages, a reciprocal contempt, an implacable hatred arose and became implanted between the two creeds, and separated them for ever.

History cannot affirm that this crusade made great progress in the civilization of Europe. The Greeks had preserved the jurisprudence of Justinian; the empire possessed wise regulations upon the levying of imposts and the administration of the public revenues; but the Latins disdained these monuments of human wisdom and of the experience of many ages; they coveted nothing the Greeks possessed but their territories and their wealth. Most of the knights took a pride in their ignorance, and amongst the spoils of Constantinople, attached no value to the ingenious productions of Greece. Amidst the conflagrations that consumed the mansions and palaces of the capital, they beheld with indifference large and valuable libraries given up to the flames. It must be confessed, however, that, in these great disasters the Muses had not to weep for the loss of any of the master-pieces they had inspired. If the conquerors knew not how to appreciate the treasures of genius, this rich deposit was not to be lost for their descendants. All the books of antiquity that were known in the time of Eustathius [A. D. 750, TRANS.], and of which that learned philosopher made the nomenclature some centuries before the fifth crusade, enriched France and Italy at the revival of letters.

We may add that the necessity for both conquerors and conquered of intercommunication must have contributed to the spreading of the Latin language among the Greeks, and that of the Greeks among the Latins. The people of Greece were obliged to learn the idiom of the clergy of Rome in order to make their petitions and complaints known; the ecclesiastics charged by the pope to convert the Greeks could not dispense with the study of the language of Plato and Demosthenes, tc teach the disciples of Photius the truths of the Roman Catholic religion.

We have spoken of the destruction of the master-pieces of sculpture; we must admit, nevertheless, that some of them escaped the barbarism of the conquerors. The Venetians, more enlightened than the other Crusaders, and born in a city constructed and embellished by the arts, caused several of the monuments of Byzantium to be transported into Italy. Four horses of bronze, which, amidst the revolutions of empires, had passed from Greece to Rome, from Rome to Constantinople, were sent to decorate the place of St. Mark: many ages after this crusade, they were doomed to be carried away from Venice, in its turn invaded by victorious armies, and again to return to the shores of the Adriatic, as eternal trophies of war, and faithful companions of victory.

The Crusaders likewise profited by several useful inventions, and transmitted them to their compatriots; and the fields and gardens of Italy and France were enriched by some plants till that time unknown in the West. Boniface sent into his marquisate some seeds of maize, which had never before been cultivated in Italy: a public document, which still exists, attests the gratitude of the people of Montferrat. The magistrates received the innocent fruits of victory with great solemnity, and, upon their altars, called down a blessing upon a production of Greece, that would one day constitute the wealth of the plains of Italy.

Flanders, Champagne, and most of the provinces of France, which had sent their bravest warriors to the crusade, fruitlessly lavished their population and their treasures upon the conquest of Byzantium. We may say that our intrepid ancestors gained nothing by this wonderful war, but the glory of having given, for a moment, masters to Constantinople, and lords to Greece. And yet these distant conquests, and this new empire, which drew from France its turbulent and ambitious princes, must have been favourable to the French monarchy. Philip Augustus must have been pleased by the absence of the great vassals of the crown, and had reason to learn with joy that the count of Flanders, a troublesome neighbour, and a not very submissive vassal, had obtained an empire in the East. The French monarchy thus derived some advantage from this crusade; but the republic of Venice profited much more by it.

This republic, which scarcely possessed a population of two hundred thousand souls, and had not the power to make its authority respected on the continent, in the first place, made use of the arms of the Crusaders, to subdue cities, of which, without their assistance, she could never have made herself mistress. By the conquest of Constantinople, she enlarged her credit and her commerce in the East, and brought under her laws some of the richest possessions of the Greek emperors. She increased the reputation of her navy, and raised herself above all the maritime nations of Europe. The Venetians, though fighting under the banners of the cross, never neglected the interests or glory of their own country, whilst the French knights scarcely ever fought for any object but personal glory and their own ambition. The republic of Venice, accustomed to calculate the advantages and expenses of war, immediately renounced all conquests the preservation of which might become burdensome; and of her new possessions in the East, only retained such as she judged necessary to the prosperity of her commerce, or the maintenance of her marine. Three years after the taking of Constantinople, the senate of Venice published an edict, by which it permitted any of the citizens to conquer the islands of the Archipelago; yielding to them the proprietorship of all the countries they might subdue. After this there soon appeared princes of Naxos, dukes of Paros, and lords of Mycone, as there had been dukes of Athens, lords of Thebes, and princes of Achaia; but these dukes and princes were only vassals of the republic. Thus Venice, more fortunate than France, made the valour and ambition of her citizens subservient to her interests.

END OF VOLUME I.

TABLE OF CONTENTS, VOL I.

BOOK I.

BIRTH OF THE CRUSADES.

A. D. 300–1095.

BOOK II.

DEPARTURE AND MARCH OF THE CRUSADERS.

A. D. 1096–1097.

BOOK III.

THE MARCH TO, AND SIEGE OF ANTIOCH.

A. D. 1097–1099.

BOOK IV.

THE SIEGE OF JERUSALEM.

A. D. 1099–1103.

BOOK V.

HISTORY OF THE KINGDOM OF JERUSALEM.

A. D. 1099–1148.

BOOK VI.

THE SECOND CRUSADE.

A. D. 1142–1148.

BOOK VII.

THE THIRD CRUSADE.

A. D. 1148–1188.

BOOK VIII.

SALADIN.

A. D. 1188–1192.

BOOK IX.

THE FOURTH CRUSADE.

A. D. 1195–1198.

BOOK X.

THE FIFTH CRUSADE.

A. D. 1198–1204.

BOOK XI.

FROM THE RESTORATION OF ISAAC TO THE DEATH OF BALDWIN.

A. D. 1198–1204.

Continued in Volume 2
Restored Special Edition

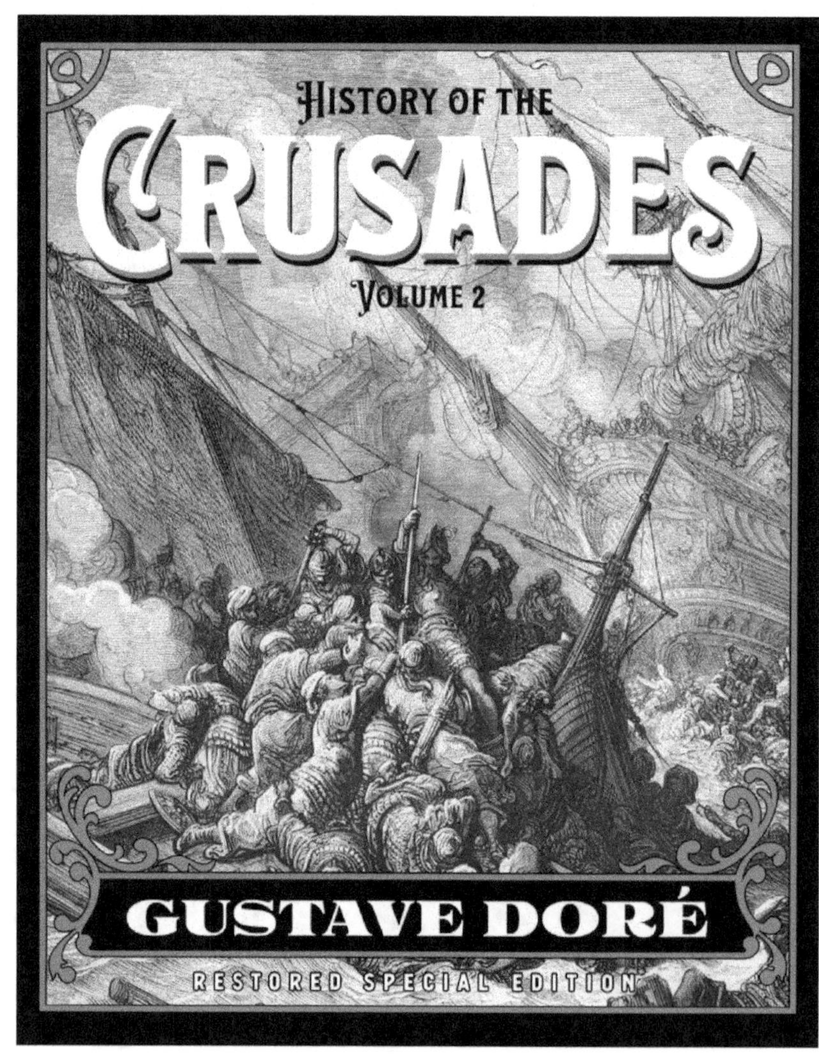

More Doré from CGR Publishing at www.CGRpublishing.com

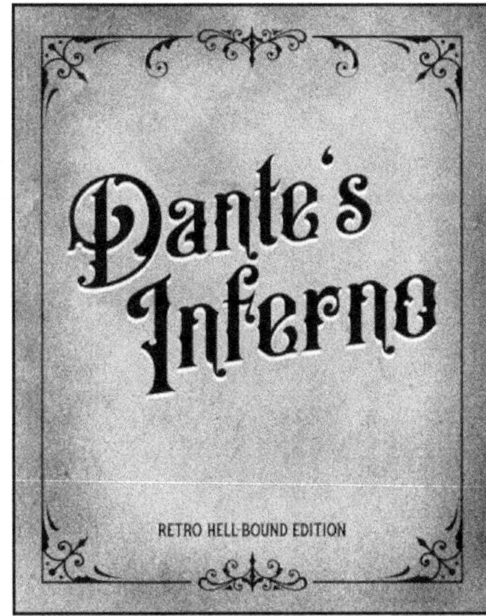

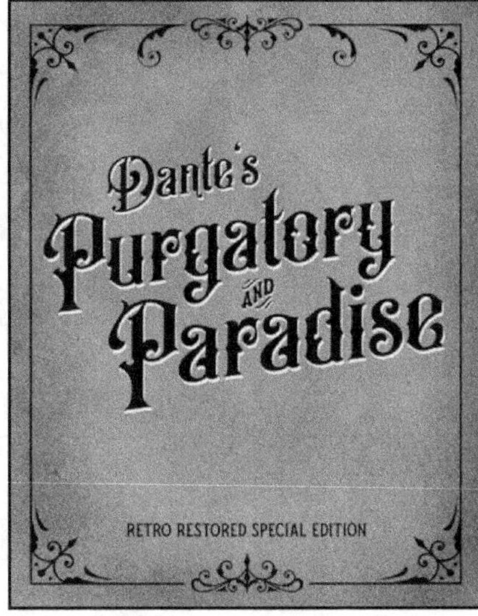

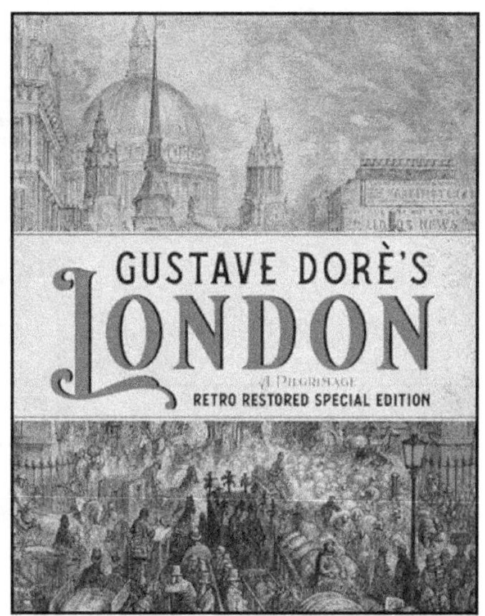

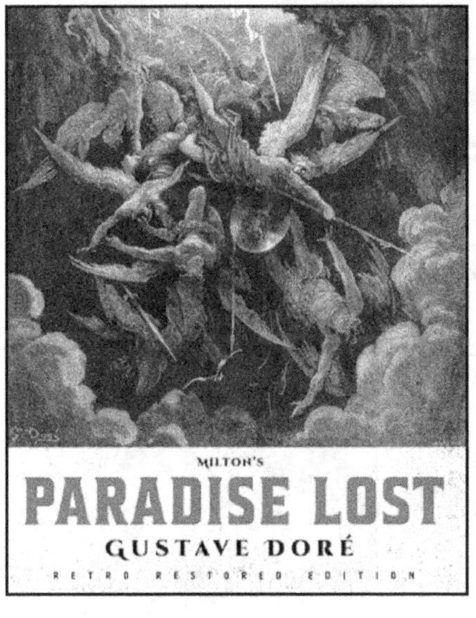

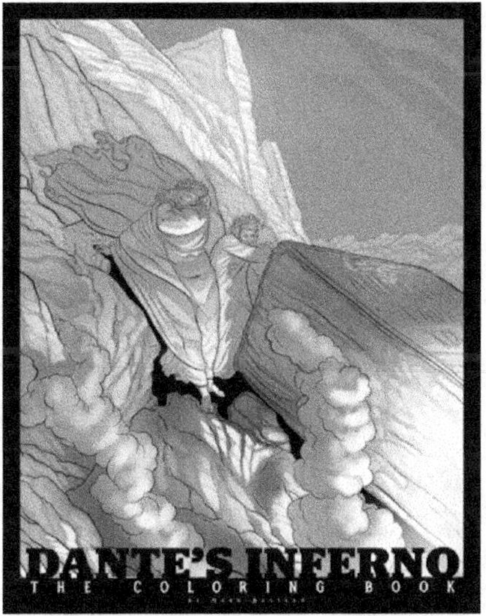

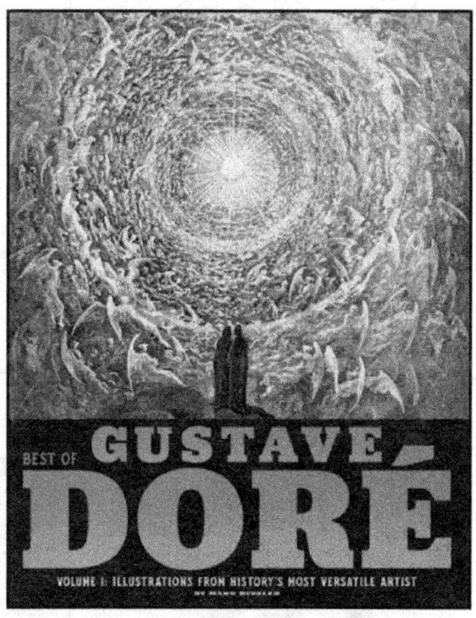

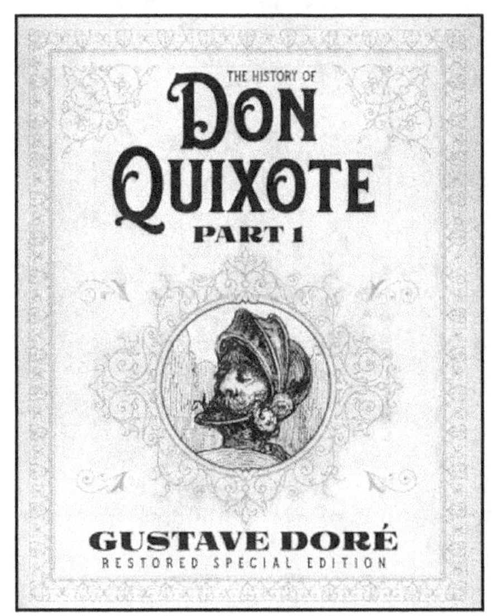

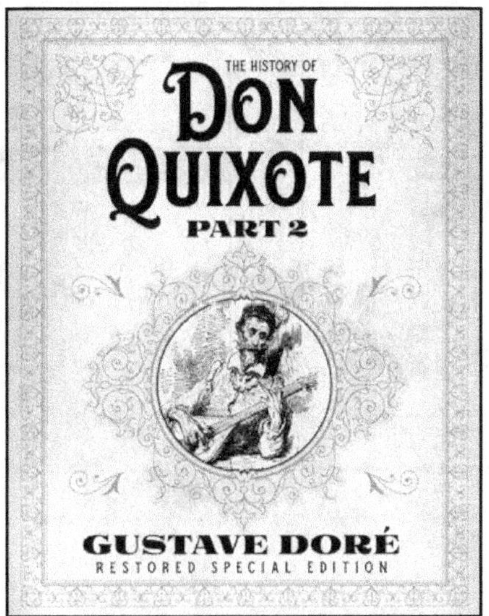

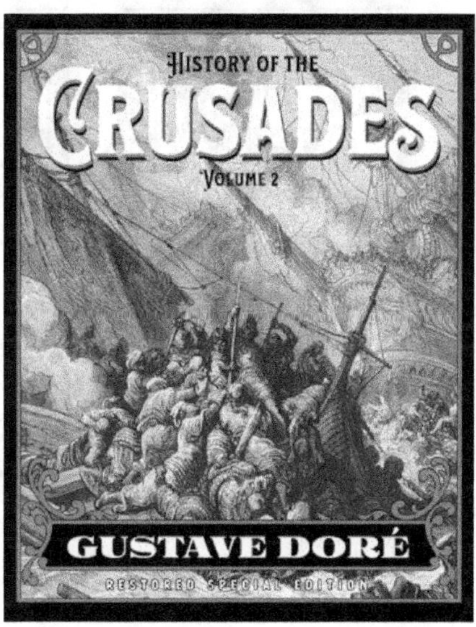

OTHER BOOKS FROM CGR PUBLISHING AT CGRPUBLISHING.COM

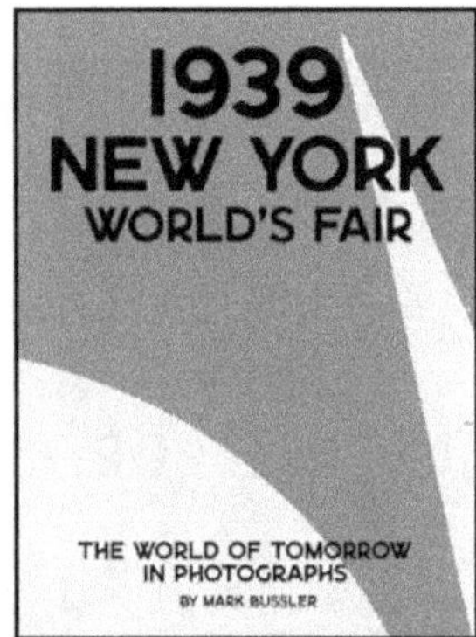

1939 New York World's Fair: The World of Tomorrow in Photographs

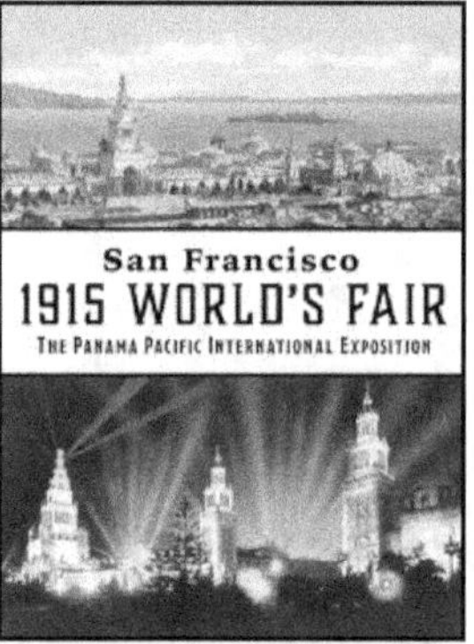

San Francisco 1915 World's Fair: The Panama-Pacific International Expo.

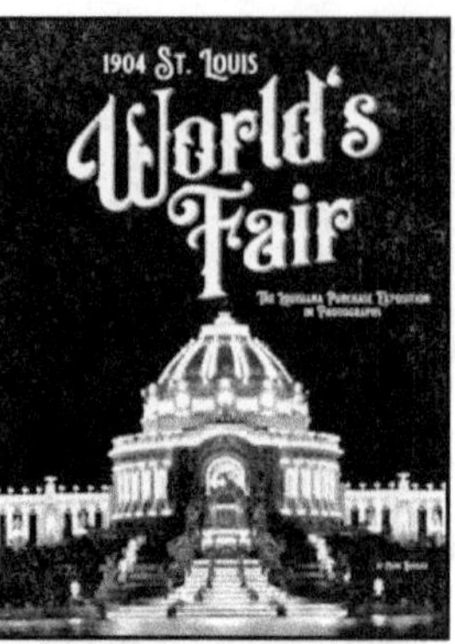

1904 St. Louis World's Fair: The Louisiana Purchase Exposition in Photographs

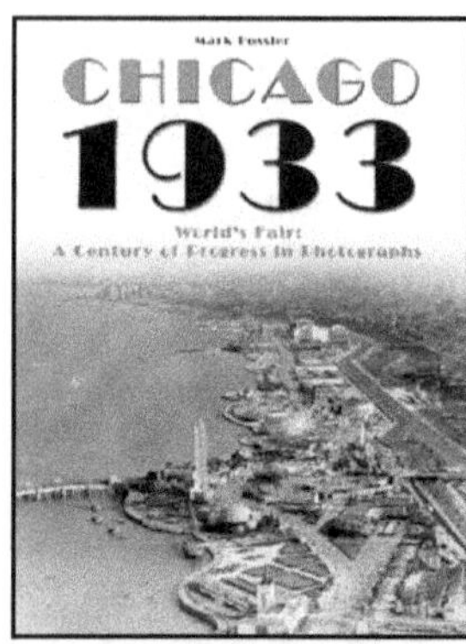

Chicago 1933 World's Fair: A Century of Progress in Photographs

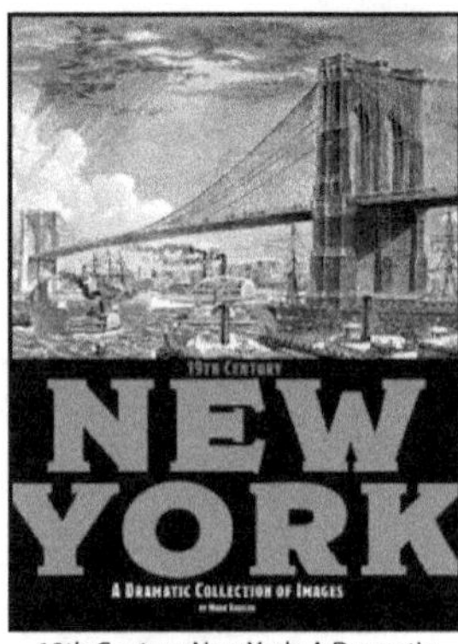

19th Century New York: A Dramatic Collection of Images

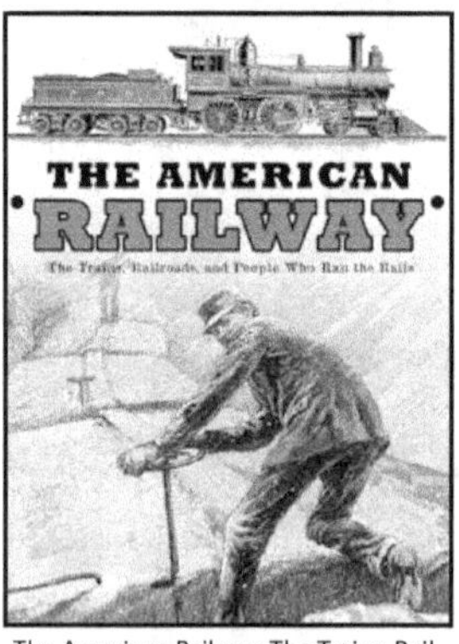

The American Railway: The Trains, Railroads, and People Who Ran the Rails

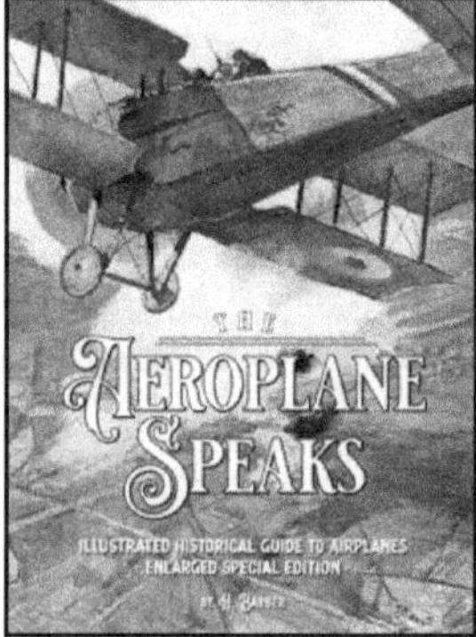

The Aeroplane Speaks: Illustrated Historical Guide to Airplanes

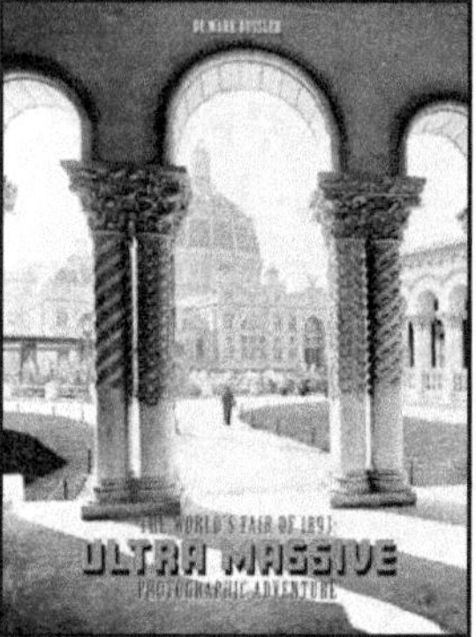

The World's Fair of 1893 Ultra Massive Photographic Adventure Vol. 1

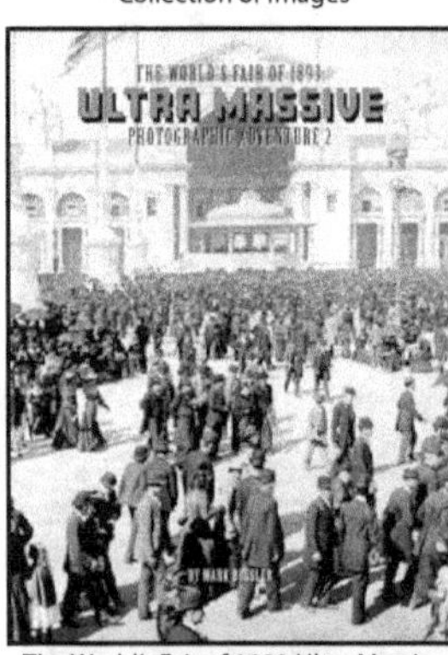

The World's Fair of 1893 Ultra Massive Photographic Adventure Vol. 2

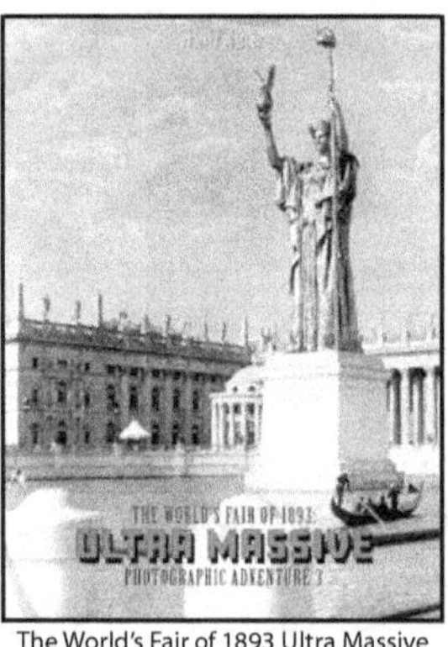

The World's Fair of 1893 Ultra Massive Photographic Adventure Vol. 3

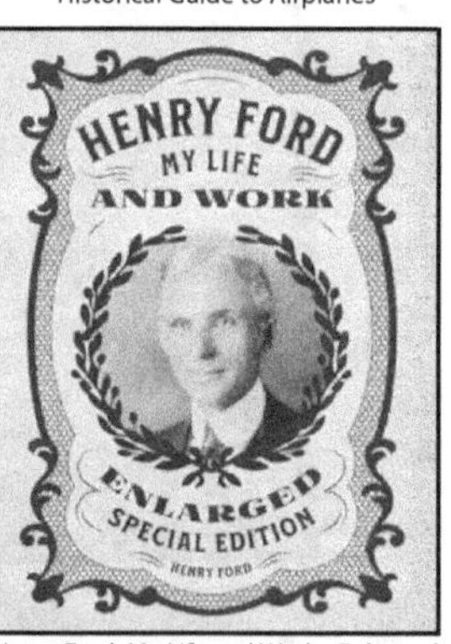

Henry Ford: My Life and Work - Enlarged Special Edition

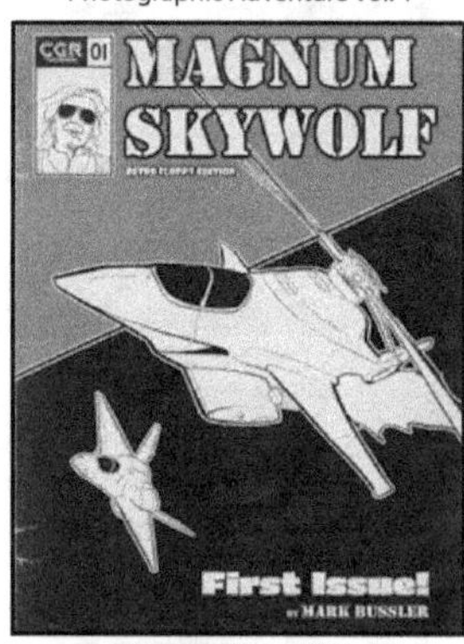

Magnum Skywolf #1

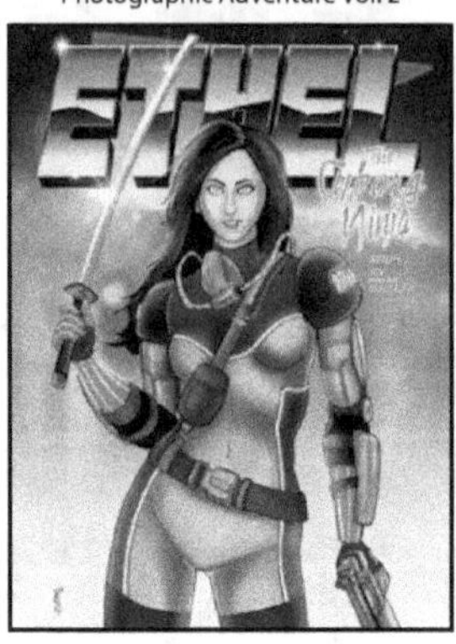

Ethel the Cyborg Ninja Book 1

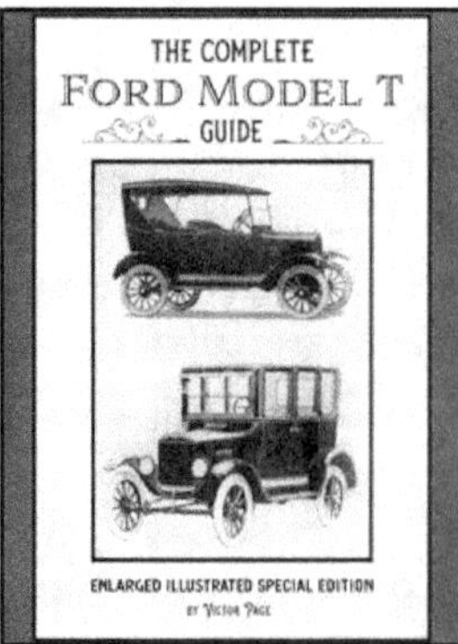

The Complete Ford Model T Guide: Enlarged Illustrated Special Edition

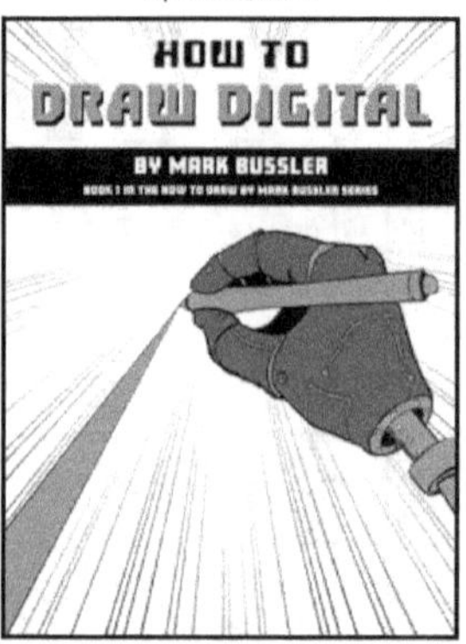

How To Draw Digital by Mark Bussler

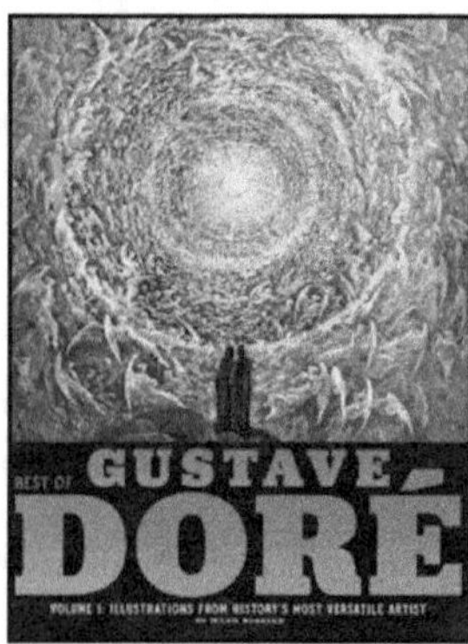

Best of Gustave Doré Volume 1: Illustrations from History's Most Versatile...

- MAILING LIST -
JOIN FOR EXCLUSIVE OFFERS

www.CGRpublishing.com/subscribe

www.ingramcontent.com/pod-product-compliance
Lightning Source LLC
LaVergne TN
LVHW061236100826
845148LV00008B/964

* 9 7 8 1 5 9 2 1 8 0 9 8 1 *